PENGUIN ENGLISH LIBRARY

THE MAJOR WORKS

SIR THOMAS BROWNE

C. A. Patrides is Professor of English and Related Literature at the University of York. He is the author of *Milton and the Christian Tradition* (1966) and *The Grand Design of God : The Literary Form of the Christian View of History* (1972), as well as editor of *Milton's Epic Poetry* (Penguin Books, 1967), *Approaches to 'Paradise Lost'* (1968), *The Cambridge Platonists* (1969), Sir Walter Ralegh's *History of the World* (1971), *The English Poems of George Herbert* (1974) and *John Milton: Selected Prose* (Penguin Books, 1974).

SIR THOMAS BROWNE

———— * ————

THE MAJOR WORKS

EDITED

WITH AN INTRODUCTION

AND NOTES BY

C. A. PATRIDES

PENGUIN BOOKS

Penguin Books Ltd, Harmondsworth, Middlesex, England
Penguin Books, 625 Madison Avenue, New York, New York 10022, U.S.A.
Penguin Books Australia Ltd, Ringwood, Victoria, Australia
Penguin Books Canada Ltd, 2801 John Street, Markham, Ontario Canada L3R 1B4,
Penguin Books (N.Z.) Ltd, 182–190 Wairau Road, Auckland 10, New Zealand

—

This selection first published 1977

—

Introduction and Notes copyright © C. A. Patrides, 1977

—

Made and printed in Great Britain by
Cox & Wyman Ltd, London, Reading and Fakenham
Set in Monotype Garamond

FOR THE HUNTLEYS:
FRANK AND TRINK

ἔνδον ἡ πηγὴ τοῦ ἀγαθοῦ

CONTENTS

THE present edition provides in the first instance the complete text of five of Browne's major works; also extracts from his colossal *Pseudodoxia Epidemica* together with the titles of the omitted chapters in order to suggest its continuity; and finally one of his numerous shorter works – 'On Dreams' – which not only displays the riches still awaiting our attention but confirms the persuasion Browne often voices elsewhere, that 'There is surely a neerer apprehension of any thing that delights us in our dreames, than in our waked senses' (below, p. 154).

Also included is Dr Samuel Johnson's *Life of Sir Thomas Browne* (1756), immediately useful because it quotes extensively from the only substantial earlier memoir – John Whitefoot's *Some Minutes for the Life of Sir Thomas Browne* (1712) – and mediately valuable in that it is the considered judgement of one major prose writer on another.

The annotator of Browne's prose is much helped by Browne himself, who frequently explains a difficult word (e.g. 'solisequious and Sun-following', 'Panoplia or compleat armour'), translates his Greek and Latin words and phrases (e.g. 'the ἐπισκιασμός and adumbration', or '*Ipsa sui pretium virtus sibi*, that vertue is her own reward, is' etc.), and places explanatory remarks in the margin (here transferred to the footnotes). Where Browne ends, however, the annotator's problems begin. The temptation to provide elaborate notes is at times irresistible; but aware that ponderous annotation of Browne's prose would interfere with his rhythms, I like to think that Gui Patin would not have included me in the just censure he directed in 1657 against a pedantic German editor of *Religio Medici*.[1] Hence my decision not to embark on the perilous seas

[1] 'Ce livre n'aurait pas besoin de tels écoliers. Personne n'était capable de traduire ce livre s'il n'avait l'esprit approchant de l'auteur, qui est gentil et éveillé. Le genre du premier auteur du livre vaut mieux que tous les commentaires, qui ne sont que la misérable pédanterie d'un jeune homme allemand qui pense être bien savant' (letter of 19 June 1657; in Bibl. §176).

of source-hunting without, and much less against, Browne's
express warrant; for I would then stand accused of that exces-
sive zeal which he discerned in yet another annotator of *Religio
Medici*, Thomas Keck in 1656.[2] Nor should the frequency with
which I call attention to widely accepted ideas be misconstrued,
since my intention is not to imply that Browne resorted to mere
commonplaces but to suggest the way his fertile imagination
transformed them into novelties.

My notes also include several of Coleridge's remarks, both
sustained and marginal. So far, however, no apology is ven-
tured for none is needed.

In quoting from the manuscripts of *Religio Medici* to suggest
earlier stages of its final text, I have normally preferred the
Pembroke version (see *P* in Abbreviations). Finally, the
appended Dictionary identifying the host of names invoked by
Browne (pp. 513 ff.) may be accepted as an effort to reduce the
proliferating notes.

A NOTE ON THE TEXT

I have throughout preferred the first editions of the works here
reprinted, except for the text of *Pseudodoxia Epidemica* where I
turned to the carefully revised 2nd edition of 1650, and the text
of the essay 'On Dreams' where I used its transcription from a
manuscript by Sir Geoffrey Keynes. Further particulars are
given in the headnotes to each work, below, pp. 57, 163, 261,
317, 389, 415.

In reprinting these texts, I have amended them in the light of
their Errata (if any), corrected the more obvious misprints and
the erroneous numbering of various sections (e.g. in *Religio
Medici*), transferred the numbers of some sections from the
margin or elsewhere to the outset of the relevant paragraphs
(e.g. in *Religio Medici*, *Pseudodoxia Epidemica* and *Christian
Morals*), reduced Browne's marginal remarks to the notes,

2. 'the learned Annotator-commentator hath parallel'd many passages
with other of Mountaignes essayes, whereas to deale clearly, when I
penned that peece I had never read 3 leaves of that Author & scarce any
more ever since' (*K*, III, 290).

expanded all contractions, and changed 'u' to 'v' where the latter is meant, and 'i' to 'j' for the same reason.

A NOTE ON ABBREVIATIONS

References in parentheses involving letters (e.g. *Browne marg.*, *K*, etc.) are expanded in the list of abbreviations, below, p. 537. References in parentheses involving numbers preceded by the symbol § (e.g. § 19, § 127, etc.) are to the numbered entries in the bibliography, below, pp. 539–58.

Biblical quotations are from the King James ('Authorised') Version of 1611, unless otherwise stated. Places of publication are given only if other than London or New York.

ACKNOWLEDGEMENTS

My foremost obligations are to the Trustees of the British Library for their permission to reprint Browne's prose from the original editions; to Faber and Faber Ltd for their permission to reprint the short essay 'On Dreams' from *The Works of Sir Thomas Browne*, edited by Sir Geoffrey Keynes (1964); and to Duke University Press for their permission to reprint extracts from *Coleridge on the Seventeenth Century*, edited by Roberta F. Brinkley (1955).

The preparation of this edition was substantially affected by several sustained studies of Browne (notably those by E. S. Merton in 1949, Joan Bennett in 1962, and Frank L. Huntley also in 1962) and the labours of the editors who preceded me in annotating one or more of his works (Dr Samuel Johnson in 1756,[3] Sir Sydney Roberts in 1927, and Frank L. Huntley in 1966, but especially W. A. Greenhill in 1881 and 1896, Norman J. Endicott in 1967, R. H. A. Robbins in 1972, and the utterly indispensable L. C. Martin in 1964). One of my greatest pleasures was to revisit the studies by Gordon Keith Chalmers, for they reminded me of his boundless generosity during my

---

3. If indeed he is the annotator of the edition of *Christian Morals* in that year. But it may well be that, while providing Browne's *Life* (below, pp. 481 ff.), he also contributed most if not all of the notes to the text.

undergraduate years at Kenyon College when he was its President.

In annotating Browne's prose I have often used extant translations. Even if I was sometimes impelled to make adjustments – especially in the translations of the Loeb Classical Library – I must acknowledge my obligation to the versions of: Aristotle, in W. D. Ross's edition (1910–1952); Cicero, by Walter Miller (1913), H. Rackam (1914), H. J. Edwards (1917), *et al.*; Hesiod, by Richard Lattimore (1959); Hippocrates, by W. H. S. Jones (1923–1931); Homer, by Richmond Lattimore (1951 and 1965); Horace, by B. J. Hayes and F. G. Plaistowe (1900), C. E. Bennett (1914), and H. Rushton Fairclough (1914); Josephus, by Ralph Marcus (1937); Justin Martyr, by Marcus Dods (1867); Juvenal, by Lewis Evans (1901) and/or G. G. Ramsay (1918); Lactantius, by William Fletcher (1871); Lucan, by J. D. Duff (1928); Lucretius, by W. H. D. Rouse (1937); Martial, by Anon. (in Bohn's Library, 1871); Minucius Felix, by Rudolph Arbesmann (1950); Ovid's *Metamorphoses*, by F. J. Miller (1916); Persius, by G. G. Ramsay (1918); Plato, by B. Jowett (4th ed., 1953); Plautus, by Paul Nixon (1916); Pliny, by John Bostock and H. T. Riley (1855); Propertius, by Walter K. Kelly (1854); Quintilian, by John S. Watson (1871); Seneca's tragedies, by Frank J. Miller (1917), and his *Moral Letters*, by E. Phillips Barker (1932); Suetonius, by Robert Graves (1957); Tertullian's *Resurrection of the Flesh*, by A. Souter (1922); Theocritus, by A. S. F. Gow (1953); Tibullus, by J. P. Postgate (1912); Virgil's *Georgics* and *Aeneid,* by C. Day Lewis (1940 and 1952), and his *Eclogues*, by T. F. Royds (1922); Xenophon, by E. C. Marchant (1923); and others.

I should finally like to record my gratitude to the staffs of the British Library, the New York Public Library, and the libraries at the University of York and New York University, for their manifold courtesies and unfailing assistance; to the authorities of New York University who in appointing me Berg Professor of English Literature for the autumn of 1974 enabled me to gain access to their city's vast resources; to Mr R. H. A. Robbins of the University of Sheffield who generously allowed me access to several notes from his forthcoming edition of *Pseudodoxia Epidemica* for the Clarendon Press; to Professors Dorothy Finkelstein of Yale University and Jason Rosenblatt of Georgetown University who lent me their knowledge of Hebrew on two occasions; to Miss Ruth Ellison of the University of York who clarified for me a number of details involving Scandinavian lore; and to Mr William Sulkin who welcomed this volume on behalf of Penguin Books and warmly supported its publication.

Yet I must end where I should have begun, with an acknowledgement of the indispensable advice of three friends in particular: Professors Frank L. Huntley of the University of Michigan and Joan Webber of the University of Washington, who suggested any number of changes which I promptly accepted, and Mr C. B. L. Barr of the York Minster Library, who by readily placing at my disposal his impressive knowledge shed abundant light on numerous passages in Latin.

University of York,   C.A.P.
1 January 1976

AN OUTLINE OF BROWNE'S LIFE

WITHIN THE CONTEXT OF
CONTEMPORARY EVENTS

[Browne thus summarized his life in a letter to John Aubrey on 14 March 1672/3:

I was borne in St Michaels Cheap in London, went to schoole at Winchester Colledge, then went to Oxford, spent some yeares in forreign parts, was admitted to bee a *Socius Honorarius* [Honorary Fellow] of the Colledge of Physitians in London. Knighted September, 1671, when the King, Queen and Court came to Norwich. Writt *Religio Medici* in English, wch was since translated into Latin [1644], French [1668], Italian [?], High and low Duch [1665]. *Pseudoxia Epidemica, or Enquiries into common and vulgar Errors,* translated into Duch 4 or 5 yeares ago [i.e. 1668]. *Hydriotaphia, or Urne buriall. Hortus Cyri, or de Quincunce.* Have some miscellaneous tracts which may bee published. (*K,* IV, 376)

See also Dr Johnson's *Life,* below, pp. 481ff.]

THE REIGN OF JAMES I (1603–1625)

1605   19 October: Browne born, the third child and first son of Thomas Browne, mercer. The Gunpowder Plot. *King Lear* first (?) acted. Bacon's *Advancement of Learning* published.

1606   *Macbeth,* Jonson's *Volpone* and Tourneur's *Revenger's Tragedy* first (?) acted. Corneille born.

1608   Milton born. Robert Cecil created Earl of Salisbury, appointed Lord Treasurer. Sylvester's translation of Du Bartas: 1st complete edition.

1609   Spenser's *Faerie Queene:* 1st folio edition. Shakespeare's *Sonnets* published.

1610   Jonson's *Alchemist* first acted; also Shakespeare's *Winter's Tale* (1611?). Galileo reports on his telescopic view of the heavens.

1611   George Abbot appointed Archbishop. The King James ('Authorised') Version of the Bible published. *The Tempest* first (?) acted. Chapman's *Iliad* completed.

1612   Death of the heir apparent Prince Henry; also of Salisbury. Robert Carr, later Earl of Somerset, in favour.

1613   Browne's father dies; his mother marries Sir Thomas Dutton

(1614?). Princess Elizabeth marries Frederick Elector Palatine. Sir Thomas Overbury murdered. Crashaw and Jeremy Taylor born.

1614 Ralegh's *History of the World* published. Webster's *Duchess of Malfi* first (?) acted.

1615 George Villiers, later Duke of Buckingham, in favour.

1616 Browne admitted to Winchester College. Death of Shakespeare. Jonson's *Works* published.

1618 Ralegh executed. Bacon appointed Lord Chancellor. The Thirty Years War (to 1648).

1619 Kepler's *De harmonice mundi* published.

1620 Settlement of first New England colony by the Pilgrim Fathers. Bacon's *Novum organum* published.

1621 Bacon impeached. Donne appointed Dean of St Paul's. Burton's *Anatomy of Melancholy* published. Marvell and La Fontaine born.

1622 Henry Vaughan and Molière born.

1623 Browne matriculated at Broadgates Hall, Oxford (i.e. Pembroke College from 1624). The 1st Shakespeare Folio published. Pascal born.

1624 Cardinal Richelieu chief minister in France.

THE REIGN OF CHARLES I (1625–1649)

1625 Death of James I; accession of Charles I who marries Henrietta Maria of France. Outbreak of the plague. Death of Webster.

1626 Browne admitted to the Degree of Bachelor of Arts at Oxford. Death of Bacon and Lancelot Andrewes. John Aubrey born.

1628 The Petition of Right. Buckingham assassinated. William Harvey's discovery of the circulation of the blood published. Bunyan born. Death of Malherbe.

1629 Browne admitted to the Degree of Master of Arts at Oxford; visits Ireland. Lancelot Andrewes's *XCVI Sermons* published. Emigrations to New England (1629 ff.).

1630 Browne departs for studies at Montpellier, Padua and Leyden (1629? 1631?). Prince Charles (later Charles II) born.

1631 Death of Donne. Dryden born.

1632 Galileo's *Dialogues concerning the Two Principal Systems of the World* published. Sir Christopher Wren, John Locke and Spinoza born.

1633 Browne admitted to the M.D. at Leyden; medical appren-
ticeship in Oxfordshire (to 1637). William Laud appointed
Archbishop. Donne's *Poems* published. Death of Herbert:
The Temple published.

1636 Advent of Cambridge Platonism (1636 ff.).

1637 Browne incorporated M.D. at Oxford, settles at Norwich.
Milton's *Masque* ('Comus') published; also Descartes's *Discourse on Method*. Death of Jonson.

1638 Milton's *Lycidas* published.

1639 First Bishops' War. Racine born.

1640 Donne's *LXXX Sermons* published. Death of Burton.
Wycherley born.

1641 Browne marries Dorothy Mileham. Second Bishops' War.
The Long Parliament (to 1660). Laud and Strafford im-
peached. Irish Rebellion. The 'Grand Remonstrance' issued.
Joseph Hall appointed Bishop of Norwich; defends epis-
copacy against Milton.

1642 *Religio Medici*: 1st and 2nd unauthorised editions; Sir
Kenelm Digby's *Observations* composed (published 1643).
Browne's son Edward born, the first of twelve children.
Charles I raises his standard at Nottingham: the Civil War
begins. Theatres closed. Death of Galileo. Newton born.

1643 *Religio Medici*: 1st authorised edition. The Westminster
Assembly of Divines. 'Solemn League and Covenant'.

1644 Milton's *Areopagitica* published.

1645 Alexander Ross attacks *Religio Medici* in *Medicus Medicatus*.
Laud executed. Rise of the New Model Army. Milton's
'minor poems' published.

1646 *Pseudodoxia Epidemica* published; also Crashaw's *Steps to the
Temple*. Episcopacy abolished.

1647 Parliamentary army occupies London.

1648 Peace of Westphalia; end of the Thirty Years War.

1649 Execution of Charles I; abolition of the monarchy and the
House of Lords. Charles II, proclaimed in Scotland,
escapes to France in 1651. Death of Crashaw.

THE INTERREGNUM (1649–1660)

1649 The Irish Rebellion crushed by Cromwell.

1650 *Pseudodoxia Epidemica*: 2nd revised edition (others in 1658,
1659, 1672).

1651 Hobbes's *Leviathan* published.

1653   The Protectorate established under Cromwell. Izaac Walton's *Compleat Angler* published.

1656   Death of Joseph Hall.

1657   Death of William Harvey.

1658   *Hydriotaphia* and *The Garden of Cypress* published. Death of Cromwell; the Protectorate passes to his son Richard.

1659   Richard Cromwell obliged to abdicate; the Protectorate ends. Purcell born.

THE REIGN OF CHARLES II (1660–1685)

1660   Charles II is recalled by Parliament. The House of Lords restored. The theatres reopened. The Royal Society founded. Defoe born.

1661   The Cavalier Parliament (to 1679). Louis XIV assumes full powers in France. Death of Saint-Amant.

1662   'Act of Uniformity'. Death of Pascal.

1664   Browne elected Fellow of the Royal College of Physicians; testifies at the witch trial at Bury St Edmunds. Vanbrugh born.

1665   Outbreak of the Great Plague (to early 1666). Death of Sir Kenelm Digby.

1666   The Great Fire of London.

1667   Browne's son Edward admitted to the M.D. at Oxford, elected to the Royal Society. *Paradise Lost* published; also Thomas Sprat's *History of the Royal Society*. Death of Jeremy Taylor. Swift born.

1670   Congreve born.

1671   Browne knighted by Charles II at Norwich. Milton's *Paradise Regained* and *Samson Agonistes* published. Shaftesbury born.

1672   Addison, Steele born.

1673   Death of Molière.

1674   Death of Milton, Herrick, Traherne.

1677   Dryden's *All for Love* first performed. Death of Spinoza.

1678   The fictitious 'Popish Plot'. Bunyan's *Pilgrim's Progress* published (Part II in 1684). Death of Marvell. Farquhar born.

1679   Death of Hobbes.

1681   Marvell's *Poems* published.

1682   19 October: death of Sir Thomas Browne on his 77th birthday.

[Browne's posthumously published works include *Certain Miscellany*

Tracts, ed. Thomas Tenison (1684); *A Letter to a Friend* (1690); *Posthumous Works* (with John Whitefoot's *Some Minutes for the Life of Sir Thomas Browne*, 1712); and *Christian Morals*, ed. John Jeffery (1716; with Samuel Johnson's *Life*, 1756).]

'ABOVE ATLAS HIS SHOULDERS':

AN INTRODUCTION
TO SIR THOMAS BROWNE

*he is a quiet and sublime Enthusiast with a strong tinge of
the Fantast, the Humorist constantly mingling with &
flashing across the Philosopher, as the darting colours in shot
silk play upon the main dye. In short, he has brains in his
Head, which is all the more interesting for a little Twist in
the Brains.*

Coleridge

I

IT was a remarkably uneventful life. Even the knighthood was
gained by default: for when Charles II on his visit to Norwich
in 1671 decided with his usual magnanimity to bestow a
knighthood on the city's mayor, the latter declined, Browne
was proposed as a substitute, and found himself a knight. Yet
half-way to that unlikely episode, Browne had already described
his life as 'a miracle of thirty yeares' – a claim dismissed by one
critic as a 'typically grandiose assertion'.[1]

But it may be that we have misread the 'miracle of thirty
yeares' as a statement of fact when it was intended in the way
Browne expressly delineates in the preface to *Religio Medici*:

There are many things delivered Rhetorically, many expressions
therein meerely Tropicall [i.e. figurative], and as they best illustrate
my intention; and therefore also there are many things to be taken
in a soft and flexible sense, and not to be called unto the rigid test
of reason. (*below, p. 60*)

Within *Religio Medici* the principle is reiterated in accordance
with the time-honoured theory that God has in the Bible 'so far
tempered the language of his utterance as to enable the weak-

1. James Winny, ed., *Religio Medici* (Cambridge, 1963), p. xvii. For
Browne's claim, see below, p. 153. Abbreviations in the notes are ex-
panded on p. 537; references in parentheses involving numbers preceded
by the symbol § (e.g. §19, §127, etc.) are to the numbered entries in the
bibliography, pp. 539–58.

ness of our nature to grasp and understand it'.[2] In Browne's
words,

unspeakable mysteries in the Scriptures are often delivered in a
vulgar and illustrative way, and being written unto man, are de-
livered, not as they truely are, but as they may bee understood.
(*below, p.* 117)

This approach is by no means characteristic of every sentence
penned by Browne. But to the extent that it is present in *Religio
Medici* in the first instance, it encompasses several implications
of fundamental importance. It suggests capitally that it is an
error readily to identify the narrative voice of *Religio Medici* with
its author, in that the thoughts and experiences recounted are
drawn less from any palpable 'fact' than from the equally pal-
pable life of Browne's imagination. In consequence, to eschew
the 'soft and flexible sense' might lead us – as it has led us – to
decline into reflections in diametric opposition to Browne's
actual intent.

The palpable life of Browne's imagination, I am suggesting,
deserves the same response we are habitually prepared to extend
to Marvell. Like Marvell, Browne refuses to be contained within
the narrow circumference we impose on him, 'the Humorist
constantly mingling with & flashing across the Philosopher'
as Coleridge sagely observed. The infinite undulations of
Browne's fertile mind dictate conclusions beyond mere
appearances, calling attention to issues further afield. As he
himself reminds us, 'Men that look upon my outside, perusing
only my condition, and fortunes, do erre in my altitude; for I
am above *Atlas* his shoulders' (below, p. 153). To ascend to
Browne's level is to sympathise with that over-enthusiastic
nineteenth-century critic who described him, with understand-
able hyperbole, as 'our most imaginative mind since Shake-
speare'.[3]

2. St Hilary of Poitiers, *De Trinitate*, VIII, 43; in *Nicene and Post-Nicene
Fathers*, 2nd series (Oxford, 1899), IX, 150. See also the formulations by
St Augustine and numerous Renaissance writers which I cite in '*Paradise
Lost* and the Theory of Accommodation', in *Bright Essence* (Salt Lake City,
1971), pp. 159–63.

3. James Russell Lowell, *Among my Books* (Boston, 1870), pp. 152–3.

II

Religio Medici – 'The Religion of a Physician' – was composed in the mid-1630s, and circulated for a time in several manuscripts before the publisher Andrew Crooke issued it in 1642 without Browne's permission. Less than distressed, Browne revised the clandestine edition and offered it to the same Crooke. Coincidentally, however, the unauthorised edition had been thrust upon Sir Kenelm Digby, 'the most accomplished cavalier of his time' according to Aubrey but (in Evelyn's judgement) 'an arrant mountebank'. Digby's hasty and rather pompous *Observations upon 'Religio Medici'* helped, initially at least, to advertise the original work. But *Religio Medici* soon commanded respect for its own sake, best evident in the array of imitations extending from *Religio Laici* – Dryden's poem as well as a treatise by Lord Herbert of Cherbury – to improbable works like *Religio Stoici*, *Religio Jurisprudentis*, and even *Religio Bibliopolæ*! (*BTB*, pp. 234 ff.). The favourable responses were indeed legion. They range from Aubrey's brief but eloquent remark ('Religio Medici . . . first opened my understanding') to the touching tribute of a Yorkshire poet in these thumping verses:

> I have not seen, (let me speak modestlie,)
> A finer Peice of Ingenuitie,
> Then in these Leaves laide out. When I survay
> This Bodie, I am rapt, and loose my way
> With wonder and Delight . . .[4]

But wonder and delight were, in some instances, rather limited. Oddly enough, Browne was even accused of being an 'atheist' – a term that in his time comprehended sceptics, agnostics, deists, and materialists.[5] Suspect among Catholics, at any rate, *Religio Medici* was placed on the Index of Prohibited Books three years

---

4. Aubrey, *Brief Lives*, ed. Oliver L. Dick, 3rd ed. (1958), p. xxviii, and *The Poems of George Daniel*, ed. A. B. Grosart (1878), I, 205; respectively.

5. Ernest A. Strathmann, 'Elizabethan Meanings of "Atheism" ', in his *Sir Walter Ralegh* (1951), Ch. III. See also D. C. Allen, 'Atheism and Atheists in the Renaissance', and P. H. Kocher, 'The Physician as Atheist', in their respective studies (§§ 1, 69).

after its publication; and equally suspect among extreme Protestants, it elicited an attack by a militant guardian of orthodoxy, Alexander Ross, whose tirades were hurled not only against Browne ('this may be indeed *religio Medici*, the religion of the House of *Medicis*, not of the Church of *England*') but against Bacon, Hobbes, and all the disciples of Copernicus.

Browne's response to Ross marks his difference from the approach of, say, Milton. Where Milton would have trampled Ross underfoot with iron sarcasm, Browne conducted himself in line with his disarming confession in *Religio Medici* that 'I have no Genius to disputes in Religion' (p. 65). Tolerant of the intolerant, he was like the Cambridge Platonists among the least contentious spirits in an age of violent strife, and among the least dogmatic in an age of aggressive and factious doctrine. Irenic by nature, he looked askance upon the claims of his contemporaries whose multiplied divisions seemed to him to undermine the Christian faith:

those who doe confine the Church of God, either to particular Nations, Churches, or Families, have made it farre narrower than our Saviour ever meant it. (*p.* 129)

True, *Religio Medici* gives the impression that its author was so detached from the upheavals of his age as to display less a disinterest than a lack of interest. Yet its preface supplies both the immediate context and the degree of personal involvement – 'the name of his Majesty defamed, the honour of Parliament depraved' (p. 59) – which Browne later elevates into a more general condemnation of 'the sinister ends of Princes, the ambition & avarice of Prelates, and the fatall corruption of times' (p. 62). The burden of the argument is borne by a personal predilection even as it was sustained by Browne's experiences on the Continent, especially his studies at Padua which, a generation after William Harvey had studied during the era of Galileo and the eminent biologist Aquapendente, was still 'famous for the Study of Physick' (i.e. medicine): cosmopolitan as it was liberal, sceptical of inflexible approaches, and consistently responsive to novel ideas. Closed minds at home would protest, and did protest, that 'we send our children beyond the Seas into *Fraunce, Italy, Spaine, Germany*; they returne not Englishmen from thence, but Frenchmen, Italians, Spaniards, Germans'.[6] But Browne would have regarded the charge as a compliment, providing *inter alia* one of the most good-natured passages in *Religio Medici* on the reprehensible culinary habits of the French (p. 133). Merely to observe the oddities of human behaviour is not very difficult, and to censure them easier still; but sympathetically to respond to multiform reality is the prerogative of the truly perceptive mind.

If the irenic disposition in *Religio Medici* could be misunderstood, so might the apparently sharp dichotomy between faith and reason. The reputed 'split' between the two[7] is certainly warranted so long as we confine ourselves to one or the other of Browne's explicit statements. Sometimes, however, one of the components in the expected opposition is quietly removed, e.g.: 'though there bee but one [world] to sense, there are two to reason; the one visible, the other invisible' (p. 104). The claim here that reason is operative equally in the physical as in the metaphysical realm, appears to contradict the role assigned to faith elsewhere. But might Browne have meant to alert us to the existence of a transcendent unity while we tend to compartmentalise human experience? For it is unlikely, we have been assured authoritatively,

It is unlikely that grace would prompt him to do one thing and reason to do another. Browne's definition of reason was not our modern one. The enlightenment left us with the view of reason as the principle of individual autonomy; for Browne, reason was *recta ratio*, first implanted by God in Adam, and still present, albeit less lustrous, in fallen man. Dimmed by the Fall, reason needs to be complemented by faith, and Browne considered it the mark of a wise man to walk in their combined light.[8]

Browne's 'reason' is the reality espoused by the Church Fathers at the invitation of the Neoplatonists, who held, according to

6. Thomas Scott, *The High-waies of God and the King* (1623), p. 60. On Padua as 'the intellectual capital of the world', see especially Stoye (§114); cf. Castiglioni (§26).

7. As averred among others by Willey (§128). See also §242.

8. John R. Mulder (§84).

St Augustine, that 'the light of the mind giving power to conceive all . . . is God that created all'.[9] Its actual description by Plotinus as 'something greater than reason, reason's Prior, as far above reason as the very object of that thought must be', is not unlike the 'Divine Sagacity' celebrated in the seventeenth century by Henry More the Cambridge Platonist, that is to say the dynamic power of mind to encompass 'the close connexion and cohesion' of the diverse aspects of the universe.[10] Granted, Browne does not always deploy 'reason' in this sense; but where he does, the term should be regarded as suggestive of the cosmic unity he constantly aspires to, a unity evident horizontally across the historical process, and vertically through the Scale of Nature.

The vertical dimension is well attested by Browne as by his contemporaries. Browne's formulation – 'there is in this Universe a Staire, or manifest Scale of creatures, rising not disorderly, or in confusion, but with a comely method and proportion' (p. 101) – appeals to the widely disseminated belief that all levels of existence are tightly knit through an elaborate hierarchical system of analogies and correspondences extending, it was said, 'from the Mushrome to the Angels'.[11] The scheme was vastly enriched by recurrent metaphoric associations with music and the circle, the one intended to sustain the persuasion that 'there is a musicke where-ever there is a harmony order or proportion' (p. 149), the other to confirm belief in the omnipresence of God 'whose center is every where, and circumference no where'.[12] Browne in resorting to these time-

9. *The City of God*, VIII, 7; trans. John Healey, revised by R. V. G. Tasker (1945). See further Robert E. Cushman, 'Faith and Reason in the Thought of St Augustine', *Church History*, XIX (1950), 271–94.

10. *The Cambridge Platonists*, ed. C. A. Patrides (1969), p. 13. The Plotinus extract is from his *Enneads*, VI, ix, 10.

11. Samuel Ward, *The Life of Faith*, 3rd ed. (1622), p. 2. See further Lovejoy (§77) as well as my extended article on 'Hierarchy and Order' (§94).

12. Quoted from the legendary Hermes Trismegistus (discussed later) in *Christian Morals*, below, p. 450. On the circle in Browne, see especially Huntley (§199), and in seventeenth-century literature: Nicolson (§86). On its wider manifestations – e.g. in architecture – consult the circular

honoured commonplaces, however, often transformed them into novelties by the unexpected twists in the course of their articulation. For instance:

I have ever beleeved, and doe now know, that there are Witches; they that doubt of these, doe not onely deny them, but Spirits; and are obliquely and upon consequence a sort, not of Infidels, but Atheists. (*below, p. 98*)

It is an astonishing utterance; but I think intentionally so. The logic is of the singular order so favoured by Browne: might not a denial of the existence of witches lead to a denial of the existence of spirits, and eventually of God? Smile though we may, Browne expresses his concern that to remove one rung from the Scale of Nature were to dismantle the entire scheme, and abrogate order. The intention, certainly, was by no means to harden hearts against the victims of misguided fanatics. 'We are no way doubtfull that there are wiches', he wrote elsewhere, 'butt have not been alwayes satisfied in the application of their wichcrafts or whether the parties under such affliction suffered from such hands'. Accordingly, when invited in 1664 to testify at the trial of two 'witches', he accepted that witchcraft was in evidence but ventured no opinion on the charge itself.[13] In theory and practice alike, his exclusive interest was to maintain the principle articulated in the penultimate paragraph of *The Garden of Cyrus*: 'All things began in order, so shall they end, and so shall they begin again; according to the ordainer of order and mystical Mathematicks of the City of Heaven' (p. 387).

The cosmic unity intimated vertically by the Scale of Nature, Browne also discerned on the horizontal plane of historical

---

patterns of Bramante's Tempietto of S. Pietro in Montorio, discussed and illustrated by Paolo Portoghesi, *Rome of the Renaissance*, trans. Pearl Sanders (1972), pp. 53 ff., and plates 17–20. The metaphoric import of music is delineated by John Hollander, *The Untuning of the Sky* (Princeton, 1961).

13. The quotation is from Browne's Commonplace Book (in *K*, III, 293). On the 1664 trial, and on Browne's views generally, see the bibliography (§§88, 187, 190; also Letts and Tyler, below, p. 547).

events. In broad outline, his approach is not distinguished by originality since it embraces another great commonplace of Occidental thought, the expressly Christian view of history as progressively apocalyptic of the Divine Purpose in a linear pattern enclosing all events from the creation to the Last Judgement.[14] Superficially observed, the pattern can be readily detected in the ever-expanding movement of the first part of *Religio Medici* that ends in 'those foure inevitable points of us all, Death, Judgement, Heaven, and Hell' (below, pp. 116 ff.). The same pattern also informs *Christian Morals,* for example the invitation to 'Look beyond the World, and before the *Æra* of *Adam*' (p. 425), as well as the memorable aphorism: 'The created World is but a small *Parenthesis* in Eternity' (p. 471). But as it is not Browne's adherence to a mere commonplace that matters, we should be cognisant of his simultaneous extension of it in a variety of directions and with an impressive opulence of detail. Perhaps most significant in this respect is his emphatic reiteration of the contrast between time which we aspire to comprehend, and the Eternal Present which we cannot. *Christian Morals* again provides the appropriate aphorism: 'The Divine Eye looks upon high and low differently from that of Man' (p. 429). Imaginatively applied in *Religio Medici*, the generalisation issues in several resonant passages whose undulating rhythms suggest the excitement of the slowly apprehended conclusion, thus:

that terrible terme *Predestination*, which hath troubled so many weake heads to conceive, and the wisest to explaine, is in respect of God no prescious determination of our estates to come, but a definitive blast of his will already fulfilled, and at the instant that he first decreed it; for to his eternitie which is indivisible, and altogether, the last Trumpe is already sounded, the reprobates in the flame, and the blessed in *Abrahams* bosome. Saint *Peter* speakes modestly, when hee saith, a thousand yeares to God are but as one day; for to speake like a Philosopher, those continued instances of time which flow into a thousand yeares, make not to him one moment; what to us is to come, to his Eternitie is present, his whole

14. This tradition-bound view is expounded in my study (§93) to which I am much indebted here.

duration being but one permanent point without succession, parts, flux, or division. (*pp. 72-3*)

Browne was utterly fascinated by the concept of the Eternal Present. After its initial formulation here, he indulges in a number of paradoxical utterances which cumulatively assert the concept by upholding the unity of the created order in the omniscient eyes of God. On such occasions the tone rises steadily as Browne's serene assurance in his own election yields to a triumphant proclamation of the contemporaneity of all events:

That which is the cause of my election, I hold to be the cause of my salvation, which was the mercy, and beneplacit of God, before I was, or the foundation of the world. *Before Abraham was, I am*, is the saying of Christ, yet is it true in some sense if I say it of my selfe, for I was not onely before my selfe, but *Adam*, that is, in the Idea of God, and the decree of that Synod held from all Eternity. And in this sense, I say, the world was before the Creation, and at an end before it had a beginning; and thus was I dead before I was alive, though my grave be *England*, my dying place was Paradise, and *Eve* miscarried of mee before she conceiv'd of *Cain*. (*pp. 131-32*)

But the vision of the confluence of what is past and passing and to come, is not the prerogative solely of the omniscient God. The same comprehensive awareness is shared by the narrator on the model of the traditional association of the creative artist and the creating Word, the Divine Logos. Just as 'God beholds all things' (p. 124), so the narrator penetrates beyond history's cunning passages to discern the pattern of time-bound yet time-less moments within the historical process, and without. Within, the sequential moments unfold in a straight line toward 'that one day, that shall include and comprehend all that went before it, wherein as in the last scene, all the Actors must enter to compleate and make up the Catastrophe of this great peece' (p. 119). Without, the artist transcends mere logic (itself a sequential mode of thought) to behold the entire play when, and especially when, time is suspended in the serenity of a nocturnal apprehension: 'I close mine eyes in security, content to take my leave of the Sunne, and sleepe unto the resurrection' (p. 157).

'I was', we have seen Browne remark, 'not onely before my selfe, but *Adam*, that is, in the Idea of God'. The concept – echoed in the 'Ideated Man' of *Christian Morals* (p. 430) – compels us to suspect Platonism, and reach for our Plotinus. But Browne wore his Platonic cloak with casual abandon, preferring a disconcerting eclecticism where we would demand absolute consistency. His approach, however, is not unlike that of his contemporaries who had also fallen under the sway of the legendary Hermes 'the Thrice Greatest' (Trismegistus), the supposed Egyptian author of widely venerated works believed to have predated Plato although actually written in the second century A.D. The Jesuit scholar Athanasius Kircher in *Oedipus Aegyptiacus* (1652) suggested the nature of the Renaissance commitment, and its implications: 'Hermes Trismegistus, the Egyptian, who first instituted the hieroglyphs, thus becoming the prince and parent of all Egyptian theology and philosophy, was the first and most ancient among the Egyptians and first rightly thought of divine things'. This imaginative tradition of a 'primitive theology of the Gentiles' had already been formulated by the Neoplatonists of fifteenth-century Florence, notably Marsilio Ficino, who looked on Hermes as 'the first author of a theology' which, merging with Zoroastrianism, was inherited by Orpheus and Pythagoras among others to find its way 'entire' into the books of 'our Plato' – 'the divine Philosopher' of Browne's own statement (p. 325). Hence the summary of Henry More in lines which he mistook (as usual) for poetry:

> Plato's school
> . . . well agrees with learned Pythagore,
> Egyptian Trismegist, and th' antique roll
> Of Chaldee wisdome, all which time hath tore
> But Plato and deep Plotin do restore.[15]

15. *Psychozoia*, I, 4; in his *Philosophical Poems*, ed. Geoffrey Bullough (Manchester, 1931), p. 2. Ficino's formulation reads: 'Prisca Gentilium Theologia, in qua Zoroaster, Mercurius, Orpheus, Aglaophemus, Pythagoras consenserunt, tota in Platonis nostri uoluminibus continetur' (*De christiana religione*, Ch. XXII; in his *Opera* [Basle, 1576], p. 25). On the entire tradition see also the bibliography (§§72, 98, 107, 111, 123).

Browne's loyalty to 'Plato's school', at best tentative, centres on three concepts alike adapted to his temperament. The first, writ large in *Religio Medici*, transmutes the hieroglyphs of Hermes into so many symbols of the mysteries of the created order in accordance with the generalisation ventured in *Christian Morals*: 'The Hand of Providence writes often by Abbreviatures, Hieroglyphicks or short Characters' (p. 428). The second concept endeavours to account for these mysteries on the basic premise that God is a single entity while 'All others doe transcend an unity, and so by consequence are many' (p. 153). This in turn suggests that history from the creation to the Last Judgement and beyond, is the history of the diversification of the One into the Many: 'As at the Creation, there was a separation of that confused masse into its species, so at the destruction thereof there shall bee a separation into its distinct individuals' (p. 120). The third concept is the familiar one of the Ideas of God, interpreted by Browne along the lines sketched by one of his contemporaries:

Philosophers and Divines call the first Images of things, as they rise up from the Fountain of eternity in the bosome of this universal and eternal Image, *Ideas*. The *Idea*, in this sense, is the first and distinct Image of each form of things in the Divine Mind.[16]

Acceptance of this commonplace led Browne not merely to 'Ideated Man' but to the more comprehensive generalisation posited early in *Religio Medici* that 'this visible world is but a picture of the invisible' (p. 74). Utterly crucial to Browne's thought, it reverberates across his several works to inform the persuasion he voices in *Hydriotaphia* that 'Life is a pure flame, and we live by an invisible Sun within us' (p. 313). In *Religio Medici*, significantly enough, the concept is articulated in terms not of theology or philosophy but of art. The 'idea', he argues, defies annihilation in that it is by nature imperishable, not subject even to the terminal fires of the final conflagration; for 'to a sensible Artist' – that is to say the creative man of sense who perceives the truth – 'the formes are not perished, but withdrawne into their incombustible part, where they lie secure'

16. Peter Sterry, *A Discourse of the Freedom of the Will* (1675), p. 49.

(p. 121). The archetype here as elsewhere is always God, himself a 'Composer', 'an excellent Artist' (pp.149 and 79).

The concepts adapted from 'Plato's school' as well as the other patterns of thought in *Religio Medici* – the Christian view of history inclusive of the Eternal Present, the Scale of Nature, the confluence of faith and reason, the all-inclusive tolerance, the irenic disposition – all these merge into an eloquent affirmation of 'the close connexion and cohesion of things', 'the common harmony' said to permeate the created order in spite of the apparent 'Antipathies and contrary faces' (p. 146). The aspiration is far from unrealistic. Fully aware that to eschew paradoxes is to deny our common experience, Browne placed them centrally within his vision of coincident opposites,[17] itself not merely paradoxical but miraculous. Miracles, we should remind ourselves, were generally regarded as the acts of God performed 'above' or 'against' nature; but Browne resolutely maintained that everything is a miracle, 'the extraordinary effect of the hand of God' (p. 95). The attitude is firmly Augustinian: 'is not the world a miracle, yet visible, and of his making? Nay, all the miracles done in this world are less than the world itself, the heaven and earth and all therein' (*The City of God*, X, 12). Miracles and paradoxes are merely apparent. A higher reality absorbs both, arresting dualistic tendencies in the reconciliation of discrepancies 'unto both beings, that is, of this World and the next' (p. 452).

III

Pseudodoxia Epidemica – 'Vulgar Errors' according to its running title – was first published in 1646 and extensively revised five times to 1672.[18] Stylistically the revisions display an increasing

17. Cf. Nicholas of Cusa's *coincidentia oppositorum*, i.e. 'that coincidence where later is one with earlier, where the end is one with the beginning, where Alpha and Omega are the same' (*De visione Dei*, X; trans. E. G. Salter, 1960).

18. The present edition reprints extracts from the 2nd edition of 1650 but includes also a chapter which Browne added in the 3rd edition of 1658 (below, pp. 216–20).

devotion to a simpler form of discourse in order to conform, so far as it was possible for Browne to conform, to the acceptable style of the dawning scientific age; while thematically his periodic amendments and substantial additions suggest an un-failing commitment to the latest developments in several fields. The colossal work is testimony to Browne's breathtaking range of interests and stupendous learning. It hardly hindered him to have known 'no lesse then six languages' as he proudly states in *Religio Medici* (p. 147) – that is to say six *modern* languages (French, Italian, Spanish, Portuguese, Dutch and Danish), not to mention Hebrew and especially Latin and Greek. Thus forti-fied he advanced through a catholic range of interests which, amply confirmed in several posthumously published tracts,[19] include in alphabetic order: anatomy, antiquities, astronomy, Biblical scholarship, botany, cartography, chemistry, cosmo-graphy, embryology, folklore, geography, history and historiography, law, literature both English and Continental,[20] medicine, mineralogy, ornithology, philology, philosophy, physiology, rhetoric, seamanship, theology, travel literature, zoology – and no doubt others. Sir Thomas Browne was, it appears, curious.

The learning displayed by *Pseudodoxia Epidemica* is not exceptional to Browne, however. Jonson, Donne, Burton, Milton, Ralegh in his appropriately entitled *History of the World*,

19. *Miscellany Tracts*, 1683 (in *K*, III, 1–120). These include *inter alia* discourses on falconry, oracular utterances and prophecy, versification, geography, topography, and *Of the Fishes eaten by our Saviour with his Disciples after his Resurrection from the Dead*; also some botanical-philological-theological *Observations upon Several Plants mentioned in Scrip-ture*, as well as a discourse on the uses *Of Garlands* ('convivial, festival, sacrificial, nuptial, honorary, funebrial').

20. The extant *Catalogue of the Libraries of the Learned Sir Thomas Brown, and Dr Edward Brown, his Son* (1710–11) includes Spenser's *Faerie Queene*, Sidney's *Arcadia*, Drayton's *Polyolbion*, Jonson's *Works*, the plays of Beaumont and Fletcher, the poems of George Herbert, and Milton's *Paradise Lost, Paradise Regained* and *Samson Agonistes* (pp. 45 ff., 52 ff.). Continental poets are led by Virgil, Dante and Tasso. The total number of items in the catalogue is nearly 2,500; but one should add, I suppose, 'some hundreds of Sermons' which were among the works Browne's daughter Elizabeth read to him in the evenings! (*K*, III, 331–2).

alike share that spectacular breadth of knowledge represented on a lower level by Samuel Purchas's inability to resist the invocation of 'seven hundred Authors, of one or other kind' (the kinds: 'Sacred, Prophane, Learned, Unlearned, Ancient, Moderne, Good, and Bad').[21] Browne's attitude to his own countless authorities is eminently pragmatic, and certainly not indiscriminate. He cites them, it has been said, 'for purposes of confirmation as for those of confutation',[22] fully cognisant that the naturalist Gesner and the anatomist Rondelet are reliable witnesses but that Aristotle, for instance, may not be accepted without qualification. Browne's view of Aristotle coincides rather with Ralegh's ('I shall never bee persuaded, that GOD hath shut up all light of Learning within the lanthorne of *Aristotles* braines') than with Dryden's more sweeping condemnation:

> The longest Tyranny that ever sway'd,
> Was what wherein our Ancestors betray'd
> Their free-born *Reason* to the *Stagirite*,
> And made his Torch their universall Light.[23]

In *Pseudodoxia Epidemica*, accordingly, Aristotle is frequently and necessarily praised as a biologist even while he is corrected in the light of a 'singular discloser of truth' like William Harvey.[24] So, too, in *Christian Morals* he is extolled as the author of *Nicomachean Ethics*, yet everywhere else – for example in *Religio Medici* (p. 77) – he is reprimanded because of his exclusive concern with the visible order. In the understatement

---

21. In *Purchas his Pilgrimage* (1613).

22. Merton (§206). Yost similarly speaks of Browne's 'intelligent acceptance of authority' (§241).

23. Ralegh, *The History of the World*, ed. C. A. Patrides (1971), p. 72, and Dryden, 'To my Honou'd Friend, Dr Charleton', ll. 1–4; respectively. Aristotle's designation derives from his birthplace Stagira in Northern Greece.

24. *Pseudodoxia Epidemica*, Book III, Ch. 28 (in *K*, II, 265). Browne with even greater enthusiasm wrote in a letter in 1646: 'be sure you make yourself master of Dr Harvey's piece *De Circul. Sang.* [i.e. *Of the Circulation of the Blood*]; which discovery I prefer to that of Columbus' (*K*, IV, 255).

of John Smith the Cambridge Platonist, Aristotle was 'not over-zealous of Religion'.[25]

'Authority' is in any case the third pillar supporting *Pseudo-doxia Epidemica*, the other two being 'experience' and 'reason'. These, alike commended in *Christian Morals* ('Joyn Sense unto Reason, and Experiment unto Speculation' [p. 439]), involve in the main the approach endorsed with equal enthusiasm in *The Garden of Cyrus* as to 'sense and ocular Observation, which seems to me the surest path, to trace the Labyrinth of Truth' (p. 386). Browne's actual scientific contributions are hardly numerous since he may only be credited with the identification of 'adipocere' (in *Hydriotaphia*, below, p. 295, note 79), and possibly with the first experiments in chemical embryology.[26] But no matter; for Browne's stature as an experimental scientist should be measured not by any immediate practical results but, as in Bacon's case, by method. This is not to say that Browne's method is an extension of Bacon's, since the catalogue of 'vulgar errors' in *Pseudodoxia Epidemica* is only nominally a response to the 'calendar of popular errors' enjoined in *The Advancement of Learning*, their respective authors differing in temperament and therefore in aim.[27] Even so Browne shares with Bacon a commitment to that 'sense and ocular Observation' patiently progressing through prejudice and misconception towards the truth. Hence Browne's omnivorous curiosity in *Pseudodoxia Epidemica*, evident also in his several letters with which he pursued his son Edward across the Continent:

Take notice of the various Animals, of places, beasts, fowles, & fishes; what the Danow [i.e. Danube] affordeth, what depth, if conveniency offers, of mines, minerall workes &c. . . .

Beside naturall things you may enquire into politicall & the government & state & subsistence of citties, townes & countries . . .

observe how the Dutch make defences agaynst sea inundations . . .

(*K*, IV, 31, 36–7, 45)

25. *Select Discourses* (1660), p. 48; cf. *The Cambridge Platonists* (as above, note 10), *passim*.

26. So Needham (§214); but his claim is disputed by Bodemer (§273).

27. Bacon's influence on Browne, accepted by Howell and Thaler but especially by Chalmers (§§232, 275, 282), is denied by Merton (§206).

– and so on. Browne himself certainly practised what he preached, whether through his ceaseless reading and voluminous correspondence, his expeditions personally to examine a whale in spite of its 'abominable scent' (p. 219), or his studies at home amidst the collected rarities seen by John Evelyn in 1671:

[the] whole house & Garden [is] a Paradise & Cabinet of rarities, & that of the best collection, especially Medails, books, Plants, natural things . . . [and] amongst other curiosities, a collection of the Eggs of all the foule & birds he could procure.[28]

Many besides Evelyn were equally impressed, witness the munificent eulogies like Robert Boyle's commendation of Browne as a trustworthy naturalist.[29]

But the naturalist who responded to the scientific spirit in *Pseudodoxia Epidemica*, was also the believer who had penned *Religio Medici*; nor were the two experiences, for Browne, mutually exclusive. We tend as a matter of course to sever the scientific mind from the religious, thinking it odd that Boyle was at once a scientist and a theologian, that Newton advanced to the forefront of science even as he laboured over commentaries on the Book of Revelation, or that in Kepler astronomy cohabited with astrology, and mathematics with superstitious mysticism. But perhaps we have not yet perceived that scientists unite what we sever, and bind what we sunder, ever conscious as they are that appearances must by definition cohere in a higher reality. So Kepler in *Harmonices mundi* (1619) had no sooner formulated the third law of planetary motion than he exploded in praise of the music of the spheres, even as his discovery of the geometric patterns of the supralunar regions was merged with a celebration of the Creator as 'Geometriæ fons ipsissimus, et, ut PLATO scripsit, *æternam exercens Geometriam*'. The implications are clearly to be observed: as Einstein said, 'without the belief in the inner harmony of the world, there could be no science'.[30] For like reasons, I would

28. Evelyn (§329).

29. See Chalmers (§275).

30. Kepler is quoted from his *Gesammelte Werke*, ed. Max Caspar (Munich, 1940), VI, 299; and Einstein, from Cecil J. Schneer, *The Search for Order* (1960), p. 368.

submit, the earth-bound naturalist of *Pseudodoxia Epidemica* cannot be distinguished from the believer who in *Religio Medici* endorses the music of the spheres (p. 149) and in *The Garden of Cyrus* remarks at length on 'how nature Geometrizeth, and observeth order in all things' (p. 356). Style apart, Browne's assumption is the assumption of Einstein: 'God does not play dice with the world'.[31]

But temperamentally incapable as Browne was to treat a grave subject gravely, the irrepressible humourist flashes across the philosopher in *Pseudodoxia Epidemica* as he did in *Religio Medici*. He approaches man's boundless credulity not so much with censorious disapproval as with sympathetic understanding. The humour on such occasions is entirely good-natured, whether he examines the belief that the sun dances on Easter Day (p. 241), or 'the other conceit that a Peacock is ashamed when he looks on his legges' (p. 222). But where credulity leads to prejudice, and prejudice to injustice, it is another matter: thus, in arguing the implausibility that the Jews 'stinck naturally' (pp. 226 ff.), he remarks on their sheer numbers in order to conclude triumphantly: 'could they be smelled out, would much advantage, not only the Church of Christ, but also the coffers of Princes'.

In another respect, however, *Pseudodoxia Epidemica* responds to the very 'vulgar errors' it censures, especially the harmless popular beliefs now lovingly reiterated only to be dismissed. Implicit at the core of *Pseudodoxia Epidemica*, in other words, is a sense of qualified despondency because fabulous yet enchanting beliefs – that the beaver when hunted bites off its testicles, that the lamprey is endowed with nine eyes, that man alone possesses an upright stature, and so on – all these must be sacrificed on the altar of demanding truth. But if Browne upholds through his rhythms what he must condemn through 'sense and ocular Observation', the final impression is of a tension arising not from divided loyalties as from calculated ambiguities – ambiguities not unlike those inherent in Spenser's dissolution of the Bower of Bliss or Milton's dismissal of the pagan deities in the *Nativity Ode*, *Lycidas* and *Paradise Lost*. *Pseudodoxia*

31. Jeremy Bernstein, *Einstein* (1973), Ch. XVI.

Epidemica is a vastly learned contribution to scientific method-
ology; but it is articulated, all too consciously, in aesthetic
terms.

IV

Hydriotaphia and *The Garden of Cyrus* were published jointly in
1658. *Hydriotaphia* – 'Urn Buriall' according to its alternative
title – has withstood much praise articulated with extravagant
rhetoric. John Addington Symonds, for instance, hailed
Browne 'as one who improvised solemn cathedral voluntaries
upon the organ of our language in its period of cumbrous and
scholastic pomp'. No less impenetrably, Charles Lamb praised
Hydriotaphia thus:

When I look at that obscure but gorgeous prose-composition . . . I
seem to myself to look into a deep abyss, at the bottom of which are
hid pearls and rich treasure; or it is like a stately labyrinth of doubt
and withering speculation, and I would invoke the spirit of the
author to lead me through it.

Thomas De Quincey also multiplied Browne's sentences to
furnish this singular example of euphonious verbiage:

What a melodious ascent as of a prelude to some impassioned re-
quiem breathing from the pomps of earth, and from the sanctities of
the grave! What a *fluctus decumanus* of rhetoric! Time expounded,
not by generations or centuries, but by the vast periods of con-
quests and dynasties; by cycles of Pharaohs and Ptolemies, Antiochi
and Arsacides! And these vast successions of time distinguished and
figured by the uproars which revolve at their inaugurations; by the
drums and tramplings rolling overhead upon the chambers of for-
gotten dead – the trepidation of time and mortality vexing, at
secular intervals, the everlasting sabbaths of the grave![32]

Modern critics are less effusive but not necessarily more perti-
nent. One attempt to account for Browne's superbly modulated

32. *Seriatim*: Symonds (§228); Lamb, as reported by Hazlitt, in the
latter's *Complete Works*, ed. P.P. Howe (1933), XVII, 124; and De
Quincey (§§185, 174). De Quincey is expressly commenting on the
passage beginning 'Now since these dead bones . . .' (below, p. 306).

rhythms in *Hydriotaphia* terminates in the suggestion that its final paragraphs may have been composed in a trance ('Did Browne possibly take laudanum? It seems very likely').[33] But potential lotos-eaters should not take this advice to heart, lest they should write like De Quincey.

Hydriotaphia according to Emerson 'smells in every word of the sepulchre'.[34] So it does; but not exclusively. Occasioned by the discovery in a field at Old Walsingham in Norfolk of some forty or fifty urns, *Hydriotaphia* is a meditation immediately on death, and mediately on immortality. It becomes in consequence 'a trial of faith', as has been said, 'an ultimate submission to an experience beyond the power of reason to embrace – a final acceptance of a faith not too easily received'.[35] The work poses the problem of evil – the incomprehensible physical evil of death – to resolve it at last through 'the concord of well-tuned sounds' which, as in Milton's *Lycidas*, subsume death within the larger vision of immortality. The prospect of death did not alarm Browne unduly, partly because his profession made death a familiar companion, but especially because he discerned in the created order evidence – 'Abbreviatures, Hieroglyphicks or short Characters' – neither of death nor immortality but of both at once. In this sense faith and reason are not distinct entities since they are merged in *Hydriotaphia* as in *Religio Medici*, and even in the casual 'Notes on Natural History', e.g.:

In bay leaves commonly used at funeralls wee unknowingly hold in our hands a singular emblem of the resurrection, for the leaves that seeme dead and drie will revive into a perfect green if theire roote bee not withered, as is observable in bay trees after hard winters, in many leaves half, in some almost wholy, withered, wherein though the alimentall & aqueous juice bee exhausted, the radicall & balsamicall humor remaining, though in a slender quantitie, is able to resurrect itself agayne: the like wee have observed in dead & withered furze. (*K*, III, 385)

33. Peter Green (§193).
34. *The Journals and Miscellaneous Notebooks*, ed. W.H. Gilman and A.R. Ferguson (Cambridge, Mass., 1963), III, 219.
35. James M. Cline (§297).

Would it perhaps suffice to describe *Hydriotaphia* as a sullen dirge *and* a solemn hymn? But at times it is neither one nor the other but unexpectedly humorous. Communal cremations, for instance, prompt Browne drily to remark whether it were advisable 'unto eight or ten bodies of men to adde one of a woman, as being more inflammable'! (p. 302). Or again, with equal gravity: 'Christians dispute how their bodies should lye in the grave. In urnall enterrment they clearly escaped this Controversie' (p. 294). The humour of *Hydriotaphia* is intended to qualify the sombre reflections within the work but also, I believe, to anticipate the tone of its companion piece, *The Garden of Cyrus*.

The Garden of Cyrus is the ultimate test of one's response to Browne. Walter Pater among others failed it; for unable to perceive in what sense the elaborate arabesques woven about the five-sided quincunx look beyond themselves, he reprimanded Browne with untoward sententiousness: 'His chimeric fancy carries him here into a kind of frivolousness'. Coleridge, on the other hand, having unerringly remarked on 'the Humorist mingling with & flashing across the Philosopher', was positively ecstatic: 'O to write a character of this man'! But the most surprising endorsement was Dr Johnson's, his admiration as vast as Browne's nominal subject is inconsequential. It is, he declared, 'a perpetual triumph of fancy to expand a scanty theme'.[36] Yet Pater's difficulties are understandable. It taxes our resources, and certainly our patience, to discern the purpose of a work which reduces the entire created order to a rhomb in order to declare it quincuncial; which twice denies that it will indulge in questionable speculations, yet on both occasions does just that, at length (pp. 329 ff., 379 ff.); and which discovers with rising enthusiasm that the number five is 'the Conjugall or wedding number', not to mention that it encompasses *inter alia* the evidently cosmic import of 'five golden mice' (pp. 380, 383). What price ingenuity?

Upon consideration, however, *The Garden of Cyrus* will be observed to demand constant awareness of the 'soft and flexible

36. *Seriatim*: Pater (§218), Coleridge (below, p. 537); and Dr Johnson (below, p. 494).

sense' commended in the preface to *Religio Medici*. For here more than anywhere else, Browne the creative artist 'plays' in the elevated sense that God the creative Word was often said to play with the order he brought into being. The well-defined tradition was summarily stated by a major scientist we encountered before. Wrote Kepler:

as the Creator played, so he also taught nature, as his image, to play; and to play the very same game that he played for her first.[37]

The divine 'play' testifies to joy, the joy of the Creator as of the created order which in Browne's vocabulary is equivalent to 'recreation', a word he invariably deploys in its twofold meaning of creation anew, and of pleasure. Accordingly *The Garden of Cyrus* opens with a revelation of the quincunx,[38] adapted from one or two excruciatingly dull treatises on agriculture (see below, p. 328, note 28). Browne's predecessors, in other words, provided the formless matter out of which he – the creator – built a remarkable edifice. The quincunx itself carries the symbolic burden which Donne, much more conservatively, discerned in crosses:

> Look downe, thou spiest out Crosses in small things;
> Looke up, thou seest birds rais'd on crossed wings;
> All the globes frame, and spheares, is nothing else
> But the Meridians crossing Parallels.
>
> ('Cross', ll. 21–4)

But while Donne's crosses are merely clever, and in any case

37. 'Wie nun Gott der Schöpffer gespielet/ also hat er auch die Natur / als sein Ebenbildt lehren spielen / und zwar eben das Spiel / das er ihr vorgespielet' (*Tertius interveniens* [Frankfurt, 1610], §126; in *Werke* [as before, note 30], IV, 246, and in W. Pauli, *The Influence of Archetypal Ideas on the Scientific Theories of Kepler*, trans. Priscilla Silz in *The Interpretation of Nature and the Psyche* [1955], p. 172). The tradition is outlined by Hugo Rahner, *Man at Play* (1965); cf. Warnke on 'Art as Play' (§124).

38. The figure derives, we have been reminded, 'from *quinqueunciae* or five-twelfths of a unit of weight of measure, and was used by the Romans to denote an arrangement of five trees in the form of a rectangle, four occupying the corners, one the centre, like the cinque-point on a die, so that a massing of quincunxes produces long rows of trees with the effect of lattice-work' (§300: see also the diagram reproduced below, p. 323).

predictable, Browne's quincunx is not only ingenious but replete with surprises, all as unlikely as the joy they intimate is unmistakable. In tone and therefore in its implications, *The Garden of Cyrus* belongs with 'The Garden' of Marvell. Each waves in its plumes the various light, playfully concerned with the created order in such a way that the whimsicality sustains the gravity, much as the unexpected levity of the last stanza of *Upon Appleton House* does not undermine the sombre issues raised but confirms them. Browne's approach, like Marvell's, is ultimately Shakespearean.

The capital concern of *The Garden of Cyrus* is to establish, as already noted, 'how nature Geometrizeth, and observeth order in all things' (above, p. 37). Ostensibly, therefore, the work focuses on 'the orderly book of nature' (below, p. 360). At the same time, mindful that 'this visible world is but a picture of the invisible' (as before, p. 31), it strains to ascend beyond the world of appearances to the realm of ideal forms. The ascent is by way of the improbable quincunx, its actual existence maintained in such an outrageous fashion that eventually it suggests another reality altogether. Numerology also intrudes, not because Browne was among the 'ancient Numerists' he invokes but because he discerned in their efforts a substantial way to confirm order in general, and the Scale of Nature in particular. As Browne's numerological absurdities mount, we are obliged to abandon the tawdry details to seek the symbolic import of 'numbryng' which John Dee had commended in 1570 as essential to the structure of the universe. Such 'numbryng' unfolds, Dee had written,

by degrees, by litle and litle, stretchyng forth, and applying some likenes of it, as first, to things Spirituall; and then, bryngyng it lower, to thynges, sensibly perceived . . .: then to the least thynges that may be seen, numerable: And at length, (most grossely), to a multitude of any corporall thynges seen, or felt.[39]

39. From Dee's prefatory address to Sir Henry Billingsley's translation of Euclid's *Elements* (1570). Critics who espouse numerology have hesitated to enroll Browne in their ranks, aware that his laughter would undermine their efforts – witness the amusing reviews of their excesses by William Nelson in *Renaissance News*, XVIII (1965), 52–7, and Douglas

Zeal for particular numbers – including the number five which Browne pursues to extinction – should be suppressed. Particular numbers confine; but where numbers generally are regarded spiritually, they assist us to perceive the cardinal meaning of the 'mysticall Mathematicks of the City of Heaven' (above, p. 27).

The Garden of Cyrus raises still other problems. Why was it attached to *Hydriotaphia*, for instance? What conceivable relationship exists between two works which, though enclosed within one volume, are so patently different in both tone and thematic patterns? Browne himself provides a solitary suggestion. *The Garden of Cyrus* follows *Hydriotaphia*, he writes, in the sense that 'the delightfull World comes after death, and Paradise succeeds the Grave' (p. 321). Authoritatively explicated, the principle at work has been said to be 'nexus through contrast': the two works are related in that

the obsession with death in one, is balanced by the celebration of life in the other. So, too, accident is opposed to design, body to soul, time to space, ignorance to knowledge, substance to form, darkness to light, mutability to immutability.[40]

Hydriotaphia and *The Garden of Cyrus* are like Milton's twin lyrics 'L'Allegro' and 'Il Penseroso', save that Milton's order is reversed with almost mathematical precision. Better still perhaps, Browne's two works are alike analogous to *Lycidas*; for if in one sense *Hydriotaphia* subsumes the problem of death within the larger vision of immortality, as claimed earlier, in another sense the problem is resolved only in *The Garden of Cyrus* which predicates (much as *Lycidas* does in its concluding ottava rima) order restored, and assurance regained.

But so much for parables. It is time to attend to style.

Bush in 'Calculus Racked Him', in his *Engaged and Disengaged* (Cambridge, Mass., 1966), pp. 58–66.

40. Frank L. Huntley (§303). A similar problem is posed by Milton's joint publication of *Paradise Regained* and *Samson Agonistes* (1671) – now also solved, notably by Balachandra Rajan in *The Prison and the Pinnacle* (Toronto, 1973), pp. 82–100.

V

An expeditious reading of Browne may tempt us to conclude that his style is uniform possibly to the point of dullness. But a careful study of his works should confirm their multiformity, and especially the extent to which the style is invariably suited to the given occasion.

The quality is not unique with Browne. Several of his contemporaries share it: Milton in particular,[41] but also Ralegh, Donne, and even Bacon, who resorts to one mode of articulation in his essays (much amended in successive editions), another in *The Advancement of Learning*, and a third in his history of Henry VII. The few examples from Browne's extensive correspondence quoted earlier (p. 35) suffice to alert us to the striking contrast between the informality of his private correspondence and the carefully wrought nature of his published works. As much is evident in the light of his strictly professional advice, for example this prescription 'for a cough and rhume':

Take a frensh barley, and hartshorne, 3 ounces, of China root one ounce, Coltsfoot a good handfull, Eringo roots 4 ounces, one ounce of Liquorish, Rosemary 3 sprigs, Cowslip flowers a handfull, sweet fennell seeds half an ounce, Raysons sliced but not stoned a pound, Currance a quarter of a pound, honey 3 pints: boyle all these in 5 gallons of water and a pint over, boyle it to 4 gallons, then work it up with yeast, like beer, when it's boyled tunne it and after it's tenn days old bottle it up.[42]

Imagine how this unlikely material would have been shaped for *Pseudodoxia Epidemica*, or indeed *The Garden of Cyrus*! For Browne laboured mightily for the desired effect, deploying a tonal range remarkable by any standards. The formal patterns of *Religio Medici*, for instance, reflect in their variable rhythms the undulations of a mind almost theatrically assertive yet self-deprecating and utterly humble. The encyclopaedic *Pseudodoxia Epidemica*, on the other hand, sweeps in a sort of staccato

41. As I argue in the introduction to my edition of *John Milton: Selected Prose* (Penguin Books, 1974).

42. R.W. Ketton-Cremer, 'Sir Thomas Browne Prescribes', *TLS*, 2 November 1971 (p. 700)

rhythm through a multiplicity of commonplaces connected, if at all, by Browne's daedalian imagination. *Hydriotaphia* and *The Garden of Cyrus* also divide in tone even as they unite in conceptual thought; for the pensive rhythms of the one are eventually overwhelmed by rhapsodies, while the tonal range of the other tends constantly toward a joyous whimsey, however serious the underlying purpose. So, too, *A Letter to a Friend* and *Christian Morals* may share several pages of nearly identical pronouncements (cf. p. 415), yet those of the first are measured and contemplative, while those of the second are aphoristic and even sententious, terse to the point of curtness, and unremittingly didactic. Browne's prose is not expansively Ciceronian nor laconically Senecan. It is both, and neither.

The tonal range of Browne's works depends on 'parallelism' as much as on his creative diction. By parallelism I mean generally the construction of sentences in emulation of Biblical precedent, especially through the provision of 'doublets' whether involving approximately synonymous words (e.g. 'ubiquitary and omnipresent', 'Basis and Pillar') or reiterated phrases (e.g. 'the mysticall way of *Pythagoras*, and the secret Magicke of numbers', or 'the corruption of these times, and the byas of present practise' – and so on).[43] The consequence of Biblical parallelism is 'rhymed thought', thus:

> When there were no depths, I was brought forth;
> When there were no fountains abounding with water...
> > (Proverbs 8.24)

> What is man, that thou art mindful of him?
> And the son of man, that thou visitest him?
> > (Psalm 8.4)

> ... I desired mercy, and not sacrifice;
> And the knowledge of God more than burnt offerings.
> > (Hosea 6.6)

> I will put my law in their inward parts,
> And write it in their hearts...   (Jeremiah 31.33)

---

43. Below, pp. 104, 159, 73, 134. Browne's 'doublets' are fully discussed by Huntley and Warren (§§198, 234).

Browne's constructive response to the Bible's literary potential is in line with the conviction he states in one of his minor tracts:

Rhetoricians and Oratours take singular notice of very many excellent passages, stately metaphors, noble tropes and elegant expressions, not to be found or parallel'd in any other Authour.[44]

The claim, in itself suggestive of the ultimate influence on Browne's prose, is echoed by any number of his contemporaries who were not prepared to dispute Donne's categorical statement that David, to whose pen the psalms were traditionally ascribed, is 'a better *Poet* than *Virgil*'. However incredible in itself, this persuasion bore impressive fruit not only in Browne's prose but in Herbert's poetry.[45]

As Biblical parallelism served Browne's purposes in one respect, his creative diction did in another. Such diction is, nominally at any rate, Latinate in the extreme – witness the following example from his short tract 'Of Garlands', which introduces at least two Latin words into English and confirms the use of five more:

The Crowns and Garlands of the Ancients were either Gestatory, such as they wore about their Heads or Necks; Purgatory, such as they carried at solemn Festivals; Pensile or Suspensory, such as they hanged about the Posts of their Houses in honour of their Gods, as of Jupiter Thyræus or Limeneus; or else they were Depository, such as they laid upon the Graves and Monuments of the dead. And these were made up after all ways of Art, Compactile, Sutile, Plectile; for which Work there were στεφανοπλόκοι, or expert Persons to contrive them after the best grace and property.

(*K*, III, 49)

44. *K*, III, 4. While endorsing the general acceptance of the Bible's influence on Browne, I cannot accept the large claims often made (e.g. by §§193, 216) about the influence of Dante. Suffice it that Browne was intimately acquainted with Dante, as he was with the Elizabethan dramatists led by Shakespeare (§§231–2). If a direct influence must be sought, I would much rather emphasize that of 'le bon Rabelais'.

45. *The Sermons of John Donne*, ed. G.R. Potter and E.M. Simpson (Berkeley, 1959), IV, 167. On Herbert's response to the Bible, see my edition of *The English Poems of George Herbert* (Everyman's University Library, 1974).

But we must take care lest we describe Browne's diction as exclusively or even predominantly Latinate. The extract from 'Of Garlands' is not the rule but the exception, since Browne normally tends to balance polysyllabic words from the Latin with monosyllabic or disyllabic words of Anglo-Saxon origin, in the manner commended by Richard Carew in *The Excellency of the English Tongue* (*c*. 1595):

the longe words that wee borrowe, being intermingled with the shorte of our owne store, make up a perfitt harmonye, by culling from out which mixture (with Iudgment) you maye frame your speech according to the matter you must worke on, maiesticall, pleasaunte, delicate, or manly, more or less, in what sorte you please.[46]

The 'perfitt harmonye' of the confluence of Latin and Anglo-Saxon defines Browne's aim equally as much as it defines Shakespeare's, e.g.:

> this my hand will rather
> The multitudinous seas incarnadine,
> Making the green one red.
>
> (*Macbeth*, II, ii, 60–62)

The harmony produced by Browne's creative diction, and the modulation promoted by parallelism, are the basic elements of the larger rhythmical animation of his paragraphs, the crucial unit. Logically, it is true, Browne's paragraphs do not always cohere; and therefore we are entitled to protest that *A Letter to a Friend* is 'an ill-coordinated patchwork', or that the reflections in *Religio Medici* are arbitrarily disposed, 'arranged in the haphazard order of rumination'.[47] But the logic of Browne's paragraphs is the logic not so much of any sequential mode of thought as of dramatic literature. Coleridge who had read the annotations on *Religio Medici* by Sir Kenelm Digby ('a pedant in his own system & opinion'), correctly observed that Digby 'ought to have considered the Religio Medici in a *dramatic* & not in a metaphysical View – as a sweet Exhibition of character & passion, & not as an Expression or Investigation of positive

46. In Williamson (§171).
47. Bennett (§176) and Winny (as above, note 1); respectively.

Truth'.[48] As with *Religio Medici*, so with Browne's other works except the didactic *Christian Morals*: each encompasses several dramatic voices which are severally 'true', just as Shakespeare's characters persuade immediately in themselves, however different the general impact of their juxtaposition might be. In other words, cognisant though we must be of the single 'sweet Exhibition of character & passion', we are also invited to recognise that Browne plays 'in one person many people', all equally convincing because they are dramatically so, yet none permitted exclusive or final authority. To deny Browne's dramatically variable tonal range would inevitably oblige us to conclude that he examines human experience 'academically and from a safe distance', that 'he speaks as an amateur and a spectator, rather than as a participant'.[49] Browne is manifestly not Donne. Save that he shares with Donne the tendency surprisingly to juxtapose heterogeneous ideas,[50] his fusion of whimsicality and gravity is rather like Marvell's as noted earlier, while his syntactical complexity is much closer to Milton's blank verse. At the same time, Browne is like Donne – as Donne is like Milton and Marvell – exceedingly partial to dramatic literature which, they all judged, best externalises not positive truth but truth in its several concurrent manifestations internal to one and the same mind.

I have argued just now against the view that the reflections in *Religio Medici* are 'arranged in the haphazard order of rumination'. Yet the claim rather accurately describes not so much the consequence of Browne's design as his actual intent. The thoughts flow freely, *apparently* disconnected, in a manner akin to the stream of consciousness technique of the modern novel; and so far, therefore, we may speak of Browne's 'series of impressions or associations, closer to the way in which mental

48. Coleridge (below, p. 537).

49. Phelps (§219).

50. Dr Johnson sensed the point of contact instinctively, for his description of Browne's style as 'a mixture of heterogeneous words, . . . terms originally appropriated to one art, and drawn by violence into the service of another' (below, p. 508), is not unlike his remark in *The Life of Cowley* that in Donne and his heirs 'the most heterogeneous ideas are yoked by violence together'.

experiences actually take place'.[51] How consciously Browne pursued this effect can be gathered from the tintinnabulary echoes in *Religio Medici* which cumulatively intimate connections beyond logic. Thoughts which in one instance are expressed casually through a seemingly accidental phrase, are later reiterated with a backward glance to their first appearance. Thus the 'definitive blast' of the Divine Will in the passage quoted earlier (p. 28), is recalled in the subsequent assertion of 'the blast of his mouth' (below, p. 105); the hope that the narrator 'may outlive a Jubilee' or fifty years (p. 112), is eventually transferred to 'the great Jubilee' of universal history (p. 119); the hell within – '*Lucifer* keeps his court in my brest, *Legion* is revived in me' (p. 125) – is echoed in the later statement of 'that unruly regiment within me that will destroy me' (p. 152); and so on. As with the details, so with the overall structure. Part I of *Religio Medici* is wedded to Part II in that they are alike structured in the light of the three cardinal virtues, the first part more concerned with faith and hope, and the second with charity, in a distinct echo of the similarly twofold divisions of formal theological treatises like Milton's *De doctrina christiana*.[52] It is clearly less than accurate to maintain that *Religio Medici* has 'no clear sense of progression', or that its second part is 'an afterthought'.[53]

We are all, Browne asserts in *Religio Medici*, 'naturally inclined unto Rhythme' (p. 150). The generalisation, as so often in Browne, is 'meerely Tropicall', and should be accepted in 'a soft and flexible sense' (as above, p. 21). Applied to his prose, it suggests above all that its 'ordered sequacious reflections'[54] mirror a reality beyond appearances, the ultimate reality of cosmic order. In this sense Browne's style may finally be described as sacramental in that its several units inclusive of words are sufficiently allusive, emblematic or ideographic to

51. Adolph (§137).

52. Huntley (§198). So, too, the 'echo' in *A Letter to a Friend* is the epistolary art of St Paul; in *Pseudodoxia Epidemica*, it is the concept of the Scale of Nature; and so on.

53. Howell and Bennett (§§254, 176); respectively.

54. Bennett (§176).

suggest the divine through the profane. The attitude is in-debted in part to the Augustinian-Protestant view of a sacra-ment as *signum visibile gratiae invisibilis*, 'the visible sign of an invisible grace'.[55] But it was wholly transformed, for Browne, under the impact of the Neoplatonic concept of the Ideas of God which provided him with opportunities imaginatively to correlate words and The Word. Words as individual realities, and the form they are obliged to yield, are never accidental but determined – even predetermined – by the artist, exactly as The Word predetermined the shape and course of the created order. Moreover, just as The Word impressed variety upon the created order, so the artist introduces variable rhythms into his prose in order to reflect the infinite beauties of the visible world and, by extension, of the invisible. Language can of course mislead, and Browne often alerts us to its perils (e.g. p. 65). But his aim in prose, like Milton's in poetry, was to discriminate between unaccommodated language which hovers on the brink of chaos, and language committed as visible sign to 'ideated' rhythm. The one partakes of the cacophonous sounds of chthonian behemoth, but the other aspires after the ultimate harmony imposed upon the sacramental universe by the arche-typal composer.

VI

Browne's reputation has never suffered any serious setbacks. While Donne was ostracised by the end of his century as Milton was at the outset of ours, and Herbert was annihilated by piety as Marvell was by nescience, Browne has remained a constant and vital presence. We have had occasion to quote the favour-able judgements of Dr Johnson and Coleridge among others. But equally suggestive of the range of responses Browne elicits, is the reaction of Melville.

Melville's enthusiasm on first reading Browne was immense. For a time, indeed, his imitation of Browne's style bordered on ventriloquism; but in the end it was Browne's thought that proved of vital importance, for he found in it elements which reflected predilections innate to himself. He admired *Pseudo-*

55. *Apud* John M. Shaw, *Christian Doctrine* (1953), p. 294.

doxia Epidemica, for instance, because it merged the scientific
and the transcendental by exploding 'vulgar errors' even as it
'heartily hugged all the mysteries in the Pentateuch' – i.e. the
first five books of the Bible.[56] Even more tellingly, Melville is
said to have regarded Browne as a kind of 'crack'd Archangel!'[57]
The remark argues an imaginatively eclectic reading of Browne,
encompassing in particular an adaptation of the concept of the
Eternal Present ('The Divine Eye looks upon high and low
differently from that of Man' [above, p. 28]) to the demands of
Moby Dick. This adaptation centres mainly on Melville's inter-
pretation of the chapter on the spermaceti whale which Browne
added to the third edition of *Pseudodoxia Epidemica* (below,
pp. 216–20). For us, I expect, the chapter testifies to Browne's
vast curiosity and his insistence of the primacy of experimental
knowledge, 'ocular Observation'. But for Melville the crucial
factor was less the obvious difference in the sizes of diminutive
man and the immense whale ('this *Leviathan*') than the striking
contrast between the whale's massive head and its limited
vision: 'that strange composure of the head, and hillock of
flesh about it', on the one hand; 'the eyes but small', on the
other. The irony is of course writ large in *Moby Dick*,[58] yet it
may not have been intended by Browne who rather delighted
constantly to shift our perspective for the reasons he suggests in
Christian Morals:

Faces look uniformly unto our Eyes: How they appear unto some
Animals of a more piercing or differing sight, who are able to dis-

56. See Matthiessen and Vande Kieft (§§335, 340).

57. As remarked in a letter by Evert A. Duyckinck, 18 March 1848;
quoted by Davis (§327).

58. Cf. 'Far back on the side of the head, . . . you will at last see a lash-
less eye, which you would fancy to be a young colt's eye; so out of all
proportion is it to the magnitude of the head . . . Moreover . . . the
peculiar position of the whale's eyes, effectively divided as they are by
many cubic feet of solid head, which towers between them like a great
mountain separating two lakes in valleys; this, of course, must wholly
separate the impressions which each independent organ imparts . . . This
peculiarity of the whale's eyes is a thing always to be borne in mind in the
fishery; and to be remembered by the reader in some subsequent scenes'
(Ch. 74).

cover the inequalities, rubbs, and hairiness of the Skin, is not without good doubt ... If things were seen as they truly are, the beauty of bodies would be much abridged. (*below, p. 443*)

Here, of course, we are no longer in the world of *Moby Dick*: we are with Gulliver his travels. It need not surprise that so many diverse minds have responded to Browne; but it should, that many more have not.

Browne's catholic appeal may be attributed largely to his invisibility, an attitude he adopted as if by anticipation of the counsel of Joyce's Stephen Dedalus that the artist should remain 'within or behind or beyond or above his handiwork, invisible, refined out of existence, indifferent, paring his finger-nails'.[59] This is not to say that we are not conscious of a definite personality in each of Browne's works. Indeed we are; but that personality is by no means identical with Dr Browne of Norwich, witness his express reminder that he was ever 'above *Atlas* his shoulders' (as before, p. 22). The implied principle must have proved an awesome burden, for it meant the subordination of his personal tragedies to his artistic integrity, even such harrowing tragedies as the deaths of eight of his twelve children. It may well be that to be vexed by contraries, as Donne was, defines the human condition; but to experience those contraries and yet transcend them, is no less an accurate definition of that condition. Browne had seen the devil at high noon and averted his gaze because as an artist he trusted that the worst might return to laughter.

We protest because such a vision appears to negate reality. But where we might be obsessed with the problem of evil, and pain, Sir Thomas Browne explored with eager thought the equally complex problem of the existence of goodness, and joy. The diverse masks he assumes in his various works while play-ing 'in one person many people', confirm through their com-mon protagonist the central role he allotted to 'recreation'. So far, certainly, it could be said of Browne's prose what Robert Frost claimed of the figure a poem makes: 'it begins in delight and ends in wisdom'. The figure, Frost added, is the same as for love.

59. *A Portrait of the Artist as a Young Man* (1956), p. 215.

SIR THOMAS BROWNE

*

THE MAJOR
WORKS

Facsimile of the title page of the 1643 edition
of *Religio Medici*

à cœlo salus

A true and full coppy of that which was most
imperfectly and Surreptitiously printed before
vnder the name of: Religio Medici.

Printed for Andrew Crooke: 1643.

Religio Medici

[Composed in the mid-1630s, *Religio Medici* – 'The Religion of a Physician' – was first published in an unauthorised edition in 1642 (hereinafter abbreviated as *UA*) and in an authorised one in 1643. See also the discussion above, pp. 23 ff.; and for further bibliographical details: below, p. 551.

The editions of 1642 and 1643 have the same engraved title page, save that the authorised edition carries the additional statement 'A true and full coppy . . .' etc. The engraving shows a man falling headlong from a rock into the sea; but his fall is arrested by a hand issuing from the clouds, confirming the man's exclamation *à cælo salus* ('from heaven, salvation'). The engraver was William Marshall, who had already ventured the portraits for Donne's *Devotions* (1643), Shakespeare's *Poems* (1640), and Bacon's *Advancement of Learning* (1640), even as he later did the portraits of Milton for the Minor Poems (1645) and Charles I for the frontispiece of *Eikon Basilike* attributed to the executed monarch (1649).]

Certainly that man were greedy of life, who should desire to live when all the world were at an end; and he must needs be very impatient, who would repine at death in the societie of all things that suffer under it. Had not almost every man suffered by the presse; or were not the tyranny thereof become universall; I had not wanted reason for complaint: but in times wherein I have lived to behold the highest perversion of that excellent invention;[1] the name of his Majesty defamed, the honour of Parliament depraved, the writings of both depravedly, anticipatively, counterfeitly imprinted; complaints may seeme ridiculous in private persons, and men of my condition may be as incapable of affronts, as hopelesse of their reparations. And truly had not the duty I owe unto the importunitie of friends, and the allegeance I must ever acknowledge unto truth prevayled with me; the inactivities of my disposition might have made these sufferings continuall, and time that brings other things to light, should have satisfied me in the remedy of its oblivion. But because things evidently false are not onely printed, but many things of truth most falsly set forth; in this latter I could not but thinke my selfe engaged: for though we have no power to redresse the former, yet in the other the reparation being within our selves, I have at present represented unto the world a full and intended copy of that Peece which was most imperfectly and surreptitiously published before.[2]

This I confesse about seven yeares past, with some others of affinitie thereto,[3] for my private exercise and satisfaction, I had at leisurable houres composed; which being communicated unto one, it became common unto many, and was by transcription successively corrupted untill it arrived in a most depraved copy at the presse. He that shall peruse that worke, and shall take notice of sundry particularities and personall expressions therein, will easily discerne the intention was not publik: and being a private exercise directed to my selfe, what is delivered

1. i.e. printing. The 'perversion' alludes to the numerous anti-royalist pamphlets of the 1630s.
2. i.e. in *UA* (see headnote, above).
3. None of these related discourses survive.

therein was rather a memoriall unto me then an example or rule unto any other: and therefore if there bee any singularitie therein correspondent unto the private conceptions of any man, it doth not advantage them; or if dissentaneous[4] thereunto, it no way overthrowes them. It was penned in such a place[5] and with such disadvantage, that (I protest) from the first setting of pen unto paper, I had not the assistance of any good booke, whereby to promote my invention or relieve my memory; and therefore there might be many reall lapses therein, which others might take notice of, and more that I suspected my selfe. It was set downe many yeares past, and was the sense of my conceptions at that time, not an immutable law unto my advancing judgement at all times, and therefore there might be many things therein plausible unto my passed apprehension, which are not agreeable unto my present selfe. There are many things delivered Rhetorically, many expressions therein meerely Tropicall,[6] and as they best illustrate my intention; and therefore also there are many things to be taken in a soft and flexible sense, and not to be called unto the rigid test of reason. Lastly all that is contained therein is in submission unto maturer discernments, and as I have declared[7] shall no further father them then the best and learned judgements shall authorize them; under favour of which considerations I have made its secrecie publike and committed the truth thereof to every ingenuous Reader.

THOMAS BROWNE

4. Contrary.
5. Probably in Oxfordshire (§ 198) – *not* near Halifax in Yorkshire as often claimed.
6. 'that speaks figuratively, or by tropes' (Blount).
7. Below, p. 132.

RELIGIO MEDICI

THE FIRST PART

1. For my Religion, though there be severall circumstances that might perswade the world I have none at all, as the generall scandall of my profession,[8] the naturall[9] course of my studies, the indifferency[10] of my behaviour, and discourse in matters of Religion, neither violently defending one, nor with that common ardour and contention opposing another; yet in despight hereof I dare, without usurpation, assume the honorable stile of a Christian: not that I meerely owe this title to the Font, my education, or Clime wherein I was borne, as being bred up either to confirme those principles my Parents instilled into my unwary understanding; or by a generall consent proceed in the Religion of my Countrey: But having, in my riper yeares, and confirmed judgement, seene and examined all, I finde my selfe obliged by the principles of Grace, and the law of mine owne reason, to embrace no other name but this; neither doth herein my zeale so farre make me forget the generall charitie I owe unto humanity, as rather to hate then pity Turkes, Infidels, and (what is worse) Jewes, rather contenting my selfe to enjoy that happy stile, then maligning those who refuse so glorious a title.

2. But because the name of a Christian is become too generall to express our faith, there being a Geography of Religions as well as Lands, and every Clime distinguished not onely by their lawes and limits, but circumscribed by their doctrines and rules of Faith; To be particular, I am of that reformed new-cast Religion, wherein I dislike nothing but the name,[11] of the same

8. Keck noted the eloquent proverb: 'It is a common speech (but onely amongst the unlearned sort) *Ubi tres medici, duo Athei*' – i.e. of every three physicians, two are atheists. But the charge was a wild exaggeration (cf. §69: Ch. XII, 'The Physician as Atheist').

9. Scientific.

10. Impartiality.

11. i.e. Protestant.

belief our Saviour taught, the Apostles disseminated, the Fathers[12] authorised, and the Martyrs confirmed; but by the sinister ends of Princes, the ambition & avarice of Prelates, and the fatall corruption of times, so decaied, impaired, and fallen from its native beauty, that it required the carefull and charitable hand of these times to restore it to its primitive integrity: Now the accidentall occasion whereon, the slender meanes whereby, the low and abject condition of the person by whom so good a worke was set on foot,[13] which in our adversaries beget contempt and scorn, fills me with wonder, and is the very same objection the insolent Pagans first cast at Christ and his Disciples.[14]

3. Yet have I not so shaken hands with those desperate Resolutions,[15] who had rather venture at large their decaied bottome, then bring her in to be new trim'd in the dock; who had rather promiscuously retaine all, then abridge any, and obstinately be what they are, then what they have beene, as to stand in diameter and swords point with them: we have reformed from them, not against them; for omitting those improperations[16] and termes of scurrility betwixt us, which onely difference our affections, and not our cause, there is between us one common name and appellation, one faith, and necessary body of principles common to us both; and therefore I am not scrupulous to converse and live with them, to enter their Churches in defect of ours, and either pray with them, or for them: I could never perceive any rationall consequence from those many texts which prohibite the children of Israel to pollute themselves with the Temples of the Heathens; we being all Christians, and not divided by such detested impieties as might prophane our prayers, or the place wherein we make them; or that a resolved

12. The Church Fathers of the first five centuries, especially St Augustine, were the guiding lights of the Reformation.

13. Luther was a miner's son.

14. Mark 6.2–3 ('From whence hath this man these things? . . . Is not this the carpenter, the son of Mary . . .' etc.).

15. 'Resolvers' (Coleridge). Browne's adverse view of Roman Catholics is soon transformed into a tolerant attitude unique by any seventeenth-century standards.

16. Reproaches.

conscience may not adore her Creator any where, especially in places devoted to his service; where if their devotions offend him, mine may please him, if theirs prophane it, mine may hallow it; Holy water and Crucifix (dangerous to the common people) deceive not my judgement, nor abuse my devotion at all: I am, I confesse, naturally inclined to that, which misguided zeale termes superstition; my common conversation I do acknowledge austere, my behaviour full of rigour, sometimes not without morosity; yet at my devotion I love to use the civility of my knee, my hat, and hand, with all those outward and sensible motions, which may expresse, or promote my invisible devotion. I should violate my owne arme rather then a Church, nor willingly deface[17] the memory[18] of Saint or Martyr. At the sight of a Crosse or Crucifix I can dispence with my hat, but scarce with the thought or memory of my Saviour; I cannot laugh at but rather pity the fruitlesse journeys of Pilgrims, or contemne the miserable condition of Friers; for though misplaced in circumstance, there is something in it of devotion: I could never heare the *Ave Marie* Bell[19] without an elevation, or thinke it a sufficient warrant, because they erred in one circumstance, for me to erre in all, that is in silence and dumbe contempt; whilst therefore they directed their devotions to her, I offered mine to God, and rectified the errours of their prayers by rightly ordering mine owne; At a solemne Procession I have wept abundantly, while my consorts, blinde with opposition and prejudice, have fallen into an accesse of scorne and laughter: There are questionlesse both in Greek, Roman, and African Churches, solemnities, and ceremonies, whereof the wiser zeales doe make a Christian use, and stand condemned by us; not as evill in themselves, but as allurements and baits of superstition to those vulgar heads that looke asquint on the face of truth, and those unstable judgements that cannot

17. Corrected from: 'I should loose mine arme rather then violate a church window, demolish an image, or deface' (*MSS.*).

18. Memorial.

19. 'A Church Bell that tolls every day at 6. and 12. of the Clocke, at the hearing whereof every one in what place soever either of house or street betakes him to his prayer, which is commonly directed to the *Virgin*' (Browne marg.).

consist in the narrow point and centre of vertue without a reele or stagger to the circumference.

4. As there were many Reformers, so likewise many reformations; every Countrey proceeding in a particular way and Method, according as their nationall interest together with their constitution and clime inclined them, some angrily and with extremitie, others calmely, and with mediocrity, not rending, but easily dividing the community, and leaving an honest possibility of a reconciliation, which though peaceable Spirits doe desire, and may conceive that revolution of time, and the mercies of God may effect; yet that judgement that shall consider the present antipathies between the two extreames, their contrarieties in condition, affection and opinion, may with the same hopes expect an union in the poles of Heaven.

5. But to difference my self neerer, & draw into a lesser circle: There is no Church whose every part so squares unto my conscience, whose articles, constitutions, and customes seeme so consonant unto reason, and as it were framed to my particular devotion, as this whereof I hold my belief, the Church of *England*, to whose faith I am a sworne subject, and therefore in a double obligation, subscribe unto her Articles, and endeavour to observe her Constitutions: whatsoever is beyond, as points indifferent, I observe according to the rules of my private reason, or the humor and fashion of my devotion, neither believing this, because *Luther* affirmed it, or disproving[20] that, because *Calvin* hath disavouched it. I condemne not all things in the Councell of *Trent*, nor approve all in the Synod of *Dort*.[21] In briefe, where the Scipture is silent, the Church is my Text; where that speakes, 'tis but my Comment: where there is a joynt silence of both, I borrow not the rules of my Religion from *Rome* or *Geneva*, but the dictates of my owne reason. It is an unjust scandall of our adversaries, and a grosse error in our selves, to compute the Nativity of our Religion from *Henry* the eight, who though he rejected the Pope, refus'd not the faith of

20. i.e. disapproving of.
21. The council at Trento in Northern Italy (1545–63), and the synod at Dordrecht in Holland (1618–19), determined the theological horizons of Catholicism and Calvinism respectively.

Rome, and effected no more then what his owne Predecessors desired and assayed in ages past, and was conceived the State of *Venice* would have attempted in our dayes.[22] It is as uncharitable a point in us to fall upon those popular scurrilities and opprobrious scoffes of the Bishop of *Rome*, whom as a temporall Prince, we owe the duty of good language: I confesse there is cause of passion betweene us; by his sentence I stand excommunicated, Heretick is the best language he affords me; yet can no eare witnesse I ever returned to him the name of Antichrist, Man of sin, or whore of *Babylon*; It is the method of charity to suffer without reaction: those usuall Satyrs,[23] and invectives of the Pulpit may perchance produce a good effect on the vulgar, whose eares are opener to Rhetorick[24] then Logick, yet doe they in no wise confirme the faith of wiser beleevers, who know that a good cause needs not to be patron'd by a passion, but can sustaine it selfe upon a temperate dispute.

6. I could never divide my selfe from any man upon the difference of an opinion, or be angry with his judgement for not agreeing with mee in that, from which perhaps within a few dayes I should dissent my selfe: I have no Genius to disputes in Religion,[25] and have often thought it wisedome to decline them, especially upon a disadvantage, or when the cause of truth might suffer in the weaknesse of my patronage: where wee desire to be informed, 'tis good to contest with men above our selves; but to confirme and establish our opinions, 'tis best to argue with judgements below our own, that the frequent spoyles and victories over their reasons may settle in our selves an esteeme, and confirmed opinion of our owne. Every man is not a proper Champion for Truth, nor fit to take up the Gantlet in the cause of Veritie: Many from the ignorance of these Maximes, and an inconsiderate zeale unto Truth, have too rashly charged the troopes of error, and remaine as Trophees

22. 'In theire quarrells with Pope Paul the fifth' (*MSS. marg.*, in *M*) – i.e. when Venice was excommunicated in 1606 for repudiating papal authority.

23. i.e. satires. See below, p. 408, note 96.

24. Consistently used in a pejorative sense, suggesting a distrust of mere language (§260).

25. On Browne's irenic disposition, see above, p. 24.

unto the enemies of Truth: A man may be in as just possession
of Truth as of a City, and yet bee forced to surrender; tis there-
fore farre better to enjoy her with peace, then to hazzard her on
a battell. If therefore there rise any doubts in my way, I doe for-
get them, or at least defer them, till my better setled judgement,
and more manly reason be able to resolve them; for I perceive
every mans owne reason is his best *Oedipus*,[26] and will upon a
reasonable truce, find a way to loose those bonds wherewith
the subtilties of errour have enchained our more flexible and
tender judgements. In Philosophy where truth seemes double-
faced, there is no man more paradoxicall then my self; but in
Divinity I love to keepe the road, and though not in an im-
plicite, yet an humble faith, follow the great wheele of the
Church, by which I move, not reserving any proper poles or
motion from the epicycle of my own braine; by this meanes I
leave no gap for Heresies, Schismes, or Errors, or which at
present, I hope I shall not injure Truth, to say, I have no taint or
tincture; I must confesse my greener studies have beene pol-
luted with two or three, not any begotten in the latter Centuries,
but old and obsolete, such as could never have been revived, but
by such extravagant and irregular heads as mine; for indeed
Heresies perish not with their Authors, but like the River
Arethusa,[27] though they lose their currents in one place, they
rise up againe in another: one generall Councell is not able to
extirpate one single Heresie, it may be canceld for the present,
but revolution of time and the like aspects from Heaven, will
restore it, when it will flourish till it be condemned againe; for
as though there were a *Metempsuchosis*,[28] and the soule of one
man passed into another 'opinions doe finde after certaine
revolutions, men and mindes like those that first begat them. To
see our selves againe wee neede not looke for *Platoes* yeare;[29]

26. Who solved the riddle of the Sphinx.

27. 'That looseth it selfe in Greece and riseth againe in Sicilie' (*MSS. marg.*, in *M*).

28. 'transmigration of the soules of men' (as below, p. 220). Cf. 'trans-
animation' (p. 467).

29. 'A revolution of certaine thousand yeares when all things should
returne unto their former estate and he be teaching againe in his schoole
as when he delivered this opinion' (Browne marg.). Cf. Plato, *Timaeus*, 39.

every man is not onely himselfe; there have beene many *Diogenes,* and as many *Timons,*[30] though but few of that name; men are lived over againe, the world is now as it was in ages past, there was none then, but there hath been some one since that parallels him, and is as it were his revived selfe.

7. Now the first of mine was that of the Arabians, that the soules of men perished with their bodies, but should yet bee raised againe at the last day; not that I did absolutely conceive a mortality of the soule; but if that were, which faith, not Philosophy hath yet throughly disproved, and that both entred the grave together, yet I held the same conceit thereof that wee all doe of the body, that it should rise againe. Surely it is but the merits of our unworthy natures, if wee sleepe in darkenesse, untill the last alarum: A serious reflex upon my owne unworthinesse did make me backward from challenging this prerogative of my soule; so I might enjoy my Saviour at the last, I could with patience be nothing almost unto eternity.[31] The second was that of *Origen,* that God would not persist in his vengeance for ever, but after a definite time of his wrath hee would release the damned soules from torture; Which error I fell into upon a serious contemplation of the great attribute of God his mercy, and did a little cherish it in my selfe, because I found therein no malice, and a ready weight to sway me from the other extream of despaire, wherunto melancholy and contemplative natures are too easily disposed.[32] A third there is which I did never positively maintaine or practice, but have often wished it had been consonant to Truth, and not offensive to my Religion, and that is the prayer for the dead;[33] whereunto

30. i.e. many cynics, and as many misanthropists.

31. The 'error' is mortalism, else psychopannychism; and widely disseminated as it was, obliged Calvin to write a treatise to refute it (1542). See §§18, 261, 272.

32. The second 'error' is known as apocatastasis ('restoration') – i.e. the eventual redemption of the damned inclusive of Satan. See §263.

33. Said by Jeremy Taylor in the seventeenth century to be 'at worst but a wrong error upon the right side of charity' (§343). Coleridge in annotating Browne observed: 'Our church with her characteristic Christian Prudence does not enjoin Prayer for the Dead, but neither does she prohibit it. In its own nature it belongs to a private aspiration; and being

I was inclined from some charitable inducements, whereby I could scarce containe my prayers for a friend at the ringing of a Bell, or behold his corpse without an oraison for his soule: 'Twas a good way me thought to be remembered by Posterity, and farre more noble then an History. These opinions I never maintained with pertinacity, or endeavoured to enveagle any mans beliefe unto mine, nor so much as ever revealed or disputed them with my dearest friends; by which meanes I neither propagated them in others, nor confirmed them in my selfe, but suffering them to flame upon their owne substance, without addition of new fuell, they went out insensibly of themselves; therefore these opinions, though condemned by lawfull Councels, were not Heresies in me, but bare Errors, and single Lapses of my understanding, without a joynt depravity of my will: Those have not only depraved understandings but diseased affections, which cannot enjoy a singularity without a Heresie, or be the author of an opinion, without they be of a Sect also; this was the villany of the first Schisme of *Lucifer*, who was not content to erre alone, but drew into his faction many Legions of Spirits; and upon this experience hee tempted only *Eve*, as well understanding the communicable nature of sin, and that to deceive but one, was tacitely and upon consequence to delude them both.[34]

8. That Heresies should arise we have the prophecy of Christ,[35] but that old ones should be abolished wee hold no prediction. That there must be heresies, is true, not onely in our Church, but also in any other: even in Doctrines hereticall there will be super-heresies, and Arians[36] not onely divided from their Church, but also among themselves: for heads that are

---

conditional, like all religious acts not expressed in Scripture, and therefore not combinable with a perfect faith, it is something between prayer and wish – an act of natural piety sublimed by Christian Hope, that shares in the light and meets the diverging rays, of Faith, though it be not contained in the Focus'.

34. The next section (#8) was not in *UA*.

35. Matthew 24.11: 'many false prophets shall rise, and shall deceive many'.

36. The disciples of Arius, who denied the divinity of Christ.

disposed unto Schisme and complexionally propense[37] to in-
novation, are naturally indisposed for a community, nor will
ever be confined unto the order or œconomy[38] of one body; and
therefore when they separate from others they knit but loosely
among themselves; nor contented with a generall breach or
dichotomie with their Church, do subdivide and mince them-
selves almost into Atomes. 'Tis true, that men of singular parts
and humors have not beene free from singular opinions and
conceits in all ages; retaining something not onely beside the
opinion of his own Church or any other, but also any particular
Author: which notwithstanding a sober judgement may doe
without offence or heresie; for there is yet after all the decrees
of counsells and the niceties of the Schooles,[39] many things
untouch'd, unimagin'd, wherein the libertie of an honest reason
may play and expatiate with security and farre without the
circle of an heresie.

9. As for those wingy mysteries in Divinity, and ayery
subtilties in Religion, which have unhing'd the braines of
better heads, they never stretched the *Pia Mater*[40] of mine; me
thinkes there be not impossibilities enough in Religion for an
active faith; the deepest mysteries ours containes, have not only
been illustrated, but maintained by syllogisme, and the rule of
reason: I love to lose my selfe in a mystery to pursue my reason
to an *oh altitudo*.[41] 'Tis my solitary recreation[42] to pose my
apprehension with those involved ænigma's and riddles of the

37. Temperamentally inclined.
38. Organisation. Also used of the divine government of the world.
39. i.e. medieval scholastic philosophy.
40. 'The inmost skin which incloseth the braine' (Bullokar). Through-
out this section, 'mystery' is used in its theological sense as 'a truth beyond
the reach of human reason but divinely revealed and hence a part of
human knowledge' (§ 260).
41. Cf. Romans 11.33: 'O the depth [in the Vulgate *O altitudo*] of the
riches both of the wisdom and knowledge of God! how unsearchable are
his judgements, and his ways past finding out!' The verse is quoted by
Bacon in *The Advancement of Learning*: 'in divinity many things must be left
abrupt, and concluded with this: *O altitudo sapientiae et scientiae Dei*!' etc.
(II, xxv, 13).
42. Browne invariably deploys 'recreation' in its twofold meaning of
creation anew, and of pleasure (§§ 31, 272). See above, p. 41.

Trinity, with Incarnation and Resurrection. I can answer all the objections of Satan, and my rebellious reason, with that odde resolution I learned of *Tertullian, Certum est quia impossibile est.*[43] I desire to exercise my faith in the difficultest point, for to credit ordinary and visible objects is not faith, but perswasion. Some beleeve the better for seeing Christ his Sepulchre, and when they have seene the Red Sea, doubt not of the miracle.[44] Now contrarily I blesse my selfe, and am thankefull that I lived not in the dayes of miracles, that I never saw Christ nor his Disciples; I would not have beene one of those Israelites that passed the Red Sea, nor one of Christs Patients, on whom he wrought his wonders; then had my faith beene thrust upon me, nor should I enjoy that greater blessing pronounced to all that believe & saw not.[45] 'Tis an easie and necessary belief to credit what our eye and sense hath examined: I believe he was dead, and buried, and rose againe; and desire to see him in his glory, rather then to contemplate him in his Cenotaphe, or Sepulchre. Nor is this much to beleeve, as we have reason, we owe this faith unto History: they only had the advantage of a bold and noble faith, who lived before his comming, who upon obscure prophesies and mysticall Types[46] could raise a beliefe, and expect apparent impossibilities.

10. 'Tis true, there is an edge in all firme beliefe, and with an easie Metaphor wee may say the sword of faith; but in these obscurities I rather use it, in the adjunct the Apostle gives it, a Buckler;[47] under which I perceive a wary combatant may lie invulnerable. Since I was of understanding to know we knew nothing, my reason hath beene more pliable to the will of faith; I am now content to understand a mystery without a rigid definition in an easie and Platonick description.[48] That allegor-

43. 'It is certain because it is impossible' (*Of the Body of Christ*, V).
44. i.e. of the crossing of the Red Sea (Exodus 14.15 ff.).
45. John 20.29.
46. i.e. prefigurations of Christ in the Old Testament. Cf. below, p. 376, note 61.
47. St Paul in Ephesians 6.16 ('the shield of faith').
48. Browne consistently opposes 'definition' – a term suggesting limitations – to mysteries, metaphors, enigmas, and the like (§ 260). 'Platonick' is used not only in the sense of a generalised mystical abstraction; it sug-

icall description of *Hermes*,⁴⁹ pleaseth mee beyond all the
Metaphysicall definitions of Divines; where I cannot satisfie my
reason, I love to humour my fancy; I had as leive you tell me
that *anima est angelus hominis, est Corpus Dei*, as *Entelechia*; *Lux
est umbra Dei*, as *actus perspicui*:⁵⁰ where there is an obscurity too
deepe for our reason, 'tis good to set downe with a description,
periphrasis,⁵¹ or adumbration; for by acquainting our reason
how unable it is to display the visible and obvious effect of
nature, it becomes more humble and submissive unto the
subtilties of faith: and thus I teach my haggard and unreclaimed
reason to stoope unto the lure of faith. I believe there was al-
ready a tree whose fruit our unhappy parents tasted, though in
the same Chapter, when God forbids it, 'tis positively said, the
plants of the field were not yet growne; for God had not caused
it to raine upon the earth.⁵² I beleeve that the Serpent (if we
shall literally understand it) from his proper forme and figure,
made his motion on his belly before the curse.⁵³ I find the triall
of the Pucellage⁵⁴ and Virginity of women, which God
ordained the Jewes,⁵⁵ is very fallible. Experience, and History
informes me, that not onely many particular women, but like-

---

gests also Plato's direct implication in the mysteries here recounted: 'it is
not improbable, he learned these and other mystical expressions in his
Learned Observations of Ægypt' (below, p. 378).

49. The description of God as 'a sphere whose centre is everywhere,
and circumference nowhere' (Browne marg., quoted in Latin) is a time-
honoured commonplace frequently quoted during the Renaissance and
certainly much favoured by Browne (§199; cf. §98). On Hermes Tris-
megistus see above, p. 30.

50. '. . . that *the soul is man's angel and God's body* [according to Para-
celsus], rather than *entelechy* [i.e. the essence of actual being, according to
Aristotle's *On the Soul*, 412a]; that *Light is the shadow of God* [according to
Ficino], rather than *actual transparency* [as in *On the Soul*, 418b] . . .' The
statements demonstrate Browne's distaste for definitions (see previous
page, note 48).

51. Circumlocution.

52. Genesis 2.5 and 17.

53. Genesis 3.14 ('upon thy belly shalt thou go') was occasionally said
to imply that, before the Fall, the serpent went upright.

54. 'Maidenhood' (Coleridge).

55. Deuteronomy 22.13 ff.

wise whole Nations have escaped the curse of childbirth, which
God seemes to pronounce upon the whole Sex;[56] yet doe I
beleeve that all this is true, which indeed my reason would
perswade me to be false; and this I think is no vulgar part of
faith to believe a thing not only above, but contrary to reason,
and against the arguments of our proper senses.

11. In my solitary and retired imagination, (*Neque enim cum
porticus aut me lectulus accepit, desum mihi*)[57] I remember I am not
alone, and therefore forget not to contemplate him and his
attributes who is ever with mee, especially those two mighty
ones, his wisedome and eternitie; with the one I recreate, with
the other I confound my understanding: for who can speake of
eternitie without a solœcisme, or thinke thereof without an
extasie? Time we may comprehend, 'tis but five dayes elder
then our selves,[58] and hath the same Horoscope with the
world; but to retire so farre backe as to apprehend a beginning,
to give such an infinite start forward, as to conceive an end in an
effence that wee affirme hath neither the one nor the other; it
puts my reason to Saint *Pauls* Sanctuary;[59] my Philosophy dares
not say the Angells can doe it; God hath not made a creature
that can comprehend him, 'tis the priviledge of his owne
nature; *I am that I am*, was his owne definition unto *Moses*;[60]
and 'twas a short one, to confound mortalitie, that durst
question God, or aske him what hee was; indeed he only is, all
others have and shall be, but in eternity there is no distinction
of Tenses; and therefore that terrible terme *Predestination*,
which hath troubled so many weake heads to conceive, and the
wisest to explaine, is in respect to God no prescious[61] deter-
mination of our estates to come, but a definitive blast of his will
already fulfilled, and at the instant that he first decreed it; for to

56. Genesis 3.16.

57. 'when I have retired to the colonnade or the couch, I do not neglect
my true interests' (adapted from Horace, *Satires*, I, iv, 133–4).

58. i.e. time came into existence on the first day of creation, while man
was made on the sixth.

59. i.e. the awareness of God's incomprehensible ways (as in Romans
11.33, above, p. 69, note 41).

60. Exodus 3.14.

61. Foreknowing. But some MSS. read 'previous'.

his eternitie which is indivisible, and altogether, the last Trumpe is already sounded, the reprobates in the flame, and the blessed in *Abrahams* bosome.[62] Saint *Peter* speakes modestly, when hee saith, a thousand yeares to God are but as one day:[63] for to speake like a Philosopher, those continued instances[64] of time which flow into thousand yeares, make not to him one moment; what to us is to come, to his Eternitie is present, his whole duration being but one permanent point without succession, parts, flux, or division.

12. There is no Attribute that adds more difficulty to the mystery of the Trinity, where though in a relative way of Father and Son, we must deny a priority. I wonder how *Aristotle* could conceive the world eternall, or how hee could make good two Eternities:[65] his similitude of a Triangle, comprehended in a square, doth somewhat illustrate the Trinitie of our soules, and that the Triple Unity of God; for there is in us not three, but a Trinity of soules, because there is in us, if not three distinct soules, yet differing faculties,[66] that can, and doe subsist apart in different subjects, and yet in us are so united as to make but one soule and substance; if one soule were so perfect as to informe three distinct bodies, that were a petty Trinity: conceive the distinct number of three, not divided nor separated by the intellect, but actually comprehended in its Unity, and that is a perfect Trinity. I have often admired the mysticall way of *Pythagoras*, and the secret Magicke of numbers;[67] Beware of Philosophy,[68] is a precept not to be received in too large a sense; for in this masse of nature there is a set of

62. i.e. Heaven (cf. Luke 16.22).

63. 2 Peter 3.8. On Browne's partiality to the concept of the Eternal Present, see above, p. 29. The most important precedent is Boethius, *The Consolation of Philosophy*, Book V, Prose IV et seq.

64. In the sense of 'instants' (*MSS.*).

65. i.e. of the visible world, and of the invisible. Aristotle maintains the world's eternity in *On the Heavens*, I, 10–12.

66. i.e. the vegetative, the sensitive, and the rational. The argument extends Aristotle's discussion in *On the Soul*, II, 3.

67. Especially the number five (see *The Garden of Cyrus*, below, pp. 317 ff.). On the lore surrounding Pythagoras consult §56.

68. Cf. Colossians 2.8: 'Beware lest any man spoil you through philosophy and vain deceit, after the tradition of men'.

things that carry in their front, though not in capitall letters, yet in stenography,[69] and short Characters, something of Divinitie, which to wiser reasons serve as Luminaries in the abysse of knowledge, and to judicious beliefes, as scales and roundles[70] to mount the pinnacles and highest pieces of Divinity. The severe Schooles shall never laugh me out of the Philosophy of *Hermes*, that this visible world is but a picture of the invisible,[71] wherein as in a pourtract, things are not truely, but in equivocall shapes; and as they counterfeit some more reall substance in that invisible fabrick.

13. That other attribute wherewith I recreate my devotion, is his wisedome, in which I am happy; and for the contemplation of this onely, do not repent me that I was bred in the way of study: The advantage I have of the vulgar, with the content and happinesse I conceive therein, is an ample recompence for all my endeavours, in what part of knowledg soever.[72] Wisedome is his most beauteous attribute, no man can attaine unto it, yet *Solomon* pleased God when hee desired it.[73] Hee is wise because hee knowes all things, and hee knoweth all things because he made them all, but his greatest knowledg is in comprehending that he made not, that is himselfe. And this is also the greatest knowledge in man. For this do I honour my own profession and embrace the counsell even of the Devill himselfe: had he read such a Lecture in Paradise as hee did at *Delphos*,[74] we had better knowne our selves, nor had we stood in feare to know him. I know he is wise in all, wonderfull in what we conceive, but far more in what we comprehend not, for we behold him

69. 'Shorthand' (Coleridge). The metaphor – like the related allusions to letters, manuscripts, and books – is fundamental to the metaphoric structure of *Religio Medici* (§198).

70. i.e. ladders and rungs.

71. On this crucial generalisation – adapted from the 'Smaragdine Table' attributed to Hermes Trismegistus – see above, p. 31.

72. The ten lines immediately following (through '. . . to know him') were not in *UA*.

73. 1 Kings 3.9–10.

74. 'Know thyself' (Browne marg., quoted in both Greek and Latin) was inscribed on the temple of the oracle at Delphi. Browne, like most of his contemporaries, habitually associates pagan deities with the devil: see below, pp. 253 ff.

but asquint upon reflex or shadow; our understanding is dimmer than *Moses* eye,[75] we are ignorant of the backparts, or lower side of his Divinity; therefore to pry into the maze of his Counsels, is not onely folly in Man, but presumption even in Angels; like us, they are his servants, not his Senators; he holds no Councell, but that mysticall one of the Trinity, wherein though there be three persons, there is but one minde that decrees, without contradiction; nor needs he any, his actions are not begot with deliberation, his wisedome naturally knowes what's best; his intellect stands ready fraught with the superlative and purest Idea's of goodnesse; consultation and election, which are two motions in us, make but one in him; his actions springing from his power, at the first touch of his will. These are Contemplations Metaphysicall, my humble speculations have another Method, and are content to trace and discover those expressions hee hath left in[76] his creatures, and the obvious effects of nature; there is no danger to profound these mysteries, no *Sanctum sanctorum*[77] in Philosophy: The world was made to be inhabited by beasts, but studied and contemplated by man: 'tis the debt of our reason wee owe unto God, and the homage wee pay for not being beasts; without this the world is still as though it had not been, or as it was before the sixt day when as yet there was not a creature that could conceive, or say there was a world. The wisedome of God receives small honour from those vulgar heads, that rudely stare about, and with a grosse rusticity admire his workes; those highly[78] magnifie him whose judicious enquiry into his acts, and deliberate research into his creatures, returne the duty of a devout and learned admiration.[79]

75. Exodus 33.23.

76. Corrected from: 'the impressions of divinity hee hath left on' (*MSS.*).

77. Holy of Holies (in the Vulgate's version of Exodus 26.33–4): 'The holiest place of the Jewes temple, where the Arke was kept, and whither none entred but the high Priest every yeere' (Bullokar).

78. Corrected from 'onely' (*MSS.*).

79. The rest of this section was not in *UA*.

Therefore,
Search while thou wilt, and let thy reason goe
To ransome truth even to the Abysse below.
Rally the scattered causes, and that line
Which nature twists be able to untwine.
It is thy Makers will, for unto none
But unto reason can he ere be knowne.
The Devills doe know thee, but those damned meteours
Build not thy glory, but confound thy creatures.
Teach my endeavours so thy workes to read,
That learning them, in thee I may proceed.
Give thou my reason that instructive flight,
Whose weary wings may on thy hands still light.
Teach me to soare aloft, yet ever so,
When neare the Sunne[80]*, to stoope againe below.*
Thus shall my humble feathers safely hover,
And though neere earth, more then the heavens discover.
And then at last, when homeward I shall drive
Rich with the spoyles of nature to my hive,
There will I sit, like that industrious flye,[81]
Buzzing thy prayses, which shall never die
Till death abrupts them, and succeeding glory
Bid me goe on in a more lasting story.

And this is almost all wherein an humble creature may endeavour to requite, and someway to retribute unto his Creator; for if not he that sayeth *Lord, Lord; but he that doth the will of the Father* shall be saved;[82] certainly our wills must bee our performances, and our intents make out our actions; otherwise our pious labours shall finde anxiety in their graves, and our best endeavours not hope, but feare a resurrection.

14. There is but one first cause, and foure second causes of all things;[83] some are without efficient, as God, others without matter, as Angels, some without forme, as the first matter,[84] but every Essence, created or uncreated, hath its finall cause, and

80. The allusion is to the myth of Icarus whose wings melted on flying close to the sun. But equally relevant is the common pun sun/Son.
81. 'used for any winged insect, particularly a bee' (§198).
82. Matthew 7.21.
83. i.e. material, formal, efficient, final (Aristotle, *Physics*, 198a 23 ff.).
84. Chaos (as below, pp. 80-81), out of which the universe was created.

some positive end both of its Essence and operation; This is the cause I grope after in the workes of nature, on this hangs the providence of God; to raise so beauteous a structure, as the world and the creatures thereof, was but his Art, but their sundry and divided operations with their predestinated ends, are from the treasury of his wisedome. In the causes, nature, and affections of the Eclipse of Sunne and Moone, there is most excellent speculation; but to profound farther, and to contemplate a reason why his providence hath so disposed and ordered their motions in that vast circle, as to conjoyne and obscure each other, is a sweeter piece of reason, and a diviner point of Philosophy; therefore sometimes, and in some things there appeares to mee as much divinity in *Galen* his Books *De usu partium*, as in *Suarez* Metaphysicks:[85] Had *Aristotle* beene as curious in the enquiry of this cause as he was of the other, hee had not left behinde him an imperfect piece of Philosophy, but an absolute tract of Divinity.[86]

15. *Natura nihil agit frustra*,[87] is the onely indisputable axiome in Philosophy; there are no *Grotesques* in nature; nor any thing framed to fill up empty cantons, and unnecessary spaces; in the most imperfect creatures, and such as were not preserved in the Arke, but having their seeds and principles in the wombe of nature, are every-where where the power of the Sun is;[88] in these is the wisedome of his hand discovered: Out of this ranke *Solomon* chose the object of his admiration,[89] indeed what rea-

85. Galen's medical treatise, especially its paean to the wisdom of God (Book III, Ch. 10), was the first endeavour to relate medicine and religion. Similar efforts during the Renaissance included the treatises by Fernel (1548), Suarez (1597) – and of course *Religio Medici* (see §254).

86. The reference is probably to the treatise *On the Heavens* (§241). Browne regards Aristotle's singular concern with the world of sense as paradigmatic of the failure to grasp the mystery at the heart of the created order (§260). See above, p. 34.

87. 'Nature does nothing in vain' (Aristotle, *On the Heavens*, 271a; *Generation of Animals*, 744a36; etc.).

88. 'It was commonly held that small animals, such as flies and mice, were spontaneously generated by the action of the sun on decaying matter; and consequently these animals had not to be included in the six-days creation' (*M*).

89. Cf. Proverbs 6.6–8.

son may not goe to Schoole to the wisedome of Bees, Aunts, and Spiders? what wise hand teacheth them to doe what reason cannot teach us? ruder heads stand amazed at those prodigious pieces of nature, Whales, Elephants, Dromidaries, and Camels; these I confesse, are the Colossus and Majestick pieces of her hand; but in these narrow Engines there is more curious Mathematicks, and the civilitie of these little Citizens, more neatly set forth the wisedome of their Maker; Who admires not *Regio-Montanus* his Fly beyond his Eagle,[90] or wonders not more at the operation of two soules in those little bodies, than but one in the trunck of a Cedar?[91] I could never content my contemplation with those generall pieces of wonders, the flux and reflux of the sea, the encrease of Nile,[92] the conversion of the Needle to the North, and have studied to match and parallel those in the more obvious and neglected pieces of Nature, which without further travell I can doe in the Cosmography of my selfe; wee carry with us the wonders, we seeke without us: There is all *Africa*, and her prodigies in us;[93] we are that bold and adventurous piece of nature, which he that studies, wisely learnes in a *compendium*, what others labour at in a divided piece and endlesse volume.[94]

16. Thus there are two bookes from whence I collect my Divinity; besides that written one of God, another of his servant Nature, that universall and publik Manuscript, that lies

90. Regiomontanus was said to have constructed an iron fly and a wooden eagle, alike capable of flight.

91. Of man's three 'souls' or faculties (above, p. 73, note 66), plants were thought to possess only one (the vegetative) and animals two (the vegetative and the sensitive).

92. 'The flood was widely held to occur on precisely the same date each year' (R).

93. Probably a reference to Church Fathers like Lactantius, who was said to have been born in Roman Africa, and St Augustine, who was Bishop of Hippo in the same (§198).

94. 'This is the true characteristic of Genius – our destiny & instinct is to unriddle the world, & he is the man of Genius who feels this instinct fresh and strong in his nature – who perceives the riddle & the mystery of all things even the commonest & needs no strange and out of the way Tales or Images to stimulate him into wonder & a deep Interest' (Coleridge).

expans'd unto the eyes of all;[95] those that never saw him in the one, have discovered him in the other: This was the Scripture and Theology of the Heathens; the naturall motion of the Sun made them more admire him, than its supernaturall station did the Children of Israel;[96] the ordinary effect of nature wrought more admiration in them, than in the other all his miracles; surely the Heathens knew better how to joyne and reade these mysticall letters, than wee Christians, who cast a more carelesse eye on these common Hieroglyphicks,[97] and disdain to suck Divinity from the flowers of nature.[98] Nor do I so forget God, as to adore the name of Nature; which I define not with the Schooles, the principle of motion and rest,[99] but, that streight and regular line, that setled and constant course the wisedome of God hath ordained the actions of his creatures, according to their severall kinds. To make a revolution every day is the nature of the Sun, because that necessary course which God hath ordained it, from which it cannot swerve, but[by]a faculty from that voyce which first did give it motion. Now this course of Nature God seldome alters or perverts, but like an excellent Artist hath so contrived his worke, that with the selfe same instrument, without a new creation hee may effect his obscurest

95. The idea inclusive of the metaphor is a commonplace adapted to Browne's purposes. Cf. Humphrey Sydenham in *Natures Overthrow* (1626), p. 2: 'Man [is] the Epitome, and *compendium* of that huge tome, that great *Manuscript* and worke of nature, wherin are written the characters of Gods omnipotencie, and power'. See also below, note 97.

96. i.e. when the sun 'stood still in the midst of heaven' (Joshua 10.13).

97. Hieroglyphs, widely accepted as symbols of hidden moral and religious meanings (§135), were thought to have been instituted by the legendary Hermes Trismegistus (above, p. 30). Metaphorically affirmed as here, they were considered to be 'the understood language of the Almightie, whose Hieroglyphical Characters, are the unnumbred Starres, the Sunne, and Moone, written on these large volumes of the firmament: written also on the earth and the seas, by the letters of all those living creatures, and plants, which inhabit and reside therein' (Ralegh, p. 86). Cf. Romans 1.19 f.: 'the invisible things of [God] ... are clearly seen, being understood by the things that are made'.

98. 'All this is very fine Philosophy, & the best & most ingenious Defence of Revelation' (Coleridge).

99. Aristotle, *Physics*, II, 1.

designes. Thus he sweetneth the water with a wood,[100] pre-serveth the creatures in the Arke, which the blast of his mouth might have as easily created: for God is like a skilfull Geo-metrician,[101] who when more easily, and with one stroke of his Compasse, he might describe, or divide a right line, had yet rather doe this in a circle or longer way, according to the constituted and forelaid principles of his art: yet this rule of his hee doth sometimes pervert, to acquaint the world with his prerogative, lest the arrogancy of our reason should question his power, and conclude he could not; & thus I call the effects of nature the works of God, whose hand & instrument she only is; and therefore to ascribe his actions unto her, is to devolve the honor of the principall agent, upon the instrument; which if with reason we may doe, then let our hammers rise up and boast they have built our houses, and our pens receive the honour of our writings. I hold there is a generall beauty in the works of God, and therefore no deformity in any kind or species of creature whatsoever: I cannot tell by what Logick we call a Toad, a Beare, or an Elephant, ugly, they being created in those outward shapes and figures which best expresse the actions of their inward formes. And having past[102] that generall visitation of God, who saw that all that he had made was good, that is, conformable to his will, which abhors deformity, and is the rule of order and beauty; there is no deformity but in monstrosity, wherein notwithstanding there is a kind of beauty, Nature so ingeniously contriving the irregular parts, as they become sometimes more remarkable than the principall Fabrick. To speake yet more narrowly, there was never any thing ugly, or

100. Exodus 15.25.

101. A commonplace notion, based on the confluence of Plato (to whom the idea is attributed by Plutarch, *Symposiacs*, VIII, 2) and the apocryphal Wisdom of Solomon 11.20 ('thou hast ordered all things in measure and number and weight'). As William Bedwell noted in 1636, 'Plato saith, That God doth alwayes worke by Geometry, that is, as the wiseman doth interpret it, ... Dispose all things by measure, and number, and weight ... Now who, I pray you, understandeth what these termes meane, but he which hath some meane skill in Geometry?' (§69). See also below, pp. 343 ff.

102. Corrected from 'past with approbation' (*MSS.*).

mis-shapen, but the Chaos; wherein notwithstanding to speake strictly, there was no deformity, because no forme, nor was it yet impregnate by the voyce of God: Now nature is not at variance with art, nor art with nature; they being both the servants of his providence: Art is the perfection of Nature: Were the world now as it was the sixt day, there were yet a Chaos: Nature hath made one world, and Art another. In briefe, all things are artificiall, for nature is the Art of God.[103]

17. This is the ordinary and open way of his providence, which art and industry have in a good part discovered, whose effects wee may foretell without an Oracle; To foreshew these is not Prophesie, but Prognostication. There is another way full of Meanders and Labyrinths, whereof the Devill and Spirits have no exact Ephemerides,[104] and that is a more particular and obscure method of his providence, directing the operations of individualls and single Essences; this we call Fortune, that serpentine and crooked line, whereby he drawes those actions his wisedome intends in a more unknowne and secret way; This cryptick and involved method of his providence have I ever admired, nor can I relate the history of my life, the occurrences of my dayes, the escapes of dangers, and hits of chance with a *Bezo las Manos*,[105] to Fortune, or a bare Gramercy to my good starres: *Abraham* might have thought the Ram in the thicket came thither by accident; humane reason would have said that meere chance conveyed *Moses* in the Arke to the sight of *Pharaohs* daughter; what a Labyrinth is there in the story of *Joseph*, able to convert a Stoick?[106] Surely there are in every mans

103. So Dante in *Of Monarchy* (II, 2) speaks of *artis divinae* 'which men generally call Nature' (§187). But the claim encompasses in particular the traditional metaphor of God as a poet (§56).

104. 'a book of Astronomy (in use among such as erect figures to cast mens nativities) by which booke is shewen how all the Planets are placed, everie day and houre of the yeare' (Bullokar).

105. Literally 'I kiss the hands': a salute. The Spanish phrase anticipates the references first to the Gunpowder Plot reportedly encouraged by Spain, and next to the defeat of the Armada in 1588 (§198).

106. The Biblical references are, *seriatim*: Genesis 22.13, Exodus 2.3 ff., and Genesis 37.2 ff. A Stoic would be converted had he realised that 'fatall necessitie' proceeds not from fate but from the 'immutable Law' of the divine will (below, p. 86).

life certaine rubs, doublings and wrenches which passe a while under the effects of chance, but at the last, well examined, prove the meere hand of God: 'Twas not dumbe chance, that to discover the Fougade or Powder plot, contrived a miscarriage in the letter.[107] I like the victory of 88. the better for that one occurrence which our enemies imputed to our dishonour, and the partiality of Fortune, to wit, the tempests and contrarietie of winds. King *Philip* did not detract from the Nation, when he said, he sent his Armado to fight with men, and not to combate with the winds. Where there is a manifest disproportion between the powers and forces of two several agents, upon a maxime of reason wee may promise the victory to the superiour; but when unexpected accidents slip in, and unthought of occurrences intervene, these must proceed from a power that owes no obedience to those axioms: where, as in the writing upon the wall,[108] we behold the hand, but see not the spring that moves it. The successe of that pety Province of Holland (of which the Grand Seigneur proudly said, That if they should trouble him as they did the Spaniard, hee would send his men with shovels and pick-axes and throw it into the Sea) I cannot altogether ascribe to the ingenuity and industry of the people,[109] but to the mercy of God, that hath disposed them to such a thriving *Genius*; and to the will of his providence, that disposeth her favour to each Countrey in their preordinate[110] season. All cannot be happy at once, for because the glory of one State depends upon the ruine of another, there is a revolution and vicissitude of their greatnesse, and must obey the swing of that wheele, not moved by intelligences,[111] but by the hand of God, whereby all Estates arise to their Zenith and verticall points, according to their predestinated periods. For the lives not onely of men, but of Commonweales, and the whole world, run not

107. i.e. by means of the letter which, sent to Lord Monteagle, resulted in the discovery of the Plot. Cf. previous page, note 105.

108. During Belshazzar's feast (Daniel 5.5).

109. The 'successe' is the independence gained by the Dutch from the Spanish in 1609. The saying of 'the Grand Seigneur' – i.e. the Ottoman emperor – may be apocryphal.

110. Foreordained.

111. The angels who were believed to move the celestial orbs.

upon an Helix[112] that still enlargeth, but on a Circle, where arriving to their Meridian, they decline in obscurity, and fall under the Horizon againe.

18. These must not therefore bee named the effects of fortune, but in a relative way, and as we terme the workes of nature. It was the ignorance of mans reason that begat this very name, and by a carelesse terme miscalled the providence of God: for there is no liberty for causes to operate in a loose and stragling way, nor any effect whatsoever, but hath its warrant from some universall or superiour cause. 'Tis not a ridiculous devotion, to say a Prayer before a game at Tables; for even in *sortilegies*[113] and matters of greatest uncertainty, there is a setled and preordered course of effects; 'tis we that are blind, not fortune: because our eye is too dim to discover the mystery of her effects, we foolishly paint her blind, & hoodwink the providence of the Almighty. I cannot justifie that contemptible Proverb, *That fooles onely are fortunate*;[114] or that insolent Paradox, *That a wise man is out of the reach of fortune*; much lesse those opprobrious Epithets of Poets, *Whore, Baud,* and *Strumpet*: 'Tis I confesse the common fate of men of singular gifts of mind, to be destitute of those of fortune; which doth not any way deject the spirit of wiser judgements, who throughly understand the justice of this proceeding; and being enriched with higher donatives, cast a more carelesse eye on these vulgar parts of felicity. 'Tis a most unjust ambition, to desire to engrosse the mercies of the Almighty, nor to be content with the goods of mind, without a possession of those of body or fortune: and 'tis an errour worse than heresie, to adore these complementall & circumstantiall pieces of felicity, and undervalue those perfections and essentiall points of happinesse, wherin we resemble our Maker. To wiser desires 'tis satisfaction enough to deserve, though not to enjoy the favours of fortune; let providence provide for fooles: 'tis not partiality, but equity in God, who deales with us but as our naturall parents; those that are able of body and mind, he leaves to their deserts; to those of weaker merits hee imparts a larger

112. Spiral.
113. Divination by casting lots.
114. Cf. the proverb 'Fortune favours fools'.

portion, and pieces out the defect of one by the excesse of the other. Thus have wee no just quarrell with Nature, for leaving us naked, or to envie the hornes, hoofs, skins, and furs of other creatures, being provided with reason, that can supply them all. Wee need not labour with so many arguments to confute judiciall Astrology; for if there be a truth therein, it doth not injure Divinity; if to be born under *Mercury* disposeth us to be witty, under *Iupiter* to be wealthy, I doe not owe a knee unto these, but unto that mercifull hand that hath ordered my indifferent and uncertaine nativity unto such benevolous aspects. Those that hold that all things were governed by fortune had not erred, had they not persisted there: The Romans that erected a Temple to Fortune, acknowledged therein, though in a blinder way, somewhat of Divinity; for in a wise supputation[115] all things begin and end in the Almighty. There is a neerer way to heaven than *Homers* chaine;[116] an easie[117] Logick may conjoyne heaven and earth in one argument, and with lesse than a Sorites[118] resolve all things into God. For though wee Christen effects by their most sensible and nearest causes, yet is God the true and infallible cause of all, whose concourse though it be generall, yet doth it subdivide it selfe into the particular actions of every thing, and is that spirit, by which each singular essence not onely subsists, but performes its operation.

19. The bad construction and perverse comment on these paire of second causes, or visible hands of God,[119] have perverted the devotion of many unto Atheisme; who forgetting the honest advisoes of faith, have listened unto the conspiracie of Passion and Reason. I have therefore alwayes endeavoured to compose those fewds and angry dissentions between affections, faith, and reason: For there is in our soule a kind of Triumvirate, or Triple government of three competitors, which distract the

115. 'counting or reckoning' (Blount).

116. The chain suspended by Zeus from heaven (*Iliad*, VIII, 18 ff.) was frequently regarded as symbolic of God's supervision of the creation's unity. Cf. §§ 251-2.

117. i.e. immediately apprehensible (§ 199).

118. 'accumulated argument' (Coleridge).

119. i.e. fortune and providence.

peace of this our Common-wealth, not lesse than did that other[120] the State of Rome.

As Reason is a rebell unto Faith, so passion unto Reason: As the propositions of Faith seeme absurd unto Reason, so the Theorems of Reason unto passion, and both unto Faith;[121] yet a moderate and peaceable discretion may so state and order the matter, that they may bee all Kings, and yet make but one Monarchy, every one exercising his Soveraignty and Prerogative in a due time and place, according to the restraint and limit of circumstance. There is, as in Philosophy, so in Divinity, sturdy doubts, and boysterous objections, wherewith the un-happinesse of our knowledge too neerely acquainteth us. More of these no man hath knowne than my selfe, which I confesse I conquered, not in a martiall posture, but on my knees.[122] For our endeavours are not onely to combate with doubts, but alwayes to dispute with the Devill; the villany of that spirit takes a hint of infidelity from our Studies, and by demonstrating a naturality in one way, makes us mistrust a miracle in another. Thus having perus'd the Archidoxis[123] and read the secret Sympathies of things, he would disswade my beliefe from the miracle of the Brazen Serpent,[124] make me conceit that image work'd by Sympathie, and was but an Ægyptian tricke to cure their diseases without a miracle. Againe, having seene some experiments of *Bitumen*, and having read farre more of *Naptha*, he whispered to my curiositie the fire of the Altar might be naturall, and bid me mistrust a miracle in *Elias* when he entrench'd the Altar round with water;[125] for that inflamable substance yeelds not easily unto water, but flames in the armes of its Antagonist: and thus would hee inveagle my beliefe to thinke the combustion of *Sodom* might be naturall, and that there was an Asphaltick and Bituminous nature in that Lake before the fire of *Gomorrha*:[126] I know that Manna is now

120. i.e. the triumvirate of Mark Antony, Octavian, and Lepidus.
121. Corrected from 'Reason', an obvious error.
122. The rest of this section was not in *UA*.
123. The title of Paracelsus's treatise on cures by means of amulets.
124. Numbers 21.9.
125. Leviticus 6.13 and 1 Kings 18.35–38.
126. Genesis 19.24–28.

plentifully gathered in *Calabria*, and *Josephus*[127] tels me in his days 'twas as plentifull in *Arabia*; the Devill therefore made the *quere*, Where was then the miracle in the dayes of *Moses*? the *Israelites* saw but that in his time, the natives of those Countries behold in ours. Thus the Devill playd at Chesse with mee, and yeelding a pawne, thought to gaine a Queen of me, taking advantage of my honest endeavours; and whilst I labour'd to raise the structure of my reason, hee striv'd to undermine the edifice of my faith.

20. Neither had these or any other ever such advantage of me, as to encline me to any point of infidelity or desperate positions of Atheisme; for I have beene these many yeares of opinion there was never any. Those that held Religion was the difference of man from beasts, have spoken probably, and proceed upon a principle as inductive[128] as the other: That doctrine of *Epicurus*, that denied the providence of God,[129] was no Atheism, but a magnificent and high-strained conceit of his Majesty, which hee deemed too sublime to minde the triviall actions of those inferiour creatures: That fatall necessitie of the Stoickes, is nothing but the immutable Law of his will. Those that heretofore denied the Divinitie of the holy Ghost, have been condemned but as Heretickes; and those that now deny our Saviour[130] (though more than Hereticks) are not so much as Atheists: for though they deny two persons in the Trinity, they hold as we do, there is but one God.

That villain and Secretary of Hell, that composed that miscreant piece of the three Impostors,[131] though divided from all Religions, and was neither Jew, Turk, nor Christian, was not a positive Atheist. I confesse every Countrey hath its *Machiavell*, every age its *Lucian*, whereof common heads must not heare,

127. In *Jewish Antiquities*, III, i, 6.

128. Persuasive.

129. In the sense that the gods are indifferent to human affairs (as reported by Diogenes Laertius, X, 139:1).

130. i.e. the Socinians.

131. 'Moses, Christ, and Mahomet' (*MSS. marg.*, in *M*). The anonymous *De tribus impostoribus* – composed long after it was first rumoured to exist and rarely if ever seen – was said to be a notorious attack on the three figures named (see §1: App.).

nor more advanced judgements too rashly venture on: 'tis the Rhetorick of Satan, and may pervext a loose or prejudicate beleefe.

21. I confesse I have perused them all, and can discover nothing that may startle a discreet beliefe: yet are there heads carried off with the wind and breath of such motives. I remember a Doctor in Physick of Italy, who could not perfectly believe the immortality of the soule, because *Galen* seemed to make a doubt thereof.[132] With another I was familiarly acquainted in France, a Divine and man of singular parts, that on the same point was so plunged and gravelled with three lines of *Seneca*,[133] that all our Antidotes, drawne from both Scripture and Philosophy, could not expell the poyson of his errour. There are a set of heads, that can credit the relations of Mariners, yet question the testimonies of Saint *Paul*; and peremptorily maintaine the traditions of *Ælian* or *Pliny*,[134] yet in Histories of Scripture, raise Quere's and objections, beleeving no more than they can parallel in humane Authors. I confesse there are in Scripture stories that doe exceed the fable of Poets, and to a captious Reader sound like *Garagantua* or *Bevis*: Search all the Legends of times past, and the fabulous conceits of these present, and 'twill bee hard to find one that deserves to carry the buckler unto *Sampson*,[135] yet is all this of an easie possibility, if we conceive a divine concourse or an influence but from the little finger of the Almighty. It is impossible that either in the discourse of man, or in the infallible voyce of God, to the weakenesse of our apprehensions, there should not appeare irregularities, contradictions, and antinomies: my selfe could shew a catalogue of doubts,[136] never yet imagined nor ques-

132. In *The Qualities of the Mind depend on the Corporeal Temperament*, III.

133. 'There is nothing after death, and death itself is nothing. Death is indivisible, destructive to the body and unsparing of the soul . . . We die wholly, and no part of us remains' (Browne marg., quoted in Latin). So Seneca in *Troades*, ll. 397, 401–2, 378–9.

134. Whose works are largely uncritical compilations.

135. i.e. to resemble Samson (Judges 14.5 ff.).

136. So Bacon had in *The Advancement of Learning* proposed a 'calendar of doubts and problems' (§190) to which Browne responded, nominally, in *Pseudodoxia Epidemica* (see above, p. 35).

tioned, as I know, which are not resolved at the first hearing, not fantastick Quere's, or objections of ayre: For I cannot heare of Atoms in Divinity. I can read the history of the Pigeon that was sent out of the Ark, and returned no more, yet not question how shee found out her mate that was left behind: That *Lazarus* was raised from the dead, yet not demand where in the interim his soule awaited; or raise a Law-case, whether his heire might lawfully detaine his inheritance, bequeathed unto him by his death; and he, though restored to life, have no Plea or title unto his former possessions. Whether *Eve* was framed out of the left side of *Adam*, I dispute not; because I stand not yet assured which is the right side of a man, or whether there be any such distinction in Nature;[137] that she was edified out of the ribbe of *Adam* I believe, yet raise no question who shall arise with that ribbe at the Resurrection. Whether *Adam* was an Hermaphrodite, as the Rabbines[138] contend upon the letter of the Text; because it is contrary to reason, there should bee an Hermaphrodite before there was a woman, or a composition of two natures, before there was a second composed. Likewise, whether the world was created in Autumne, Summer, or Spring; because it was created in them all; for whatsoever Signe the Sun possesseth, those foure seasons are actually existent: It is the nature of this Luminary to distinguish the severall seasons of the yeare, all which it makes at one time in the whole earth, and successive in any part thereof.[139] There are a bundle of curiosities, not onely in Philosophy but in Divinity, proposed and discussed by men of most supposed abilities, which indeed are not worthy our vacant houres, much lesse our serious studies; Pieces onely fit to be placed in *Pantagruels* Library, or bound up with *Tartaretus de modo Cacandi*.[140]

137. The question was later taken up in *Pseudodoxia Epidemica*, IV, 5 ('Of the right and left Hand').

138. i.e. rabbis, or Jewish authorities on law and doctrine generally.

139. Further discussed in *Pseudodoxia Epidemica*, VI, 2 ('Of mens Enquiries in what season or point of the Zodiack it [the world] began . . .').

140. 'Browne is adopting Rabelais's jibe at Tartaretus, who was a doctor of the Sorbonne notorious for his refinements on the subtleties of Duns Scotus' (§196). The title of the reputed treatise involves (as a Latin dictionary tactfully reports) 'to go to stool'.

22. These are niceties that become not those that peruse so serious a Mystery. There are others more generally questioned and called to the Barre, yet me thinkes of an easie, and possible truth. 'Tis ridiculous to put off, or drowne the generall Flood of *Noah* in that particular inundation of *Deucalion*: that there was a Deluge once, seemes not to mee so great a miracle, as that there is not one alwayes. How all the kinds of Creatures, not only in their owne bulks, but with a competency of food & sustenance, might be preserved in one Arke, and within the extent of three hundred cubits, to a reason that rightly examines it, will appeare very foesible.[141] There is another secret, not contained in the Scripture, which is more hard to comprehend, & put the honest Father[142] to the refuge of a Miracle; and that is, not onely how the distinct pieces of the world, and divided Ilands should bee first planted by men, but inhabited by Tygers, Panthers and Beares. How *America* abounded with beasts of prey, and noxious Animals, yet contained not in it that necessary creature, a Horse, is very strange. By what passage those, not onely Birds, but dangerous and unwelcome Beasts came over: How there bee creatures there, which are not found in this triple Continent;[143] all which must needs bee strange unto us, that hold but one Arke, and that the creatures began their progresse from the mountaines of *Ararat*.[144] They who to salve[145] this would make the Deluge particular, proceed upon a Principle that I can no way grant; not onely upon the negative of holy Scriptures, but of mine owne reason, whereby I can make it probable, that the world was as well peopled in the time of *Noah* as in ours, and fifteene hundred yeares to people the world, as full a time for them as foure thousand yeares since have beene to us.[146] There are other assertions and common

141. Corrected from 'forcible' (*MSS.*), no doubt because of St Augustine's discussion of the matter in *The City of God*, XV, 27.

142. St Augustine (ibid., XVI, 7).

143. i.e. Europe, Asia, and Africa.

144. Where Noah's ark landed after the Flood (Genesis 8.4).

145. Smooth over; as in 'to salve (save) the phenomena', i.e. resolve apparent contradictions.

146. The Flood was believed to have occurred 1500 years after the creation, itself dated *c.* 4000 B.C. (see below, p. 439, note 31). The question

tenents drawn from Scripture, and generally beleeved as
Scripture; whereunto, notwithstanding, I would never betray
the libertie of my reason. 'Tis a postulate to me, that *Methusalem*
was the longest liv'd of all the children of *Adam*, and no man
will bee able to prove it; when from the processe of the Text I
can manifest it may be otherwise.[147] That *Judas* perished by
hanging himself, there is no certainety in Scripture, though in
one place it seemes to affirme it, and by a doubtfull word hath
given occasion to translate it; yet in another place, in a more
punctuall description, it makes it improbable, and seemes to
overthrow it.[148] That our Fathers, after the Flood, erected the
Tower of *Babell*, to preserve themselves against a second
Deluge, is generally opinioned and beleeved; yet is there
another intention of theirs expressed in Scripture:[149] Besides, it
is improbable from the circumstance of the place, that is, a
plaine in the land of *Shinar*. These are no points of Faith, and
therefore may admit a free dispute. There are yet others, and
those familiarly concluded from the Text, wherein (under
favour) I see no consequence. The Church of Rome confidently
proves the opinion of Tutelary Angels, from that answer when
Peter knockt at the doore, *'Tis not he but his Angel*; that is, might
some say, his Messenger, or some body from him; for so the
Originall signifies;[150] and is as likely to be the doubtfull

is reconsidered, with other matters here discussed, in *Pseudodoxia Epidemica* (VI, 6; VII, 3, 6, and 11).

147. The next few lines read (in P only) thus: 'That Judas hanged himselfe, tis an absurdity, and an affirmative that is not expressed in the text, but quite contrarie to the words and their externall construction. With this paradoxe I remember I netled an angrie Jesuite who had that day let this fall in his sermon, who afterwards, upon a serious perusall of the text, confessed my opinion, and prooved a courteous friend to mee, a stranger, and noe enemy; These . . .'

148. Matthew 27.5 and Acts 1.18. The former provides the 'doubtfull word' $\dot{a}\pi\dot{\eta}\gamma\xi\alpha\tau o$, meaning 'hanged himself' as well as 'was strangled' (M).

149. The 'opinioned' view is by Josephus, *Jewish Antiquities*, I, iv, 2; the contrary intention is in Genesis 11.4 ('let us build us . . . a tower, whose top may reach unto heaven; and let us make us a name, lest we be scattered abroad').

150. Acts 12.11, where *angelos* could indeed mean 'messenger'.

Families[151] meaning. This exposition I once suggested to a young Divine, that answered upon this point, to which I remember the *Franciscan* Opponent replyed no more, but, That it was a new and no authentick interpretation.

23. These are but the conclusions, and fallible discourses of man upon the word of God, for such I doe beleeve the holy Scriptures; yet were it of man, I could not choose but say, it was the singularest, and superlative Piece that hath been extant since the Creation; were I a Pagan, I should not refraine the Lecture of it; and cannot but commend the judgement of *Ptolomy*, that thought not his Library compleate without it: the Alcoran of the Turks[152] (I speake without prejudice) is an ill composed Piece, containing in it vaine and ridiculous errours in Philosophy, impossibilities, fictions, and vanities beyond laughter, maintained by evident and open Sophismes, the policy of Ignorance, deposition of Universities, and banishment of Learning, that hath gotten foot by armes and violence; This[153] without a blow hath disseminated it selfe through the whole earth. It is not unremarkable what *Philo* first observed, That the Law of *Moses* continued two thousand yeares without the least alteration;[154] whereas, we see, the Lawes of other Common-weales doe alter with occasions; and even those that pretended their originall from some Divinity, to have vanished without trace or memory. I beleeve, besides *Zoroaster*, there were divers that writ before *Moses*,[155] who notwithstanding have suffered the common fate of time. Mens Workes have an age like themselves; and though they out-live their Authors, yet have they a stint and period to their duration: This onely[156] is a Worke too hard for the teeth of time, and cannot perish but in the generall flames, when all things shall confesse their ashes.

24. I have heard some with deepe sighs lament the lost lines of

151. i.e. congregations (R).
152. i.e. the Koran of the Moslems.
153. i.e. the Bible.
154. Philo, *Life of Moses*, II, 3.
155. St Augustine in *The City of God*, XV, 23, sceptically mentions works ascribed to Enoch.
156. i.e. the Bible.

Cicero; others with as many groanes deplore the combustion of the Library of *Alexandria*; for my owne part, I thinke there be too many in the world, and could with patience behold the urne and ashes of the *Vatican*, could I with a few others recover the perished leaves of *Solomon*. I would not omit a Copy of *Enochs* Pillars, had they many neerer Authors than *Josephus*, or did not relish somewhat of the Fable.[157] Some men have written more than others have spoken; *Pineda* quotes more Authors in one worke, than are necessary in a whole world.[158] Of those three great inventions in *Germany*,[159] there are two which are not without their incommodities, and 'tis disputable whether they exceed not their use and commodities. 'Tis not a melancholy *Utinam*[160] of mine owne, but the desires of better heads, that there were a general Synod; not to unite the incompatible difference of Religion, but for the benefit of learning, to reduce it as it lay at first in a few and solid Authors; and to condemne to the fire those swarms and millions of *Rhapsodies*, begotten onely to distract and abuse the weaker judgements of Scholars, and to maintaine the Trade and Mystery of Typographers.

25. I cannot but wonder with what exceptions the *Samaritanes* could confine their beliefe to the *Pentateuch*, or five Books of *Moses*.[161] I am ashamed at the Rabbinicall Interpretation of the Jews, upon the Old Testament, as much as their defection from the New: and truely it is beyond wonder, how that contemptible and degenerate issue of *Jacob*, once so devoted to Ethnick[162] Superstition, and so easily seduced to the Idolatry of their Neighbours, should now in such an obstinate and peremptory beliefe, adhere unto their owne Doctrine, expect impossibilities,

157. Enoch's Pillars were said to have contained inscriptions of all the achievements to his time; but see previous page, note 155.

158. '*Pineda* in his *Monarcia Ecclesiastica* quotes one thousand and fortie Authors' (Browne marg.).

159. 'Gunnes, printing. The Mariners compasse' (*MSS. marg.*).

160. i.e. exclamation (literally, 'Oh that!).

161. 'The Samaritan version of the Pentateuch, not printed till 1645, was known to differ slightly from the standard Massoretic version of the Jews' (R).

162. i.e. pagan.

and in the face and eye of the Church persist without the least hope of conversion: This is a vice in them, that were a vertue in us; for obstinacy in a bad cause, is but constancy in a good. And herein I must accuse those of my own Religion; for there is not any of such a fugitive faith, such an unstable belief, as a Christian; none that do so oft transforme themselves, not unto severall shapes of Christianity and of the same Species, but unto more unnaturall and contrary formes, of Jew and Mahometan, that from the name of Saviour can condescend to the bare terme of Prophet; and from an old beliefe that he is come, fall to a new expectation of his comming: It is the promise of Christ to make us all one flock; but how and when this union shall be, is as obscure to me as the last day. Of those foure members of Religion[163] wee hold a slender proportion; there are I confesse some new additions, yet small to those which accrew to our Adversaries, and those only drawne from the revolt of Pagans, men but of negative impieties, and such as deny Christ, but because they never heard of him: But the Religion of the Jew is expressly against the Christian, and the Mahometan against both; for the Turke, in the bulke hee now stands, he is beyond all hope of conversion; if hee fall asunder there may be conceived hopes, but not without strong improbabilities. The Jew is obstinate in all fortunes; the persecution of fifteene hundred yeares hath but confirmed them in their errour: they have already endured whatsoever may be inflicted, and have suffered, in a bad cause, even to the condemnation of their enemies. Persecution is a bad and indirect way to plant Religion; It hath beene the unhappy method of angry devotions, not onely to confirme honest Religion, but wicked Heresies, and extravagant opinions. It was the first stone and Basis of our Faith, none can more justly boast of persecutions, and glory in the number and valour of Martyrs; for, to speake properly, those are true and almost onely examples of fortitude: Those that are fetch'd from the field, or drawne from the actions of the Campe, are not oft-times so truely precedents of valour as audacity, and at the best attaine but to some bastard piece of fortitude. If wee

163. i.e. pagan, Jewish, Christian, and Mohammedan.

shall strictly examine the circumstances and requisites which
Aristotle requires to true and perfect valour,[164] we shall finde
the name onely in his Master *Alexander*, and as little in that
Romane Worthy, *Julius Cæsar*; and if any, in that easie and
active way, have done so nobly as to deserve that name, yet in
the passive and more terrible piece these[165] have surpassed, and
in a more heroicall way may claime the honour of that Title.
'Tis not in the power of every honest faith to proceed thus
farre, or passe to Heaven through the flames; every one hath
it not in that full measure, nor in so audacious and resolute
a temper, as to endure those terrible tests and trialls, who
notwithstanding in a peaceable way doe truely adore their
Saviour, and have (no doubt) a faith acceptable in the eyes of
God.

26. Now as all that die in warre are not termed Souldiers, so
neither can I properly terme all those that suffer in matters of
Religion Martyrs. The Councell of *Constance* condemnes *John
Husse* for an Heretick, the Stories of his owne party stile him a
Martyr; He must needs offend the Divinity of both, that sayes[166]
hee was neither the one nor the other: There are many (question-
lesse) canonized on earth, that shall never be Saints in Heaven;
and have their names in Histories and Martyrologies, who in
the eyes of God, are not so perfect Martyrs as was that wise
Heathen *Socrates*, that suffered on a fundamentall point of
Religion, the Unity of God. I have often pitied the miserable
Bishop that suffered in the cause of *Antipodes*; yet cannot
choose but accuse him of as much madnesse, for exposing his
living on such a trifle, as those of ignorance and folly that con-
demned him.[167] I think my conscience will not give me the lie;
if I say, there are not many extant that in a noble way feare the
face of death lesse than my selfe, yet from the morall duty I owe
to the Commandement of God, and the naturall respects that I

164. In *Nicomachean Ethics*, III, 6–9.
165. i.e. the Christian martyrs.
166. Corrected from: 'What false Divinity is it if I say' (*MSS.*).
167. 'Virgilius' (*MSS. marg.*): Bishop of Salzburg, deprived for a time
of his See because his theory of antipodes was thought to imply the
existence of another world.

tender unto the conservation of my essence and being, I would
not perish upon a Ceremony, Politick points, or indifferency:
nor is my beleefe of that untractable temper, as not to bow at
their obstacles, or connive at matters wherein there are not
manifest impieties: The leaven therefore and ferment of all, not
onely Civill, but Religious actions, is wisedome; without which,
to commit our selves to the flames is Homicide, and (I feare) but
to passe through one fire into another.

27. That Miracles are ceased, I can neither prove, nor abso-
lutely deny, much lesse define the time and period of their cessa-
tion; that they survived Christ, is manifest upon record of
Scripture; that they out-lived the Apostles also, and were
revived at the conversion of Nations, many yeares after, we can-
not deny, if wee shall not question those Writers whose
testimonies wee doe not controvert, in points that make for our
owne opinions; therefore that may have some truth in it that is
reported by the Jesuites of their Miracles in the Indies, I
could wish it were true, or had any other testimony then their
owne Pennes: they may easily beleeve those Miracles abroad,
who daily conceive a greater at home; the transmutation of
those visible elements into the body and blood of our
Saviour:[168] for the conversion of water into wine, which he
wrought in *Cana*, or what the Devill would have had him done
in the wildernesse, of stones into Bread,[169] compared to this,
will scarce deserve the name of a Miracle: Though indeed, to
speake properly, there is not one Miracle greater than another,
they being the extraordinary effect of the hand of God, to
which all things are of an equall facility; and to create the world
as easie as one single creature. For this is also a miracle, not
onely to produce effects against, or above Nature, but before
Nature; and to create Nature as great a miracle, as to contra-
dict or transcend her. Wee doe too narrowly define the power
of God, restraining it to our capacities. I hold that God can doe
all things, how he should work contradictions I do not under-
stand, yet dare not therefore deny. I cannot see why the Angel
of God should question *Esdras* to recall the time past, if it

168. i.e. according to the Catholic doctrine of transubstantiation.
169. John 2.1–10 and Matthew 4.1–3, respectively.

were beyond his owne power;[170] or that God should pose[171] mortalitie in that, which hee was not able to performe himselfe. I will not say God cannot, but hee will not performe many things, which wee plainely affirme he cannot: this I am sure is the mannerliest proposition, wherein notwithstanding I hold no Paradox. For strictly his power is the same with his will, and they both with all the rest doe make but one God.[172]

28. Therefore that Miracles have beene I doe beleeve, that they may yet bee wrought by the living I doe not deny: but have no confidence in those which are fathered on the dead; and this hath ever made me suspect the efficacy of reliques, to examine the bones, question the habits and appertinencies of Saints, and even of Christ himselfe: I cannot conceive why the Crosse that *Helena* found and whereon Christ himself died should have power to restore others unto life; I excuse not *Constantine* from a fall off his horse, or a mischiefe from his enemies, upon the wearing those nayles on his bridle which our Saviour bore upon the Crosse in his hands: I compute among your *Piæ fraudes*,[173] nor many degrees before consecrated swords and roses, that which *Baldwin* King of Jersualem return'd the *Genovese* for their cost and paines in his warre, to wit the ashes of *John* the Baptist. Those that hold the sanctitie of their soules doth leave behind a tincture and sacred facultie on their bodies, speake naturally of Miracles, and doe not salve the doubt. Now one reason I tender so little devotion unto reliques is, I think, the slender and doubtfull respect I have alwayes held unto Antiquities: for that indeed which I admire is farre before antiquity, that is Eternity, and that is God himselfe; who though hee be stiled the Antient of dayes,[174] cannot receive the adjunct of antiquity, who was before the world, and shall be after it, yet is not older then it: for in his yeares there is no

---

170. 2 Esdras 4.5: 'Then said he unto me, Go thy way, weigh me the weight of the fire, or measure me the blast of the wind, or call me again the day that is past'.
171. Puzzle.
172. The next section (#28) was not in *UA*.
173. Pious frauds.
174. Daniel 7.9.

Climacter,[175] his duration is eternity, and farre more venerable then antiquitie.

29. But above all things, I wonder how the curiositie of wiser heads could passe that great and indisputable miracle, the cessation of Oracles: and in what swoun their reasons lay, to content themselves and sit downe with such far-fetch't and ridiculous reasons as *Plutarch* alleadgeth for it.[176] The Jewes that can beleeve the supernaturall solstice of the Sunne in the dayes of *Joshua*,[177] have yet the impudence to deny the Eclipse, which every Pagan confessed at his death:[178] but for this, it is evident beyond all contradiction, the Devill himselfe confessed it.[179] Certainly it is not a warrantable curiosity, to examine the verity of Scripture by the concordance of humane history, or seek to confirme the Chronicle of *Hester* or *Daniel*, by the authority of *Magasthenes* or *Herodotus*. I confesse I have had an unhappy curiosity this way, till I laughed my selfe out of it with a piece of *Justine*, where hee delivers that the children of *Israel* for being scabbed were banished out of Egypt.[180] And truely since I have understood the occurrences of the world, and know in what counterfeit shapes & deceitfull vizzards times present represent on the stage things past; I doe beleeve them little more than things to come. Some have beene of my opinion, and endevoured to write the History of their own lives; wherein *Moses* hath outgone them all, and left not onely the story of his life, but as some will have it of his death also.[181]

30. It is a riddle to me, how this story of Oracles hath not worm'd out of the world that doubtfull conceit, of Spirits and Witches; how so many learned heads should so farre forget their Metaphysicks, and destroy the Ladder and scale of

175. i.e. climacteric, a critical period in man's life. See below, pp. 231 ff.
176. In his treatise *The Cessation of the Oracles*. On the background to Browne's discourse – and to Milton's version in the *Nativity Ode* (ll. 145 ff.) – see §292. See also below, pp. 253 ff.

177. As above, p. 79, note 96.   178. i.e. Christ's (Luke 23.44–5).
179. 'In his Oracle to *Augustus*' (Browne marg.), quoted in Browne's translation below, p. 254. The prophecy is attributed to the devil as the inspirer of pagan oracles (as above, p. 74, note 74).

180. Justin, XXXVI, ii, 12.
181. In Deuteronomy 34.5–8.

creatures,[182] as to question the existence of Spirits: for my part,
I have ever beleeved, and doe now know, that there are
Witches; they that doubt of these, doe not onely deny them,
but Spirits; and are obliquely and upon consequence a sort, not
of Infidels, but Atheists.[183] Those that to confute their in-
credulity desire to see apparitions, shall questionlesse never
behold any, nor have the power to be so much as Witches; the
Devill hath them already in a heresie as capitall as Witchcraft,
and to appeare to them, were but to convert them: Of all the
delusions wherewith he deceives mortalitie, there is not any
that puzleth mee more than the Legerdemain of *Changelings*; I
doe not credit those transformations of reasonable creatures
into beasts, or that the Devill hath a power to transpeciate a
man into a horse, who tempted Christ (as a triall of his Divini-
tie) to convert but stones into bread. I could beleeve that
Spirits use with man the act of carnality, and that in both sexes; I
conceive they may assume, steale, or contrive a body, wherein
there may be action enough to content decrepit lust, or passion
to satisfie more active veneries,[184] yet in both, without a
possibility of generation: and therefore that opinion, that
Antichrist should be borne of the Tribe of *Dan* by conjunction
with the Devill, is ridiculous, and a conceit fitter for a Rabbin
than a Christian. I hold that the Devill doth really possesse some
men, the spirit of melancholy others, the spirit of delusion
others; that as the Devill is concealed and denyed by some, so
God and good Angels are pretended[185] by others, whereof the
late defection of the Maid of Germany hath left a pregnant
example.[186]

182. Cf. the fuller formulation below, p. 101: 'there is in this Universe a
Staire . . .' etc.
183. 'A strange kind of *Atheisme* to deny witches!' exclaimed Alexander
Ross in 1645: 'is there such a strict relation between *witches* and *spirits*, that
hee that denies the one must needs deny the other?' But Browne's premise
is Henry More's: '*No Spirit, no God*' (*The Cambridge Platonists*, ed. C.A.
Patrides [1969], p. 32). See especially above, p. 27.
184. Sexual desires.
185. Affected.
186. 'That lived without meate upon the Smell of a Rose' (*MSS. marg.*).
The 'Maid' was the impostor Eva Flegen of Mörs, who claimed to have
fasted from 1597 for no less than thirty years (§244).

31. Againe, I beleeve that all that use sorceries, incantations, and spells, are not Witches, or as we terme them, Magicians; I conceive there is a traditionall Magicke, not learned immediately from the Devill, but at second hand from his Schollers; who having once the secret betrayed, are able, and doe emperically practice without his advice, they both proceeding upon the principles of nature: where actives aptly conjoyned to disposed passives,[187] will under any Master produce their effects. Thus I thinke at first a great part of Philosophy was Witchcraft, which being afterward derived to one another, proved but Philosophy, and was indeed no more but the honest effects of Nature: What invented by us is Philosophy, learned from him is Magicke. Wee doe surely owe the discovery of many secrets to the discovery of good and bad Angels. I could never passe that sentence of *Paracelsus* without an asterisk or annotation; *Ascendens constellatum multa revelat, quærentibus magnalia naturæ*, i.e. *opera Dei.*[188] I doe thinke that many mysteries ascribed to our owne inventions, have beene the courteous revelations of Spirits; for those noble essences in heaven beare a friendly regard unto their fellow natures on earth; and therefore beleeve that those many prodigies and ominous prognostickes which fore-run the ruines of States, Princes, and private persons, are the charitable premonitions of good Angels, which more carelesse enquiries terme but the effects of chance and nature.

32. Now besides these particular and divided Spirits, there may be (for ought I know) an universall and common Spirit to the whole world.[189] It was the opinion of *Plato*, and it is yet of the *Hermeticall* Philosophers; if there be a common nature that unites and tyes the scattered and divided individuals into one species, why may there not bee one that unites them all? However, I am sure there is a common Spirit that playes within us,

187. 'Actives' are heat and cold; 'passives', moisture and dryness (*M*).
188. 'A star in the ascendant reveals many things to those who seek the marvels of nature, that is, the works of God'. 'Thereby', a marginal note explains, 'is meant our good Angel appointed us from our nativity'.
189. i.e. the world soul according to Plato's *Timaeus* (41d–e), here related to the soul of man as the 'common Spirit that playes within us' (§198).

yet makes no part of us, and that is the Spirit of God, the fire and scintillation of that noble and mighty Essence, which is the life and radicall heat of spirits, and those essences that know not the vertue of the Sunne, a fire quite contrary to the fire of Hell: This is that gentle heate that brooded on the waters, and in six dayes hatched the world;[190] this is that irradiation that dispells the mists of Hell, the clouds of horrour, feare, sorrow, despaire; and preserves the region of the mind in serenity: whosoever feels not the warme gale and gentle ventilation of this Spirit (though I feele his pulse) I dare not say he lives; for truely without this, to mee there is no heat under the Tropick; nor any light, though I dwelt in the body of the Sunne.

> *As when the labouring Sun hath wrought his track,*
> *Up to the top of lofty Cancers back,*
> *The ycie Ocean cracks, the frozen pole*
> *Thawes with the heat of the Celestiall coale;*
> *So when thy absent beames begin t'impart*
> *Againe a Solstice on my frozen heart,*
> *My winters ov'r, my drooping spirits sing,*
> *And every part revives into a Spring.*
> *But if thy quickning beames a while decline,*
> *And with their light blesse not this Orbe of mine,*
> *A chilly frost surpriseth every member,*
> *Ane in the midst of June, I feele December.[191]*
> *O how this earthly temper doth debase*
> *The noble Soule, in this her humble place!*
> *Whose wingy nature ever doth aspire,*
> *To reach that place whence first it tooke its fire.*
> *These flames I feele, which in my heart doe dwell,*
> *Are not thy beames, but take their fire from Hell:*
> *O quench them all, and let thy light divine*
> *Be as the Sunne to this poore Orbe of mine.*

190. 'The Spirit of God played ['moved' in *AV*] upon the waters, Genesis 1.2' (*MSS. marg.*, quoted in Latin). Cf. *Paradise Lost*, I, 19–22: 'Thou ... Dove-like satst brooding on the vast Abyss / And mad'st it pregnant'.

191. Inserted here (*MSS.*): '*Keepe still in my Horizon, for to mee, | Tis not the Sunne that makes the day, but thee*'. The lines occur in the poem below, p. 156.

> *And to thy sacred Spirit convert those fires,*
> *Whose earthly fumes choake my devout aspires.*

33. Therefore for Spirits I am so farre from denying their existence, that I could easily beleeve, that not onely whole Countries, but particular persons have their Tutelary, and Guardian Angels: It is not a new opinion of the Church of *Rome*, but an old one of *Pythagoras* and *Plato*;[192] there is no heresie in it, and if not manifestly defin'd in Scripture, yet is it an opinion of a good and wholesome use in the course and actions of a mans life, and would serve as an *Hypothesis* to salve many doubts, whereof common Philosophy affordeth no solution: Now if you demand my opinion and Metaphysicks of their natures, I confesse them very shallow, most of them in a negative way, like that of God; or in a comparative, betweene our selves and fellow creatures; for there is in this Universe a Staire, or manifest Scale of creatures, rising not disorderly, or in confusion, but with a comely method and proportion:[193] betweene creatures of meere existence and things of life, there is a large disproportion of nature; betweene plants and animals or creatures of sense, a wider difference; between them and man, a farre greater: and if the proportion hold on, betweene man and Angels there should bee yet a greater.[194] We doe not comprehend their natures, who retaine the first definition of *Porphyry*,[195] and distinguish them from our selves by immortality; for before his fall, man also was immortall; yet must wee needs affirme that he had a different essence from the Angels: having therefore no certaine knowledge of their natures, 'tis no bad method of the Schooles, whatsoever perfection we finde obscurely in our selves, in a more compleate and absolute way to ascribe unto them. I beleeve they have an extemporary

192. So Diogenes Laertius (VIII, 32) on Pythagoras; and Plato, *Phaedo*, 107d.

193. See above, p. 26.

194. The differences notwithstanding, Browne affirms the continuity of the hierarchical universe, in line with the common belief that there is 'no *vacuum*, or vacuity in the world' (Michael Sendigovius, *A New Light*, trans. J. French [1650], p. 88). See below, p. 103, note 205.

195. 'A rational and immortal essence' (*MSS. marg.*, quoted in Latin).

knowledge, and upon the first motion of their reason doe what we cannot without study or deliberation;[196] that they know things by their formes, and define by specificall difference, what we describe by accidents and properties;[197] and therefore probabilities to us may bee demonstrations unto them; that they have knowledge not onely of the specificall, but numericall formes of individualls, and understand by what reserved[198] difference each single *Hypostasis*[199] (besides the relation to its species) becomes its numericall selfe. That as the Soule hath a power to move the body it informes, so there's a Faculty to move any, though informe none; ours upon restraint of time, place, and distance; but that invisible hand that conveyed *Habakkuk* to the Lions den, or *Philip* to *Azotus*,[200] infringeth this rule, and hath a secret conveyance, wherewith mortality is not acquainted; if they have that intuitive knowledge, whereby as in reflexion they behold the thoughts of one another, I cannot peremptorily deny but they know a great part of ours. They that to refute the Invocation of Saints, have denied that they have any knowledge of our affaires below, have proceeded too farre, and must pardon my opinion, till I can thoroughly answer that piece of Scripture, *At the conversion of a sinner the Angels of heaven rejoyce.*[201] I cannot with those in that great Father securely interpret the worke of the first day, *Fiat lux,*[202] to the creation of Angels, though (I confesse) there is not any creature that hath so neare a glympse of their nature, as light in

196. The angels' 'intuitive knowledge' (mentioned later) is also affirmed in Milton's discrimination between the 'discoursive' reason of men, and the 'intuitive' of the angels (*Paradise Lost*, V, 487–90).

197. The 'specificall difference' is the innate characteristic of a given species; 'accidents and properties' are all external appearances and attributes.

198. Peculiar.

199. Being, entity, person; but also 'person of the Trinity' (Coleridge) in the sense that the angels intuitively comprehend the relations within the triune Godhead.

200. So the apocryphal book of Bel and the Dragon, 36 and 39, and Acts 8.39–40; respectively.

201. Luke 15.10.

202. 'Let there be light' (Genesis 1.3). The 'great Father' is St Augustine.

the Sunne and Elements; we stile it a bare accident,[203] but where it subsists alone, 'tis a spirituall Substance, and may bee an Angel: in briefe, conceive light invisible, and that is a Spirit.

34. These are certainly the Magisteriall & master pieces of the Creator, the Flower (or as we may say) the best part of nothing,[204] actually existing, what we are but in hopes, and probabilitie, we are onely that amphibious piece betweene a corporall and spirituall essence, that middle forme that linkes those two together, and makes good the method of God and nature, that jumps not from extreames, but unites the incompatible distances by some middle and participating natures;[205] that wee are the breath and similitude of God, it is indisputable, and upon record of holy Scripture,[206] but to call our selves a Microcosme, or little world, I thought it onely a pleasant trope of Rhetorick, till my neare judgement and second thoughts told me there was a reall truth therein: for first wee are a rude masse, and in the ranke of creatures, which onely are, and have a dull kinde of being not yet priviledged with life, or preferred[207] to sense or reason; next we live the life of plants, the life of animals, the life of men, and at last the life of spirits, running on in one mysterious nature those five kinds of existences, which comprehend the creatures not onely of the world, but of the Universe;[208] thus is man that great and true *Amphibium*, whose nature is disposed to live not onely like other creatures in divers elements, but in divided and distinguished worlds; for

203. Non-essential quality (R).

204. The angels are the best part of the creation *ex nihilo* ('out of nothing'). But Browne is probably being as playful as Donne was in 'Aire and Angels'. See also below, p. 105.

205. 'God hath joyned all things in the world, *per media*, by middles; as first, hee hath coupled the *earth* and *water* by *slime*; so the *ayre* and the *water* by *vapours* ...' etc. (John Weemes, *The Pourtraiture of the Image of God* [1627], p. 49; in §95). Cf. above, p. 101, note 194.

206. Genesis 1.26 and 2.7.

207. Elevated.

208. Sir Walter Ralegh detailed at some length the basis of the common claim: 'because in the little frame of mans body there is a representation of the Universall, and (by allusion) a kind of participation of all the parts therof, therefore was man called *Microcosmus*, or the little world ...' (Ralegh, pp. 126 f.).

though there bee but one to sense, there are two to reason; the
one visible, the other invisible,[209] whereof *Moses* seemes to have
left noe[210] description, and of the other so obscurely, that some
parts thereof[211] are yet in controversie; and truely for the first
chapters of *Genesis*, I must confesse a great deale of obscurity,
though Divines have to the power of humane reason en-
deavoured to make all goe in a literall meaning, yet those
allegoricall interpretations are also probable, and perhaps the
mysticall method of *Moses* bred up in the Hieroglyphicall
Schooles of the Egyptians.[212]

35. Now for that immateriall world, me thinkes wee need not
wander so farre as the first moveable,[213] for even in this
materiall fabricke the spirits walke as freely exempt from the
affection of time, place, and motion, as beyond the extreamest
circumference: doe but extract from the corpulency of bodies,
or resolve things beyond their first matter, and you discover
the habitation of Angels, which if I call the ubiquitary, and
omnipresent essence of God, I hope I shall not offend Divinity;
for before the Creation of the world God was really all things.
For the Angels hee created no new world, or determinate man-
sion, and therefore they are every where where is his essence,
and doe live at a distance even in himselfe: that God made all
things for man, is in some sense true, yet not so farre as to
subordinate the creation of those purer creatures unto ours,
though as ministring spirits they doe, and are willing to fulfill
the will of God in these lower and sublunary[214] affaires of
man; God made all things for himselfe,[215] and it is impossible hee
should make them for any other end than his owne glory; it is

209. See above, p. 25.
210. The negative is added from *P* by Sanna (below, p. 551), as required
by the sense. 'Whereof' refers to the invisible world; 'the other', to the
visible.
211. 'The element of fire' (*MSS. marg.*) which Moses failed to mention
in Genesis 1.
212. Acts 7.22: 'Moses was learned in all the wisdom of the Egyptians'.
213. *Primum mobile*, the outermost sphere of Ptolemaic cosmology.
214. i.e. earthly (literally 'below the moon').
215. Proverbs 16.4.

all he can receive, and all that is without himselfe; for honour being an externall adjunct, and in the honourer rather than in the person honoured, it was necessary to make a creature, from whom hee might receive this homage, and that is in the other world Angels, in this, man; which when we neglect, we forget the very end of our creation, and may justly provoke God, not onely to repent that hee hath made the world, but that hee hath sworne hee would not destroy it.[216] That there is but one world, is a conclusion of faith. *Aristotle* with all his Philosophy hath not beene able to prove it, and as weakely that the world was eternall; that dispute much troubled the penne of the antient Philosophers, but *Moses* decided that question, and all is salved with the new terme of a creation, that is, a production of something out of nothing; and what is that? Whatsoever is opposite to something or more exactly, that which is truely contrary unto God: for he onely is, all others have an existence, with dependency and are something but by a distinction;[217] and herein is Divinity conformant unto Philosophy, and generation not onely[218] founded on contrarieties, but also creation; God being all things is contrary unto nothing out of which were made all things, and so nothing became something, and *Omneity* informed *Nullity* into an essence.[219]

36. The whole Creation is a mystery, and particularly that of man, at the blast of his mouth were the rest of the creatures made, and at his bare word they started out of nothing: but in the frame of man (as the text describes it)[220] he played the sensible operator, and seemed not so much to create, as make him; when hee had separated the materials of other creatures, there consequently resulted a forme and soule, but having raised the wals of man, he was driven to a second and harder creation of a

216. i.e. by flood (Genesis 9.9 ff.).
217. Qualification. The rest of this section was not in *UA*.
218. i.e. not only generation.
219. 'An excellent *Burlesque* on some parts of the Schoolmen, tho' I fear an unintentional one' (Coleridge). 'Omneity' literally means allness; and 'nullity', nothingness.
220. Genesis 2.7: 'God formed man of the dust of the ground, and breathed into his nostrils the breath of life'.

substance like himselfe, an incorruptible and immortall soule.
For these two affections[221] we have the Philosophy, and opinion
of the Heathens, the flat affirmative of *Plato*, and not a negative
from *Aristotle*:[222] there is another scruple cast in by Divinity
(concerning its production) much disputed in the *Germane*
auditories, and with that indifferency and equality of arguments,
as leave the controversie undetermined. I am not of *Paracelsus*
minde[223] that boldly delivers a receipt to make a man without
conjunction, yet cannot but wonder at the multitude of heads
that doe deny traduction,[224] having no other argument to
confirme their beliefe, then that Rhetoricall sentence, and
Antimetathesis of *Augustine, Creando infunditur, infundendo
creatur*:[225] either opinion will consist well enough with religion,
yet I should rather incline to this, did not one objection haunt
mee, not wrung from speculations and subtilties, but from
common sense, and observation, not pickt from the leaves of
any author, but bred amongst the weeds and tares of mine owne
braine. And this is a conclusion from the equivocall[226] and
monstrous productions in the copulation of man with beast;
for if the soule of man bee not transmitted and transfused in the
seed of the parents, why are not those productions meerely
beasts, but have also an impression and tincture of reason in as
high a measure as it can evidence it selfe in those improper
organs ? Nor truely can I peremptorily deny, that the soule in
this her sublunary estate, is wholly and in all acceptions inorgan-
icall,[227] but that for the performance of her ordinary actions, is
required not onely a symmetry and proper disposition of

221. i.e. the soul's incorruptibility and immortality.
222. Plato, *Phaedrus*, 24c; Aristotle, *On the Soul*, II, 4, and III, 5.
223. In *The Nature of Things*, I.
224. 'Traducianism' proposes that the soul is transmitted by the parents
to the children; 'creationism', that each soul is created anew at concep-
tion or birth.
225. 'In creation it is infused, in infusion it is created'. The quotation
appears to derive from Peter Lombard, *Sentences*, II, xxvii, 2 (R). Anti-
metathesis: 'a figure in Rhetorick where one word is inverted upon
another' (*MSS. marg.*).
226. Uncertain, dubious.
227. i.e. not dependent on any bodily organ.

Organs, but a Crasis[228] and temper correspondent to its operations; yet is not this masse of flesh and visible structure the instrument and proper corps of the soule, but rather of sense, and that the hand of reason.[229] In our study of Anatomy there is a masse of mysterious Philosophy, and such as reduced the very Heathens to Divinitie; yet amongst all those rare discoveries, and curious pieces I finde in the fabricke of man, I doe not so much content my selfe, as in that I finde not, that is no Organe or instrument for the rationall soule; for in the braine, which wee tearme the seate of reason, there is not any thing of moment more than I can discover in the cranie of a beast:[230] and this is a sensible and no inconsiderable argument of the inorganity of the soule, at least in that sense we usually so receive it. Thus we are men, and we know not how, there is something in us, that can be without us, and will be after us, though it is strange that it hath no history, what it was before us, nor cannot tell how it entred in us.[231]

37. Now for these wals of flesh, wherein the soule doth seeme to be immured before the Resurrection,[232] it is nothing but an elementall composition, and a fabricke that must fall to ashes; *All flesh is grasse*,[233] is not onely metaphorically, but literally true, for all those creatures we behold, are but the hearbs of the field, digested into flesh in them, or more remotely carnified[234] in our selves. Nay further, we are what we all abhorre, *Antropophagi* and Cannibals, devourers not onely of men, but of our selves; and that not in an allegory, but a positive truth; for all this masse of flesh which wee behold, came in at our mouths: this frame wee looke upon, hath beene upon our trenchers; In briefe, we have devoured our selves. I cannot beleeve the wisedome of *Pythagoras* did ever positively, and in a literall sense, affirme his *Metempsychosis*, or impossible transmigration of the

228. Blend.

229. i.e. the soul is the instrument of reason, as the body is that of the senses.

230. The rest of the sentence (to 'so receive it') was not in *UA*.

231. 'Truly sublime and in Sir T. Brown's best manner' (Coleridge).

232. Corrected from 'Restauration' (*MSS.*). Cf. above, p. 67, note 32.

233. Isaiah 40.6.

234. Made into flesh.

soules of men into beasts: of all Metamorphoses or trans-
migrations, I beleeve onely one, that is of *Lots* wife, for that of
Nabuchodonosor proceeded not so farre;[235] In all others I con-
ceive there is no further verity then is contained in their impli-
cite sense and morality: I beleeve that the whole frame of a
beaste doth perish, and is left in the same state after death, as
before it was materialled unto life; that the soules of men know
neither contrary nor corruption, that they subsist beyond the
body, and outlive death by the priviledge of their proper
natures, and without a miracle; that the soules of the faithfull, as
they leave earth, take possession of Heaven: that those appari-
tions, and ghosts of departed persons are not the wandring
soules of men, but the unquiet walkes of Devils, prompting
and suggesting us unto mischiefe, bloud, and villany, instilling,
& stealing into our hearts, that the blessed spirits are not at rest
in their graves, but wander solicitous of the affaires of the
world; that those phantasmes appeare often, and doe frequent
Cemiteries, charnall houses, and Churches, it is because those
are the dormitories of the dead, where the Devill like an insolent
Champion beholds with pride the spoyles and Trophies of his
victory in *Adam*.

38. This is that dismall conquest we all deplore, that makes us
so often cry (O) *Adam, quid fecisti?*[236] I thanke God I have not
those strait ligaments, or narrow obligations to the world, as to
dote on life, or be convulst and tremble at the name of death:
Not that I am insensible of the dread and horrour thereof, or by
raking into the bowells of the deceased, continuall sight of
Anatomies, Skeletons, or Cadaverous reliques, like Vespilloes,
or Grave-makers, I am become stupid, or have forgot the
apprehension of mortality, but that marshalling all the horrours,
and contemplating the extremities thereof, I finde not any thing
therein able to daunt the courage of a man, much lesse a well
resolved Christian. And therefore am not angry at the errour of
our first parents, or unwilling to beare a part of this common

235. The one was changed into a pillar of salt (Genesis 19.26); the
other's hair was 'grown like eagles' feathers, and his nails like birds' claws'
(Daniel 4.33).
236. 'O Adam, what hast thou done?' (2 Esdras 7.48; cf. Genesis 3.13).

fate, and like the best of them to dye, that is, to cease to breathe, to take a farewell of the elements, to be a kinde of nothing for a moment, to be within one instant of a spirit. When I take a full view and circle of my selfe, without this reasonable moderator, and equall piece of justice, Death, I doe conceive my selfe the miserablest person extant; were there not another life that I hope for,[237] all the vanities of this world should not intreat a moments breath from me; could the Devill worke my beliefe to imagine I could ever dye, I would not out-live that very thought; I have so abject a conceit of this common way of existence, this retaining to the Sunne and Elements, I cannot thinke this is to be a man, or to live according to the dignitie of humanity; in expectation of a better I can with patience embrace this life, yet in my best meditations doe often defie death;[238] I honour any man that contemnes it, nor can I highly love any that is afraid of it; this makes me naturally love a Souldier, and honour those tattered and contemptible Regiments that will die at the command of a Sergeant. For a Pagan there may be some motives to bee in love with life, but for a Christian to be amazed at death, I see not how hee can escape this Dilemma, that he is too sensible of this life, or hopelesse[239] of the life to come.

39. Some Divines count *Adam* 30 yeares old at his creation, because they suppose him created in the perfect age and stature of man;[240] and surely wee are all out of the computation of our age, and every man is some moneths elder than hee bethinkes him; for we live, move, have a being, and are subject to the actions of the elements, and the malice of diseases in that other world, the truest Microcosme, the wombe of our mother; for besides that generall and common existence wee are conceived

237. Discussed more fully below, pp. 130 ff.

238. Corrected from 'desire death' (*MSS.*). Also inserted here (*MSS.*): 'It is a symptome of Melancholy to be afraid of death, and yet sometimes to desire it; this latter I have often discovered in my selfe, and thinke noe man ever desired life as I have sometimes Death;'

239. Corrected from 'too carelesse' (*MSS.*), in line with the emphasis here on hope (cf. below, p. 133, note 1).

240. See below, p. 454, note 26. Cf. Browne's own age (mentioned below, pp. 112 and 153).

to hold in our Chaos, and whilst wee sleepe within the bosome of our causes, wee enjoy a being and life in three distinct worlds, wherein we receive most manifest graduations: In that obscure world and wombe of our mother, our time is short, computed by the Moone; yet longer than the dayes of many creatures that behold the Sunne, our selves being not yet without life, sense, and reason,[241] though for the manifestation of its actions, it awaits the opportunity of objects; and seemes to live there but in its roote and soule of vegetation: entring afterwards upon the scene of the world, wee arise up and become another creature, performing the reasonable actions of man, and obscurely manifesting that part of Divinity in us, but not in complement and perfection, till we have once more cast our secondine,[242] that is, this slough of flesh, and are delivered into the last world, that is, that ineffable place of *Paul*, that proper *ubi*[243] of spirits. The smattering I have of the Philosophers stone, (which is something more than the perfect exaltation of gold)[244] hath taught me a great deale of Divinity, and instructed my beliefe, how that immortall spirit and incorruptible substance of my soule may lye obscure, and sleepe a while within this house of flesh. Those strange and mysticall transmigrations that I have observed in Silkewormes, turn'd my Philosophy into Divinity. There is in these workes of nature, which seeme to puzle reason, something Divine, and hath more in it then the eye of a common spectator doth discover.[245]

241. i.e. being potentially in possession of our three 'souls' (as above, p. 73, note 66).

242. 'That skinne wherein the childe is wrapped in the mothers wombe' (Cockeram).

243. Place. St Paul 'was caught up into paradise, and heard unspeakable words, which it is not lawful for a man to utter' (2 Corinthians 12.4).

244. i.e. refining of gold. Cf. Ben Jonson's *The Alchemist*.

245. Inserted here (P only): 'I have therefore forsaken those strict definitions of Death, by privation of life, extinction of naturall heate, separation &c. of soule and body, and have fram'd one in hermeticall way unto my owne fancie; *est mutatio ultima, qua perficitur nobile illud extractum Microcosmi* [i.e. death is the final change, by which that noble portion of the microcosm is perfected], for to mee that consider things in a naturall and experimentall way, man seemes to bee but a digestion or a preparative way unto that last and glorious Elixar which lies imprison'd in the chaines of flesh'.

40. I am naturally bashfull, nor hath conversation, age, or travell, beene able to effront, or enharden me,[246] yet I have one part of modesty, which I have seldome discovered in another, that is (to speake truly) I am not so much afraid of death, as ashamed thereof; tis the very disgrace and ignominy of our natures, that in a moment can so disfigure us that our nearest friends, Wife, and Children stand afraid and start at us. The Birds and Beasts of the field that before in a naturall feare obeyed us, forgetting all allegiance begin to prey upon us. This very conceite hath in a tempest disposed and left me willing to be swallowed up in the abysse of waters; wherein I had perished, unseene, unpityed, without wondring eyes, teares of pity, Lectures of mortality, and none had said, *quantum mutatus ab illo!*[247] Not that I am ashamed of the Anatomy of my parts, or can accuse nature for playing the bungler in any part of me, or my owne vitious life for contracting any shamefull disease upon me, whereby I might not call my selfe as wholesome a morsell for the wormes as any.

41. Some upon the courage of a fruitfull issue, wherein, as in the truest Chronicle, they seem to outlive themselves, can with greater patience away with death. This conceit and counterfeit subsisting in our progenies[248] seemes to mee a meere fallacy, unworthy the desires of a man, that can but conceive a thought of the next world; who, in a nobler ambition, should desire to live in his substance in Heaven rather than his name and shadow in the earth. And therefore at my death I meane to take a totall adieu of the world, not caring for a Monument, History, or Epitaph, not so much as the bare memory of my name to be found any where but in the universall Register of God:[249] I am not yet so Cynicall, as to approve the Testament of *Diogenes*,[250]

246. i.e. to make me less bashful or more bold.

247. 'How terribly changed from that!' (*Aeneid*, II, 274). Said of Hector, whose shade Aeneas meets in Hades.

248. i.e. in our children: the 'fruitfull issue' just mentioned. On man's futile efforts to survive on earth, see further *Hydriotaphia* (below, pp. 261 ff.).

249. The Book of Life (Revelation 20.15).

250. 'Who willed his friend not to bury him, but to hang him up with a staffe in his hand to fright away the Crowes' (Browne marg.). So Cicero, *Tusculan Disputations*, I, 43.

nor doe I altogether allow that *Rodomontado* of *Lucan*;

> *Cælo tegitur, qui non habet urnam.*
> He that unburied lies wants not his Herse,
> For unto him a tombe's the Universe.[251]

But commend in my calmer judgement, those ingenuous intentions that desire to sleepe by the urnes of their Fathers, and strive to goe the nearest way unto corruption. I doe not envie the temper of Crowes and Dawes,[252] nor the numerous and weary dayes of our Fathers before the Flood. If there bee any truth in Astrology, I may outlive a Jubilee,[253] as yet I have not seene one revolution of *Saturne*,[254] nor hath my pulse beate thirty yeares, and yet excepting one, have seene the Ashes, and left underground, all the Kings of *Europe*, have beene contemporary to three Emperours, foure Grand Signiours, and as many Popes;[255] mee thinkes I have outlived my selfe, and begin to bee weary of the Sunne, I have shaked hands with delight in my warme blood and Canicular dayes,[256] I perceive I doe Anticipate the vices of age, the world to mee is but a dreame, or mockshow, and wee all therein but Pantalones[257] and Antickes to my severer contemplations.

42. It is not, I confesse, an unlawfull Prayer to desire to surpasse the dayes of our Saviour, or wish to out-live that age wherein he thought fittest to dye,[258] yet, if (as Divinity affirmes) there shall be no gray hayres in Heaven, but all shall rise in the perfect state of men, we doe but out-live those perfections in this world, to be recalled unto them, by a greater miracle in the next,

251. Lucan, *Pharsalia*, VII, 819.
252. Alike long-lived.
253. 'The Jewish computacion for 50 yeares' (*MSS. marg.*, in *M*).
254. 'The planet of Saturne makes his revolution once in 30 yeares' (*MSS. marg.*, in *M*).
255. The (German) emperors are Rudolph II, Matthias, and Ferdinand II; the four Ottoman emperors: Ahmed I, Mustapha I, Osman II, and Murad IV; and the four Popes: Leo XI, Paul V, Gregory XV, and Urban VIII. The exception is Christian IV of Denmark (d. 1648).
256. '*Dogdayes*. Certain dayes in July and August, so called of the Starre *Canis*, the Dogge: which then rising with the Sun, doeth greatly increase the heate thereof' (Bullokar).
257. 'A french word for Anticks' (*MSS. marg.*, in *M*).
258. Traditionally said to have been thirty-three (cf. Luke 3.23).

and run on here but to be retrograde hereafter. Were there any hopes to out-live vice, or a point to be super-annuated from sin, it were worthy our knees to implore the dayes of *Methuselah*. But age doth not rectifie, but incurvate[259] our natures, turning bad dispositions into worser habits, and (like diseases) brings on incurable vices; for every day as we grow weaker in age, we grow stronger in sinne, and the number of our dayes doth but make our sinnes innumerable. The same vice committed at sixteene, is not the same, though it agree in all other circumstances, at forty, but swels and doubles from the circumstance of our ages, wherein besides the constant and inexcusable habit of transgressing, the maturity of our Judgement cuts off pretence unto excuse or pardon: every sin, the oftner it is committed, the more it acquireth in the quality of evill; as it succeeds in time, so it precedes in degrees of badnesse, for as they proceed they ever multiply, and like figures in Arithmeticke, the last stands for more than all that went before it:[260] And though I thinke no man can live well once but hee that could live twice, yet for my owne part, I would not live over my houres past, or beginne againe the thred of my dayes: not upon *Cicero*'s ground, because I have lived them well,[261] but for feare I should live them worse: I find my growing Judgement dayly instruct me how to be better, but my untamed affections and confirmed vitiosity makes mee dayly doe worse; I finde in my confirmed age the same sinnes I discovered in my youth, I committed many then because I was a child, and because I commit them still I am yet an Infant. Therefore I perceive a man may bee twice a child before the dayes of dotage, and stand in need of *Æsons* bath[262] before threescore.

259. Bend.

260. The rest of this section, and the whole of the next (#43), were not in *UA*. Inserted here instead (*MSS*.): 'The course and order of my life would bee a verie death unto others; I use my selfe to all diets, aires, humours, hunger, thirst, heate; [when] cold, I cure not my selfe by heate; when sicke, not by physicke; those that understand how I live may justly say I regard not life, nor stand in feare of Death'.

261. *On Old Age*, XXIII (84).

262. Which rejuvenated him at Medea's intercession (Ovid, *Metamorphoses*, VII, 159 ff.).

43. And truely there goes a great deale of providence to produce a mans life unto threescore; there is more required than an able temper for those yeeres; though the radicall humour containe in it sufficient oyle for seventie, yet I perceive in some it gives no light past thirtie; men assigne not all the causes of long life that write whole bookes thereof. They that found themselves on the radicall balsome or vitall sulphur[263] of the parts, determine not why *Abel* liv'd not so long as *Adam*. There is therefore a secret glome or bottome[264] of our dayes; 'twas his wisedome to determine them, but his perpetuall and waking providence that fulfils and accomplisheth them, wherein the spirits, our selves, and all the creatures of God in a secret and disputed way doe execute his will. Let them not therefore complaine of immaturitie that die about thirty, they fall but like the whole world, whose solid and well composed substance must not expect the duration and period of its constitution, when all things are compleated in it, its age is accomplished, and the last and generall fever may as naturally destroy it before six thousand,[265] as me before forty, there is therfore some other hand that twines the thread of life than that of nature; wee are not onely ignorant in Antipathies and occult qualities, our ends are as obscure as our beginnings, the line of our dayes is drawne by night, and the various effects therein by a pencill that is invisible; wherein though wee confesse our ignorance, I am sure we doe not erre, if wee say, it is the hand of God.

44. I am much taken with two verses of *Lucan*, since I have beene able not onely, as we doe at Schoole, to construe, but understand:

> *Victurosque Dei celant ut vivere durent,*
> *Felix esse mori.*

> *We're all deluded, vainely searching wayes,*
> *To make us happy by the length of dayes;*
> *For cunningly to make's protract this breath,*
> *The Gods conceale the happines of Death.*

263. Regarded as one of the ultimate constituents of matter.
264. i.e. ball or skein (of thread).
265. The generally accepted limit of the world's history (see below, p. 308, note 18).

There be many excellent straines in that Poet, wherewith his Stoicall Genius hath liberally supplyed him; and truely there are singular pieces in the Philosophy of *Zeno*, and doctrine of the Stoickes, which I perceive, delivered in a Pulpit, passe for currant Divinity: yet herein are they in extreames, that can allow a man to be his owne *Assassine*, and so highly extoll the end and suicide of *Cato*; this is indeed not to feare death, but yet to bee afraid of life. It is a brave act of valour to contemne death, but where life is more terrible than death, it is then the truest valour to dare to live, and herein Religion hath taught us a noble example: For all the valiant acts of *Curtius*, *Scevola* or *Codrus*, do not parallel or match that one of *Job*;[266] and sure there is no torture to[267] the racke of a disease, nor any Poynyards in death it selfe like those in the way or prologue unto it. *Emori nolo, sed me esse mortuum nihil curo*, I would not die, but care not to be dead.[268] Were I of *Cæsars* Religion I should be of his desires, and wish rather to goe off at one blow, then to be sawed in peeces by the grating torture of a disease.[269] Men that looke no further than their outsides thinke health an appertinance unto life, and quarrell with their constitutions for being sick; but I that have examined the parts of man, and know upon what tender filaments that Fabrick hangs, doe wonder that we are not alwayes so; and considering the thousand dores that lead to death doe thanke my God that we can die but once. 'Tis not onely the mischiefe of diseases, and the villanie of poysons that make an end of us, we vainly accuse the fury of Gunnes, and the new inventions of death; 'tis in the power of every hand to destroy us, and wee are beholding unto every one wee meete hee doth not kill us. There is therefore but one comfort left, that though it be in the power of the weakest arme to take away life, it is not in the strongest to deprive us of death: God would not exempt himselfe from that,[270] the misery of immortality in the flesh, he undertooke not that was in it immortall. Certainly there

266. Who refused to 'curse God, and die' (Job 2.9–10).
267. i.e. compared to.
268. Cicero, *Tusculan Disputations*, I, 8.
269. The rest of this section was not in *UA*.
270. i.e. from death (during his incarnate life on earth).

is no happinesse within this circle of flesh, nor is it in the
Opticks of these eyes to behold felicity; the first day of our
Jubilee is death; the devill hath therefore fail'd of his desires;
wee are happier with death than we should have beene without
it: there is no misery but in himselfe where there is no end of
misery; and so indeed in his own sense, the Stoick[271] is in the
right. Hee forgets that hee can die who complaines of misery,
wee are in the power of no calamitie while death is in our
owne.

45. Now besides this literall and positive kinde of death,
there are others whereof Divines make mention, and those I
thinke, not meerely Metaphoricall, as Mortification, dying unto
sin and the world; therefore, I say, every man hath a double
Horoscope, one of his humanity, his birth; another of his
Christianity, his baptisme, and from this doe I compute or
calculate my Nativitie, not reckoning those *Horæ combustæ*,[272]
and odde dayes, or esteeming my selfe any thing, before I was
my Saviours, and inrolled in the Register of Christ: Whosoever
enjoyes not this life, I count him but an apparition, though he
weare about him the sensible affections of flesh. In these morall
acceptions,[273] the way to be immortall is to die daily, nor can I
thinke I have the true Theory of death, when I contemplate a
skull, or behold a Skeleton with those vulgar imaginations it
casts upon us; I have therefore enlarged that common *Memento
mori*,[274] into a more Christian memorandum, *Memento quatuor
novissima*,[275] those foure inevitable points of us all, Death,
Judgement, Heaven, and Hell. Neither did the contemplations
of the Heathens rest in their graves, without a further thought
of *Radamanth* or some judiciall proceeding after death, though
in another way, and upon suggestion of their naturall reasons. I

271. Seneca, *Of Providence*, VI, 7.

272. 'That tyme when the moone is in conjunction and obscured by the
Sunne, the Astrologers call horæ combustæ' (*MSS. marg.*, in *M*).

273. Symbolic senses (R).

274. 'Remember you are to die'.

275. 'Remember the four last things'. The eschatological discourse to
the end of Part I (p. 132) adapts several traditional concepts (§96). Cf. the
sermon in Joyce's *Portrait of the Artist as a Young Man*, itself indebted to a
late seventeenth-century treatise (see *MP*, LVII [1960], 172–98).

cannot but marvaile from what *Sibyll* or Oracle they stole the prophesy of the worlds destruction by fire, or whence *Lucan* learned to say,

> *Communis mundo superest rogus, ossibus astra*
> *Misturus.*
> There yet remaines to th' world one common fire,
> Wherein our bones with stars shall make one pyre.[276]

I beleeve the world growes neare its end, yet is neither old nor decayed, nor will ever perish upon the ruines of its owne principles.[277] As the worke of Creation was above nature, so is its adversary, annihilation; without which the world hath not its end, but its mutation. Now what force should bee able to consume it thus farre, without the breath of God, which is the truest consuming flame, my Philosophy cannot informe me. Some[278] beleeve there went not a minute to the worlds creation, nor shal there go to its destruction; those six dayes so punctually described, make not to them one moment, but rather seem to manifest the method and Idea of the great worke of the intellect of God,[279] than the manner how hee proceeded in its operation. I cannot dreame that there should be at the last day any such Judiciall proceeding, or calling to the Barre, as indeed the Scripture seemes to imply,[280] and the literall commentators doe conceive: for unspeakable mysteries in the Scriptures are often delivered in a vulgar and illustrative way, and being written unto man, are delivered, not as they truely are, but as they may bee understood;[281] wherein notwithstanding the different interpretations according to different capacities may stand

276. Lucan, *Pharsalia*, VII, 814–15.

277. An important qualification to the widespread belief in the world's ever-increasing decay (see §53). *Hydriotaphia* also dwells on the 'great mutations of the world' (below, pp. 261 ff.), while *The Garden of Cyrus* provides the broader context.

278. 'I' (*MSS.*), changed to 'Some' because the passage departs from the literal interpretation of Genesis 1.

279. So Milton's God beholds the newly created world 'how good, how fair, / Answering his great Idea' (*Paradise Lost*, VII, 556–7). See above, p. 31.

280. Matthew 24.2 ff., 2 Peter 3.7 ff., etc.

281. On the theory of accommodation operative here, see above, p. 21 f.

firme with our devotion, nor bee any way prejudiciall to each single edification.

46. Now to determine the day and yeare of this inevitable time, is not onely convincible[282] and statute madnesse, but also manifest impiety; How shall we interpret *Elias* 6000. yeares, or imagine the secret communicated to a Rabbi, which God hath denyed unto his Angels?[283] It had beene an excellent quære, to have posed the devill of *Delphos*,[284] and must needs have forced him to some strange amphibology; it hath not onely mocked the predictions of sundry Astrologers in ages past, but the prophecies of many melancholy heads in these present, who neither understanding reasonably things past or present, pretend a knowledge of things to come, heads ordained onely to manifest the incredible effects of melancholy, and to fulfill old prophesies,[285] rather than be the authors of new. 'In those dayes there shall come warres and rumours of warres',[286] to me seemes no prophesie, but a constant truth, in all times verified since it was pronounced: There shall bee signes in the Moone and Starres, how comes he then like a theefe in the night,[287] when he gives an item of his comming? That common signe drawne from the revelation of Antichrist[288] is as obscure as any; in our common compute he hath beene come these many yeares,[289] but for my owne part to speake freely, I am halfe of opinion that Antichrist is the Philosophers stone in Divinity, for the discovery and invention whereof, though there be prescribed

282. i.e. convictable.

283. Matthew 24.36: 'Of that day and hour knoweth no man, no, not the angels of heaven'. On the prophecy attributed to 'Elias' (Elijah), see below, p. 439, note 31.

284. 'The Oracle of Apollo' at Delphi (*MSS. marg.*, in *M*).

285. 'In those dayes there shall come lyers and false prophets' (Browne marg.). As above, p. 68, note 35.

286. Matthew 24.6.

287. Luke 21.25 and 1 Thessalonians 5.2, respectively.

288. 'that man of sin . . ., the son of perdition; who . . . as God sitteth in the temple God, shewing himself that he is God' (2 Thessalonians 2.3–4; cf. 1 John 2.18).

289. A discreet reference to the numerous Protestant identifications of the Antichrist with the Pope.

rules, and probable inductions, yet hath hardly any man attained the perfect discovery thereof. That generall opinion that the world growes neere its end, hath possessed all ages past as neerely as ours; I am afraid that the Soules that now depart, cannot escape that lingring expostulation of the Saints under the Altar, *Quousque Domine? How long, O Lord?*[290] and groane in the expectation of the great Jubilee.[291]

47. This is the day that must make good that great attribute of God, his Justice, that must reconcile those unanswerable doubts that torment the wisest understandings, and reduce those seeming inequalities, and respective[292] distributions in this world, to an equality and recompensive Justice in the next. This is that one day, that shall include and comprehend all that went before it, wherein as in the last scene, all the Actors must enter to compleate and make up the Catastrophe of this great peece. This is the day whose memory hath onely power to make us honest in the darke, and to bee vertuous without a witnesse. *Ipsa sui pretium virtus sibi*, that vertue is her owne reward,[293] is but a cold principle, and not able to maintaine our variable resolutions in a constant and setled way of goodnesse. I have practised that honest artifice of *Seneca*, and in my retired and solitary imaginations, to detaine me from the foulenesse of vice, have fancyed to my selfe the presence of my deare and worthiest friends,[294] before whom I should lose my head, rather than be vitious, yet herein I found that there was nought but morall honesty, and this was not to be vertuous for his sake who must reward us at the last. I have tryed if I could reach that great resolution of his,[295] to be honest without a thought of Heaven or Hell; and indeed I found upon a naturall inclination, an inbred loyalty unto vertue, that I could serve her without a livery, yet not in that resolved and venerable way, but that the

290. Revelation 6.9–10.

291. The earlier specific reference (above, p. 112, note 253) is now transmuted into the Day of Judgement.

292. Discriminating, partial.

293. A proverbial utterance phrased among others by Seneca, *On the Happy Life*, IX, 4.

294. Seneca, *Moral Letters*, XXV, 5–6; quoting Epicurus.

295. ibid., CXIII, 31.

frailty of my nature, upon an easie temptation, might be induced to forget her. The life therefore and spirit of all our actions, is the resurrection, and stable apprehension, that our ashes shall enjoy the fruit of our pious endeavours; without this, all Religion is a Fallacy, and those impieties of *Lucian*, *Euripedes*,[296] and *Julian* are no blasphemies, but subtile verities, and Atheists have beene the onely Philosophers.[297]

48. How shall the dead arise, is no question of my faith; to beleeve onely possibilities, is not faith, but meere Philosophy; many things are true in Divinity, which are neither inducible by reason, nor confirmable by sense, and many things in Philosophy confirmable by sense, yet not inducible by reason. Thus it is impossible by any solid or demonstrative reasons to perswade a man to beleeve the conversion of the Needle to the North; though this be possible, and true, and easily credible, upon a single experiment unto the sense. I beleeve that our estranged and divided ashes shall unite againe, that our separated dust after so many pilgrimages and transformations into the parts of mineralls, Plants, Animals, Elements, shall at the voyce of God returne into their primitive shapes; and joyne againe to make up their primary and predestinate formes. As at the Creation, there was a separation of that confused masse[298] into its species, so at the destruction thereof there shall bee a separation into its distinct individuals. As at the Creation of the world, all the distinct species that wee behold, lay involved in one masse, till the fruitfull voyce of God separated this united multitude into its severall species: so at the last day, when these corrupted reliques shall be scattered in the wildernesse of formes, and seeme to have forgot their proper habits, God by a powerfull voyce shall command them backe into their proper shapes, and call them out by their single individuals: Then shall appeare the fertilitie of *Adam*, and the magicke of that sperme that hath dilated into so many millions.[299] I have often beheld

296. Whose 'impieties' include a sustained effort to discredit the traditional gods. Cf. below, p. 311, note 32.

297. 'That is, if nothing remaine after this life' (Keck).

298. Chaos (as above, p. 76, note 84).

299. Inserted here (*MSS.*): 'What is made to bee immortall, nature

as a miracle, that artificiall resurrection and revivification of *Mercury*, how being mortified[300] into thousand shapes, it assumes againe its owne, and returns into its numericall selfe. Let us speake naturally, and like Philosophers, the formes of alterable bodies in these sensible corruptions perish not; nor, as wee imagine, wholly quit their mansions, but retire and contract themselves into their secret and unaccessible parts, where they may best protect themselves from the action of their Antagonist. A plant or vegetable consumed to ashes, to a contemplative and schoole[301] Philosopher seemes utterly destroyed, and the forme to have taken his leave for ever: But to a sensible Artist[302] the formes are not perished, but withdrawne into their incombustible part, where they lie secure from the action of that devouring element. This is made good by experience, which can from the ashes of a plant revive the plant, and from its cinders recall it into its stalk and leaves again.[303] What the Art of man can doe in these inferiour pieces, what blasphemy is it to affirme the finger of God cannot doe in these more perfect and sensible structures ? This is that mysticall Philosophy, from whence no true Scholler becomes an Atheist, but from the visible effects of nature, growes up a reall Divine, and beholds not in a dreame, as *Ezekiel*,[304] but in an ocular and visible object the types of his resurrection.

49. Now, the necessary Mansions of our restored selves are those two contrary and incompatible places wee call Heaven

cannot nor will the voice of God destroy; these bodies wee behold to perish were in their created natures immortall, and liable to death but accidentally, and upon forfeit; therefore they owe not that naturall homage unto death, as other creatures, but may bee restored to immortality by a lesser miracle, and by a bare and easie revocation of the curse returne immortall;'

300. Dissolved in acid.

301. i.e. scholastic (cf. above, p. 69, note 39).

302. i.e. the creative man of sense who perceives the truth (as above, p. 31). Corrected from 'suttle' (*MSS.*).

303. 'This was, I believe, some lying Boast of Paracelsus, which the good Sir T. Brown has swallowed for a Truth' (Coleridge). Not quite; for Browne appears to have consulted an actual if misinterpreted experiment (*M*).

304. Ezekiel 37.1 ff.

and Hell; to define them, or strictly to determine what and where these are, surpasseth my Divinity. That elegant Apostle[305] which seemed to have a glimpse of Heaven, hath left but a negative description thereof; Which neither eye hath seen, nor eare hath heard, nor can enter into the heart of man: he was translated out of himself to behold it, but being returned into himselfe could not expresse it. Saints *Johns* description by Emeralds, Chrysolites, and pretious stones,[306] is too weake to expresse the materiall Heaven we behold. Briefely therefore, where the soule hath the full measure, and complement of happinesse, where the boundlesse appetite of that spirit remaines compleatly satisfied, that it can neither desire addition nor alteration, that I thinke is truely Heaven: and this can onely be in the enjoyment of that essence, whose infinite goodnesse is able to terminate the desires of it selfe, and the unsatiable wishes of ours; whereever God will thus manifest himselfe, there is Heaven, though within the circle of this sensible world. Thus the soule of man may bee in Heaven any where, even within the limits of his owne proper body, and when it ceaseth to live in the body, it may remaine in its owne soule, that is its Creator. And thus wee may say that Saint *Paul*, whether in the body, or out of the body, was yet in Heaven.[307] To place it in the Empyreall, or beyond the tenth Spheare,[308] is to forget the worlds destruction; for when this sensible world shall bee destroyed, all shall then be here as it is now there, an Empyreall Heaven, a *quasi* vacuitie, when to aske where Heaven is, is to demand where the presence of God is, or where wee have the glory of that happy vision. *Moses* that was bred up in all the learning of the *Egyptians*, committed a grosse absurdity in Philosophy, when with these eyes of flesh he desired to see God,[309] and petitioned his Maker, that is truth it selfe, to a contradiction. Those that imagine Heaven and Hell

305. St Paul, whose verses are quoted next (1 Corinthians 2.9 and 2 Corinthians 12.4: see above, p. 110, note 243).
306. Revelation 21.19–21.
307. 2 Corinthians 12.2.
308. Which enclosed the moving spheres of Ptolemaic cosmology. Heaven was said to be situated beyond it.
309. Exodus 33.17 ff. See also above, p. 104, note 212.

neighbours, and conceive a vicinity between those two extreames, upon consequence of the Parable, where *Dives* discoursed with *Lazarus*[310] in *Abrahams* bosome, do too grossely conceive of those glorified creatures, whose eyes shall easily out-see the Sunne, and behold without a Perspective,[311] the extremest distances: for if there shall be in our glorified eyes, the faculty of sight & reception of objects I could thinke the visible species[312] there to be in as unlimitable a way as now the intellectuall. I grant that two bodies placed beyond the tenth Spheare, or in a vacuity, according to *Aristotles* Philosophy,[313] could not behold each other, because there wants a body or Medium to hand and transport the visible rayes of the object unto the sense; but when there shall be a generall defect of either Medium to convey, or light to prepare & dispose that Medium, and yet a perfect vision, wee must suspend the rules of our Philosophy, and make all good by a more absolute piece of Opticks.

50. I cannot tell how to say that fire is the essence of hell, I know not what to make of Purgatory, or conceive a flame that can either prey upon, nor purifie the substance of a soule; those flames of sulphure mentioned in the Scriptures,[314] I take not to be understood of this present Hell,[315] but of that to come, where fire shall make up the complement of our tortures, & have a body or subject wherein to manifest its tyranny: Some who have had the honour to be textuarie[316] in Divinity, are of opinion it shall be the same specificall fire with ours. This is hard to conceive, yet can I make good how even that may prey upon our bodies, and yet not consume us: for in this materiall world, there are bodies that persist invincible in the powerfullest flames, and though by the action of fire they fall into ignition and liquation,[317] yet will they never suffer a destruction: I

310. Luke 16.19 ff.
311. Telescope.
312. i.e. external appearances.
313. *On the Soul*, II, 7.
314. Revelation 21.8, etc.
315. See the next section (#51).
316. Authoritative.
317. i.e. they burn and melt.

would gladly know how *Moses* with an actuall fire calcin'd,[318] or burnt the golden Calfe into powder: for that mysticall mettle of gold, whose solary and celestial nature I admire, exposed unto the violence of fire, grows onely hot and liquifies, but consumeth not: so when the consumable and volatile pieces of our bodies shall be refined into a more impregnable and fixed temper like gold, though they suffer from the action of flames, they shall never perish, but lie immortall in the armes of fire. And surely if this frame must suffer onely by the action of this element, there will many bodies escape, and not onely Heaven, but earth will not bee at an end, but rather a beginning; For at present it is not earth, but a composition of fire, water, earth, and aire; but at that time spoyled of these ingredients, it shall appeare in a substance more like it selfe, its ashes. Philosophers that opinioned the worlds destruction by fire, did never dreame of annihilation, which is beyond the power of sublunary causes; for the last and proper action of that element is but vitrification or a reduction of a body into Glasse; & therefore some of our Chymicks[319] facetiously affirm, that at the last fire all shall be crystallized & reverberated[320] into glasse, which is the utmost action of that element. Nor need we fear this term 'annihilation' or wonder that God will destroy the workes of his Creation: for man subsisting, who is, and will then truely appeare a Microcosme, the world cannot bee said to be destroyed. For the eyes of God, and perhaps also of our glorified selves, shall as really behold and contemplate the world in its Epitome or contracted essence, as now it doth at large and in its dilated substance.[321] In the seed of a Plant to the eyes of God, and to the understanding of man, there exists, though in an invisible way, the perfect leaves, flowers, and fruit thereof: (for things that are in *posse* to the sense, are actually existent to the understanding.) Thus God beholds all things, who contemplates as fully his

318. 'Calcination a chymicall terme for the reduction of a minerall into powder' (*MSS. marg.*, in *M*). The Biblical reference is Deuteronomy 9.21.

319. i.e. chemists; but here more properly alchemists.

320. i.e. altered by heat.

321. i.e. the universe at large (the macrocosm) which is reflected in the 'little compendium' or microcosm of man. Cf. above, p. 103, note 208.

workes in their Epitome, as in their full volume, and beheld as amply the whole world in that little compendium of the sixth day, as in the scattered and dilated pieces of those five before.

51. Men commonly set forth the torments of Hell by fire, and the extremity of corporall afflictions, and describe Hell in the same method that *Mahomet* doth Heaven. This indeed makes a noyse, and drums in popular eares: but if this be the terrible piece thereof, it is not worthy to stand in diameter with Heaven, whose happinesse consists in that part that is best able to comprehend it, that immortall essence, that translated divinity and colony of God, the soule.[322] Surely though wee place Hell under earth, the Devils walke and purlue is about it; men speake too popularly who place it in those flaming mountaines,[323] which to grosser apprehensions represent Hell. The heart of man is the place the devill dwels in; I feele sometimes a hell within my selfe, *Lucifer* keeps his court in my brest, *Legion*[324] is revived in me. There are as many hels as *Anaxagoras* conceited worlds: there was more than one hell in *Magdalen*, when there were seven devils; for every devill is an hell unto himselfe: hee holds enough of torture in his owne *ubi*, and needs not the misery of circumference to afflict him, and thus a distracted conscience here is a shadow or introduction unto hell hereafter; Who can but pity the mercifull intention of those hands that doe destroy themselves? the devill were it in his power would doe the like, which being impossible his miseries are endlesse, and he suffers most in that attribute wherein he is impassible,[325] his immortality.

52. I thanke God, and with joy I mention it, I was never afraid of Hell, nor never grew pale at the description of that place; I have so fixed my contemplations on Heaven, that I have almost forgot the Idea of Hell, and am afraid rather to lose the joyes of the one than endure the misery of the other; to be deprived of them is a perfect hell, & needs me thinkes no addition to compleate our afflictions; that terrible terme hath never

322. The rest of this section was not in *UA*.
323. i.e. volcanoes.
324. The host of demonic spirits (cf. Mark 5.9).
325. Beyond harm.

detained me from sin, nor do I owe any good action to the name thereof: I feare God, yet am not afraid of him, his mercies make me ashamed of my sins, before his judgements afraid thereof: these are the forced and secondary method of his wisedome, which he useth but as the last remedy, and upon provocation, a course rather to deterre the wicked, than incite the vertuous to his worship. I can hardly thinke there was ever any scared into Heaven, they goe the fairest way to Heaven, that would serve God without a Hell, other Mercentaries that crouch unto him in feare of Hell, though they terme themselves the servants, are indeed but the slaves of the Almighty.

53. And to be true, and speake my soule, when I survey the occurrences of my life, and call into account the finger of God, I can perceive nothing but an abysse and masse of mercies, either in generall to mankind, or in particular to my selfe; and whether out of the prejudice of my affection, or an inverting and partiall conceit of his mercies, I know not, but those which others terme crosses, afflictions, judgements, misfortunes, to me who enquire farther into them than their visible effects, they both appeare, and in event have ever proved the secret and dissembled favours of his affection. It is a singular piece of wisedome to apprehend truly, and without passion the workes of God, and so well to distinguish his justice from his mercy, as not to miscall those noble attributes; yet it is likewise an honest piece of Logick so to dispute and argue the proceedings of God, as to distinguish even his judgements into mercies. For God is mercifull unto all, because better to the worst, than the best deserve, and to say he punisheth none in this world, though it be a Paradox, is no absurdity. To one that hath committed murther, if the Judge should say, onely ordaine a Fine,[326] it were a madnesse to call this a punishment, and to repine at the sentence, rather than admire the clemency of the Judge. Thus our offences being mortall, and deserving not onely death, but damnation, if the goodnesse of God be content to traverse and passe them over with a losse, misfortune, or disease; what frensie were it to terme this a punishment, rather than an extremity of mercy, and to groane under the rod of his judge-

326. Corrected from 'boxe of the eare' (P).

ments, rather than admire the Scepter of his mercies? Therefore to adore, honour, and admire him, is a debt of gratitude due from the obligation of our nature, states, and conditions; and with these thoughts, he that knowes them best, will not deny that I adore him; that I obtaine Heaven, and the blisse thereof, is accidentall, and not the intended worke of my devotion, it being a felicitie I can neither thinke to deserve, nor scarse in modesty to expect. For these two ends of us all, either as rewards or punishments, are mercifully ordained and disproportionally disposed unto our actions, the one being so far beyond our deserts, the other so infinitely below our demerits.

54. There is no salvation to those that beleeve not in Christ, that is, say some, since his Nativity, and as Divinity affirmeth, before also; which makes me much apprehend the end of those honest Worthies and Philosophers which died before his Incarnation. It is hard to place those soules in Hell whose worthy lives doe teach us vertue on earth; methinks amongst those many subdivisions of hell, there might have bin one Limbo left for these:[327] What a strange vision will it be to see their poeticall fictions converted into verities, & their imagined & fancied Furies, into reall Devils? how strange to them will sound the History of *Adam*, when they shall suffer for him they never heard of? when they derive their Genealogy from the Gods, shall know they are the unhappy issue of sinfull man? It is an insolent part of reason to controvert the works of God, or question the justice of his proceedings; Could humility teach others, as it hath instructed me, to contemplate the infinite and incomprehensible distance betwixt the Creator and the creature, or did wee seriously perpend that one Simile of Saint *Paul, Shall the vessell say to the Potter, Why hast thou made me thus?*[328] it would prevent these arrogant disputes of reason, nor would wee argue the definitive sentence of God, either to Heaven or Hell. Men that live according to the right rule and law of reason, live but in their owne kinde, as beasts doe in theirs; who justly obey the prescript of their natures, and therefore cannot

327. The passage is said to have been 'obviously inspired' by Dante, *Inferno*, IV, 31–45 (§220). On 'perpend' see below, p. 166, note 3.
328. Cf. Romans 9.20–21.

reasonably demand a reward of their actions, as onely obeying the naturall dictates of their reason. It will therefore, and must at last appeare, that all salvation is through Christ; which verity I feare these great examples of vertue must confirme, and make it good, how the perfectest actions of earth have no title or claime unto Heaven.

55. Nor truely doe I thinke the lives of these or of any other were ever correspondent, or in all points conformable unto their doctrines; it is evident that *Aristotle* transgressed the rule of his owne Ethicks;[329] the Stoicks that condemne passion, and command a man to laugh in *Phalaris* his Bull, could not endure without a groane a fit of the stone or collick. The *Scepticks* that affirmed they know nothing, even in that opinion confute themselves, and thought they knew more than all the world beside. *Diogenes* I hold to bee the most vainegglorious man of his time, and more ambitious in refusing all honours, than *Alexander* in rejecting none. Vice and the Devill put a fallacie upon our reasons and provoking us too hastily to run from it, entangle and profound us deeper in it. The Duke of *Venice*, that weds himselfe unto the Sea, by a ring of Gold,[330] I will not argue of prodigality, because it is a solemnity of good use and consequence in the State. But the Philosopher[331] that threw his money into the Sea to avoyd avarice, was a notorious prodigal. There is no road or ready way to vertue, it is not an easie point of art to disentangle our selves from this riddle, or web of sin: To perfect vertue, as to Religion, there is required a Panoplia or compleat armour,[332] that whilst we lye at close ward against one vice we lye open to the vennie[333] of another: And indeed wiser discretions that have the thred of reason to conduct them, offend without a pardon; whereas under heads[334] may stumble without dishonour. There goe so many circumstances to piece

329. *Nicomachean Ethics*, VIII, x, 1–3, which was said to have been contradicted in Aristotle's relationship with the tyrant Hermias.

330. The annual ritual of Venice's marriage to the sea celebrated her bountiful seaborne empire.

331. Crates the Cynic (as reported by Diogenes Laertius, VI, 87).

332. Cf. Ephesians 6.13: 'take unto you the whole armour of God' etc.

333. Hit or thrust (in fencing).

334. Persons of inferior intelligence.

up one good action, that it is a lesson to be good, and wee are forced to be vertuous by the booke. Againe, the practice of men holds not an equall pace, yea, and often runnes counter to their Theory; we naturally know what is good, but naturally pursue what is evill:[335] the Rhetoricke wherewith I perswade another cannot perswade my selfe: there is a depraved appetite in us, that will with patience heare the learned instructions of Reason; but yet performe no farther than agrees to its owne irregular Humour. In briefe, we all are monsters, that is, a composition of man and beast, wherein we must endeavour to be as the Poets fancy that wise man *Chiron*,[336] that is, to have the Region of Man above that of Beast, and sense to sit but at the feete of reason. Lastly, I doe desire with God, that all, but yet affirme with men, that few shall know salvation, that the bridge is narrow, the passage straite unto life;[337] yet those who doe confine the Church of God, either to particular Nations, Churches, or Families, have made it farre narrower than our Saviour ever meant it.[338]

56. The vulgarity of those judgements that wrap the Church of God in *Strabo*'s cloake and restraine it unto Europe,[339] seeme to mee as bad Geographers as *Alexander*, who thought hee had conquer'd all the world when hee [had] not subdued the halfe of any part thereof: For wee cannot deny the Church of God both in Asia and Africa, if we doe not forget the peregrinations of the Apostles, the death of their Martyrs, the sessions of many, and even in our reformed[340] judgement lawfull councells held in those parts in the minoritie and nonage of ours: nor must a few differences more remarkable in the eyes of man than perhaps in the judgement of God, excommunicate from heaven

335. Cf. Romans 7.19: 'the good that I would, I do not: but the evil which I would not, that I do'.

336. 'Chiron, a Centaure' (*MSS. marg.*, in *M*).

337. Cf. 1 Timothy 2.3-4 ('God . . . will have all men to be saved') and Matthew 7.14 ('straight is the gate, and narrow is the way, which leadeth unto life, and few there be that find it').

338. The next section was not in *UA*.

339. Strabo's *Geography* (II, v, 14) likens the known inhabited world to a short cloak spread out (R).

340. i.e. Protestant.

one another, much lesse those Christians who are in a manner all Martyrs, maintaining their faith in the noble way of persecution, and serving God in the fire, whereas we honour him but in the Sunshine. 'Tis true we all hold there is a number of Elect[341] and many to be saved, yet take our opinions together, and from the confusion thereof there will be no such thing as salvation, nor shall any one be saved; for first the Church of *Rome* condemneth us, wee likewise them, the Sub-reformists and Sectaries[342] sentence the Doctrine of our Church as damnable, the Atomist, or Familist[343] reprobates all these, and all these them againe. Thus whilst the mercies of God doth promise us heaven, our conceits and opinions exclude us from that place. There must be therefore more than one Saint *Peter*, particular Churches and Sects usurpe the gates of heaven, and turne the key against each other, and thus we goe to heaven against each others wills, conceits and opinions, and with as much uncharity as ignorance, doe erre I feare in points, not onely of our own, but on[e] anothers salvation.

57. I beleeve many are saved who to man seeme reprobated, and many are reprobated, who in the opinion and sentence of man, stand elected; there will appeare at the last day, strange, and unexpected examples, both of his justice and his mercy, and therefore to define either is folly in man, and insolency, even in the devils; those acute and substill spirits, in all their sagacity, can hardly divine who shall be saved, which if they could prognostick,[344] their labour were at an end; nor need they compasse the earth, seeking whom they may devoure. Those who upon a rigid application of the Law, sentence *Solomon* unto damnation,[345] condemne not onely him, but themselves, and

341. Mark 13.20 ('the elect . . . whom he hath chosen'), etc.

342. i.e. reformers who demand further reformation, and dissenters.

343. 'Atomist' could be a reference to the fundamentalist sect of the Adamites, or may simply mean 'materialist'. The 'Familist' is a member of the Family of Love, a revolutionary sect of mystics.

344. Foretell. In the preceding lines, Browne 'must have had before his mind' not only Matthew 8.11–12 ('many shall come from the east and west . . . in the kingdom of heaven') but its expansion by Dante in *Paradiso*, XIX, 103 ff., and XX, 133 ff. (§220).

345. i.e. in that he was not baptised. Cf. Romans 2.12.

the whole world; for by the letter, and written Word[346] of God,
we are without exception in the state of death, but there is a
prerogative of God, and an arbitrary pleasure above the letter
of his owne Law, by which alone wee can pretend unto salva-
tion, and through which *Solomon* might be as easily saved as
those who condemne him.

58. The number of those who pretend unto salvation, and
those infinite swarmes who thinke to passe through the eye of
this Needle,[347] have much amazed me. That name and com-
pellation of *little Flocke*,[348] doth not comfort but deject my
devotion, especially when I reflect upon mine owne un-
worthinesse, wherein, according to my humble apprehensions,
I am below them all. I beleeve there shall never be an Anarchy
in Heaven, but as there are Hierarchies amongst the Angels,[349]
so shall there be degrees of priority amongst the Saints. Yet is it
(I protest) beyond my ambition to aspire unto the first rankes,
my desires onely are, and I shall be happy therein, to be but the
last man, and bring up the Rere in Heaven.

59. Againe, I am confident, and fully perswaded, yet dare not
take my oath of my salvation; I am as it were sure, and do
beleeve, without all doubt, that there is such a City as *Con-
stantinople*, yet for me to take my oath thereon, were a kinde of
perjury, because I hold no infallible warrant from my owne
sense to confirme me in the certainty thereof. And truely,
though many pretend an absolute certainty of their salvation,
yet when an humble soule shall contemplate her owne un-
worthinesse, she shall meete with many doubts and suddainely
finde how little[350] wee stand in need of the precept of Saint *Paul,
Worke out your salvation with feare and trembling.*[351] That which is
the cause of my election, I hold to be the cause of my salvation,
which was the mercy, and beneplacit[352] of God, before I was, or

346. Corrected from 'law' (*MSS.*).
347. Matthew 19.24: 'It is easier for a camel to go through the eye of a
needle, than for a rich man to enter the kingdom of God'.
348. Luke 12.32.
349. Widely accepted by Protestants in principle, even as the traditional
division into nine orders was consistently opposed (§94).
350. Corrected from 'much' (*P*; *K*).   351. Philippians 2.12.
352. Good pleasure, gracious purpose.

the foundation of the world. *Before Abraham was, I am*, is the saying of Christ,[353] yet is it true in some sense[354] if I say it of my selfe, for I was not onely before my selfe, but *Adam*, that is, in the Idea of God, and the decree of that Synod held from all Eternity.[355] And in this sense, I say, the world was before the Creation, and at an end before it had a beginning;[356] and thus was I dead before I was alive, though my grave be *England*, my dying place was Paradise, and *Eve* miscarried of mee before she conceiv'd of *Cain*.

60. Insolent zeales that doe decry good workes and rely onely[357] upon faith, take not away merit: for depending upon the efficacy of their faith, they enforce the condition of God, and in a more sophisticall way doe seeme to challenge Heaven. It was decreed by God, that onely those that lapt in the water like dogges, should have the honour to destroy the *Midianites*,[358] yet could none of those justly challenge, or imagine hee deserved that honour thereupon. I doe not deny, but that true faith, and such as God requires, is not onely a marke or token, but also a meanes of our Salvation, but where to finde this, is as obscure to me, as my last end. And if our Saviour could object unto[359] his owne Disciples & favourites, a faith, that to the quantity of a graine of Mustard seed, is able to remove mountaines; surely that which wee boast of, is not any thing, or at the most, but a remove from nothing. This is the Tenor of my beleefe, wherein, though there be many things singular, and to the humour of my irregular selfe, yet, if they square not with maturer Judgements, I disclaime them, and doe no further father them, than the learned and best Judgements shall authorize them.

353. John, 8.58.

354. 'in some sense' was not in *UA*.

355. i.e. the council of the triune Godhead in Genesis 1.26 ('Let *us* make man in *our* image'). On 'the Idea of God' see above, p. 31.

356. The rest of this section was not in *UA*.

357. 'onely' (not in *UA*) was added here to suggest Browne's reluctance to side with Protestant zealots ('zeales') who proclaimed justification solely by faith (*sola fide*) at the expense of good works ('merit').

358. Judges 7.4–7.

359. Place before. Cf. Matthew 17.20.

THE SECOND PART

1. Now for that other Vertue of Charity,[1] without which
Faith is a meer notion, and of no existence, I have ever en-
deavoured to nourish the mercifull disposition, and humane
inclination I borrowed from my Parents, and regulate it to the
written and prescribed Lawes of Charity; and if I hold the true
Anatomy of my selfe, I am delineated & naturally framed to
such a piece of vertue: for I am of a constitution so generall,
that it consorts, and sympathizeth with all things; I have no
antipathy, or rather Idio-syncrasie,[2] in dyet, humour, ayre, any
thing; I wonder not at the *French*, for their dishes of frogges,
snailes, and toadstooles, nor at the Jewes for Locusts and
Grasse-hoppers, but being amongst them, make them my
common viands; and I finde they agree with my stomach as well
as theirs; I could digest a Sallad gathered in a Church-yard, as
well as in a Garden. I cannot start at the presence of a Serpent,
Scorpion, Lizard, or Salamander; at the sight of a Toad, or
Viper, I finde in me no desire to take up a stone to destroy
them. I feele not in my selfe those common antipathies that I
can discover in others: Those nationall repugnances doe not
touch me, nor doe I behold with prejudice the *French*, *Italian*,
Spaniard, or *Dutch*; but where I finde their actions in ballance
with my Countreymens, I honour, love, and embrace them in
the same degree; I was borne in the eighth Climate,[3] but seeme
for to bee framed, and constelled unto all; I am no Plant that
will not prosper out of a Garden. All places, all ayres make
unto me one Country; I am in *England*, every where, and under
any meridian; I have beene shipwrackt,[4] yet am not enemy with
the sea or winds; I can study, play, or sleepe in a tempest. In
briefe, I am averse from nothing, my conscience would give mee
the lie if I should say I absolutely detest or hate any essence but

1. The casual reminder that Part II is to be concerned with charity,
alerts us in retrospect to the concern of Part I with the other two cardinal
virtues, faith and hope. See above, p. 49.
2. 'peculiar temperament' (Coleridge).
3. i.e. England. 'Climate' is a belt of the earth's surface contained
between two parallels of latitude (*OED*).
4. On his return from a visit to Ireland in 1629.

the Devill, or so at least abhorre any thing but that wee might come to composition. If there be any among those common objects of hatred I doe contemne and laugh at, it is that great enemy of reason, vertue and religion, the multitude, that numerous piece of monstrosity, which taken asunder seeme men, and the reasonable creatures of God; but confused together, make but one great beast, & a monstrosity more prodigious than Hydra; it is no breach of Charity to call these fooles, it is the stile all holy Writers have afforded them, set downe by *Solomon* in canonicall Scripture,[5] and a point of our faith to beleeve so. Neither in the name of multitude doe I onely include the base and minor sort of people; there is a rabble even amongst the Gentry, a sort of Plebeian heads, whose fancy moves with the same wheele as these; men in the same Levell with Mechanickes,[6] though their fortunes doe somewhat guild their infirmities, and their purses compound for their follies. But as in casting account, three or foure men together come short in account of one man placed by himself below them:[7] So neither are a troope of these ignorant Doradoes,[8] of that true esteeme and value, as many a forlorne person, whose condition doth place them below their feet. Let us speake like Politicians, there is a Nobility without Heraldry, a naturall dignity, whereby one man is ranked with another, another Filed before him, according to the quality of his desert, and preheminence of his good parts.[9] Though the corruption of these times, and the byas of present practise wheele another way, thus it was in the first and primitive Common-wealths, and is yet in the integrity and Cradle of well-ordered polities, till corruption getteth ground, ruder desires labouring after that which wiser considerations contemn, every one having a liberty to amasse &

5. Proverbs 1.7 ('fools despise wisdom and instruction'), etc. Denunciations of the multitude, commonplace in Browne's age, include an outburst by the saintly Lancelot Andrewes (§262).

6. The uneducated.

7. The reference is probably to the standard abacus with two banks of beads, above and below; so that 'three or foure men [i.e. gentlemen] together come short' of the one below, who is worth five (§258).

8. Rich men (literally the gilded ones).

9. The social hierarchy here, parallels the cosmic one above (p. 101).

heape up riches, and they a license or faculty to doe or purchase any thing.

2. This generall and indifferent temper of mine, doth more neerely dispose mee to this noble vertue. It is a happinesse to be borne and framed unto vertue, and to grow up from the seeds of nature, rather than the inoculation and forced graftes of education; yet if we are directed only by our particular Natures, and regulate our inclinations by no higher rule than that of our reasons, we are but Moralists; Divinity will still call us Heathens. Therfore this great worke of charity, must have other motives, ends, and impulsions: I give no almes[10] to satisfie the hunger of my Brother, but to fulfill and accomplish the Will and Command of my God; I draw not my purse for his sake that demands it, but his that enjoyned it; I relieve no man upon the Rhetorick of his miseries, nor to content mine own commiserating disposition, for this is still but morall charity, and an act that oweth more to passion than reason. Hee that relieves another upon the bare suggestion and bowels of pity, doth not this so much for his sake as for his own: for by compassion we make anothers misery our own, & so by relieving them, we relieve our selves also. It is as erroneous a conceite to redresse other mens misfortunes upon the common considerations of mercifull natures, that it may bee one day our own case, for this is a sinister and politick kind of charity, whereby we seem to bespeak the pities of men, in the like occasions; and truly I have observed that those professed Eleemosynaries,[11] though in a croud or multitude, doe yet direct and place their petitions on a few and selected persons; there is surely a Physiognomy, which those experienced and Master Mendicants observe, whereby they instantly discover a mercifull aspect, and will single out a face, wherein they spy the signatures and markes of mercy: for there are mystically in our faces certaine characters which carry in them the motto of our Soules, wherein he that cannot read *A.B.C.* may read our natures. I hold moreover that there is a Phytognomy,[12] or Physiognomy, not onely

10. The 1678 edition was the first to add 'only' after 'almes'.
11. Beggars.
12. Vegetable physiognomy, as Browne makes clear.

of men, but of Plants, and Vegetables; and in every one of them, some outward figures which hang as signes or bushes of their inward formes. The finger of God hath left an inscription upon all his workes, not graphicall or composed of Letters, but of their severall formes, constitutions, parts, and operations, which aptly joyned together doe make one word that doth expresse their natures. By these Letters God cals the Starres by their names, and by this Alphabet *Adam* assigned to every creature a name peculiar to its Nature.[13] Now there are besides these Characters in our faces, certaine mysticall figures[14] in our hands, which I dare not call meere dashes, strokes, *a la volèe*, or at randome, because delineated by a pencill, that never workes in vaine; and hereof I take more particular notice, because I carry that in mine owne hand, which I could never read of, nor discover in another. *Aristotle*, I confesse, in his acute, and singular booke of Physiognomy,[15] hath made no mention of Chiromancy, yet I beleeve the *Egyptians*, who were neerer addicted to those abstruse and mysticall sciences, had a knowledge therein, to which those vagabond and counterfeit *Egyptians*[16] did after pretend, and perhaps retained a few corrupted principles, which sometimes might verifie their prognostickes.

It is the common wonder of all men, how among so many millions of faces, there should be none alike; Now contrary, I wonder as much how there should be any; he that shall consider how many thousand severall words have beene carelesly and without study composed out of 24. Letters;[17] withall how many hundred lines there are to be drawn in the fabrick of one man; shall easily finde that this variety is necessary: And it will bee very hard that they shall so concur as to make one portract like another. Let a Painter carelesly limbe out a Million of faces, and you shall finde them all different, yea let him have his copy[18] before him, yet after all his art there will remaine a sensible

13. Psalm 147–4 and Genesis 2.19–20, respectively.

14. Corrected from 'lines and figures' (*MSS.*).

15. i.e. the apocryphal *Physiognomica* (§241).

16. i.e. gipsies.

17. Here reduced from twenty-six because i/j and u/v were commonly regarded as single letters.

18. i.e. model.

distinction; for the patterne or example of every thing is the perfectest in that kind, whereof wee still come short, though wee transcend or goe beyond it, because herein it is wide and agrees not in all points unto its Copy.[19] Nor doth the similitude of creatures disparage the variety of nature, nor any way confound the workes of God. For even in things alike, there is diversitie, and those that doe seeme to accord doe manifestly disagree. And thus is Man like God, for in the same things that wee resemble him, wee are utterly different from him. There was never any thing so like another, as in all points to concurre, there will ever some reserved difference slip in, to prevent the Identity, without which, two severall things would not be alike, but the same, which is impossible.

3. But to returne from Philosophy to Charity, I hold not so narrow a conceit of this vertue, as to conceive that to give almes, is onely to be Charitable, or thinke a piece of Liberality can comprehend the Totall of Charity; Divinity hath wisely divided the act thereof into many branches, and hath taught us in this narrow way, many pathes unto goodnesse; as many wayes as we may doe good, so many wayes we may bee Charitable; there are infirmities, not onely of body, but of soule, and fortunes, which doe require the mercifull hand of our abilities. I cannot contemn a man for ignorance but behold him with as much pity as I doe *Lazarus*.[20] It is no greater Charity to cloath his body, then apparell the nakednesse of his Soule. It is an honourable object to see the reasons of other men weare our Liveries, and their borrowed understandings doe homage to the bounty of ours. It is the cheapest way of beneficence, and like the naturall charity of the Sunne illuminates another without obscuring it selfe. To be reserved and caitif in this part of goodnesse, is the sordidest piece of covetousnesse, and more contemptible than the pecuniary avarice. To this (as calling my selfe a Scholler) I am obliged by the duty of my condition, I make not therefore my head a grave, but a treasure of knowledge; I intend no Monopoly, but a Community in learning; I

19. i.e. the copy made necessarily diverges from *the* Copy or ultimate 'patterne' which is the Idea of God (as above, p. 31).

20. i.e. the beggar 'full of sores' in the parable (Luke 16.20).

study not for my owne sake onely, but for theirs that study not for themselves. I envy no man that knowes more than my selfe, but pity them that know lesse. I instruct no man as an exercise of my knowledge, or with an intent rather to nourish and keepe it alive in mine owne head, than beget and propagate it in his; and in the midst of all my endeavours there is but one thought that dejects me, that my acquired parts must perish with my selfe, nor can bee Legacyed among my honoured Friends. I cannot fall out or contemne a man for an errour, or conceive why a difference in opinion should divide an affection: for controversies, disputes, and argumentations, both in Philosophy, and in Divinity, if they meete with discreet and peaceable natures, doe not infringe the Lawes of Charity. In all disputes so much[21] as there is of passion, so much there is of nothing to the purpose, for then reason like a bad hound spends upon a false sent, and forsakes the question first started. And this is one reason why controversies are never determined, for though they be amply proposed, they are scarse at all handled, they doe so swell with unnecessary Digressions, and the Parenthesis on the party, is often as large as the maine discourse upon the Subject. The Foundations of Religion are already established, and the principles of Salvation subscribed unto by all, there remaines not many controversies worth a passion, and yet never any disputed without, not onely in Divinity, but in inferiour Arts: What a $B\alpha\tau\rho\alpha\chi o\mu\nu o\mu\alpha\chi i\alpha$,[22] and hot skirmish is betwixt *S.* and *T.* in *Lucian*?[23] How doth Grammarians hack and flash for the Genitive case in *Jupiter*?[24] How doe they breake their owne pates to salve that of *Priscian*?[25] *Si foret in terris, rideret Democritus.*[26] Yea, even amongst wiser militants,

21. The 1643 edition punctuates: 'the Lawes of Charity in all disputes; so much' etc. I follow the reading in *MSS.*, *E*, *M*, *K*.

22. 'Battle of the Frogs and the Mice', the title of the mock-heroic poem formerly attributed to Homer.

23. i.e. the mock trial of the relative claims of the Greek letters Sigma and Tau, in Lucian's *Consonants at Law*.

24. 'Whether *Jovis* or *Jupiteris*' (Browne marg.).

25. The proverbial 'To break Priscian's head' was said of any violation of the rules of grammar.

26. 'Were Democritus still on earth, he would laugh'. So Horace, *Epistles*, II, i, 194.

how many wounds have beene given, and credits slaine for the poore victory of an opinion or beggerly conquest of a distinction? Schollers are men of peace, they beare no armes, but their tongues are sharper then *Actius* his razor,[27] their pens carry farther, and give a lowder report than thunder; I had rather stand in the shock of a Basilisco[28] than in the fury of a mercilesse Pen. It is not meere zeale to Learning, or devotion to the Muses, that wiser Princes Patron the Arts, and carry an indulgent aspect unto Schollers, but a desire to have their names eternized by the memory of their writings, and a feare of the revengefull pen of succeeding ages: for these are the men,[29] that when they have played their parts, and had their *exits*, must step out and give the morall of their Scenes, and deliver unto posterity an Inventory of their vertues and vices. And surely there goes a great deale of conscience to the compiling of an History, there is no reproach to the scandall of a Story; It is such an Authenticke kinde of falsehood that with authority belies our good names to all Nations and Posteritie.

4. There is another offence unto Charity, which no Author hath ever written of, and few take notice of, and that's the reproach, not of whole professions, mysteries and conditions, but of whole nations, wherein by opprobrious Epithets wee miscall each other, and by an uncharitable Logicke from a disposition in a few conclude a habit in all.

> *Le mutin Anglois, et le bravache Escossois;*
> *Le bougre Italien, et le fol Francois;*
> *Le poultron Romaine, le larron de Gascongne,*
> *L'Espagnol superbe, et l' Aleman yurongne.*[30]

Saint *Paul* that cals the *Cretians* lyers, doth it but indirectly and

27. 'That cutt a whetstone in two' (*MSS. marg.*, in *M*). So Livy, I, 36.
28. Large cannon, named after the fatal (but fabled) basilisk.
29. i.e. the scholars. The personal pronouns immediately following, refer to the princes.
30. 'The rebellious Englishman, and the swaggering Scot; the Italian bugger, and the mad Frenchman; the cowardly Roman, and the thieving Gascon; the arrogant Spaniard, and the drunken German'. The lines adapt Sonnet LXVIII in Du Bellay's *Les Regrets* (§270).

upon quotation of their owne Poet.[31] It is as bloody a thought in one way as *Neroes*[32] was in another. For by a word wee wound a thousand, and at one blow assassine the honour of a Nation. It is as compleate a piece of madnesse to miscall and rave against the times, or thinke to recall men to reason, by a fit of passion: *Democritus* that thought to laugh the times into goodnesse, seemes to mee as deeply Hypochondriack, as *Heraclitus* that bewailed them; it moves not my spleene to behold the multitude in their proper humours, that is, in their fits of folly and madnesse, as well understanding that Wisedome is not prophan'd[33] unto the World, and 'tis the priviledge of a few to be vertuous. They that endeavour to abolish vice destroy also vertue, for contraries, though they destroy one another, are yet the life of one another.[34] Thus vertue (abolish vice) is an Idea; againe, the communitie of sinne doth not disparage goodnesse; for when vice gaines upon the major part, vertue, in whom it remaines, becomes more excellent, and being lost in some, multiplies its goodnesse in others which remaine untouched, and persists intire in the generall inundation. I can therefore behold vice without a Satyre content onely, with an admonition, or instructive reprehension; for Noble natures, and such as are capable of goodnesse, are railed into vice, that might as easily bee admonished into vertue; and we should be all so farre the Orators of goodnesse, as to protect her from the power of vice, and maintaine the cause of injured truth. No man can justly censure or condemne another, because indeed no man truely knowes another. This I perceive in my selfe, for I am in the darke to all the world, and my nearest friends behold mee but in a cloud, those that know mee but superficially, thinke lesse of me than I doe of my selfe; those of my neere acquaintance thinke more; God, who truely knowes me, knowes that I am nothing, for hee onely beholds me, and all the world, who

31. Titus 1.12, quoting Epimenides.

32. Most likely Caligula's, who wished that the Romans might have had a single neck so that it could be severed at a stroke.

33. Corrected from 'hereditary' (*MSS.*).

34. Cf. Milton, *Areopagitica* (1644): 'that which purifies us is triall, and triall is by what is contrary' etc. (*Selected Prose*, ed. C.A. Patrides, Penguin Books [1974], p. 213).

lookes not on us through a derived ray, or a trajection of a sensible species,[35] but beholds the substance without the helpes of accidents, and the formes of things, as wee their operations. Further, no man can judge another, because no man knowes himselfe; for we censure others but as they disagree from that humour which wee fancy laudable in our selves, and commend others but for that wherein they seeme to quadrate[36] and consent with us. So that in conclusion, all is but that we all condemne, selfe-love. 'Tis the generall complaint of these times, and perhaps of those past, that charity growes cold; which I perceive most verified in those which most doe manifest the fires and flames of zeale; for it is a vertue that best agrees with coldest natures, and such as are complexioned for humility: But how shall we expect charity towards others, when we are uncharitable to our selves? Charity begins at home, is the voyce of the world, yet is every man his greatest enemy, and as it were, his owne executioner. *Non occides,*[37] is the Commandement of God, yet scarse observed by any man; for I perceive every man is his owne *Atropos,* and lends a hand to cut the thred of his owne dayes. *Cain* was not therefore the first murtherer, but *Adam,* who brought in death;[38] whereof hee beheld the practise and example in his owne sonne *Abel,* and saw that verified in the experience of another; which faith could not perswade him in the Theory of himselfe.

5. There is I thinke[39] no man that apprehends his owne miseries lesse than my selfe, and no man that so neerely apprehends anothers. I could lose an arme without a teare, and with few groans, mee thinkes, be quartered into pieces; yet can I weepe most seriously at a Play, and receive with a true passion, the counterfeit griefes of those knowne and professed impostures.[40] It is a barbarous part of inhumanity to adde unto any

35. i.e. transmission to the mind of a material object's image; hence 'derived' (reflected).

36. To square or agree.

37. 'Thou shalt not kill' (Exodus 20.13).

38. Browne's contemporaries did not hesitate similarly to denounce Adam as history's 'first Criminal' (§95).

39. 'I thinke' was not in *UA.*

40. A variant of 'impostors' (*MSS.*).

afflicted parties misery, or endeavour to multiply in any man, a
passion, whose single nature is already above his patience; this
was the greatest affliction of *Job,* and those oblique expostu-
lations of his friends[41] a deeper injury than the downe-right
blowes of the Devill. It is not the teares of our owne eyes onely,
but of our friends also, that doe exhaust the current of our
sorrowes, which falling into many streames, runne more
peaceably, and is contented with a narrower channel. It is an
act within the power of charity, to translate a passion out of one
breast into another, and to divide a sorrow almost out of it
selfe; for an affliction like a dimension[42] may be so divided, as
if not indivisible, at least to become insensible. Now with my
friend I desire not to share or participate, but to engrosse his
sorrowes, that by making them mine owne, I may more easily
discusse them; for in mine owne reason, and within my selfe I
can command that, which I cannot entreate without my selfe,
and within the circle of another. I have often thought those
Noble paires and examples of friendship not so truely Histories
of what had beene, as fictions of what should be, but I now per-
ceive nothing in them, but possibilities, nor any thing in the
Heroick examples of *Damon* and *Pythias, Achilles* and *Patroclus,*
which mee thinkes upon some grounds I could not performe
within the narrow compasse of my selfe. That a man should
lay down his life for his friend, seemes strange to vulgar affec-
tions, and such as confine themselves within that worldly prin-
ciple, Charity beginnes at home. For mine owne part I could
never remember the relations that I held unto my selfe, nor the
respect that I owe unto mine owne nature, in the cause of God,
my Country, and my Friends. Next to these three, I doe em-
brace my selfe; I confesse I doe not observe that order that the
Schooles ordaine our affections, to love our Parents, Wifes,
Children, and then our Friends, for excepting the injunctions
of Religion, I doe not find in my selfe such a necessary and
indissoluble Sympathy to all those of my bloud. I hope I do

41. In Job 4-5, 8, 11, etc.
42. i.e. like anything measurable.

not breake the fifth Commandement,[43] if I conceive I may love my friend before the nearest of my bloud, even those to whom I owe the principles of life; I never yet cast a true affection on a Woman,[44] but I have loved my Friend as I do vertue, my soule, my God. From hence me thinkes I doe conceive how God loves man, what happinesse there is in the love of God. Omitting all other, there are three most mysticall unions; Two natures in one person;[45] three persons in one nature; one soule in two bodies. For though indeed they bee really divided, yet are they so united, as they seeme but one, and make rather a duality then two distinct soules.

6. There are wonders in true affection, it is a body of *Ænigmaes*, mysteries and riddles, wherein two so become one, as they both become two; I love my friend before my selfe, and yet me thinkes I do not love him enough; some few months hence my multiplyed affection will make me beleeve I have not loved him at all, when I am from him, I am dead till I bee with him, when I am with him, I am not satisfied, but would still be nearer him: united soules are not satisfied with embraces, but desire to be truely each other, which being impossible, their desires are infinite, and must proceed without a possibility of satisfaction. Another misery there is in affection, that whom we truely love like our owne, wee forget their lookes, nor can our memory retaine the Idea of their faces; and it is no wonder, for they are our selves, and our affections makes their lookes our owne. This noble affection fals not on vulgar and common constitutions, but on such as are mark'd for vertue; he that can love his friend with this noble ardour, will in a competent degree affect all. Now if wee can bring our affections to looke beyond the body, and cast an eye upon the soule, wee have found out the true object, not onely of friendship but charity; and the greatest happinesse that wee can bequeath the soule, is that wherein we

43. 'Honour thy father and thy mother' (Exodus 20.12).
44. See below, p. 148. Coleridge responded to this sentence with a lengthy and passionate outburst ('I loved *one* Woman; & believe that such a Love of such a Woman is the highest Friendship' etc.).
45. i.e. the divine and the human in Christ.

all doe place our last felicity, Salvation, which though it bee not
in our power to bestow, it is in our charity, and pious invoca-
tions to desire, if not procure, and further. I cannot contentedly
frame a Prayer for my selfe in particular, without a catalogue for
my friends, nor request a happinesse wherein my sociable dis-
position doth not desire the fellowship of my neighbour. I never
heare the Toll of a passing Bell, though in my mirth, without my
prayers and best wishes for the departing spirit; I cannot goe to
cure the body of my Patient, but I forget my profession, and
call unto God for his soule; I cannot see one say his Prayers, but
in stead of imitating him, I fall into a supplication[46] for him,
who perhaps is no more to mee than a common nature: and if
God hath vouchsafed an eare to my supplications, there are
surely many happy that never saw me, and enjoy the blessing of
mine unknowne devotions. To pray for enemies, that is, for their
salvation, is no harsh precept, but the practise of our daily and
ordinary devotions. I cannot beleeve the story of the Italian,[47]
our bad wishes and uncharitable[48] desires proceed no further
than this life; it is the Devill, and the uncharitable votes of
Hell, that desire our misery in the world to come.

7. To doe no injury, nor take none, was a principle, which to
my former yeares, and impatient affections, seemed to containe
enough of morality, but my more setled yeares and Christian
constitution have fallen upon severer resolutions. I can hold
there is no such thing as injury, that if there be, there is no such
injury as revenge, and no such revenge as the contempt of an
injury; that to hate another, is to maligne himselfe, that the
truest way to love another, is to despise our selves. I were un-
just unto mine owne conscience, if I shoul say I am at variance
with any thing like my selfe, I finde there are many pieces in this
one fabricke of man; this frame is raised upon a masse of Anti-
pathies: I am one mee thinkes, but as the world; wherein not-
withstanding there are a swarme of distinct essences, and in

46. Corrected from 'zealous oration' (*MSS.*).
47. 'who after he had inveigled his enemy to disclaime his faith for the
redemption of his life, did presently poyniard him, to prevent repentance,
and assure his eternall death' (*Pseudodoxia Epidemica*, VII, 19).
48. Corrected from 'malevolous' (*MSS.*).

them another world of contrarieties; wee carry private and domesticke enemies within, publike and more hostile adversaries without. The Devill that did but buffet Saint *Paul*,[49] playes mee thinkes at sharpe[50] with me: Let mee be nothing if within the compasse of my selfe, I doe not find the battell of *Lepanto*,[51] passion against reason, reason against faith, faith against the Devill, and my conscience against all. There is another man within mee that's angry with mee, rebukes, commands, and dastards mee.[52] I have no conscience of Marble to resist the hammer of more heavie offences, nor yet so soft and waxen, as to take the impression of each single peccadillo or scape of infirmity: I am of a strange beliefe, that it is as easie to be forgiven some sinnes, as to commit some others. For my originall sinne, I hold it to be washed away in my Baptisme; for my actuall transgressions, I compute and reckon with God, but from my last repentance, Sacrament or generall absolution: And therefore am not terrified with the sinnes or madnesse of my youth. I thanke the goodnesse of God I have no sinnes that want a name, I am not singular in offences, my transgressions are Epidemicall, and from the common breath of our corruption.[53] For there are certaine tempers of body, which matcht with an humorous depravity of mind, doe hatch and produce viciosities, whose newnesse and monstrosity of nature admits no name; this was the temper of that Lecher that carnald with a Statua,[54] and the constitution of *Nero* in his Spintrian[55] recreations. For the heavens are not onely fruitfull in new and unheard of starres,[56] the earth in plants and animals, but mens minds also in villany and vices; now the dulnesse of my reason,

49. 2 Corinthians 12.7.

50. i.e. with unbated sword.

51. The decisive naval battle against the Turkish fleet on 7 October 1571.

52. i.e. renders me a coward.

53. The ten lines immediately following (to '. . . any of these') were not in *UA*.

54. i.e. copulated with a statue.

55. 'pertaining to . . . monstrous actions of lust' (Blount; *OED*). The allusion is to the Emperor Tiberius (Claudius Nero Caesar), as reported by Suetonius, *Tiberius*, XLIII.

56. i.e. discovered by Galileo (1610).

and the vulgarity[57] of my disposition, never prompted my invention, nor sollicited my affection unto any of these; yet even those common and *quotidian*[58] infirmities that so necessarily attend me, and doe seeme to bee my very nature, have so dejected me, so broken the estimation that I should have otherwise of my selfe, that I repute my selfe the most abjectest piece of mortality: Divines prescribe a fit of sorrow to repentance, there goes indignation, anger, sorrow, hatred, into mine, passions of a contrary nature, which neither seeme to sute with this action, nor my proper constitution. It is no breach of charity to our selves to be at variance with our vices, nor to abhorre that part of us, which is an enemy to the ground of charity, our God; wherein wee doe but imitate our great selves the world,[59] whose divided Antipathies and contrary faces doe yet carry a charitable regard unto the whole by their particular discords, preserving the common harmony, and keeping in fetters those powers, whose rebellions once Masters,[60] might bee the ruine of all.

8. I thanke God, amongst those millions of vices I doe inherit and hold from *Adam*, I have escaped one, and that a mortall enemy to charity, the first and father sin, not only of man, but of the devil, Pride, a vice whose name is comprehended in a Monosyllable, but in its nature not circumscribed with a world;[61] I have escaped it in a condition that can hardly avoid it: those petty acquisitions and reputed perfections that advance and elevate the conceits of other men, adde no feathers unto mine; I have seene a Grammarian toure,[62] and plume himselfe over a single line in *Horace*, and shew more pride in the construction of one Ode,[63] than the Author in the composure

57. Ordinariness.
58. Daily.
59. The macrocosm (cf. above, p. 103, note 208).
60. i.e. once the rebellions are masters.
61. '*Pride* is a more subtle sin then you conceive', replied Ross in 1645: 'pride intrudes it selfe amongst our best workes: And have you not pride, in thinking you have no pride?' But that is precisely Browne's (*not* the narrator's) point; and he makes much of it in what ensues.
62. i.e. tower.
63. i.e. in the way an ode is constructed.

of the whole book. For my owne part, besides the *Jargon* and
Patois of severall Provinces, I understand no lesse then six
Languages,[64] yet I protest I have no higher conceit of my selfe
than had our Fathers before the confusion of *Babel*, when there
was but one Language in the world, and none to boast himselfe
either Linguist or Criticke. I have not onely seene severall
Countries, beheld the nature of their climes, the Chorography[65]
of their Provinces, Topography of their Cities, but understood
their severall Lawes, Customes and Policies; yet cannot all this
perswade the dulnesse of my spirit unto such an opinion of my
self, as I behold in nimbler & conceited heads, that never looked
a degree beyond their nests. I know the names, and somewhat
more, of all the constellations in my Horizon, yet I have seene
a prating Mariner that could onely name the Poynters[66] and the
North Starre, out-talke mee, and conceit himselfe a whole
Spheare above mee. I know most of the Plants of my Country
and of those about mee; yet me thinkes I do not know so many
as when I did but know an hundred, and had scarcely ever
Simpled[67] further than Cheap-side: for indeed heads of capa-
city, and such as are not full with a handfull, or easie measure of
knowledg, thinke they know nothing, till they know all, which
being impossible, they fall upon the opinion of *Socrates*, and
onely know they know not any thing.[68] I cannot thinke that
Homer pin'd away upon the riddle of the Fisherman,[69] or that
Aristotle, who understood the uncertainty of knowledge, and
confessed so often the reason of man too weake for the workes
of nature, did ever drowne himselfe upon the flux and reflux of
Euripus:[70] wee doe but learne to day, what our better advanced
judgements will unteach to morrow: and *Aristotle* doth but
instruct us as *Plato* did him; that is, to confute himselfe. I have

64. Enumerated above, p. 33 (cf. §195).
65. 'The description of a countrey' (Cockeram).
66. The two stars in the Great Bear pointing nearly to the Pole Star.
67. Gathered simples (medicinal herbs).   68. Plato, *Apology*, 21d.
69. *Pseudodoxia Epidemica*, VII, 13, dismisses the legend that Homer
wasted to death because unable to solve a riddle.
70. 'That Aristotle drowned himselfe in Euripus as despairing to re-
solve the cause of its reciprocation, or ebbe and flow seven times a day . . .
is generally beleeved amongst us' (ibid.).

runne through all sorts, yet finde no rest in any, though our first studies & *junior* endeavors may stile us Peripateticks, Stoicks, or Academicks, yet I perceive the wisest heads prove at last, almost all Scepticks, and stand like *Janus* in the field of knowledge.[71] I have therefore on common and authentick Philosophy I learned in the Schooles, whereby I discourse and satisfie the reason of other men, another more reserved and drawne from experience, whereby I content mine owne. *Solomon* that complained of ignorance in the height of knowledge,[72] hath not onely humbled my conceits, but discouraged my endeavours. There is yet another conceit that hath sometimes made me shut my bookes; which tels mee it is a vanity to waste our dayes in the blind pursuit of knowledge, it is but attending a little longer, and wee shall enjoy that by instinct and infusion[73] which we endeavour at here by labour and inquisition: it is better to sit downe in a modest ignorance, & rest contented with the naturall blessing of our owne reasons, then buy the uncertaine knowledge of this life, with sweat and vexation, which death gives every foole gratis, and is an accessary of our glorification.

9. I was never yet once, and commend their resolutions who never marry twice,[74] not that I disallow of second marriage; as neither in all cases of Polygamy, which considering some times and the unequall number of both sexes may bee also necessary. The whole world[75] was made for man, but the twelfth part of man for woman: man is the whole world and the breath of God, woman the rib and crooked piece of man. I could be content[76] that we might procreate like trees, without conjunction, or that there were any way to perpetuate the world without this triviall and vulgar way of coition; It is the foolishest act a wise man

71. Here and in all subsequent references to Janus (see below, p. 524), cf. the fundamental principle articulated earlier: 'In Philosophy . . . truth seemes double-faced' (above, p. 66).   72. Ecclesiastes 8.16–17.

73. Cf. the angels' 'intuitive knowledge', above, p. 102, note 196.

74. Corrected from: 'I was never yet once, and am resolv'd never to bee married twice' (*MSS.*). *Religio Medici*, written when Browne was single, was published after his first and only marriage (1641).

75. Corrected from 'woman' (*MSS.*; *K*).

76. Corrected from 'I could wish' (*MSS.*).

commits in all his life, nor is there any thing that will more deject his coold imagination, when hee shall consider what an odde and unworthy piece of folly hee hath committed;[77] I speake not in prejudice, nor am averse from that sweet sexe, but naturally amorous of all that is beautifull; I can looke a whole day with delight upon a handsome picture, though it be but of an Horse. It is my temper, & I like it the better, to affect all harmony, and sure there is musicke even in the beauty, and the silent note which *Cupid* strikes, farre sweeter than the sound of an instrument. For there is a musicke where-ever there is a harmony, order or proportion; and thus farre we may maintain the musick of the spheares; for those well ordered motions, and regular paces, though they give no sound unto the eare, yet to the understanding they strike a note most full of harmony.[78] Whatsoever is harmonically composed, delights in harmony; which makes me much distrust the symmetry of those heads which declaime against all[79] Church musicke. For my selfe, not only from my obedience but my particular genius, I doe imbrace it; for even that vulgar and Taverne Musicke, which makes one man merry, another mad, strikes in mee a deepe fit of devotion, and a profound contemplation of the first Composer,[80] there is something in it of Divinity more than the eare discovers.[81] It is an Hieroglyphicall and shadowed lesson of the

77. The sentiment was first censured by James Howell in 1645, who thought 'it was a most unmanly thing' in Browne 'to wish that ther wer a way to propagat the world otherwise than by conjunction with women' (*Epistolæ Ho-Elianæ*, 3rd ed. [1655], I, 308). Other censures followed, e.g. Dr Johnson's, below, p. 489. But the lighthearted tone of the passage suggests that Browne again deploys his 'soft and flexible sense' (see above, p. 21).

78. So Hermes Trismegistus affirmed that God is 'by nature a musician, and . . . works harmony in the universe at large' (*Hermetica*, ed. Walter Scott [Oxford, 1924], I, 274–7). The concept is of great antiquity and equal popularity throughout the Renaissance.

79. Corrected from 'our' (*MSS.*).

80. 'the first Composer' is a correction of 'my Maker' (*MSS.*).

81. The passage, according to De Quincey, 'though chiefly remarkable for its sublimity, has also a philosophic value, inasmuch as it points to the true theory of musical effects' (*Confessions of an English Opium-Eater* [1821], Part II).

whole world, and Creatures of God, such a melody to the eare, as the whole world well understood, would afford the understanding. In briefe, it is a sensible fit of that Harmony, which intellectually sounds in the eares of God. I will not say with *Plato*, the Soule is an Harmony,[82] but harmonicall, and hath its neerest sympathy unto musicke:[83] thus some, whose temper of body agrees, and humours the constitution of their soules, are borne Poets, though indeed all are naturally inclined unto Rhythme. This made *Tacitus* in the very first line of his Story, fall upon a verse;[84] and *Cicero*, the worst of Poets, but declayming for a Poet, falls in the very first sentence upon a perfect Hexameter.[85] I feele not in me those sordid, and unchristian desires of my profession, I doe not secretly implore and wish for Plagues, rejoyce at Famines, revolve Ephemerides,[86] and Almanacks, in expectation of malignant Aspects, fatall conjunctions,[87] and Eclipses: I rejoyce not at unwholsome Springs, nor unseasonable Winters; my Prayer goes with the Husbandmans; I desire every thing in its proper season, that neither men nor the times bee out of temper. Let mee be sicke my selfe, if sometimes the malady of my patient be not a disease unto me, I desire rather to cure his infirmities than my owne necessities, where I do him no good me thinkes it is scarce honest gaine, though I confesse 'tis but the worthy salary of our wellintended endeavours: I am not onely ashamed, but heartily sorry, that besides death, there are diseases incurable, yet not for my own sake, or that they be beyond my art, but for the general cause & sake of humanity whose common cause I apprehend as mine own: And to speak more generally, those three Noble professions which al civil Common wealths doe

82. *Phaedo*, 86b–d.
83. Inserted here (*MSS*.): 'it unties the ligaments of my frame, takes mee to peeces, dilates mee out of my selfe, and by degrees (mee thinkes) resolves mee into heaven'.
84. In his *Annals*: 'Urbem Romam in principio Reges habuere' (Browne marg.).
85. 'Pro Archia Poeta': In qua me non inficior mediocriter esse' (Browne marg.).
86. i.e. ponder over astronomical calendars (cf. above, p. 81, note 104).
87. i.e. of heavenly bodies, said to effect disasters on earth.

honour, are raised upon the fall of *Adam*, & are not any exempt from their infirmities; there are not onely diseases incurable in Physicke,[88] but cases indissoluble in Lawes, Vices incorrigible in Divinity: if general Councells may erre, I doe not see why particular Courts should be infallible, their perfectest rules are raised upon the erroneous reasons of Man, and the Lawes of one, doe but condemn the rules of another; as *Aristotle* oft-times the opinions of his predecessours, because, though agreeable to reason, yet were not consonant to his owne rules, and the Logicke of his proper principles. Againe, to speake nothing of the sinne against the Holy Ghost,[89] whose cure not onely, but whose nature is unknowne; I can cure the gout or stone in some, sooner than Divinity, Pride, or Avarice in others. I can cure vices by Physicke, when they remaine incurable by Divinity, and shall obey my pils, when they contemne their[90] precepts. I boast nothing, but plainely say, we all labour against our owne cure, for death is the cure of all diseases. There is no Catholicon or universall remedy I know but this, which thogh nauseous to queasie stomachs, yet to prepared appetites is Nectar and a pleasant potion of immortality.

10. For my conversation,[91] it is like the Sunne's with all men, and with a friendly aspect to good and bad. Me thinkes there is no man bad, and the worst, best; that is, while they are kept within the circle of those qualities, wherein they are good: there is no mans minde of such discordant and jarring a temper to which a tuneable disposition may not strike a harmony. *Magnæ virtutes nec minora vitia*,[92] it is the posie of the best natures, and may bee inverted on the worst; there are in the most depraved and venemous dispositions, certaine pieces that remaine untoucht; which by an Antiperistasis[93] become more excellent, or by the excellency of their antipathies are able to preserve them-

88. i.e. medicine (as above, p. 24).

89. Matthew 12.31, Mark 3.29, Luke 12.10.

90. i.e. the divines'.

91. Conduct. In Milton's *Doctrine and Discipline of Divorce* (1643) the word suggests society, association with others.

92. 'Great virtues, nor lesser vices'.

93. Contrast.

selves from the contagion of their enemy vices, and persist entire beyond the generall corruption. For it is also thus in natures. The greatest Balsames doe lie enveloped in the bodies of most powerfull Corrosives; I say moreover, and I ground upon experience, that poysons containe within themselves their owne Antidote, and that which preserves them from the venom of themselves; without which they were not deletorious to others onely, but to themselves also. But it is the corruption that I feare within me, not the contagion of commerce without me. 'Tis that unruly regiment within me that will destroy me, 'tis I that doe infect my selfe, the man without a Navell[94] yet lives in me; I feele that originall canker corrode and devoure me, and therefore *Defenda me Dios de me*, Lord deliver me from my selfe,[95] is a part of my Letany, and the first voyce of my retired imaginations. There is no man alone, because every man is a *Microcosme*, and carries the whole world about him; *Nunquam minus solus quam cum solus*,[96] though it bee the Apophthegme of a wise man, is yet true in the mouth of a foole; for indeed, though in a Wildernesse, a man is never alone, not onely because hee is with himselfe, and his owne thoughts, but because he is with the devill, who ever consorts with our solitude, and is that unruly rebell that musters up those disordered motions, which accompany our sequestred imaginations: And to speake more narrowly, there is no such thing as solitude, nor any thing that can be said to be alone, and by it selfe, but God, who is his owne circle, and can subsist by himselfe, all others besides their dissimilar and Heterogeneous parts, which in a manner multiply their natures, cannot subsist without the concourse[97] of God, and the society of that hand which doth uphold their natures. In briefe, there can be nothing truely alone, and by its self, which is not truely one, and such is onely

94. 'Adam, whom I conceave to want a navill, because he was not borne of a woman' (*MSS. marg.*, in *M*). Added Keck: 'the Author meanes . . . by a metonymie originall sin'.

95. The line is said to have been borrowed from Antonio de Guevara's *Epistolas familiares* (§ 245).

96. 'Never less lonely than when he was alone' (Cicero, *On Duties*, III, i, 1).

97. Co-operation.

God: All others doe transcend an unity, and so by consequence are many.

11. Now for my life, it is a miracle of thirty yeares, which to relate, were not a History, but a peece of Poetry, and would sound to common eares like a fable; for the world, I count it not an Inne, but an Hospitall, and a place, not to live, but to die in. The world that I regard is my selfe, it is the Microcosme of mine owne frame,[98] that I cast mine eye on; for the other, I use it but like my Globe, and turne it round sometimes for my recreation. Men that look upon my outside, perusing onely my condition, and fortunes, do erre in my altitude; for I am above *Atlas* his shoulders.[99] The earth is a point not onely in respect of the heavens above us, but of that heavenly and celestiall part within us: that masse of flesh that circumscribes me, limits not my mind: that surface that tells the heavens it hath an end,[100] cannot perswade me I have any; I take my circle to be above three hundred and sixty,[101] though the number of the Arke do measure my body, it comprehendeth not my minde: whilst I study to finde how I am a Microcosme or little world, I finde my selfe something more than the great. There is surely a peece of Divinity in us, something that was before the Elements, and owes no homage unto the Sun. Nature tels me I am the Image of God as well as Scripture;[102] he that understands not thus much, hath not his introduction or first lesson, and is yet to begin the Alphabet of man. Let me not injure the felicity of others, if I say I am as happy as any, *Ruat cœlum Fiat voluntas tua*,[103] salveth all; so that whatsoever happens, it is but what our daily prayers

98. See above, p. 103, note 208.

99. See above, pp. 22 and 52. The thirteen lines immediately following (to '. . . the Alphabet of man') were not in *UA*.

100. i.e. the external appearance of the earth's finite sphere, as seen from the heavens beyond.

101. i.e. degrees in the earth's circle: 'the number of the Arke' (arc) mentioned next.

102. Genesis 1.26–7, etc.

103. 'Though the heavens fall, thy will be done' (cf. the concluding sentence, below, p. 161). Inserted just before the Latin phrase (*MSS*.): 'I have that in mee can convert poverty into riches, transforme adversity into prosperity; I am more invulnerable then Achilles, fortune hath not one place to hit mee;'

desire. In briefe, I am content, and what should providence
adde more? Surely this is it wee call Happinesse, and this doe I
enjoy, with this I am happy in a dreame, and as content to enjoy
a happinesse in a fancie as others in a more apparent truth and
reality. There is surely a neerer apprehension of any thing that
delights us in our dreames, than in our waked senses;[104] without
this I were unhappy, for my awaked judgement discontents me,
ever whispering unto me, that I am from my friend, but my
friendly dreames in the night requite me, and make me thinke I
am within his armes. I thanke God for my happy dreames, as I
doe for my good rest, so there is a satisfaction in them unto
reasonable desires, and such as can be content with a fit of
happinesse; and surely it is not a melancholy conceite to thinke
we are all asleepe in this world, and that the conceits of this life
are as meare dreames to those of the next, as the Phantasmes of
the night, to the conceit of the day. There is an equall delusion
in both, and the one doth but seeme to bee the embleme or
picture of the other; we are somewhat more than our selves in
our sleepes, and the slumber of the body seemes to bee but the
waking of the soule. It is the ligation[105] of sense, but the liberty
of reason, and our awaking conceptions doe not match the
fancies of our sleepes. At my Nativity, my ascendant was the
earthly signe of *Scorpius*.[106] I was borne in the Planetary houre of
Saturne, and I think I have a peece of that Leaden Planet in
me.[107] I am no way facetious, nor disposed for the mirth and
galliardize[108] of company, yet in one dreame I can compose a
whole Comedy, behold the action, apprehend the jests, and

104. Inserted here (*MSS.*): 'with this I can bee a king without a crowne,
rich without a stiver, in heaven though on earth, enjoy my friend, and
embrace him at a distance, when I cannot behold him,' See further *On
Dreams*, below, pp. 473 ff.

105. Binding.

106. The 'ascendant' is the zodiacal constellation just emerging; and
Scorpio, the eighth sign of the zodiac. Browne was born on 19 October.

107. The 'melancholy' temperament of individuals so born, was re-
garded as indicative of thoughtfulness and imagination – an attitude
characteristic of the Florentine Neoplatonists, especially since Ficino was
(like Plato) conveniently born under Saturn (§253).

108. Gaiety.

laugh my selfe awake at the conceits thereof; were my memory as faithfull as my reason is then fruitfull, I would never study but in my dreames, and this time also would I chuse for my devotions, but our grosser memories have then so little hold of our abstracted understandings, that they forget the story, and can only relate to our awaked soules, a confused & broken tale of that that hath passed. *Aristotle*, who hath written a singular tract of sleepe, hath not me thinkes throughly defined it, nor yet *Galen*, though hee seeme to have corrected it;[109] for those *Noctambuloes* and night-walkers, though in their sleepe, doe yet enjoy the action of their senses: wee must therefore say that there is something in us that is not in the jurisdiction of *Morpheus*; and that those abstracted and ecstaticke soules doe walke about in their owne corps, as spirits with the bodies they assume, wherein they seeme to heare, see, and feele, though indeed the organs are destitute of sense, and their natures of those faculties that should informe them. Thus it is observed that men sometimes upon the houre of their departure, doe speake and reason above themselves. For then the soule begins to bee freed from the ligaments of the body, begins to reason like her selfe, and to discourse in a straine above mortality.[110]

12. We tearme sleepe a death, and yet it is waking that kils us, and destroyes those spirits that are the house of life. 'Tis indeed a part of life that best expresseth death, for every man truely lives so long as hee acts his nature, or someway makes good the faculties of himselfe: *Themistocles* therefore that slew his Souldier in his sleepe[111] was a mercifull executioner, 'tis a kinde of punishment the mildnesse of no lawes hath invented; I wonder the fancy of *Lucan* and *Seneca*[112] did not discover it. It is

109. Aristotle, *Of Sleep and Waking*, I (where sleep is said to be 'a sort of lack of notion' [R]); Galen, *Of Muscular Motion*, II, 4 (see Browne's paraphrase in the next sentence). The phrase 'me thinkes' was not in *UA* (cf. above, p. 141, note 39).

110. Cf. Plotinus on 'reason's Prior' (above, p. 26). The eight opening lines of the next section (to '. . . discover it') were not in *UA*.

111. The story is actually related of Iphicrates and/or Epaminondas; in Frontinus, *Strategematon*, III, xii, 2–3 (*G1*).

112. Who, forced by Nero to commit suicide, were permitted to select the manner of their death.

that death by which we may be literally said to die daily, a death
which *Adam* died before his mortality; a death whereby we live
a middle and moderating point betweene life and death; in fine,
so like death, I dare not trust it without my prayers, and an
halfe adiew unto the world,[113] and take my farewell in a Col-
loquy with God.

> *The night is come like to the day,*
> *Depart not thou great God away.*
> *Let not my sinnes, blacke as the night,*
> *Eclipse the lustre of thy light.*
> *Keepe still in my Horizon, for to me,*
> *The Sunne makes not the day, but thee.*[114]
> *Thou whose nature cannot sleepe,*
> *On my temples centry keepe;*
> *Guard me 'gainst those watchfull foes,*
> *Whose eyes are open while mine close.*
> *Let no dreames my head infest,*
> *But such as* Jacobs *temples blest.*[115]
> *While I doe rest, my soule advance,*
> *Make my sleepe a holy trance:*
> *That I may, my rest being wrought,*
> *Awake into some holy thought.*
> *And with as active vigour runne*
> *My course, as doth the nimble Sunne.*
> *Sleepe is a death, O make me try,*
> *By sleeping what it is to die.*
> *And as gently lay my head*
> *On my Grave, as now my bed.*
> *How ere I rest, great God let me*
> *Awake againe at last with thee.*
> *And thus assur'd, behold I lie*
> *Securely, or to wake or die.*

113. The rest of the sentence reads (*MSS.*): 'And truly 'tis a fit time for
our devotion, and therefore I cannot laie downe my head without an
Orizon [i.e. oration], and take my farewell in a colloquie with God'.

114. '*thou*, says the *grammar*; THEE, says the *Rhyme*, and a Poet of
course is naturally *partial* to the latter' (Coleridge). The poem has been
often praised, and once favourably compared with Herrick's verses
(§176).

115. i.e. the dream of the ladder to Heaven (Genesis 28.12 ff.).

These are my drowsie dayes, in vaine
I doe now wake to sleepe againe.
O come that houre, when I shall never
Sleepe againe, but wake for ever!

This is the dormitive[116] I take to bedward, I need no other
Laudanum than this to make me sleepe; after which I close mine
eyes in security, content to take my leave of the Sunne, and
sleepe unto the resurrection.

13. The method I should use in distributive justice, I often
observe in commutative, and keepe a Geometricall proportion
in both,[117] whereby becomming equable to others, I become
unjust to my selfe, and supererogate[118] in that common prin-
ciple, Doe unto others as thou wouldest be done unto thy
selfe.[119] I was not borne unto riches, neither is it I thinke[120] my
Starre to be wealthy; or if it were, the freedome of my minde,
and franknesse of my disposition, were able to contradict and
crosse my fates: for to me avarice seemes not so much a vice,
as a deplorable piece of madnesse; to conceive our selves
Urinals, or bee perswaded that wee are dead, is not so ridicu-
lous, nor so many degrees beyond the power of Hellebore,[121] as
this. The opinions of theory and positions of men are not so
voyd of reason as their practised conclusion: some have held
that Snow is blacke, that the earth moves, that the soule is ayre,
fire, water,[122] but all this is Philosophy, and there is no *delirium*,

116. 'The name of an extract, wherewith wee use to provoke sleepe'
(*MSS. marg.*, in *M*).

117. In transactions, distributive justice provides for payments in
arithmetical progression; in rewards, commutative justice provides for
payments several times what may be deserved ('Geometricall proportion').
Thus Aristotle, *Nicomachean Ethics*, V, 3 (*M*).

118. Do more than is required.

119. Luke 6.31.

120. 'I thinke' was not in *UA* (cf. above, p. 141, note 39).

121. Believed to cure the insane, and recommended (by Horace, *Satires*,
II, iii, 82) for the avaricious.

122. 'Snow is blacke': said to have been the opinion of Anaxagoras (so
Cicero, *Academic Questions*, II, xxx, 10); 'the earth moves': apparently dis-
missive of the Copernican theory, but tolerated later as a hypothesis (see
below, p. 160, note 139); 'the soule is ayre, fire, water': said to have been
upheld by Diogenes, Democritus, and Hippon, respectively (so Aristotle,
On the Soul, I, 2).

if we doe but speculate[123] the folly and indisputable dotage of avarice to that subterraneous Idoll,[124] and God of the earth. I doe confesse I am an Atheist, I cannot perswade my selfe to honour that the world adores; whatsoever vertue its prepared substance may have within my body, it hath no influence nor operation without; I would not entertaine a base designe, or an action that should call mee villaine, for the Indies, and for this onely doe I love and honour my owne soule, and have mee thinkes, two armes too few to embrace my selfe. *Aristotle* is too severe, that will not allow us to bee truely liberall without wealth, and the bountifull hand of fortune;[125] if this be true, I must confesse I am charitable onely in my liberall intentions, and bountifull well-wishes. But if the example of the Mite[126] bee not onely an act of wonder, but an example of the noblest charity,[127] surely poore men may also build Hospitals, and the rich alone have not erected Cathedralls. I have a private method which others observe not, I take the opportunity of my selfe to do good, I borrow occasion of charity from mine owne necessities, and supply the wants of others, when I am in most neede my selfe;[128] for it is an honest stratagem to take advantage of our selves, and so to husband the act of vertue, that where they are defective in one circumstance, they may repay their want, and multiply their goodnesse in another. I have not *Peru*[129] in my desires, but a competence, and abilitie to performe those good workes to which hee[130] hath inclined my nature. Hee is rich, who hath enough to bee charitable, and it is hard to bee so poore, that a noble minde may not finde a way to this peece of goodnesse. *Hee that giveth to the poore lendeth to the Lord;*[131]

123. Reflect upon.

124. i.e. gold.

125. *Nicomachean Ethics*, I, viii, 15; but cf. IV, i, 19.

126. i.e. the poor widow who contributed 'two mites, which make a farthing' (Mark 12.42 ff.).

127. The rest of the sentence reads (*MSS.*): 'I can justly boast I am as charitable as some who have built hospitalls, or erected Cathedralls'.

128. Inserted here (*MSS.*): 'when I am reduc'd to the last tester [i.e. head-piece], I love to divide it to [*or* with] the poore;'

129. i.e. its famous silver mines.

130. i.e. God.

131. Proverbs 19.17.

there is more Rhetorick in that one sentence than in a Library of
Sermons, and indeed if those sentences were understood by the
Reader, with the same Emphasis as they are delivered by the
Author, wee needed not those Volumes of instructions, but
might bee honest by an Epitome. Upon this motive onely I can-
not behold a Begger without relieving his necessities with my
purse, or his soule with my prayers; these scenicall and acciden-
tall differences betweene us cannot make mee forget that
common and untoucht part of us both; there is under these
Centoes[132] and miserable outsides, these mutilate and semi-
bodies, a soule of the same alloy with our owne, whose
Genealogy is God as well as ours, and in as faire a way to
salvation, as our selves. Statists[133] that labour to contrive a
Common-wealth without poverty, take away the object of
charity, not understanding onely[134] the Common-wealth of a
Christian, but forgetting the prophecy of Christ.[135]

14. Now there is another part of charity, which is the Basis
and Pillar of this, and that is the love of God, for whom wee love
our neighbour: for this I thinke charity, to love God for him-
selfe, and our neighbour for God. All that is truely amiable is
God, or as it were a divided piece of him, that retaines a reflex or
shadow of himselfe. Nor is it strange that wee should place
affection on that which is invisible, all that wee truely love is
thus, what wee adore under affection of our senses, deserves not
the honour of so pure a title. Thus wee adore vertue, though to
the eyes of sense shee bee invisible. Thus that part of our noble
friends that wee love, is not that part that we embrace, but that
insensible part that our armes cannot embrace.[136] God being
all goodnesse, can love nothing but himselfe, hee loves us but
for that part which is as it were himselfe, and the traduction[137]

132. Patched garments.
133. Political theorists.
134. i.e. not only not understanding.
135. 'The poore ye shall have alwayes with you' (*MSS. marg.*: an un-
likely adaptation of Luke 6.20). Coleridge protested vigorously: 'O, for
shame! for shame! – is there no object of charity but abject Poverty?' etc.
136. 'Embrace' or 'inbrace': also 'buckle on (as a shield is buckled on
to the arm)' (§176).
137. Offspring (cf. above, p. 106, note 224).

of his holy Spirit. Let us call to assize the lives of our parents, the affection of our wives and children, and they are all dumbe showes,[138] and dreames, without reality, truth, or constancy; for first there is a strong bond of affection betweene us and our parents, yet how easily dissolved? We betake our selves to a woman, forgetting our mothers in a wife, and the wombe that bare us in that that shall beare our image. This woman blessing us with children, our affections leaves the levell it held before, and sinkes from our bed unto our issue and picture of posterity, where affection holds no steady mansion. They growing up in yeares desire our ends, or applying themselves to a woman, take a lawfull way to love another better than our selves. Thus I perceive a man may bee buried alive, and behold his grave in his owne issue.

15. I conclude therefore and say, there is no happinesse under (or as *Copernicus*[139] will have it, above) the Sunne, nor any Crambe[140] in that repeated veritie and burthen of all the wisedom of *Solomon, All is vanitie and vexation of spirit;*[141] there is no felicity in that the world adores. *Aristotle* whilst hee labours to refute the Idea's of *Plato*, fals upon one himselfe: for his *summum bonum,*[142] is a *Chimera*, and there is no such thing as his Felicity. That wherein God himselfe is happy, the holy Angels are happy, in whose defect the Devils are unhappy; that dare I call happinesse: whatsoever conduceth unto this, may with an easie Metaphor deserve that name; whatsoever else the world termes happines, is to me a story out of *Pliny*, an apparition, or neat delusion, wherein there is no more of happinesse than the name. Blesse mee in this life with but the peace of my conscience, command of my affections, the love of thy selfe and my dearest

138. i.e. mimes.

139. 'Who holds the Sunne is the center of the World' (*MSS. marg.*, in *M*). Browne was clearly not impressed by the Copernican theory, but unlike the majority of his contemporaries, he refused either to condemn it or treat it 'with contempt and ridicule' (as Dr Johnson claimed, below, p. 491): see further *Pseudodoxia Epidemica*, below, p. 184. The theory was not confirmed as an 'ocular' fact until Newton (§282).

140. Distasteful repetition.

141. Ecclesiastes 1.14, 2.11, etc.

142. i.e. chiefest good (*Nicomachean Ethics*, I, 6 ff.).

friends,[143] and I shall be happy enough to pity *Cæsar*. These are O Lord the humble desires of my most reasonable ambition and all I dare call happinesse on earth: wherein I set no rule or limit to thy hand or providence, dispose of me according to the wisedome[144] of thy pleasure. Thy will bee done, though in my owne undoing.[145]

143. Corrected from 'the love of my dearest friend' (*MSS.*).

144. Corrected from 'justice' (*MSS.*).

145. Corrected from 'in my owne damnation' (*MSS.*). Cf. Matthew 26.42.

Pseudodoxia Epidemica

[*Pseudodoxia Epidemica*: *or, Enquiries into Very many Received Tenents, and commonly Presumed Truths* was first published in 1646; five other editions followed, each carefully revised and/or augmented, to 1672. The title page carries a quotation, in Latin, from Julius Scaliger: 'To cull from books what authors have reported is exceedingly dangerous; true knowledge of things themselves is out of the things themselves' [§ 190]. See also the discussion above, pp. 32 ff.; and for further biographical details: below, p. 553.

The selections here reprinted are from the second edition of 1650 ('Corrected and much Enlarged by the Author'), except for one chapter borrowed from the third edition of 1658 (see pp. 216–20). The titles of all omitted chapters are given as part of the text in order to preserve its continuity. I have also reproduced Browne's marginal notes – but not those by 'some strange hand' which, as we are told in the prefatory remarks by 'N.N.', merely 'invite or fix the Readers eye upon some things (among as many other omitted) which he thought observable'. As 'N.N.' sagely adds, the Reader would be well advised 'never [to] judge of the Authours Sense solely by the Note in the Margin, but (and that principally,) by reflexion, and consideration of the Text it self'.]

SELECTIONS

Would Truth dispense, we could be content, with Plato, that knowledge were but Remembrance; that Intellectuall acquisition were but Reminiscentiall evocation, and new impressions but the colourishing of old stamps which stood pale in the soul before. For, what is worse, knowledge is made by oblivion; and to purchase a clear and warrantable body of Truth, we must forget and part with much we know. Our tender Enquiries taking up Learning at large, and together with true and assured notions, receiving many, wherein our reviewing judgements doe finde no satisfaction; and therefore in this Encyclopædie and round of knowledge, like the great and exemplary wheeles of heaven, we must observe two Circles: that while we are daily carried about, and whirled on by the swinge and rapt of the one, we may maintain a naturall and proper course, in the slow and sober wheele of the other. And this we shall more readily perform, if we timely survey our knowledge; impartially singling out those encroachments, which junior compliance and popular credulity hath admitted. Whereof at present we have endeavoured a long and serious Adviso; proposing not only a large and copious List, but from experience and reason attempting their decisions.

And first we crave exceeding pardon in the audacity of the Attempt; humbly acknowledging a work of such concernment unto Truth, and difficulty in it self, did well deserve the conjunction of many heads: And surely more advantageous had it been unto Truth, to have fallen into the endeavours of some cooperating advancers, that might have performed it to the life, and added authority thereto: which the privacie of our condition, and unequall abilities cannot expect. Whereby notwithstanding we have not been diverted, nor have our solitary attempts been so discouraged, as to despair the favourable look of Learning upon our single and unsupported endeavours.

Nor have we let fall our Penne, upon discouragement of contradiction, unbelief, and difficulty of disswasion from radicated[1] beliefs, and points of high prescription; although we are very sensible how hardly teaching years doe learn, what roots old age contracteth into

---

1. Rooted, established.

errors, and how such as are but *Acorns* in our younger brows, grow Oaks in our elder heads, and become inflexible unto the powerfullest arm of reason. Although we have also beheld, what cold requitals others have found in their severall redemptions of Truth; and how their ingenious enquiries have been dismissed with censure, and obloquie of singularities.

Some consideration we hope from the course of our Profession; which though it leadeth us into many Truths that passe undiscerned by others, yet doth it disturb their communications, and much interrupt the office of our Pens in their well intended transmissions: and therefore surely in this work attempts will exceed performances: it being composed by snatches of time, as medicall vacations, and the fruitlesse importunity of Uroscopy[2] would permit us. And therefore also perhaps it hath not found that regular and constant stile, those infallible experiments, and those assured determinations, which the subject sometime requireth, and might be expected from others, whose quiet doors and unmolested hours afford no such distractions. Although who shall indifferently perpend[3] the exceeding difficulty, which either the obscurity of the subject, or unavoidable paradoxologie[4] must often put upon the Attemptor, will easily discern, a work of this nature is not to be performed upon one legge, and should smell of oyle[5] if duly and deservedly handled.

Our first intentions considering the common interest of Truth, resolved to propose it unto the Latine republicke and equall judges of Europe; but owing in the first place this service unto our Countrey, and therein especially unto its ingenious Gentry, we have declared our self in a Language best conceived. Although I confesse, the quality of the Subject will sometimes carry us into expressions beyond meer English apprehensions; and indeed if elegancie still proceedeth, and English Pens maintain that stream we have of late observed to flow from many, we shall within few years be fain to learn Latine to understand English, and a work will prove of equall facility in either. Nor have we addressed our Penne or stile unto the people, (whom Books doe not redresse, and are this way incapable of reduction) but unto the knowing

2. 'Inspection of Urines' (Browne marg.).
3. 'examine or consider diligently' (Blount).
4. 'speaking by, or of Paradoxes' (Blount, citing Browne).
5. i.e. study under lamplight.

and leading part of Learning; as well understanding (at least probably hoping) except they be watered from higher regions, and fructifying meteors of knowledge, these weeds must lose their alimentall sappe and wither of themselves; whose conserving influence, could our endeavours prevent, we should trust the rest unto the sythe of Time, and hopefull dominion of Truth.

We hope it will not be unconsidered, that we finde no open tract, or constant manuduction[6] in this Labyrinth; but are oft-times fain to wander in the America and untravelled parts of Truth; For though not many years past, Dr Primrose hath made a learned and full Discourse of vulgar Errors in Physick, yet have we discussed but two or three thereof. Scipio Mercurij hath also left an excellent Tract in Italian concerning popular Errors; but confining himself only unto those in Physick, he hath little conduced unto the generality of our Doctrine. Laurentius Joubertus, by the same Title led our expectation into thoughts of great relief; whereby notwithstanding we reaped no advantage; it answering scarce at all the promise of the inscription. Nor perhaps (if it were yet extant) should we finde any farther Assistance from that ancient piece of Andreas, pretending the same Title.[7] And therefore we are often constrained to stand alone against the strength of opinion; and to meet the Goliah and Giant of Authority, with contemptible pibbles, and feeble arguments, drawn from the scrip and slender stock of our selves. Nor have we indeed scarce named any Author whose Name we doe not honour; and if detraction could invite us, discretion surely would contain us from any derogatory intention, where highest Pens and friendliest eloquence must fail in commendation.

And therefore also we cannot but hope the equitable considerations and candour of reasonable mindes. We cannot expect the frown of Theologie herein; nor can they which behold the present state of things, and controversie of points so long received in Divinity, condemn our sober enquiries in the doubtfull appertinancies of Arts, and Receptaries[8] of Philosophy. Surely Philologers and Criticall Discoursers, who look beyond the shell and obvious exteriours of things, will not be angry with our narrower explorations. And we cannot doubt, our brothers in Physick (whose knowledge in Naturals will lead

6. 'guiding by the hand' (Blount).
7. The treatise *On False Beliefs* (Browne marg., quoted in Greek).
8. Accepted (but not proven) notions.

*them into a nearer apprehension of many things delivered) will friendly
accept, if not countenance our endeavours. Nor can we conceive, it may
be unwelcome unto those honoured Worthies, who endeavour the
advancement of Learning:*[9] *as being likely to finde a clearer progres-
sion, when so many rubbes are levelled, and many untruths taken off,
which passing as principles with common beliefs, disturb the tran-
quillity of Axiomes, which otherwise might be raised. And wise men
cannot but know, that Arts and Learning want this expurgation: and
if the course of truth be permitted unto its self, like that of Time and
uncorrected computations, it cannot escape many errours, which dura-
tion still enlargeth.*

*Lastly, We are not Magisteriall in opinions, nor have we Dictator-
like obtruded our conceptions; but in the humility of Enquiries or
disquisitions, have only proposed them unto more ocular discerners.*[10]
*And therefore opinions are free, and open it is for any to think or
declare the contrary. And we shall so farre encourage contradiction, as
to promise no disturbance, or reoppose any Penne, that shall Fallaciously
refute us; that shall only lay hold of our lapses, single out Digressions,
Corollaries, or Ornamentall conceptions, to evidence his own in as in-
different truths. And shall only take notice of such, whose experi-
mentall and judicious knowledge shall solemnly look upon it; not only
to destroy of ours, but to establish of his own, not to traduce or extenu-
ate, but to explain and dilucidate, to adde and ampliate, according to
the laudable custome of the Ancients in their sober promotions of
Learning. Unto whom notwithstanding, we shall not contentiously
rejoin, or only to justifie our own, but to applaud or confirm his
maturer assertions; and shall conferre what is in us unto his name and
honour; Ready to be swallowed in any worthy enlarger: as having
acquired our end, if any way, or under any name we may obtain a
worke, so much desired, and yet desiderated of Truth.*

THOMAS BROWNE.

9. i.e. like Bacon. See above, p. 35.

10. Cf. the 'ocular Observation' commended in *The Garden of Cyrus*,
below, p. 386.

THE FIRST BOOK:

OR,

GENERALL PART

CHAP. I. *Of the Causes of Common Errors*

The first and father cause of common Error, is the common infirmity of humane nature; of whose deceptible[1] condition, although perhaps there should not need any other eviction, then the frequent errors we shall our selves commit, even in the expresse declarement hereof: Yet shall we illustrate the same from more infallible constitutions, and persons presumed as farre from us in condition, as time, that is our first and in-generated[2] fore-fathers. From whom as we derive our being, and the severall wounds of constitution: so may we in some manner excuse our infirmities in the depravity of those parts, whose traductions[3] were pure in them, and their originals but once removed from God. Who notwithstanding (if posterity may take leave to judge of the fact, as they are assured to suffer in the punishment) were grossely deceived in their perfection; and so weakly deluded in the clarity of their understanding, that it hath left no small obscurity in ours, how error should gain upon them.

For first, They were deceived by Satan; and that not in an invisible insinuation, but an open and discoverable apparition, that is, in the form of a Serpent;[4] whereby although there were many occasions of suspition, and such as could not easily escape a weaker circumspection, yet did the unwary apprehension of Eve take no advantage thereof. It hath therefore seemed strange unto some, she should be deluded by a Serpent, or subject her

1. Apt to be deceived.
2. i.e. not born but created: Adam and Eve. Hence, in the next sentence, the 'wounds of constitution', i.e. the transmitted effects of the Fall of Man.
3. Transmissions (cf. above, p. 106, note 224).
4. See Genesis 2–3. *Paradise Lost* (1667) may usefully be read in the light of Browne's remarks in this chapter.

reason to a beast, which God had subjected unto hers. It hath empuzzeled the enquiries of others to apprehend, and enforced them unto strange conceptions, to make out how without fear or doubt she could discourse with such a creature, or hear a Serpent speak, without suspition of imposture. The wits of others, have been so bold as to accuse her simplicity in receiving his temptation so coldly; and when such specious effects of the fruit were promised, as to make them like gods, not to desire, at least not to wonder he pursued not that benefit himself. And had it been their own case would perhaps have replied, If the taste of this fruit maketh the eaters like gods, why remainest thou a beast? If it maketh us but like gods, we are so already. If thereby our eyes shall be opened hereafter, they are at present quick enough to discover thy deceit, and we desire them no opener to behold our own shame. If to know good and evil be our advantage, although we have free will unto both, we desire to perform but one; we know 'tis good to obey the Commandment of God, but evil if we transgresse it.

They were deceived by one another, and in the greatest disadvantage of delusion, that is the stronger by the weaker: For Eve presented the fruit, and Adam received it from her. Thus the Serpent was cunning enough to begin the deceit in the weaker; and the weaker of strength, sufficient to consummate the fraud in the stronger. Art and fallacy was used unto her, a naked offer proved sufficient unto him: so his superstruction was his ruine, and the fertility of his sleep,[5] an issue of death unto him. And although the condition of sex and posteriority of creation[6] might somewhat extenuate the error of the woman: Yet was it very strange and inexcusable in the man; especially if as some affirm, he was the wisest of all men since; or if as others have conceived, he was not ignorant of the fall of the Angels, and had thereby example and punishment to deterre him.

They were deceived from themselves, and their own apprehensions; for Eve either mistook or traduced the Commandment of God. Of every tree of the garden thou maiest freely eat, but of the tree of knowledge of good and evil thou shalt not eat,

5. i.e. Eve.
6. i.e. Eve's creation after Adam's.

for in the day thou eatest thereof, thou shalt surely die.[7] Now
Eve upon the question of the Serpent returned the precept in
different tearms, You shall not eat of it, neither shall you touch
it lest perhaps you die. In which delivery, there were no lesse
then two mistakes, or rather additionall mendacities; for the
commandment forbid not the touch of the fruit, and positively
said ye shall surely die; but the extenuating replied, *ne forte
moriamini*, lest perhaps ye die. For so in the vulgar translation[8] it
runneth, and so is it expressed in the Thargum or Paraphrase of
Jonathan.[9] And therefore although it be said, and that very truly
that the devil was a liar from the beginning, yet was the woman
herein the first expresse beginner; and falsified twice before the
reply of Satan. And therefore also to speak strictly, the sin of the
fruit was not the first offence, they first transgressed the rule of
their own reason, and after, the Commandment of God.

They were deceived through the conduct of their senses, and
by temptations from the object it self; whereby although their
intellectuals[10] had not failed in the theory of truth, yet did the
inservient and brutall[11] faculties controle the suggestion of
reason: Pleasure and profit already overswaying the instruc-
tions of honesty, and sensuality perturbing the reasonable com-
mands of vertue. For so is it delivered in the text; That when the
woman saw that the tree was good for food, and that it was
pleasant unto the eye, and a tree to be desired to make one wise,
she took of the fruit thereof and did eat.[12] Now hereby it
appeareth, that Eve before the fall, was by the same and beaten
way of allurements inveigled, whereby her posterity hath been
deluded ever since; that is those three delivered by St John, the
lust of the flesh, the lust of the eye, and the pride of life;[13]
wherein indeed they seemed as weakly to fail as their debilitated

7. Genesis 2.16–17.
8. i.e. the Vulgate.
9. Targums ('interpretations') were Aramaic paraphrases of the Old
Testament; they include the one by Jonathan, in official use by the third
century A.D.
10. The faculty of reason: understanding.
11. i.e. servile and bestial: faculties of the lower order.
12. Genesis 3.6.
13. 1 John 2.16.

posterity, ever after. Whereof notwithstanding some in their imperfections, have resisted more powerfull temptations; and in many moralities condemned the facility of their seductions.

Again, They might for ought we know, be still deceived in the unbelief of their mortality, even after they had eat of the fruit. For Eve observing no immediate execution of the curse, she delivered the fruit unto Adam; who after the taste thereof, perceiving himself still to live, might yet remain in doubt, whether he had incurred death; which perhaps he did not indubitably beleeve, untill he was after convicted in the visible example of Abel. For he that would not beleeve the menace of God at first, it may be doubted whether before an ocular example he beleeved the curse at last. And therefore they are not without all reason, who have disputed the fact of Cain, that is although he purposed to mischief, whether he intended to murther his brother; or designed that, whereof he had not beheld an example in his own kinde; there might be somewhat in it that he would not have done, or desired undone, when he brake forth as desperately as before he had done uncivilly; My iniquity is greater then can be forgiven me.[14]

Some nicities I confesse there are which extenuate, but many more that aggravate this delusion; which exceeding the bounds of our Discourse, and perhaps our satisfaction, we shall at present passe over. And therefore whether the sinne of our first parents were the greatest of any since, whether the transgression of Eve seducing, did not exceed that of Adam seduced, or whether the resistibility of his reason did not equivalence the facility of her seduction, we shall referre it unto the Schoolman.[15] Whether there were not in Eve as great injustice in deceiving her husband, as imprudence in being deceived her self, especially if foretasting the fruit, her eyes were opened before his, and she knew the effect of it, before he tasted of it, we leave it unto the Morallist. Whether the whole relation be not Allegoricall, that is, whether the temptation of the man by the woman, be not the seduction of the rationall, and higher parts by the inferiour and feminine faculties: or whether the

14. Cf. Genesis 4.13–14.
15. As above, p. 69, note 39.

tree in the middest of the garden, were not that part in the centre of the body, on which was afterward the appointment of circumcision in males, we leave it unto the Thalmudist. Whether there were any policie in the devil to tempt them before conjunction, or whether the issue before tentation[16] might in justice have suffered with those after, we leave it unto the Lawyer. Whether Adam foreknew the advent of Christ, or the reparation of his error by his Saviour; how the execution of the curse should have been ordered, if after Eve had eaten, Adam had yet refused. Whether if they had tasted the tree of life before that of good and evil, they had yet suffered the curse of mortality; or whether the efficacie of the one had not overpowred the penalty of the other, we leave it unto God. For he alone can truly determine these and all things else; who as he hath proposed the world unto our disputation, so hath he reserved many things unto his own resolution; whose determinations we cannot hope from flesh; but must with reverence suspend unto that great day, whose justice shall either condemn our curiosities, or resolve our disquisitions.

Lastly, Man was not only deceiveable in his integrity, but the Angels of light in all their clarity. He that said he would be like the highest[17] did erre if in some way he conceived not himself so already; but in attempting so high an effect from himself, he mis-understood the nature of God, and held a false apprehension of his own; whereby vainly attempting not only insolencies, but impossibilities, he deceived himself as low as hell. In brief, there is nothing infallible but God, who cannot possibly erre. For things are really true as they correspond unto his conception; and have so much of verity, as they hold of conformity unto that intellect, in whose Idea they had their first determinations.[18] And therefore being the rule, he cannot be irregular; nor being truth it self, conceiveably admit the impossible society of error.

16. i.e. temptation.
17. Lucifer (see below, p. 449, note 8).
18. On the Ideas of God, see above, p. 31.

CHAP. II. *A further illustration of the same*

CHAP. III. *Of the second cause of Popular Errors; the erroneous disposition of the people*

Having thus declared the fallible nature of man even from his first production, we have beheld the generall cause of error. But as for popular errors, they are more neerly founded upon an erroneous inclination of the people; as being the most deceptible part of mankinde, and ready with open arms to receive the encroachments of error. Which condition of theirs although deduceable from many grounds, yet shall we evidence it, but from a few, and such as most neerly and undeniably declare their natures.

How unequall discerners of truth they are, and openly exposed unto error, will first appear from their unqualified intellectuals, unable to umpire the difficulty of its dissentions. For error to speak strictly, is a firm assent unto falsity. Now whether the object whereunto they deliver up their assent be true or false, they are incompetent judges.

For the assured truth of things is derived from the principles of knowledge, and causes, which determine their verities. Whereof their uncultivated understandings, scarce holding any theory, they are but bad discerners of verity; and in the numerous track of error, but casually do hit the point and unity of truth.

Their understanding is so feeble in the discernment of falsities, and averting the errors of reason, that it submitteth unto the fallacies of sense, and is unable to rectifie the error of its sensations. Thus the greater part of mankinde having but one eye of sence and reason,[19] conceive the earth farre bigger then the Sun, the fixed Stars lesser then the Moon, their figures plain, and their spaces equidistant. For thus their sence informeth them, and herein their reason cannot rectifie them; and

19. Sense is throughout understood to be 'what is open to verification by our eyes and senses through observation and experiment'; and reason, 'the faculty by which man is able to grasp the laws governing the divinely created universe' (§59).

therefore hopelesly continuing in their mistakes, they live and die in their absurdities; passing their daies in perverted apprehensions, and conceptions of the world, derogatory unto God, and the wisdome of the creation.

Again, Being so illiterate in point of intellect, and their sense so incorrected, they are farther indisposed ever to attain unto truth, as commonly proceeding in those waies, which have most reference unto sense, and wherein there lieth most notable and popular delusion.

For being unable to weild the intellectuall arms of reason, they are fain to betake themselves unto wasters and the blunter weapons of truth; affecting the grosse and sensible waies of doctrine, and such as will not consist with strict and subtile reason. Thus unto them a piece of Rhetorick is a sufficient argument of Logick, an Apologue[20] of Æsope, beyond a Syllogisme in Barbara;[21] parables then propositions, and proverbs more powerfull then demonstrations. And therefore are they led rather by example, then precept; receiving perswasions from visible inducements, before intellectual instructions. And therefore also they judge of humane actions by the event; for being uncapable of operable circumstances, or rightly to judge the prudentiality of affairs, they only gaze upon the visible successe, and thereafter condemn or cry up the whole progression. And so from this ground in the Lecture of holy Scripture, their apprehensions, are commonly confined unto the literall sense of the text; from whence have ensued the grosse and duller sort of heresies. For not attaining the deuteroscopy, and second intention of the words, they are fain to omit their superconsequencies, coherencies, figures, or tropologies,[22] and are not sometime perswaded by fire beyond their literalities. And therefore also things invisible, but unto intellectuall discernments, to humour the grossenesse of their comprehensions, have been degraded from their proper forms,

20. 'Fable' (Browne marg.).

21. A syllogism of which the major and minor premises, and the conclusion, are universal affirmatives: e.g. 'all animals are mortal, all men are animals, therefore all men are mortal' (*OED*).

22. 'figurative speakynge' (Elyot; cf. above, p. 60, note 6).

and God himself dishonoured into manuall[23] expressions. And so likewise being unprovided, or unsufficient for higher speculations, they will alwaies betake themselves, unto sensible representations, and can hardly be restrained the dulnesse of Idolatry. A sinne or folly not only derogatory unto God, but men; overthrowing their reason, as well as his divinity. In brief, a reciprocation, or rather an Inversion of the creation; making God one way, as he made us another; that is, after our Image, as he made us after his.

Moreover, their understanding thus weak in it self, and perverted by sensible delusions, is yet farther impaired by the dominion of their appetite; that is, the irrationall and brutall part of the soul, which lording it over the sovereign faculty, interrupts the actions of that noble part, and choaks those tender sparks, which Adam hath left them of reason. And therefore they do not only swarm with errors, but vices depending thereon. Thus they commonly affect no man any farther than he deserts his reason, or complies with their aberrancies. Hence they embrace not vertue for it self, but its reward; and the argument from pleasure or utility is farre more powerfull, then that from vertuous honesty; which Mahomet and his contrivers well understood, when he set out the felicity of his heaven, by the contentments of flesh, and the delights of sense: slightly passing over the accomplishment of the soul, and the beatitude of that part which earth and visibilities too weakly affect.[24] But the wisdom of our Saviour, and the simplicity of his truth proceeded another way; defying the popular provisions of happinesse from sensible expectations; placing his felicity in things removed from sense, and the intellectuall enjoyment of God. And therefore the doctrine of the one was never afraid of Universities, or endeavoured the banishment of learning like the other. And though Galen doth sometime nibble at Moses, and beside the Apostate Christian,[25] some Heathens have questioned his Philosophicall part or treaty of the Creation: Yet is there surely no reasonable Pagan, that will

23. Physical or human.
24. See also above, p. 91.
25. 'Julian' (Browne marg.).

not admire the rationall and well grounded precepts of Christ; whole life as it was conformable unto his doctrine, so was that unto the highest rules of reason; and must therefore flourish in the advancement of learning, and the perfection of parts best able to comprehend it.

Again, Their individuall imperfections being great, they are moreover enlarged by their aggregation; and being erroneous in their single numbers once hudled together, they will be error it self. For being a confusion of knaves and fools, and a farraginous[26] concurrence of all conditions, tempers, sex, and ages; it is but naturall if their determinations be monstrous, and many waies inconsistent with truth. And therefore wise men have alwaies applauded their own judgement, in the contradiction of that of the people; and their soberest adversaries, have ever afforded them the stile of fools and mad men;[27] and to speak impartially, their actions have often made good these Epithites. Had Orestes been Judge, he would not have acquitted that Lystrian rabble of madnesse,[28] who upon a visible miracle, falling into so high a conceit of Paul and Barnabas, that they termed the one Jupiter, the other Mercurius; that they brought oxen and garlands, and were hardly restrained, from sacrificing unto them; did notwithstanding suddenly after fall upon Paul, and having stoned him, drew him for dead out of the city. It might have hazarded the sides of Democritus, had he been present at that tumult of Demetrius;[29] when the people flocking together in great numbers, some cried one thing, and some another, and the assembly was confused, and the most part knew not wherefore they were come together; notwithstanding, all with one voice for the space of two hours cried out, Great is Diana of the Ephesians. It had overcome the patience of Job, as it did the meeknesse of Moses, and would surely have mastered any, but the longanimity and lasting sufferance of God, Had they beheld the mutiny in the wilder-

26. Indiscriminate.

27. See above, p. 134, note 5.

28. In Acts 14.11 ff.: Orestes is here cast in the role of a madman because haunted by the Erinyes.

29. In Acts 19.23 ff. On Democritus see below, p. 520.

nesse; when after ten great miracles in Egypt, and some in the same place, they melted down their stolen ear-rings into a calf,[30] and monstrously cried out, These are thy gods O Israel, that brought thee out of the land of Egypt. It much accuseth the impatiencie of Peter, who could not endure the staves of the multitude, and is the greatest example of lenity in our Saviour,[31] when he desired of God forgivenesse unto those, who having one day brought him into the City in triumph, did presently after, act all dishonour upon him, and nothing could be heard but *Crucifige* in their courts. Certainly he that considereth these things in Gods peculiar people, will easily discern how little of truth, there is in the waies of the multitude; and though sometimes they are flattered with that Aphorisme,[32] will hardly beleeve the voice of the people to be the voice of God.

Lastly, Being thus divided from truth in themselves, they are yet farther removed by advenient[33] deception. For true it is (and I hope shall not offend their vulgarities,) if I say they are daily mocked into error by subtler devisors, and have been expresly deluded, by all professions and ages. Thus the Priests of Elder time, have put upon them many incredible conceits, not only deluding their apprehensions, with Ariolation,[34] South-saying, and such oblique Idolatries; but winning their credulities unto the literall and down-right adorement of Cats, Lizards and Beetles. And thus also in some Christian Churches, wherein is presumed an irreprovable truth, if all be true that is suspected, or half what is related, there have not wanted, many strange deceptions, and some thereof are still confessed by the name of Pious fraudes. Thus Theudas an Impostor was able to lead away four thousand into the wildernesse, and the delusions of Mahomet almost the fourth part of mankinde. Thus all heresies how grosse soever, have found a welcome with the people. For thus, many of the Jews were wrought into belief, that Herod

30. Cf. Exodus 12.35.
31. 'Peter having a sword drew it, and smote the high priest's servant, and cut off his right ear . . . Then said Jesus unto Peter, Put up thy sword into the sheath' (John 18.10–11).
32. i.e. 'The Voice of the people is the voice of God'.
33. Adventitious, superadded.
34. 'foretelling, sooth-saying' (Blount).

was the Messias; and David George of Leyden and Arden, were not without a party amongst the people, who maintained the same opinion of themselves almost in our daies.

Physitians (many at least that make profession thereof) beside divers lesse discoverable waies of fraud, have made them beleeve, there is the book of fate, or the power of Aarons brestplate[35] in Urines. And therefore hereunto they have recourse as unto the Oracle of life, the great determinator of virginity, conception, fertility, and the inscrutable infirmities of the whole body. For as though there were a seminality in Urine, or that like the seed it carried with it the Idea of every part, they foolishly conceive we visibly behold therein the Anatomy of every particle, and can thereby indigitate their affections; and running into any demands expect from us a sudden resolution in things wherein the devil of Delphos[36] would demurre, and we know hath taken respite of some daies to answer easier questions.

Saltimbancoes, Quacksalvers and Charlatans, deceive them in lower degrees. Were Æsop alive, the Piazza and Pont Neuf[37] could not but speak their fallacies; mean while there are too many, whose cries cannot conceale their mischiefs. For their Impostures are full of cruelty, and worse then any other; deluding not only unto pecuniary defraudations, but the irreparable deceit of death.

Astrologers, which pretend to be of Cabala with the starres (such I mean as abuse that worthy enquiry;)[38] have not been wanting in their deceptions. Who having wonne their belief unto principles whereof they make great doubt themselves, have made them beleeve that arbitrary events below, have necessary causes above; whereupon their credulities assent unto any prognosticks, and daily swallow the predictions of men, which considering the independencie of their causes, and

35. Said to have possessed magical powers. See Exodus 28.15 ff.

36. Apollo's oracle: see above, p. 74, note 74.

37. 'Places in Venice and Paris, where mountebanks play their pranks' (Browne marg.).

38. Cabbala, the esoteric theosophy of medieval Judaism, was endorsed by numerous Renaissance thinkers including Browne. Its abuses were equally numerous.

contingencie in their events, are only in the prescience of God.

Fortune tellers, Juglers, Geomancers,[39] and the like incantatory impostors, though commonly men of inferiour rank, and from whom without illumination they can expect no more then from themselves, do daily and professedly delude them. Unto whom (what is deplorable in men and Christians) too many applying themselves; betwixt jest and earnest, betray the cause of truth, and insensibly make up the legionary body of error.

Statistes and Politicians, unto whom *Ragione di Stato*,[40] is the first considerable, as though it were their businesse to deceive the people, as a Maxime, do hold, that truth is to be concealed from them; unto whom although they reveale the visible design, yet do they commonly conceale the capitall intention. And therefore have they alway been the instruments of great designes, yet seldome understood the true intention of any; accomplishing the drifts of wiser heads, as inanimate and ignorant Agents the generall designe of the world; who though in some latitude of sense, and in a naturall cognition perform their proper actions, yet do they unknowingly concurre unto higher ends, and blindely advance the great intention of nature. Now how farre they may be kept in ignorance, a great example there is in the people of Rome, who never knew the true and proper name of their own City. For beside that common appellation received by the Citizens, it had a proper and secret name concealed from them: *Cujus alterum nomen dicere secretis Ceremoniarum nefas habetur*,[41] saith Plinie; lest the name thereof being discovered unto their enemies, their Penates[42] and Patronall gods, might be called forth by charms and incantations. For according unto the tradition of Magitians, the tutelary spirits will not remove at common appellations, but at the proper names of things whereunto they are protectors.

Thus having been deceived by themselves, and continually

39. Practitioners of geomancy, 'divination by points and circles made on the earth, or by opening of the earth' (Blount).

40. 'Reason of State'.

41. 'Whose other name the hallowed mysteries of the sacred rites forbid us to mention' (Pliny, III, v, 65).

42. Roman household gods.

deluded by others, they must needs be stuffed with errors, and even over-runne with these inferiour falsities; whereunto whosoever shall resigne their reasons, either from the root of deceit in themselves, or inability to resist such triviall ingannations[43] from others; although their condition and fortunes may place them many Spheres above the multitude, yet are they still within the line of vulgarity, and Democraticall enemies of truth.

CHAP. IV. *Of the nearer and more Immediate Causes of popular errours, both in the wiser and common sort, Misapprehension, Fallacy, or false diduction, Credulity, Supinity, adherence unto Antiquitie, Tradition and Authoritie*

The first is a mistake, or a conception of things, either in their first apprehensions, or secondary relations. So Eve mistook the Commandment, either from the immediate injunction of God, or from the secondary narration of her husband. So might the Disciples mistake our Saviour, in his answer unto Peter, concerning the death of John, as is delivered, John 21. Peter seeing John, saith unto Jesus, Lord, and what shall this man doe? Jesus saith, If I will, that he tarry till I come, what is that unto thee? Then went this saying abroad among the brethren, that that Disciple should not die.[44] Thus began the conceit and opinion of the Centaures, that is, in the mistake of the first beholders, as is declared by Servius; when some young Thessalians on horseback were beheld afarre off, while their horses watered, that is, while their heads were depressed, they were conceived by the first spectators, to be but one animall; and answerable hereunto have their pictures been drawn ever since.

And as simple mistakes commonly beget fallacies, so men rest not in false apprehensions, without absurd and inconsequent diductions; from fallacious foundations, and misapprehended mediums, erecting conclusions no way inferrible from their premises. Now the fallacies whereby men deceive others, and are deceived themselves, the Ancients, have divided into

43. 'Deceptions' (Browne marg.).
44. John 21.21-23.

Verball and Reall. Of the Verball, and such as conclude from mistakes of the word, although there be no lesse then six, yet are there but two thereof worthy our notation; and unto which the rest may be referred: that is the fallacies of Æquivocation and Amphibologie; which conclude from the ambiguity of some one word, or the ambiguous syntaxis of many put together. From this fallacy arose that calamitous error of the Jews, misapprehending the Prophesies of their Messias, and expounding them alwaies unto literall and temporall expectations. By this way many errors crept in and perverted the doctrine of Pythagoras, whilest men received his precepts in a different sense from his intention; converting Metaphors into proprieties, and receiving as literrall expressions, obscure and involved truths. . . .

The circle of this fallacy is very large, and herein may be comprised all Ironicall mistakes; for intended expressions receiving inverted significations; all deductions from metaphors, parables, allegories, unto reall and rigid interpretations. Whereby have risen not only popular errors in Philosophy, but vulgar and senselesse heresies in Divinity; as will be evident unto any that shall examine their foundations, as they stand related by Epiphanius, Austin, or Prateolus. . . .

CHAP. V. *Of Credulity and Supinity*

A third cause of common Errors is the Credulity of men, that is, an easie assent, to what is obtruded, or a beleeving at first ear what is delivered by others. This is a weaknesse in the understanding, without examination assenting unto things, which from their natures and causes doe carry no perswasion; whereby men often swallow falsities for truths, dubiosities for certainties, fesibilities for possibilities, and things impossible as possibilities themselves. Which, though a weaknesse of the Intellect, and most discoverable in vulgar heads, yet hath it sometime fallen upon wiser brains, and great advancers of truth. Thus many wise Athenians so far forgot their Philosophy, and the nature of humane production, that they descended unto beliefs, the originall of their Nation was from the Earth, and had no other beginning then from the seminality and womb of their great Mother. Thus is it not without wonder, how those learned Arabicks so tamely delivered up their belief unto the absurdities of the Alcoran. How the noble Geber, Avicenna and Almanzor, should rest satisfied in the nature and causes of earthquakes, delivered from the doctrine of their Prophet; that is, from the motion of a great Bull, upon whose hornes all the earth is poised. How their faiths could decline so low, as to concede their generations in heaven, to be made by the smell of a citron, or that the felicity of their Paradise should consist in a Jubile of copulation, that is a coition of one act prolonged unto fifty years.[45] Thus is it almost beyond wonder, how the belief of reasonable creatures, should ever submit unto Idolatry: and the credulity of those men scarce credible (without presumption of a second fall) who could beleeve a Deity in the work of their own hands. For although in that ancient and diffused adoration of Idols, unto the Priests and subtiler heads, the worship perhaps might be symbolicall, and as those Images some way related unto their deities; yet was the Idolatry direct and down-right in the people; whose credulity is illimitable; who may be made beleeve that any thing is God; and may be made beleeve there is no God at all.

And as Credulity is the cause of Error, so incredulity often-times of not enjoying truth; and that not only an obstinate incredulity, whereby we will not acknowledge assent unto what is reasonably inferred, but any Academicall reservation in matters of easie truth, or rather scepticall infidelity against the evidence of reason and sense. For these are conceptions befalling wise men, as absurd as the apprehensions of fools, and the credulity of the people which promiscuously swallow any thing. For this is not only derogatory unto the wisdom of God, who hath proposed the world unto our knowledge, and thereby the notion of himself, but also detractory unto the intellect, and

45. The passage is adapted from Bellonius (see §210). Geber *et al*. are added as representatives of Mohammedanism.

sense of man expressedly disposed for that inquisition. And therefore *hoc tantum scio quod nihil scio*,[46] is not to be received in an absolute sense, but is comparatively expressed unto the number of things whereof our knowledge is ignorant; nor will it acquit the insatisfaction of those which quarrell with all things, or dispute of matters concerning whose verities we have conviction from reason, or decision from the inerrable and requisite conditions of sense. And therefore if any affirm the earth doth move, and will not beleeve with us, it standeth still; because he hath probable reasons for it, and I no infallible sense nor reason against it, I will not quarrell with his assertion.[47] But if like Zeno he shall walk about, and yet deny there is any motion in nature, surely that man was constituted for Anticera,[48] and were a fit companion for those, who having a conceit they are dead, cannot be convicted into the society of the living.

The fourth is a supinity or neglect of enquiry, even in matters whereof we doubt; rather beleeving, then going to see, or doubting with ease and gratis, then beleeving with difficulty or purchase; whereby, either from a temperamentall inactivity we are unready to put in execution the suggestions or dictates of reason; or by a content and acquiescence in every species of truth, we embrace the shadow thereof, or so much as may palliate its just and substantiall acquirements. Had our forefathers sat down in these resolutions, or had their curiosities been sedentary, who pursued the knowledge of things through all the corners of nature, the face of truth had been obscure unto us, whose lustre in some part their industries have revealed.

Certainly the sweat of their labours was not salt unto them, and they took delight in the dust of their endeavours. For questionlesse in knowledge there is no slender difficulty, and truth which wise men say doth lye in a well, is not recoverable but by exantlation.[49] It were some extenuation of the curse, if *in*

---

46. The Socratic 'I only know that I know nothing' (cf. *Apology*, 21–3).

47. See also above, p. 160, note 139.

48. i.e. Anticyra: 'a place famous for the growth of Hellebore, a place supposed to cure madness' (Coleridge).

49. 'The act of drawing up, as a bucket from a well' (Coleridge).

sudore vultus tui,[50] were confinable unto corporall exercitations, and there still remained a Paradise or unthorny place of knowledge. But now our understandings being eclipsed, as well as our tempers infirmed, we must betake our selves to waies of reparation, and depend upon the illumination of our endeavours. For thus we may in some measure repair our primary ruines,[51] and build our selves men again. And though the attempts of some have been precipitous, and their enquiries so audacious as to come within command of the flaming swords, and lost themselves in attempts above humanity; yet have the enquiries of most defected by the way, and tyred within the sober circumference of knowledge.

And this is the reason why some have transcribed any thing; and although they cannot but doubt thereof, yet neither make experiment by sense or enquiry by reason, but live in doubts of things whose satisfaction is in their own power; which is indeed the inexcusable part of our ignorance, and may perhaps fill up the charge of the last day. For not obeying the dictates of reason, and neglecting the cries of truth, we fail not only in the trust of our undertakings, but in the intention of man it self. Which although more veniall unto ordinary constitutions, and such as are not framed beyond the capacity of beaten notions, yet will it inexcusably condemn some men, who having received excellent endowments, have yet sat down by the way, and frustrated the intention of their habilities. For certainly as some men have sinned, in the principles of humanity, and must answer, for not being men, so others offend if they be not more; *Magis extra vitia quam cum virtutibus*,[52] would commend those, These are not excusable without an Excellency. For great constitutions, and such as are constellated unto knowledge, do nothing till they outdoe all; they come short of themselves if they go not beyond others, and must not sit down under the degree of worthies. God expects no lustre from the minor stars,

50. Genesis 3.19 (Vulgate): 'in the sweat of thy face' (*AV*).
51. Cf. Milton, *Of Education* (1644): 'The end then of learning is to repair the ruines of our first Parents' etc. (*Selected Prose*, ed. C.A. Patrides, Penguin Books [1974], p. 182).
52. Rather without vice than with virtue.

but if the Sun should not illuminate all, it were a sin in Nature. *Ultimus bonorum*,[53] will not excuse every man, nor is it sufficient for all to hold the common levell; Mens names should not only distinguish them: A man should be something that men are not, and individuall in somewhat beside his proper nature. Thus while it exceeds not the bounds of reason and modesty, we cannot condemn singularity. *Nos numerus sumus*,[54] is the motto of the multitude, and for that reason are they fools. For things as they recede from unity, the more they approach to imperfection, and deformity; for they hold their perfection in their simplicities, and as they nearest approach unto God.

Now as there are many great wits to be condemned, who have neglected the increment of Arts, and the sedulous pursuit of knowledge; so are there not a few very much to be pittied, whose industry being not attended with naturall parts, they have sweat to little purpose, and rolled the stone in vain. Which chiefly proceedeth from naturall incapacity, and geniall indisposition, at least to those particulars whereunto they apply their endeavours. And this is one reason why though Universities be full of men, they are oftentimes empty of learning. Why as there are some which do much without learning, so others but little with it, and few that attain to any measure of it. For many heads that undertake it, were never squared nor timbred for it. There are not only particular men, but whole nations indisposed for learning; whereunto is required not only education, but a pregnant Minerva and teeming constitution. For the wisdome of God hath divided the Genius of men according to the different affairs of the world, and varied their inclinations according to the variety of Actions to be performed therein. Which they who consider not, rudely rushing upon professions and waies of life unequall to their natures; dishonour not only themselves and their functions, but pervert the harmony of the whole world. For if the world went on as God hath ordained it, and were every one implied in points concordant to their Natures; Professions, Arts and Common-

53. The last of the good.
54. 'We are but ciphers' (Horace, *Epistles*, I, ii, 27).

wealths would rise up of themselves; nor needed we a Lanthorn to finde a man in Athens.[55]

CHAP. VI. *Of adherence unto Antiquity*

But the mortallest enemy unto knowledge, and that which hath done the greatest execution upon truth, hath been a peremptory adhesion unto Authority, and more especially the establishing of our belief upon the dictates of Antiquity. For (as every capacity may observe) most men of Ages present, so superstitiously do look on Ages past, that the authorities of the one, exceed the reasons of the other. Whose persons indeed being farre removed from our times, their works, which seldome with us passe uncontrouled, either by contemporaries or immediate successors, are now become out of the distance of envies: And the farther removed from present times, are conceived to approach the nearer unto truth it self. Now hereby methinks we manifestly delude our selves, and widely walk out of the track of truth.

For first, men hereby impose a thraldome on their times, which the ingenuity of no age should endure, or indeed the presumption of any did ever yet enjoin. Thus Hippocrates about 2000. year agoe, conceived it no injustice, either to examine or refute the doctrines of his predecessors: Galen the like, and Aristotle most of any. Yet did not any of these conceive themselves infallible, or set down their dictates as verities irrefragable;[56] but when they either deliver their own inventions, or reject other mens opinions, they proceed with Judgement and Ingenuity, establishing their assertion, not only with great solidity, but submitting them also unto the correction of future discovery.

Secondly, Men that adore times past, consider not that those times were once present, that is, as our own are at this instant, and we our selves unto those to come, as they unto us at present; as we relye on them, even so will those on us, and magnifie us

55. As Diogenes did, searching with a lantern at daytime for an honest man.
56. 'Undeniable' (Cockeram).

hereafter, who at present condemn our selves. Which very absurdity is daily committed amongst us even in the esteem and censure of our own times. And to speak impartially, old men from whom we should expect the greatest example of wisdome, do most exceed in this point of folly; commending the daies of their youth, they scarce remember, at least well understood not; extolling those times their younger years have heard their fathers condemn, and condemning those times the gray heads of their posterity shall commend. And thus is it the humour of many heads to extoll the daies of their fore-fathers, and declaim against the wickednesse of times present. Which notwithstanding they cannot handsomely doe, without the borrowed help and satyres of times past; condemning the vices of their times, by the expressions of vices in times which they commend, which cannot but argue the community of vice in both. Horace therefore, Juvenall and Perseus were no prophets, although their lines did seem to indigitate and point at our times. There is a certain list of vices committed in all ages, and declaimed against by all Authors, which will last as long as humane nature; or digested into common places may serve for any theme, and never be out of date untill Dooms day.

Thirdly, The testimonies of Antiquity and such as passe oraculously amongst us, were not if we consider them alwaies so exact, as to examine the doctrine they delivered. For some, and those the acutest of them, have left unto us many things of falsity, controulable, not only by criticall and collective reason, but common and countrey observation ... Other Authors write often dubiously, even in matters wherein is expected a strict and definitive truth; extenuating their affirmations, with *aiunt, ferunt, fortasse*,[57] As Dioscorides, Galen, Aristotle, and many more. Others by hear say; taking upon trust most they have delivered; whose volumes are meer collections, drawn from the mouthes or leaves of other Authors; as may be observed in Plinie, Ælian, Athenæus, and many more. Not a few transcriptively; subscribing their names unto other mens endeavours, and meerly transcribing almost all they have

57. i.e. 'so they say', 'they assert', 'perhaps'.

written. The Latines transcribing the Greeks, the Greeks and Latines each other. . . .

Fourthly. While we so eagerly adhear unto Antiquity, and the accounts of elder times, we are to consider the fabulous condition thereof; and that we shall not deny if we call to minde the mendacity of Greece, from whom we have received most relations, and that a considerable part of Ancient times, was by the Greeks themselves termed μυθικόν, that is, made up or stuffed out with fables. And surely the fabulous inclination of those daies, was greater then any since; which swarmed so with fables, and from such slender grounds, took hintes for fictions, poysoning the world ever after; wherein, how far they exceeded, may be exemplified from Palæphatus, in his book of fabulous narrations. That fable of Orpheus, who by the melody of his musick, made woods and trees to follow him, was raised upon a slender foundation; for there were a crew of mad women, retired unto a mountain, from whence being pacified by his Musick, they descended with boughs in their hands, which unto the fabulosity of those times, proved a sufficient ground to celebrate unto all posterity the Magick of Orpheus harp, and its power to attract the senselesse trees about it. . . .

Fiftly, We applaud many things delivered by the Ancients, which are in themselves but ordinary, and come short of our own conceptions. Thus we usually extoll, and our Orations cannot escape the sayings of the wise men of Greece. *Nosce teipsum* of Thales: *Nosce tempus* of Pittacus: *Nihil nimis* of Cleobulus;[58] which notwithstanding to speak indifferently, are but vulgar precepts in Morality, carrying with them nothing above the line, or beyond the extemporary sententiosity of common conceits with us. Thus we magnifie the Apothegmes, or reputed replies of wisdom, whereof many are to be seen in Laertius, more in Lycosthenes, not a few in the second book of Macrobius, in the salts of Cicero, Augustus, and the Comicall wits of those times: in most whereof there is not much to admire and are me thinks exceeded, not only in the replies of wise men, but the passages of society and urbanities of our times. And

58. 'Know thyself', 'Know the [right] time', and 'Nothing too much'; respectively.

thus we extoll their adages or proverbs; and Erasmus hath taken great pains to make collections of them; whereof notwithstanding the greater part will, I beleeve, unto indifferent judges be esteemed no extraordinaries; and may be paralleled, if not exceeded, by those of more unlearned nations, and many of our own.

Sixtly, We urge authorities, in points that need not, and introduce the testimony of ancient writers, to confirm things evidently beleeved, and whereto no reasonable hearer but would assent without them; such as are; *Nemo mortalium omnibus horis sapit. Virtute nil præstantius, nil pulchrius. Omnia vincit amor. Præclarum quiddam veritas.*[59] All which, although things known and vulgar, are frequently urged by many men, and though triviall verities in our mouthes, yet noted from Plato, Ovid, or Cicero, they become reputed elegancies. . . .

Lastly, While we so devoutly adhere unto Antiquity in some things, we doe not consider we have deserted them in severall others. For they indeed have not only been imperfect, in the conceit of some things, but either ignorant or erroneous in many more. They understood not the motion of the eight sphear from West to East, and so conceived the longitude of the starres invariable. They conceived the torrid Zone unhabitable, and so made frustrate the goodliest part of the earth. But we now know 'tis very well empeopled, and the habitation thereof esteemed so happy, that some have made it the proper seat of Paradise; and been so farre from judging it unhabitable, that they have made it the first habitation of all. Many of the Ancients denied the Antipodes, and some unto the penality of contrary affirmations; but the experience of our enlarged navigations, can now assert them beyond all dubitation. Having thus totally relinquisht them in some things, it may not be presumptuous, to examine them in others; but surely most unreasonable to adhere to them in all, as though they were infallible or could not erre in any.

59. 'No mortal man is worse all the time', 'Nothing is more excellent than virtue', 'Love conquers all', and 'Truth is a splendid thing'; respectively.

CHAP. VII. *Of Authority*

Nor is only a resolved prostration unto Antiquity a powerfull enemy unto knowledge, but any confident adherence unto Authority, or resignation of our judgements upon the testimony of Age or Author whatsoever.

For first, To speak generally an argument from Authority to wiser examinations, is but a weaker kinde of proof, it being but a topicall probation, and as we term it, an artificiall argument, depending upon a naked asseveration: wherein neither declaring the causes, affections or adjuncts of what we beleeve, it carrieth not with it the reasonable inducements of knowledge; and therefore *Contra negantem principia, Ipse dixit*, or *Oportet discentem credere*,[60] although postulates very accommodable unto Junior indoctrinations; yet are their authorities but temporary, and not to be imbraced beyond the minority of our intellectuals. For our advanced beliefs are not to be built upon dictates, but having received the probable inducements of truth, we become emancipated from testimoniall ingagements, and are to erect upon the surer base of reason.

Secondly, Unto reasonable perpensions[61] it hath no place in some Sciences, small in others, and suffereth many restrictions, even where it is most admitted. It is of no validity in the Mathematicks, especially the mother part thereof Arithmetick and Geometry. For these Sciences concluding from dignities and principles known by themselves, receive not satisfaction from probable reasons, much lesse from bare and peremptory asseverations ... In naturall Philosophy more generally pursued amongst us, it carrieth but slender consideration; for that also proceeding from setled principles, therein is expected a satisfaction from scientificall progressions, and such as beget a sure or rationall belief. For if Authority might have made out the assertions of Philosophy, we might have held, that snow

60. '[It is pointless to argue with one who] denies first principles', 'He himself said so [i.e. made an unsupported assertion]', and 'The pupil must believe [what his master tells him]'; respectively.
61. Diligent examinations (cf. above, p. 166, note 3).

was black, that the sea was but the sweat of the earth, and many of the like absurdities . . .[62]

In Morality, Rhetorick, Law and History, there is I confesse a frequent and allowable use of testimony; and yet herein I perceive, it is not unlimitable, but admitteth many restrictions. Thus in law both Civill and Divine, that is only esteemed a legall testimony, which receives comprobation from the mouths of at least two witnesses; and that not only for prevention of calumny, but assurance against mistake; whereas notwithstanding the solid reason of one man, is as sufficient as the clamor of a whole Nation; and with imprejudicate apprehensions begets as firm a belief as the authority or aggregated testimony of many hundreds. For reason being the very root of our natures, and the principles there of common unto all; what is against the laws of true reason, or the unerring understanding of any one, if rightly apprehended, must be disclaimed by all Nations, and rejected even by mankinde. . . .

CHAP. VIII. *A brief enumeration of Authors*[63]

CHAP. IX. *Of the same*[64]

CHAP. X. *Of the last and common promoter of false Opinions, the endeavours of Satan*

But beside the infirmities of humane nature, the seed of error within our selves, and the severall waies of delusion from each other, there is an invisible Agent, and secret promoter without us, whose activity is undiscerned, and plaies in the dark upon us; and that is the first contriver of Error, and professed opposer of Truth, the devil. For though permitted unto his proper principles, Adam perhaps would have sinned without the suggestion of Satan, and from the transgressive infirmities of himself might have erred alone, as well as the Angels before

62. See above, p. 157, note 122.

63. The omitted chapter is devoted to authors 'not to be swallowed at large'. They include Aelian, Albertus Magnus, Athenaeus, Herodotus, Solinus, *et al*.

64. The omitted chapter previews 'common errors' discussed more fully later, e.g. the griffin (pp. 208 f.), the phoenix (see pp. 210 ff.), etc.

him. And although also there were no devil at all, yet is there now in our natures a confessed sufficiency unto corruption; and the frailty of our own Oeconomie,[65] were able to betray us out of truth; yet wants there not another Agent, who taking advantage hereof, proceedeth to obscure the diviner part, and efface all tract of its traduction: To attempt a particular of all his wiles, is too bold an Arithmetick for man: what most considerably concerneth his popular and practised waies of delusion, he first deceiveth mankinde in five main points concerning God and himself.

And first his endeavours have ever been, and they cease not yet to instill a belief in the minde of man, There is no God at all. And this he specially labours to establish in a direct and literall apprehension; that is, that there is no such reality existent, that the necessity of his entity dependeth upon ours, and is but a Politicall Chymera; That the naturall truth of God is an artificiall erection of man, and the Creator himself but a subtile invention of the creature. Where he succeeds not thus high, he labours to introduce a secondary and deductive Atheisme; that although, men concede there is a God, yet should they deny his providence; and therefore assertions have flown about, that he intendeth only the care of the species or common natures, but letteth loose the guard of individuals, and single existencies therein: That he looks not below the Moon, but hath designed the regiment of sublunary affairs unto inferiour deputations. To promote which apprehensions or empuzzell their due conceptions, he casteth in the notions of fate, destiny, fortune, chance and necessity; tearms commonly misconceived by vulgar heads, and their propriety sometime perverted by the wisest. Whereby extinguishing in mindes the compensation of vertue and vice, the hope and fear of heaven or hell; they comply in their actions unto the drift of his delusions, and live like creatures below the capacity of either. . . .

Again, To render our errours more monstrous (and what unto miracle sets forth the patience of God,) he hath endeavoured to make the world beleeve, that he was God himself; and failing of his first attempt to be but like the highest in

65. As above, p. 69, note 38.

heaven, he hath obtained with men to be the same on earth; and hath accordingly assumed the annexes of divinity, and the prerogatives of the Creator, drawing into practice the operation of miracles, and the prescience of things to come. Thus hath he in a specious way wrought cures upon the sick: plaied over the wondrous acts of Prophets, and counterfeited many miracles of Christ and his Apostles. Thus hath he openly contended with God; And to this effect his insolency was not ashamed to play a solemne prize with Moses;[66] wherein although his performance were very specious, and beyond the common apprehension of any power below a Deity, yet was it not such as could make good his Omnipotency. For he was wholly confounded in the conversion of dust into lice.[67] An act Philosophy can scarce deny to be above the power of Nature, nor upon a requisite predisposition beyond the efficacy of the Sun. Wherein notwithstanding the head of the old Serpent was confessedly too weak for Moses hand, and the arm of his Magicians too short for the finger of God.

Thus hath he also made men beleeve that he can raise the dead; that he hath the key of life and death, and a prerogative above that principle which makes no regression from privations. The Stoicks that opinioned the souls of wise men, dwelt about the Moon, and those of fools wandred about the earth, advantaged the conceit of this effect; wherein the Epicureans, who held that death was nothing, nor nothing after death, must contradict their principles to be deceived. Nor could the Pythagorian or such as maintained the transmigration of souls give easie admittance hereto: for holding that separated souls, successively supplied other bodies; they could hardly allow the raising of souls from other worlds, which at the same time, they conceived conjoined unto bodies in this. More inconsistent with these opinions, is the error of Christians, who holding the dead doe rest in the Lord, doe yet beleeve they are at the lure of the devil; that he who is in bonds himself commandeth the fetters of the dead, and dwelling in the bottomlesse lake, the

66. i.e. when the transformation of Moses's rod into a serpent was matched by the magicians' similar acts (Exodus 7.10–12).
67. Exodus 8.17.

blessed from Abrahams bosome, that can beleeve the reall resurrection of Samuel; or that there is any thing but delusion, in the practice of Necromancy[68] and popular conception of Ghosts.

He hath moreover endeavoured the opinion of Deity, by the delusion of Dreams, and the discovery of things to come in sleep, above the prescience of our waked senses. In this expectation he perswaded the credulity of elder times to take up their lodging before his temple, in skinnes of their own sacrifices: till his reservednesse had contrived answers, whose accomplishments were in his power, or not beyond his presagement. Which way, although it hath pleased Almighty God, sometimes to reveale himself, yet was the proceeding very different. For the revelations of heaven are conveied by new impressions, and the immediate illumination of the soul; whereas the deceiving spirit, by concitation of humors, produceth his conceited phantasmes; or by compounding the species already residing, doth make up words which mentally speak his intentions.[69]

But above all other he most advanced his Deity in the solemn practice of Oracles, wherein in severall parts of the world, he publikely professed his divinity; but how short they flew of that spirit, whose omniscience they would resemble, their weaknesse sufficiently declared. . . .[70]

Again, Such is the mystery of his delusion, that although he labour to make us beleeve that he is God, and supremest nature whatsoever, yet would he also perswade our beliefs, that he is lesse then Angels or men; and his condition not only subjected unto rationall powers, but the action of things which have no efficacy on our selves. Thus hath he inveigled no small part of the world into a credulity of artificiall Magick: That there is an Art, which without compact commandeth the powers of hell; whence some have delivered the polity of spirits, and left an account even to their Provinciall dominions; that they stand in awe of charmes, spells and conjurations, that he is afraid of

68. 'Divination by the dead' (Browne marg.).

69. See also *On Dreams*, below, pp. 473 ff.

70. The rest of this paragraph previews the fuller discussion later, pp. 253 ff.

letters and characters, of notes and dashes, which set together
doe signifie nothing; and not only in the dictionary of man, but
the subtiler vocabulary of Satan. ... Whereof having once
begot in our mindes an assured dependence, he makes us rely
on powers which he but precariously obeies; and to desert those
true and only charmes which hell cannot withstand.

Lastly, To lead us farther into darknesse, and quite to lose us
in this maze of error, he would make men beleeve there is no
such creature as himself, and that he is not only subject unto
inferiour creatures but in the rank of nothing. Insinuating into
mens mindes there is no devill at all, and contriveth accordingly,
many waies to conceale or indubitate his existency. Wherein
beside that he anihilates the blessed Angels and spirits in the
rank of his creation; he begets a security of himself and a care-
lesse eye unto the last remunerations. And therefore hereto he
inveigleth, not only Sadduces and such as retain unto the
Church of God, but is also content that Epicurus, Democritus
or any heathen should hold the same. And to this effect he
maketh men beleeve that apparitions, and such as confirm his
existence are either deceptions of sight, or melancholy deprave-
ments of phancy: Thus when he had not only appeared but
spake unto Brutus; Cassius the Epicurian was ready at hand to
perswade him, it was but a mistake in his weary imagination,
and that indeed there were no such realities in nature.[71] Thus he
endeavours to propagate the unbelief of witches,[72] whose con-
cession infers his coexistency; by this means also he advanceth
the opinion of totall death, and staggereth the immortality of
the soul: for, such as deny there are spirits subsistent without
bodies, will with more difficulty affirm the separated existence
of their own. ...

And thus how strangely he possesseth us with errors may
clearly be observed; deluding us into contradictory and incon-
sistent falsities; whilest he would make us beleeve, That there
is no God. That there are many. That he himself is God. That he
is lesse then Angels or Men. That he is nothing at all. ...

71. Plutarch, *Brutus*, XXXVI.
72. i.e. the lack of belief in witches. See also above, pp. 27 and 98.

Chap. XI. *A Further Illustration*

Now although these waies of delusions, most Christians have escaped, yet are there many other whereunto we are daily betrayed; and these we meet with in obvious occurrents of the world, wherein he induceth us, to ascribe effects unto causes of no cognation; and distorting the order and theory of causes perpendicular to their effects, he draws them aside unto things whereto they runne parallel, and in their proper motions would never meet together.

Thus doth he sometime delude us in the conceits of Starres and Meteors, beside their allowable actions ascribing effects thereunto of independent causations. Thus hath he also made the ignorant sort beleeve that naturall effects immediately and commonly proceed from supernaturall powers; and these he usually derives from heaven, his own principality the air, and meteors therein; which being of themselves, the effects of naturall and created causes, and such as upon a due conjunction of actives and passives, without a miracle must arise unto what they appear; are alwaies looked on by ignorant spectators as supernaturall spectacles, and made the causes or signes of most succeeding contingencies. To behold a Rain-bow in the night, is no prodigy unto a Philosopher. Then eclipses of Sun or Moon, nothing is more naturall. . . .

He deludeth us also by Philters, Ligatures, Charmes, ungrounded Amulets, Characters, and many superstitious waies in the cure of common diseases; seconding herein the expectation of men with events of his own contriving. Which while some unwilling to fall directly upon Magick, impute unto the power of imagination, or the efficacy of hidden causes, he obtains a bloudy advantage; for thereby he begets not only a false opinion, but such as leadeth the open way of destruction. In maladies admitting naturall reliefs, making men rely on remedies, neither of reall operation in themselves, nor more then seeming efficacy in his concurrence. Which whensoever he pleaseth to withdraw, they stand naked unto the mischief of their diseases; and revenge the contempt of the medicines of the earth which God hath created for them. And therefore when neither miracle is expected, nor connexion of cause unto effect from naturall grounds concluded; however it be sometime successefull, it cannot be safe to rely on such practises, and desert the known and authentick provisions of God. In which rank of remedies, if nothing in our knowledge or their proper power be able to relieve us, we must with patience submit unto that restraint, and expect the will of the Restrainer. . . .

Again, Although his delusions run highest in points of practice, whose errors draw on offensive or penall enormities, yet doth he also deal in points of speculation, and things whose knowledge terminates in themselves; whose cognition although it seems indifferent, and therefore its aberration directly to condemn no man; yet doth he hereby preparatively dispose us unto errors, and deductively deject us into destructive conclusions.

That the Sun, Moon and Stars are living creatures, endued with soul and life, seems an innocent error, and a harmlesse digression from truth; yet hereby he confirmed their idolatry, and made it more plausibly embraced. For wisely mistrusting that reasonable spirits would never firmly be lost in the adorement of things inanimate, and in the lowest form fo Nature; he begat an opinion that they were living creatures, and could not decay for ever.

That spirits are corporeall, seems at first view a conceit derogative unto himself, and such as he should rather labour to overthrow; yet hereby he establisheth the doctrine of Lustrations, Amulets and Charmes, as we have declared before. . . .

THE SECOND BOOK:

OF SUNDRY POPULAR TENETS CONCERNING MINERALL, AND VEGETABLE BODIES, GENERALLY HELD FOR TRUTH; WHICH EXAMINED, PROVE EITHER FALSE, OR DUBIOUS

THE THIRD BOOK:

OF DIVERS POPULAR AND RECEIVED TENETS
CONCERNING ANIMALS, WHICH EXAMINED,
PROVE EITHER FALSE OR DUBIOUS

CHAP. I. *Of the Elephant*

The first shall be of the Elephant; whereof there generally passeth an opinion it hath no joints; and this absurdity is seconded with another, that being unable to lie down, it sleepeth against a tree; which the Hunters observing doe saw almost asunder; whereon the beast relying, by the fall of the tree falls also down it self, and is able to rise no more. Which conceit is not the daughter of later times, but an old and gray-headed error, even in the daies of Aristotle, as he delivereth in his book, *de incessu animalium*; and stand successively related by severall other Authors; by Diodorus Siculus, Strabo, Ambrose, Cassiodore, Solinus and many more. Now herein me thinks men much forget themselves, not well considering the absurdity of such assertions.

For first, they affirm it hath no joints, and yet concede it walks and moves about; whereby they conceive there may be a progression or advancement made in motion without inflexion of parts. Now all progression or animall locomotion being (as Aristotle teacheth) performed *tractu & pulsu*; that is, by drawing on, or impelling forward some part which was before in station, or at quiet; where there are no joints or flexures, neither can there be these actions; and this is true, not only in Quadrupedes, Volatils and Fishes, which have distinct and prominent organs of motion, legs, wings and fins; but in such also as perform their progression by the trunck, as Serpents, Wormes and Leeches; whereof though some want bones, and all extended articulations, yet have they arthriticall analogies;[1] and by the motion of fibrous and musculous parts, are able to make progression. Which to conceive in bodies inflexible, and

1. 'Jointlike parts' (Browne marg.). See also Dr Johnson, below, p. 508.

without all protrusion of parts, were to expect a race from Hercules his pillars; or hope to behold the effects of Orpheus his harp; when Trees found joints, and danced after his musick.

Again, While men conceive they never lie down, and enjoy not the position of rest, ordained unto all pedestrious animals, hereby they imagin (what reason cannot conceive) that an animall of the vastest dimension and longest duration, should live in a continuall motion, without that alternity and vicissitude of rest whereby all others continue; and yet must thus much come to passe, if we opinion they lie not down and enjoy no decumbence[2] at all. For station is properly no rest, but one kinde of motion, relating unto that which Physitians (from Galen) doe name extensive or tonicall; that is, an extension of the muscles and organs of motion maintaining the body at length or in its proper figure; wherein although it seem to be unmoved, it is neverthelesse not without all motion; for in this position the muscles are sensibly extended, and labour to support the body; which permitted unto its proper gravity, would suddenly subside and fall unto the earth, as it happeneth in sleep, diseases and death. From which occult action and invisible motion of the muscles in station (as Galen declareth) proceed more offensive lassitudes then from ambulation.[3] And therefore the Tyranny of some have tormented men, with long and enforced station; and though Ixion and Sisiphus which alwaies moved, doe seem to have the hardest measure; yet was not Titius favoured, that lay extended upon Caucasus; and Tantalus suffered somewhat more then thirst, that stood perpetually in hell. Thus Mercurialis in his Gymnasticks justly makes standing one kinde of exercise; and Galen when we lye down, commends unto us middle figures; that is, not to lye directly, or at length, but somewhat inflected, that the muscles may be at rest; for such as he termeth Hypobolemaioi or figures of excesse, either shrinking up or stretching out, are wearisome positions, and such as perturb the quiet of those parts. Now various parts doe variously discover these indolent and quiet positions; some in right lines, as the wrists; some at right

2. 'Lying or sitting down' (Blount).
3. 'walking' (Cockeram).

angles, as the cubit; others at oblique angles, as the fingers and the knees: all resting satisfied in postures of moderation, and none enduring the extremity of flexure or extension.

Moreover men herein doe strangely forget the obvious relations of history, affirming they have no joints, whereas they daily reade of severall actions which are not performable without them. They forget what is delivered by Xiphilinus, and also by Suetonius in the lives of Nero and Galba, that Elephants have been instructed to walk on ropes, in publike shews before the people; which is not easily performed by man, and requireth not only a broad foot, but a pliable flexure of joints, and commandible disposure of all parts of progression. They passe by that memorable place in Curtius, concerning the Elephant of King Porus, *Indus qui Elephantem regebat, descendere eum ratus, more solito procumbere jussit in genua, cæteri quoque (ita enim instituti erant) demisere corpora in terram.*[4] They remember not the expression of *Osorius de rebus gestis Emanuelis*, when he speaks of the Elephant presented to Leo the tenth, *Pontificem ter genibus flexis, & demisso corporis habitu venerabundus salutavit.*[5] But above all, they call not to minde that memorable shew of Germanicus, wherein twelve Elephants danced unto the sound of musick, and after laid them down in the Tricliniums, or places of festivall Recumbency.

They forget the Etymologie of the Knee, approved by some Grammarians.[6] They disturb the position of the young ones in the wombe: which upon extension of leggs is not easily conceiveable; and contrary unto the generall contrivance of nature. Nor doe they consider the impossible exclusion thereof, upon extension and rigour of the leggs.

Lastly, They forget or consult not experience; whereof not many years past, we have had the advantage in England, by an Elephant shewn in many parts thereof; not only in the posture of standing, but kneeling and lying down. Whereby although

4. 'The Indian who controlled the elephant, intending to dismount, in the usual way ordered it to go down on its knees, and all the others let their bodies down on the ground, because they had been trained to do so'.

5. 'It greeted the bishop with veneration, kneeling three times and keeping itself in a lowly position'.

6. 'γόνο [knee] from γωνία [angle]' (Browne marg.).

the opinion at present be well suppressed, yet from some strings of tradition, and fruitfull recurrence of error, it is not improbable, it may revive in the next generation again; this being not the first that hath been seen in England; for (besides some other since) as Polydore Virgil relateth, Lewis the French King sent one to Henry the third; and Emanuel of Portugall another to Leo the tenth into Italy; where notwithstanding the error is still alive and epidemicall, as with us.

The hint and ground of this opinion might be the grosse and somewhat Cylindricall[7] composure of the legs, the equality and lesse perceptible disposure of the joints, especially in the four legs of this Animall; they appearing when he standeth, like pillars of flesh, without any evidence of articulation. The different flexure and order of the joints might also countenance the same; being not disposed in the Elephant, as they are in other quandrupedes, but carry a nearer conformity into those of man; that is; the bought of the fore-legs not directly backward, but laterally and somewhat inward; but the hough or suffraginous[8] flexure behinde rather outward. Contrary unto many other quadrupedes, and such as can scratch the ear with the hinder foot, as Horses, Camels, Deer, Sheep and Dogges; for their fore legs bend like our legs, and their hinder legs like our arms, when we move them to our shoulders. But quadrupedes oviparous, as Frogs, Lizards, Crocodiles, have their joints and motive flexures more analogously framed unto ours; and some among viviparous; that is, such thereof as can bring their fore-feet and meat therein into their mouthes, as most can doe that have the clavicles or coller-bones; whereby their breasts are broader, and their shoulders more asunder, as the Ape, the Monkey, the Squirrell and some others. If therefore any shall affirm the joints of Elephants are differently framed from most of other quadrupedes, and more obscurely and grossely almost then any; he doth herein no injury unto truth. But if *à dicto secundum quid ad dictum simpliciter,*[9] he affirmeth also they have no articulations at all; he incurs the controllment

7. 'Round, pillar-like' (Browne marg.).
8. Pertaining to the hocks of animals.
9. 'to infer an absolute truth from a qualified premise' (E).

of reason, and cannot avoid the contradiction also of sense.

As for the manner of their venation,[10] if we consult historicall experience, we shall finde it to be otherwise then as is commonly presumed, by sawing away of trees. The accounts whereof are to be seen at large in *Johannes Hugo, Edwardus Lopez, Garcias ab Horto, Cadamustus* and many more.

Other concernments there are of the Elephant, which might admit of discourse; and if we should question the teeth of Elephants, that is, whether they be properly so termed, or might not rather be called horns; it were no new enquiry of mine, but a paradox as old as Oppianus. Whether as Pliny and divers since affirm, that Elephants are terrefied, and make away upon the grunting of Swine, *Garcias ab Horto* may decide, who affirmeth upon experience they enter their stalls, and live promiscuously in the woods of Malavar. That the situation of the genitalls is averse,[11] and their copulation like that of Camels, as Pliny hath also delivered, is not to be received; for we have beheld that part in a different position; and their coition is made by supersaliency[12] like that of Horses, as we are informed by some who have beheld them in that act. That some Elephants have not only written whole sentences, as Ælian ocularly testifieth, but have also spoken, as Oppianus delivereth, and Christophorus a Costa particularly relateth; although it sound like that of Achilles Horse in Homer, we doe not conceive impossible: nor beside the affinity of reason in this Animall any such intollerable incapacity in the organs of divers quadrupedes, whereby they might not be taught to speak, or become imitators of speech like birds. Strange it is how the curiosity of men that have been active in the instruction of beasts, have never fallen upon this artifice; and among those many paradoxicall and unheard of imitations, should not attempt to make one speak. The Serpent that spake unto Eve, the Dogs and Cats, that usually speak unto Witches, might afford some encouragement. And since broad and thick chops are required in birds that speak, since lips and teeth are also organs of speech; from

10. 'huntyng' (Elyot).
11. In the rear.
12. 'leaping or jumping upon' (Blount, citing Browne).

these there is also an advantage in quadrupedes; and a proximity of reason in Elephants and Apes above them all. Since also an Echo will speak without any mouth at all, articulately returning the voice of man, by only ordering the vocall spirit in concave and hollow places; whether the musculous and motive parts about the hollow mouthes of beasts, may not dispose the passing spirit into some articulate notes, seems a querie of no great doubt.

CHAP. II. *Of the Horse*

CHAP. III. *Of the Dove*

CHAP. IV. *Of the Bever*

That a Bever to escape the Hunter, bites off his testicles or stones, is a tenent very ancient; and hath had thereby advantage of propagation. For the same we finde in the Hieroglyphicks of the Ægyptians; in the Apologue of Æsope, an Author of great antiquity, who lived in the beginning of the Persian Monarchy, and in the time of Cyrus; the same is touched by Aristotle in his Ethicks, but seriously delivered by Ælian, Pliny and Solinus; with the same we meet with in Juvenall, who by an handsome and metricall expression more welcomely engrafts it in our junior memories

>   ——imitatus Castora, qui se
> Eunuchum ipse facit, cupiens evadere damno
> Testiculorum, adeo medicatum intelligit inguen,[13]

it hath been propagated by Emblems; and some have been so bad Grammarians, as to be deceived by the name, deriving *Castor à castrando*; whereas, the proper Latine word is *Fiber*; and *Castor*, but borrowed from the Greek, so called *quasi γάστωρ*, that is, *Animal ventricosum*, from his swaggy and prominent belly.[14]

13. 'imitating the beaver, who makes a eunuch of himself, hoping to escape by the sacrifice of his testicles; well does he know their medicinal properties' (Juvenal, XII, 34–6).

14. i.e. the Latin for beaver is *fiber* as well as *castor*; the latter derives from the Greek κάστωρ [*kastor*], itself related not to 'castrated' but to 'pot-bellied' (γαστρώδης).

Herein therefore to speak compendiously, we first presume to affirm, that from a strict enquiry, we cannot maintain the evulsion or biting off any parts; and this is declarable from the best and most professed Writers; for though some have made use hereof in a Morall or Tropicall way, yet have the professed discoursers by silence deserted, or by experience rejected this assertion. Thus was it in ancient times discovered, and experimentally refuted by one Sestius a Physitian, as it stands related by Pliny; by Dioscorides, who plainly affirms that this tradition is false; by the discoveries of modern Authors, who have expressly discoursed hereon, as Aldrovandus, Mathiolus, Gelnerus, Bellonius; by Olaus *Magnus*, Peter Martyr and divers others; who have described the manner of their venations in America; they generally omitting this way of their escape, and have delivered severall other, by which they are daily taken.

The originall of the conceit was probably Hieroglyphicall; which after became Mythologicall unto the Greeks, and so set down by Æsop; and by processe of tradition, stole into a totall verity, which was but partially true, that is in its covert sense and morality. Now why they placed this invention upon the Bever (beside the Medicall and Merchantable commodity of *castoreum* or parts conceived to be bitten away) might be the sagacity and wisdome of that animall; which indeed from the works it performes, and especially its artifice in building, is very strange, and surely not to be matched by any other. . . .

CHAP. V. *Of the Badger*

That a Brock or Badger hath the legs of one side shorter then of the other, though an opinion perhaps not very ancient, is yet very generall; received not only by theorists and unexperienced beleevers, but assented unto by most who have the opportunity to behold and hunt them daily. Which notwithstanding upon enquiry I finde repugnant unto the three determinators of truth, Authority, Sense and Reason. For first, Albertus *magnus* speaks dubiously, confessing he could not confirm the verity hereof; but Aldrovand affirmeth plainly, there can be no such inequality observed. And for my own part, upon indifferent enquiry, I cannot discover this difference; although the regardible side be defined, and the brevity by most imputed unto the left.

Again, It seems no easie affront unto reason, and generally repugnant unto the course of nature; for if we survey the totall set of animals, we may in their legs, or organs of progression, observe an equality of length, and parity of numeration; that is, not any to have an odde leg, or the supporters and movers of one side not exactly answered by the other. Although the hinder may be unequall unto the fore and middle legs, as in Frogs, Locusts and Grashoppers; or both unto the middle, as in some beetles, and spiders, as is determined by Aristotle *de incessu animalium*. Perfect and viviparous quadrupeds, so standing in their position of pronenesse, that the opposite joints of neighbour legs consist in the same plane; and a line descending from their navell intersects at right angles the axis of the earth. It happeneth often I confesse that a Lobster hath the chely or great claw of one side longer then the other; but this is not properly their legs, but a part of apprehension, and whereby they hold or seize upon their prey; for the legs and proper parts of progression are inverted backward, and stand in a position opposite unto these.

Lastly, The monstrosity is ill contrived, and with some disadvantage; the shortnesse being affixed unto the legs of one side, which might have been more tolerably placed upon the thwart or Diagoniall[15] movers; for the progression of quadrupeds being performed *per Diametrum*, that is the crosse legs moving or resting together, so that two are alwaies in motion, and two in station at the same time; the brevity had been more tolerable in the crosse legs. For then the motion and station had been performed by equall legs; whereas herein they are both performed by unequall organs, and the imperfection becomes discoverable at every hand.

Chap. VI. *Of the Beare*

Chap. VII. *Of the Basilisk*

15. 'Diagonion, a line drawn from the crosse angles' (Browne marg.).

CHAP. VIII. *Of the Wolfe*

CHAP. IX. *Of Deere*

CHAP. X. *Of the Kingfisher*

CHAP. XI. *Of Griffins*

That there are Griffins in Nature, that is, a mixt and dubious Animall, in the fore-part resembling an Eagle, and behinde, the shape of a Lion, with erected eares, four feet, and a long taile, many affirm, and most, I perceive, deny not. The same is averred by Ælian, Solinus, Mela and Herodotus, countenanced by the name sometimes found in Scripture, and was an Hieroglyphick of the Egyptians.

Notwithstanding we finde most diligent enquiries to be of a contrary assertion; for beside that Albertus and Pliny have disallowed it, the learned Aldrovandus hath in a large discourse rejected it; Mathias Michovius who writ of those Northern parts wherein men place these Griffins, hath positively concluded against it; and if examined by the doctrine of Animals, the invention is monstrous, nor much inferiour unto the figment of Sphynx, Chimæra and Harpies. For though some species there be of middle and participating natures, that is, of bird and beast, as Bats and some few others, yet are their parts so conformed and set together, that we cannot define the beginning or end of either; there being a commixtion of both in the whole, rather then an adaptation or cement of the one unto the other.

Now for the word γρύψ or Gryps, sometimes mentioned in Scripture, and frequently in humane Authors, properly understood, it signifies some kinde of Eagle or Vulture; from whence the Epithete Grypus for an hooked or Aquiline nose. Thus when the Septuagint makes use of this word, Tremellius and our Translation hath rendred it the Ossifrage;[16] which is one kinde of Eagle. And although the Vulgar translation, and that annexed unto the Septuagint retain the word *Gryps*, which in ordinary and school-construction is commonly rendred a Griffin; yet cannot the Latine assume any other sense then the

16. Leviticus 11.13 (Browne marg.).

Greek, from whence it is borrowed. And though the Latine *Gryphes* be altered somewhat by the addition of an h, or aspiration of the letter π, yet is not this unusuall; so what the Greeks call τρόπαιον, the Latines will call *Trophæum*, and that person which in the Gospel is named Κλεότας, the Latines will render *Cleophas*. And therefore the quarrell of Origen was injust and his conception erroneous, when he conceived the food of Griffins forbidden by the Law of Moses; that is, poeticall Animals, and things of no existence. And therefore when in the Hecatombs[17] and mighty oblations of the Gentiles, it is delivered they sacrificed Gryphes or Griffins; hereby we may understand some stronger sort of Eagles. And therefore also when its said in Virgil of an improper match, or Mopsus marrying Nysa, *Jungentur jam gryphes equis*;[18] we need not hunt after other sense, then that strange unions shall be made, and differing natures be conjoined together.

As for the testimonies of ancient Writers, they are but derivative, and terminate all in one Aristeus a Poet of Proconesus; who affirmed that neer the Arimaspi, or one eyed Nation, Griffins defended the mines of gold. But this as Herodotus delivereth, he wrote by hearsay; and Michovius who hath expressely written of those parts plainly affirmeth, there is neither gold nor Griffins in that countrey, nor any such Animall extant; for so doth he conclude, *Ego vero contra veteres authores, Gryphes nec in illa septentrionis, nec in aliis orbis partibus inveniri affirmarim.*[19]

Lastly, Concerning the Hieroglyphicall authority, although it neerest approacheth the truth, it doth not inferre its existency; the conceit of the Griffin properly taken being but a symbolicall phancy, in so intolerable a shape including allowable morality. So doth it well make out the properties of a Guardian, or any person entrusted; the ears implying attention, the wings celerity of execution, the Lion-like shape, courage and audacity, the hooked bill, reservance and tenacity. It is also an Embleme of

17. 'sacrifices, wherein were kylled a hundred beastes' (Elyot).

18. 'Horses will now mate with griffins' (*Eclogues*, VIII, 27).

19. 'In opposition to ancient writers I would affirm that griffins are to be found neither in that northern region nor in other parts of the world'.

THE MAJOR WORKS

valour and magnanimity, as being compounded of the Eagle and Lion, the noblest Animals in their kindes; and so is it appliable unto Princes, Presidents, Generals, and all heroick Commanders; and so is it also born in the Coat-armes of many noble Families of Europe.

CHAP. XII. *Of the Phœnix*

That there is but one Phœnix in the world, which after many hundred years burneth it self, and from the ashes thereof ariseth up another, is a conceit not new or altogether popular, but of great Antiquity; not only delivered by humane Authors, but frequently expressed by holy Writers; by Cyril, Epiphanius and others, by Ambrose in his Hexameron, and Tertul. in his Poem *de Judicio Domini*, but more agreeably unto the present sense, in his excellent Tract, *de Resur. carnis*. [*I mean that bird, special to the east, famous for its solitary character, miraculous in its after-history, which gladly puts itself to death and renews itself, passing away and appearing again by a death which is a birth, a second time a phœnix where now there is none, a second time the very creature that no longer exists, another and yet the same*].[20] The Scripture also seems to favour it, particularly that of Job 21. in the Interpretation of Beda, *Dicebam in nidulo meo moriar, & sicut Phœnix multiplicabo dies*:[21] and Psalme 31. δίκαιος ὡς φοῖνιξ ἀνθήσει, *vir justus ut Phœnix florebit*,[22] as Tertullian renders it, and so also expounds it in his book before alledged.

All which notwithstanding, we cannot presume the existence of this Animall; nor dare we affirm there is any Phœnix in Nature. For, first there wants herein the definitive confirmator and test of things uncertain, that is, the sense of man. For though many Writers have much enlarged hereon, there is not any ocular describer, or such as presumeth to confirm it upon aspection:[23] And therefore Herodotus that led the story unto

20. *The Resurrection of the Flesh*, XIII: in Browne's text quoted in Latin.
21. 'I used to say, "I will die in my little nest and multiply my days like the phoenix"'.
22. Psalm 91 [92].12, which the *AV* renders 'The righteous shall flourish like *the palm tree*' (in the Septuagint: *the phoenix*).
23. Beholding.

PSEUDODOXIA EPIDEMICA

the Greeks, plainly saith, he never attained the sight of any, but
only in the picture.

Again, Primitive Authors, and from whom the stream of
relations is derivative, deliver themselves very dubiously; and
either by a doubtfull parenthesis, or a timerous conclusion
overthrow the whole relation ... Moreover, Such as have
naturally discoursed hereon, have so diversly, contrarily, or
contradictorily delivered themselves, that no affirmative from
thence can reasonably be deduced. For most have positively
denied it, and they which affirm and beleeve it, assign this name
unto many, and mistake two or three in one ... Nor are men
only at variance in regard of the Phœnix it self, but very dis-
agreeing in the accidents ascribed thereto: for some affirm it
liveth three hundred, some five, others six, some a thousand,
others no lesse then fifteen hundred years; some say it liveth
in Æthiopia, others in Arabia, some in Ægypt, others in
India, and some in Utopia; for such must that be which is des-
cribed by Lactantius; that is, which neither was singed in the
combustion of Phaeton, or overwhelmed by the inundation of
Deucaleon.

Lastly, Many Authors who have discoursed hereof, have so
delivered themselves, and with such intentions, we cannot
from thence deduce a confirmation. For some have written
Poetically as Ovid, Mantuan, Lactantius, Claudian and others:
Some have written mystically, as Paracelsus in his book *de
Azoth*, or *de ligno & linea vitæ*; and as severall Hermeticall
Philosophers, involving therein the secret of their Elixir, and
enigmatically expressing the nature of their great work. Some
have written Rhetorically, and concessively, not controverting
but assuming the question, which taken as granted advantaged
the illation. So have holy men made use hereof as farre as thereby
to confirm the Resurrection; for discoursing with heathens who
granted the story of the Phœnix, they induced the Resurrection
from principles of their own, and positions received among
themselves. Others have spoken Emblematically and Hiero-
glyphically; and so did the Ægyptians, unto whom the Phœnix
was the Hieroglyphick of the Sunne. And this was probably
the ground of the whole relation; succeeding ages adding

fabulous accounts, which laid together built up this singularity, which every pen proclaimeth. . . .

CHAP. XIII. *Frogges, Toades and Toad-stone*

CHAP. XIV. *Of the Salamander*

CHAP. XV. *Of the Amphisbæna*

CHAP. XVI. *Of the Viper*

CHAP. XVII. *Of Hares*

CHAP. XVIII. *Of Molls*

CHAP. XIX. *Of Lampries*

Whether Lampries have nine eies, as is received, we durst refer it unto Polyphemus, who had but one, to judge it. An error concerning eies, occasioned by the error of eies; deduced from the appearance of divers cavities or holes on either side, which some call eies that carelessly behold them; and is not only refutable by experience, but also repugnant unto reason. For beside the monstrosity they fasten unto Nature, in contriving many eies, who hath made but two unto any animall, that is, one of each side, according to the division of the brain; it were a superfluous and inartificiall act to place and settle so many in one plane; for the two extreams would sufficiently perform the office of sight without the help of the intermediate eies, and behold as much as all seven joined together. For the visible base of the object would be defined by these two; and the middle eies although they behold the same thing, yet could they not behold so much thereof as these; so were it no advantage unto man to have a third eie, between those two he hath already; and the fiction of Argus seems more reasonable then this; for though he had many eies, yet were they placed in circumference and positions of advantage.

Again, These cavities which men call eies are seated out of the head, and where the Gils of other fish are placed; containing no organs of sight, nor having any communication with the brain. Now all sense proceeding from the brain, and that being placed (as Galen observeth) in the upper part of the body, for the fitter situation of the eies, and conveniency required unto sight; it is not reasonable to imagine that they are any where else, or deserve that name which are seated in other parts. And therefore we relinquish as fabulous what is delivered of Sternopthalmi, or men with eies in their breast; and when it is said by Solomon, A wise mans eies are in his head,[24] it is to be taken in a second sense, and affordeth no objection. True it is that the eies of animals are seated with some difference, but all whatsoever in the head, and that more forward then the ear or hole of hearing. In quadrupedes, in regard of the figure of their heads, they are placed at some distance; in latirostrous[25] and flat-bild birds they are more laterally seated; and therefore when they look intently they turn one eie upon the object, and can convert their heads to see before and behinde, and to behold two opposite points at once. But at a more easie distance are they situated in man, and in the same circumference with the ear; for if one foot of the compasse be placed upon the Crown, a circle described thereby will intersect, or passe over both the eares.

The error in this conceit consists in the ignorance of these cavities, and their proper use in nature; for this is a particular disposure of parts, and a peculiar conformation whereby these holes and sluces supply the defect of Gils, and are assisted by the conduit in the head; for like cetaceous animals and Whales, the Lamprey hath a fistula, spout or pipe at the back part of the head, whereat it spurts out water. Nor is it only singular in this formation, but also in many other; as in defect of bones, whereof it hath not one; and for the spine or back-bone, a cartilaginous substance without any spondyles, processes or protuberance whatsoever. As also in the provision which Nature hath made for the heart; which in this animall is very strangely secured, and lies immured in a cartilage or gristly substance. And lastly, in the colour of the liver; which is in the male of an excellent grasse green; but of a deeper colour in the female, and will communicate a fresh and durable verdure.

24. Ecclesiastes 2.14.
25. Broad-beaked.

CHAP. XX. *Of Snayles*

CHAP. XXI. *Of the Cameleon*

CHAP. XXII. *Of the Oestridge*

CHAP. XXIII. *Of the Unicorns horn*

Great account and much profit is made of Unicorns horn, at least of that which beareth the name thereof; wherein not-withstanding, many I perceive suspect an Imposture, and some conceive there is no such animall extant.[26] Herein therefore to draw up our determinations, beside the severall places of Scripture mentioning this animall (which some perhaps may contend to be only meant of the Rhinoceros)[27] we are so far from denying there is any Unicorn at all, that we affirm there are many kindes thereof. In the number of Quadrupedes, we will concede no lesse then five; that is, the Indian Oxe, the Indian Asse, the Rhinoceros, the Oryx, and that which is more eminently termed *Monoceros*, or *Unicornis*: Some in the list of fishes; as that described by Olaus, Albertus and others: and some unicorns we will allow even among insects; as those four kindes of nasicornous[28] Beetles described by Mussetus.

Secondly, Although we concede there be many Unicornes, yet are we still to seek; for whereunto to affix this horn in question, or to determine from which thereof we receive this magnified medicine, we have no assurance, or any satisfactory decision. For although we single out one, and eminently thereto assign the name of the Unicorn, yet can we not be secure what creature is meant thereby, what constant shape it holdeth, or in what number to be received. For as far as our endeavours dis-

26. As late as 1661, some members of the Royal Society appear to have credited the unicorn's existence (§176). Alexander Ross provided a description: it 'hath the proportion and bignesse of a Horse, the head, legges and feet of a Stagge, and the mane of a Horse; he hath a horn in his forehead' etc. (in *Arcana Microcosmi* [1651], pp. 188 ff.).

27. 'Some doubt to be made what *re'em* signifieth in Scripture' (Browne marg.). True enough; for *re'em* (in Deuteronomy 33.17, Job 39.9–10, Psalms 22.21 and 92.10, etc.) appears as 'unicorn' in *AV* (a literal translation of the Septuagint) but as 'unicorn' or 'rhinocerus' in the Vulgate.

28. 'that hath a horn on the nose' (Blount, citing Browne).

cover, this animall is not uniformly described, but differently set forth by those that undertake it. . . .

Thirdly, Although we were agreed what animall this was, or differed not in its description, yet would this also afford but little satisfaction; for the horne we commonly extoll, is not the same with that of the Ancients; for that in the description of Ælian and Pliny was black; this which is shewed amongst us is commonly white, none black; and of those five which Scaliger beheld, though one spadiceous, or of a light red, and two inclining to red, yet was there not any of this complexion among them.

Fourthly, What horns soever they be which passe amongst us, they are not surely the horns of any one kinde of animall, but must proceed from severall sorts of Unicorns. . . .

Fifthly, Although there be many Unicorns, and consequently many horns, yet many there are which bear that name, and currantly passe among us, which are no horns at all. . . .

Sixtly, Although we were satisfied we had the Unicornes horn, yet were it no injury unto reason to question the efficacy thereof, or whether those vertues pretended doe properly belong unto it. For what we observe (and it escaped not the observation of Paulus Jovius many years past) none of the Ancients ascribed any medicinall or antidotall vertue unto the Unicorns horn; and that which Ælian extolleth, who was the first and only man of the Ancients who spake of the medicall vertue of any Unicorn, was the horn of the Indian Asse; whereof, saith he, the Princes of those parts make bowles and drink therein, as preservatives against poison, Convulsions and the Falling-sicknesse. Now the description of that horn is not agreeable unto that we commend; for that (saith he) is red above, white below, and black in the middle; which is very different from ours, or any to be seen amongst us. And thus, though the description of the Unicorn be very ancient, yet was there of old no vertue ascribed unto it; and although this amongst us receive the opinion of the same vertue, yet is it not the same horn whereunto the Ancients ascribed it. . . . Since therefore there be many Unicornes; Since that whereto we appropriate a horn is so variously described, that it seemeth either never to have been seen by two persons, or not to have been one animall; Since though they agreed in the description of the animall, yet is not the horn we extoll the same with that of the Ancients; Since what hornes soever they be that passe among us, they are not the hornes of one, but severall animals: Since many in common use and high esteem are no hornes at all: Since if they were true hornes, yet might their vertues be questioned: Since though we allowed some vertues, yet were not others to be received; with what security a man may rely on this remedy, the mistresse of fools hath already instructed some, and to wisdome (which is never too wise to learn) it is not too late to consider.

CHAP. XXIV. *That all Animals of the Land, are in their kinde in the Sea*

CHAP. XXV. *Concerning the common course in Diet, in making choice of some Animals, and abstaining from eating others*

ADDENDUM[29]

CHAP. XXVI. *Of Sperma-Ceti, and the Sperma-Ceti Whale*

What Sperma-Ceti is, men might justly doubt, since the learned *Hofmannus* in his work of Thirty years, saith plainly, *Nescio quid sit.*[30] And therefore need not wonder at the variety of opinions; while some conceived it to be *flos maris*, and many, a bituminous substance floating upon the sea.

That it was not the spawn of the Whale, according to vulgar conceit, or nominal appellation, Phylosophers have always doubted; not easily conceiving the Seminal humour of Animals, should be inflammable; or of a floating nature.

That it proceedeth from the Whale, beside the relation of

29. Chapter XXVI was added in the 3rd edition (1658); and retained in the next one (also 1658), it was removed from the 5th edition (1659). Its importance for Melville is noted above, p. 51.

30. 'I do not know what it is'. The entire sentence is included in the Extracts prefixed to *Moby Dick*.

Clusius and other learned observers, was indubitably determined, not many years since by a Sperma-Ceti Whale, cast on our coast of *Norfolk*.[31] Which, to lead on further inquiry, we cannot omit to inform. It contained no less then sixty foot in length, the head somewhat peculiar, with a large prominency over the mouth; teeth only in the lower Jaw, received into fleshly sockets in the upper. The Weight of the largest about two pound: No gristly[32] substances in the mouth, commonly called Whale-bones; Only two short finns seated forwardly on the back; the eyes but small, the pizell[33] large, and prominent. A lesser Whale of this kind above twenty years ago, was cast up on the same shore.[34]

The description of this Whale seems omitted by *Gesner, Rondeletius,* and the first Editions of *Aldrovandus*; but described in the latin impression of *Pareus,* in the Exoticks of *Clusius,* and the natural history of *Nirembergius,* but more amply in the Icons and figures of *Johnstonus.*

Mariners (who are not the best Nomenclators) called it a *Jubartas,* or rather *Gibbartus.* Of the same appellation we meet with one in *Rondeletius,* called by the *French* Gibbar, from its round and gibbous[35] back. The name *Gibbarta* we find also given unto one kind of *Greenland* Whales: But this of ours seemed not to answer the Whale of that denomination; but more agreeable unto the *Trumpa* or Sperma-Ceti Whale: according to the account of our *Greenland* describers in *Purchas.* And maketh the third among the eight remarkable Whales of that Coast.

Out of the head of this Whale, having been dead divers daies, and under putrifaction, flowed streams of oyl and Sperma-Ceti; which was carefully taken up and preserved by the Coasters. But upon breaking up, the Magazin of Sperma-Ceti, was found in the head lying in foulds and courses, in the bigness of goose eggs, encompassed with large flakie substances,

31. 'Near *Wells*' (Browne marg.).
32. Cartilaginous.
33. Penis.
34. 'Near *Hunstanton*' (Browne marg.).
35. Hump-shaped.

as large as a mans head, in form of hony-combs, very white and full of oyl.

Some resemblance or trace hereof there seems to be in the *Physiter* or *Capidolio* of *Rondeletius*; while he delivers, that a fatness more liquid then oyl, runs from the brain of that animal; which being out, the Reliques are like the skales of *Sardinos* pressed into a mass; which melting with heat, are again concreted by cold. And this many conceive to have been the fish which swallowed *Jonas*. Although for the largeness of the mouth, and frequency in those seas, may possibly be the *Lamia*.[36]

Some part of the Sperma-Ceti found on the shore was pure, and needed little depuration;[37] a great part mixed with fetid oyl, needing good preparation, and frequent expression, to bring it to a flakie consistency. And not only the head, but other parts contained it. For the carnous parts being roasted, the oyl dropped out, an axungious[38] and thicker part subsiding; the oyl it self contained also much in it, and still after many years some is obtained from it.

Greenland Enquirers seldom meet with a Whale of this kind: and therefore it is but a contingent Commodity, not reparable from any other. It flameth white and candent like Champhire,[39] but dissolveth not in *aqua fortis*, like it. Some lumps containing about two ounces, kept ever since in water, afford a fresh, and flosculous[40] smell. Well prepared and separated from the oyl, it is of a substance unlikely to decay, and may outlast the oyl required in the Composition of *Mathiolus*.

Of the large quantity of oyl, what first came forth by expression from the *Sperma-Ceti*, grew very white and clear, like that of Almonds or Ben. What came by decoction[41] was red. It was found to spend much in the vessels which contained it: It freezeth or coagulateth quickly with cold, and the newer

36. A genus of shark.
37. Refining.
38. Lard-like, greasy.
39. i.e. camphor.
40. Of the savour of flowers.
41. Extraction.

soonest. It seems different from the oyl of any other animal,
and very much frustrated the expectation of our soap-boylers,
as not incorporating or mingling with their lyes. But it mixeth
well with painting Colours, though hardly drieth at all.
Combers of wool made use hereof, and Country people for cuts,
aches and hard tumors. It may prove of good Medical use; and
serve for a ground in compounded oyls and Balsams. Distilled,
it affords a strong oyl, with a quick and piercing water. Upon
Evaporation it gives a balsame, which is better performed[42]
with Turpentine distilled with *Sperma-Ceti.*

Had the abominable scent permitted, enquirie had been
made into that strange composure of the head, and hillock of
flesh about it. Since the workmen affirmed, they met with
Sperma-Ceti before they came to the bone, and the head yet pre-
served, seems to confirm the same. The sphincters inserving
unto[43] the Fistula or spout, might have been examined, since
they are so notably contrived in other cetaceous Animals; as
also the Larynx or Throtle, whether answerable unto that of
Dolphins and Porposes in the strange composure and figure
which it maketh. What figure the stomack maintained in this
Animal of one jaw of teeth, since in Porposes which abound in
both, the ventricle is trebly divided, and since in that formerly
taken nothing was found but weeds and a Loligo.[44] The heart,
lungs, and kidneys, had no escaped; wherein are remarkable
differences from Animals of the land, likewise what humor the
bladder contained, but especially the seminal parts, which might
have determined the difference of that humor, from this which
beareth its name.

In vain it was to rake for Ambergreece in the panch of this
Leviathan, as *Greenland* discoverers, and attests[45] of experience
dictate, that they sometimes swallow great lumps thereof in the
Sea; insufferable fetour denying that enquiry. And yet if, as
Paracelsus encourageth, Ordure makes the best Musk, and from

42. Finished.
43. i.e. the contractile muscular ring conducive to.
44. Squid.
45. Evidences.

the most fetid substances may be drawn the most odoriferous Essences; all that had not *Vespasians* Note,[46] might boldly swear, here was a subject fit for such extractions.

CHAP. XXVI. *Compendiously of sundry Tenents concerning other Animals, which examined prove either false or dubious*

1. And first from great Antiquity, and before the Melody of Syrens, the Musicall note of Swans hath been commended, and that they sung most sweetly before their death. For thus we reade in Plato, that from the opinion of Metempsuchosis, or transmigration of the soules of men into the bodies of beasts most sutable unto their humane condition, after his death, Orpheus the Musician became a Swan. Thus was it the bird of Apollo the god of Musick by the Greeks; and an Hieroglyphick of Musick among the Ægyptians, from whom the Greeks derived the conception; hath been the affirmation of many Latines, and hath not wanted assertors almost from every Nation.

All which notwithstanding, we finde this relation doubtfully received by Ælian, as an hearsay account by Bellonius, as a false one by Pliny; expresly refuted by Myndius in Athenæus; and severely rejected by Scaliger . . . Authors also that countenance it, speak not satisfactorily of it. Some affirming they sing not till they die; some that they sing, yet die not. Some speak generally, as though this note were in all; some but particularly, as though it were only in some; some in places remote, and where we can have no triall of it; others in places where every experience can refute it; as Aldrovandus upon relation, delivered, concerning the Musick of the Swans on the river of Thames near London.

Now that which countenanceth, and probably confirmeth this opinion, is the strange and unusuall conformation of the winde pipe, or vocall organ in this animall: observed first by Aldrovandus, and conceived by some contrived for this intention: for in its length it farre exceedeth the gullet; and hath

46. Who had imposed a tax on the city urinals but, as he pointed out, the proceeds were not at all offensive (Suetonius, *Vespasian*, XXIII).

in the chest a sinuous revolution, that is, when it ariseth from the lungs, it ascendeth not directly unto the throat, but ascending first into a capsulary reception of the breast bone, by a Serpentine and Trumpet recurvation it ascendeth again into the neck; and so by the length thereof a great quantity of air is received, and by the figure thereof a musicall modulation effected. But to speak indifferently, this formation of the Weazon,[47] is not peculiar unto the Swan, but common also unto the Platea or Shovelard, a bird of no Musicall throat; And as Aldrovandus confesseth may thus be contrived in the Swan to contain a larger stock of air, whereby being to feed on weeds at the bottom, they might the longer space detain their heads under water. But were this formation peculiar, or had they unto this effect an advantage from this part: yet have they a known and open disadvantage from another; that is, a flat bill. For no Latirostrous[48] animall (whereof neverthelesse there are no slender numbers) were ever commended for their note, or accounted among those animals which have been instructed to speak.

When therefore we consider the dissention of Authors, the falsity of relations, the indisposition of the Organs, and the immusicall note of all we ever beheld or heard of; if generally taken and comprehending all Swans, or of all places, we cannot assent thereto. Surely he that is bit with a Tarantula, shall never be cured by this Musick; and with the same hopes we expect to hear the harmony of the Spheres.

2. That there is a speciall propriety in the flesh of Peacocks rost or boiled, to preserve a long time incorrupted, hath been the assertion of many; stands yet confirmed by Austin, *De Civitate Dei*; by Gygas Sempronius, in Aldrovandus, and the same experiment we can confirm our selves, in the brawn or fleshy parts of Peacocks so hanged up with thred, that they touch no place whereby to contract a moisture; and hereof we have made triall both in summer and winter. The reason, some, I perceive, attempt to make out from the siccity and drinesse of its flesh, and some are content to rest in a secret propriety

47. i.e. weasand: windpipe.
48. As above, p. 213, note 25.

thereof. As for the siccity of the flesh, it is more remarkable in other animals, as Eagles, Hawkes, and birds of prey; That it is a propriety or agreeable unto none other, we cannot with reason admit: for the same preservation, or rather incorruption we have observed in the flesh of Turkeys, Capons, Hares, Partridge, Venison, suspended freely in the air, and after a year and a half, dogs have not refused to eat them.

As for the other conceit that a Peacock is ashamed when he looks on his legges, as is commonly held, and also delivered by Cardan; beside what hath been said against it by Scaliger, let them beleeve that hold specificall[49] deformities; or that any part can seem unhansome to their eies, which hath appeared good and beautifull unto their makers. The occasion of this conceit, might first arise from a common abservation, that when they are in their pride, that is, advance their train, if they decline their neck to the ground, they presently demit and let fall the same: which indeed they cannot otherwise do; for contracting their body, and being forced to draw in their foreparts, to establish the hinder in the elevation of the train; if the foreparts depart and incline to the ground, the hinder grow too weak, and suffer the train to fall. And the same in some degree is also observable in Turkeys. . . .

CHAP. XXVII. *Of some others*

49. i.e. peculiar to a species.

THE FOURTH BOOK:

OF MANY POPULAR AND RECEIVED TENENTS CONCERNING MAN, WHICH EXAMINED, PROVE EITHER FALSE OR DUBIOUS

CHAP. I. *Of the erectnesse of Man*

That onely Man hath an erect figure, and for to behold and look up toward heaven, according to that of the Poet,

> *Pronaque cum spectant animalia cætera terram,*
> *Os homini sublime dedit, cælumque tueri*
> *Jussit, & erectos ad sydera tollere vultus,*[1]

is a double assertion, whose first part may be true; if we take erectnesse strictly, and so as Galen hath defined it; for they only, saith he, have an erect figure, whose spine and thigh-bone are carried in right lines; and so indeed of any we yet know, Man only is erect. For the thighes of other animals doe stand at angles with their spine, and have rectangular positions in birds, and perfect Quadrupeds; nor doth the Frog, though stretched out, or swimming, attain the rectitude of man, or carry its thigh without all angularity. And thus is it also true that man only sitteth, if we define sitting to be a firmation of the body upon the Ischias:[2] wherein if the position be just and

1. Ovid, *Metamorphoses*, I, 84–6; freely translated by Arthur Golding (1567) thus:

> where all other beasts behold the ground with grovelling eie,
> He gave to Man a stately looke replete with majestie.
> And willde him to behold the Heaven wyth countnance cast on hie,
> To marke and understand what things were in the starrie skie.

Cf. Milton, *Paradise Lost*, VII, 506–10; and Donne: 'Wee attribute but one privilege and advantage to Mans body above other moving creatures, that he is not as others, groveling, but of an erect, of an upright form, naturally built, and disposed to the contemplation of *Heaven* . . .' (*Devotions upon Emergent Occasions* [1624], ed. John Sparrow [Cambridge, 1923], p. 10). See §291.

2. The lowest part of the *os innominatum*, the bone on which the body rests when sitting.

naturall, the thigh-bone lieth at right angles to the spine, and the leg bone or tibia to the thigh. For others when they seem to sit, as Dogs, Cats, or Lions, doe make unto their spine acute angles with their thigh, and acute to the thigh with their shank. Thus is it likewise true, what Aristotle alledgeth in that Problem; why man alone suffereth pollutions in the night? because man only lieth upon his back; if we define not the same by every supine position, but when the spine is in rectitude with the thigh, and both with the armes lie parallell to the Horizon; so that a line through their navel will passe through the Zenith and centre of the earth; and so cannot other animals lie upon their backs; for though the spine lie parallell with the Horizon, yet will their legs incline, and lie at angles unto it. And upon these three divers positions in man, wherein the spine can only be at right lines with the thigh, arise those remarkable postures, prone, supine and erect; which are but differenced in situation or in angular postures upon the back, the belly and the feet.

But if erectnesse be popularly taken, and as it is largely opposed unto pronenesse, or the posture of animals looking downwards, carrying their venters or opposite part to the spine directly towards the earth, it may admit of question. For though in Serpents and Lizards we may truly allow a pronenesse, yet Galen acknowledgeth that perfect Quadrupeds, as Horses, Oxen and Camels, are but partly prone, and have some part of erectnesse. And birds or flying animals, are so farre from this kinde of pronenesse, that they are almost erect; advancing the head and breast in their progression, and only prone in the act of volitation. And if that be true which is delivered of the Penguin or *Anser Magellanicus*, often described in Maps about those Straits, that they go erect like men, and with their breast and belly doe make one line perpendicular unto the axis of the earth; it will make up the exact erectnesse of man. Nor will that insect come very short which we have often beheld, that is, one kinde of Locust which stands not prone, or a little inclining upward, but in a large erectnesse; elevating alwaies the two fore legs, and sustaining it self in the middle of the other four; by Zoographers[3] called *mantis*, and by the common people of

3. 'Describers of Animals' (Browne marg.).

Province, *Prega Dio*,[4] the Prophet and praying Locust; as being generally found in the posture of supplication, or such as resembleth ours, when we lift up our hands to heaven.

As for the end of this erection, to look up toward heaven; though confirmed by severall testimonies, and the Greek Etymology of man,[5] it is not so readily to be admitted; and as a popular and vain conceit was anciently rejected by Galen; who in his third, *De usu partium*, determines, that man is erect because he was made with hands, and was therewith to exercise all Arts, which in any other figure he could not have performed; as he excellently declareth in that place, where he also proves that man could have been made neither Quadruped nor Centaur.

And for the accomplishment of this intention, that is, to look up and behold the heavens, man hath a notable disadvantage in the eyelid; whereof the upper is farre greater than the lower, which abridgeth the sight upwards; contrary to those of birds, who herein have the advantage of man: Insomuch that the learned Plempius is bold to affirm that if he had had the formation of the eyelids, he would have contrived them quite otherwise.

The ground and occasion of this conceit was a literall apprehension of a figurative expression in Plato, as Galen thus delivers; To opinion that man is erect to look up and behold the heavens, is a conceit only fit for those that never saw the fish Uranoscopus, that is, the Beholder of heaven; which hath its eyes so placed, that it lookes up directly to heaven; which man doth not, except he recline, or bend his head backward: and thus to look up to heaven, agreeth not only unto Men, but Asses; to omit birds with long necks, which look not only upwards, but round about at pleasure; and therefore men of this opinion understood not Plato when he said that men doth *Sursum aspicere*;[6] for thereby was not meant to gape, or look upward with the eye, but to have his thoughts sublime; and not only to behold, but speculate their nature, with the eye of the understanding.

4. The Italian name for the praying mantis. 'Province' is Provence.
5. ἄνθρωπος (man) is said to derive from ἄνω (upwards) and θρώσκω (leap).
6. i.e. man looks up, heavenward.

Now although Galen in this place makes instance but in one, yet are there other fishes, whose eies regard the heavens, as Plane, and cartilagineous fishes, as pectinals, or such as have their bones made laterally like a comb; for when they apply themselves to sleep or rest upon the white side, their eies on the other side look upward toward heaven. For birds, they generally carry their heads erectly like man, and have advantage in their upper eyelid; and many that have long necks, and bear their heads somewhat backward, behold farre more of the heavens, and seem to look above the æquinoxiall circle; and so also in many Quadrupeds, although their progression be partly prone, yet is the sight of their eye direct, not respecting the earth but heaven; and makes an higher arch of altitude then our own. The position of a Frogge with his head above water exceedeth these; for therein he seemes to behold a large part of the heavens, and the acies[7] of his eye to ascend as high as the Tropick; but he that hath beheld the posture of a Bittor, will not deny that it beholds almost the very Zenith.[8]

CHAP. II. *Of the Heart*

CHAP. III. *Of Pleurisies*

CHAP. IV. *Of the Ring-finger*

CHAP. V. *Of the right and left Hand*

CHAP. VI. *Of Swimming*

CHAP. VII. *Concerning Weight*

CHAP. VIII. *Of the passage of Meat and Drink*

CHAP. IX. *Of Sneezing*

CHAP. X. *Of the Jews*

That Jews stinck naturally, that is, that in their race and nation there is an evil savour, is a received opinion we know not how to admit; although concede many questionable points, and dis-

7. Sight (see below, p. 373, note 50).
8. 'Point of heaven over our heads' (Browne marg.).

pute not the verity of sundry opinions which are of affinity hereto. We will acknowledge that certain odours attend on animals, no lesse then certain colours; that pleasant smels are not confined unto vegetables, but found in divers animals, and some more richly then in plants. And though the Probleme of Aristotle enquire why none smels sweet beside the Parde?[9] yet later discoveries adde divers sorts of Monkeys, the Civet Cat and Gazela, from which our Musk proceedeth. We confesse that beside the smell of the species, there may be Individuall odours, and every man may have a proper and peculiar savour; which although not perceptible unto man, who hath this sense, but weak, yet sensible unto Dogs, who hereby can single out their Masters in the dark. We will not deny that particular men have sent forth a pleasant savour, as Theophrastus and Plutarch report of Alexander the great, and Tzetzes and Cardan doe testifie of themselves. That some may also emit an unsavoury odour, we have no reason to deny; for this may happen from the quality of what they have taken; the Fætor[10] whereof may discover it self by sweat and urine, as being unmasterable by the naturall heat of man, not to be dulcified[11] by concoction beyond an unsavoury condition: the like may come to passe from putrid humors, as is often discoverable in putrid and malignant fevers. And sometime also in grosse and humid bodies even in the latitude of sanity; the naturall heat of the parts being insufficient for a perfect and through-digestion, and the errors of one concoction not rectifiable by another: but that an unsavoury odour is gentilitious or nationall unto the Jews, if rightly understood, we cannot well concede; nor will the information of reason or sense induce it.

For first, Upon consult of reason, there will be found no easie assurance for to fasten a materiall or temperamentall propriety upon any nation; there being scarce any condition (but what depends upon clime) which is not exhausted or obscured from the commixture of introvenient[12] nations either by commerce

9. i.e. leopard. The work cited is the pseudo-Aristotelian *Problems*.
10. 'yll savour' (Elyot).
11. Sweetened.
12. 'coming in' (Blount).

or conquest; much more will it be difficult to make out this affection in the Jews, whose race however pretended to be pure, must needs have suffered inseparable commixtures with nations of all sorts, not only in regard of their proselytes, but their universall dispersion; some being posted from severall parts of the earth, others quite lost, and swallowed up in those nations where they planted. For the tribes of Reuben, Gad, part of Manasses and Naphthali, which were taken by Assur, and the rest at the sacking of Samaria which were led away by Salmanasser into Assyria, and after a year and half arrived at Arsereth, as is delivered in Esdras,[13] these I say never returned, and are by the Jews as vainly expected as their Messias. Of those of the tribe of Juda and Benjamin, which were led captive into Babylon by Nebuchadnezzar, many returned unto Zorobabel; the rest remained, and from thence long after upon invasion of the Saracens, fled as far as India; where yet they are said to remain, but with little difference from the Gentiles.

The Tribes that returned to Judea, were afterward widely dispersed; for beside sixteen thousand which Titus sent to Rome unto the triumph of his father Vespasian, he sold no lesse then an hundred thousand for slaves; not many years after Adrian the Emperour, who ruined the whole Countrey, transplanted many thousands into Spain, from whence they dispersed into divers Countreys, as into France and England, but were banished after from both: from Spain they dispersed into Africa, Italy, Constantinople, and the dominions of the Turke, where they remain as yet in very great numbers. And if (according to good relations) where they may freely speak it, they forbear not to boast that there are at present many thousand Jews in Spain, France and England, and some dispensed withall, even to the degree of Priesthood; it is a matter very considerable, and could they be smelled out, would much advantage, not only the Church of Christ, but also the coffers of Princes.

Now having thus lived in severall Countries, and alwaies in subjection, they must needs have suffered many commixtures, and we are sure they are not exempted from the common con-

13. 2 Esdras 14.45.

tagion of Venery[14] contracted first from Christians. Nor are fornications unfrequent between them both; there commonly passing opinions of invitement, that their Women desire copulation with them, rather then their own Nation, and affect Christian carnality above circumcised venery. It being therefore acknowledged, that some are lost, evident that others are mixed, and scarce probable that any are distinct, it will be hard to establish this quality upon the Jews, unlesse we also transferre the same, unto those whose generations are mixed, whose genealogies are Jewish, and naturally derived from them.

Again, If we concede a Nationall unsavourinesse in any people, yet shall we finde the Jews lesse subject hereto then any, and that in those regards which most powerfully concurre to such effects, that is, their diet and generation. As for their diet, whether in obedience unto the precepts of reason, or the injunctions of parsimony, therein they are very temperate, seldome offending in ebriety or excesse of drink, nor erring in gulosity or superfluity of meats. . . . So that observing a spare and simple diet, whereby they prevent the generation of crudities; and fasting often whereby they might also digest them; they must be lesse inclinable unto this infirmity then any other Nation, whose proceedings are not so reasonable to avoid it.

As for their generations and conceptions (which are the purer from good diet,) they become more pure and perfect by the strict observation of their Law; upon the injunctions whereof, they severely observe the times of Purification, and avoid all copulation, either in the uncleannesse of themselves, or impurity of their Women. A rule, I fear, not so well observed by Christians; whereby not only conceptions are prevented, but if they proceed, so vitiated and defiled, that durable inquinations,[15] remain upon the birth; which, when the conception meets with these impurities, must needs be very potent; since in the purest and most fair conceptions, learned men derive the cause of Pox and Meazles, from principles of that

14. 'lechery, fleshly wantonnesse' (Blount).
15. Disgraces.

nature; that is, the menstruous impurities in the mothers bloud, and virulent tinctures contracted by the Infant, in the nutriment of the wombe.

Lastly, Experience will convict it; for this offensive odor is no way discoverable in their Synagogues where many are, and by reason of their number could not be concealed: nor is the same discernible in commerce or conversation with such as are cleanly in Apparell, and decent in their Houses. Surely the Viziars and Turkish Basha's[16] are not of this opinion; who as Sir Henry Blunt informeth, doe generally keep a Jew of their private Counsell. And were this true, the Jews themselves doe not strictly make out the intention of their Law; for in vain doe they scruple to approach the dead, who livingly are cadaverous, or fear any outward pollution, whose temper pollutes themselves. And lastly, were this true, our opinion is not impartiall; for unto converted Jews who are of the same seed, no man imputeth this unsavoury odor; as though Aromatized by their conversion, they amitted their sent[17] with their Religion, and smelt no longer then they savoured of the Jew.

Now the ground that begat or propagated this assertion, might be the distastfull aversenesse of the Christian from the Jew, from the villany of that fact, which made them abominable and stinck in the nostrils of all men. Which reall practice, and metaphoricall expression, did after proceed into a literall construction; but was a fraudulent illation; for such an evil savour their father Jacob acknowledged in himself, when he said, his sons had made him stinck in the land,[18] that is, to be abominable unto the inhabitants thereof. Now how dangerous it is in sensible things to use metaphoricall expressions unto the people, and what absurd conceits they will swallow in their literals; an impatient example we have in our own profession; who having called an eating Ulcer by the name of a Wolfe, common apprehension conceives a reality therein; and against our selves ocular affirmations are pretended to confirm it. . . .

16. i.e. pashas.
17. i.e. lost their scent.
18. Genesis 34.30.

CHAP. XI. *Of Pigmies*

CHAP. XII. *Of the great Climactericall year, that is, Sixty three*

Certainly the eies of the understanding, and those of the sense are differently deceived in their greatest objects; the sense apprehending them in lesser magnitudes then their dimensions require; so it beholdeth the Sunne, the Starres, and the Earth it self; but the understanding quite otherwise; for that ascribeth unto many things farre larger horizons then their due circumscriptions require; and receiveth them with amplifications which their reality will not admit: Thus hath it fared with many Heroes and most worthy persons, who being sufficiently commendable from true and unquestionable merits, have received advancement from falsehood and the fruitfull stock of fables. Thus hath it happened unto the Starres and luminaries of heaven; who being sufficiently admirable in themselves, have been set out by effects no way dependant on their efficiencies, and advanced by amplifications to the questioning of their true endowments. Thus is it not improbable it hath also fared with number; which though wonderfull in it self, and sufficiently magnifiable from its demonstrable affections, hath yet received adjections from the multiplying conceits of men, and stands laden with additions which its equity will not admit.

And so perhaps hath it happened unto the number 7 and 9, which multiplied into themselves doe make up Sixty three, commonly esteemed the great Climactericall of our lives; for the daies of men are usually cast up by Septenaries, and every seventh year conceived to carry some altering character with it, either in the temper of body, minde, or both. But among all other, three are most remarkable, that is 7 times 7 or fourty nine, 9 times 9 or eighty one, and 7 times 9 or the year of Sixty three; which is conceived to carry with it the most considerable fatality; and consisting of both the other numbers was apprehended to comprise the vertue of either; is therefore expected and entertained with fear, and esteemed a favour of fate to passe it over. Which notwithstanding many suspect to be but a

Panick terrour, and men to fear they justly know not what; and to speak indifferently, I finde no satisfaction, nor any sufficiency in the received grounds to establish a rationall feare.

Now herein to omit Astrologicall considerations (which are but rarely introduced) the popular foundation whereby it hath continued, is first, the extraordinary power and secret vertue conceived to attend these numbers; whereof we must confesse there have not wanted not onely especiall commendations, but very singular conceptions. Among Philosophers, Pythagoras seemes to have plaied the leading part, which was long after continued by his disciples, and the Italick Schoole. The Philosophy of Plato, and most of the Platonists abounds in numerall considerations; above all Philo the learned Jew, hath acted this part even to superstition; bestowing divers pages in summing up every thing which might advantage this number. Which notwithstanding when a serious Reader shall perpend, he will hardly finde any thing that may convince his judgement, or any further perswade, then the lenity of his belief, or prejudgement of reason inclineth.

For first, Not only the number of 7 and 9 from considerations abstruse have been extolled by most, but all or most of the other digits have been as mystically applauded; for the number of One and Three have not been only admired by the Heathens, but from adorable grounds, the unity of God, and mystery of the Trinity admired by many Christians. The number of four stands much admired not only in the quaternity of the Elements, which are the principles of bodies, but in the letters of the Name of God, which in the Greek, Arabian, Persian, Hebrew and Ægyptian, consisteth of that number; and was so venerable among the Pythagoreans, that they swore by the number four. That of six hath found many leaves in its favour; not only for the daies of the Creation, but its naturall consideration, as being a perfect number, and the first that is compleated by its parts; that is, the sixt, the half, and the third, 1. 2. 3. which drawn into a summe make six: The number of Ten hath been as highly extolled, as containing even, odde, long and plain, quadrate and cubicall numbers; and Aristotle observed with admiration, that Barbarians as well as Greeks, did use a numeration unto Ten; which being so generall was not to be judged casuall, but to have a foundation in nature. So that not only 7 and 9, but all the rest have had their Elogies, as may be observed at large in Rhodiginus, and in severall Writers since: every one extolling number, according to his subject, and as it advantaged the present discourse in hand.[19]

Again, They have been commended not only from pretended grounds in nature, but from artificiall, casuall or fabulous foundations: so have some endeavoured to advance their admiration, from the 9 Muses, from the 7 Wonders of the World, and from the 7 Gates of Thebes; in that 7 Cities contended for Homer, in that there are 7 Starres in Ursa minor, and 7 in Charles wayne or Plaustrum of Ursa major. Wherein indeed although the ground be naturall, yet either from constellations or their remarkable parts, there is the like occasion to commend any other number; the number 5 from the Starres in Sagitta, 3 from the girdle of Orion, and 4 from Equiculus, Crusero, or the feet of the Centaure; yet are such as these clapt in by very good Authors, and some not omitted by Philo. . . .

As for the Criticall daies (such I mean wherein upon a decertation[20] between the disease and nature, there ensueth a sensible alteration, either to life or death,) the reasons thereof are rather deduced from Astrology, then Arithmetick; for accounting from the beginning of the disease, and reckoning on unto the seventh day, the Moon will be in a Tetragonall or Quadrate aspect, that is, 4 signes removed from that wherein the disease began; in the fourteenth day it will be in an opposite aspect; and at the end of the third septenary Tetragonall again; as will most graphically appear in the figures of Astrologers, especially Lucas Gauricus. . . .

Lastly, Though many things have been delivered by Authors concerning number, and they transferred unto the advantage of their nature, yet are they oft times otherwise to be understood, then as they are vulgarly received in active and causall consider-ations; they being many times delivered Hieroglyphically,.

19. Including *The Garden of Cyrus* which extols the number five (below, pp. 317 ff.).
20. Strife.

Metaphorically, Illustratively, and not with reference unto action or causality. True it is, that God made all things in number, weight and measure,[21] yet nothing by them or through the efficacy of either. Indeed our daies, actions and motions being measured by time (which is but motion measured) what ever is observable in any, fals under the account of some number; which notwithstanding cannot be denominated the cause of those events. So doe we injustly assign the power of Action even unto Time it self; nor doe they speak properly who say that Time consumeth all things; for Time is not effective, nor are bodies destroyed by it, but from the action and passion of their Elements in it; whose account it only affordeth; and measuring out their motion, informs us in the periods and termes of their duration, rather then effecteth or Physically produceth the same. . . .

All which perpended, it may be easily perceived with what insecurity of truth we adhere unto this opinion; ascribing not only effects depending on the naturall period of time unto arbitrary calculations, and such as vary at pleasure; but confirming our tenets by the uncertain account of others and our selves. There being no positive or indisputable ground where to begin our compute; that if there were, men have been severall waies mistaken; the best in some latitude, others in greater, according to the different compute of divers states, the short and irreconcilable years of some, the exceeding error in the naturall frame of others, and the lapses and false deductions of ordinary accountants in most.

Which duly considered, together with a strict account and criticall examen of reason, will also distract the witty determinations of Astrology. That Saturn the enemy of life, comes almost every seventh year, unto the quadrate or malevolent place, unto that where it begun: that as the Moon about every seventh day ariveth unto a contrary signe, so Saturne, which remaineth about as many years, as the Moon doth daies in one signe, and holdeth the same consideration in years as the Moon in daies; doth cause these periculous[22] periods. Which together

21. See above, p. 80, note 101.
22. Perilous.

with other Planets, and profection of the Horoscope, unto the seventh house, or opposite signes every seventh year; oppresseth living natures, and causeth observable mutations, in the state of sublunary things. . . .

CHAP. XIII. *Of the Canicular or Dog-daies*

THE FIFTH BOOK:

OF MANY THINGS QUESTIONABLE AS THEY ARE COMMONLY DESCRIBED IN PICTURES

Another mistake there may be in the Picture of our first Parents, who after the manner of their posterity are both delineated with a Navell. And this is observable not only in ordinary and stained peeces, but in the Authentick draughts of Urbin, Angelo and others.[1] Which notwithstanding cannot be allowed, except we impute that unto the first cause, which we impose not on the second; or what we deny unto nature, we impute unto Naturity[2] it self; that is, that in the first and most accomplished peece, the Creator affected superfluities, or ordained parts without all use or office.

For the use of the Navell is to continue the infant unto the Mother, and by the vessels thereof to convey its aliment and sustentation. The vessels whereof it consisteth, are the umbilicall vein, which is a branch of the Porta,[3] and implanted in the liver of the Infant; two Arteries likewise arising from the Iliacall branches, by which the Infant receiveth the purer portion of bloud and spirits from the mother; and lastly, the Urachos or ligamentall passage derived from the bottome of the bladder, whereby it dischargeth the waterish and urinary part of its aliment. Now upon the birth when the Infant forsaketh the

1. i.e. not only in stained glass but in the engravings of Raphael, Michelangelo, *et al.*

2. Nature's underlying creative power. Cf. below, p. 238, note 7.

3. The *vena porta* or great vein conveying blood to the liver (*OED*).

wombe, although it dilacerate,[4] and break the involving
membranes, yet doe these vessels hold, and by the mediation
thereof the Infant is connected unto the wombe, not only before,
but a while also after the birth. These therefore the midwife
cutteth off, contriving them into a knot close unto the body of
the Infant; from whence ensueth that tortuosity or complicated
nodosity we usually call the Navell; occasioned by the collig-
ation[5] of vessels before mentioned. Now the Navell being a part,
not precedent, but subsequent unto generation, nativity or
parturition,[6] it cannot be well imagined at the creation or
extraordinary formation of Adam, who immediately issued
from the Artifice of God; nor also that of Eve; who was not
solemnly begotten, but suddenly framed, and anomalously
proceeded from Adam.

And if we be led into conclusions that Adam had also this
part, because we behold the same in our selves, the inference is
not reasonable; for if we conceive the way of his formation, or
of the first animals, did carry in all points a strict conformity
unto succeeding productions, we might fall into imaginations
that Adam was made without Teeth; or that he ran through
those notable alterations in the vessels of the heart, which the
Infant suffereth after birth: we need not dispute whether the
egge or Bird were first; and might conceive that Dogges were
created blinde, because we observe they are litered so with us.
Which to affirm, is to confound, at least to regulate creation
unto generation, the first Acts of God, unto the second of
Nature, which were determined in that generall indulgence,
Encrease and multiply, produce or propagate each other; that
is, not answerably in all points, but in a prolonged method
according to seminall progression. For the formation of things
at first was different from their generation after; and although it
had nothing to precede it, was aptly contrived for that which
should succeed it. And therefore though Adam were framed
without this part, as having no other wombe then that of his
proper principles, yet was not his posterity without the same:

4. 'teare in peeces' (Cockeram).
5. Conjunction.
6. 'being in labor, with childe' (Blount).

for the seminality of his fabrick contained the power thereof; and was endued with the science[7] of those parts whose predestinations upon succession it did accomplish.

All the Navell therefore and conjunctive part we can suppose in Adam, was his dependency on his Maker, and the connexion he must needs have unto heaven, who was the Sonne of God. For holding no dependence on any preceding efficient but God; in the act of his production there may be conceived some connexion, and Adam to have been in a moment all Navell with his Maker. And although from his carnality and corporall existence, the conjunction seemeth no nearer then of causality and effect; yet in his immortall and diviner part he seemed to hold a nearer coherence, and an umbilicality even with God himself. And so indeed although the propriety of this part be found but in some animals, and many species there are which have no Navell at all; yet is there one link and common connexion, one generall ligament, and necessary obligation of all whatever unto God. Whereby although they act themselves at distance, and seem to be at loose; yet doe they hold a continuity with their Maker. Which catenation or conserving union when ever his pleasure shall divide, let goe, or separate; they shall fall from their existence, essence, and operations; in brief, they must retire unto their primitive nothing, and shrink into that Chaos again. . . .

They who hold the egge was before the Bird, prevent this doubt in many other animals, which also extendeth unto them; for Birds are nourished by umbilicall vessels, and the Navell is manifest sometimes a day or two after exclusion; the same is probable in all oviparous exclusions, if the lesser part of egges must serve for the formation, the greater part for nutriment. The same is made out in the egges of Snakes; and is not improbable in the generation of Porwiggles or Tadpoles; and may be also true in some vermiparous exclusions; although (as we have observed the daily progresse thereof) the whole Maggot is little enough to make a Flye, without any part remaining.

7. Knowledge. By 'seminality' Browne appeals to 'plastic' nature (see below, p. 347, note 24).

Certainly of all men that suffered from the confusion of Babel, the Ægyptians found the best evasion; for, though words were confounded, they invented a language of things, and spake unto each other by common notions in Nature. Whereby they discoursed in silence; and were intuitively understood from the theory of their Expresses. For they assumed the shapes of animals common unto all eies; and by their conjunctions and compositions were able to communicate their conceptions, unto any that coapprehended the Syntaxis [8] of their natures. This many conceive to have been the primitive way of writing, and of greater antiquity then letters; and this indeed might Adam well have spoken, who understanding the nature

8. 'order in construction' (Elyot).

of things, had the advantage of naturall expressions; which the Ægyptians but taking upon trust, upon their own or common opinion; from conceded mistakes they authentically promoted errors; describing in their Hieroglyphicks creatures of their own invention; or from known and conceded animals, erecting significations not inferrible from their natures.

And first, Although there were more things in Nature then words which did expresse them; yet even in these mute and silent discourses, to expresse complexed significations, they took a liberty to compound and piece together creatures of allowable formes into mixtures inexistent. Thus began the descriptions of Griphins, Basilisks, Phenix, and many more; which Emblematists and Heralds have entertained with significations answering their institutions; Hieroglyphically adding Martegres, Wivernes, Lion-fishes, with divers others. Pieces of good and allowable invention unto the prudent Spectator, but are lookt on by vulgar eyes as literall truths, or absurd impossibilities; whereas, indeed they are commendable inventions, and of laudable significations.

Again, Beside these pieces fictitiously set down, and having no copy in Nature; they had many unquestionably drawn, of inconsequent signification, nor naturally verifying their intention. We shall instance but in few, as they stand recorded by Orus. The male sex they expressed by a Vulture, because of Vultures all are females, and impregnated by the winde; which authentically transmitted hath passed many pens, and became the assertion of Aelian, Ambrose, Basil, Isidore, Tzetzes, Philes, and others. Wherein notwithstanding what injury is offered unto the Creation in this confinement of sex, and what disturbance unto Philosophy in the concession of windy conceptions, we shall not here declare. By two dragmes they thought it sufficient to signifie an heart; because the heart at one year weigheth two dragmes, that is, a quarter of an ounce, and unto fifty years annually encreaseth the weight of one dragme; after which in the same proportion it yearly decreaseth; so that the life of a man doth not naturally extend above an hundred; and this was not only a popular conceit, but consentaneous[9]

9. 'agreable' (Elyot).

unto their Physicall principles, as Heurnius hath accounted it.

A woman that hath but one childe, they expresse by a Lionesse; for that conceiveth but once. Fecundity they set forth by a Goat, because but seven daies old, it beginneth to use coition. The abortion of a woman they describe by an Horse kicking a Wolfe; because a Mare will cast her fole if she tread in the track of that animall. Deformity they signifie by a Bear; and an unstable man by an Hyæna, because that animall yearly exchangeth its sex. A woman delivered of a female childe, they imply by a Bull looking over his left shoulder; because if in coition a Bull part from a Cow on that side, the Calf will prove a female.

All which with many more, how farre they consent with truth, we shall not disparage our Reader to dispute; and though some way allowable unto wiser conceits, who could distinctly receive their significations; yet carrying the majesty of Hieroglyphicks, and so transmitted by Authors, they crept into a belief with many, and favourable doubt with most. And thus, I fear, it hath fared with the Hieroglyphicall symboles of Scripture; which excellently intended in the species of things sacrificed, in the prohibited meats, in the dreams of Pharaoh, Joseph, and many other passages; are oft times wrackt beyond their symbolizations, and inlarg'd into constructions disparaging their true intentions.

CHAP. XXI. *Compendiously of many questionable Customes, Opinions, Pictures, Practises, and Popular Observations*

16. We shall not, I hope, disparage the Resurrection of our Redeemer, if we say the Sun doth not dance on Easter day. And though we would willingly assent unto any sympatheticall exultation, yet cannot conceive therein any more than a Tropicall[10] expression. Whether any such notion there were in that day wherein Christ arised, Scripture hath not revealed, which hath been punctually in other records concerning solary miracles: and the Areopagite that was amazed at the Eclipse, took no notice of this. And if metaphoricall expressions go

10. Figurative (as above, p. 60, note 6).

farre, we may be bold to affirm, not only that one Sunne danced, but two arose that day: That light appeared at his nativity, and darknesse at his death, and yet a light at both; for even that darknesse was a light unto the Gentiles illuminated by that obscurity. That 'twas the first time the Sunne set above the Horizon; that although there were darknesse above the earth there was light beneath it, nor dare we say that hell was dark if he were in it. . . .

CHAP. XXI. *Of some others*

1. That temperamentall dignotions,[11] and conjecture of prevalent humours, may be collected from spots in our nails, we are not averse to concede. But yet not ready to admit sundry divinations, vulgarly raised upon them. Nor doe we observe it verified in others, what Cardan discovered as a property in himself: to have found therein some signes of most events that ever happened unto him. Or that there is much considerable in that doctrine of Cheiromancy,[12] that spots in the top of the nailes doe signifie things past; in the middle, things present; and at the bottome, events to come. That white spots presage our felicity, blew ones our misfortunes. That those in the nail of the thumb have significations of honour, those in the forefinger of riches, and so respectively in other fingers, (according to Planeticall relations, from whence they receive their names) as Tricassus hath taken up, and Pictiolus well rejecteth.

We shall not proceed to querie, what truth there is in Palmistrie, or divination from those lines in our hands, of high denomination. Although if any thing be therein, it seems not confinable unto man; but other creatures are also considerable: as is the forefoot of the Moll, and especially of the Monkey; wherein we have observed the table line, that of life, and of the liver. . . .

11. i.e. distinguishing characteristics of temperament.
12. '*Chiromancer*, a Palmester, or one who tells fortunes by the lines of ones hand' (Blount).

THE SIXTH BOOK:

OF SUNDRY COMMON OPINIONS
COSMOGRAPHICALL AND HISTORICALL

It is evident not only in the generall frame of Nature, that things most manifest unto sense, have proved obscure unto the understanding: But even in proper and appropriate objects, wherein we affirm the sense cannot erre, the faculties of reason most often fail us. Thus of colours in generall, under whose glosse and vernish all things are seen, no man hath yet beheld the true nature; or positively set down their incontroulable causes. . . . Their generall or first natures being thus obscure, there will be greater difficulties in their particular discoveries; for being farther removed from their simplicities they fall into more complexed considerations; and so require a subtiler act of reason to distinguish and call forth their natures. Thus although a man understood the generall nature of colours, yet were it no easie probleme to resolve, Why Grasse is green? Why Garlick, Molyes, and Porrets[1] have white roots, deep green leaves, and black seeds? Why severall docks, and sorts of Rhubarb with yellow roots, send forth purple flowers? Why also from Lactary or milky plants which have a white and lacteous juice dispersed through every part, there arise flowers blue and yellow? Moreover beside the specificall and first digressions ordained from the Creation, which might be urged to salve[2] the variety in every species; Why shall the Marvaile of Peru produce its flowers of different colours, and that not once, or constantly, but every day and variously? Why Tulips of one colour produce some of another, and running through almost all, should still escape a blue? And lastly, Why some men, yea and they a mighty and considerable part of mankinde, should first acquire and still retain the glosse and tincture of blacknesse? which whoever strictly enquires, shall finde no lesse of darknesse in the cause, then blacknesse in the effect it self; there arising unto examination no such satisfactory and unquarrellable reasons, as may confirm the causes generally received; which are but two in number: The heat and scorch of the Sunne; or the curse of God on Cham and his posterity. . . .

If the fervor of the Sunne, or intemperate heat of clime did solely occasion this complexion, surely a migration or change thereof might cause a sensible, if not a totall mutation; which notwithstanding experience will not admit. For Negroes transplanted although into cold and flegmatick habitations, continue their hue both in themselves, and also their generations; except they mix with different complexions; whereby notwithstanding there only succeeds a remission of their

1. Scallions.
2. See above, p. 89, note 145.

tinctures; there remaining unto many descents a full shadow of their originals; and if they preserve their copulations entire they still maintain their complexions; as is very remarkable in the dominions of the Grand Signior,[3] and most observable in the Moores in Brasilia, which transplanted about an hundred years past, continue the tinctures of their fathers unto this day. And so likewise fair or white people translated into hotter Countries receive not impressions amounting to this complexion, as hath been observed in many Europeans who have lived in the land of Negroes: and as Edvardus Lopes testifieth of the Spanish plantations, that they retained their native complexions unto his daies. . . .

Thus having evinced, at least made dubious, the Sunne is not the Authour of this blacknesse; how, and when this tincture first began is yet a riddle, and positively to determine it surpasseth my presumption. . . . However therefore this complexion was first acquired, it is evidently maintained by generation, and by the tincture of the skin as a spermaticall part traduced from father unto son: so that they which are strangers contract it not, and the Natives which transmigrate omit it not without commixture, and that after divers generations. And this affection (if the story were true) might wonderfully be confirmed, by what Maginus and others relate of the Emperour of Æthiopia, or Prester John, who derived from Solomon is not yet descended into the hue of his Countrey, but remains a Mulatto, that is, of a Mongrill complexion unto this day. Now although we conceive this blacknesse to be seminall, yet are we not of Herodotus conceit, that their seed is black. An opinion long ago rejected by Aristotle, and since by sence and enquiry. His assertion against the Historian was probable, that all seed was white; that is without great controversie in viviparous Animals, and such as have Testicles, or preparing vessels wherein it receives a manifest dealbation.[4] And not only in them, but (for ought I know) in Fishes, not abating the seed of Plants; whereof though the skin and covering be black, yet is the seed and fructifying part not so: as may be observed in the seeds of Onyons, Pyonie, and Basill. Most controvertible it seems in the spawn of Frogs, and Lobsters, whereof notwithstanding at the very first the spawn is white, contracting by degrees a blacknesse, answerable in the one unto the colour of the shell, in the other unto the Porwigle or Tadpole; that is, that Animall which first proceedeth from it. And thus may it also be in the generation and sperm of Negroes; that being first and in its naturals white, but upon separation of parts, accidents before invisible become apparent; there arising a shadow or dark efflorescence in the outside; whereby not only their legitimate and timely births, but their abortions are also duskie, before they have felt the scorch and fervor of the Sunne.

CHAP. XI. *Of the same*

A second opinion there is, that this complexion was first a curse of God derived unto them from Cham, upon whom it was inflicted for discovering the nakednesse of Noah.[5] Which notwithstanding is sooner affirmed then proved, and carrieth with it sundry improbabilities. For first, if we derive the curse on Cham, or in generall upon his posterity, we shall Benegroe a greater part of the earth then ever was so conceived; and not only paint the Æthiopians, and reputed sonnes of Cush, but the people also of Ægypt, Arabia, Assyria, and Chaldea; for by his race were these Countries also peopled. And if concordantly unto Berosus, the fragment of Cato *de Originibus*, some things of Halicarnasseus, Macrobius, and out of them of Leandro and Annius, we shall conceive of the travels of Camese or Cham; we may introduce a generation of Negroes as high as Italy; which part was never culpable of deformity, but hath produced the magnified examples of beauty. . . .

Lastly, Whereas men affirm this colour was a Curse, I cannot make out the propriety of that name, it neither seeming so to them, nor reasonably unto us; for they take so much content therein, that they esteem deformity by other colours, describing the Devil, and terrible objects, White. And if we seriously con-

5. Genesis 9.20–25.

sult the definitions of beauty, and exactly perpend what wise men determine thereof, we shall not apprehend a curse, or any deformity therein. For first, some place the essence thereof in the proportion of parts; conceiving it to consist in a comely commensurability of the whole unto the parts, and the parts between themselves; which is the determination of the best and learned Writers. Now hereby the Moors are not excluded from beauty; there being in this description no consideration of colours, but an apt connexion and frame of parts and the whole. Others there be, and those most in number, which place it not only in proportion of parts, but also in grace of colour. But to make Colour essentiall unto Beauty, there will arise no slender difficulty; For Aristotle in two definitions of pulchritude, and Galen in one, have made no mention of colour. Neither will it agree unto the Beauty of Animals; wherein notwithstanding there is an approved pulchritude. Thus horses are handsome under any colour, and the symmetry of parts obscures the consideration of complexions. Thus in concolour animals and such as are confined unto one colour, we measure not their Beauty thereby; for if a Crow or Black-bird grow white, we generally account it more pretty; And even in monstrosity descend not to opinion of deformity. By this way likewise the Moores escape the curse of deformity; there concurring no stationary colour, and sometimes not any unto Beauty.

The Platonick contemplators reject both these descriptions founded upon parts and colours, or either; as M. Leo the Jew hath excellently discoursed in his Genealogy of Love: defining Beauty a formall grace, which delights and moves them to love which comprehend it. This grace say they, discoverable outwardly, is the resplendor and Raye of some interiour and invisible Beauty, and proceedeth from the forms of compositions amiable. Whose faculties if they can aptly contrive their matter, they beget in the subject an agreeable and pleasing beauty; if over-ruled thereby, they evidence not their perfections, but runne into deformity. For seeing that out of the same materials, Thersites and Paris, Beauty and monstrosity[6] may be contrived; the forms and operative faculties introduce and determine their

6. The one corresponding to Paris, the other to Thersites.

perfections. Which in naturall bodies receive exactnesse in every kinde, according to the first Idea of the Creator,[7] and in contrived bodies the phancy of the Artificer. And by this consideration of Beauty, the Moores also are not excluded, but hold a common share therein with all mankinde.

Lastly, in whatsoever its Theory consisteth, or if in the generall, we allow the common conceit of symmetry and of colour, yet to descend unto singularities, or determine in what symmetry or colour it consisted, were a slippery designation. For Beauty is determined by opinion, and seems to have no essence that holds one notion with all; that seeming beauteous unto one, which hath no favour with another; and that unto every one, according as custome hath made it naturall, or sympathy and conformity of mindes shall make it seem agreeable. Thus flat noses seem comely unto the Moore, an Aquiline or hawked one unto the Persian, a large and prominent nose unto the Romane; but none of all these are acceptable in our opinion. Thus some think it most ornamentall to wear their Bracelets on their Wrests, others say it is better to have them about their Ancles; some think it most comely to wear their Rings and Jewels in the Ear, others will have them about their Privities; a third will not think they are compleat except they hang them in their lips, cheeks or noses. Thus Homer to set off Minerva calleth her $\gamma\lambda\alpha\nu\kappa\tilde{\omega}\pi\iota\varsigma$, that is, gray or light-blue eyed: now this unto us seems farre lesse amiable then the black. Thus we that are of contrary complexions accuse the blacknesse of the Mores as ugly: But the Spouse in the Canticles excuseth this conceit, in that description of hers, I am black, but comely.[8] And howsoever Cerberus, and the furies of hell be described by the Poets under this complexion, yet in the beauty of our Saviour blacknesse is commended, when it is said, his locks are bushie and black as a Raven.[9] So that to inferre this as a curse, or to reason it as a deformity, is no way reasonable; the two foundations of beauty, Symmetry and complexion, receiving such various apprehensions; that no deviation will be expounded so

7. See above, p. 31.
8. Song of Solomon ('Canticle of Canticles') 1.5.
9. ibid. 5.11.

high as a curse or undeniable deformity, without a manifest and confessed degree of monstrosity.

Lastly, It is a very injurious method unto Philosophy, and a perpetuall promotion of ignorance, in points of obscurity, nor open unto easie considerations, to fall upon a present refuge unto Miracles; or recurre unto immediate contrivance from the insearchable hands of God. Thus in the conceit of the evil odor of the Jews,[10] Christians without a farther research into the verity of the thing, or enquiry into the cause, draw up a judgement upon them from the passion of their Saviour. Thus in the wondrous effects of the clime of Ireland, and the freedom from all venemous creatures, the credulity of common conceit imputes this immunity unto the benediction of St Patrick, as Beda and Gyraldus have left recorded. Thus the Asse having a peculiar mark of a crosse made by a black list down his back, and another athwart, or at right angles down his shoulders; common opinion ascribes this figure unto a peculiar signation; since that beast had the honour to bear our Saviour on his back. Certainly this is a course more desperate then Antipathies, Sympathies or occult qualities; wherein by a finall and satisfactive discernment of faith, we lay the last and particular effects upon the first and generall cause of all things; whereas in the other, we doe but palliate our determinations; untill our advanced endeavours doe totally reject, or partially salve their evasions.

CHAP. XII. *A digression concerning Blacknesse*

CHAP. XIII. *Of Gypsies*

CHAP. XIV. *Of some others*

10. Discussed earlier, pp. 226 ff.

THE SEVENTH BOOK:

CONCERNING MANY HISTORICALL TENENTS GENERALLY RECEIVED, AND SOME DEDUCED FROM THE HISTORY OF HOLY SCRIPTURE

CHAP. I. *Of the Forbidden Fruit*

CHAP. II. *That a Man hath one Rib lesse then a Woman*

That a Man hath one Rib lesse then a Woman, is a common conceit derived from the history of Genesis, wherein it stands delivered, that Eve was framed out of a Rib of Adam; whence 'tis concluded the sex of man still wants that rib our Father lost in Eve. And this is not only passant with the many, but was urged against Columbus in an Anatomy of his at Pisa; where having prepared the Sceleton of a Woman that chanced to have thirteen ribs on one side, there arose a party that cried him down, and even unto oathes affirmed, this was the rib wherein a woman exceeded. Were this true, it would autoptically[1] silence that dispute out of which side Eve was framed; it would determine the opinion of Oleaster, that she was made out of the ribs of both sides; or such as from the expression of the Text maintain there was a plurality required, and might indeed decry the parabolicall[2] exposition of Origen, Cajetan, and such as fearing to concede a monstrosity, or mutilate the integrity of Adam; preventively conceive the creation of thirteen ribs.

But this will not consist with reason or inspection. For if we survey the Sceleton of both sexes, and therein the compage[3] of bones, we shall readily discover that men and women have four and twenty ribs; that is, twelve on each side; seven greater annexed unto the Sternon, and five lesser which come short thereof; wherein if it sometimes happen that either sex exceed, the conformation is irregular, deflecting from the common rate

1. By actual inspection.
2. 'Of or belonging to a Parable' (Blount).
3. 'close joyning' (Blount, citing Browne).

or number, and no more inferrible upon mankinde, then the monstrosity of the son of Rapha, or the vitious excesse in the number of fingers and toes. And although some difference there be in figure, and the female *os inominatum*[4] be somewhat more protuberant, to make a fairer cavity for the Infant; the coccyx sometime more reflected to give the easier delivery, and the ribs themselves seem a little flatter, yet are they equall in number. And therefore while Aristotle doubteth the relations made of Nations, which had but seven ribs on a side, and yet delivereth that men have generally no more then eight; as he rejecteth their history, so can we not accept of his Anatomy. . . .

CHAP. III. *Of Methuselah*

What hath been every where opinion'd, by all men, and in all times, is more then Paradoxicall to dispute; and so that Methuselah was the longest liver of all the posterity of Adam[5] we quietly beleeve: but that he must needs be so, is perhaps below Paralogy[6] to deny. For hereof there is no determination from the Text; wherein it is only particular'd he was the longest liver of all the Patriarchs whose age is there expressed; but that he outlived all others we cannot well conclude. For of those nine whose death is mentioned before the floud, the Text expresseth that Enoch was the shortest liver; who saw but three hundred sixty five years. But to affirm from hence, none of the rest, whose age is not expressed, did die before that time; is surely an illation whereto we cannot assent.

Again, Many persons there were in those daies of longevity, of whose age notwithstanding there is no account in Scripture; as of the race of Cain, the wives of the nine Patriarches, with all the sons and daughters that every one begat; whereof perhaps some persons might outlive Methuselah; the Text intending only the masculine line of Seth, conduceable unto the Geneal-

---

4. See above, p. 223, note 2.
5. He died at the age of 969 (Genesis 5.27).
6. i.e. paralogism: faulty reasoning.

ogy of our Saviour, and the antediluvian Chronology. And therefore we must not contract the lives of those which are left in silence by Moses. . . .

Now that conception that no man did ever attain unto a thousand years, because none should ever be one day old in the sight of the Lord, unto whom according to that of David, A thousand years are but one day;[7] doth not advantage Methuselah. And being deduced from a popular expression, which will not stand a Metaphysicall and strict examination, is not of force to divert a serious enquirer. For unto God a thousand years are no more then one moment,[8] and in his sight Methuselah lived no nearer one day then Abel, for all parts of time are alike unto him, unto whom none are referrible; and all things present, unto whom nothing is past or to come. And therefore, although we be measured by the Zone of time, and the flowing and continued instants thereof, do weave at last a line and circle about the eldest; yet can we not thus commensurate the sphere of Trismegistus;[9] or sum up the unsuccessive and stable duration of God.

CHAP. IV. *That there was no Rainbow before the Floud*

CHAP. V. *Of Sem, Ham, and Japhet*

CHAP. VI. *That the Tower of Babel was erected against a second Deluge*

CHAP. VII. *Of the Mandrakes of Leah*

CHAP. VIII. *Of the three Kings of Collein*

CHAP. IX. *Of the food of John the Baptist, Locusts and wilde honey*

CHAP. X. *That John the Evangelist should not die*

CHAP. XI. *More compendiiously of some others*

7. Psalm 90.4.
8. As above, p. 73, note 63.
9. As above, p. 71, note 49.

CHAP. XII. *Of the cessation of Oracles*

That Oracles ceased or grew mute at the coming of Christ, is best understood in a qualified sense and not without all latitude; as though precisely there were none after, nor any decay before. For (what we must confesse unto relations of Antiquity) some pre-decay is observable from that of Cicero urged by Baronius; *Cur isto modo jam oracula Delphis non eduntur, non modo nostra ætate, sed jam diu, ut nihil possit esse contemptius.*[10] That during his life they were not altogether dumb, is deduceable from Suetonius in the life of Tiberius, who attempting to subvert the Oracles adjoining unto Rome, was deterred by the Lots or Chances which were delivered at Preneste. After his death we meet with many; Suetonius reports, that the Oracle of Antium forewarned Caligula to beware of Cassius, who was one that conspired his death. Plutarch[11] enquiring why the Oracles of Greece ceased, excepteth that of Lebadia; and in the same place Demetrius affirmeth the Oracles of Mopsus and Amphilochus were much frequented in his daies. In brief, histories are frequent in examples, and there want not some even to the reign of Julian.

What therefore may consist with history; by cessation of Oracles with Montacutius we may understand their intercision,[12] not abscission or consummate desolation; their rare delivery, not totall dereliction: and yet in regard of divers Oracles, we may speak strictly, and say there was a proper Cessation. Thus may we reconcile the accounts of times, and allow those few and broken Divinations, whereof we reade in story and undeniable Authors. For that they received this blow from Christ, and no other causes alledged by the Heathens; from oraculous confession they cannot deny; whereof upon record there are some very remarkable. The first that Oracle of Delphos delivered unto Augustus.

---

10. 'Nothing can be more contemptible than that the oracles are not given out at Delphi in this way, not only in our time but for a long time since'. On the legend and its several manifestations, see §292.
11. As above, p. 97, note 176.
12. 'cutting off in the midst' (Blount).

Me puer Hebræus Divos Deus ipse gubernans
Cedere sede jubet, tristemque redire sub orcum;
Aris ergo dehinc tacitus discedito nostris.

An Hebrew childe, a God all gods excelling,
To hell again commands me from this dwelling.
Our Altars leave in silence, and no more
A resolution e're from hence implore.

A second recorded by Plutarch, of a voice that was heard to cry
unto Mariners at the Sea, *Great Pan is dead*; which is a relation
very remarkable, and may be read in his defect of Oracles. A
third reported by Eusebius in the life of his magnified Con-
stantine; that about that time Apollo mourned, declaring his
Oracles were false, and that the righteous upon earth did
hinder him from speaking truth. And a fourth related by
Theodoret, and delivered by Apollo Daphnes unto Julian,
upon his Persian Expedition, that he should remove the bodies
about him, before he could return an answer, and not long after
his Temple was burnt with Lightning.

All which were evident and convincing acknowledgements
of that power which shut his[13] lips; and restrained that delusion
which had reigned so many Centuries. But as his malice is
vigilant, and the sinnes of men doe still continue a toleration of
his mischiefs, he resteth not, nor will he ever cease to circum-
vent the sonnes of the first deceived; and therefore expelled his
Oracles and solemn Temples of delusion, he runnes into cor-
ners, exercising minor trumperies, and acting his deceits in
Witches, Magicians, Diviners, and such inferiour seducers.
And yet (what is deplorable) while we apply our selves thereto,
and affirming that God hath left to speak by his Prophets,
expect in doubtfull matters a resolution from such spirits;
while we say the devil is mute, yet confesse that these can
speak; while we deny the substance, yet practise the effect; and
in the denied solemnity maintain the equivalent efficacy; in
vain we cry that Oracles are down; Apollo's altar still doth
smoke; nor is the fire of Delphos out unto this day.

Impertinent it is unto our intention to speak in generall of

13. i.e. Satan's.

Oracles, and many have well performed it. The plainest of others was that recorded by Herodotus and delivered unto Crœsus; who as a triall of his omniscience sent unto distant Oracles; and so contrived with the messengers, that though in severall places, yet at the same time they should demand what Crœsus was then a doing. Among all others the Oracle of Delphos only hit it; returning answer, he was boyling a Lamb with a Tortoyse, in a brazen vessell with a cover of the same metall. The stile is haughty in Greek, though somewhat lower in Latine,

> *Æquoris est spatium & numerus mihi notus arenæ,*
> *Mutum percipio, fantis nihil audio vocem.*
> *Venit ad hos sensus nidor testudinis acris,*
> *Quæ semel agninâ coquitur cum carne labete,*
> *Aere infra strato, & stratum cui desuper æs est.*

> I know the space of Sea, the number of the sand,
> I hear the silent, mute I understand.
> A tender Lamb joyned with Tortoise flesh,
> Thy Master King of Lydia now doth dresse.
> The sent thereof doth in my nostrils hover
> From brazen pot closed with brazen cover.

Hereby indeed he acquired much wealth and more honour, and was reputed by Crœsus as a Diety: and yet not long after, by a vulgar fallacy he deceived his favourite and greatest friend of Oracles into an irreparable overthrow by Cyrus. And surely the same successe are likely all to have that rely or depend upon him;[14] 'twas the first play he practised on mortality, and as time hath rendred him more perfect in the Art, so hath the inveteratenesse of his malice more ready in the execution. 'Tis therefore the sovereign degree of folly, and a crime not only against God, but also our own reasons, to expect a favour from the devil, whose mercies are more cruell then those of Polyphemus; for he devours his favourites first, and the nearer a man approacheth, the sooner he is scorched by Moloch. In brief, his favours are deceitfull and double-headed, he doth apparent good, for reall and convincing evil after it; and exalteth us up to the top of the Temple, but to humble us down from it.

14. i.e. Satan.

CHAP. XIII. *Of the death of Aristotle*

CHAP. XIV. *Of the wish of Philoxenus*

CHAP. XV. *Of the Lake Asphaltites*

CHAP. XVI. *Of divers other relations*

1. The relation of Averroes and now common in every mouth, of the woman that conceived in a bath, by attracting the sperme or seminall effluxion of a man admitted to bath in some vicinity unto her, I have scarce faith to beleeve; and had I been of the Jury, should have hardly thought I had found the father in the person that stood by her. 'Tis a new and unseconded way in History to fornicate at a distance; and much offendeth the rules of Physick, which say, there is no generation without a joynt emission, nor only a virtuall but corporall and carnall contaction. . . .

2. The relation of Lucillius, and now become common, concerning Crassus the grandfather of Marcus the wealthy Roman, that he never laughed but once in all his life, and that was at an Asse eating Thistles, is something strange. For, if an indifferent and unridiculous object could draw his habituall austerenesse unto a smile; it will be hard to beleeve he could with perpetuity resist the proper motives thereof. For the act of laughter which is a sweet contraction of the muscles of the face, and a pleasant agitation of the vocall organs, is not meerly voluntary; or totally within the jurisdiction of our selves: but as it may be constrained by corporall contraction in any, and hath been enforced in some even in their death; so the new unusuall or unexpected jucundities, which present themselves to any man in his life; at some time or other will have activity enough to excitate the earthiest soul, and raise a smile from most composed tempers. . . .

3. The same conceit there passeth concerning our blessed Saviour, and is sometimes urged as an high example of gravity. And this is opinioned, because in holy Scripture it is recorded he sometimes wept, but never that he laughed. Which howsoever granted, it will be hard to conceive how he passed his

younger years and childhood without a smile; if as Divinity affirmeth, for the assurance of his humanity unto men, and the concealment of his Divinity from the devil, he passed this age like other children, and so proceeded untill he evidenced the same. And surely no danger there is to affirm the act or performance of that, whereof we acknowledge the power and essentiall property; and whereby indeed he most neerly convinced the doubt of his humanity. Nor need we be afraid to ascribe that unto the incarnate Sonne, which sometimes is attributed unto the uncarnate Father; of whom it is said, He that dwelleth in the heavens shall laugh the wicked to scorn.[15] For, a laugh there is of contempt or indignation, as well as of mirth and Jocosity; And that our Saviour was not exempted from the ground hereof, that is, the passion of anger, regulated and rightly ordered by reason, the Schools doe not deny: and besides the experience of the money-changers, and Dove-sellers in the Temple, is testified by St John when he saith, the speech of David was fulfilled in our Saviour. . . .[16]

CHAP. XVII. *Of some others*

5. The story of the wandring Jew is very strange, and will hardly obtain belief; yet is there a formall account thereof set down by Matthew Paris, from the report of an Armenian Bishop; who came into this kingdome about four hundred years ago, and had often entertained this wanderer at his Table. That he was then alive, was first called Cartaphilus, was keeper of the Judgement Hall, whence thrusting out our Saviour with expostulation for his stay, was condemned to stay untill his return; was after baptized by Ananias, and by the name of Joseph; was thirty years old in the daies of our Saviour, remembred the Saints that arised with him, the making of the Apostles Creed, and their severall perigrinations. Surely were this true, he might be an happy arbitrator in many Christian controversies; but must impardonably condemn the obstinacy

15. Psalm 2.4.
16. John 2.17, quoting Psalm 69.9 ('the zeal of thine house hath eaten me up').

of the Jews, who can contemn the Rhetorick of such miracles, and blindely behold so living and lasting conversions.

6. Clearer confirmations must be drawn for the history of Pope Joane, who succeeded Leo the fourth, and preceded Benedict the third, then any we yet discover. And since it is delivered with *aiunt* and *ferunt*[17] by many; since the learned Leo Allatius hath discovered, that ancient copies of Martinus Polonus, who is chiefly urged for it, had not this story in it; since not only the stream of Latine Historians have omitted it, but Photius the Patriarch, Metrophanes Smyrnæus, and the exasperated Greeks have made no mention of it, but conceded Benedict the third Successor unto Leo the fourth; he wants not grounds that doubts it. . . .

8. Who can but pity the vertuous Epicurus,[18] who is commonly conceived to have placed his chief felicity in pleasure and sensuall delights, and hath therefore left an infamous name behinde him? How true, let them determine who reade that he lived seventy years, and wrote more books then any Philosopher but Chrysippus, and no lesse then three hundred, without borrowing from any Author. That he was contented with bread and water, and when he would dine with Jove, and pretend unto epulation,[19] he desired no other addition then a piece of Cytheridian cheese.[20] That shall consider the words of Seneca, *Non dico, quod plerique nostrorum, sectam Epicuri flagitiorum magistrum esse: sed illud dico, male audite infamis est, & immerito.*[21] Or shall reade his life, his Epistles, his Testament in Laertius; who plainly names them calumnies, which are commonly said against them.

The ground hereof seems a misapprehension of his opinion, who placed his felicity not in the pleasures of the body, but the minde, and tranquillity thereof, obtained by wisdome and

17. As above, p. 188, note 57.
18. Cf. below, p. 304. The present section is said to be 'the first pointed defence in English of Epicurus's position' (§54).
19. Feasting.
20. See below, p. 436, note 1.
21. 'I do not say, as do most of our sect, that the school of Epicurus is an academy of vice, but I say it has a bad name, is of ill repute, and yet undeservedly' (*On the Happy Life*, XIII, 2).

vertue, as is most clearly determined in his Epistle unto Menæceus. Now how this opinion was first traduced by the Stoicks, how it afterwards became a common belief, and so taken up by Authors of all ages, by Cicero, Plutarch, Clemens, Ambrose and others; the learned pen of Gassendus[22] hath discovered.

CHAP. XVIII. *More briefly of some others*

CHAP. XIX. *Of some Relations whose truth we fear*[23]

22. In *The Life and death of Epicurus*, 1647 (Browne marg.).

23. *Pseudodoxia Epidemica* terminates with a quotation, in Latin, from Lactantius's *Institutes*, I, 23 (first quoted in the 2nd edition of 1650): 'the first step towards wisdom is to understand what is false'.

Hydriotaphia

[*Hydriotaphia, Urne-Buriall, or, A Discourse of the Sepulchrall Urnes lately found in Norfolk* was first published jointly with *The Garden of Cyrus* in 1658. See also the discussion above, pp. 38 ff.; and for further bibliographical details: below, p. 554.]

THOMAS Le GROS

*When the Funerall pyre was out, and the last valediction over, men took a
lasting adieu of their interred Friends, little expecting the curiosity of
future ages should comment upon their ashes, and having no old experience
of the duration of their Reliques, held no opinion of such after consider-
ations.*

*But who knows the fate of his bones, or how often he is to be buried?
who hath the Oracle of his ashes, or whether they are to be scattered? The
Reliques of many lie like the ruines of* Pompeys,[2] *in all parts of the
earth; And when they arrive at your hands, these may seem to have
wandered far, who in a direct*[3] *and* Meridian Travell, *have but few miles
of known Earth between your self and the Pole.*

That the bones of Theseus *should be seen again in Athens,*[4] *was not
beyond conjecture,*[5] *and hopeful expectation; but that these*[6] *should arise
so opportunely to serve your self, was an hit of fate and honour beyond
prediction.*

*We cannot but with these Urnes might have the effect of Theatrical
vessels, and great* Hippodrome *Urnes in* Rome;[7] *to resound the
acclamations and honour due unto you. But these are sad and sepulchral
Pitchers, which have no joyful voices; silently expressing old mortality,
the ruines of forgotten times, and can only speak with life, how long in*

1. A close friend who lived in Crostwick Hall north of Norwich; son of
Sir Charles Le Gros, himself a patient of Browne's.

2. 'The Sons of Pompey are covered by the soils of Asia and Europe;
Pompey himself by that of Africa' (Browne marg., quoting the Latin of
Martial, V, lxxiv, 1–2).

3. 'Little directly, but Sea between your house and *Greenland*' (Browne
marg.). Crostwick Hall (above, note 1) is less than twenty miles from the
coast.

4. 'Brought back by *Cimon*' (Browne marg.). So Plutarch, *Cimon*, VIII,6.

5. The word is much favoured in this treatise, even as *The Garden of
Cyrus* favours 'discern' and 'discover' (§198).

6. i.e. in the discovered urns.

7. 'The great Urnes in the *Hippodrome* at *Rome* conceived to resound the
voices of people at their shows' (Browne marg.).

this corruptible frame, some parts may be uncorrupted; yet able to out-
last bones long unborn, and noblest pyle[8] among us.

We present not these as any strange sight or spectacle unknown to your
eyes, who have beheld the best of Urnes, and noblest variety of Ashes;
Who are your self no slender master of Antiquities, and can daily com-
mand the view of so many Imperiall faces;[9] Which raiseth your thoughts
unto old things, and consideration of times before you, when even living
men were Antiquities; when the living might exceed the dead, and to
depart this world, could not be properly said, to go unto the greater
number.[10] And so run up your thoughts upon the ancient of dayes, the
Antiquities truest object, unto whom the eldest parcels are young, and
earth it self an Infant; and without Ægyptian account[11] makes but small
noise in thousands.

We were hinted by the occasion, not catched the opportunity to write of
old things, or intrude upon the Antiquary. We are coldly drawn unto
discourses of Antiquities, who have scarce time before us to comprehend
new things, or make out learned Novelties. But seeing they arose as they
lay, almost in silence among us, at least in short account suddenly passed
over; we were very unwilling they should die again, and be buried twice
among us.

Beside, to preserve the living, and make the dead to live, to keep men out
of their Urnes, and discourse of humane fragments in them, is not im-
pertinent unto our profession; whose study is life and death, who daily
behold examples of mortality, and of all men least need artificial
memento's, *or coffins by our bed side, to minde us of our graves.*

'Tis time to observe Occurrences, and let nothing remarkable escape
us; The Supinity of elder dayes hath left so much in silence, or time hath
so martyred the Records, that the most industrious heads do finde no
easie work to erect a new Britannia.[12]

8. Raynham Hall in Norfolk, built by Inigo Jones in 1630, 'worthily
possessed by that true Gentleman Sir *Horatio Townshend*, my honored
Friend' (Browne marg.).

9. i.e. on Roman coins.

10. 'Joined the great majority' (Browne marg., quoting the Latin of
Petronius, *Satyricon*, XLII, 5).

11. 'Which makes the world so many years old' (Browne marg.) – i.e.
several times the estimates current during the Renaissance (see below,
p. 439, note 31).

12. 'Wherein M. *Dugdale* hath excellently well endeavoured, and worthy

'Tis opportune to look back upon old times, and contemplate our Forefathers. Great examples grow thin, and to be fetched from the passed world. Simplicity flies away, and iniquity comes at long strides upon us. We have enough to do to make up our selves from present and passed times, and the whole stage of things scarce serveth for our instruction. A compleat peece of vertue must be made up from the Centos of all ages, as all the beauties of Greece could make but one handsome Venus.[13]

When the bones of King Arthur were digged up,[14] the old Race might think, they beheld therein some Originals of themselves; Unto these of our Urnes none here can pretend relation, and can only behold the Reliques of those persons, who in their life giving the Laws unto their predecessors, after long obscurity, now lye at their mercies. But remembring the early civility they brought upon these Countreys, and forgetting long passed mischiefs; We mercifully preserve their bones, and pisse not upon their ashes.[15]

In the offer of these Antiquities we drive not at ancient Families, so long out-lasted by them; We are farre from erecting your worth upon the pillars of your Fore-fathers, whose merits you illustrate. We honour your old Virtues, conformable unto times before you, which are the Noblest Armoury. And having long experience of your friendly conversation, void of empty Formality, full of freedome, constant and Generous Honesty, I look upon you as a Gemme of the Old Rock,[16] and must professe my self even to Urne and Ashes,

Norwich
May 10 [1658]

Your ever faithfull Friend,
and Servant,
THOMAS BROWNE

---

to be countenanced by ingenuous and noble persons' (Browne marg.). The reference is to Sir William Dugdale's antiquarian labours, worthy of Camden's classic *Britannia* (1586 ff.).

13. Actually Helen (according to Cicero, *On Invention*, II, 1). 'Centos' means patched garments.

14. In the time of Henry II, according to Camden's *Britannia* (Browne marg.).

15. Horace, *The Art of Poetry*, 471.

16. 'The most outstanding diamond comes from ancient rock' (Browne marg., in Latin).

HYDRIOTAPHIA

URNE-BURIALL

OR,

A BRIEF DISCOURSE OF THE SEPULCHRALL
URNES LATELY FOUND IN NORFOLK

CHAPTER I

In the deep discovery of the Subterranean world, a shallow part
would satisfie some enquirers; who, if two or three yards were
open about the surface, would not care to rake the bowels of
Potosi,[1] and regions towards the Centre. Nature hath furnished
one part of the Earth, and man another. The treasures of time
lie high, in Urnes, Coynes, and Monuments, scarce below the
roots of some vegetables. Time hath endlesse rarities, and
shows of all varieties; which reveals old things in heaven,
makes new discoveries in earth, and even earth it self a dis-
covery. That great Antiquity *America* lay buried for a thousand
years; and a large part of the earth is still in the Urne unto us.

Though if *Adam* were made out of an extract of the Earth,[2]
all parts might challenge a restitution, yet few have returned
their bones farre lower then they might receive them;[3] not
affecting the graves of Giants, under hilly and heavy coverings,
but content with lesse then their owne depth, have wished their
bones might lie soft, and the earth be light upon them; Even
such as hope to rise again, would not be content with centrall
interrment, or so desperately to place their reliques as to lie
beyond discovery, and in no way to be seen again; which happy
contrivance hath made communication with our forefathers,

1. 'The rich [in silver] Mountain of *Peru*' (Browne marg.). Cf. above,
p. 158, note 129.
2. According to tradition, Adam was formed of dust from the four
quarters of the earth. Hence the four letters of his name – in Greek at any
rate: 'Α (νατολὴ), Δ (ύσις), ''Α (ρκτος), Μ (εσημβρία).
3. i.e. from the earth's surface which nourished them.

and left unto our view some parts, which they never beheld themselves.

Though earth hath engrossed the name yet water hath proved the smartest grave; which in forty dayes[4] swallowed almost mankinde, and the living creation; Fishes not wholly escaping, except the Salt Ocean were handsomely contempered[5] by a mixture of the fresh Element.

Many have taken voluminous pains to determine the state of the soul upon disunion; but men have been most phantasticall in the singular contrivances of their corporall dissolution: whilest the sobrest Nations have rested in two wayes, of simple inhumation and burning.

That carnall interment or burying, was of the elder date, the old examples of *Abraham*[6] and the Patriarchs are sufficient to illustrate; And were without competition, if it could be made out, that *Adam* was buried near *Damascus*, or Mount *Calvary*, according to some Tradition. God himself, that buried but one, was pleased to make choice of this way, collectible from Scripture-expression, and the hot contest between Satan and the Arch-Angel, about discovering the body of *Moses*.[7] But the practice of Burning was also of great Antiquity, and of no slender extent. For (not to derive the same from *Hercules*)[8] noble descriptions there are hereof in the Grecian Funerals of *Homer*, In the formall Obsequies of *Patroclus*, and *Achilles*;[9] and somewhat elder in the *Theban* warre, and solemn combustion of *Meneceus*, and *Archemorus*,[10] contemporary unto *Jair* the Eighth Judge of *Israel*.[11] Confirmable also among the *Trojans*, from the Funerall Pyre of *Hector*, burnt before the gates of *Troy*, And the burning of *Penthisilea* the *Amazonean Queen*:[12] and long continuance of that practice, in the inward Countries of *Asia*;

4. During the Flood (Genesis 7.17 ff.).
5. Moderated.
6. Genesis 25.9.
7. Deuteronomy 34.6 in the light of Jude 9.
8. Who is said to have cremated the warrior Argeus.
9. *Iliad*, XXIII, 161 ff.; *Odyssey*, XXIV, 65 ff.
10. Statius, *Thebaid*, XII, 60 ff., and VI, 1 ff.
11. Judges 10.3–5.
12. *Iliad*, XXIV, 782 ff.

while as low as the Reign of *Julian*, we finde that the King of *Chionia*[13] burnt the body of his Son, and interred the ashes in a silver Urne.

The same practice extended also farre West,[14] and besides *Herulians*, *Getes*, and *Thracians*,[15] was in use with most of the *Celtæ*, *Sarmatians*, *Germans*, *Gauls*, *Danes*, *Swedes*, *Norwegians*; not to omit some use thereof among *Carthaginians* and *Americans*: Of greater Antiquity among the *Romans* then most opinion, or *Pliny*[16] seems to allow. For (beside the old Table Laws of burning[17] or burying within the City, of making the Funerall fire with plained wood, or quenching the fire with wine.) *Manlius* the Consul burnt the body of his Son: *Numa* by speciall clause of his Will, was not burnt but buried; And *Remus* was solemnly buried, according to the description of *Ovid*.[18]

Cornelius Sylla was not the first whose body was burned in *Rome*, but of the *Cornelian* Family, which being indifferently, not frequently used before; from that time spread, and became the prevalent practice. Not totally pursued in the highest runne[19] of Cremation; For when even Crows were funerally burnt, *Poppæa* the Wife of *Nero* found a peculiar grave enterment.[20] Now as all customes were founded upon some bottome of Reason, so there wanted not grounds for this; according to severall apprehensions of the most rationall dissolution. Some being of the opinion of *Thales*, that water was the originall of all things, thought it most equall to submit into the principle of putrefaction, and conclude in a moist relentment. Others conceived it most natural to end in fire, as due unto the master principle in the composition, according to the doctrine of

13. 'Gumbrates King of *Chionia* a Countrey near *Persia*. Ammianus Marcellinus' (Browne marg.).

14. So Arnoldus Montanus on cremation, as supported by the scholars Giraldi and Kirchmann (Browne marg.).

15. i.e. of eastern Europe.

16. In his *Natural History*, X, 60.

17. In the Roman code of the Twelve Tables (Browne marg., quoted in Latin).

18. 'Finally a flame was applied to the pyre' (Browne marg., quoting the Latin of Ovid, *Fasti*, IV, 856).

19. Currency, popularity (R).

20. Tacitus, *Annals*, XVI, 6.

Heraclitus. And therefore heaped up large piles, more actively to waft them toward that Element, whereby they also declined a visible degeneration into worms, and left a lasting parcell of their composition.

Some apprehended a purifying virtue in fire, refining the grosser commixture, and firing out the Æthereall particles so deeply immersed in it. And such as by tradition or rationall conjecture held any hint of the finall pyre of all things; or that this Element at last must be too hard for all the rest; might conceive most naturally of the fiery dissolution. Others pretending no natural grounds, politickly declined the malice of enemies upon their buried bodies. Which consideration led *Sylla* unto this practise; who having thus served the body of *Marius,* could not but fear a retaliation upon his own; entertained after in the Civill wars, and revengeful contentions of *Rome.*

But as many Nations embraced, and many left it indifferent, so others too much affected, or strictly declined this practice. The *Indian Brachmans* seemed too great friends unto fire, who burnt themselves alive, and thought it the noblest way to end their dayes in fire; according to the expression of the Indian, burning himself at *Athens,*[21] in his last words upon the pyre unto the amazed spectators, *Thus I make my selfe Immortall.*

But the *Chaldeans* the great Idolaters of fire, abhorred the burning of their carcasses, as a pollution of that Deity. The *Persian Magi* declined it upon the like scruple, and being only sollicitous about their bones, exposed their flesh to the prey of Birds and Dogges. And the *Persees* now in *India,* which expose their bodies unto Vultures, and endure not so much as *feretra* or Beers of Wood, the proper Fuell of fire, are led on with such niceties. But whether the ancient *Germans* who burned their dead, held any such fear to pollute their Deity of *Herthus,* or the earth, we have no Authentick conjecture.

The Ægyptians were afraid of fire, not as a Deity, but a

21. 'And therefore the Inscription of his Tomb was made accordingly' (Browne marg.). The source here is Nicholas of Damascus as reported by Perucci, one of the three scholars liberally used throughout this chapter (see previous page, note 14).

devouring Element, mercilessly consuming their bodies, and leaving too little of them; and therefore by precious Embalments, depositure in dry earths, or handsome inclosure in glasses, contrived the notablest wayes of integrall conservation. And from such Ægyptian scruples imbibed by *Pythagoras*, it may be conjectured that *Numa* and the Pythagoricall Sect first waved the fiery solution.

The *Scythians* who swore by winde and sword, that is, by life and death, were so farre from burning their bodies, that they declined all interrment, and made their graves in the ayr: And the *Ichthyophagi* or fish-eating Nations about Ægypt, affected the Sea for their grave: Thereby declining visible corruption, and restoring the debt of their bodies. Whereas the old Heroes in *Homer*, dreaded nothing more than water or drowning; probably upon the old opinion of the fiery substance of the soul, only extinguishable by that Element; And therefore the Poet emphatically implieth the totall destruction of this kinde of death, which happened to *Ajax Oileus*.[22]

The old *Balearians*[23] had a peculiar mode, for they used great Urnes and much wood, but no fire in their burials, while they bruised the flesh and bones of the dead, crowded them into Urnes, and laid heapes of wood upon them. And the *Chinois*[24] without cremation or urnall interrment of their bodies, make use of trees and much burning, while they plant a Pine-tree by their grave, and burn great numbers of printed draughts of slaves and horses over it, civilly content with their companies in effigie, which barbarous Nations exact unto reality.

Christians abhorred this way of obsequies, and though they stickt not to give their bodies to be burnt in their lives, detested that mode after death; affecting rather a depositure than absumption,[25] and properly submitting unto the sentence of God, to return not unto ashes but unto dust againe, conformable

22. 'Which Magius reads ἐξαπόλωλε' (Browne marg.). The Greek adapts a word from *Odyssey*, IV, 511, to justify 'totall destruction'.

23. So Diodorus Siculus, V, 18 (Browne marg.).

24. So Ramusius (Browne marg.).

25. i.e. preferring rather to be placed (in the grave) than to be destroyed (by fire).

unto the practice of the Patriarchs, the terrment of our Saviour, of *Peter*, *Paul*, and the ancient Martyrs. And so farre at last declining promiscuous enterrment with Pagans, that some have suffered Ecclesiastical censures,[26] for making no scruple thereof.

The *Musselman* beleevers will never admit this fiery resolution. For they hold a present trial from their black and white Angels in the grave; which they must have made so hollow, that they may rise upon their knees.

The Jewish Nation, though they entertained the old way of inhumation, yet sometimes admitted this practice. For the men of *Jabesh* burnt the body of *Saul*.[27] And by no prohibited practice to avoid contagion or pollution, in time of pestilence, burnt the bodies of their friends.[28] And when they burnt not their dead bodies, yet sometimes used great burnings neare and about them, deducible from the expressions concerning *Jehoram*, *Sedechias*, and the sumptuous pyre of *Asa*:[29] And were so little averse from Pagan burning, that the Jews lamenting the death of *Cæsar* their friend, and revenger on *Pompey*, frequented the place where his body was burnt for many nights together.[30] And as they raised noble Monuments and *Mausolæums* for their own Nation,[31] so they were not scrupulous in erecting some for others, according to the practice of *Daniel*, who left that lasting sepulchrall pyle in *Echbatana*, for the *Medean* and *Persian* Kings.[32]

But even in times of subjection and hottest use,[33] they conformed not unto the *Romane* practice of burning; whereby the Prophecy was secured concerning the body of Christ, that it

26. Bishop Martialis, as reported by Cyprian (Browne marg.).

27. 1 Samuel 31.12.

28. Amos 6.10 (Browne marg.).

29. Jeremiah 34.5, 2 Chronicles 16.14 and 21.19.

30. So Suetonius, *Julius*, LXXXIV, 5 (Browne marg.).

31. 'As that magnificent Monument erected by Simon' (Browne marg.): 1 Maccabees 1.13.

32. ' "A wonderfully made work" [quoted in Greek from Josephus, *Jewish Antiquities*, X, xi, 7], whereof the Jewish Priest had alwayes the custody unto *Josephus* his dayes' (Browne marg.).

33. Most violent treatment (R).

should not see corruption, or a bone should not be broken;[34] which we beleeve was also providentially prevented, from the Souldiers spear and nails that past by the little bones both in his hands and feet: Not of ordinary contrivance, that it should not corrupt on the Crosse, according to the Laws of *Romane* Crucifixion, or an hair of his head perish, though observable in Jewish customes, to cut the hairs of Malefactors.

Nor in their long co-habitation with Ægyptians, crept into a custome of their exact embalming, wherein deeply slashing the muscles, and taking out the brains and entrails, they had broken the subject[35] of so entire a Resurrection, nor fully answered the types of *Enoch*, *Eliah*, or *Jonah*,[36] which yet to present or restore, was of equall facility unto that rising power, able to break the fasciations[37] and bands of death, to get clear out of the Cere-cloth, and an hundred pounds of oyntment, and out of the Sepulchre before the stone was rolled from it.

But though they embraced not this practice of burning, yet entertained they many ceremonies agreeable unto *Greeke* and *Romane* obsequies. And he that observeth their funerall Feasts, their Lamentations at the grave, their musick, and weeping mourners; how they closed the eyes of their friends, how they washed, anointed, and kissed the dead; may easily conclude these were not meere Pagan-Civilities. But whether that mournfull burthen, and treble calling out after *Absalom*,[38] had any reference unto the last conclamation,[39] and triple valediction, used by other Nations, we hold but a wavering conjecture.

Civilians[40] make sepulture but of the Law of Nations, others doe naturally found it and discover it also in animals. They that

34. Psalm 16.10, Acts 2.31, John 19.36.
35. Substance, material (*OED*; *M*).
36. Types or prefigurations of the Resurrection in that the first two were translated to heaven, and the last was delivered from the whale's body.
37. Bandages.
38. 'O Absolom, Absolom, Absolom. 2 Samuel 18.33' (Browne marg.).
39. 'shout or noise of many together' (Blount).
40. 'experts in those thinges, that appertayne to the ministration of a common weale' (Elyot).

are so thick skinned[41] as still to credit the story of the *Phœnix*, may say something for animall burning: More serious conjectures finde some examples of sepulture in Elephants, Cranes, the Sepulchrall Cells of Pismires and practice of Bees; which civill society carrieth out their dead, and hath exequies, if not interrments.

CHAPTER II

The Solemnities, Ceremonies, Rites of their Cremation or enterrment, so solemnly delivered by Authours, we shall not disparage our Reader to repeat. Only the last and lasting part in their Urns, collected bones and Ashes, we cannot wholly omit, or decline that Subject, which occasion lately presented, in some discovered among us.

In a Field of old *Walsingham*, not many moneths past, were digged up between fourty and fifty Urnes,[1] deposited in a dry and sandy soile, not a yard deep, nor farre from one another: Not all strictly of one figure, but most answering these described: Some containing two pounds of bones, distinguishable in skulls, ribs, jawes, thigh-bones, and teeth, with fresh impressions of their combustion. Besides the extraneous substances like peeces of small boxes, or combes handsomely wrought, handles of small brasse instruments, brazen nippers, and in one some kinde of *Opale*.[2]

Near the same plot of ground, for about six yards compasse were digged up coals and incinerated substances, which begat conjecture that this was the *Ustrina* or place of burning their

41. Obtuse rather than insensitive (§ 176). Browne is probably thinking of Ross who vigorously defended the existence of the phoenix in 1651 (as he did that of the unicorn: above, p. 214, note 26).

1. The accompanying plate appears in the 1st edition at the outset of *Hydriotaphia*, immediately after the epistle dedicatory (above, p. 265). The quotation from Propertius (IV, xi, 14) reads: 'I am a weight that may be lifted with five fingers' – where the reference to five contains, in anticipation of *The Garden of Cyrus*, 'the merest hint of the quincunx' (§ 198).

2. 'In one sent me by my worthy friend Dr *Thomas Witherley* of *Walsingham*' (Browne marg.). See further below, p. 280.

En Sum quod digitis Quinque Levatur onus propert:

[See page opposite, note 1]

bodies or some sacrificing place unto the *Manes*, which was properly below the surface of the ground, as the *Aræ* and Altars unto the gods and *Heroes* above it.[3]

That these were the Urnes of *Romanes* from the common custome and place where they were found, is no obscure conjecture, not farre from a *Romane* Garrison, and but five Miles from *Brancaster*, set down by ancient Record under the name of *Brannodunum*.[4] And where the adjoyning Towne, containing seven Parishes, in no very different sound, but Saxon Termination, still retains the Name of *Burnham*, which being an early station, it is not improbable the neighbour parts were filled with habitations, either of *Romanes* themselves, or *Brittains Romanised*, which observed the *Romane* customes.

Nor is it improbable that the *Romanes* early possessed this Countrey;[5] for though we meet not with such strict particulars of these parts, before the new Institution of *Constantine*, and military charge of the Count of the *Saxon* shore, and that about the *Saxon* Invasions, the *Dalmatian* Horsemen were in the Garrison of *Brancaster*: Yet in the time of *Claudius*, *Vespasian*, and *Severus*, we finde no lesse then three Legions dispersed through the Province of *Brittain*. And as high[6] as the Reign of *Claudius* a great overthrow was given unto the *Iceni*, by the *Romane* Lieutenant *Ostorius*. Not long after the Countrey was so molested, that in hope of a better state, *Prasutagus* bequeathed his Kingdome unto *Nero* and his Daughters; and *Boadicea* his Queen fought the last decisive Battle with *Paulinus*.[7] After which time and Conquest of *Agricola* the Lieutenant of *Vespasian*, probable it is they wholly possessed this Countrey, ordering it into Garrisons or Habitations, best suitable with their securities. And so some *Romane* Habitations, not improb-

---

3. *Manes* are the spirits of the dead; *aræ* are altars for demigods or heroes, and *altaria*, for gods.

4. The urns were in fact Saxon, not Roman (see §298). Browne later recognises that some 'might somewhat doubt' whether the urns did not belong 'unto our *Brittish*, *Saxon*, or *Danish* Forefathers' (below, p. 281).

5. i.e. county.

6. As early.

7. Tacitus, *Annals*, XIV, 31–8.

able in these parts, as high as the time of *Vespasian*, where the *Saxons* after seated, in whose thin-fill'd Mappes we yet finde the Name of *Walsingham*. Now if the *Iceni* were but *Gammadims*, *Anconians*, or men that lived in an Angle wedge or Elbow of *Brittain*, according to the Originall Etymologie, this countrey will challenge the Emphaticall appellation, as most properly making the Elbow or Iken of *Icenia*.[8]

That *Britain* was notably populous is undeniable, from that expression of *Cæsar*.[9] That the *Romans* themselves were early in no small Numbers, Seventy Thousand with their associats slain by *Boadicea*, affords a sure account. And though many *Roman* habitations are now unknowne, yet some by old works, Rampiers,[10] Coynes, and Urnes doe testifie their Possessions. Some Urnes have been found at *Castor*, some also about *South-creake*, and not many years past, no lesse then ten in a Field at *Buxton*,[11] not near any recorded Garison. Nor is it strange to finde *Romane* Coynes of Copper and Silver among us; of *Vespasian, Trajan, Adrian, Commodus, Antoninus, Severus*, &c. But the greater number of *Dioclesian, Constantine, Constans, Valens*, with many of *Victorinus Posthumius, Tetricus*, and the thirty Tyrants in the Reigne of *Gallienus*; and some as high as *Adrianus* have been found about *Thetford*, or *Sitomagus*, mentioned in the itinerary of *Antoninus*, as the way from *Venta* or *Castor* unto *London*.[12] But the most frequent discovery is made

8. The Gammadims (Ezekiel 27.11) were thought to be the inhabitants of Anconia (from the Greek ἀγκών, 'bend of the elbow'). Hence Norfolk's 'Emphaticall appellation' (*G2*).

9. 'The population is innumerable; the farm-buildings are found very close together, being very like those of the Gauls' (Browne marg., quoting the Latin of Caesar, *Gallic War*, V, 12).

10. i.e. ramparts.

11. 'In the ground of my worthy Friend *Rob. Jegon* Esq. wherein some things contained were preserved by the most worthy Sir *William Paston*, Bt.' (Browne marg.).

12. 'From *Castor* to *Thetford* the Romanes accounted thirty two miles, and from thence observed not our common road to *London*, but passed by *Combretonium ad Ansam, Canonium, Cæsaromagus* [i.e. Ipswich, Dedham, Kelvedon, Chelmsford], &c. by *Bretenham, Coggeshall, Chelmeford, Burntwood*, &c.' (Browne marg.). Castor is Caistor St Edmunds (Venta Icenorum); but Sitomagus is Stowmarket, not Thetford.

at the two *Casters* by *Norwich* and *Yarmouth*,[13] at *Burghcastle* and *Brancaster*.[14]

Besides, the *Norman, Saxon* and *Danish* peeces of *Cuthred, Canutus, William, Matilda*,[15] and others, som *Brittish* Coynes of gold have been dispersedly found; And no small number of silver peeces near *Norwich*;[16] with a rude head upon the obverse, and an ill formed horse on the reverse, with Inscriptions *Ic. Duro. T.* whether implying *Iceni, Dutotriges, Tascia,* or *Trinobantes,* we leave to higher conjecture. Vulgar Chronology will have *Norwich* Castle as old as *Julius Cæsar;* but his distance from these parts, and its *Gothick* form of structure, abridgeth such Antiquity. The *British* Coyns afford conjecture of early habitation in these parts, though the City of *Norwich* arose from the ruines of *Venta*,[17] and though perhaps not without some habitation before, was enlarged, builded, and nominated by the *Saxons.* In what bulk or populosity it stood in the old East-angle Monarchy, tradition and history are silent. Considerable it was in the *Danish* Eruptions, when *Sueno* burnt *Thetford* and *Norwich,* and *Ulfketel* the Governour thereof, was able to make some resistance, and after endeavoured to burn the *Danish* Navy.[18]

How the *Romanes* left so many Coynes in Countreys of their Conquests, seems of hard resolution, except we consider how they buried them under ground, when upon barbarous invasions they were fain to desert their habitations in most part of their Empire, and the strictnesse of their laws forbidding to

13. 'Most at *Caster* by *Yarmouth,* found in a place called *East-bloudyburgh furlong,* belonging to Mr *Thomas Wood,* a person of civility, industry and knowledge in this way, who hath made observation of remarkable things about him, and from whom we have received divers Silver and Copper Coynes' (Browne marg.).

14. 'Belonging to that Noble Gentleman, and true example of worth Sir *Ralph Hare* Baronet, my honoured Friend' (Browne marg.).

15. 'A peece of *Maud* [i.e. Matilda] the Empresse said to be found in *Buckenham* Castle with this Inscription, *Elle n'a elle*' (Browne marg.). The reference is probably to a coin; but the inscription is meaningless.

16. 'At *Thorpe*' (Browne marg.).

17. Norwich replaced Venta (previous page, note 12), but on a different site.

18. So the *Chronicon Brompton Abbatis Jornalensis* (Browne marg.).

transfer them to any other uses; Wherein the *Spartans* were singular, who to make their Copper money[19] uselesse, con-tempered it with vinegar. That the *Brittains* left any, some wonder; since their money was iron, and Iron rings before *Cæsar*;[20] and those of after stamp[21] by permission, and but small in bulk and bignesse; that so few of the *Saxons* remain, because overcome by succeeding Conquerours upon the place, their Coynes by degrees passed into other stamps, and the marks of after ages.

Then the time of these Urnes deposited, or precise Antiquity of these Reliques, nothing of more uncertainty. For since the Lieutenant of *Claudius* seems to have made the first progresse into these parts, since *Boadicea* was overthrown by the Forces of *Nero*, and *Agricola* put a full end to these Conquests; it is not probable the Countrey was fully garrison'd or planted before; and therefore however these Urnes might be of later date, not likely of higher Antiquity.

And the succeeding Emperours desisted not from their Conquests in these and other parts; as testified by history and medall inscription yet extant. The Province of *Brittain* in so divided a distance from *Rome,* beholding the faces [of] many Imperiall persons, and in large account no fewer then *Cæsar, Claudius, Britannicus, Vespasian, Titus, Adrian, Severus, Commodus, Geta,* and *Caracalla.*

A great obscurity herein, because no medall or Emperours Coyne enclosed, which might denote the date of their enterr-ments. Observable in many Urnes, and found in those of *Spittle* Fields by *London,*[22] which contained the Coynes of *Claudius, Vespasian, Commodus, Antoninus,* attended with Lacrymatories,[23] Lamps, Bottles of Liquor, and other appurtenances of affec-tionate superstition, which in these rurall interrements were wanting.

Some uncertainty there is from the period or term of burn-

19. In Plutarch, *Lycurgus,* IX (Browne marg.), the money is iron, not copper.

20. Caesar, *Gallic War,* V, 12, also mentions other metals.

21. Later mintage (R).

22. 'Stowe Survey of *London*' (Browne marg.).

23. Tear-bottles' (as below, p. 286).

ing, or the cessation of that practise. *Macrobius* affirmeth it was disused in his dayes. But most agree, though without authentick record, that it ceased with the *Antonini*. Most safely to be understood after the Reigne of those Emperours, which assumed the name of *Antoninus*, extending unto *Heliogabalus*. Not strictly after *Marcus*; for about fifty years later we finde the magnificent burning, and consecration of *Severus*;[24] and if we so fix this period or cessation, these Urnes will challenge above thirteen hundred years.

But whether this practise was onely then left by Emperours and great persons, or generally about *Rome*, and not in other Provinces, we hold no authentick account. For after *Tertullian*, in the dayes of *Minucius* it was obviously objected upon Christians, that they condemned the practise of burning.[25] And we finde a passage in *Sidonius*,[26] which asserteth that practise in *France* unto a lower account. And perhaps not fully disused till Christianity fully established, which gave the finall extinction of these sepulchrall Bonefires.

Whether they were the bones of men or women or children, no authentick decision from ancient custome in distinct places of buriall. Although not improbably conjectured, that the double Sepulture or burying place of *Abraham*,[27] had in it such intension. But from exility[28] of bones, thinnesse of skulls, smallnesse of teeth, ribbes, and thigh-bones; not improbable that many thereof were persons of *minor* age, or women. Confirmable also from things contained in them: In most were found substances resembling Combes, Plates like Boxes, fastened with Iron pins, and handsomely overwrought like the necks or Bridges of Musicall Instruments, long brasse plates overwrought like the handles of neat implements, brazen nippers to pull away hair, and in one a kinde of *Opale* yet maintaining a blewish colour.

Now that they accustomed to burn or bury with them, things

24. Septimius Severus (d. 211). See further below, p. 285, note 8.

25. 'They denounce funeral pyres and condemn cremation' (Browne marg., quoting the Latin of Minucius Felix, *Octavius*, XI, 4).

26. Sidonius Apollinaris, *Letters*, III, 3 (Browne marg.).

27. Genesis 23.9 (Browne suppl., quoting the Vulgate).

28. 'smalness' (Blount).

wherein they excelled, delighted, or which were dear unto
them, either as farewells unto all pleasure, or vain apprehen-
sion that they might use them in the other world, is testified by
all Antiquity. Observable from the Gemme or Berill Ring upon
the finger of *Cynthia*, the Mistresse of *Propertius*, when after her
Funerall Pyre her Ghost appeared unto him.[29] And notably
illustrated from the Contents of that *Romane* Urne preserved by
Cardinall *Farnesse*,[30] wherein besides great number of Gemmes
with heads of Gods and Goddesses, were found an Ape of
Agath, a Grashopper, an Elephant of Ambre, a Crystall Ball,
three glasses, two Spoones, and six Nuts of Crystall. And be-
yond the content of Urnes, in the Monument of *Childerick* the
first,[31] and fourth King from *Pharamond*, casually discovered
three years past at *Tournay*, restoring unto the world much gold
richly adorning his Sword, two hundred Rubies, many hundred
Imperial Coyns, three hundred golden Bees, the bones and
horseshoe of his horse enterred with him, according to the
barbarous magnificence of those dayes in their sepulchral
Obsequies. Although if we steer by the conjecture of many and
Septuagint expression; some trace thereof may be found even
with the ancient Hebrews, not only from the Sepulcrall treasure
of *David*, but the circumcision knives which *Josuah* also buried.[32]

Some men considering the contents of these Urnes, lasting
peeces and toyes included in them, and the custome of burning
with many other Nations, might somewhat doubt whether all
Urnes found among us, were properly *Romane* Reliques, or
some not belonging unto our *Brittish*, *Saxon*, or *Danish* Fore-
fathers.

In the form of Buriall among the ancient *Brittains*, the large
Discourses of *Cæsar*, *Tacitus*, and *Strabo* are silent: For the dis-
covery whereof, with other particulars, we much deplore the
losse of that Letter which *Cicero* expected or received from his
Brother *Quintus*, as a resolution of *Brittish* customes;[33] or the

29. Propertius, *Elegies*, IV, vii, 9.
30. As reported in Vegenère's edition of Livy (Browne marg.).
31. As reported by Chifflet (Browne marg.).
32. Joshua 24.30 (31) according to the Septuagint.
33. Cicero, *Letters to Quintus*, II, xv (xvi), 4.

account which might have been made by *Scribonius Largus* the Physician, accompanying the Emperour *Claudius*, who might have also discovered that frugall Bit of the Old *Brittains*, which in the bignesse of a Bean could satisfie their thirst and hunger.[34]

But that the *Druids* and ruling Priests used to burn and bury, is expressed by *Pomponius*; That *Bellinus* the Brother of *Brennus*, and King of *Brittains* was burnt, is acknowledged by *Polydorus*.[35] That they held that practise in *Gallia*, *Cæsar* expresly delivereth.[36] Whether the *Brittains* (probably descended from them, of like Religion, Language and Manners) did not sometimes make use of burning; or whether at least such as were after civilized unto the *Romane* life and manners, conformed not unto this practise, we have no historicall assertion or deniall. But since from the account of *Tacitus*[37] the *Romanes* early wrought so much civility upon the Brittish stock, that they brought them to build Temples, to wear the Gowne, and study the *Romane* Laws and language, that they conformed also unto their religious rites and customes in burials, seems no improbable conjecture.

That burning the dead was used in *Sarmatia*, is affirmed by *Gaguinus*, that the *Sueons* and *Gothlanders*[38] used to burne their Princes and great persons, is delivered by *Saxo* and *Olaus*; that this was the old *Germane* practice, is also asserted by *Tacitus*. And though we are bare in historicall particulars of such obsequies in this Island, or that the *Saxons*, *Jutes*, and *Angles* burnt their dead, yet came they from parts where 'twas of ancient practise; the *Germanes* using it, from whom they were descended. And even in *Jutland* and *Sleswick* in *Anglia Cymbrica*,[39] Urnes with bones were found not many years before us.

But the *Danish* and Northern Nations have raised an *Æra* or

34. So Dio Cassius, LXXII, 12 (Browne marg.).

35. 'As also by *Amandus Zierexensis* in *Historia*, and *Pineda* in his *Universa historia*. Spanish' (Browne suppl., correcting the inadvertent introduction of this phrase into the text of the 1st edition).

36. In *Gallic War*, VI, 16.

37. In *Agricola*, XXI.

38. i.e. Swedes and Goths. 'Sarmatia' is the area extending across N.E. Europe.

39. A district in Schleswig (R).

point of compute from their Custome of burning their dead:[40] Some deriving it from *Unguinus,* some from *Frotho* the great; who ordained by Law, that Princes and Chief Commanders should be committed unto the fire, though the common sort had the common grave enterrment. So *Starkatterus* that old *Heroe* was burnt, and *Ringo* royally burnt the body of *Harald* the King slain by him.

What time this custome generally expired in that Nation, we discern no assured period; whether it ceased before Christianity, or upon their Conversion, by *Ausgarius* the Gaul in the time of *Ludovicus Pius* the Sonne of *Charles* the great, according to good computes; or whether it might not be used by some persons, while for a hundred and eighty years Paganisme and Christianity were promiscuously embraced among them, there is no assured conclusion. About which times the *Danes* were busie in *England,* and particularly infested this Countrey: Where many Castles and strong holds, were built by them, or against them, and great number of names and Families still derived from them. But since this custome was probably disused before their Invasion or Conquest, and the *Romanes* confessedly practised the same, since their possession of this Island, the most assured account will fall upon the *Romanes,* or *Brittains Romanized.*

However certain it is, that Urnes conceived of no *Romane* Originall, are often digged up both in *Norway,* and *Denmark,* handsomely described, and graphically represented by the Learned Physician *Wormius,*[41] And in some parts of *Denmark* in no ordinary number, as stands delivered by Authours exactly describing those Countreys.[42] And they contained not only bones, but many other substances in them, as Knives, peeces of Iron, Brasse and Wood, and one of *Norwaye* a brasse guilded Jewes-harp.

Nor were they confused or carelesse in disposing the noblest

40. 'Roisold, Brendetiide, Ildtyde' (Browne add.), each signifying the Age of Burning.

41. In his *Danica Monumenta* (Browne marg.). Wormius is the principal authority for these paragraphs.

42. So Cypraeus (Browne marg.).

sort, while they placed large stones in circle about the Urnes, or bodies which they interred: Somewhat answerable unto the Monument of *Rollrich* stones in *England*, or sepulcrall Monument probably erected by *Rollo*, who after conquered *Normandy*. Where 'tis not improbable somewhat might be discovered. Mean while to what Nation or person belonged that large Urne found at *Ashburie*, containing mighty bones, and a Buckler; What those large Urnes found at little *Massingham*,[43] or why the *Angelsea* Urnes are placed with their mouths downward, remains yet undiscovered.

CHAPTER III

Playstered and whited Sepulchres, were anciently affected in cadaverous, and corruptive Burials; And the rigid Jews were wont to garnish the Sepulchres of the righteous;[1] *Ulysses* in *Hecuba*[2] cared not how meanly he lived, so he might finde a noble Tomb after death. Great Princes affected great Monuments, And the fair and larger Urnes contained no vulgar ashes, which makes that disparity in those which time discovereth among us. The present Urnes were not of one capacity, the largest containing above a gallon, Some not much above half that measure; nor all of one figure, wherein there is no strict conformity, in the same or different Countreys; Observable from those represented by *Casalius*, *Bosio*, and others, though all found in *Italy*. While many have handles, ears, and long necks, but most imitate a circular figure, in a sphericall and round composure; whether from any mystery, best duration or capacity, were but a conjecture. But the common form with necks was a proper figure, making our last bed like our first; nor much unlike the Urnes of our Nativity, while we lay in the nether part of the Earth,[3] and inward vault of our Microcosme.[4]

43. 'In Norfolk' (Browne marg.). Three other marginal notes in this paragraph specify Browne's sources as Camden, Twyne, and Holinshed.

1. Matthew 23.29 (Browne marg.).

2. Euripides, *Hecuba*, ll. 317–20 (Browne marg.).

3. Psalm 63.9 (Browne marg.).

4. See above, p. 103, note 208.

Many Urnes are red, these but of a black colour, somewhat smooth, and dully sounding, which begat some doubt, whether they were burnt, or only baked in Oven or Sunne: According to the ancient way, in many bricks, tiles, pots, and testaceous[5] works; and as the word *testa*[6] is properly to be taken, when occurring without addition: And chiefly intended by *Pliny*, when he commendeth bricks and tiles of two years old, and to make them in the spring. Nor only these concealed peeces, but the open magnificence of Antiquity, ran much in the Artifice of Clay. Hereof the house of *Mausolus* was built, thus old *Jupiter* stood in the Capitoll, and the *Statua* of *Hercules* made in the Reign of *Tarquinius Priscus*, was extant in *Plinies* dayes. And such as declined burning or Funerall Urnes, affected Coffins of Clay, according to the mode of *Pythagoras*, and was preferred by *Varro*.[7] But the spirit of great ones was above these circumscriptions, affecting copper, silver, gold, and *Porphyrie* Urnes, wherein *Severus* lay, after a serious view and sentence on that which should contain him.[8] Some of these Urnes were thought to have been silvered over, from sparklings in several pots, with small Tinsell parcels; uncertain whether from the earth, or the first mixture in them.

Among these Urnes we could obtain no good account of their coverings; Only one seemed arched over with some kinde of brickwork. Of those found at *Buxton*[9] some were covered with flints, some in other parts with tiles; those at *Yarmouth Caster*, were closed with *Romane* bricks. And some have proper earthen covers adapted and fitted to them. But in the *Homerical* Urne of *Patroclus*,[10] whatever was the solid Tegument,[11] we finde the immediate covering to be a purple peece of silk: And such as had no covers might have the earth closely pressed into them, after which disposure were probably some of these, wherein we

5. 'that whiche hath a shelle' (Elyot).
6. 'a sharde [fragment] of a potte or tyle, also an erthen pot' (Elyot).
7. So Pliny, XXXV, 45 and 49.
8. 'Thou shalt hold that man whom the world could not hold' (Browne marg., quoting the Greek of Dio Cassius, LXXVII, xv, 4; R).
9. See above, p. 277.
10. *Iliad*, XXIII, 254.
11. 'coverynge or cover' (Elyot).

found the bones and ashes half mortered unto the sand and sides of the Urne; and some long roots of Quich, or Dogs-grass wreathed about the bones.

No Lamps, included Liquors, Lachrymatories, or Tear-bottles attended these rurall Urnes, either as sacred unto the *Manes*, or passionate expressions of their surviving friends. While with rich flames, and hired tears they solemnized their Obsequies, and in the most lamented Monuments made one part of their Inscriptions.[12] Some finde sepulchrall Vessels containing liquors, which time hath incrassated[13] into gellies. For beside these Lachrymatories, notable Lamps, with Vessels of Oyles and Aromaticall Liquors attended noble Ossuaries. And some yet retaining a Vinosity[14] and spirit in them, which if any have tasted they have farre exceeded the Palats of Antiquity. Liquors not to be computed by years of annuall Magistrates, but by great conjunctions and the fatall periods Kingdomes.[15] The draughts of Consulary date,[16] were but crude unto these, and *Opimian* Wine[17] but in the must unto them.

In sundry Graves and Sepulchres, we meet with Rings, Coynes, and Chalices; Ancient frugality was so severe, that they allowed no gold to attend the Corps, but only that which served to fasten their teeth.[18] Whether the *Opaline* stone in this Urne[19] were burnt upon the finger of the dead, or cast into the fire by some affectionate friend, it will consist with either custome. But other incinerable substances were found so fresh, that they could feel no sindge from fire. These upon view were judged to be wood, but sinking in water and tried by the fire, we found them to be bone or Ivory. In their hardnesse and yellow colour

12. 'With tears they laid out [the corpse]' (Browne marg., in Latin).

13. 'made thick or gross' (Blount).

14. i.e. vinous quality. The detail is reported by Lazius (Browne marg.).

15. 'About five hundred years. *Plato*' (Browne marg.). Cf. *The Republic*, VIII, 546.

16. i.e. dated by the consuls in office at the time of vintage (R).

17. The celebrated wine of 121 B.C., in the consulate of Opimius, as reported by Petronius, XXXIV, 6 (Browne marg.).

18. As reported in the Twelve Tables (Browne marg.). Cf. above, p. 269, note 17.

19. See above, pp. 274 and 280.

they most resembled Box, which in old expressions found the Epithete of Eternall,[20] and perhaps in such conservatories[21] might have passed uncorrupted.

That Bay-leaves were found green in the Tomb of *S. Humbert*,[22] after an hundred and fifty years, was looked upon as miraculous. Remarkable it was unto old Spectators, that the Cypresse of the Temple of *Diana*, lasted so many hundred years: The wood of the Ark and Olive Rod of *Aaron*[23] were older at the Captivity. But the Cypresse of the Ark of *Noah*, was the greatest vegetable Antiquity, if *Josephus*[24] were not deceived, by some fragments of it in his dayes. To omit the Moore-logs, and Firre-trees found under-ground in many parts of *England*; the undated ruines of windes, flouds or earthquakes; and which in *Flanders* still shew from what quarter they fell, as generally lying in a North-East position.[25]

But though we found not these peeces to be Wood, according to first apprehension, yet we missed not altogether of some woody substance; For the bones were not so clearly pickt, but some coals were found amongst them; A way to make wood perpetuall, and a fit associat for metall, whereon was laid the foundation of the great *Ephesian* Temple, and which were made the lasting tests of old boundaries and Landmarks; Whilest we look on these, we admire not Observations of Coals found fresh, after four hundred years.[26] In a long deserted habitation,[27] even Egge-shels have been found fresh, not tending to corruption.

In the Monument of King *Childerick*, the Iron Reliques were found all rusty and crumbling into peeces. But our little Iron pins which fastened the Ivory works, held well together, and lost not their Magneticall quality, though wanting a tenacious moisture for the firmer union of parts, although it be hardly

20. So Pliny, XVI, 78 (Browne marg.).
21. '*Conservatory*, a place to preserve, or keep things in' (Blount).
22. So Casalius (Browne marg.).
23. Hebrews 9.4.
24. In *Jewish Antiquities*, I, iii, 5; XX, ii, 2.
25. So Goropius (Browne marg.).
26. So Biringuccio (Browne marg.).
27. 'At Elmeham' (Browne marg.).

drawn into fusion, yet that metall soon submitteth unto rust and dissolution. In the brazen peeces we admired not the duration but the freedome from rust, and ill savour; upon the hardest attrition, but now exposed unto the piercing Atomes of ayre; in the space of a few moneths, they begin to spot and betray their green entrals. We conceive not these Urnes to have descended thus naked as they appear, or to have entred their graves without the old habit of flowers. The Urne of *Philopœmen* was so laden with flowers and ribbons, that it afforded no sight of it self.[28] The rigid *Lycurgus* allowed Olive and Myrtle. The *Athenians* might fairly except against the practise of *Democritus* to be buried up in honey; as fearing to embezzle a great commodity of their Countrey, and the best of that kinde in *Europe*. But *Plato* seemed too frugally politick, who allowed no larger Monument then would contain four Heroick Verses, and designed the most barren ground for sepulture:[29] Though we cannot commend the goodnesse of that sepulchrall ground, which was set at no higher rate then the mean salary of *Judas*.[30] Though the earth had confounded[31] the ashes of these Ossuaries, yet the bones were so smartly burnt, that some thin plates of brasse were found half melted among them: whereby we apprehend they were not of the meanest carcasses, perfunctorily fired as sometimes in military, and commonly in pestilence, burnings; or after the manner of abject corps, hudled forth and carelesly burnt, without the Esquiline Port at *Rome*;[32] which was an affront continued[33] upon *Tiberius*, while they but half burnt his body,[34] and in the Amphitheatre, according to the custome in notable Malefactors; whereas *Nero* seemed not so much to feare his death, as that his head should be cut off, and his body not burnt entire.[35]

28. Plutarch, *Philopoemen*, XXI, 3.

29. *Laws*, 958e.

30. Matthew 27. 5–8.

31. Mingled.

32. Where the bodies of those held in contempt were burnt or thrown to the dogs (R).

33. 'contrived' (the word is a pen-and-ink correction in a copy of the 1st edition; M).

34. Suetonius, *Tiberius*, LXXV, 3 (Browne marg.).

35. Suetonius, *Nero*, XLIX, 4.

Some finding many fragments of sculs in these Urnes, sus-
pected a mixture of bones; In none we searched was there cause
of such conjecture, though sometimes they declined not that
practise; The ashes of *Domitian* were mingled with those of
Julia, of *Achilles* with those of *Patroclus*:[36] All Urnes contained
not single ashes; Without confused burnings they affectionately
compounded their bones; passionately endeavouring to con-
tinue their living Unions. And when distance of death denied
such conjunctions, unsatisfied affections, conceived some satis-
faction to be neighbours in the grave, to lye Urne by Urne, and
touch but in their names. And many were so curious to continue
their living relations, that they contrived large, and family
Urnes, wherein the Ashes of their nearest friends and kindred
might successively be received,[37] at least some parcels thereof,
while their collaterall memorials lay in *minor* vessels about
them.

Antiquity held too light thoughts from Objects of mortality,
while some drew provocatives of mirth from Anatomies, and
Juglers shewed tricks with Skeletons.[38] When Fidlers made not
so pleasant mirth as Fencers, and men could sit with quiet
stomacks while hanging was plaied before them.[39] Old con-
siderations made few *memento's* by sculs and bones upon their
monuments. In the Ægyptian Obelisks and Hieroglyphicall
figures it is not easie to meet with bones. The sepulchrall Lamps
speak nothing lesse then sepulture; and in their literall draughts
prove often obscene and antick peeces: Where we finde *D.M.*[40]
it is obvious to meet with sacrificing *patera's,*[41] and vessels of

36. Suetonius, *Domitian,* XVII, 3 (Browne marg.); and *Odyssey,* XXIV,
76–7.

37. 'S[ee] the most learned and worthy Mr *M. Casaubon* upon *Antoninus*'
(Browne marg.).

38. Petronius, XXXIV.

39. ' *Ἀγχώνην παίζειν* [i.e. The Hanging game]. A barbarous pastime
at Feasts, when men stood upon a rolling Globe, with their necks in a
Rope fastned to a beame, and a knife in their hands, ready to cut it when
the stone was rolled away, wherein if they failed they lost their lives to the
laughter of their spectators' (Browne marg.). So Athenaeus, IV, 155.

40. '*Diis manibus*' (Browne marg.) – i.e. 'To the gods of the under-
world': the common way that Roman funerary inscriptions began.

41. Dishes used in libations at sacrifices.

libation, upon old sepulchrall Monuments. In the Jewish
Hypogæum[42] and subterranean Cell at *Rome*, was little observable
beside the variety of Lamps, and frequent draughts of the holy
Candlestick.[43] In authentick draughts of *Anthony* and *Jerome*,[44]
we meet with thigh-bones and deaths heads; but the cemiteriall
Cels of ancient Christians and Martyrs, were filled with
draughts of Scripture Stories; not declining the flourishes of
Cypresse, Palmes, and Olive; and the mysticall Figures of Pea-
cocks, Doves and Cocks. But iterately[45] affecting the pourtraits
of *Enoch*, *Lazarus*, *Jonas*, and the Vision of *Ezechiel*,[46] as hopefull
draughts, and hinting imagery of the Resurrection; which is the
life of the grave, and sweetens our habitations in the Land of
Moles and Pismires.

Gentile Inscriptions precisely delivered the extent of mens
lives, seldome the manner of their deaths, which history it self so
often leaves obscure in the records of memorable persons. There
is scarce any Philosopher but dies twice or thrice in *Laertius*;
Nor almost any life without two or three deaths in *Plutarch*;
which makes the tragicall ends of noble persons more favour-
ably resented[47] by compassionate Readers, who finde some relief
in the Election of such differences.

The certainty of death is attended with uncertainties, in time,
manner, places. The variety of Monuments hath often obscured
true graves: and *Cenotaphs* confounded Sepulchres. For beside
their reall Tombs, many have found honorary and empty
Sepulchres. The variety of *Homers* Monuments made him of
various Countreys. *Euripides* had his Tomb in *Attica*, but his
sepulture in *Macedonia*,[48] And *Severus* found his real Sepulchre in
Rome, but his empty grave in *Gallia*.[49]

42. Vault. As reported by Bosio (Browne marg.).

43. Exodus 25.31 ff.

44. Of whom the first lived in a tomb, and the second frequented the
Roman catacombs.

45. Repeatedly.

46. Ezekiel 37.1 ff.

47. Felt.

48. So Pausanias (Browne marg.). 'Attica' corrects the erroneous
'Africa' of the 1st edition.

49. So Lampridius (Browne marg.).

He that lay in a golden Urne[50] eminently above the Earth, was not like to finde the quiet of these bones. Many of these Urnes were broke by a vulgar discoverer in hope of inclosed treasure. The ashes of *Marcellus* were lost above ground, upon the like account.[51] Where profit hath prompted, no age hath wanted such miners. For which the most barbarous Expilators found the most civill Rhetorick.[52] Gold once out of the earth is no more due unto it; What was unreasonably committed to the ground is reasonably resumed from it: Let Monuments and rich Fabricks, not Riches adorn mens ashes. The commerce of the living is not to be transfered unto the dead: It is not injustice to take that which none complains to lose, and no man is wronged where no man is possessor.

What virtue yet sleeps in this *terra damnata*[53] and aged cinders, were petty magick to experiment; These crumbling reliques and long-fired particles superannate such expectations: Bones, hairs, nails, and teeth of the dead, were the treasures of old Sorcerers. In vain we revive such practices; Present superstition too visibly perpetuates the folly of our Fore-fathers, wherein unto old Observation this Island was so compleat, that it might have instructed *Persia*.[54]

Plato's historian of the other world,[55] lies twelve dayes incorrupted, while his soul was viewing the large stations of the dead. How to keep the corps seven dayes from corruption by anointing and washing, without exenteration, were an hazardable peece of art, in our choisest practise. How they made distinct separation of bones and ashes from fiery admixture, hath found no historicall solution. Though they seemed to make a distinct collection, and overlooked not *Pyrrhus* his toe.[56] Some

50. The Emperor Trajan (Browne marg.).
51. So Plutarch, *Marcellus*, XXX, 2–3 (Browne marg.).
52. 'The Commission of the *Gothish* King *Theodoric* for finding out sepulchrall treasure' (Browne marg.); so Cassiodorus in *Variae*. 'Expilators' are plunderers.
53. Literally, 'damned earth': in alchemy, the residue after calcination.
54. Pliny, XXX, 4 (Browne marg.).
55. Er, in *The Republic*, X, 614b.
56. 'Which could not be burnt' (Browne suppl.). So Pliny, VII, 2.

provision they might make by fictile[57] Vessels, Coverings, Tiles, or flat stones, upon and about the body. And in the same Field, not farre from these Urnes, many stones were found under ground, as also by carefull separation of extraneous matter, composing and raking up the burnt bones with forks, observable in that notable lump of *Galvanus*.[58] *Marlianus*, who had the sight of the *Vas Ustrinum*, or vessell wherein they burnt the dead, found in the Esquiline Field at *Rome*, might have afforded clearer solution. But their insatisfaction herein begat that remarkable invention in the Funerall Pyres of some Princes, by incombustible sheets made with a texture of *Asbestos*, incremable[59] flex, or Salamanders wool, which preserved their bones and ashes incommixed.

How the bulk of a man should sink into so few pounds of bones and ashes, may seem strange unto any who considers not its constitution, and how slender a masse will remain upon an open and urging fire of the carnall composition. Even bones themselves reduced into ashes, do abate a notable proportion. And consisting much of a volatile salt, when that is fired out, make a light kind of cinders. Although their bulk be disproportionable to their weight, when the heavy principle of Salt is fired out, and the Earth almost only remaineth; Observable in sallow, which makes more Ashes then Oake; and discovers the common fraud of selling Ashes by measure, and not by ponderation.

Some bones make best Skeletons,[60] some bodies quick and speediest ashes: Who would expect a quick flame from Hydropicall *Heraclitus*?[61] The poysoned Souldier when his Belly brake, put out two pyres in *Plutarch*.[62] But in the plague of *Athens*,[63] one private pyre served two or three Intruders; and

57. 'made of erthe' (Elyot).
58. Decorated with representations of ancient funeral rites (R).
59. Incombustible.
60. 'Old bones according to *Lyserus*. Those of young persons not tall nor fat according to [*Realdus*] *Columbus*' (Browne marg.).
61. Who died from dropsy, as reported by Diogenes Laertius.
62. Plutarch, *Tiberius Gracchus*, XIII, 4–5 (Browne marg.).
63. Thucydides, II, lii, 4 (Browne marg.).

the *Saracens* burnt in large heaps, by the King of *Castile*,[64] shewed how little Fuell sufficeth. Though the Funerall pyre of *Patroclus* took up an hundred foot, a peece of an old boat burnt *Pompey*;[65] And if the burthen of *Isaac*[66] were sufficient for an holocaust, a man may carry his owne pyre.

From animals are drawn good burning lights, and good medicines against burning; Though the seminall humour seems of a contrary nature to fire, yet the body compleated proves a combustible lump, wherein fire findes flame even from bones, and some fuell almost from all parts. Though the Metropolis of humidity[67] seems least disposed unto it, which might render the soulls of these Urnes lesse burned then other bones. But all flies or sinks before fire almost in all bodies: When the common ligament is dissolved, the attenuable[68] parts ascend, the rest subside in coal, calx or ashes.

To burn the bones of the King of *Edom*[69] for Lyme, seems no irrationall ferity;[70] But to drink of the ashes of dead relations,[71] a passionate prodigality. He that hath the ashes of his friend, hath an everlasting treasure: where fire taketh leave, corruption slowly enters; In bones well burnt, fire makes a wall against it self; experimented in copels, and tests[72] of metals, which consist of such ingredients. What the Sun compoundeth, fire analyseth, not transmuteth. That devouring agent leaves almost allwayes a morsell for the Earth, whereof all things are but a colonie; and which, if time permits, the mother Element will have in their primitive masse again.

He that looks for Urnes and old sepulchrall reliques, must not seek them in the ruines of Temples; where no Religion anciently

64. So Valla (Browne marg.).

65. *Iliad*, XXIII, 164 (Browne marg., quoting the original Greek), and Plutarch, *Pompey*, LXXX, 2.

66. Genesis 22.6: 'the wood of the burnt offering [laid] upon Isaac'.

67. 'The brain. *Hippocrates*' (Browne marg.).

68. Capable of being made thinner.

69. Amos 2.1 (Browne marg.).

70. 'cruelty, fierceness' (Blount).

71. 'As *Artemisia* of her Husband *Mausolus*' (Browne marg.).

72. Earthenware vessels; cf. above, p. 285, note 6.

placed them. These were found in a Field, according to ancient custome, in noble or private buriall; the old practise of the *Canaanites*, the Family of *Abraham*, and the burying place of *Josua*,[73] in the borders of his possessions; and also agreeable unto *Roman* practice to bury by high-wayes, whereby their Monuments were under eye: Memorials of themselves, and *memento's* of mortality into living passengers; whom the Epitaphs of great ones were fain to beg to stay and look upon them. A language though sometimes used, not so proper in Church-Inscriptions.[74] The sensible Rhetorick of the dead, to exemplarity of good life, first admitted the bones of pious men, and Martyrs within Church-wals; which in succeeding ages crept into promiscuous practise. While *Constantine* was peculiarly favoured to be admitted unto the Church Porch; and the first thus buried in *England*[75] was in the dayes of *Cuthred*.

Christians dispute how their bodies should lye in the grave. In urnall enterrment they clearly escaped this Controversie: Though we decline the Religious consideration, yet in cemiteriall and narrower burying places, to avoid confusion and crosse position, a certain posture were to be admitted; Which even Pagan civility observed.[76] The *Persians* lay North and South, The *Megarians* and *Phœnicians* placed their heads to the East: The *Athenians*, some think, towards the West, which Christians still retain. And *Beda* will have it to be the posture of our Saviour. That he was crucified with his face towards the West, we will not contend with tradition and probable account; But we applaud not the hand of the Painter, in exalting his Crosse so high above those on either side; since hereof we finde no authentick account in history, and even the crosses found by *Helena* pretend no such distinction from longitude[77] or dimension.

73. Genesis 23.5–20 and 49.29–32, and Joshua 24.30.

74. *'Siste viator'* (Browne marg.) – i.e. 'Stop passerby': a variation on Cicero's rendering of Simonides's inscription at Thermopylae.

75. Archbishop Cuthbert, buried in Canterbury Cathedral in 758.

76. So Kirchmann (Browne marg.), one of the major sources for these paragraphs (cf. above, p. 269, note 14).

77. 'length' (Bullokar). On St Helena see also above, p. 96.

To be knav'd[78] out of our graves, to have our sculs made drinking-bowls, and our bones turned into Pipes, to delight and sport our Enemies, are Tragicall abominations, escaped in burning Burials.

Urnall enterrments, and burnt Reliques lye not in fear of worms, or to be an heritage for Serpents; In carnall sepulture, corruptions seem peculiar unto parts, and some speak of snakes out of the spinall marrow. But while we suppose common wormes in graves, 'tis not easie to finde any there; few in Church-yards above a foot deep, fewer or none in Churches, though in fresh decayed bodies. Teeth, bones, and hair, give the most lasting defiance to corruption. In an Hydropicall body ten years buried in a Church-yard, we met with a fat concretion,[79] where the nitre of the Earth, and the salt and lixivious[80] liquor of the body, had coagulated large lumps of fat, into the consistence of the hardest castle-soap; whereof part remaineth with us. After a battle with the *Persians* the *Roman* Corps decayed in few dayes, while the *Persian* bodies remained dry and uncorrupted. Bodies in the same ground do not uniformly dissolve, nor bones equally moulder; whereof in the opprobrious disease[81] we expect no long duration. The body of the Marquesse of *Dorset* seemed sound and handsomely cereclothed, that after seventy eight years was found uncorrupted.[82] Common Tombs preserve

78. Corrected by some editors to 'gnaw'd'. But Browne may have been thinking of the graveyard scene in *Hamlet*, e.g. 'That skull had a tongue in it, . . . How the knave jowls it to the ground' (V, i, 78–9; §298).

79. i.e. adipocere or grave wax, 'the insoluble fatty acids left as a residue of the pre-existing fats of animals, and produced by the slow hydrolysis of the fats in the wet ground' (§190). This is generally regarded as Browne's 'one notable scientific discovery' (ibid.), well in advance of its rediscovery by Fourcroy in the eighteenth century (see especially §§296, 298).

80. Alkaline.

81. i.e. syphilis.

82. 'Of *Thomas* Marquesse of *Dorset*, whose body being buried 1530 was [in] 1608 upon the cutting open of the Cerecloth found perfect and nothing corrupted, the flesh not hardened, but in colour, proportion, and softnesse like an ordinary corps newly to be interred. Burtons *descript. of Leicestershire*' (Browne marg.).

not beyond powder: A firmer consistence and compage[83] of parts might be expected from Arefaction,[84] deep buriall or charcoal. The greatest Antiquities of mortall bodies may remain in putrified bones, whereof, though we take not in the pillar of *Lots* wife, or Metamorphosis of *Ortelius*,[85] some may be older then Pyramids, in the putrified Reliques of the generall inundation. When *Alexander* opened the Tomb of *Cyrus*, the remaining bones discovered his proportion, whereof urnall fragments afford but a bad conjecture, and have this disadvantage of grave enterrments, that they leave us ignorant of most personall discoveries. For since bones afford not only rectitude and stability, but figure unto the body; It is no impossible Physiognomy to conjecture at fleshy appendencies;[86] and after what shape the muscles and carnous parts might hang in their full consistences. A full spread *Cariola*[87] shews a well-shaped horse behinde, handsome formed sculls, give some analogie of fleshy resemblance. A criticall view of bones makes a good distinction of sexes. Even colour is not beyond conjecture; since it is hard to be deceived in the distinction of *Negro*'s sculls.[88] *Dantes* Characters[89] are to be found in sculls as well as faces. *Hercules* is not onely known by his foot. Other parts make out their comproportions, and inferences upon whole or parts. And since the dimensions of the head measure the whole body, and the figure

83. Joining together.

84. '*Arefactio*, to make drie' (Elyot).

85. 'In his Map of *Russia*' (Browne marg.), which shows in the east a group of natives turned to stone (*G2*). On Lot's wife see Genesis 19.26.

86. i.e. appendages.

87. 'That part in the Skeleton of an Horse, which is made by the hanch-bones' (Browne suppl.).

88. 'For their extraordinary thickness' (Browne suppl.).

89. 'The Poet Dante in his view of Purgatory [XXIII, 31–3], found gluttons so meagre, and extenuated, that he conceited them to have been in the Siege of Jerusalem, and that it was easie to have discovered *Homo* or *Omo* in their faces: M being made by the two lines of their cheeks, arching over the Eyebrows to the nose, and their sunk eyes making O O which makes up *Omo*.

> *Parean l'occhiaie anella senza gemme:*
> *Che nel viso degli huomini legge huomo,*
> *Ben'havria quivi conosciuto l'emme.'* (Browne marg.)

thereof gives conjecture of the principall faculties; Physiog-
nomy outlives our selves, and ends not in our graves.

Severe contemplators observing these lasting reliques, may
think them good monuments of persons past, little advantage to
future beings. And considering that power which subdueth all
things unto it self, that can resume the scattered Atomes, or
identifie[90] out of any thing, conceive it superfluous to expect a
resurrection out of Reliques. But the soul subsisting, other
matter clothed with due accidents, may salve the individuality:
Yet the Saints we observe arose from graves and monuments,
about the holy City.[91] Some think the ancient Patriarchs so
earnestly desired to lay their bones in *Canaan*,[92] as hoping to
make a part of that Resurrection, and though thirty miles from
Mount *Calvary*, at least to lie in that Region, which should pro-
duce the first-fruits of the dead. And if according to learned con-
jecture, the bodies of men shall rise where their greatest Reliques
remain, many are not like to erre in the Topography of their
Resurrection, though their bones or bodies be after translated
by Angels into the field of *Ezechiels* vision, or as some will order
it, into the Valley of Judgement, or *Jehosaphat*.[93]

CHAPTER IV

Christians have handsomely glossed the deformity of death, by
careful consideration of the body, and civil rites which take of
brutall terminations. And though they conceived all reparable
by a resurrection, cast not off all care of enterrment. And since
the ashes of Sacrifices burnt upon the Altar of God, were care-
fully carried out by the Priests, and deposed in a clean field;[1]
since they acknowledged their bodies to be the lodging of
Christ, and temples of the holy Ghost,[2] they devolved not all
upon the sufficiency of soul existence; and therefore with long

90. i.e. assert identities.
91. Cf. Matthew 27.52–3.
92. Genesis 49.29.
93. So Tirinus in annotating Ezekiel 31.1 ff. (Browne marg.).
1. Leviticus 4.12.
2. 1 Corinthians 6.19.

services and full solemnities concluded their last Exequies, wherein to all distinctions the Greek devotion seems most pathetically ceremonious.[3]

Christian invention hath chiefly driven at Rites, which speak hopes of another life, and hints of a Resurrection. And if the ancient Gentiles held not the immortality of their better part, and some subsistence after death; in severall rites, customes, actions and expressions, they contradicted their own opinions: wherein *Democritus* went high, even to the thought of a resurrection, as scoffingly recorded by *Pliny*.[4] What can be more expresse than the expression of *Phocyllides*?[5] Or who would expect from *Lucretius* a sentence of *Ecclesiastes*?[6] Before *Plato* could speak, the soul had wings in *Homer*, which fell not, but flew out of the body into the mansions of the dead; who also observed that handsome distinction of *Demas* and *Soma*, for the body conjoyned to the soul and body separated from it.[7] *Lucian* spoke much truth in jest, when he said, that part of *Hercules* which proceeded from *Alchmena* perished, that from *Jupiter* remained immortall.[8] Thus *Socrates* was content that his friends should bury his body, so they would not think they buried *Socrates*, and regarding only his immortall part, was indifferent to be burnt or buried.[9] From such Considerations *Diogenes* might contemn Sepulture. And being satisfied that the soul could not perish, grow carelesse of corporall enterrment.

3. i.e. the Eastern Orthodox ritual of burial appears especially to move the emotions.

4. 'Just like the promise that he shall come to life again, which was made by Democritus; who, however, never has come to life again himself. Out upon it! What downright madness it is, to suppose that life is to recommence after death!' (Browne marg., quoting the Latin of Pliny, VII, lv, 189).

5. 'We hope that perhaps the remains of the departed may return from the earth into the light' (Browne marg., quoted in Greek: R).

6. 'That which once came from earth, to earth returns' (Browne marg., quoting the Latin of Lucretius, II, 999–1000). Cf. Ecclesiastes 12.7: 'Then shall the dust return to the earth which was before the earth'.

7. *Odyssey*, XI, 222. 'Demas' and 'soma' are the living and the dead body, respectively.

8. Lucian, *Hermotimus*, VII.

9. Plato, *Phaedo*, 115e (Browne marg.).

The *Stoicks* who thought the souls of wise men had their habitation about the *moon*, might make slight account of subterraneous deposition; whereas the *Pythagorians* and transcorporating Philosophers,[10] who were to be often buried, held great care of their enterrment. And the Platonicks rejected not a due care of the grave, though they put their ashes to unreasonable expectations, in their tedious term of return and long set revolution.[11]

Men have lost their reason in nothing so much as their religion, wherein stones and clouts make Martyrs; and since the religion of one seems madnesse unto another, to afford an account or rationall of old Rites, requires no rigid Reader; That they kindled the pyre aversly, or turning their face from it, was an handsome Symbole of unwilling ministration; That they washed their bones with wine and milk, that the mother wrapt them in Linnen, and dryed them in her bosome, the first fostering part, and place of their nourishment; That they opened their eyes towards heaven, before they kindled the fire, as the place of their hopes or originall, were no improper Ceremonies. Their last valediction thrice uttered by the attendants[12] was also very solemn, and somewhat answered by Christians, who thought it too little, if they threw not the earth thrice upon the enterred body. That in strewing their Tombs the *Romans* affected the Rose, the Greeks *Amaranthus* and myrtle; that the Funerall pyre consisted of sweet fuell, Cypresse, Firre, Larix,[13] Yewe, and Trees perpetually verdant, lay silent expressions of their surviving hopes: Wherein Christians which deck their Coffins with Bays have found a more elegant Embleme. For that tree seeming dead, will restore it self from the root, and its dry and exuccous[14] leaves resume their verdure again; which if we mistake not, we have also observed in furze. Whether the planting of yewe in Churchyards, hold not its originall from ancient

10. i.e. philosophers who upheld the transmigration of souls.

11. Cf. the Platonic year (above, p. 66, note 29).

12. 'Farewell, farewell, farewell. We shall follow you in the order in which nature permits' (Browne marg., in Latin).

13. i.e. larch.

14. i.e. exsuccous: sapless. See the passage quoted on p. 39.

Funerall rites, or as an Embleme of Resurrection from its
perpetual verdure, may also admit conjecture.

They made use of Musick to excite or quiet the affections of
their friends, according to different harmonies. But the secret
and symbolicall hint was the harmonical nature of the soul;
which delivered from the body, went again to enjoy the primi-
tive harmony of heaven, from whence it first descended; which
according to its progresse traced by antiquity, came down by
Cancer, and ascended by *Capricornus*.[15]

They burnt not children before their teeth appeared, as
apprehending their bodies too tender a morsell for fire, and
that their gristly bones would scarce leave separable reliques
after the pyrall combustion. That they kindled not fire in their
houses for some dayes after, was a strict memoriall of the late
afflicting fire. And mourning without hope, they had an happy
fraud against excessive lamentation, by a common opinion that
deep sorrows disturbed their ghosts.[16]

That they buried their dead on their backs, or in a supine
position, seems agreeable unto profound sleep, and common
posture of dying; contrary to the most naturall way of birth;
Nor unlike[17] our pendulous posture, in the doubtfull state of
the womb. *Diogenes* was singular, who preferred a prone situa-
tion in the grave, and some Christians[18] like neither, who
decline the figure of rest, and make choice of an erect posture.

That they carried them out of the world with their feet
forward, not inconsonant unto reason: As contrary unto the
native posture of man, and his production first into it. And also
agreeable unto their opinions, while they bid adieu unto the
world, not to look again upon it; whereas *Mahometans* who
think to return to a delightfull life again, are carried forth with
their heads forward, and looking toward their houses.

They closed their eyes as parts which first die or first discover

15. The exit and entrance of heaven, according to Macrobius, *On 'The
Dream of Scipio'*, I, 12 (M).
16. 'Hurt not my spirit' (Browne marg.. quoting the Latin of Tibullus,
I, i, 67).
17. 'And unlike' (the reading of E)? 'Nor like' (K)?
18. 'Russians, &c.' (Browne marg.).

the sad effects of death. But their iterated clamations[19] to excitate their dying or dead friends, or revoke them unto life again, was a vanity of affection; as not presumably ignorant of the criticall tests of death, by apposition of feathers, glasses, and reflexion of figures, which dead eyes represent not; which however not strictly verifiable in fresh and warm *cadavers*, could hardly elude the test, in corps of four or five dayes.[20]

That they suck'd in the last breath of their expiring friends, was surely a practice of no medicall institution, but a loose opinion that the soul passed out that way, and a fondnesse of affection from some *Pythagoricall* foundation, that the spirit of one body passed into another;[21] which they wished might be their own.

That they powred oyle upon the pyre, was a tolerable practise, while the intention rested in facilitating the accension;[22] But to place good *Omens* in the quick and speedy burning, to sacrifice unto the windes for a dispatch in this office, was a low form of superstition.

The *Archimime* or *Jester* attending the Funerall train, and imitating the speeches, gesture, and manners of the deceased, was too light for such solemnities, contradicting their Funerall Orations, and dolefull rites of the grave.

That they buried a peece of money with them as a Fee of the *Elysian Ferriman*,[23] was a practise full of folly. But the ancient custome of placing coynes in considerable Urnes, and the present practise of burying medals in the Noble Foundations of *Europe*, are laudable wayes of historicall discoveries, in actions, persons, Chronologies; and posterity will applaud them.

We examine not the old Laws of Sepulture, exempting certain persons from buriall or burning. But hereby we apprehend that these were not the bones of persons Planet-struck[24] or burnt with fire from Heaven: No Reliques of Traitors to their

19. i.e. reiterated calls.
20. 'At least by some difference from living Eyes' (Browne suppl.).
21. As reported by Perucci (Browne marg.).
22. Kindling.
23. i.e. Charon, who ferried the dead across the river Styx to Hades for the price of an obol.
24. i.e. said to have been killed by a malign planet's influence.

Countrey, Self-killers, or Sacrilegious Malefactors; Persons in old apprehension unworthy of the *earth*; condemned unto the *Tartara's*[25] of Hell, and bottomlesse pit of *Pluto*, from whence there was no redemption.

Nor were only many customes questionable in order to their Obsequies, but also sundry practises, fictions, and conceptions, discordant or obscure, of their state and future beings; whether unto eight or ten bodies of men to adde one of a woman, as being more inflammable, and unctuously constituted for the better pyrall combustion, were any rationall practise: Or whether the complaint of *Perianders* Wife[26] be tolerable, that wanting her Funerall burning she suffered intolerable cold in Hell, according to the constitution of the infernall house of *Pluto*, wherein cold makes a great part of their tortures; it cannot passe without some question.

Why the Female Ghosts appear unto *Ulysses*,[27] before the *Heroes* and masculine spirits? Why the *Psyche* or soul of *Tiresias* is of the masculine gender;[28] who being blinde on earth sees more then all the rest in hell; Why the Funerall Suppers consisted of Egges, Beans, Smallage, and Lettuce, since the dead are made to eat *Asphodels*[29] about the *Elyzian* medows? Why since there is no Sacrifice acceptable, nor any propitiation for the Covenant of the grave; men set up the Deity of *Morta*,[30] and fruitlesly adored Divinities without ears? it cannot escape some doubt.

The dead seem all alive in the humane *Hades* of *Homer*, yet cannot well speak, prophesie, or know the living, except they drink bloud, wherein is the life of man. And therefore the souls of *Penelope*'s Paramours conducted by *Mercury* chirped like bats

25. i.e. the lowest of low regions (the double plural of Tartarus). 'Pluto' in the next line, and in the next paragraph, corrects the erroneous 'Plato' of the 1st edition.

26. Melissa, in Herodotus, V, 92.

27. *Odyssey*, XI, 225 ff.

28. As Homer's grammar suggests in *Odyssey*, XI, 90 (Browne suppl., quoting the Greek).

29. 'In Lucian' (Browne marg.).

30. See below, p. 397, note 34.

and those which followed *Hercules* made a noise but like a flock of birds.[31]

The departed spirits know things past and to come, yet are ignorant of things present. *Agamemnon* foretels what should happen unto *Ulysses*, yet ignorantly enquires what is become of his own Son. The Ghosts are afraid of swords in *Homer*, yet *Sybilla* tels *Æneas* in *Virgil*, the thin habit of spirits was beyond the force of weapons. The spirits put off their malice with their bodies, and *Cæsar* and *Pompey* accord in Latine Hell, yet *Ajax* in *Homer* endures not a conference with *Ulysses*: And *Deiphobus* appears all mangled in *Virgils* Ghosts, yet we meet with perfect shadows among the wounded ghosts of *Homer*.[32]

Since *Charon* in *Lucian* applauds his condition among the dead, whether it be handsomely said of *Achilles*, that living contemner of death, that he had rather be a Plowmans servant then Emperour of the dead?[33] How *Hercules* his soul is in hell, and yet in heaven, and *Julius* his soul in a Starre, yet seen by *Æneas* in hell, except the Ghosts were but Images and shadows of the soul, received in higher mansions, according to the ancient division of body, soul, and image or *simulachrum* of them both.[34] The particulars of future beings must needs be dark unto ancient Theories, which Christian Philosophy yet determines but in a Cloud of opinions. A Dialogue between two Infants in the womb concerning the state of this world, might handsomely illustrate our ignorance of the next, whereof methinks we yet discourse in *Platoes* denne,[35] and are but *Embryon* Philosophers.

Pythagoras escapes in the fabulous hell of *Dante*, among that swarm of Philosophers, wherein whilest we meet with *Plato* and

31. The paragraph draws on Homer (*Odyssey*, XI, 141 ff., and XXIV, 6–9), and Leviticus 17.11 and 14.

32. The paragraph draws on Homer (*Odyssey*, XI, 48–50, 443–61, and 543–64), Virgil (*Aeneid*, VI, 494–7), and Dante (*Inferno*, X, 97–108).

33. Cf. Lucian's dialogue *Charon*; and *Odyssey*, XI, 485–91.

34. *Odyssey*, XI, 601–4; Horace, *Odes*, I, xii, 46–8; and *Aeneid*, VI, 826 ff.

35. The Cave in *The Republic*, VII, 514 ff.

Socrates, *Cato* is to be found in no lower place then Purgatory.[36] Among all the set, *Epicurus* is most considerable, whom men make honest without an *Elyzium*, who contemned life without encouragement of immortality, and making nothing after death, yet made nothing of the King of terrours.[37]

Were the happinesse of the next world as closely apprehended as the felicities of this, it were a martyrdome to live; and unto such as consider none hereafter, it must be more then death to dye, which makes us amazed at those audacities, that durst be nothing, and return into their *Chaos* again. Certainly such spirits as could contemn death, when they expected no better being after, would have scorned to live had they known any. And therefore we applaud not the judgment of *Machiavel*,[38] that Christianity makes men cowards, or that with the confidence of but half dying, the despised virtues of patience and humility, have abased the spirits of men, which Pagan principles exalted, but rather regulated the wildenesse of audacities, in the attempts, grounds, and eternall sequels of death; wherein men of the boldest spirits are often prodigiously temerarious. Nor can we extenuate the valour of ancient Martyrs, who contemned death in the uncomfortable scene of their lives, and in their decrepit Martyrdomes did probably lose not many moneths of their dayes, or parted with life when it was scarce worth the living. For (beside that long time past holds no consideration unto a slender time to come) they had no small disadvantage from the constitution of old age, which naturally makes men fearfull; And complexionally superannuated[39] from the bold and couragious thoughts of youth and fervent years. But the contempt of death from corporall animosity,[40] promoteth not our felicity. They may sit in the *Orchestra*, and noblest Seats of Heaven, who have held up shaking hands in the fire, and humanely contended for glory.[41]

36. *Inferno*, IV (Browne marg.), where Pythagoras is not in fact mentioned, and *Purgatorio*, I, 31 ff. But 'escapes' may mean 'escapes notice' or 'escapes condemnation' (*G2*).

37. On Epicurus see also above, p. 258.   38. In *Discourses*, II, 2.

39. i.e. temperamentally outgrown.

40. High spirits, courage, bravery (*OED*; §176).

41. Cf. below, p. 405.

Mean while *Epicurus* lyes deep in *Dante*'s hell,[42] wherein we meet with Tombs enclosing souls which denied their immortalities. But whether the virtuous heathen, who lived better then he spake, or erring in the principles of himself, yet lived above Philosophers of more specious Maximes, lye so deep as he is placed; at least so low as not to rise against Christians, who beleeving or knowing that truth, have lastingly denied it in their practise and conversation, were a quæry too sad to insist on.

But all or most apprehensions rested in Opinions of some future being, which ignorantly or coldly beleeved, begat those perverted conceptions, Ceremonies, Sayings, which Christians pity or laugh at. Happy are they, which live not in that disadvantage of time, when men could say little for futurity, but from reason. Whereby the noblest mindes fell often upon doubtfull deaths, and melancholly Dissolutions; With these hopes *Socrates* warmed his doubtfull spirits, against that cold potion, and *Cato* before he durst give the fatall stroak spent part of the night in reading the immortality of *Plato*,[43] thereby confirming his wavering hand unto the animosity of that attempt.

It is the heaviest stone that melancholy can throw at a man, to tell him he is at the end of his nature; or that there is no further state to come, unto which this seemes progressionall, and otherwise made in vaine; Without this accomplishment the naturall expectation and desire of such a state, were but a fallacy in nature, unsatisfied Considerators would quarrell the justice of their constitutions, and rest content that *Adam* had fallen lower, whereby by knowing no other Originall, and deeper ignorance of themselves, they might have enjoyed the happinesse of inferiour Creatures; who in tranquility possesse their Constitutions, as having not the apprehension to deplore their own natures. And being framed below the circumference of these hopes, or cognition of better being, the wisedom of God hath necessitated their Contentment: But the superiour ingredient and obscured part of our selves,[44] whereto all present felicities afford no resting contentment, will be able at last to

42. *Inferno*, X, 13–15.
43. i.e. the *Phaedo*. So Plutarch in *Cato Minor*, LXVIII, 2, and LXX, 1.
44. i.e. the soul.

tell us we are more then our present selves; and evacuate such hopes in the fruition of their own accomplishments.

CHAPTER V

Now since these dead bones have already out-lasted the living ones of *Methuselah*, and in a yard under ground, and thin walls of clay, out-worn all the strong and specious buildings above it; and quietly rested under the drums and tramplings of three conquests;[1] What Prince can promise such diuturnity[2] unto his Reliques, or might not gladly say,

Sic ego componi versus in ossa velim.[3]

Time which antiquates Antiquities, and hath an art to make dust of all things, hath yet spared these *minor* Monuments. In vain we hope to be known by open and visible conservatories,[4] when to be unknown was the means of their continuation and obscurity their protection: If they dyed by violent hands, and were thrust into their Urnes, these bones become considerable, and some old Philosophers would honour them,[5] whose souls they conceived most pure, which were thus snatched from their bodies; and to retain a stranger propension[6] unto them: whereas they weariedly left a languishing corps, and with faint desires of re-union. If they fell by long and aged decay, yet wrapt up in the bundle of time, they fall into indistinction,[7] and make but one blot with Infants. If we begin to die when we live, and long life be but a prolongation of death; our life is a sad composition; We live with death, and die not in a moment.

1. i.e. the Anglo-Saxon, the Danish, and the Norman (always assuming the urns to have been Roman). On this paragraph cf. De Quincey's 'annotation', above, p. 38.

2. 'Long continuance' (Bullokar).

3. 'Thus, when naught is left of me but bones, would I be laid to rest' (Tibullus, III, ii, 26).

4. As above, p. 287, note 21.

5. So the *Oracula magica* with the scholia by Psellus and Gemistus Plethon (Browne marg.).

6. 'proneness, propensity' (Blount).

7. i.e. undistinguishableness.

How many pulses made up the life of *Methuselah*, were work for *Archimedes*: Common Counters summe up the life of *Moses* his man.[8] Our dayes become considerable like petty sums by minute accumulations; where numerous fractions make up but small round numbers; and our dayes of a span long make not one little finger.[9]

If the nearnesse of our last necessity, brought a nearer conformity unto it, there were a happinesse in hoary hairs, and no calamity in half senses. But the long habit of living indisposeth us for dying; When Avarice makes us the sport of death; When even *David* grew politickly cruell; and *Solomon* could hardly be said to be the wisest of men.[10] But many are too early old, and before the date of age. Adversity stretcheth our dayes, misery makes *Alcmenas* nights,[11] and time hath no wings unto it. But the most tedious being is that which can unwish it self, content to be nothing, or never to have been, which was beyond the *male*-content of *Job*, who cursed not the day of his life, but his Nativity: Content to have so farre been, as to have a Title to future being; Although he had lived here but in an hidden state of life, and as it were an abortion.[12]

What Song the *Syrens* sang, or what name *Achilles* assumed when he hid himself among women, though puzling Questions[13] are not beyond all conjecture. What time the persons of these Ossuaries entred the famous Nations of the dead,[14] and slept with Princes and Counsellours,[15] might admit a wide solution. But who were the proprietaries of these bones, or

8. 'In the Psalme of *Moses*' (Browne marg.): i.e. Psalm 90.10. The reference to Archimedes involves his directions in *The Sand Reckoner* for numbering the grains of sand in the universe.

9. 'According to the ancient Arithmetick of the hand wherein the little finger of the right hand contracted, signified an hundred. Pierius in *Hieroglyph*.' (Browne marg.).

10. 2 Samuel 8.2 and 1 Kings 11.1 ff.

11. 'One night as long as three' (Browne marg.) so that Zeus could enjoy her the more.

12. Job 3.1 ff.

13. 'The puzling questions of Tiberius unto Grammarians' as reported by Suetonius, *Tiberius*, LXX (Browne add.). See also below, p. 438, note 22.

14. *Odyssey*, X, 526 (Browne add.).

15. Job 3.13–15 (Browne add.).

what bodies these ashes made up, were a question above Antiquarism. Not to be resolved by man, nor easily perhaps by spirits, except we consult the Provinciall Guardians, or tutellary Observators.[16] Had they made as good provision for their names, as they have done for their Reliques, they had not so grosly erred in the art of perpetuation. But to subsist in bones, and be but Pyramidally extant, is a fallacy in duration. Vain ashes, which in the oblivion of names, persons, times, and sexes, have found unto themselves, a fruitlesse continuation, and only arise unto late posterity, as Emblemes of mortall vanities; Antidotes against pride, vain-glory, and madding vices. Pagan vain-glories which thought the world might last for ever, had encouragement for ambition, and finding no *Atropos* unto the immortality of their Names, were never dampt with the necessity of oblivion. Even old ambitions had the advantage of ours, in the attempts of their vain-glories, who acting early, and before the probable Meridian of time,[17] have by this time found great accomplishment of their designes, whereby the ancient *Heroes* have already out-lasted their Monuments, and Mechanicall preservations. But in this latter Scene of time we cannot expect such Mummies unto our memories, when ambition may fear the Prophecy of *Elias*,[18] and *Charles* the fifth can never hope to live within two *Methusela's* of *Hector*.[19]

And therefore restlesse inquietude for the diuturnity of our memories unto present considerations, seems a vanity almost out of date, and superanuated peece of folly. We cannot hope to live so long in our names, as some have done in their persons,

16. Cf. above, p. 101: 'not onely whole Countries, but particular persons have their Tutellary, and Guardian Angels'.

17. About 1000 B.C., the mid-point of the world's history (see next note).

18. 'That the world may last but six thousand years' (Browne marg.) – i.e. from 4000 B.C. to A.D. 2000. See also below, p. 439, note 31.

19. 'Hectors fame lasting above two lives of *Methuselah* [2 × 969 or 1938 years], before that famous Prince was extant' (Browne marg.); so the fame of Charles V (b. 1500) can only extend some 500 years before the expected end of the world.

one face of *Janus* holds no proportion unto the other. 'Tis too late to be ambitious. The great mutations of the world are acted, or time may be too short for our designes. To extend our memories by Monuments, whose death we dayly pray for,[20] and whose duration we cannot hope, without injury to our expectations, in the advent of the last day, were a contradiction to our beliefs. We whose generations are ordained in this setting part of time, are providentially taken off from such imaginations. And being necessitated to eye the remaining particle of futurity, are naturally constituted unto thoughts of the next world, and cannot excusably decline the consideration of that duration, which maketh Pyramids pillars of snow, and all that's past a moment.

Circles and right lines limit and close all bodies, and the mortall right-lined circle,[21] must conclude and shut up all. There is no antidote against the *Opium* of time, which temporally considereth all things; Our Fathers finde their graves in our short memories, and sadly tell us how we may be buried in our Survivors. Grave-stones tell truth scarce fourty years:[22] Generations passe while some trees stand, and old Families last not three Oaks. To be read by bare Inscriptions like many in *Gruter*,[23] to hope for Eternity by Ænigmaticall Epithetes, or first letters of our names, to be studied by Antiquaries, who we were, and have new Names given us like many of the Mummies,[24] are cold consolations unto the Students of perpetuity, even by everlasting Languages.

To be content that times to come should only know there was such a man, not caring whether they knew more of him, was a

20. i.e. in the Lord's prayer, 'Thy Kingdom come'.
21. 'θ The character of death' (Browne marg.). The Greek letter *theta* (θ) is the initial of *thanatos* or death: 'a theta described upon the judges' tessera or ballot was a mark for death or capital punishment' (*SJ*).
22. 'Old ones being taken up, and other bodies laid under them' (Browne marg.).
23. Gruterus's *Ancient Inscriptions* (Browne marg.).
24. 'Which men show in several Countries, giving them what Names they please; and unto some the Names of the old Ægyptian Kings out of Herodotus' (Browne suppl.).

frigid ambition in *Cardan*:[25] disparaging his horoscopal inclination and judgement of himself, who cares to subsist like *Hippocrates* Patients, or *Achilles* horses in *Homer*,[26] under naked nominations, without deserts and noble acts, which are the balsame of our memories, the *Entelechia*[27] and soul of our subsistences. To be namelesse in worthy deeds exceeds an infamous history. The *Canaanitish* woman lives more happily without a name, then *Herodias* with one.[28] And who had not rather have been the good theef, then *Pilate*?

But the iniquity of oblivion blindely scattereth her poppy, and deals with the memory of men without distinction to merit of perpetuity. Who can but pity the founder of the Pyramids? *Herostratus* lives that burnt the Temple of *Diana*, he is almost lost that built it;[29] Time hath spared the Epitaph of *Adrians* horse, confounded that of himself. In vain we compute our felicities by the advantage of our good names, since bad have equall durations; and *Thersites* is like to live as long as *Agamemnon*. Who knows whether the best of men be known? or whether there be not more remarkable persons forgot, then any that stand remembred in the known account of time? without the favour of the everlasting Register the first man had been as unknown as the last, and *Methuselahs* long life had been his only Chronicle.

Oblivion is not to be hired: The greater part must be content to be as though they had not been, to be found in the Register of God, not in the record of man. Twenty seven Names make up the first story,[30] and the recorded names ever since contain not one living Century. The number of the dead long exceedeth all that shall live. The night of time far surpasseth the day, and who

25. 'I want it to be known that I exist, I do not wish it to be known what [sort of person] I am' (Browne marg., quoting Cardan's Latin, itself an adaptation of a phrase in Seneca's *On Benefits*, VII, 19).

26. The patients are named as medical cases in several Hippocratic treatises. On Achilles's horses see *Iliad*, XVI, 149–52.

27. As above, p. 71, note 50.

28. The one offered water to Christ (Matthew 15.22 ff.), while the other demanded the head of John the Baptist (14.6 ff.).

29. Chersiphon (according to Pliny, XXXVI, 21).

30. 'Before the flood' (Browne suppl.).

knows when was the Æquinox?[31] Every houre addes unto that
current Arithmetique, which scarce stands one moment. And
since death must be the *Lucina* of life, and even Pagans[32] could
doubt whether thus to live, were to dye. Since our longest
Sunne sets at right descensions, and makes but winter arches,[33]
and therefore it cannot be long before we lie down in darknesse,
and have our light in ashes.[34] Since the brother of death[35] daily
haunts us with dying *memento*'s, and time that grows old it self,
bids us hope no long duration: Diuturnity is a dream and folly
of expectation.

Darknesse and light divide the course of time, and oblivion
snares with memory, a great part even of our living beings; we
slightly remember our felicities, and the smartest stroaks of
affliction leave but short smart upon us. Sense endureth no
extremities, and sorrows destroy us or themselves. To weep
into stones are fables. Afflictions induce callosities,[36] miseries
are slippery, or fall like snow upon us, which notwithstanding is
no unhappy stupidity. To be ignorant of evils to come, and
forgetfull of evils past, is a mercifull provision in nature, where-
by we digest the mixture of our few and evil dayes, and our
delivered senses not relapsing into cutting remembrances, our
sorrows are not kept raw by the edge of repetitions. A great part
of Antiquity contented their hopes of subsistency with a trans-
migration of their souls. A good way to continue their mem-
ories, while having the advantage of plurall successions, they
could not but act something remarkable in such variety of be-
ings, and enjoying the fame of their passed selves, make
accumulation of glory unto their last durations. Others rather
then be lost in the uncomfortable night of nothing, were

31. Referring to the widespread belief in nature's decay (see §53).

32. 'Euripides' (Browne marg.), in a fragment from a lost play quoted
by Plato, *Gorgias*, 492e.

33. i.e. our longest possible life is but as a winter's day (R).

34. 'According to the custome of the Jewes, who place a lighted
waxcandle in a pot of ashes by the corps' (Browne suppl.), as reported by
Leon of Modena.

35. i.e. sleep (cf. below, p. 475). In Greek mythology, death and sleep
are the children of Night.

36. i.e. callousness.

content to recede into the common being, and make one particle of the publick soul of all things, which was no more then to return into their unknown and divine Originall again. Ægyptian ingenuity was more unsatisfied, contriving[37] their bodies in sweet consistences, to attend the return of their souls. But all was vanity, feeding the winde,[38] and folly. The Ægyptian Mummies, which *Cambyses* or time hath spared, avarice now consumeth. Mummie[39] is become Merchandise, *Mizraim* cures wounds, and *Pharaoh* is sold for balsoms.

In vain do individuals hope for Immortality, or any patent from oblivion, in preservations below the Moon: Men have been deceived even in their flatteries above the Sun, and studied conceits to perpetuate their names in heaven. The various Cosmography of that part hath already varied the names of contrived constellations; *Nimrod* is lost in *Orion*, and *Osyris* in the Dogge-starre. While we look for incorruption in the heavens, we finde they are but like the Earth; Durable in their main bodies, alterable in their parts: whereof beside Comets and new Stars, perspectives begin to tell tales.[40] And the spots that wander about the Sun, with *Phaetons* favour, would make clear conviction.

There is nothing strictly immortall, but immortality; whatever hath no beginning may be confident of no end. All others have a dependent being, and within the reach of destruction, which is the peculiar of that necessary essence that cannot destroy it self; And the highest strain of omnipotency to be so powerfully constituted, as not to suffer even from the power of it self. But the sufficiency of Christian Immortality frustrates all earthly glory, and the quality of either state after death, makes a folly of posthumous memory. God who can only destroy our souls, and hath assured our resurrection, either of our bodies or names hath directly promised no duration. Wherein there is so

37. Changed to 'continuing' (*K*): a conjectural reading.

38. Ecclesiastes 1.14 (Browne marg.).

39. As a drug (*M*).

40. Telescopes ('perspectives') had in Browne's time confirmed what had been observed by the naked eye, that comets and novae intruded upon the very regions above the moon declared by Aristotle to have been 'incorruptible' (*On the Heavens*, II, 1). Cf. §69.

much of chance that the boldest Expectants have found un-
happy frustration; and to hold long subsistence, seems but a
scape in oblivion. But man is a Noble Animal, splendid in
ashes, and pompous in the grave, solemnizing Nativities and
Deaths with equall lustre, nor omitting Ceremonies of bravery,
in the infamy of his nature.

Life is a pure flame, and we live by an invisible Sun within us.
A small fire sufficeth for life, great flames seemed too little after
death, while men vainly affected precious pyres, and to burn
like *Sardanapalus*, but the wisedom of funerall Laws[41] found the
folly of prodigall blazes, and reduced undoing fires, unto the
rule of sober obsequies, wherein few could be so mean as not to
provide wood, pitch, a mourner, and an Urne.[42]

Five Languages secured not the Epitaph of *Gordianus*;[43] The
man of God lives longer without a Tomb then any by one,
invisibly interred by Angels, and adjudged to obscurity, though
not without some marks directing humane discovery. *Enoch*
and *Elias* without either tomb or buriall, in an anomalous state
of being, are the great Examples of perpetuity, in their long and
living memory, in strict account being still on this side death,
and having a late part yet to act upon this stage of earth.[44] If in
the decretory term of the world[45] we shall not all dye but be
changed, according to received translation; the last day will
make but few graves; at least quick Resurrections will anti-
cipate lasting Sepultures; Some Graves will be opened before
they be quite closed, and *Lazarus* be no wonder. When many
that feared to dye shall groane that they can dye but once, the
dismall state is the second and living death,[46] when life puts

41. Cicero, *On the Laws*, II, 23 (59).

42. According to the epitaph of Rufus and Veronica in Gruterus, 'From
their goods no more was found than was sufficient to pay for the pyre and
pitch for cremating their bodies, and for the hired female mourner and
the urn' (Browne marg., quoting the epitaph in Latin). On Gruterus see
above, p. 309, note 23.

43. 'In Greek, Latine, Hebrew, Ægyptian, Arabick, defaced by *Licinus*
the Emperor' (Browne suppl.).

44. Enoch and Elijah were sometimes identified with the 'two witnesses'
of Revelation 11.3 ff. who are yet to come.

45. i.e. the Last Judgement.

46. Revelation 20. 14 and 21. 8. See below, p. 445, note 48.

despair on the damned; when men shall wish the coverings of Mountaines, not of Monuments, and annihilation shall be courted.

While some have studied Monuments, others have studiously declined them: and some have been so vainly boisterous, that they durst not acknowledge their Graves; wherein *Alaricus* seems most subtle, who had a River turned to hide his bones at the bottome.[47] Even *Sylla* that thought himself safe in his Urne, could not prevent revenging tongues, and stones thrown at his Monument. Happy are they whom privacy makes innocent, who deal so with men in this world, that they are not afraid to meet them in the next, who when they dye, make no commotion among the dead, and are not toucht with that poeticall taunt of *Isaiah*.[48]

Pyramids, *Arches*, *Obelisks*, were but the irregularities of vain-glory, and wilde enormities of ancient magnanimity. But the most magnanimous resolution rests in the Christian Religion, which trampleth upon pride, and sets on the neck of ambition, humbly pursuing that infallible perpetuity, unto which all others must diminish their diameters, and be poorly seen in Angles of contingency.[49]

Pious spirits who passed their dayes in raptures of futurity, made little more of this world, then the world that was before it, while they lay obscure in the Chaos of pre-ordination, and night of their fore-beings. And if any have been so happy as truly to understand Christian annihilation, extasis, exolution, lique-faction, transformation, the kisse of the Spouse, gustation of God, and ingression into the divine shadow, they have already had an handsome anticipation of heaven; the glory of the world is surely over, and the earth in ashes unto them.[50]

To subsist in lasting Monuments, to live in their productions,

47. According to Jordandes (Browne marg.).
48. Isaiah 14.4–17 (Browne marg.).
49. '*Angulus contingentiæ*, the least of Angles' (Browne marg.).
50. The rhythm of the mystical phrases is distinctly Browne's, but the phrases themselves are commonplace. 'Exolution' intimates the soul's release; 'the Spouse' is the Church (in the light of the Song of Solomon); 'ingression into the divine shadow' suggests entry into the paradoxical state wherein *Lux est umbra Dei* (as above, p. 71); etc.

to exist in their names, and prædicament[51] of *Chymera*'s, was large satisfaction unto old expectations, and made one part of their *Elyzjums*. But all this is nothing in the Metaphysicks of true belief. To live indeed is to be again our selves, which being not only an hope but an evidence in noble beleevers; 'Tis all one to lye in St *Innocents* Church-yard,[52] as in the Sands of *Ægypt*: Ready to be any thing, in the extasie of being ever, and as content with six foot as the Moles of *Adrianus*.[53]

Lucan

Tabesne cadavera solvat
An rogus haud refert.[54]

51. 'A term in logic, meaning that which is predicated or asserted' (§176).

52. 'In Paris where bodies soon consume' (Browne marg.). John Evelyn noted on 1 April 1644: 'I tooke a turne in St Inocents Church-yard where the story of the devouring quality of the ground (consuming Bodys in 24 houres), the Vast Charnells of Bones, Tombs, Piramids and sepultures tooke up much of my time' (*Diary*, ed. E.S. de Beer [Oxford, 1955], II, 131).

53. 'A stately *Mausoleum* or sepulchral pyle built by *Adrianus* in *Rome*, where now standeth the Castle of St. *Angelo*' (Browne marg.).

54. 'It matters not whether the corpses are burnt on the pyre or decompose with time' (Lucan, *Civil War*, VII, 809–10).

The Garden of Cyrus

[*The Garden of Cyrus, or The Quincunciall, Lozenge, or Net-work Plantations of the Ancients, Artificially, Naturally, Mystically Considered*, was first published jointly with *Hydriotaphia* in 1658. See also the discussion above, pp. 40 ff.; and for further bibliographical details: below, p. 554.]

NICHOLAS BACON

OF GILLINGHAM ESQUIRE.[1]

Had I not observed that Purblinde men have discoursed well of sight, and some without issue, excellently of Generation;[2] I that was never master of any considerable garden, had not attempted this Subject. But the Earth is the Garden of Nature, and each fruitfull Countrey a Paradise. Dioscorides *made most of his Observations in his march about with* Antonius; *and* Theophrastus *raised his generalities chiefly from the field.*

Beside we write no Herball, nor can this Volume deceive you, who have handled the massiest thereof: who know that three Folio's are yet too little, and how New Herbals fly from America *upon us, from persevering Enquirers, and old in those singularities, we expect such Descriptions.[3] Wherein* England *is now so exact, that it yeelds not to other Countreys.[4]*

We pretend not to multiply vegetable divisions by Quincuncial and Reticulate[5] plants; or erect a new Phytology.[6] The Field of knowledge hath been so traced, it is hard to spring any thing new. Of old things we write something new, If truth may receive addition, or envy will have any thing new; since the Ancients knew the late Anatomicall discoveries, and Hippocrates *the Circulation.[7]*

You have been so long out of trite learning, that 'tis hard to finde a

1. Grandson of Sir Nicholas Bacon, the premier baronet who was half-brother to Sir Francis Bacon. In the 1st edition this dedication appears immediately after the one to Le Gros (above, pp. 263–5).
2. Two marginal notes here refer to Plempius, Cabeus, and Harvey.
3. The herbals 'from *America*' may allude to the work of Hernandes. Three marginal notes here also refer to Besler, Bauhin, and 'My worthy friend M. *Goodier* an ancient and learned botanist'.
4. 'As in *London* and divers parts, whereof we mention none, lest we seem to omit any' (Browne marg.).
5. i.e. five-leaved and net-like.
6. i.e. botany.
7. Harvey's discovery was sometimes said to have been anticipated by Hippocrates.

subject proper for you; and if you have met with a Sheet upon this, we have missed our intention. In this multiplicity of writing, bye and barren Themes are best fitted for invention; Subjects so often discoursed confine the Imagination, and fix our conceptions unto the notions of fore-writers. Beside, such Discourses allow excursions, and venially admit of collaterall truths, though at some distance from their principals. Wherein if we sometimes take wide liberty, we are not single, but erre by great example.[8]

He that will illustrate the excellency of this order, may easily fail upon so spruce a Subject, wherein we have not affrighted the common Reader with any other Diagramms, then of it self;[9] *and have industriously declined illustrations from rare and unknown plants.*

Your discerning judgement so well acquainted with that study, will expect herein no mathematicall truths, as well understanding how few generalities and U finita's[10] *there are in nature. How* Scaliger *hath found exceptions in most Universals of* Aristotle *and* Theophrastus. *How Botanicall Maximes must have fair allowance, and are intolerably currant,*[11] *if not intolerably over-ballanced by exceptions.*

You have wisely ordered your vegetable delights, beyond the reach of exception. The Turks who passt their dayes in Gardens here, will have Gardens also hereafter, and delighting in Flowers on earth, must have Lillies and Roses in Heaven. In Garden Delights 'tis not easie to hold a Mediocrity; that insinuating pleasure is seldome without some extremity. The Antients venially delighted in flourishing Gardens; Many were Florists that knew not the true use of a Flower; And in Plinies *dayes none had directly treated of that Subject. Some commendably affected Plantations of venemous Vegetables,*[12] *some confined their delights unto single plants, and* Cato *seemed to dote upon Cabbage; While the*

8. Two works by Hippocrates (Browne marg.) have digressions on sexual intercourse and tonsillitis, respectively.

9. See the diagram reproduced on p. 323 where the quotation from Quintilian (VIII, iii, 9) reads: 'What is more beautiful than the well-known quincunx which, in whatever direction you view it, presents straight lines?' Both diagram and quotation are borrowed from Curtius and della Porta (see below, p. 328, note 28).

10. 'Rules without exceptions' (Browne marg.) – i.e. the rule in Latin grammar that all final *u*'s are long (*M*).

11. i.e. valid.

12. e.g. Attalus (as below, p. 328, note 21).

*Ingenuous delight of Tulipists, stands saluted with hard language, even by
their own Professors.*[13]

*That in this Garden Discourse, we range into extraneous things, and
many parts of Art and Nature, we follow herein the example of old
and new Plantations, wherein noble spirits contented not themselves with
Trees, but by the attendance of Aviaries, Fish Ponds, and all variety of
Animals, they made their gardens the Epitome of the earth, and some
resemblance of the secular shows of old.*

*That we conjoyn these parts of different Subjects, or that this should
succeed the other; Your judgement will admit without impute of
incongruity; Since the delightfull World comes after death, and Paradise
succeeds the Grave.*[14] *Since the verdant state of things is the Symbole of
the Resurrection, and to flourish in the state of Glory, we must first be
sown in corruption.*[15] *Beside the antient practise of Noble Persons, to
conclude in Garden-Graves, and Urnes themselves of old, to be wrapt up
in flowers and garlands.*

Nullum sine venia placuisse eloquium,[16] *is more sensibly under-
stood by Writers, then by Readers; nor well apprehended by either, till
works have hanged out like* Apelles *his Pictures;*[17] *wherein even com-
mon eyes will finde something for emendation.*

*To wish all Readers of your abilities, were unreasonably to multiply
the number of Scholars beyond the temper of these times. But unto this
ill-judging age, we charitably desire a portion of your equity, judgement,
candour, and ingenuity; wherein you are so rich, as not to lose by
diffusion. And being a flourishing branch of that Noble Family,*[18] *unto
which we owe so much observance, you are not new set, but long rooted in*

13. Lauremberg and others, who speak of 'tulipomania' (Browne
marg.).

14. On this solitary hint of the relationship between *Hydriotaphia* and
The Garden of Cyrus, see above, p. 43.

15. 1 Corinthians 15.42.

16. 'Eloquence has never been accepted without a measure of con-
donement' (Browne marg., adapted from Seneca, *Moral Letters*, CXIV,
12).

17. Apelles used to hide behind his paintings to hear the remarks of
the public (Pliny, XXXV, xxxvi, 84–5).

18. 'Of the most worthy Sr. *Edmund Bacon*, prime Baronet, my true and
noble Friend' (Browne marg.). He was the son and heir of Sir Nicholas
(above, p. 319, note 1).

such perfection; whereof having had so lasting confirmation in your
worthy conversation, constant amity, and expression; and knowing you a
serious Student in the highest arcana's *of* Nature; *with much excuse we*
bring these low delights, and poor maniples[19] *to your Treasure.*

Norwich *May* 1.
[1658]

Your affectionate Friend
and Servant,
THOMAS BROWNE

19. Handfuls.

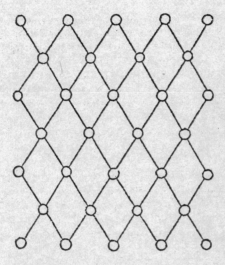

Quid Quincunce speciosius, qui, in quam cunqz partem spectaueris, rectus est: Quintilian:∥

[See p. 320, note 9]

THE GARDEN OF CYRUS

OR,

THE QUINCUNCIALL, LOZENGE, OR NET-WORK PLANTATIONS OF THE ANCIENTS, ARTIFICIALLY, NATURALLY, MYSTICALLY CONSIDERED

CHAPTER I[1]

That *Vulcan* gave arrows unto *Apollo* and *Diana* the fourth day after their Nativities, according to Gentile Theology, may passe for no blinde apprehension of the Creation of the Sunne and Moon, in the work of the fourth day; When the diffused light contracted into Orbes, and shooting rayes, of those Luminaries.[2] Plainer Descriptions there are from Pagan pens, of the creatures of the fourth day; While the divine Philosopher unhappily omitteth the noblest part of the third;[3] And *Ovid* (whom many conceive to have borrowed his description from *Moses*) coldly deserting the remarkable account of the text, in three words,[4] describeth this work of the third day; the vegetable creation, and first ornamentall Scene of nature; the primitive food of animals, and first story of Physick,[5] in Dietetical conservation.

For though Physick may pleade high, from that medicall act of God, in casting so deep a sleep upon our first Parent; And Chirurgery[6] finde its whole art, in that one passage concerning

1. The running title of Chapters I–III (to p. 364) is 'Cyrus-Garden, Or The Quincunx Naturally Considered'. Cf. below, p. 364, note 1.
2. Genesis 1.14 ff.
3. Genesis 1.12: 'And the earth brought forth grass, and herb yielding after his kind, and the tree yielding fruit'. The 'Philosopher' is 'Plato in *Timæo*' (Browne marg.).
4. '*fronde tegi silvas*' (Browne marg.). From Ovid, *Metamorphoses*, I, 44: 'He ordered the woods to be covered with leaves'.
5. i.e. medicine.
6. i.e. surgery: 'διαίρεσις [dissection], in opening the flesh. ἐξαίρεσις — [extraction], in taking out the rib. σύνθεσις [synthesis] in closing up the part again' (Browne marg.). Cf. Genesis 2.21–2.

the Rib of *Adam*, yet is there no rivality with[7] Garden contrivance and Herbery. For if Paradise were planted the third day of the Creation, as wiser Divinity concludeth, the Nativity thereof was too early for Horoscopie; Gardens were before Gardiners, and but some hours after the earth.[8]

Of deeper doubt is its Topography, and locall designation, yet being the primitive garden, and without much controversie seated in the East;[9] it is more then probable the first curiosity, and cultivation of plants, most flourished in those quarters. And since the Ark of *Noah* first toucht upon some mountains of *Armenia*,[10] the planting art arose again in the East, and found its revolution not far from the place of its Nativity, about the Plains of those Regions. And if *Zoroaster* were either *Cham*, *Chus*, or *Mizraim*, they were early proficients therein, who left (as *Pliny* delivereth) a work of Agriculture.[11]

However the account of the Pensill or hanging gardens of *Babylon*, if made by *Semiramis*, the third or fourth from *Nimrod*, is of no slender antiquity; which being not framed upon ordinary levell of ground, but raised upon pillars, admitting under-passages, we cannot accept as the first *Babylonian* Gardens; But a more eminent progress and advancement in that art, then any that went before it: Somewhat answering or hinting the old Opinion concerning Paradise it self, with many conceptions[12] elevated, above the plane of the Earth.

Nebuchodonosor whom some will have to be the famous *Syrian* King of *Diodorus*, beautifully repaired that City; and so magnificently built his hanging gardens; that from succeeding Writers he had the honour of the first.[13] From whence over-

7. i.e. rivalry with: opposition to.

8. i.e. while man was created on the sixth day, the earth – and gardens – were made on the third.

9. 'For some there is [doubt] from the ambiguity of the word *Mikedem* [the Hebrew of Genesis 8.2], whether *ab oriente* [from the East] or *a principio* [from the beginning]' (Browne marg.).

10. Ararat (Genesis 8.4).

11. The work is by Mago of Carthage (as reported by Pliny, XVIII, 3), here conflated with the 'magus' Zoroaster.

12. i.e. according to several theories.

13. Diodorus Siculus and other writers (e.g. Josephus) attribute the Hanging Gardens to a Syrian king who reigned subsequent to Semiramis.

looking *Babylon*, and all the Region about it, he found no cir-
cumscription to the eye of his ambition, till over-delighted with
the bravery of this Paradise; in his melancholy metamorphosis,[14]
he found the folly of that delight, and a proper punishment, in
the contrary habitation, in wilde plantations and wandrings of
the fields.

The *Persian* Gallants who destroyed this Monarchy, main-
tained their Botanicall bravery. Unto whom we owe the very
name of Paradise:[15] wherewith we meet not in Scripture before
the time of *Solomon*, and conceived originally *Persian*. The word
for that disputed Garden, expressing in the Hebrew no more
then a Field enclosed, which from the same Root is content to
derive a garden and a Buckler.

Cyrus the elder brought up in Woods and Mountains, when
time and power enabled, pursued the dictate of his education,
and brought the treasures of the field into rule and circum-
scription. So nobly beautifying the hanging Gardens of
Babylon, that he was also thought to be the authour thereof.

Ahasuerus (whom many conceive to have been *Artaxerxes
Longi-manus*) in the Countrey and City of Flowers,[16] and in an
open Garden, entertained his Princes and people, while *Vasthi*
more modestly treated the Ladies within the Palace thereof.

But if (as some opinion) King *Ahasuerus* were *Artaxerxes
Mnemon*, that found a life and reign answerable unto his great
memory, our magnified *Cyrus* was his second[17] Brother: who
gave the occasion of that memorable work, and almost miracu-
lous retrait of *Xenophon*.[18] A person of high spirit and honour,
naturally a King, though fatally prevented by the harmlesse
chance of *post*-geniture: Not only a Lord of Gardens, but a
manuall planter thereof: disposing his trees like his armies in
regular ordination.[19] So that while old *Laertas* hath found a

14. 'he was driven from men, and . . . his hairs were grown like eagles'
feathers, and his nails like birds' claws' (Daniel 4.33).

15. From the Old Persian *pairidaëza*, enclosure or park.

16. Shushan (Browne marg.), described in Esther 1.5 ff.

17. i.e. his next younger: 'Plutarch in the life of *Artaxerxes*' (Browne
marg.).

18. In his *Anabasis*.

19. Cf. Marvell, *Upon Appleton House*, stanzas 39 ff.

name in *Homer* for pruning hedges, and clearing away thorns and bryars;[20] while King *Attalus* lives for his poysonous plantations of *Aconites*, Henbane, Hellebore, and plants hardly admitted within the walls of Paradise;[21] While many of the Ancients do poorly live in the single names of Vegetables;[22] All stories do look upon *Cyrus*, as the splendid and regular planter.

According whereto *Xenophon* describeth his gallant plantation at *Sardis*, thus rendred by *Strebæus. Arbores pari intervallo sitas, rectos ordines, & omnia perpulchre in Quincuncem directa.*[23] Which we shall take for granted as being accordingly rendred by the most elegant of the *Latines*;[24] and by no made term, but in use before by *Varro*. That is the rows and orders so handsomly disposed; or five trees so set together, that a regular angularity, and through prospect, was left on every side, Owing this name not only unto the Quintuple number of Trees, but the figure declaring that number. Which being doubled at the angle, makes up the Letter *x*, that is the Emphaticall decussation,[25] or fundamentall figure.

Now though in some ancient and modern practice the *area* or decussated plot, might be a perfect square, answerable to a *Tuscan Pedestall*,[26] and the *Quinquernio* or Cinque-point of a dye; wherein by Diagonall lines the intersection was rectangular;[27] accomodable unto Plantations of large growing Trees; and we must not deny our selves the advantage of this order; yet shall we chiefly insist upon that of *Curtius* and *Porta*,[28] in their brief

20. *Odyssey*, XXIV, 223 ff.

21. Plutarch, *Demetrius*, XX, 2. Cf. below, p. 454, note 29.

22. Cf. Phalaris, etc.; also flowers like Iris and Hyacinth.

23. Xenophon, *Oeconomicus*, IV, 21, reports that Lysander on a visit to the palace at Sardis admired 'the beauty of the trees in it, the accuracy of the spacing, the straightness of the rows, the [quincuncial] regularity of the angles' (Browne marg., quoted in Greek).

24. Cicero, *On Old Age*, XVII (Browne marg.).

25. i.e. intersection: crossing to form the figure X. The quincunx (see above, p. 41, note 38) is 'doubled at the angle' in that two V's (in Roman numerals) constitute an X – itself the Greek letter *chi* (as in 'Jesus Christos').

26. The pillar base in the 'Tuscan' architectural order.

27. Corrected from 'regular'.

28. So Curtius and della Porta (Browne marg.), the principal sources throughout Chapter I (§300).

description hereof. Wherein the *decussis* is made within a longilaterall square,[29] with opposite angles, acute and obtuse at the intersection; and so upon progression making a *Rhombus* or Lozenge figuration, which seemeth very agreeable unto the Originall figure; Answerable whereunto we observe the decussated characters in many consulary Coynes, and even in those of *Constantine* and his Sons, which pretend their pattern in the Sky;[30] the crucigerous Ensigne carried this figure, not transversly or rectangularly intersected, but in a decussation, after the form of an *Andrean* or *Burgundian* cross,[31] which answereth this description.

Whereby the way we shall decline the old Theme, so traced by antiquity of crosses and crucifixion: Whereof some being right,[32] and of one single peece without traversion or transome,[33] do little advantage our subject. Nor shall we take in the mysticall *Tau*, or the Crosse of our blessed Saviour,[34] which having in some descriptions an *Empedon*[35] or crossing foot-stay, made not one single transversion. And since the Learned *Lipsius* hath made some doubt even of the Crosse of St *Andrew*, since some Martyrologicall Histories deliver his death by the generall Name of a crosse, and *Hippolitus* will have him suffer by the sword; we should have enough to make out the received Crosse of that Martyr. Nor shall we urge the *labarum*, and famous Standard of *Constantine*, or make further use thereof, then as the first Letters in the Name of our Saviour Christ,[36] in use among Christians, before the dayes of *Constantine*, to be observed in Sepulchral Monuments of Martyrs,[37] in the Reign of *Adrian*,

29. i.e. the X shape is made within a rectangle.

30. The allusion is to the 'crucigerous' or cross-bearing sign – the labarum – seen by Constantine the Great while marching against Rome (A.D. 312).

31. Also X-shaped.

32. i.e. upright.

33. Cross-piece.

34. The Greek letter 'T' was frequently regarded as symbolic of the Cross.

35. Footrest.

36. 'X' and 'P' (in Greek) often merged as in the *labarum* (above, note 30).

37. As those of Marius and Alexander (Browne marg.).

and *Antoninus*; and to be found in the Antiquities of the Gentiles, before the advent of Christ, as in the Medall of King *Ptolomy*, signed with the same characters, and might be the beginning of some word or name, which Antiquaries have not hit on.

We will not revive the mysterious crosses of *Ægypt*, with circles on their heads, in the breast of *Serapis*, and the hands of their Geniall spirits, not unlike the character of *Venus*,[38] and looked on by ancient Christians, with relation unto Christ. Since however they first began, the Ægyptians thereby expressed the processe and motion of the spirit of the world, and the diffusion thereof upon the Celestiall and Elementall nature; implyed by a circle and right-lined intersection. A secret in their Telesmes[39] and magicall Characters among them. Though he that considereth the plain crosse[40] upon the head of the Owl in the Laterane Obelisk, or the crosse erected upon a picher diffusing streams of water into two basins, with sprinkling branches in them, and all described upon a two-footed Altar, as in the Hieroglyphicks of the brazen Table of *Bembus*;[41] will hardly decline all thought of Christian signality in them.

We shall not call in the Hebrew *Tenupha*, or ceremony of their Oblations, waved by the Priest unto the four quarters of the world, after the form of a crosse;[42] as in the peace-offerings. And if it were clearly made out what is remarkably delivered from the Traditions of the Rabbins, that as the Oyle was powred coronally or circularlly upon the head of Kings, so the High-Priest was anointed decussatively or in the form of a X; though it could not escape a typicall thought[43] of Christ, from mysticall considerators; yet being the conceit is Hebrew, we should rather expect its verification from Analogy in that language, then to confine the same unto the unconcerned Letters of

38. i.e. the sign ♀. Cf. below, p. 379, note 75.

39. i.e. talismans.

40. 'Wherein the lower part is somewhat longer', as noted by Upton and Aureo (Browne marg.).

41. The altar is described by Casalius and Bosio (Browne marg.); the 'brazen Table' is Bembo's collection of hieroglyphs in bronze.

42. Ezekiel 48.10.

43. i.e. a thought involving 'types' or prefigurations. Cf. below, p. 333, note 61.

Greece, or make it out by the characters of *Cadmus* or *Palamedes*.

Of this Quincunciall Ordination the Ancients practised much discoursed little; and the Moderns have nothing enlarged; which he that more nearly considereth, in the form of its square *Rhombus*, and decussation, with the severall commodities, mysteries, parallelismes, and resemblances, both in Art and Nature, shall easily discern the elegancy of this order.

That this was in some wayes of practice in diverse and distant Nations, hints or deliveries there are from no slender Antiquity. In the hanging Gardens of *Babylon*, from *Abydenus*, *Eusebius*, and others, *Curtius* describeth this Rule of decussation.⁴⁴ In the memorable Garden of *Alcinous* anciently conceived an originall phancy, from Paradise, mention there is of well contrived order; For so hath *Didymus* and *Eustathius* expounded the emphatical word.⁴⁵ *Diomedes* describing the Rurall possessions of his father, gives account in the same Language of Trees orderly planted.⁴⁶ And *Ulysses* being a boy was promised by his Father fourty Figge-trees, and fifty rows of Vines producing all kinde of grapes.⁴⁷

That the Eastern Inhabitants of *India*, made use of such order, even in open Plantations, is deducible from *Theophrastus*; who describing the trees whereof they made their garments, plainly delivereth that they were planted κατ' ὄρχους,⁴⁸ and in such order that at a distance men would mistake them for Vineyards. The same seems confirmed in *Greece* from a singular expression in *Aristotle*⁴⁹ concerning the order of Vines, delivered by a military term representing the orders of Souldiers, which also confirmeth the antiquity of this form yet used in vineall plantations.

44. 'That decussation presented a pleasant and delightful appearance' (Browne marg., quoting the Latin of Curtius from a statement reported by Eusebius).

45. i.e. ὄρχατος, 'orchard', literally 'row of trees' (*Odyssey*, VII, 112).

46. *Iliad*, XIV, 123.

47. *Odyssey*, XXIV, 341; according to the explication by Favorinus and Philoxenus (Browne marg.).

48. 'In rows' (Theophrastus, *On Plants*, IV, iv, 8, and vii, 7–8).

49. 'συστάδας ἀμπέλων' (Browne marg., quoted from *Politics*, VII, x, 5): suggestive of the quincunx in the planting of vines.

That the same was used in Latine plantations is plainly confirmed from the commending penne of *Varro, Quintilian,* and handsome Description of *Virgil.*[50]

That the first Plantations not long after the Floud were disposed after this manner, the generality and antiquity of this order observed in Vineyards, and Wine plantations, affordeth some conjecture. And since from judicious enquiry, *Saturn* who divided the world between his three sonnes, who beareth a Sickle in his hand, who taught the plantations of Vines, the setting, grafting of trees, and the best part of Agriculture, is discovered to be *Noah,*[51] whether this early dispersed Husbandry in Vineyards, had not its Originall in that Patriarch, is no such Paralogicall[52] doubt.

And if it were clear that this was used by *Noah* after the Floud, I could easily beleeve it was in use before it; Not willing to fix [to] such ancient inventions no higher originall then *Noah*; Nor readily conceiving those aged *Heroes,* whose diet was vegetable, and only, or chiefly consisted in the fruits of the earth, were much deficient in their splendid cultivations; or after the experience of fifteen hundred years, left much for future discovery in Botanicall Agriculture. Nor fully perswaded that Wine was the invention of *Noah,* that fermented Liquors, which often make themselves, so long escaped their Luxury or experience; that the first sinne of the new world[53] was no sin of the old. That *Cain* and *Abel* were the first that offered Sacrifice; or because the Scripture is silent that *Adam* or *Isaac* offered none at all.

Whether *Abraham* brought up in the first planting Countrey, observed not some rule hereof, when he planted a grove at *Beer-sheba*; or whether at least a like ordination were not in the

50. 'Give your rows more elbow-room; but see that the alleys of trees are planted there in squares with equal precision' (Browne marg., quoted in Latin from Virgil's *Georgics,* II, 277–8). On Quintilian see above, p. 320, note 9.

51. The identification had been ventured by Bochart among others (*G2*).

52. 'unreasonable' (as Dr Johnson noted, below, p. 508).

53. Drunkenness (Genesis 9.21), the first offence recorded after the Flood (*G2*).

Garden of *Solomon*,[54] probability may contest. Answerably unto the wisedom of that eminent Botanologer,[55] and orderly disposer of all his other works. Especially since this was one peece of Gallantry, wherein he pursued the specious[56] part of felicity, according to his own description.[57] I made me Gardens and Orchards, and planted Trees in them of all kindes of fruit. I made me Pools of water, to water therewith the wood that bringeth forth Trees, which was no ordinary plantation, if according to the *Targam*, or *Chaldee Paraphrase*, it contained all kindes of Plants, and some fetched as far as *India*; And the extent thereof were from the wall of *Jerusalem* unto the water of *Siloah*.[58]

And if *Jordan* were but *Jaar Eden*, that is, the River of *Eden*, *Genesar* but *Gansar* or the Prince of Gardens; and it could be made out, that the Plain of *Jordan* were watered not comparatively, but causally, and because it was the Paradise of God, as the Learned *Abramas* hinteth, he was not far from the Prototype and originall of Plantations. And since even in Paradise it self, the tree of knowledge was placed in the middle of the Garden, whatever was the ambient[59] figure, there wanted not a centre and rule of decussation. Whether the groves and sacred Plantations of Antiquity, were not thus orderly placed, either by *quaternio's*,[60] or quintuple ordinations, may favourably be doubted. For since they were so methodicall in the constitutions of their temples, as to observe the due scituation, aspect, manner, form, and order in Architectonicall relations, whether they were not as distinct in their groves and Plantations about them, in form and *species*[61] respectively unto their Deities, is not without probability of conjecture. And in their groves of the Sunne this was a fit number, by multiplication to denote the

54. On Abraham's grove see Genesis 21.33; on Solomon's garden, the Song of Solomon.
55. i.e. botanist; here, God.
56. 'beautiful or graceful in appearance' (Blount).
57. In Ecclesiastes 2.5–6, quoted next.
58. Cf. Nehemiah 3.15.
59. 'environing, encompassing' (Blount).
60. i.e. patterns of four. Cf. 'square-orders' (below, p. 368).
61. 'figure or image' (Elyot).

dayes of the year; and might Hieroglyphically speak as much, as the mysticall *Statua* of *Janus*[62] in the Language of his fingers. And since they were so criticall in the number of his[63] horses, the strings of his Harp, and rayes about his head, denoting the orbes of heaven, the Seasons and Moneths of the Yeare; witty Idolatry would hardly be flat in other appropriations.

CHAPTER II

Not was this only a form of practise in Plantations, but found imitation from high Antiquity, in sundry artificiall contrivances and manuall operations. For to omit the position of squared stones, *cuneatim* or *wedgwise* in the Walls of *Roman* and *Gothick* buildings; and the *lithostrata* or figured pavements of the ancients, which consisted not all of square stones, but were divided into triquetrous[1] segments, honey-combs, and sexangular figures, according to *Vitruvius*;[2] The squared stones and bricks in ancient fabricks, were placed after this order. And two above or below conjoyned by a middle stone or *Plinthus*, observable in the ruines of *Forum Nervæ*, the *Mausoleum* of *Augustus*, the Pyramid of *Cestius*, and the sculpture draughts[3] of the larger Pyramids of Ægypt. And therefore in the draughts of eminent fabricks, Painters do commonly imitate this order in the lines of their description.

In the Laureat draughts[4] of sculpture and picture, the leaves and foliate works are commonly thus contrived, which is but in imitation of the *Pulvinaria*,[5] and ancient pillow-work, observable in *Ionick* peeces, about columns, temples and altars. To omit many other analogies, in Architectonicall draughts, which art it self is founded upon fives,[6] as having its subject, and most gracefull peeces divided by this number.

62. 'Which King *Numa* set up with his fingers so disposed that they numerically denoted 365' (Browne marg., referring to Pliny, XXXIV, 16).
  63. i.e. the sun's – and so Apollo's.
  1. Triangular.   2. In *Of Architecture*, VII, i, 3–4.
  3. Engraved drawings.   4. Laurel patterns.
  5. 'Couches used for the images of gods in Roman antiquity' (§219).
  6. A marginal note refers to the five parts of a building, the five types of column, and the five means of spacing columns.

The Triumphal Oval, and Civicall Crowns of Laurel, Oake, and Myrtle, when fully made, were pleated after this order. And to omit the crossed Crowns of Christian Princes; what figure that was which *Anastatius* described upon the head of *Leo* the third; or who first brought in the Arched Crown; That of Charles the great, (which seems the first remarkably closed Crown,) was framed after this manner;[7] with an intersection in the middle from the main crossing barres, and the interspaces, unto the frontal circle, continued[8] by handsome network-plates, much after this order. Whereon we shall not insist, because from greater Antiquity, and practice of consecration, we meet with the radiated, and starry Crown, upon the head of *Augustus*, and many succeeding Emperors. Since the Armenians and Parthians had a peculiar royall Capp; And the Grecians from *Alexander* another kinde of diadem. And even Diadems themselves were but fasciations,[9] and handsome ligatures, about the heads of Princes; nor wholly omitted in the mitrall Crown, which common picture seems to set too upright and forward upon the head of *Aaron*:[10] Worne sometimes singly, or doubly by Princes, according to their Kingdomes; and no more to be expected from two Crowns at once, upon the head of *Ptolemy*.[11] And so easily made out when historians tell us, some bound up wounds, some hanged themselves with diadems.

The beds of the antients were corded somewhat after this fashion: That is not directly, as ours at present, but obliquely, from side to side, and after the manner of network; whereby they strengthened the spondæ or bedsides, and spent less cord in the work: as is demonstrated by *Blancanus*.

And as they lay in crossed beds, so they sat upon seeming crosselegg'd seats: in which form the noblest thereof were framed: Observable in the triumphall seats, the *sella curulis*, or *Ædyle Chayres*, in the coyns of *Cestius*, *Sylla*, and *Julius*. That they

7. So Chifflet (Browne marg.; *M*).
8. Contained.
9. Bands (cf. above, p. 273, note 37).
10. i.e. the 'common picture' or illustration of Exodus 28 (in the Geneva Bible of 1560).
11. 1 Maccabees 11.13 (Browne marg.).

sat also crossed legg'd many noble draughts declare; and in this figure the sitting gods and goddesses are drawn in medalls and medallions.[12] And beside this kinde of work in Retiarie[13] and hanging textures, in embroderies, and eminent needle-works; the like is obvious unto every eye in glass-windows. Nor only in Glassie contrivances, but also in Lattice and Stone-work, conceived in the Temple of *Solomon*; wherein the windows are termed *fenestræ reticulatæ*,[14] or lights framed like nets. And agreeable unto the Greek expression concerning Christ in the Canticles, looking through the nets, which ours hath rendered, he looketh forth at the windows, shewing himselfe through the lattesse;[15] that is, partly seen and unseen, according to the visible and invisible side of his nature. To omit the noble reticulate work, in the chapiters of the pillars of *Solomon*, with Lillies, and Pomegranats upon a network ground; and the *Craticula* or grate through which the ashes fell in the altar of burnt offerings.[16]

That the networks and nets of antiquity were little different in the form from ours at present, is confirmable from the nets in the hands of the Retiarie gladiators, the proper combatants with the secutores.[17] To omit the ancient Conopeion[18] or gnatnet, of the Ægyptians, the inventors of that Artifice: the rushey labyrinths of *Theocritus*;[19] the nosegaynets, which hung from the head under the nostrils of Princes; and that uneasie metaphor of *Reticulum Jecoris*, which some expound the lobe, we the caule above the liver.[20] As for that famous network of *Vulcan*, which inclosed *Mars* and *Venus*, and caused that unextinguishable laugh in heaven;[21] since the gods themselves could not discern

12. 'The larger sort of Medals' (Browne suppl.).

13. Net-like.

14. Translated from the Septuagint version of Ezekiel 41.16: θυρίδες δικτυωταί (Browne marg.).

15. Song of Solomon ('Canticle of Canticles') 2.9, in *AV* (Browne marg.).

16. 1 Kings 7.17–20 and Exodus 27.4

17. i.e. the gladiators armed with swords (cf. below, p. 427, note 45).

18. i.e. mosquito-net.

19. Cf. the 'pots of woven rush' in his *Idylls*, XXI, 11.

20. Leviticus 3.4 (Browne suppl.).

21. *Odyssey*, VIII, 326 (Browne marg., quoting the Greek).

it, we shall not prie into it; Although why *Vulcan* bound them, *Neptune* loosed them, and *Apollo* should first discover them, might afford no vulgar mythologie. Heralds have not omitted this order or imitation thereof, whiles they Symbollically adorn their Scuchions with Mascles Fusils and Saltyrs,[22] and while they disposed the figures of Ermins, and vaired[23] coats in this Quincuncial method.

The same is not forgot by Lapidaries[24] while they cut their gemms pyramidally, or by æquicrural[25] triangles. Perspective pictures, in their Base, Horison, and lines of distances, cannot escape these Rhomboidall decussations. Sculptors[26] in their strongest shadows, after this order do draw their double Haches.[27] And the very *Americans* do naturally fall upon it, in their neat and curious textures, which is also observed in the elegant artifices of *Europe*. But this is no law unto the woof of the neat *Retiarie* Spider, which seems to weave without transversion,[28] and by the union of right lines to make out a continued surface, which is beyond the common art of Textury, and may still nettle *Minerva*[29] the Goddesse of that mystery. And he that shall hatch the little seeds, either found in small webs, or white round Egges, carried under the bellies of some Spiders, and behold how at their first production in boxes, they will presently fill the same with their webbs, may observe the early, and untaught finger of nature, and how they are natively provided with a stock, sufficient for such Texture.

The Rurall charm against *Dodder, Tetter,*[30] and strangling weeds, was contrived after this order, while they placed a chalked Tile at the four corners, and one in the middle of their

22. Heraldic lozenge-patterns.
23. i.e. vairy: in heraldry, the colours of the coats' fur.
24. '*Lapidarie*. One that selleth or polisheth precious stones: a Jeweller' (Bullokar).
25. Isosceles (below, p. 371, note 35).
26. Engravers.
27. Cross-shading (R).
28. Turning across or athwart.
29. 'As in the contention between *Minerva* and *Arachne* [i.e. Spider]' (Browne marg.). 'Textury' is weaving.
30. White bryony or tetterberry (R).

fields, which though ridiculous in the intention, was rationall in the contrivance, and a good way to diffuse the magick through all parts of the *Area*.

Somewhat after this manner they ordered the little stones in the old game of *Pentalithismus*, or casting up five stones to catch them on the back of their hand. And with some resemblance hereof, the *Proci* or Prodigall Paramours disposed their men, when they played at *Penelope*.[31] For being themselves an hundred and eight, they set fifty four stones on either side, and one in the middle, which they called *Penelope*, which he that hit was master of the game.

In Chesse-boards and Tables[32] we yet finde Pyramids and Squares, I wish we had their true and ancient description, farre different from ours, or the *Chet mat*[33] of the *Persians*, which might continue[34] some elegant remarkables, as being an invention as High as *Hermes* the Secretary of *Osyris*, figuring the whole world, the motion of the Planets, with Eclipses of Sunne and Moon.[35]

Physicians are not without the use of this decussation in severall operations, in ligatures and union of dissolved continuities. Mechanicks make use hereof in forcipall[36] Organs, and Instruments of Incision; wherein who can but magnifie the power of decussation, inservient[37] to contrary ends, solution and consolidation, union, and division, illustrable from *Aristotle* in the old *Nucifragium* or Nutcracker, and the Instruments of Evulsion,[38] compression or incision; which consisting of two *Vectes* or armes, converted towards each other, the innitency[39] and stresse being made upon the *hypomachlion* or

31. Eustathius commenting on *Odyssey*, I, 401 (Browne marg.).
32. Backgammon.
33. 'Chec-mate' in some copies (*G2*).
34. Contain (as above, p. 335, note 8).
35. Cf. Plato, *Phaedrus*, 274e–d (Browne marg.). 'High', as so often in Browne, means 'ancient'. On Hermes Trismegistus see above, p. 79, note 97.
36. Forceps-like.
37. Subservient (§ 176).
38. 'plucking up' (Blount).
39. Pressure.

fulciment[40] in the decussation and greater compression is made by the union of two impulsors.[41]

The *Roman Batalia*[42] was ordered after this manner, whereof as sufficiently known *Virgil* hath left but an hint, and obscure intimation.[43] For thus were the maniples and cohorts of the *Hastati*, *Principes* and *Triarii*[44] placed in their bodies, wherein consisted the strength of the *Roman* battle. By this Ordination they readily fell into each other; the *Hastati* being pressed, handsomely retired into the intervalls of the *principes*, these into

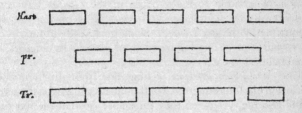

that of the *Triarii*, which making as it were a new body, might joyntly renew the battle, wherein consisted the secret of their successes. And therefore it was remarkably singular in the battle of *Africa*,[45] that *Scipio* fearing a rout from the Elephants of the Enemy, left not the *Principes* in their alternate distances, whereby the Elephants passing the vacuities of the *Hastati*, might have run upon them, but drew his battle into right order, and leaving the passages bare, defeated the mischief intended by the Elephants. Out of this figure were made too remarkable

40. Fulcrum (§176).

41. Impelling forces.

42. 'In the disposure of the Legions in the Wars of the Republike, before the division of the Legion into ten Cohorts by the Emperours' (Browne marg.). So Salmasius.

43. In *Georgics*, II, 279–81: 'in war . . . a legion deploys by companies from column of route into line across an open plain, and the ranks are dressed by the right'.

44. The front, second, and reserve lines, respectively.

45. At Zama in 202 B.C., against the Carthaginians (Livy, XXX, xxxii, 10 ff.).

forms of Battle, the *Cuneus* and *Forceps*, or the sheare and wedge battles, each made of half a *Rhombus*, and but differenced by position. The wedge invented to break or work into a body, the *forceps* to environ and defeat the power thereof, composed out of the selectest Souldiery and disposed into the form of an V, wherein receiving the wedge, it inclosed it on both sides. After this form the famous *Narses* ordered his battle against the *Franks*, and by this figure the *Almans* were enclosed, and cut in peeces.[46]

The *Rhombus* or Lozenge figure so visible in this order, was also a remarkable form of battle in the *Grecian* Cavalry,[47] observed by the *Thessalians*, and *Philip* King of *Macedon*, and frequently by the *Parthians*, As being most ready to turn every way, and best to be commanded, as having its ductors, or Commanders at each Angle.

The *Macedonian Phalanx* (a long time thought invincible) consisted of a long square.[48] For though they might be sixteen in Rank and file, yet when they shut close, so that the fixt pike advanced before the first ranck, though the number might be square, the figure was oblong, answerable unto the Quincunciall quadrate of *Curtius*. According to this square *Thucydides* delivers, the *Athenians* disposed their battle against the *Lacedemonians* brickwise,[49] and by the same word the Learned *Guellius*[50] expoundeth the quadrate of *Virgil*, after the form of a brick or tile.

And as the first station and position of trees, so was the first habitation of men, not in round Cities, as of later foundation; For the form of *Babylon* the first City was square, and so shall also be the last, according to the description of the holy City in the Apocalyps.[51] The famous pillars of *Seth* before the floud, had also the like foundation, if they were but *antidiluvian*

46. Narses defeated the Franks in 553; Julian, the 'Almans' (Germans) in 357.

47. So Aelian (Browne marg.).

48. i.e. rectangle.

49. ἐν πλαισίῳ (Browne marg., quoted from Thucydides, VI, lxvii, 1): suggestive of hollow rectangles used in moulding bricks.

50. Commenting on *Georgics*, II, 278 (Browne marg.).

51. Revelation 21.16. On Babylon see Herodotus, I, 178.

Obelisks,[52] and such as *Cham* and his *Ægyptian* race, imitated after the Flood.

But *Nineveh* which Authours acknowledge to have exceeded *Babylon*, was of a longilaterall[53] figure, ninety-five Furlongs broad, and an hundred and fifty long, and so making about sixty miles in circuit, which is the measure of three dayes journey, according unto military marches, or castrensiall mansions.[54] So that if *Jonas* entred at the narrower side, he found enough for one dayes walk to attain the heart of the City, to make his Proclamation.[55] And if we imagine a City extending from *Ware* to *London*,[56] the expression will be moderate of six score thousand Infants,[57] although we allow vacuities, fields, and intervals of habitation as there needs must be when the monument of *Ninus* took up no lesse then ten furlongs.

And, though none of the seven wonders, yet a noble peece of Antiquity, and made by a Copy exceeding all the rest, had its principall parts disposed after this manner, that is, the Labyrinth of *Crete*, built upon a long quadrate, containing five large squares, communicating by right inflections, terminating in the centre of the middle square, and lodging of the *Minotaur*, if we conform unto the description of the elegant medall thereof in *Agostino*.[58] And though in many accounts we reckon grosly by the square, yet is that very often to be accepted as a long sided quadrate, which was the figure of the Ark of the Covenant, the table of the Shew-bread, and the stone wherein the names of the twelve Tribes were engraved,[59] that is, three in a row, naturally making a longilaterall Figure, the perfect quadrate being made by nine.

What figure the stones themselves maintained, tradition and

52. 'Obelisks being erected upon a square base' (Browne suppl.). The sentence draws on Josephus, *Jewish Antiquities*, I, ii, 3.

53. Rectangular. So Diodorus Siculus, II, iii, 2–3 (Browne marg.).

54. Areas from one camp to another.

55. Jonah 3.4.

56. About twenty-five miles.

57. Jonah 4.11.

58. In his treatise on medals (Browne marg.).

59. Genesis 6.15, Exodus 25–23 and 28.17–21, respectively.

Scripture are silent, yet Lapidaries in precious stones affect a Table or long square, and in such proportion, that the two laterall, and also the three inferiour Tables are equall unto the superiour, and the angles of the laterall Tables, contain and constitute the *hypothenusæ*, or broader sides subtending.[60]

That the Tables of the Law were of this figure, general imitation and tradition hath confirmed; yet are we unwilling to load the shoulders of *Moses*[61] with such massie stones as some pictures lay upon them, since 'tis plainly delivered that he came down with them in his hand; since the word strictly taken implies no such massie hewing, but cutting, and fashioning of them into shape and surface; since some will have them Emeralds, and if they were made of the materials of Mount *Sina*, not improbable that they were marble: Since the words were not many, the letters short of seven hundred, and the Tables written on both sides required no such capacity.

The beds of the Ancients were different from ours at present, which are almost square, being framed ob-long, and about a double unto their breadth; not much unlike the *area*, or bed of this Quincuncial quadrate. The single beds of *Greece* were six foot, and a little more in length, three in breadth; the Giant-like bed of *Og*, which had four cubits of bredth, nine and a half in length,[62] varied not much from this proportion. The Funeral bed of King *Cheops*, in the greater Pyramid, which holds seven in length, and four foot in bredth, had no great difformity from this measure; And whatsoever were the bredth, the length could hardly be lesse, of the tyrannical bed of *Procrustes*, since in a shorter measure he had not been fitted with persons for his cruelty of extension.[63] But the old sepulchral bed, or *Amazonian* Tomb in the market-place of *Megara*,[64] was in the form of a Lozenge; readily made out by the composure of the body. For the arms not lying fasciated or wrapt up after the *Grecian*

60. Extended.
61. Who carried them down Mount Sinai (Exodus 32.15).
62. As described in Deuteronomy 3.11.
63. i.e. stretching, as he was wont to do.
64. So Plutarch, *Theseus*, XXVII (Browne marg.).

manner, but in a middle distention,[65] the including lines will strictly make out that figure.

CHAPTER III

Now although this elegant ordination of vegetables, hath found coincidence or imitation in sundry works of Art, yet is it not also destitute of naturall examples,[1] and though overlooked by all, was elegantly observable, in severall works of nature.

Could we satisfie our selves in the position of the lights above, or discover the wisedom of that order so invariably maintained in the fixed Stars of heaven; Could we have any light, why the stellary part of the first masse, separated into this order, that the Girdle of *Orion* should ever maintain its line, and the two Starres in *Charles*'s Wain never leave pointing at the Pole-Starre, we might abate the *Pythagoricall* Musick of the Spheres, the sevenfold Pipe of *Pan*;[2] and the strange Cryptography of *Gaffarell* in his Starrie Booke of Heaven.[3]

But not to look so high as Heaven or the single Quincunx of the *Hyades* upon the head of *Taurus*, the Triangle, and remarkable *Crusero*[4] about the foot of the *Centaur*; observable rudiments there are hereof in subterraneous concretions, and bodies in the Earth; in the *Gypsum* or *Talcum Rhomboides*, in the Favaginites or honey-comb-stone, in the *Asteria* and *Astroites*, and in the crucigerous[5] stone of S. *Iago* of *Gallicia*.

The same is observably effected in the *Julus*, *Catkins*, or pendulous excrescencies of severall Trees, of Wallnuts, Alders, and Hazels, which hanging all the Winter, and maintaining their Net-worke close, by the expansion thereof are the early fore-

65. i.e. half-stretched.

1. In the liberal examples provided by Browne the naturalist hereafter, his marginal notes – and annotation generally – are reduced to a minimum.

2. On the one, cf. above, p. 149; on the other: Virgil, *Eclogues*, II, 36–7 ('I have a pipe of seven unequal hemlock-stems compacted. Damoetas gave it to me').

3. His treatise *Unheard-of Curiosities* (English trans., 1650).

4. The Southern Cross.

5. Cross-bearing (as above, p. 329, note 30).

tellers of the Spring, discoverable also in long Pepper, and elegantly in the *Julus* of *Calamus Aromaticus*, so plentifully growing with us in the first palmes of Willowes, and in the Flowers of Sycamore, Petasites, Asphodelus, and *Blattaria*, before explication.[6] After such order stand the flowery Branches in our best spread *Verbascum*, and the seeds about the spicous[7] head or torch of *Tapsas Barbatus*, in as fair a regularity as the circular and wreathed order will admit, which advanceth one side of the square, and makes the same Rhomboidall.

In the squamous[8] heads of *Scabious*, *Knapweed*, and the elegant *Jacea Pinea*, and in the Scaly composure of the *Oak-Rose*, which some years most aboundeth. After this order hath Nature planted the Leaves in the Head of the common and prickled Artichoak; wherein the black and shining Flies do shelter themsleves, when they retire from the purple Flower about it; The same is also found in the pricks, sockets, and impressions of the seeds, in the pulp or bottome thereof; wherein do elegantly stick the Fathers of their Mother.[9] To omit the Quincunciall Specks on the top of the Miscle-berry, especially that which grows upon the *Tilia* or Lime-Tree. And the remarkable disposure of those yellow fringes about the purple Pestill of *Aaron*, and elegant clusters of Dragons, so peculiarly secured by nature, with an *umbrella* or skreening Leaf about them.

The Spongy leaves of some Sea-wracks, Fucus, Oaks, in their severall kindes, found about the Shoar, with ejectments of the Sea, are over-wrought with Net-work elegantly containing this order, which plainly declareth the naturality of this texture; And how the needle of nature delighteth to work, even in low and doubtful vegetations.

The *Arbustetum* or Thicket on the head of the Teazell, may be observed in this order: And he that considereth that fabrick so regularly palisadoed,[10] and stemm'd with flowers of the royall

6. 'unfolding or opening' (Bullokar).

7. Pointed, spiky.

8. Scaly.

9. i.e. the seeds – an expression from the *Greek Anthology* (Browne marg.).

10. Spiked.

colour; in the house of the solitary maggot, may finde the Seraglio of *Solomon*,[11] And contemplating the calicular shafts, and uncous disposure[12] of their extremities, so accommodable unto the office of abstersion,[13] not condemne as wholly improbable the conceit of those who accept it, for the herbe *Borith*.[14] Where by the way, we could with much inquiry never discover any transfiguration, in this abstemious insect, although we have kept them long in their proper houses, and boxes. Where some wrapt up in their webbs, have lived upon their own bowels, from September unto July.

In such a grove doe walke the little creepers about the head of the burre. And such an order is observed in the aculeous[15] prickly plantation, upon the heads of several common thistles, remarkably in the notable palisadoes[16] about the flower of the milk-Thistle; and he that inquireth into the little bottome[17] of the globe-thistle, may finde that gallant bush arise from a scalpe of like disposure.

The white umbrella or medicall bush of Elder, is an Epitome of this order: arising from five main stemms Quincuncially disposed, and tollerably maintained in their subdivisions. To omit the lower observations in the seminal spike of Mercurie, weld, and Plantane.

Thus hath nature ranged the flowers of Santfoyne, and French honey suckle; and somewhat after this manner hath ordered the bush in *Jupiters* beard, or houseleek; which old superstition set on the tops of houses, as a defensative against lightening, and thunder. The like in Fenny Seagreen or the water Souldier; which, though a militarie name from Greece, makes out the Roman order.

A like ordination there is in the favaginous[18] Sockets, and

11. 'There being a single Maggot found almost in every head' (Browne suppl.). Solomon had 700 wives and 300 concubines (1 Kings 11.3).

12. i.e. crooked arrangement.

13. Cleansing, scouring.

14. Jeremiah 2.22 (Browne marg.).

15. 'prycke or stynge' (Elyot).

16. 'pointed Stakes' (Blount).

17. As above, p. 114, note 264.

18. Cellular, like a honeycomb.

Lozenge seeds of the noble flower of the Sunne. Wherein in Lozenge figured boxes nature shuts up the seeds, and balsame which is about them.

But the Firre and Pinetree from their fruits doe naturally dictate this position. The Rhomboidall protuberances in Pineapples maintaining this Quincuncial order unto each other, and each Rhombus in it selfe. Thus are also disposed the triangular foliations, in the conicall fruit of the firre tree, orderly shadowing and protecting the winged seeds below them.

The like so often occurreth to the curiosity of observers, especially in spicated seeds and flowers, that we shall not need to take in the single Quincunx of Fuchsius in the grouth of the masle fearn, the seedie disposure of Gramen Ischemon, and the trunk or neat Reticulate work in the codde of the Sachell palme.

For even in very many round stalk plants, the leaves are set after a Quintuple ordination, the first leaf answering the fifth, in lateral disposition. Wherein the leaves successively rounding the stalke, in foure at the furthest the compass is absolved,[19] and the fifth leafe or sprout, returns to the position of the other fift before it; as in accounting upward is often observable in furze, pellitorye, Ragweed, the sproutes of Oaks, and thorns upon pollards, and very remarkably in the regular disposure of the rugged excrescencies in the yearly shoots of the Pine.

But in square stalked plants, the leaves stand respectively[20] unto each other, either in crosse or decussation to those above or below them, arising at crosse positions; whereby they shadow not each other, and better resist the force of winds, which in a parallel situation, and upon square stalkes would more forcibly bear upon them.

And to omit, how leaves and sprouts, which compasse not the stalk, are often set in a Rhomboides, and making long, and short Diagonals, doe stand like the leggs of Quadrupeds when they goe: Nor to urge the thwart enclosure and furdling[21] of flowers, and blossomes, before explication, as in the multiplyed

19. i.e. the circuit is completed (R).
20. i.e. in symmetric relation.
21. Folding.

leaves of Pionie; And the Chiasmus[22] in five leaved flowers, while one lies wrapt about the staminous beards, the other foure obliquely shutting and closing upon each other; and how even flowers which consist of foure leaves, stand not ordinarily in three and one, but two, and two crossewise unto the Stylus;[23] even the Autumnal budds, which awaite the returne of the sun, doe after the winter solstice multiply their calicular leaves, making little Rhombuses, and network figures, as in the Sycamore and Lilac.

The like is discoverable in the original production of plants, which first putting forth two leaves, those which succeed, bear not over each other, but shoot obliquely or crossewise, untill the stalke appeareth; which sendeth not forth its first leaves without all order unto them; and he that from hence can discover in what position the two first leaves did arise, is no ordinary observator.

Where by the way, he that observeth the rudimental spring of seeds, shall finde strict rule, although not after this order. How little is required unto effectual generation, and in what diminutives the plastick principle[24] lodgeth, is exemplified in seeds, wherein the greater mass affords so little comproduction. In Beanes the leaf and root sprout from the Germen, the main sides split, and lye by, and in some pull'd up near the time of blooming we have found the pulpous sides intire or little wasted. In Acorns the nebb dilating splitteth the two sides, which sometimes lye whole, when the Oak is sprouted two handfuls. In Lupins these pulpy sides do sometimes arise with the stalk in a resemblance of two fat leaves. Wheat and Rye will grow up, if after they have shot some tender Roots, the adhering pulp be taken from them. Beanes will prosper though a part be cut away, and so much set as sufficeth to contain and keep the Germen close. From this superfluous pulp in unkindely, and

22. Crosswise arrangement.

23. i.e. 'the stemme' (as below p. 361).

24. i.e. the 'plastic' power permeating the entire created order. The reference, one of the earliest in the seventeenth century, was to form part of the endeavours to combat the emerging materialism by asserting a Principle beyond appearances (see §63).

wet years, may arise that multiplicity of little insects, which infest the Roots and Sprouts of tender Graines and pulses.[25]

In the little nebbe or fructifying principle, the motion is regular, and not transvertible,[26] as to make that ever the leaf, which nature intendeth the root; observable from their conversion,[27] until they attain their right position, if seeds be set inversedly.[28]

In vain we expect the production of plants from different parts of the seed, from the same *corculum*[29] or little original proceed both germinations; and in the power of this slender particle lye many Roots and sprouts, that though the same be pull'd away, the generative particle with renew them again, and proceed to a perfect plant; And malt may be observed to grow, though the Cummes[30] be fallen from it.

The seminall nebbe hath a defined and single place, and not extended unto both extremes. And therefore many too vulgarly conceive that Barley and Oats grow at both ends; For they arise from one *punctilio*[31] or generative nebbe, and the Speare sliding under the husk, first appeareth nigh the toppe. But in Wheat and Rye being bare the sprouts are seen together. If Barley unhulled would grow, both would appear at once. But in this and Oatmeal the nebbe is broken away, which makes them the milder food, and lesse apt to raise fermentation in Decoctions.

Men taking notice of what is outwardly visible, conceive a sensible priority in the Root. But as they begin from one part, so they seem to start and set out upon one signall of nature. In Beans yet soft, in Pease while they adhere unto the Cod,[32] the rudimentall Leafe and Root are discoverable. In the seeds of Rocket and Mustard, sprouting in Glasses of water, when the one is manifest the other is also perceptible. In muddy waters apt to breed *Duckweed*, and Periwinkles, if the first and rudi-

25. 'pease, beanes, lupines, and such other Graine' (Bullokar).
26. Athwart (cf. above, p. 337, note 28).
27. 'turning' (as below, p. 372).
28. i.e. invertedly, upside down.
29. Literally 'little heart'.
30. i.e. comes: radicles on malted barley.
31. 'very little point' (Blount).
32. The pod or seed-vessel of a plant.

mentall stroaks[33] of Duckweed be observed, the Leaves and Root anticipate not each other. But in the Date-stone the first sprout is neither root nor leaf distinctly, but both together; For the Germination being to passe through the narrow Navell and hole about the midst of the stone, the generative germ is faine to enlengthen it self, and shooting out about an inch, at that distance divideth into the ascending and descending portion.

And though it be generally thought that Seeds will root at that end, where they adhere to their Originals, and observable it is that the nebbe sets most often next the stalk, as in Grains, Pulses, and most small Seeds, yet is it hardly made out in many greater plants. For in Acornes, Almonds, Pistachios, Wallnuts, and accuminated[34] shells, the germ puts forth at the remotest part of the pulp. And therefore to set Seeds in that posture, wherein the Leaf and Roots may shoot right without contortion, or forced circumvolution, which might render them strongly rooted, and straighter, were a Criticisme[35] in Agriculture. And nature seems to have made some provision hereof in many from their figure, that as they fall from the tree they may lye in Positions agreeable to such advantages.

Beside the open and visible Testicles of plants, the seminall powers lie in great part invisible, while the Sun findes polypody[36] in stone-wals, the little stinging Nettle, and nightshade in barren sandy High-wayes, *Scurvy-grasse* in *Greeneland*, and unknown plants in earth brought from remote Countries. Beside the known longevity of some Trees, what is the most lasting herb, or seed, seems not easily determinable. Mandrakes upon known account have lived near an hundred yeares. Seeds found in Wilde-Fowls Gizards have sprouted in the earth. The Seeds of Marjorane and *Stramonium*[37] carelesly kept, have grown after seven years. Even in Garden-plots long fallow, and digged up, the seeds of *Blattaria*[38] and yellow henbane,

33. Lightly impressed lines.
34. Pointed.
35. Nice point.
36. Fern.
37. The purple thorn-apple.
38. 'an herbe, calso called *Verbascon*' (Elyot). See above, p. 344.

after twelve years burial have produced themselves again.

That bodies are first spirits *Paracelsus* could affirm, which in the maturation of Seeds and fruits, seems obscurely implied by *Aristotle*,[39] when he delivereth, that the spirituous parts are converted into water, and the water into earth, and attested by observation in the maturative progresse of Seeds, wherein at first may be discerned a flatuous[40] distension of the husk, afterwards a thin liquor, which longer time digesteth into a pulp or kernell observable in Almonds and large Nuts. And some way answered in the progressionall perfection of animall semination, in its spermaticall maturation, from crude pubescency unto perfection. And even that seeds themselves in their rudimentall discoveries, appear in foliaceous surcles,[41] or sprouts within their coverings, in a diaphonous gellie, before deeper incrassation,[42] is also visibly verified in Cherries, Acorns, Plums.

From seminall considerations, either in reference unto one another, or distinction from animall production, the holy Scripture describeth the vegetable creation;[43] And while it divideth plants but into Herb and Tree, though it seemeth to make but an accidental division, from magnitude, it tacitely containeth the naturall distinction of vegetables, observed by Herbarists, and comprehending the four kinds.[44] For since the most naturall distinction is made from the production of leaf or stalk, and plants after the two first seminall leaves, do either proceed to send forth more leaves, or a stalk, and the folious and stalky emission distinguisheth herbs and trees, in a large acception[45] it compriseth all Vegetables, for the frutex and suffrutex[46] are under the progression of trees, and stand

39. *Meteorologica*, IV, 3, with Cabeus's commentary (Browne marg.). Coleridge in a long note found the opinion of Paracelsus (in *Philosophia sagax*, I, 3) 'defensible'.
40. 'full of blowing or windiness' (Blount) – i.e. inflated.
41. Small leaf-like shoots.
42. Thickening (cf. above, p. 286, note 13).
43. In Genesis 1.11.
44. Enumerated below, p. 380, note 7.
45. i.e. acceptation.
46. i.e. the shrub or bush, and the half-shrub.

Authentically differenced, but from the accidents of the stalk.

The Æquivocall production of things[47] under undiscerned principles, makes a large part of generation, though they seem to hold a wide univocacy[48] in their set and certain Originals, while almost every plant breeds its peculiar insect, most a Butterfly, moth or fly, wherein the Oak seems to contain the largest seminality, while the Julus,[49] Oak-apple, pill, woolly tuft, foraminous roundles upon the leaf, and grapes under ground make a Fly with some difference. The great variety of Flyes lyes in the variety of their originals, in the seeds of Caterpillars or Cankers there lyeth not only a Butterfly or Moth, but if they be sterill or untimely cast, their production is often a Fly, which we have also observed from corrupted and mouldred Egges, both of Hens and Fishes; To omit the generation of Bees out of the bodies of dead Heifers, or what is strange yet well attested, the production of Eeles in the backs of living Cods and Perches.

The exiguity[50] and smallnesse of some seeds extending to large productions is one of the magnalities[51] of nature, somewhat illustrating the work of the Creation, and vast production from nothing. The true seeds of Cypresse[52] and Rampions are indistinguishable by old eyes. Of the seeds of Tobacco a thousand make not one grain. The disputed seeds of Harts tongue, and Maidenhair, require a greater number. From such undiscernable seminalities arise spontaneous productions. He that would discern the rudimentall stroak of a plant, may behold it in the Originall of Duckweed, at the bignesse of a pins point,

47. i.e. the 'spontaneous productions' referred to below. 'Written before Harvey's *ab ovo omnia* [i.e. Everything begins from the egg]. Since his work, and Leuenhoke's microscopium, the question is settled in Physics; but whether in metaphysics, is not quite so clear' (Coleridge).

48. Oneness, agreement.

49. 'a little worme with many fete, bredynge in vynes & okes' (Elyot). 'These and more to be found upon our Oaks; not well described by any till the Edition of [Bauhin's] *Theatrum Botanicum*' (Browne suppl.).

50. Littleness.

51. From *magnalia*: 'great things to be wondred at. As *Magnalia Dei* (mentioned *Act.* 2.11) the great works of God' (Blount).

52. So Laurenberg (Browne marg.).

from convenient water in glasses, wherein a watchfull eye may also discover the puncticular[53] Originals of Periwincles and Gnats.

That seeds of some Plants are lesse then any animals, seems of no clear decision; That the biggest of Vegetables exceedeth the biggest of Animals, in full bulk, and all dimensions, admits exception in the Whale, which in length and above ground measure, will also contend with tall Oakes. That the richest odour of plants, surpasseth that of Animals may seem of some doubt, since animall-musk, seems to excell the vegetable, and we finde so noble a scent in the Tulip-Fly, and Goat-Beetle.[54]

Now whether seminall nebbes hold any sure proportion unto seminall enclosures, why the form of the germe doth not answer the figure of the enclosing pulp, why the nebbe is seated upon the solid, and not the channeld side of the seed as in grains, why since we often meet with two yolks in one shell, and sometimes one Egge within another, we do not oftener meet with two nebbes in one distinct seed: why since the Egges of a Hen laid at one course, do commonly out-weigh the bird, and some moths coming out of their cases, without assistance of food, will lay so many Egges as to out weigh their bodies, trees rarely bear their fruit, in that gravity or proportion: Whether in the germination of seeds according to *Hippocrates*,[55] the lighter part ascendeth, and maketh the sprout, the heaviest tending downward frameth the root; Since we observe that the first shoot of seeds in water, will sink or bow down at the upper and leafing end: Whether it be not more rational Epicurisme to contrive whole dishes out of the nebbes and spirited particles of plants, then from the Gallatures and treddles[56] of Egges; since that part is found to hold no seminal share in Oval Generation,[57] are quæries which might enlarge but must conclude this digression.

53. Minute (cf. above, p. 348, note 31).
54. 'The long and tender green Capricornus rarely found, we could never meet with but two' (Browne marg.).
55. In *Children by Nature*, XXII.
56. Germs (in both cases).
57. i.e. the production of the egg.

And though not in this order, yet how nature delighteth in this number, and what consent and coordination there is in the leaves and parts of flowers, it cannot escape our observation in no small number of plants. For the calicular or supporting and closing leaves, do answer the number of the flowers, especially in such as exceed not the number of Swallows Egges;[58] as in Violets, Stichwort, Blossomes, and flowers of one leaf have often five divisions, answered by a like number of calicular leaves; as *Gentianella*, *Convolvulus*, Bell-flowers. In many the flowers, blades, or staminous shootes and leaves are all equally five, as in cockle, mullein and *Blattaria*; Wherein the flowers before explication are pentagonally wrapped up, with some resemblance of the *blatta* or moth from whence it hath its name: But the contrivance of nature is singular in the opening and shutting of Bindeweeds, performed by five inflexures,[59] distinguishable by pyramidicall figures, and also different colours.

The rose at first is thought to have been of five leaves, as it yet groweth wilde among us; but in the most luxuriant, the calicular leaves do still maintain that number. But nothing is more admired then the five Brethren[60] of the Rose, and the strange disposure of the Appendices or Beards, in the calicular leaves thereof, which in despair of resolution is tolerably salved from this contrivance, best ordered and suited for the free closure of them before explication. For those two which are smooth, and of no beard are contrived to lye undermost, as without prominent parts, and fit to be smoothly covered; the other two which are beset with Beards on either side, stand outward and uncovered, but the fifth or half-bearded leaf is covered on the bare side but on the open side stands free, and bearded like the other.

Besides a large number of leaves have five divisions, and may be circumscribed by a *Pentagon* or figure of five Angles, made by right lines from the extremity of their leaves, as in Maple, Vine, Figge-Tree: But five-leaved flowers are commonly disposed circularly about the *Stylus*; according to the higher Geometry of

58. 'Which exceed not five' (Browne suppl.).
59. Turns inwards.
60. i.e. the five leaves of the calyx (*OED*; *M*).

nature, dividing a circle by five *radii*, which concurre not to make Diameters, as in Quadrilaterall and sexangular[61] Intersections.

Now the number of five is remarkable in every circle, not only as the first sphærical number,[62] but the measure of sphærical motion. For sphærical bodies move by fives,[63] and every globular figure placed upon a plane, in direct volutation, returns to the first point of contaction in the fifth touch, accounting by the Axes of the Diameters or Cardinall points of the four quarters thereof. And before it arriveth unto the same point again, it maketh five circles equall unto it self, in each progresse from those quarters, absolving an equall circle.

By the same number doth nature divide the circle of the Sea-Starre, and in that order and number disposeth those elegant Semi-circles, or dentall sockets and egges in the Sea Hedge-hogge. And no mean Observations hereof there is in the Mathematicks of the neatest Retiary Spider, which concluding in fourty four Circles, from five Semidiameters beginneth that elegant texture.

And after this manner doth lay the foundation of the circular branches of the Oak, which being five-cornered, in the tender annual sprouts, and manifesting upon incision the signature of a Starre, is after made circular, and swel'd into a round body: Which practice of nature is become a point of art, and makes two Problemes in *Euclide*.[64] But the Bramble which sends forth shoots and prickles from its angles, maintains its pentagonnall figure, and the unobserved signature of a handsome porch within it. To omit the five small buttons dividing the Circle of the Ivy-berry, and the five characters in the Winter stalk of the Walnut, with many other Observables, which cannot escape the eyes of signal discerners; Such as know where to finde

61. i.e. hexagonal.
62. i.e. 5 multiplied by itself yields figures ending in 5 – e.g. 5, 25, 125, etc. (*M*).
63. Hereafter the argument is: 'when a circle or sphere is rolled forward on a plane it covers its own area five times by the time it regains its original position' (*M*, citing Bovillus).
64. *Elements*, IV, 11 (Browne marg.).

Ajax his name in *Delphinium*, or *Aarons* Mitre in Henbane.[65]

Quincuncial forms and ordinations, are also observable in animal figurations. For to omit the hioides or throat-bone of animals, the *furcula* or *merry-thought* in birds, which supporteth the *scapulæ*, affording a passage for the windepipe and the gullet, the wings of Flyes, and disposure of their legges in their first formation from maggots, and the position of their horns, wings and legges, in their *Aurelian*[66] cases and swadling clouts: The back of the *Cimex Arboreus*, found often upon Trees and lesser plants, doth elegantly discover the *Burgundian* decussation; And the like is observable in the belly of the *Notonecton*, or water-Beetle, which swimmeth on its back, and the handsome Rhombusses of the Sea-poult, or Weazell, on either side the Spine.

The sexangular Cels in the Honeycombs of Bees, are disposed after this order, much there is not of wonder in the confused Houses of Pismires, though much in their busie life and actions, more in the edificial[67] Palaces of Bees and Monarchical spirits; who make their combs six-corner'd, declining a circle, whereof many stand not close together, and compleatly fill the *area* of the place; But rather affecting a six-sided figure, whereby every cell affords a common side unto six more, and also a fit receptacle for the Bee it self, which gathering into a Cylindrical Figure, aptly enters its sexangular house, more nearly approaching a circular Figure, then either doth the Square or Triangle. And the Combes themselves so regularly contrived, that their mutual intersections make three Lozenges at the bottome of every Cell; which severally regarded make three Rows of neat Rhomboidall Figures, connected at the angles, and so continue three several chains throughout the whole comb.

As for the *Favago* found commonly on the Sea shoar, though named from an honey-comb, it but rudely makes out the resemblance, and better agrees with the round Cels of humble

65. *Delphinium* or larkspur may have been the flower marked AI AI (for AIAS or Ajax, according to Ovid, *Metamorphoses*, XIII, 395–8); henbane was thought to resemble Aaron's mitre (Exodus 28.36–9).
66. Pertaining to a chrysalis (*aurelia*).
67. Pertaining to 'the art of building' (Blount).

Bees. He that would exactly discern the shop of a Bees mouth, need observing eyes, and good augmenting glasses; wherein is discoverable one of the neatest peeces in nature, and must have a more piercing eye then mine; who findes out the shape of Buls heads, in the guts of Drones pressed out behinde, according to the experiment of *Gomesius*; wherein notwithstanding there seemeth somewhat which might incline a pliant fancy to credulity of similitude.

A resemblance hereof there is in the orderly and rarely disposed Cels, made by Flyes and Insects, which we have often found fastened about small sprigs, and in those cottonary[68] and woolly pillows, which sometimes we meet with fastened unto Leaves, there is included an elegant Net-work Texture, out of which come many small Flies. And some resemblance there is of this order in the Egges of some Butterflies and moths, as they stick upon leaves, and other substances; which being dropped from behinde, nor directed by the eye, doth neatly declare how nature Geometrizeth, and observeth order in all things.[69]

A like correspondency in figure is found in the skins and outward teguments of animals, whereof a regardable part are beautiful by this texture. As the backs of several Snakes and Serpents, elegantly remarkable in the *Aspis*, and the Dartsnake, in the Chiasmus and larger decussations upon the back of the Rattlesnake, and in the close and finer texture of the *Mater formicarum*, or snake that delights in Ant-hils; whereby upon approach of outward injuries, they can raise a thicker Phalanx on their backs, and handsomely contrive themselves into all kindes of flexures: Whereas their bellies are commonly covered with smooth semi-circular divisions, as best accommodable unto their quick and gliding motion.

This way is followed by nature in the peculiar and remarkable tayl of the Bever, wherein the scaly particles are disposed, somewhat after this order, which is the plainest resolution of the wonder of *Bellonius*, while he saith, with incredible Artifice hath Nature framed the tayl or Oar of the Bever: where by the

68. i.e. cotton-like.
69. See above, pp. 37 and 42.

way we cannot but wish a model of their houses, so much extolled by some Describers: wherein since they are so bold as to venture upon three stages, we might examine their Artifice in the contignations,[70] the rule and order in the compartitions;[71] or whether that magnified structure be any more then a rude rectangular pyle or meer hovell-building.

Thus works the hand of nature in the feathery plantation about birds. Observable in the skins of the breast,[72] legs and Pinions of Turkies, Geese, and Ducks, and the Oars or finny feet of Water-Fowl: And such a naturall Net is the scaly covering of Fishes, of Mullets, Carps, Tenches, &c. even in such as are excoriable[73] and consist of smaller scales, as Bretts, Soals, and Flounders. The like Reticulate grain is observable in some *Russia* Leather. To omit the ruder Figures of the ostracion, the triangular or cunny fish, or the pricks of the Sea-Porcupine.

The same is also observable in some part of the skin of man, in habits of neat texture, and therefore not unaptly compared unto a Net: We shall not affirm that from such grounds, the Ægyptian Embalmers imitated this texture yet in their linnen folds the same is still observable among their neatest Mummies, in the figures of *Isis* and *Osyris*, and the Tutelary spirits in the Bembine Table.[74] Nor is it to be over-looked how *Orus*, the Hieroglyphick of the world is described[75] in a Net-work covering, from the shoulder to the foot. And (not to enlarge upon the cruciated character of *Trismegistus*, or handed crosses,[76] so often occurring in the Needles of *Pharaoh*, and Obelisks of

70. Conjoining of structures.

71. 'By *Compartition*, Architects understand a graceful and useful distribution of the whole ground-plot' (Blount).

72. 'Elegantly conspicuous on the inside of the stripped skins of Dive-Fowl, of the Cormorant, Goshonder, Weasell, Loon, &c.' (Browne marg.).

73. From *excorio*: 'to plucke off the skynne' (Elyot).

74. The 'brasen Table' (above, p. 330, note 41).

75. By Kircher (above, p. 30).

76. The 'cruciated character' is the Greek letter X, said to have been invented by Hermes Trismegistus; 'handed crosses' are the pre-Christian crosses with handles, thus: ♀.

Antiquity) the *Statuæ Isiacæ*, Teraphims,[77] and little Idols, found about the Mummies, do make a decussation or *Jacobs Crosse*, with their armes, like that on the head of *Ephraim* and *Manasses*,[78] and this *decussis*[79] is also graphically described between them.

This Reticulate or Net-work was also considerable in the inward parts of man, not only from the first *subtegmen* or warp of his formation, but in the netty *fibres* of the veins and vessels of life; wherein according to common Anatomy the right and transverse *fibres* are decussated, by the oblique *fibres*; and so must frame a Reticulate and Quincunciall Figure by their Obliquations,[80] Emphatically extending that Elegant expression of Scripture, Thou hast curiously embroydered me, thou hast wrought me up after the finest way of texture, and as it were with a Needle.[81]

Nor is the same observable only in some parts, but in the whole body of man, which upon the extension of arms and legges, doth make out a square, whose intersection is at the genitals. To omit the phantastical Quincunx in *Plato* of the first Hermaphrodite or double man, united at the Loynes, which *Jupiter* after divided.[82]

A rudimentall resemblance hereof there is in the cruciated and rugged folds of the *Reticulum*, or Net-like Ventricle of ruminating horned animals, which is the second in order, and culinarily called the Honey-comb. For many divisions there are in the stomack of severall animals; what number they maintain in the *Scarus* and ruminating Fish, common description, or our own experiment hath made no discovery. But in the Ventricle of *Porpuses* there are three divisions. In many Birds a crop,

77. i.e. statues of Isis, and household idols (Genesis 31.19), respectively.

78. Genesis 48.13–14.

79. The crossed figure X (as above, p. 328, note 25).

80. 'turning away or aside' (Blount).

81. Adapted from Psalm 139.14.

82. The first allusion is attested by Vitruvius in *Of Architecture*, III, i, 13, as well as by Leonardo's well-known drawing of Vitruvian Man; the second is in Plato's *Symposium*, 189–91.

Gizard, and little receptacle before it; but in Cornigerous[83] animals, which chew the cudd, there are no less then four of distinct position and office.[84]

The *Reticulum* by these crossed cels, makes a further digestion, in the dry and exuccous[85] part of the Aliment received from the first Ventricle. For at the bottome of the gullet there is a double Orifice; What is first received at the mouth descendeth into the first and greater stomack, from whence it is returned into the mouth again; and after a fuller mastication, and salivous mixture, what part thereof descendeth again, in a moist and succulent body, it slides down the softer and more permeable Orifice, into the Omasus or third stomack; and from thence conveyed into the fourth, receives its last digestion. The other dry and exuccous part after rumination by the larger and stronger orifice beareth into the first stomack, from thence into the *Reticulum*, and so progressively into the other divisions. And therefore in Calves newly calved, there is little or no use of the two first Ventricles, for the milk and liquid aliment slippeth down the softer Orifice, into the third stomack; where making little or no stay, it passeth into the fourth, the seat of the *Coagulum*, or Runnet, or that division of stomack which seems to bear the name of the whole, in the Greek translation[86] of the Priests Fee, in the Sacrifice of Peace-offerings.

As for those Rhomboidal Figures made by the Cartilagineous parts of the Wezon, in the Lungs of great Fishes, and other animals, as *Rondeletius* discovered, we have not found them so to answer our figure as to be drawn into illustration; Something we expected in the more discernable texture of the lungs of frogs, which notwithstanding being but two curious bladders not weighing above a grain, we found interwoven with veins not observing any just order. More orderly situated are those cretaceous and chalky concretions found sometimes in the bignesse of a small fech[87] on either side their spine; which being

83. Horned.

84. i.e. the four stomachs of ruminating animals (Browne suppl., named in Greek and Latin).

85. Sapless (as above, p. 299. note 14).

86. i.e. the Septuagint, on Leviticus 7.31.

87. i.e. vetch: the bean-like fruit, or the plant itself.

not agreeable unto our order, nor yet observed by any, we shall not here discourse on.

But had we found a better account and tolerable Anatomy, of that prominent jowle of the *Sperma Ceti* Whale, then questuary[88] operation, or the stench of the last cast upon our shoar,[89] permitted, we might have perhaps discovered some handsome order in those Net-like seases[90] and sockets, made like honeycombs, containing that medicall matter.

Lastly, The incession or locall motion[91] of animals is made with analogy unto this figure, by decussative diametrals, Quincunciall Lines and angles. For to omit the enquiry how Butterflies and breezes[92] move their four wings, how birds and fishes in ayre and water move by joynt stroaks of opposite wings and Finnes, and how salient[93] animals in jumping forward seem to arise and fall upon a square base; As the station of most Quadrupeds, is made upon a long square, so in their motion they make a Rhomboides; their common progression being performed Diametrally, by decussation and crosse advancement of their legges, which not observed begot that remarkable absurdity in the position of the legges of *Castors* horse[94] in the Capitol. The Snake which moveth circularly makes his spires in like order, the convex and concave spirals answering each other at alternate distances; in the motion of man the armes and legges observe this thwarting position, but the legges alone do move Quincuncially by single angles with some resemblance of an V measured by successive advancement from each foot, and the angle of indenture great or lesse, according to the extent or brevity of the stride.

Studious Observators may discover more analogies in the orderly book of nature, and cannot escape the Elegancy of her hand in other correspondencies. The Figures of nails and

88. i.e. quaestuary: money-making.
89. 'Described in our *Pseudo. Epidem.*' (Browne marg.): see above, p. 217.
90. Containers (*M*).
91. i.e. locomotion, movement.
92. Gadflies.
93. Leaping.
94. Both its left legs are on the ground.

crucifying appurtenances, are but precariously made out in the *Granadilla* or flower of Christs passion: And we despair to behold in these parts that handsome draught of crucifixion in the fruit of the *Barbado* Pine.⁹⁵ The seminal Spike of *Phalaris*, or great shaking grasse, more nearly answers the tayl of a Rattle-Snake, then many resemblances in *Porta*: And if the man *Orchis* of *Columna*⁹⁶ be well made out, it excelleth all analogies. In young Wallnuts cut athwart, it is not hard to apprehend strange characters; and in those of somewhat elder growth, handsome ornamental draughts about a plain crosse. In the root of *Osmond* or Water fern, every eye may discern the form of a Half Moon, Rain-bow, or half the character of Pisces.⁹⁷ Some finde Hebrew, Arabick, Greek, and Latine Characters in Plants; In a common one among us we seem to read *Aiaia, Viviu, Lelil*.⁹⁸

Right lines and circles make out the bulk of plants; In the parts thereof we finde Helicall or spirall roundles, voluta's,⁹⁹ conicall Sections, circular Pyramids, and frustums of *Archimedes*;¹⁰⁰ And cannot overlook the orderly hand of nature, in the alternate succession of the flat and narrower sides in the tender shoots of the Ashe, or the regular inequality of bignesse in the five-leaved flowers of Henbane, and something like in the calicular leaves of *Tutson*. How the spots of *Persicaria* do manifest themselves between the sixt and tenth ribbe. How the triangular capp in the stemme or *stylus* of Tuleps doth constantly point at three outward leaves. That spicated flowers do open first at the stalk. That white flowers have yellow thrums or knops. That the nebbe of Beans and Pease do all look downward, and so presse not upon each other; And how the seeds of many pappous or downy flowers lockt up in sockets after a gomphosis or *mortis*-articulation,¹⁰¹ diffuse themselves circularly into

95. i.e. banana, not pineapple.
96. i.e. the testicle-like plant described by Colonna.
97. Whose zodiacal sign is ♓.
98. Dr Henry Power had asked Browne 'In what plant these tearmes are Inscribed' (*K*, IV, 264) but the question is yet to be answered.
99. i.e. volutes, the spiral scrolls ornamenting Ionic capitals.
100. i.e. the conic sections described by Archimedes.
101. i.e. fixing in place.

branches of rare order, observable in *Tragopogon* or Goats-beard, comformable to the Spiders web, and the *Radii* in like manner telarely[102] inter-woven.

And how in animall natures, even colours hold correspondencies, and mutuall correlations. That the colour of the Caterpillar will shew again in the Butterfly, with some latitude is allowable. Though the regular spots in their wings seem but a mealie adhesion, and such as may be wiped away, yet since they come in this variety, out of their cases, there must be regular pores in those parts and membranes, defining such Exudations.

That *Augustus* had native notes on his body and belly,[103] after the order and number in the Starres of *Charles wayne*, will not seem strange unto astral Physiognomy, which accordingly considereth moles in the body of man, or Physicall Observators, who from the position of moles in the face, reduce them to rule and correspondency in other parts. Whether after the like method medicall conjecture may not be raised, upon parts inwardly affected; since parts about the lips are the critical fears of Pustules[104] discharged in Agues; And serophulous tumours about the neck do so often speak the like about the Mesentery,[105] may also be considered.

The russet neck in young Lambs[106] seems but adventitious, and may owe its tincture to some contaction[107] in the womb; But that if sheep have any black or deep russet in their faces, they want not the same about their legges and feet; That black Hounds have mealy mouths and feet; That black Cows which have any white in their tayls, should not misse of some in their bellies; and if all white in their bodies, yet if black-mouth'd, their ears and feet maintain the same colour, are correspondent tinctures not ordinarily failing in nature, which easily unites the accidents of extremities, since in some generations she trans-

102. Like a spider's web.

103. Suetonius, *Augustus*, LXXX (Browne marg.), speaks of the emperor's birthmarks.

104. Blisters.

105. 'a skyn the whiche doth tye the guttes together' (Boorde; *OED*).

106. 'To be observed in white young Lambs, which afterward vanisheth' (Browne suppl.).

107. i.e. contact.

mutes the parts themselves, while in the *Aurelian*[108] *Meta-morphosis* the head of the canker becomes the Tayl of the Butterfly. Which is in some way not beyond the contrivance of Art, in submersions and Inlays, inverting the extremes of the plant, and fetching the root from the top, and also imitated in handsome columnary work, in the inversion of the extremes; wherein the Capitel, and the Base, hold such near correspondency.

In the motive parts of animals may be discovered mutuall proportions; not only in those of Quadrupeds, but in the thigh-bone, legge, foot-bone, and claws of Birds. The legs of Spiders are made after a sesqui-tertian proportion,[109] and the long legs of some locusts, double unto some others. But the internodial parts[110] of Vegetables, or spaces between the joints, are contrived with more uncertainty; though the joints themselves in many plants, maintain a regular number.

In vegetable composure, the unition[111] of prominent parts seems most to answer the *Apophyses*[112] or processes of Animall bones, whereof they are the produced parts or prominent explantations.[113] And though in the parts of plants which are not ordained for motion, we do not expect correspondent Articulations; yet in the setting on of some flowers, and seeds in their sockets, and the lineal commissure[114] of the pulpe of severall seeds, may be observed some shadow of the Harmony; some show of the Gomphosis or *mortis*-articulation.

As for the Diarthrosis[115] or motive Articulation, there is expected little Analogy, though long-stalked leaves doe move by long lines, and have observable motions, yet are they made by outward impulsion, like the motion of pendulous bodies,

108. As above, p. 355, note 66.
109. i.e. after the ratio $1\frac{1}{3}$:1 – 'which contains as much as another, and a third more' (Blount).
110. i.e. the parts between the nodes.
111. i.e. union.
112. Natural protuberances.
113. i.e. the swellings or prominent outgrowths.
114. Merging.
115. The motion of one bone upon another.

while the parts themselves are united by some kinde of *symphysis*[116] unto the stock.

But standing vegetables, void of motive-Articulations, are not without many motions. For beside the motion of vegetation upward, and of radiation unto all quarters, that of contraction, dilatation, inclination, and contortion, is discoverable in many plants. To omit the rose of *Jericho*, the ear of Rye, which moves with change of weather, and the Magical spit, made of no rare plants,[117] which windes before the fire, and rosts the bird without turning.

Even Animals near the Classis of plants, seem to have the most restless motions. The Summer-worm of Ponds and plashes makes a long waving motion; the hair-worm seldome lies still. He that would behold a very anomalous motion, may observe it in the Tortile and tiring stroaks of Gnatworms.[118]

CHAPTER IV[1]

As for the delights, commodities, mysteries, with other concernments of this order, we are unwilling to fly them over, in the short deliveries of *Virgil*, *Varro*, or others, and shall therefore enlarge with additionall ampliations.

By this position they had a just proportion of Earth, to supply an equality of nourishment. The distance being ordered, thick or thin, according to the magnitude or vigorous attraction of the plant, the goodnesse, leannesse, or propriety of the soyle, and therefore the rule of *Solon*,[2] concerning the territory of *Athens*, not extendible unto all; allowing the distance of six foot unto common Trees, and nine for the Figge and Olive.

They had a due diffusion of their roots on all or both sides,

116. Union, fusion.

117. i.e. hazelwood, which itself turns and twists (*E*).

118. 'Found often in some form of red maggot in the standing waters of Cisterns in the Summer' (Browne marg.). 'Tiring' means drawing or pulling.

1. The running title of Chapters IV–V is 'Cyrus-Garden, Or The Quincunx Mistically Considered'. Cf. above, p. 325, note 1.

2. Plutarch, *Solon*, XXIII, 6.

whereby they maintained some proportion to their height, in Trees of large radication.[3] For that they strictly make good their profundeur or depth unto their height, according to common conceit, and that expression of *Virgil*,[4] though confirmable from the plane Tree in *Pliny*,[5] and some few examples, is not to be expected from the generallitie of Trees almost in any kinde, either of side-spreading, or tap-roots: Except we measure them by lateral and opposite diffusions; nor commonly to be found in *minor* or hearby plants; If we except Sea-holly, Liquorish, Sea-rush, and some others.

They had a commodious radiation in their growth; and a due expansion of their branches, for shadow or delight. For trees thickly planted, do runne up in height and branch with no expansion, shooting unequally or short, and thinne upon the neighbouring side. And therefore Trees are inwardly bare, and spring, and leaf from the outward and Sunny side of their branches.

Whereby they also avoided the perill of συνολεθρισμός[6] or one tree perishing with another, as it happeneth oft-times from the sick *effluviums*[7] or entanglements of the roots, falling foul with each other. Observable in Elmes set in hedges, where if one dieth the neighbouring Tree prospereth not long after.

In this situation divided into many intervals and open unto six passages, they had the advantage of a fair perflation[8] from windes, brushing and cleansing their surfaces, relaxing and closing their pores unto due perspiration. For that they afford large *effluviums* perceptible from odours, diffused at great distances, is observable from Onyons out of the earth; which though dry, and kept until the spring, as they shook forth large and many leaves, do notably abate of their weight. And mint

3. i.e. of extensive roots.

4. 'High as its head is carried into the sky, so deep do its roots go down toward Hades' (Browne marg., quoting the Latin of *Aeneid*, IV, 445–56).

5. *Natural History*, XII, v, 9.

6. Probably συνολεθρία (συν + ὀλεθρία), joint or shared destruction.

7. Issuing forth.

8. Ventilation. The 'six passages' are: two from the sides intersecting at right angles, two from the corners making X's, one from the earth, one from the air (*H*).

growing in glasses of water, until it arriveth unto the weight of an ounce, in a shady place, will sometimes exhaust a pound of water.

And as they send forth much, so may they receive somewhat in: For beside the common way and road of reception by the root, there may be a refection and imbibition from without; For gentle showrs refresh plants, though they enter not their roots; And the good and bad *effluviums* of Vegetables, promote or debilitate each other. So *Epithymum*⁹ and *Dodder*, rootlesse and out of the ground, maintain themselves upon Thyme, Savory, and plants, whereon they hang. And *Ivy* divided from the root, we have observed to live some years, by the cirrous¹⁰ parts commonly conceived but as tenacles and holdfasts unto it. The stalks of mint cropt from the root stripped from the leaves, and set in *glasses* with the root end upward, & out of the water, we have observed to send forth sprouts and leaves without the aid of roots, and *scordium*¹¹ to grow in like manner, the leaves set downward in water. To omit severall Sea-plants, which grow on single roots from stones, although in very many there are side-shoots and *fibres*, beside the fastening root.

By this open position they were fairly exposed unto the rayes of Moon and Sunne, so considerable in the growth of Vegetables. For though Poplars, Willows, and severall Trees be made to grow about the brinks of *Acharon*,¹² and dark habitations of the dead; Though some plants are content to grow in obscure Wells; wherein also old Elme pumps afford sometimes long bushy sprouts, not observable in any above-ground: And large fields of Vegetables are able to maintain their verdure at the bottome and shady part of the Sea; yet the greatest number are not content without the actual rayes of the Sunne, but bend, incline, and follow them; As large lists of solisequious and Sun-following plants. And some observe the method of its motion in their owne growth and conversion twining towards the West by the South, as Bryony, Hops,

9. A variety of dodder.
10. Hairy.
11. i.e. water germander.
12. i.e. the river Acheron (*Odyssey*, X, 509–10).

Woodbine, and several kindes of Bindeweed, which we shall
more admire; when any can tell us, they observe another
motion, and Twist by the North at the *Antipodes*. The same
plants rooted against an erect North-wall full of holes, will
finde a way through them to look upon the Sunne. And in
tender plants from mustard seed, sown in the winter, and in a
pot of earth placed inwardly[13] against a South-window, the
tender stalks of two leaves arose not erect, but bending towards
the window, nor looking much higher then the Meridian Sun.
And if the pot were turned they would work themselves into
their former declinations,[14] making their conversion by the
East. That the Leaves of the Olive and some other Trees
solstitially[15] turn, and precisely tell us, when the Sun is entred
Cancer,[16] is scarce expectable in any Climate; and *Theophrastus*
warily observes it;[17] Yet somewhat thereof is observable in our
own, in the leaves of Willows and Sallows, some weeks after
the Solstice. But the great *Convolvulus* or white-flower'd
Bindweed observes both motions of the Sunne, while the flower
twists Æquinoctionally[18] from the left hand to the right,
according to the daily revolution; The stalk twineth ecliptic-
ally[19] from the right to the left, according to the annual conver-
sion.

Some commend the exposure of these orders unto the
Western gales, as the most generative and fructifying breath of
heaven. But we applaud the Husbandry of *Solomon*, whereto
agreeth the doctrine of *Theophrastus*. Arise O North-winde, and
blow thou South upon my garden, that the spices thereof may
flow out;[20] For the North-winde closing the pores, and shutting
up the *effluviums*, when the South doth after open and relax

13. i.e. in a room.

14. 'bending downeward' (Bullokar).

15. i.e. at the summer solstice (see next note).

16. i.e. on Midsummer Day.

17. In *On Plants*, I, x, 1.

18. 'that is toward the Eastern or Western points' (*Pseudodoxia Epi-
demica*, II, 2).

19. i.e. in the direction of the sun's (apparent) annual motion.

20. Song of Solomon 4.16; cf. Theophrastus on the impact of winds, in
On Plants, IV, i, 4.

them; the Aromatical gummes do drop, and sweet odours fly actively from them. And if his garden had the same situation, which mapps, and charts afford it, on the East side of *Jerusalem*, and having the wall on the West; these were the windes, unto which it was well exposed.

By this way of plantation they encreased the number of their trees, which they lost in *Quarternio*'s, and square-orders, which is a commodity[21] insisted on by *Varro*, and one great intent of nature, in this position of flowers and seeds in the elegant formation of plants, and the former Rules observed in naturall and artificiall Figurations.

Whether in this order and one Tree in some measure breaking the cold, and pinching gusts of windes from the other, trees will not better maintain their inward circles, and either escape or moderate their excentricities,[22] may also be considered. For the circles in Trees are naturally concentricall, parallell unto the bark, and unto each other, till frost and percing windes contract and close them on the weatherside, the opposite semicircle widely enlarging, and at a comely distance, which hindreth ofttimes the beauty and roundnesse of Trees, and makes the Timber lesse serviceable; whiles the ascending juyce not readily passing, settles in knots and inequalities. And therefore it is no new course of Agriculture, to observe the native position of Trees according to North and South in their transplantations.

The same is also observable underground in the circinations[23] and sphærical rounds of Onyons, wherein the circles of the Orbes are ofttimes larger, and the meridionall lines stand wider upon one side then the other. And where the largenesse will make up the number of planetical Orbes, that of *Luna*, and the lower planets excede the dimensions of *Saturne*, and the higher:[24]

21. Suitable arrangement; in Varro, *On Agriculture*, I, vii, 2. On *'quaternio's'* see above, p. 333, note 60.

22. Literally 'deviations from the circular form'. Cf. 'eccentricall' in the next paragraph.

23. Spherical layers (R).

24. 'In a lop-sided onion of seven or more rings, those closer to the centre on one side are larger than those farthest from the centre on the other' (H).

Whether the like be not verified in the Circles of the large roots of Briony and Mandrakes, or why in the knotts of Deale or Firre the Circles are often eccentricall, although not in a plane, but vertical and right position, deserves a further enquiry.

Whether there be not some irregularity of roundnesse in most plants according to their position? Whether some small compression of pores be not perceptible in parts which stand against the current of waters, as in Reeds, Bullrushes, and other vegetables toward the streaming quarter,[25] may also be observed, and therefore such as are long and weak, are commonly contrived into a roundnesse of figure, whereby the water presseth lesse, and slippeth more smoothly from them, and even in flags of flat-figured leaves, the greater part obvert[26] their sharper sides unto the current in ditches.

But whether plants which float upon the surface of the water, be for the most part of cooling qualities, those which shoot above it of heating vertues, and why? whether *Sargasso* for many miles floating upon the Western Ocean, or Sea-lettuce, and Phasganium at the bottome of our Seas, make good the like qualities? Why Fenny waters afford the hottest and sweetest plants, as Calamus, Cyperus, and Crowfoot, and mudd cast out of ditches most naturally produceth Arsmart, Why plants so greedy of water so little regard oyl? Why since many seeds contain much oyle within them, they endure it not well without, either in their growth or production? Why since Seeds shoot commonly under ground, and out of the ayre, those which are let fall in shallow glasses, upon the surface of the water, will sooner sprout then those at the bottome? And if the water be covered with oyle, those at the bottome will hardly sprout at all, we have not room to conjecture.

Whether Ivy would not lesse offend the Trees in this clean ordination, and well kept paths, might perhaps deserve the question. But this were a quæry only unto some habitations, and little concerning *Cyrus* or the Babylonian territory; wherein by no industry *Harpalus* could make Ivy grow: And *Alexander* hardly found it about those parts to imitate the pomp of

25. i.e. upstream.
26. Turn.

Bacchus.[27] And though in these Northern Regions we are too much acquainted with one Ivy, we know too little of another, whereby we apprehend not the expressions of Antiquity, the Splenetick medicine of *Galen,*[28] and the Emphasis of the Poet, in the beauty of the white Ivy.[29]

The like concerning the growth of Misseltoe, which dependeth not only of the *species,* or kinde of Tree, but much also of the Soil. And therefore common in some places, not readily found in others, frequent in *France,* not so common in *Spain,* and scarce at all in the Territory of *Ferrara*: Nor easily to be found where it is most required upon Oaks, lesse on Trees continually verdant. Although in some places the Olive escapeth it not, requiting its detriment, in the delightfull view of its red Berries; as *Clusius* observed in *Spain,* and *Bellonius* about *Hierusalem.* But this Parasiticall plant suffers nothing to grow upon it, by any way of art; nor could we ever make it grow where nature had not planted it; as we have in vain attempted by inocculation and incision,[30] upon its native or forreign stock. And though there seem nothing improbable in the seed, it hath not succeeded by sation[31] in any manner of ground, wherein we had no reason to despair, since we reade of vegetable horns, and how Rams horns will root about *Goa.*[32]

But besides these rurall commodities, it cannot be meanly delectable in the variety of Figures, which these orders open, and closed do make. Whilest every inclosure makes a *Rhombus,* the figures obliquely taken a Rhomboides, the intervals

27. Theophrastus, *On Plants,* IV, iv, 1, and Plutarch, *Alexander,* XXXV; respectively.

28. *Of the Temperaments and Powers of Simples,* VII (Browne marg.), where Galen gives a prescription for splenetic patients.

29. 'fairer than the white ivy' (Browne marg., quoting the Latin of Virgil, *Eclogues,* VII, 38).

30. i.e. insition: engrafting (*OED*).

31. '*Satio,* the acte of sowinge of corne' (Elyot).

32. Linschoten, *Discourse of Voyages,* I, 61 (Browne marg.). The Royal Society was to express an interest in the reputed 'horns taking root and growing about Goa', only to discover that 'it was a jeer put upon the Portugues, because the women of Goa are counted much given to lechery' (§187).

bounded with parallell lines, and each intersection built upon a square, affording two Triangles or Pyramids vertically conjoyned;[33] which in the strict Quincunciall order doe oppositely make acute and blunt Angles.

And though therein we meet not with right angles, yet every Rhombus containing four Angles equall unto four right, it virtually contains four right. Nor is this strange unto such as observe the naturall lines of Trees, and parts disposed in them. For neither in the root doth nature affect this angle, which shooting downward for the stability of the plant, doth best effect the same by Figures of Inclination; Nor in the Branches and stalky leaves, which grow most at acute angles; as declining from their head the root, and diminishing their Angles with their altitude: Verified also in lesser Plants, whereby they better support themselves, and bear not so heavily upon the stalk: So that while near the root they often make an Angle of seventy parts,[34] the sprouts near the top will often come short of thirty. Even in the nerves and master veins of the leaves the acute angle ruleth; the obtuse but seldome found, and in the backward part of the leaf, reflecting and arching about the stalk. But why ofttimes one side of the leaf is unequall unto the other, as in Hazell and Oaks, why on either side the master vein the lesser and derivative channels stand not directly opposite, nor at equall angles, respectively unto the adverse side, but those of one part do often exceed the other, as the Wallnut and many more deserves another enquiry.

Now if for this order we affect coniferous and tapering Trees, particularly the Cypresse, which grows in a conicall figure; we have found a Tree not only of great Ornament, but in its Essentials of affinity unto this order. A solid Rhombus being made by the conversion of two Equicrurall Cones, as *Archimedes* hath defined.[35] And these were the common Trees about *Babylon*, and the East, whereof the Ark was made; and *Alexander* found no Trees so accomodable to build his Navy; And this

33. i.e. joined by their apexes.
34. i.e. degrees.
35. On conic sections (as before, p. 361, note 100). An 'Equicrurall' cone is an isosceles (as above, p. 337, note 25).

we rather think to be the Tree mentioned in the Canticles, which stricter Botanology will hardly allow to be Camphire.[36]

And if delight or ornamentall view invite a comely disposure by circular amputations,[37] as is elegantly performed in Hawthorns; then will they answer the figures made by the conversion of a Rhombus, which maketh two concentricall Circles; the greater circumference being made by the lesser angles, the lesser by the greater.

The Cylindrical figure of Trees is virtually contained and latent in this order. A Cylinder or long round being made by the conversion or turning of a Parallelogram, and most handsomely by a long square, which makes an equall, strong and lasting figure in Trees, agreeable unto the body and motive parts of animals, the greatest number of Plants, and almost all roots, though their stalks be angular, and of many corners, which seem not to follow the figure of their Seeds; Since many angular Seeds send forth round stalks, and sphæricall seeds arise from angular spindles,[38] and many rather conform unto their Roots, as the round stalks of bulbous Roots, and in tuberous Roots stemmes of like figure. But why since the largest number of Plants maintain a circular Figure, there are so few with teretous or longround leaves; why coniferous Trees are tenuifolious or narrowleafed, why Plants of few or no joynts have commonly round stalks, why the greatest number of hollow stalks are round stalks; or why in this variety of angular stalks the quadrangular most exceedeth, were too long a speculation; Mean while obvious experience may finde, that in Plants of divided leaves above, nature often beginneth circularly in the two first leaves below, while in the singular plant of Ivy, she exerciseth a contrary Geometry, and beginning with angular leaves below, rounds them in the upper branches.

Nor can the rows in this order want delight, as carrying an aspect answerable unto the *dipteros hypæthros*, or double order of columns open above; the opposite ranks of Trees standing like

36. Genesis 6.14; Arrian, VII, 19; and Song of Solomon ('Canticles') 1.14 – respectively.

37. Pruning in circular fashion.

38. Stalks.

pillars in the *Cavedia*[39] of the Courts of famous buildings, and the *Portico*'s of the *Templa subdialia*[40] of old; Somewhat imitating the *Peristylia* or Cloyster buildings, and the *Exedræ*[41] of the Ancients, wherein men discoursed, walked and exercised; For that they derived the rule of Columnes from Trees, especially in their proportionall diminutions, is illustrated by *Vitruvius*[42] from the shafts of Firre and Pine. And though the inter-arboration do imitate the *Areostylos*, or thin order,[43] not strictly answering the proportion of intercolumniations;[44] yet in many Trees they will not exceed the intermission[45] of the Columnes in the Court of the Tabernacle;[46] which being an hundred cubits long, and made up by twenty pillars, will afford no lesse then intervals of five cubits.

Beside, in this kinde of aspect the sight being not diffused but circumscribed between long parallels and the ἐπισκιασμὸς[47] and adumbration from the branches, it frameth a penthouse over the eye, and maketh a quiet vision: And therefore in diffused and open aspects, men hollow their hand above their eye, and make an artificiall brow, whereby they direct the dispersed rayes of sight, and by this shade preserve a moderate light in the chamber of the eye; keeping the *pupilla*[48] plump and fair, and not contracted or shrunk as in light and vagrant[49] vision.

And therefore providence hath arched and paved the great house of the world, with colours of mediocrity, that is, blew and green, above and below the sight, moderately terminating the *acies*[50] of the eye. For most plants, though green above-

39. Inner halls of Roman houses.
40. Open-air temples (*subdialia* is synonymous with *hypæthros*).
41. Arcades with recesses.
42. In *On Architecture*, V, i, 3.
43. With thinly spaced columns.
44. 'the space betweene pilars' (Elyot).
45. Spacing.
46. Exodus 27.9–11.
47. Shading.
48. i.e. the eye's pupil.
49. Unshaded (R).
50. 'that parte of the eie, whych is called the syghte . . . Also the front of an hoste, at the joynynge of battayle' (Elyot).

ground, maintain their Originall white below it, according to the candour[51] of their seminall pulp, and the rudimental leaves do first appear in that colour; observable in Seeds sprouting in water upon their first foliation. Green seeming to be the first supervenient, or above-ground complexion of Vegetables, separable in many upon ligature or inhumation,[52] as Succory, Endive, Artichoaks, and which is also lost upon fading in the Autumn.

And this is also agreeable unto water it self, the alimental vehicle of plants, which first altereth into this colour; And containing many vegetable seminalities,[53] revealeth their Seeds by greennesse; and therefore soonest expected in rain or standing water, not easily found in distilled or water strongly boiled; wherein the Seeds are extinguished by fire and decoction, and therefore last long and pure without such alteration, affording neither uliginous coats,[54] grantworms, Acari, hair-worms, like crude and common water; And therefore most fit for wholsome beverage, and with malt makes Ale and Beer without boyling. What large water-drinkers some Plants are, the Canary-Tree and Birches in some Northern Countries, drenching the Fields about them do sufficiently demonstrate. How water it self is able to maintain the growth of Vegetables, and without extinction of their generative or medicall vertues; Beside the experiment of *Helmonts* tree,[55] we have found in some which have lived six years in glasses. The seeds of Scurvy-grasse growing in waterpots, have been fruitfull in the Land; And *Asarum*[56] after a years space, and once casting its leaves in water, in the second leaves, hath handsomely performed its vomiting operation.

Nor are only dark and green colors, but shades and shadows contrived through the great Volume of nature, and trees or-

51. Brilliant whiteness.
52. i.e. burying under ground.
53. i.e. seminal principles (of growth).
54. Slimy covers.
55. Helmont had planted a willow's stem in sterilised earth; watered only with rain or distilled water, its weight multiplied over thirty times within five years.
56. Used as an emetic.

dained not only to protect and shadow others, but by their shades and shadowing parts, to preserve and cherish themselves. The whole radiation or branchings shadowing the stock and the root, the leaves, the branches and fruit, too much exposed to the windes and scorching Sunne. The calicular leaves inclose the tender flowers, and the flowers themselves lye wrapt about the seeds, in their rudiment and first formations, which being advanced the flowers fall away; and are therefore contrived in variety of figures, best satisfying the intention; Handsomely observable in hooded and gaping flowers, and the Butterfly bloomes of leguminous plants, the lower leaf closely involving the rudimental Cod,[57] and the alary or wingy divisions embracing or hanging over it.

But Seeds themselves do lie in perpetual shades, either under the leaf, or shut up in coverings; And such as lye barest, have their husks, skins, and pulps about them, wherein the nebbe and generative particle lyeth moist and secured from the injury of Ayre and Sunne. Darknesse and light hold interchangeable dominions, and alternately rule the seminal state of things. Light unto *Pluto* is darknesse unto *Jupiter*.[58] Legions of seminall *Idæa*'s lye in their second Chaos and *Orcus* of *Hipocrates*; till putting on the habits of their forms, they shew themselves upon the stage of the world, and open dominion of *Jove*. They that held the Stars of heaven were but rayes and flashing glimpses of the Empyreall light, through holes and perforations of the upper heaven, took of the natural shadows of stars,[59] while according to better discovery the poor Inhabitants of the Moone have but a polary life, and must passe half their dayes in the shadow of that Luminary.

Light that makes things seen, makes some things invisible, were it not for darknesse and the shadow of the earth, the noblest part of the Creation had remained unseen, and the Stars in heaven as invisible as on the fourth day,[60] when they

57. As above, p. 348, note 32.

58. 'Orcus's light is Jupiter's darkness, Orcus's darkness is Jupiter's light': Hippocrates (Browne marg., quoted in Latin).

59. i.e. dispenses with natural occultations or eclipses. So Hevelius in his study of the moon (Browne marg.).

60. As above, p. 325, note 2.

were created above the Horizon, with the Sun, or there was not an eye to behold them. The greatest mystery of Religion is expressed by adumbration, and in the noblest part of Jewish Types, we finde the Cherubims shadowing the Mercy-seat:[61] Life it self is but the shadow of death, and souls departed but the shadows of the living: All things fall under this name. The Sunne it self is but the dark *simulachrum*,[62] and light but the shadow of God.[63]

Lastly, It is no wonder that this Quincunciall order was first and still affected as gratefull unto the Eye: For all things are seen Quincuncially; For at the eye the Pyramidal rayes from the object, receive a decussation, and so strike a second base upon the *Retina* or hinder coat, the proper organ of Vision; wherein the pictures from objects are represented, answerable to the paper, or wall in the dark chamber;[64] after the decussation of the rayes at the hole of the hornycoat, and their refraction upon the Christalline humour, answering the *foramen* of the window, and the *convex* or burning-glasses, which refract the rayes that enter it. And if ancient Anatomy would hold, a like disposure there was of the optick or visual nerves in the brain, wherein Antiquity conceived a concurrence by decussation. And this not only observable in the Laws of direct Vision, but in some part also verified in the reflected rayes of sight. For making the angle of incidence equal to that of reflexion, the visuall raye returneth Quincuncially, and after the form of a V, and the line of reflexion being continued unto the place of vision, there ariseth a semi-decussation, which makes the object seen in a perpendicular unto it self, and as farre below the reflectent, as it

61. The Incarnation was prefigured 'by types / And shadowes', as Milton was to write in *Paradise Lost* (XII, 232–3; cf. above, p. 70). Hence, *inter alia*, 'the cherubims of glory shadowing the mercy-seat' of the Tabernacle (Hebrews 9.5) prefigured the advent of Christ (Luke 1.35: 'the power of the Highest shall overshadow thee').

62. Image.

63. Cf. above, p. 71: '*Lux est umbra Dei*'.

64. i.e. the *camera obscura*. The paragraph describes accepted theories of vision, both modern and ancient, involving patterns diagrammatically represented as > ('the decussation') and >— ('semi-decussation').

is from it above; observable in the Sun and Moon beheld in water.

And this is also the law of reflexion in moved[65] bodies and sounds, which though not made by decussation, observe the rule of equality between incidence and reflexion; whereby whispering places are framed by Ellipticall arches laid side-wise; where the voice being delivered at the *focus* of one extrem-ity, observing an equality unto the angle of incidence, it will reflect upon the *focus* of the other end, and so escape the ears of the standers in the middle.

A like rule is observed in the reflection of the vocall and sonorous line in Ecchoes, which cannot therefore be heard in all stations. But happening in woody plantations, by waters, and able to return some words; if reacht by a pleasant and well-dividing[66] voice, there may be heard the loftest notes in nature.

And this not only verified in the way of sence, but in ani-mall[67] and intellectuall receptions. Things entring upon the intellect by a Pyramid from without, and thence into the memory by another from within, the common decussation being in the understanding as is delivered by *Bovillus*.[68] Whether the intellectual and phantastical[69] lines be not thus rightly disposed, but magnified diminished, distorted, and ill placed in the Mathematicks of some brains, whereby they have irregular apprehensions of things, perverted notions, concep-tions, and incurable hallucinations, were no unpleasant specu-lation.

And if Ægyptian Philosophy may obtain, the scale of influences was thus disposed, and the genial spirits of both worlds, do trace their way in ascending and descending Pyramids, mystically apprehended in the Letter X, and the open Bill and stradling Legges of a Stork, which was imitated by that Character.

65. i.e. by a force strong enough to make them rebound (*M*).
66. Well-tuned (*R*).
67. i.e. animate, and therefore spiritual.
68. In his treatise *Of Perception* (Browne marg.). Bovillus makes his point with a diagram of several crossing lines (see *M*).
69. i.e. fantastical: pertaining to vision.

Of this Figure *Plato*[70] made choice to illustrate the motion of the soul, both of the world and man; while he delivereth that God divided the whole conjunction length-wise, according to the figure of a Greek X, and then turning it about reflected it into a circle; By the circle implying the uniform motion of the first Orb, and by the right lines, the planetical and various motions within it. And this also with application unto the soul of man, which hath a double aspect, one right, whereby it beholdeth the body, and objects without; another circular and reciprocal, whereby it beholdeth it self. The circle declaring the motion of the individisible soul, simple, according to the divinity of its nature, and returning into it self; the right lines respecting the motion pertaining unto sense, and vegetation, and the central decussation, the wondrous connexion of the severall faculties conjointly in one substance. And so conjoyned the unity and duality of the soul, and made out the three substances so much considered by him; That is, the indivisible or divine, the divisible or corporeal, and that third, which was the *Systasis*[71] or harmony of those two, in the mystical decussation.

And if that were clearly made out which *Justin Martyr* took for granted, this figure hath had the honour to characterize and notifie[72] our blessed Saviour, as he delivereth in that borrowed expression from *Plato*; *Decussavit eum in universo*,[73] the hint whereof he would have *Plato* derive from the figure of the brazen Serpent,[74] and to have mistaken the Letter X for T, whereas it is not improbable, he learned these and other mystical expressions in his Learned Observations of Ægypt, where he

70. *Timaeus*, 36b–d; merged in the next paragraph with Justin Martyr's *First Apology*, LXX. The argument must be visualised, for it involves not only Christ's initial in Greek (X) and the Cross (+ *or* T) but patterns which, made by the intersecting circles if rotated on a vertical axis, pass through the Greek letter *theta* (θ) representing *thanatos* or death (cf. above, p. 309, note 21; and §198).

71. Union. Also 'communication between a man and a god'.

72. 'make knowne' (Bullokar).

73. 'He placed him crosswise in the universe'. So Justin Martyr (above, note 70), who attributes the statement to Plato.

74. Numbers 21.8–9.

might obviously behold the Mercurial characters,[75] the handed crosses, and other mysteries not throughly understood in the sacred Letter X, which being derivative from the Stork, one of the ten sacred animals, might be originally Ægyptian, and brought into *Greece* by *Cadmus* of that Countrey.

CHAPTER V

To enlarge this contemplation unto all the mysteries and secrets, accomodable unto this number, were inexcusable Pythagorisme,[1] yet cannot omit the ancient conceit of five surnamed the number of justice;[2] as justly dividing between the digits, and hanging in the centre of Nine, described by square numeration, which angularly divided will make the decussated number;[3] and so agreeable unto the Quincunciall Ordination, and rowes divided by Equality, and just *decorum*, in the whole com-plantation; And might be the Originall of that common game among us,[4] wherein the fifth place is Soveraigne, and carrieth the chief intention. The Ancients wisely instructing youth, even in their recreations unto virtue, that is, early to drive at the middle point and Central Seat of justice.

Nor can we omit how agreeable unto this number an handsome division is made in Trees and Plants, since *Plutarch*,[5] and the Ancients have named it the Divisive Number, justly

75. Cf. 'the mysterious crosses of *Ægypt*', above, p. 330. 'Mercurial' refers to both Hermes (Mercurius) Trismegistus [cf. the handed crosses ♀, above, p. 357, note 76] and the sign of the planet Mercury ☿ (*G2*).

1. i.e. the mystical import of numbers according to Pythagoras and his disciples.

2. δίκη (Browne marg.): *dike* or justice.

3. A marginal note provides the diagram ⋰ which 'by square numeration' becomes $\begin{smallmatrix} 1 & 2 & 3 \\ 4 & 5 & 6 \\ 7 & 8 & 9 \end{smallmatrix}$ with the number five 'hanging in the centre of Nine'.

4. i.e. nine-pins (*M*).

5. In *The Cessation of the Oracles*.

dividing the Entities of the world,[6] many remarkable things in it, and also comprehending the generall division of Vegetables.[7] And he that considers how most blossomes of Trees, and greatest number of Flowers, consist of five leaves; and therein doth rest the setled rule of nature; So that in those which exceed there is often found, or easily made a variety; may readily discover how nature rests in this number, which is indeed the first rest and pause of numeration in the fingers, the naturall Organs thereof. Nor in the division of the feet of perfect animals doth nature exceed this account. And even in the joints of feet, which in birds are most multiplied, surpasseth not this number; So progressionally making them out in many,[8] that from five in the fore-claw she descendeth unto two in the hindemost; And so in fower feet[9] makes up the number of joynts, in the five fingers or toes of man.

Not to omit the Quintuple section of a Cone,[10] of handsome practise in Ornamentall Garden-plots, and in some way discoverable in so many works of Nature; In the leaves, fruits, and seeds of Vegetables, and scales of some Fishes, so much considerable in glasses,[11] and the optick doctrine; wherein the learned may consider the Crystalline humour[12] of the eye in the cuttle fish and *Loligo*.

He that forgets not how Antiquity named this the Conjugall or wedding number,[13] and made it the Embleme of the most remarkable conjunction, will conceive it duely appliable unto

6. i.e. the four constituents of matter – 'fire, water, earth, and aire' (as above, p. 124) – and the quintessence (ether).

7. '*Arbor, frutex, suffrutex, herba,* and that fifth which comprehendeth the *fungi* and *tubera*' (Browne marg.). Cf. above, p. 350, note 46.

8. 'As Herns, Bitterns, and long claw'd Fowls' (Browne suppl.).

9. i.e. claws.

10. Ellipse, parabola, hyperbola, circle, triangle (Browne marg., named in Latin).

11. i.e. microscopes.

12. i.e. lens.

13. Cf. Plutarch, *The E at Delphi*: 'the beginning and ground of even numbers is Two, and of odde, Three . . .: which being joined together is engendered Five, . . . worthily named Γάμος, that is to say, Mariage; because the even number hath some resemblance to the female, and the odde, a reference to the male' (Holland's translation, 1603; in *M*).

this handsome Oeconomy,[14] and vegetable combination; May hence apprehend the allegoricall sence of that obscure expression of *Hesiod*,[15] and afford no improbable reason why *Plato* admitted his Nuptiall guests by fives, in the kindred of the married couple.[16]

And though a sharper mystery might be implied in the Number of the five wise and foolish Virgins, which were to meet the Bridegroom,[17] yet was the same agreeable unto the Conjugall Number, which ancient Numerists[18] made out by two and three, the first parity and imparity, the active and passive digits, the materiall and formall principles in generative Societies. And not discordant even from the customes of the *Romans,* who admitted but five Torches in their Nuptiall solemnities.[19] Whether there were any mystery or not implied, the most generative animals were created on this day,[20] and had accordingly the largest benediction: And under a Quintuple consideration, wanton Antiquity considered the Circumstances of generation, while by this number of five they naturally divided the Nectar of the fifth Planet.[21]

The same number in the Hebrew mysteries and Cabalistical accounts was the character of Generation;[22] declared by the Letter *He*, the fifth in their Alphabet; According to that Cabalisticall *Dogma*: If *Abram* had not had this Letter added unto his Name[23] he had remained fruitlesse, and without the

14. As above, p. 69, note 38.

15. 'Beware of all fifth days; they are harsh and angry' – in *Works and Days*, 802 (Browne marg.).

16. *Laws*, VI (Browne marg.).

17. Matthew 25.1.

18. i.e. numerologists. On Browne's attitude to numerology see above pp. 42-3.

19. So Plutarch (Browne marg.).

20. i.e. the fifth of the creation (Genesis 1.20–23).

21. i.e. Venus: 'the lips that Venus has imbued with the quintessence of her own nectar' (Browne suppl., quoting the Latin of Horace, *Odes*, I, xiii, 15–16).

22. According to Archangelus Burgonovus (Browne marg.) in his defence of the cabalistic or esoteric Judaeo-Christian doctrines of Pico (§178).

23. i.e. the letter 'h', when Abram was renamed Abraham (Genesis 17.5).

power of generation: Not onely because hereby the number of his Name attained two hundred fourty eight, the number of the affirmative precepts, but because as increated natures there is a male and female, so in divine and intelligent productions, the mother of Life and Fountain of souls in Cabalisticall Technology is called *Binah*; whose Seal and Character was *He*. So that being sterill before, he received the power of generation from that measure and mansion in the Archetype; and was made comformable unto *Binah*. And upon such involved considerations, the ten of *Sarai* was exchanged into five.[24] If any shall look upon this as a stable number, and fitly appropriable unto Trees, as Bodies of Rest and Station, he hath herein a great Foundation in nature, who observing much variety in legges and motive Organs of Animals, as two, four, six, eight, twelve, fourteen, and more, hath passed over five and ten, and assigned them unto none.[25] And for the stability of this Number, he shall not want the sphericity of its nature, which multiplied in it self, will return into its own denomination, and bring up the reare of the account. Which is also one of the Numbers that makes up the mysticall Name of God, which consisting of Letters denoting all the sphæricall Numbers, ten, five, and six;[26] Emphatically sets forth the Notion of *Trismegistus*, and that intelligible Sphere, which is the Nature of God.[27]

Many Expressions by this Number occurre in Holy Scripture, perhaps unjustly laden with mysticall Expositions, and little concerning our order. That the Israelites were forbidden to eat the fruit of their new planted Trees, before the fifth yeare,[28] was very agreeable unto the naturall Rules of Husbandry: Fruits being unwholsome and lash,[29] before the fourth, or fifth Yeare.

24. i.e. the letter 'iod' (the tenth of the Hebrew alphabet) was changed to 'h' (the fifth) when Sarai became Sarah (Genesis 17.15).

25. 'Or very few' (Browne marg., mentioning a spider with ten legs noted by Clusius and de Laet – 'If perfectly described', he adds).

26. The three Hebrew letters in Yahweh ('Jehovah') denote the three numbers mentioned.

27. As above, p. 71, note 49.

28. Leviticus 19.23–5.

29. Watery.

In the second day or Feminine part of five, there was added no approbation.[30] For in the third or masculine day, the same is twice repeated;[31] and a double benediction inclosed both Creations, whereof the one, in some part was but an accomplishment of the other. That the Trespasser was to pay a fifth part above the head or principall,[32] makes no secret in this Number, and implied no more then one part above the principall; which being considered in four parts, the additionall forfeit must bear the Name of a fift. The five golden mice[33] had plainly their determination from the number of the Princes; That five should put to flight an hundred[34] might have nothing mystically implyed; considering a rank of Souldiers could scarce consist of a lesser number. Saint *Paul* had rather speak five words in a known then ten thousand in an unknowne tongue:[35] That is as little as could well be spoken. A simple proposition consisting of three words and a complexed one not ordinarily short of five.[36]

More considerable there are in this mysticall account, which we must not insist on. And therefore why the radicall Letters[37] in the Pentateuch, should equall the number of the Souldiery of the Tribes;[38] Why our Saviour in the Wildernesse fed five thousand persons with five Barley Loaves, and again, but four

30. i.e. that the second day of creation was 'good' – the benediction mentioned in every other instance (Genesis 1.6–8). On the number two as 'Feminine', see above, p. 380, note 13.

31. i.e. that it was 'good' (Genesis 1.10 and 12).

32. Leviticus 6.5.

33. i.e. the 'trespass offering' of 'five golden mice, according to the number of the lords of the Philistines' (1 Samuel 6.4).

34. Leviticus 6.5 ('five of you shall chase an hundred').

35. 1 Corinthians 14.19.

36. The ensuing seven paragraphs reduced Coleridge to ecstasy: 'Quincunxes in Heaven above, Quincunxes in Earth below, & Quincunxes in the water beneath the Earth; Quincunxes in Deity, Quincunxes in the mind of man, Quincunxes in optic nerves, in Roots of Trees, in leaves, in petals, in every thing!'

37. The consonants in the roots of Hebrew words.

38. The Pentateuch or first five books of the Bible were said to contain just over 600,000 'radicall Letters'; and the warriors of Israel, to have been nearly as many (Numbers 1.46).

thousand with no lesse then seven of Wheat?[39] Why *Joseph*
designed five changes of Rayment unto *Benjamin*? and *David*
took just five pibbles out of the Brook against the Pagan
Champion?[40] We leave it unto Arithmeticall Divinity, and
Theologicall explanation.

Yet if any delight in new Problemes, or think it worth the
enquiry, whether the Criticall Physician hath rightly hit the
nominall notation of Quinque;[41] Why the Ancients mixed five
or three but not four parts of water unto their Wine: And
Hippocrates observed[42] a fifth proportion in the mixture of
water with milk, as in *Dysenteries* and bloudy fluxes. Under what
abstruse foundation Astrologers do Figure the good or bad
Fate from our Children, in good Fortune, or the fifth house of
their Celestriall Schemes.[43] Whether the Ægyptians described a
Starre by a Figure of five points, with reference unto the five
Capitall aspects,[44] whereby they transmit their Influences, or
abstruser Considerations? Why the Cabalisticall Doctors, who
conceive the whole *Sephiroth*, or divine emanations to have
guided the ten-stringed Harp of *David*, whereby he pacified the
evil spirit of *Saul*, in strict numeration doe begin with the
Perihypate Meson, or si fa ut, and so place the Tiphereth
answering C fol fa ut, upon the fifth string:[45] Or whether this
number be oftener applied unto bad things and ends, then good
in holy Scripture, and why? He may meet with abstrusities of
no ready resolution.

If any shall question the rationality of that Magick, in the cure
of the blind man by *Serapis*, commanded to place five fingers on

39. John 6.9–10 and Matthew 15.34–8, respectively.
40. Genesis 45.22 and 1 Samuel 17.40, respectively.
41. Scaliger – 'the Criticall Physician' or literary doctor – had claimed
that the Latin word for five derives from the Greek of 'four and one'
(Browne marg.).
42. In *Epidemics*, VII, 3.
43. ''Αγαθὴ τύχη, or *bona fortuna*, the name of the fifth house' (Browne
marg.). The celestial regions were divided into twelve 'houses'.
44. 'Conjunct, opposite, sextile, trigonal, tetragonal' (Browne marg.).
45. The Biblical episode (1 Samuel 16.23) elicited many elaborate dis-
courses as by Mersenne (quoted in *M*).

his Altar, and then his hand on his Eyes ?[46] Why since the whole Comœdy is primarily and naturally comprised in four parts,[47] and Antiquity permitted not so many persons to speak in one Scene, yet would not comprehend the same in more or lesse then five acts?[48] Why amongst Sea-starres nature chiefly delighteth in five points ? And since there are found some of no fewer then twelve, and some of seven, and nine, there are few or none discovered of six or eight ? If any shall enquire why the Flowers of *Rue* properly consist[ing] of four Leaves, The first and third Flower have five ? Why since many Flowers have one leaf or none, as *Scaliger* will have it, diverse three, and the greatest number consist of five divided from their bottomes; there are yet so few of two: or why nature generally beginning or setting out with two opposite leaves at the Root, doth so seldome conclude with that order and number at the Flower ? he shall not passe his hours in vulgar speculations.

If any shall further quæry why magneticall Philosophy[49] excludeth decussations, and needles transversly placed do naturally distract their verticities ?[50] Why Geomancers[51] do imitate the Quintuple Figure, in their Mother Characters of Acquisition and Amission,[52] &c. somewhat answering the Figures in the Lady or speckled Beetle ? With what Equity, Chiromantical conjecturers[53] decry these decussations in the Lines and Mounts of the hand ? What that decussated Figure intendeth in the medall of *Alexander* the Great ?[54] Why the Goddesses sit commonly crosse-legged in ancient draughts,

46. According to an inscription printed by Gruterus (*G2*).

47. i.e. the four parts of any dramatic poem (Browne marg., naming the terms in Greek).

48. Horace, *The Art of Poetry*, 189–90.

49. i.e. the science of magnetism.

50. i.e. turn away their vertices so that, in pointing north, they avoid the decussation.

51. As above, p. 180, note 39.

52. 'loss' (Blount).

53. As above, p. 242, note 12.

54. Referring to a coin illustrated by Agostino (as above, p. 341, note 58).

Since *Juno* is described in the same as a veneficial[55] posture to
hinder the birth of *Hercules*? If any shall doubt why at the
Amphidromicall Feasts,[56] on the fifth day after the Childe was
born presents were sent from friends, of *Polipusses*, and Cuttle-
fishes? Why five must be only left in that Symbolicall mutiny
among the men of *Cadmus*?[57] Why *Proteus* in *Homer* the Symbole
of the first matter, before he setled himself in the midst of his
Sea-monsters, doth place them out by fives?[58] Why the fifth
years Oxe was acceptable Sacrifice unto *Jupiter*?[59] Or why the
Noble *Antoninus* in some sence doth call the soul it self a
Rhombus?[60] He shall not fall on trite or triviall disquisitions.
And these we invent and propose unto acuter enquirers,
nauseating crambe verities[61] and questions over-queried. Flat
and flexible truths are beat out by every hammer; but *Vulcan*
and his whole forge sweat to work out *Achilles* his armour.[62] A
large field is yet left unto sharper discerners to enlarge upon this
order, to search out the *quaternio's*[63] and figured draughts of this
nature, and moderating the study of names, and meer nomen-
clature of plants, to erect generalities, disclose unobserved
proprieties, not only in the vegetable shop, but the whole
volume of nature; affording delightful Truths, confirmable by
sense and ocular Observation,[64] which seems to me the surest
path, to trace the Labyrinth of Truth. For though discursive
enquiry and rationall conjecture, may leave handsome gashes
and flesh-wounds; yet without conjunction of this expect no
mortal or dispatching blows unto errour.

55. i.e. venefical: malignant. The myth is described in 'draughts' (draw-
ings) and related by Ovid, *Metamorphoses*, IX, 298–300.
56. The ancient Amphidromia at the naming of a child.
57. Ovid, *Metamorphoses*, III, 126.
58. *Odyssey*, IV, 412.
59. *Iliad*, II, 403, and VII, 315.
60. Marcus Aurelius, *Meditations*, XI, 12; etc.
61. i.e. nauseated by stale truths.
62. *Iliad*, XVIII, 468 ff.
63. i.e. the Pythagorean tetrad ($1+2+3+4 = 10$), suggestive of the
totality of things and their underlying design. See §56.
64. i.e. experimental knowledge, the 'experience' and 'reason' com-
mended in *Pseudodoxia Epidemica* (see above, p. 35).

But the Quincunx of Heaven[65] runs low, and 'tis time to close the five ports of knowledge;[66] We are unwilling to spin out our awaking thoughts into the phantasmes of sleep, which often continueth præcogitations;[67] making Cables of Cobwebbes and Wildernesses of handsome Groves. Beside *Hippocrates*[68] hath spoke so little and the Oneirocriticall Masters,[69] have left such frigid Interpretations from plants, that there is little encouragement to dream of Paradise it self. Nor will the sweetest delight of Gardens afford much comfort in sleep; wherein the dulnesse of that sense shakes hands with delectable odours; and though in the Bed of *Cleopatra*,[70] can hardly with any delight raise up the ghost of a Rose.

Night which Pagan Theology could make the daughter of *Chaos*,[71] affords no advantage to the description of order: Although no lower then that Masse can we derive its Genealogy. All things began in order, so shall they end, and so shall they begin again; according to the ordainer of order and mystical Mathematicks of the City of Heaven.

Though *Somnus* in *Homer* be sent to rowse up *Agamemnon*,[72] I finde no such effects in these drowsy approaches of sleep. To keep our eyes open longer were but to act our *Antipodes*.[73] The Huntsmen are up in *America*, and they are already past their first sleep in *Persia*.[74] But who can be drowsie at that howr

65. 'Hyades near the Horizon about midnight at that time', i.e. the beginning of March (Browne marg.). Hyades is the cluster of five stars in the vicinity of Pleiades.

66. i.e. the five senses.

67. Previous thoughts.

68. In *On Dreams* (Browne marg.).

69. 'Artemidorus & Apomazar' (Browne marg.): see below, p. 476, note 5.

70. 'strewed with roses' (Browne marg.).

71. Hesiod, *Theogony*, 123.

72. *Iliad*, II, 6, where Zeus sends not sleep but a dream (somnium).

73. 'Think thou', exclaimed Coleridge, 'that there ever was such a reason given before for going to bed at midnight, to wit, that if we did not, we should be acting the part of our ANTIPODES!!'

74. ' – what Life, what Fancy! Does the whimsical Knight give us thus a dish of strong green Tea, & call it an *Opiate*?' (Coleridge).

which freed us from everlasting sleep? or have slumbring thoughts at that time, when sleep it self must end, and as some conjecture all shall awake again?

A Letter to a Friend

[*A Letter to a Friend, upon occasion of the Death of his Intimate Friend* was first published posthumously in 1690. Originally thought to have been written in the early 1670s (e.g. §190), the work is now generally accepted as having been composed not long after December 1656. At that time, it has been established, Browne addressed the *Letter* to Sir John Pettus on the occasion of Robert Loveday's death of consumption at the age of thirty-five (see §§314–15).]

Give me leave to wonder that News of this nature should have such heavy Wings, that you should hear so little concerning your dearest Friend, and that I must make that unwilling Repetition to tell you, *Ad portam rigidos calces extendit*,[1] that he is Dead and Buried, and by this time no Puny among the mighty Nations of the Dead; for tho he left this World not very many days past, yet every hour you know largely addeth unto that dark Society; and considering the incessant Mortality of Mankind, you cannot conceive there dieth in the whole Earth so few as a thousand an hour.

Altho at this distance you had no early Account or Particular of his Death; yet your Affection may cease to wonder that you had not some secret Sense or Intimation thereof by Dreams, thoughtful Whisperings, Mercurisms, Airy Nuncio's, or sympathetical Insinuations, which many seem to have had at the Death of their dearest Friends: for since we find in that famous Story, that Spirits themselves were fain to tell their Fellows at a distance, that the great *Antonio* was dead;[2] we have a sufficient Excuse for our Ignorance in such Particulars, and must rest content with the common Road, and *Appian* way of Knowledge by Information. Tho the uncertainty of the End of this World hath confounded all Humane Predictions; yet they who shall live to see the Sun and Moon darkned, and the Stars to fall from Heaven, will hardly be deceived in the Advent of the last Day; and therefore strange it is, that the common Fallacy of consumptive Persons, who feel not themselves dying, and therefore still hope to live, should also reach their Friends in perfect Health and Judgment. That you should be so little

1. Persius, III, 105: 'He stretches out his heels cold and stark towards the door'.
2. The reference is not to Plutarch's story ('the great Pan is dead') but to George Sandys's report in 1621 that the death of 'one Antonio called the Rich' was foretold by 'a voice' (§321). Browne's preference for Sandys's account may have been dictated by the fact that the daughter of Sir John Pettus (see headnote, above) had married into the Sandys family.

acquainted with *Plautus*'s sick Complexion,[3] or that almost an *Hippocratical*[4] Face should not alarum you to higher fears, or rather despair of his Continuation in such an emaciated State, wherein medical Predictions fail not, as sometimes in acute Diseases, and wherein 'tis as dangerous to be sentenced by a Physician as a Judge.

Upon my first Visit I was bold to tell them who had not let fall all hopes of his Recovery, That in my sad Opinion he was not like to behold a Grashopper, much less to pluck another Fig; and in no long time after seemed to discover that odd mortal Symptom in him not mention'd by *Hippocrates*, that is, to lose his own Face and look like some of his near Relations; for he maintained not his proper Countenance, but looked like his Uncle, the Lines of whose Face lay deep and invisible in his healthful Visage before: for as from our beginning we run through variety of Looks, before we come to consistent and settled Faces; so before our End, by sick and languishing Alterations, we put on new Visages: and in our Retreat to Earth, may fall upon such Looks which from community of seminal Originals were before latent in us.

He was fruitlessly put in hope of advantage by change of Air, and imbibing the pure Aerial Nitre of these Parts;[5] and therefore being so far spent, he quickly found *Sardinia* in *Tivoli*,[6] and the most healthful Air of little effect, where Death had set her Broad Arrow;[7] for he lived not unto the middle of *May*, and confirmed the Observation of *Hippocrates*[8] of that mortal time

3. Plautus, *The Captives*, 647–8: 'thin face, sharp nose, complexion fair, black eyes, hair a little reddish, waving, and curled'.

4. 'moribund' (§176). The allusion is to Hippocrates's description (in *Prognostics*, II) of the dying man.

5. i.e. East Anglia. Air containing nitre was said to be conducive to health (M).

6. 'When death comes, Sardinia is in the midst of Tivoli' (Browne marg., quoting the Latin of Martial, *Epigrams*, IV, 60, 5–6). Sardinia was regarded as unhealthy.

7. 'In the King's Forests they set the Figure of a broad Arrow upon Trees that are to be cut down' (Browne marg.).

8. In *Epidemics*, VI, vii, 9 (Browne marg.).

of the Year when the Leaves of the Fig-tree resemble a Daw's Claw. He is happily seated who lives in Places whose Air, Earth, and Water, promote not the Infirmities of his weaker Parts, or is early removed into Regions that correct them. He that is tabidly inclined, were unwise to pass his days in *Portugal:* Cholical Persons will find little Comfort in *Austria* or *Vienna:* He that is Weak-legg'd must not be in Love with *Rome*, nor an infirm Head with *Venice* or *Paris*. Death hath not only particular Stars in Heaven, but malevolent Places on Earth, which single out our Infirmities, and strike at our weaker Parts; in which Concern, passager and migrant Birds have the great Advantages; who are naturally constituted for distant Habitations, whom no Seas nor Places limit, but in their appointed Seasons will visit us from *Greenland* and Mount *Atlas*, and as some think, even from the *Antipodes*.[9]

Tho we could not have his Life, yet we missed not our desires in his soft Departure, which was scarce an Expiration; and his End not unlike his Beginning, when the salient Point[10] scarce affords a sensible motion, and his Departure so like unto Sleep, that he scarce needed the civil Ceremony of closing his Eyes; contrary unto the common way wherein Death draws up, Sleep lets fall the Eye-lids. With what strift[11] and pains we came into the World we know not; but 'tis commonly no easie matter to get out of it: yet if it could be made out, that such who have easie Nativities have commonly hard Deaths, and contrarily; his Departure was so easie, that we might justly suspect his Birth was of another nature, and that some *Juno* sat cross-legg'd at his Nativity.[12]

Besides his soft Death, the incurable state of his Disease might somewhat extenuate your Sorrow, who know that Monsters but seldom happen, Miracles more rarely, in Physick.[13] *Angelus Victorius* gives a serious Account of a Consump-

9. So Belonnius (Browne marg.).
10. The heart as first seen in embryos (*M*).
11. Striving.
12. See above, p. 386, note 55.
13. '*Monstra contingunt in medicina. Hippoc.* Strange and rare Escapes there happen sometimes in Physic' (Browne marg.).

tive, Hectical, Pthysical Woman, who was suddenly cured by the Intercession of *Ignatius*.[14] We read not of any in Scripture who in this case applied unto our Saviour, tho some may be contained in that large Expression, That *he went about Galilee healing all manner of Sickness, and all manner of Diseases*.[15] Amulets, Spells, Sigils and Incantations, practised in other Diseases, are seldom pretended in this; and we find no Sigil in the Archidoxis[16] of *Paracelsus* to cure an extreme Consumption or *Marasmus*, which if other Diseases fail, will put a period unto long Livers, and at last make dust of all. And therefore the *Stoicks* could not but think that the firy Principle would wear out all the rest, and at last make an end of the World, which notwithstanding without such a lingring period the Creator may effect at his Pleasure: and to make an end of all things on Earth, and our Planetical System of the World, he need but put out the Sun.

I was not so curious to entitle the Stars unto any concern of his Death, yet could not but take notice that he died when the Moon was in motion from the Meridian; at which time, an old *Italian* long ago would persuade me, that the greatest part of Men died: but herein I confess I could never satisfie my Curiosity; altho from the time of Tides in Places upon or near the Sea, there may be considerable Deductions; and *Pliny* hath an odd and remarkable Passage concerning the Death of Men and Animals upon the Recess or Ebb of the Sea.[17] However, certain it is he died in the dead and deep part of the Night, when *Nox* might be most apprehensibly said to be the Daughter of Chaos, the Mother of Sleep and Death, according to old Genealogy;[18] and so went out of this World about that hour when our blessed Saviour entred it, and about what time many conceive he will return again unto it. *Cardan* hath a peculiar and no hard Obser-

14. So Angelus Victorius (Browne marg.).

15. Matthew 4.23 (Browne marg.).

16. The *Archidoxis magica* (as above, p. 85, note 123).

17. 'Aristotle adds that no animal dies except when the tide is ebbing. The observation has been often made on the ocean of Gaul; but it has only been found true with respect to man' (Browne marg., quoting the Latin of Pliny, II, ci, 220).

18. As in Hesiod, *Theogony*, 212.

vation from a Man's Hand, to know whether he was born in the day or night, which I confess holdeth in my own. And *Scaliger* to that purpose hath another from the tip of the Ear.[19] Most Men are begotten in the Night, most Animals in the Day; but whether more Persons have been born in the Night or the Day, were a Curiosity undecidable, tho more have perished by violent Deaths in the Day; yet in natural Dissolutions both Times may hold an Indifferency, at least but contingent[20] Inequality. The whole course of Time runs out in the Nativity and Death of Things; which whether they happen by Succession or Coincidence, are best computed by the natural, not artificial Day.

That *Charles* the Fifth was Crowned upon the day of his Nativity, it being in his own power so to order it, makes no singular Animadversion; but that he should also take King *Francis* Prisoner upon that day, was an unexpected Coincidence, which made the same remarkable. *Antipater* who had an Anniversary Feast[21] every Year upon his Birth day, needed no Astrological Revolution to know what day he should dye on.[22] When the fixed Stars have made a Revolution unto the points from whence they first set out, some of the Ancients thought the World would have an end;[23] which was a kind of dying upon the day of its Nativity. Now the Disease prevailing and swiftly advancing about the time of his Nativity, some were of Opinion, that he would leave the World on the day he entred into it: but this being a lingring Disease, and creeping softly on, nothing critical was found or expected, and he died not before fifteen days after. Nothing is more common with Infants than to dye on the day of their Nativity, to behold the worldly Hours and but the Fractions thereof; and even to perish before their

---

19. 'The hanging part of the ear is called the lobe. Not every ear has this part: those who are born at night do not have it, but those who are born in the day do, for the most part' (Browne marg., quoting the Latin of Scaliger's commentary on Aristotle).

20. Accidental.

21. 'fever' (*MSS.*: *M, K, E*).

22. So Pliny, VII, 52

23. See above, p. 66, note 29.

Nativity in the hidden World of the Womb, and before their
good Angel is conceived to undertake them.[24] But in Persons
who out-live many Years, and when there are no less than three
hundred sixty five days to determine their Lives in every Year;
that the first day should make the last, that the Tail of the Snake
should return into its Mouth precisely at that time, and they
should wind up upon the day of their Nativity,[25] is indeed a
remarkable Coincidence, which tho Astrology hath taken
witty pains to salve, yet hath it been very wary in making Pre-
dictions of it.

In this consumptive Condition and remarkable Extenuation
he came to be almost half himself, and left a great part behind
him which he carried not to the Grave. And tho that Story of
Duke *John Ernestus Mansfield*[26] be not so easily swallowed, that
at his Death his Heart was found not to be so big as a Nut; yet
if the Bones of a good Sceleton weigh little more than twenty
pounds, his Inwards and Flesh remaining could make no Bouff-
age,[27] but a light bit for the Grave. I never more lively beheld
the starved Characters of *Dante*[28] in any living Face; an Arus-
pex[29] might have read a Lecture upon him without Exentera-
tion,[30] his Flesh being so consumed that he might, in a manner,
have discerned his Bowels without opening of him: so that to
be carried *sextâ cervice*[31] to the Grave, was but a civil unnecessity;
and the Complements of the Coffin might out-weigh the
Subject of it.

24. See above, p. 99, note 188.

25. 'According to the *Egyptian* Hieroglyphick' (Browne marg.). Cf.
Pierius: 'The snake eats its own tail to show the immortality of its
generations and to demonstrate that the beginning is turned to the end
and the end turned back to the beginning' (*M*). Browne himself was to
die on his birthday, 19 October 1682.

26. So Knolles on the Duke John Ernestus (Browne marg.).

27. Satisfying meal.

28. 'In the Poet *Dante* his description' (Browne marg.): *Purgatorio*,
XXIII, 28. Cf. above, p. 296, note 89.

29. 'he that telleth of thinges to come by lokynge in beastes bowelles'
(Elyot).

30. Taking out the entrails.

31. Carried by six (Juvenal, *Satires*, I, 64).

Omnibus Ferrarius[32] in mortal Dysenteries of Children looks for a Spot behind the Ear; in consumptive Diseases some eye the Complexion of Moals; *Cardan* eagerly views the Nails, some the Lines of the Hand, the Thenar or Muscle of the Thumb; some are so curious as to observe the depth of the Throat-pit, how the proportion varieth of the Small of the Legs unto the Calf, or the compass of the Neck unto the Circumference of the Head: but all these, with many more, were so drowned in a mortal Visage and last Face of *Hippocrates*,[33] that a weak Physiognomist might say at first eye, This was a Face of Earth, and that *Morta*[34] had set her Hard-Seal upon his Temples, easily perceiving what *Caricatura*[35] Draughts Death makes upon pined Faces, and unto what an unknown degree a Man may live backward.[36]

Tho the Beard be only made a distinction of Sex and sign of masculine Heat by *Ulmus*,[37] yet the Precocity and early growth thereof in him, was not to be liked in reference unto long Life. *Lewis*, that virtuous but unfortunate King of *Hungary*, who lost his Life at the Battel of *Mohacz*, was said to be born without a Skin, to have bearded at Fifteen, and to have shewn some gray Hairs about Twenty; from whence the Diviners conjectured, that he would be spoiled of his Kingdom, and have but a short Life: But Hairs make fallible Predictions, and many Temples early gray have out-lived the Psalmist's Period.[38] Hairs which have most amused me have not been in the Face or Head but on the Back, and not in Men but Children, as I long ago observed in that Endemial Distemper of little Children in *Languedock*, called the *Morgellons*,[39] wherein they critically break out with

32. In his treatise *Concerning the Diseases of Children*, 1577 (Browne marg.).
33. As above, p. 392, note 4.
34. '*Morta*, the Deity of Death or Fate' (Browne marg.).
35. 'When Mens Faces are drawn with resemblance to some other Animals, the *Italians* call it, to be drawn in *Caricatura*' (Browne marg.).
36. i.e. retrogressively.
37. In his treatise *Concerning the Use of the Human Beard* (Browne marg.).
38. 'The Life of a Man is Three-score and Ten' (Browne marg.): Psalm 90.10.
39. The rare disease variously known as Les Crinons, Masclous, or Masquelons (for details see §317).

harsh Hairs on their Backs, which takes off the unquiet Symptoms of the Disease, and delivers them from Coughs and Convulsions.

The *Egyptian* Mummies that I have seen, have had their Mouths open, and somewhat gaping, which affordeth a good opportunity to view and observe their Teeth, wherein 'tis not easie to find any wanting or decayed: and therefore in *Egypt*, where one Man practised but one Operation, or the Diseases but of single Parts, it must needs be a barren Profession to confine unto that of drawing of Teeth, and little better than to have been Tooth-drawer unto King *Pyrrhus*, who had but two in his Head.[40] How the *Bannyans* of *India* maintain the Integrity of those Parts, I find not particularly observed; who notwithstanding have an Advantage of their Preservation by abstaining from all Flesh, and employing their Teeth in such Food unto which they may seem at first framed, from their Figure and Conformation: but sharp and corroding Rheums[41] had so early mouldred those Rocks and hardest parts of his Fabrick, that a Man might well conceive that his Years were never like to double or twice tell over his Teeth.[42] Corruption had dealt more severely with them, than sepulchral Fires and smart Flames with those of burnt Bodies of old; for in the burnt Fragments of Urns which I have enquired into, altho I seem to find few Incisors or Shearers, yet the Dog Teeth and Grinders do notably resist those Fires.

In the Years of his Childhood he had languished under the Disease of his Country, the Rickets; after which notwithstanding many I have seen become[43] strong and active Men; but whether any have attained unto very great Years the Disease is scarce so old as to afford good Observation. Whether the Children of the *English* Plantations be subject unto the same Infirmity, may be worth the observing. Whether Lameness and

40. 'His upper and lower Jaw being solid, and without distinct rows of Teeth' (Browne marg.): cf. Plutarch's life of Pyrrhus, III.

41. According to Picotus (Browne marg.).

42. 'Twice tell over his Teeth never live to threescore Years' (Browne marg.).

43. 'many I have seen become' (*MSS.*: *K*; *E*): 'many have been become' (1690 ed.: *M*).

Halting do still encrease among the Inhabitants of *Rovigno* in *Istria*, I know not; yet scarce twenty Years ago Monsieur *du Loyr*[44] observed, that a third part of that People halted: but too certain it is, that the Rickets encreaseth among us; the Small-Pox grows more pernicious than the Great: the Kings Purse knows that the King's Evil grows more common.[45] *Quartan* Agues are become no Strangers in *Ireland*; more common and mortal in *England:* and tho the Ancients gave that Disease very good Words,[46] yet now that Bell makes no strange sound which rings out for the Effects thereof.[47]

Some think there were few Consumptions in the Old World, when Men lived much upon Milk; and that the ancient Inhabitants of this Island were less troubled with Coughs when they went naked, and slept in Caves and Woods, than Men now in Chambers and Feather-beds. *Plato* will tell us,[48] that there was no such Disease as a Catarrh in *Homer*'s time, and that it was but new in *Greece* in his Age. *Polydore Virgil* delivereth that Pleurisies were rare in *England*, who lived but in the days of *Henry* the Eighth. Some will allow no Diseases to be new, others think that many old ones are ceased; and that such which are esteemed new, will have but their time: However, the Mercy of God hath scattered the great heap of Diseases, and not loaded any one Country with all: some may be new in one Country which have been old in another. New Discoveries of the Earth discover new Diseases: for besides the common swarm, there are endemial and local Infirmities proper unto certain Regions, which in the whole Earth make no small number: and if *Asia, Africa*, and *America* should bring in their List, *Pandoras* Box would swell, and there must be a strange Pathology.

44. In *Les Voyages* (1654).
45. When persons were touched for the King's Evil [scrofula], a gold medal was hung round each patient's neck (*G1*).
46. 'Most carefree and easy' (Browne marg., quoted in Greek and Latin): as remarked by Hippocrates, *Epidemics*, I, iii, 11.
47. 'The bell rarely tolls for a fourth-day fever' (Browne marg., quoting the Latin of a popular saying). The daily services were at the first, third, sixth and ninth hours.
48. In *The Republic*, III, 405d.

Most Men expected to find a consumed Kell,[49] empty and
bladder-like Guts, livid and marbled Lungs, and a withered
Pericardium in this exuccous[50] Corps: but some seemed too
much to wonder that two Lobes of his Lungs adhered unto his
side; for the like I had often found in Bodies of no suspected
Consumptions or difficulty of Respiration. And the same more
often happeneth in Men than other Animals; and some think,
in Women than in Men: but the most remarkable I have met
with, was in a Man,[51] after a Cough of almost fifty Years, in
whom all the Lobes adhered unto the Pleura,[52] and each Lobe
unto another; who having also been much troubled with the
Gout, brake the Rule of *Cardan*,[53] and died of the Stone in the
Bladder. *Aristotle* makes a Query,[54] Why some Animals cough
as Man, some not, as Oxen. If coughing be taken as it consisteth
of a natural and voluntary motion, including Expectoration and
spitting out, it may be as proper unto Man as bleeding at the
Nose; otherwise we find that *Vegetius* and Rural Writers[55] have
not left so many Medicines in vain against the Coughs of Cattel;
and Men who perish by Coughs dye the Death of Sheep, Cats
and Lyons: and tho Birds have no Midriff, yet we meet with
divers Remedies in *Arrianus*[56] against the Coughs of Hawks.
And tho it might be thought, that all Animals who have Lungs
do cough; yet in cetaceous[57] Fishes, who have large and strong
Lungs, the same is not observed; nor yet in oviparous[58] Quad-
rupeds: and in the greatest thereof, the Crocodile, altho we read
much of their Tears, we find nothing of that motion.

49. The membrane investing the intestines (*M*).

50. Sapless (as above, p. 299, note 14).

51. 'So A.F.' (Browne marg.). *K* reads '*A.J.*', identified as Sir Arthur
Jenny (*K*, III, 301).

52. Ribs.

53. 'Cardan in his *Encomium Podagræ* [Praise of Gout] reckoneth this
among the *Dona Podagræ* [Gifts of Gout], that they are delivered thereby
from the Pthysis and Stone in the Bladder' (Browne marg.).

54. In the pseudo-Aristotelian *Problems*, X, 1.

55. i.e. writers on agriculture.

56. An error for Aldrovandi (*M*)?

57. 'belonging to Whales or such like great fishes' (Blount).

58. 'Birds, Beasts, or Fishes that breed eggs or spawn' (Blount, citing
Browne). Cf. above, p. 203.

From the Thoughts of Sleep, when the Soul was conceived nearest unto Divinity, the Ancients erected an Art of Divination, wherein while they too widely expatiated in loose and inconsequent Conjectures, *Hippocrates*[59] wisely considered Dreams as they presaged Alterations in the Body, and so afforded hints toward the preservation of Health, and prevention of Diseases; and therein was so serious as to advise Alteration of Diet, Exercise, Sweating, Bathing and Vomiting; and also so religious, as to order Prayers and Supplications unto respective Deities, in good Dreams unto *Sol, Jupiter cœlestis, Jupiter opulentus, Minerva, Mercurius,* and *Apollo;* in bad unto *Tellus* and the Heroes.

And therefore I could not but take notice how his Female Friends were irrationally curious so strictly to examine his Dreams, and in this low state to hope for the Fantasms of Health. He was now past the healthful Dreams of the Sun, Moon, and Stars in their Clarity and proper Courses. 'Twas too late to dream of Flying, of Limpid Fountains, smooth Waters, white Vestments, and fruitful green Trees, which are the Visions of healthful Sleeps, and at good distance from the Grave.

And they were also too deeply dejected that he should dream of his dead Friends, inconsequently divining, that he would not be long from them; for strange it was not that he should sometimes dream of the dead whose Thoughts run always upon Death: beside, to dream of the dead, so they appear not in dark Habits, and take nothing away from us, in *Hippocrates*[60] his Sense was of good signification: for we live by the dead, and every thing is or must be so before it becomes our Nourishment. And *Cardan,* who dream'd that he discoursed with his dead Father in the Moon, made thereof no mortal Interpretation: and even to dream that we are dead, was no condemnable Fantasm in old *Oneirocriticism,*[61] as having a signification of

59. In *On Dreams* (Browne marg.). The more 'scientific' attitude of Hippocrates is here contrasted to interpretations of dreams ventured by Artemidorus, whose *Oneirocriticon* is 'mainly a source book of ancient superstition' (§125).

60. ibid.

61. See below, p. 476, note 5.

Liberty, vacuity from Cares, exemption and freedom from Troubles, unknown unto the dead.

Some Dreams I confess may admit of easie and feminine Exposition: he who dream'd that he could not see his right Shoulder, might easily fear to lose the sight of his right Eye; he that before a Journey dream'd that his Feet were cut off, had a plain warning not to undertake his intended Journey. But why to dream of Lettuce should presage some ensuing Disease, why to eat Figs should signifie foolish Talk, why to eat Eggs great Trouble, and to dream of Blindness should be so highly commended, according to the *Oneirocritical* Verses of *Astrampsychus* and *Nicephorus*, I shall leave unto your Divinaton.

He was willing to quit the World alone and altogether, leaving no Earnest behind him for Corruption or Aftergrave, having small content in that common satisfaction to survive or live in another, but amply satisfied that his Disease should dye with himself, nor revive in a Posterity to puzzle Physick, and make sad *Memento*'s of their Parent hereditary. Leprosie awakes not sometimes before Forty, the Gout and Stone often later; but consumptive and tabid Roots sprout more early, and at the fairest make seventeen Years of our Life doubtful before that Age.[62] They that enter the World with original Diseases as well as Sin, have not only common Mortality but sick Traductions[63] to destroy them, make commonly short Courses, and live not at length but in Figures; so that a sound *Cæsarean* Nativity[64] may out-last a natural Birth, and a Knife may sometimes make way for a more lasting fruit than a Midwife; which makes so few Infants now able to endure the old Test of the River,[65] and many to have feeble Children who could scarce have been married at *Sparta*, and those provident States who studied strong and healthful Generations; which happen but contingently in mere *pecuniary* Matches, or Marriages made by the

62. Hippocrates claims that man declines most between his eighteenth and his thirty-fifth year (*Aphorisms*, V, 9).

63. Transmissions (cf. above, p. 106, note 224).

64. 'A sound Child cut out of the Body of the Mother' (Browne marg.).

65. 'We take our children young to the river and harden them in the painful, ice-cold water' (Browne marg., quoting the Latin of *Aeneid*, IX, 603–4).

Candle,[66] wherein notwithstanding there is little redress to be hoped from an Astrologer or a Lawyer, and a good discerning Physician were like to prove the most successful Counsellor.

Julius Scaliger, who in a sleepless Fit of the Gout could make two hundred Verses in a Night, would have but five plain Words upon his Tomb.[67] And this serious Person,[68] tho no *minor* Wit, left the Poetry of his Epitaph unto others; either unwilling to commend himself, or to be judged by a Distich, and perhaps considering how unhappy great Poets have been in versifying their own Epitaphs; wherein *Petrarcha*, *Dante*, and *Ariosto*, have so unhappily failed, that if their Tombs should out-last their Works, Posterity would find so little of *Apollo* on them, as to mistake them for Ciceronian Poets.[69]

In this deliberate and creeping progress unto the Grave, he was somewhat too young, and of too noble a mind, to fall upon that stupid Symptom observable in divers Persons near their Journeys end, and which may be reckoned among the mortal Symptoms of their last Disease; that is, to become more narrow minded, miserable and tenacious, unready to part with any thing when they are ready to part with all, and afraid to want when they have no time to spend; mean while Physicians, who know that many are mad but in a single depraved Imagination, and one prevalent Decipiency;[70] and that beside and out of such single Deliriums a Man may meet with sober Actions and good Sense in *Bedlam;* cannot but smile to see the Heirs and concerned Relations, gratulating themselves in the sober departure of their Friends; and tho they behold such mad covetous Passages, content to think they dye in good Understanding, and in their sober Senses.

Avarice, which is not only Infidelity but Idolatry, either from

66. i.e. like those auction-sales where bids were received so long as a small candle still burned (*G1*; *M*).

67. 'Julius Caesar Scaliger his remains' (Browne marg., quoting the Latin in Joseph Scaliger's biography of his father).

68. i.e. Robert Loveday (see headnote, above, p. 389).

69. Cf. '*Cicero*, the worst of Poets' (above, p. 150).

70. i.e. desipiency: 'when the sick person speak and doth idly; dotage' (Blount).

covetous Progeny or questuary[71] Education, had no Root in his Breast, who made good Works the Expression of his Faith, and was big with desires unto publick and lasting Charities; and surely where good Wishes and charitable Intentions exceed Abilities, Theoretical Beneficency may be more than a Dream. They build not Castles in the Air who would build Churches on Earth; and tho they leave no such Structures here, may lay good Foundations in Heaven. In brief, his Life and Death were such, that I could not blame them who wished the like, and almost to have been himself; almost, I say; for tho we may wish the prosperous Appurtenances of others, or to be an other in his happy Accidents; yet so intrinsical is every Man unto himself, that some doubt may be made, whether any would exchange his Being, or substantially become another Man.

He had wisely seen the World at home and abroad, and thereby observed under what variety Men are deluded in the pursuit of that which is not here to be found. And altho he had no Opinion of reputed Felicities below, and apprehended Men widely out in the estimate of such Happiness; yet his sober contempt of the World wrought no *Democritism* or *Cynicism*, no laughing or snarling at it, as well understanding there are not Felicities[72] in this World to satisfie a serious Mind; and therefore to soften[73] the stream of our Lives, we are fain to take in the reputed Contentations of this World, to unite with the Crowd in their Beatitudes, and to make our selves happy by Consortion, Opinion, or Co-existimation:[74] for strictly to separate from received and customary Felicities, and to confine unto the rigor of Realities, were to contract the Consolation of our Beings unto too uncomfortable[75] Circumscriptions.

Not to fear Death, nor desire it,[76] was short of his Resolution: to be dissolved, and be with Christ, was his dying ditty. He conceived his Thred long, in no long course of Years, and

71. As above, p. 360, note 88.
72. 'Felicities': 'real Felicities enough' (*MSS.*: *M*).
73. 'soften': 'sweeten' (*MSS.*: *M*).
74. Co-existence.
75. 'unto too uncomfortable': 'into to narrowe' (*MSS.*: *M*).
76. Martial, *Epigrams*, X, xlvii, 13 (Browne marg., quoted in Latin).

when he had scarce out-lived the second Life of *Lazarus*;[77] esteeming it enough to approach the Years of his Saviour,[78] who so ordered his own humane State, as not to be old upon Earth.

But to be content with Death may be better than to desire it: a miserable Life may make us wish for Death, but a virtuous one to rest in it; which is the Advantage of those resolved Christians, who looking on Death not only as the sting, but the period and end of Sin, the Horizon and Isthmus between this Life and a better, and the Death of this World but as a Nativity of another, do contentedly submit unto the common Necessity, and envy not *Enoch* or *Elias*.

Not to be content with Life is the unsatisfactory state of those which destroy themselves;[79] who being afraid to live, run blindly upon their own Death, which no Man fears by Experience: and the *Stoicks* had a notable Doctrine to take away the fear thereof; that is, In such Extremities to desire that which is not to be avoided, and wish what might be feared; and so made Evils voluntary, and to suit with their own Desires, which took off the terror of them.

But the ancient Martyrs were not encouraged by such Fallacies; who, tho they feared not Death were afraid to be their own Executioners; and therefore thought it more Wisdom to crucifie their Lusts than their Bodies, to circumcise than stab their Hearts, and to mortifie than kill themselves.[80]

His willingness to leave this World about that Age when most Men think they may best enjoy it, tho paradoxical unto worldly Ears, was not strange unto mine, who have so often observed, that many, tho old, oft stick fast unto the World, and

77. 'Who upon some Accounts, and Tradition, is said to have lived 30 Years after he was raised by our Saviour. *Baronius*' (Browne marg.). Baronius had quoted the account of Epiphanius.

78. As above, p. 112, note 258.

79. 'In the Speech of *Vulteius* in *Lucan* [IV, 486–7], animating his Souldiers in a great struggle to kill one another ... [:] "All fear is over do but resolve to dye, and make your Desires meet Necessity" ' (Browne marg.).

80. On the Stoic and Christian attitudes to death – and life – see also above, p. 304.

seem to be drawn like *Cacus*'s Oxen,[81] backward with great strugling and reluctancy unto the Grave. The long habit of Living makes meer Men more hardly to part with Life, and all to be nothing, but what is to come. To live at the rate of the old World, when some could scarce remember themselves young, may afford no better digested Death than a more moderate period. Many would have thought it an Happiness to have had their lot of Life in some notable Conjunctures of Ages past; but the uncertainty of future Times hath tempted few to make a part in Ages to come. And surely, he that hath taken the true Altitude of Things, and rightly calculated the degenerate state of this Age, is not like to envy those that shall live in the next, much less three or four hundred Years hence, when no Man can comfortably imagine what Face this World will carry: and therefore since every Age makes a step unto the end of all things and the Scripture affords so hard a Character of the last Times;[82] quiet Minds will be content with their Generations, and rather bless Ages past than be ambitious of those to come.

Tho Age had set no Seal upon his Face, yet a dim Eye might clearly discover Fifty in his Actions; and therefore since Wisdom is the gray Hair, and an unspotted Life old Age; altho his Years came short, he might have been said to have held up with longer Livers, and to have been *Solomon*'s Old Man.[83] And surely if we deduct all those days of our Life which we might wish unlived, and which abate the comfort of those we now live; if we reckon up only those days which God hath accepted of our Lives, a Life of good Years will hardly be a span long: the Son in this sense may out-live the Father, and none be climaterically old.[84] He that early arriveth unto the Parts and Prudence of Age, is happily old without the uncomfortable Attendants of it; and 'tis superfluous to live unto gray Hairs when in a precocious Temper we anticipate the Virtues of them.

81. In *Aeneid*, VIII, 209.
82. Especially in the Book of Revelation, whose 'signs' of the age preceding the Last Judgement were widely said to have been fulfilled by the seventeenth century.
83. Wisdom of Solomon 4.9 (Browne marg.).
84. i.e. old at sixty-three, one's climacteric year (above, pp. 231 ff.).

In brief, he cannot be accounted young who out-liveth the old Man. He that hath early arrived unto the measure of a perfect Stature in Christ, hath already fulfilled the prime and longest Intention of his Being: and one day lived after the perfect Rule of Piety, is to be preferred before sinning Immortality.

Although he attained not unto the Years of his Predecessors, yet he wanted not those preserving Virtues which confirm the thread of weaker Constitutions. Cautelous[85] Chastity and crafty Sobriety were far from him; those Jewels were Paragon, without Flaw, Hair, Ice, or Cloud in him: which affords me an hint to proceed in these good Wishes and few *Memento's* unto you.[86]

Tread softly and circumspectly in this funambulous[87] Track and narrow Path of Goodness: pursue Virtue virtuously;[88] be sober and temperate, not to preserve your Body in a sufficiency to wanton Ends; not to spare your Purse; not to be free from the Infamy of common Transgressors[89] that way, and thereby to balance or palliate obscure and closer[90] Vices; nor simply to enjoy Health: by all which you may leaven good Actions, and render Virtues disputable:[91] but in one Word, that you may truly serve God; which every Sickness will tell you, you cannot well do without Health. The sick mans Sacrifice is but a lame Oblation.[92] Pious Treasures laid up in healthful days, excuse the defect of sick Non-performances; without which we must needs look back with Anxiety upon the lost opportunities of

85. 'Deceitfull' (Cockeram).

86. Nearly all the paragraphs from the next one to the end of the *Letter* (p. 414) reappear in *Christian Morals* (see below, pp. 417 ff.).

87. Rope-walking.

88. 'virtuously': 'for itself or at least for the noblest ends that attend it' (*MSS.*: *M*).

89. 'not to be free from the Infamy of common Transgressors': 'not to procure the name of a sober & temperate person & so to bee out of the list of common offenders' (*MSS.*: *M*).

90. 'palliate obscure and closer': 'observe thy closer & hidden' (*MSS.*: *M*).

91. 'render Virtues disputable': 'tread away from true virtue' (*MSS.*: *M*).

92. 'Oblation': 'offering. Remember thy creator in the dayes of thy youth & lay up a treasure of pietie in thy healthfull dayes. & conserve thy health in the first place for that intention.' (*MSS.*: *M*).

Health; and may have cause rather to envy than pity the Ends of penitent Malefactors, who go with clear parts unto the last Act of their Lives; and in the integrity of their Faculties return their Spirit unto God that gave it.

Consider whereabout thou art in *Cebes* his Table, or that old philosophical Pinax of the Life of Man;[93] whether thou art still in the Road of Uncertainties; whether thou hast yet entred the narrow Gate, got up the Hill and asperous[94] way which leadeth unto the House of Sanity, or taken that purifying Potion from the hand of sincere Erudition, which may send thee clear and pure a way unto a virtuous and happy Life.

In this virtuous Voyage let not disappointment cause Despondency, nor difficulty Despair: think not that you are sailing from *Lima* to *Manillia*, wherein thou may'st tye up the Rudder, and sleep before the Wind;[95] but expect rough Seas, Flaws, and contrary Blasts; and 'tis well if by many cross Tacks and Verings thou arrivest at thy Port. Sit not down in the popular Seats and common Level of Virtues, but endeavour to make them Heroical. Offer not only Peace-Offerings but Holocausts unto God. To serve him singly, to serve our selves, were too partial a piece of Piety, nor likely to place us in the highest Mansions of Glory.

He that is chaste and continent, not to impair his Strength, or terrified by Contagion, will hardly be heroically virtuous. Adjourn not that Virtue unto those Years when *Cato* could lend out his Wife, and impotent Satyrs write Satyrs[96] against Lust: but be chaste in thy flaming days, when *Alexander* dared not trust his Eyes upon the fair Daughters of *Darius*, and when so many Men think there is no other way but *Origen*'s.[97]

93. The *Pinax* commonly attributed to Socrates's pupil Cebes, but actually written in the first century A.D.

94. Rough.

95. 'Through the Pacific Sea, with a constant Gale from the East' (Browne marg.).

96. i.e. satirists write satires. Seventeenth-century spelling permits the ambiguity in formal definitions of *satyr*: 'a Monster having a body like a man, but all hairy, with legges and feet like a Goat; it is also a biting verse' (Cockeram).

97. 'Who is said to have Castrated himself' (Browne marg.: as below, p. 418, note 5).

Be charitable before Wealth makes thee covetous, and lose not the Glory of the Mite.[98] If Riches increase, let thy Mind hold pace with them; and think it not enough to be liberal, but munificent. Tho a Cup of cold Water from some hand may not be without its Reward; yet stick not thou for Wine and Oyl for the Wounds of the distressed: and treat the Poor as our Saviour did the Multitude, to the Relicks of some Baskets.

Trust not to the Omnipotency of Gold, or say unto it, Thou art my Confidence: Kiss not thy Hand when thou beholdest that terrestrial Sun, nor bore thy Ear unto its Servitude. A Slave unto Mammon makes no Servant unto God: Covetousness cracks the Sinews of Faith, numbs the Apprehension of any thing above Sense, and only affected with the certainty of things present, makes a peradventure of Things to come; lives but unto one World, nor hopes but fears another; makes our own Death sweet unto others, bitter unto our selves; gives a dry Funeral, Scenical Mourning, and no wet Eyes at the Grave.

If Avarice be thy Vice, yet make it not thy Punishment: miserable Men commiserate not themselves, bowelless unto themselves, and merciless unto their own Bowels. Let the fruition of Things bless the possession of them, and take no satisfaction in dying but living rich: for since thy good Works, not thy Goods, will follow thee; since Riches are an Appurtenance of Life, and no dead Man is rich, to famish in Plenty, and live poorly to dye rich, were a multiplying improvement in Madness, and Use upon Use in Folly.

Persons lightly dip'd, not grain'd in generous Honesty, are but pale in Goodness, and faint hued in Sincerity: but be thou what thou virtuously art, and let not the Ocean wash away thy Tincture: stand magnetically upon that Axis where prudent Simplicity hath fix'd thee, and let no Temptation invert the Poles of thy Honesty: and that Vice may be uneasie, and even monstrous unto thee, let iterated good Acts, and long confirmed Habits, make Vertue natural, or a second Nature in thee. And since few or none prove eminently vertuous but from some advantageous Foundations in their Temper and natural

98. 'Mite': the reading in *Christian Morals* (below, p. 418); but the 1st edition of 1690 reads 'Mitre'.

Inclinations; study thy self betimes, and early find, what Nature bids thee to be, or tells thee what thou may'st be. They who thus timely descend into themselves, cultivating the good Seeds which Nature hath set in them, and improving their prevalent Inclinations to Perfection, become not Shrubs, but Cedars in their Generation; and to be in the form of the best of the Bad, or the worst of the Good, will be no satisfaction unto them.

Let not the Law of thy Country be the *non ultra*[99] of thy Honesty, nor think that always good enough which the Law will make good. Narrow not the Law of Charity, Equity, Mercy; joyn Gospel Righteousness with Legal Right; be not a meer *Gamaliel* in the Faith; but let the Sermon in the Mount be thy *Targum*[100] unto the Law of *Sinai*.

Make not the Consequences of Vertue the Ends thereof: be not beneficent for a Name or Cymbal of Applause, nor exact and punctual in Commerce, for the Advantages of Trust and Credit, which attend the Reputation of just and true Dealing; for such Rewards, tho unsought for, plain Virtue will bring with her, whom all Men honour, tho they pursue not. To have other bye ends in good Actions, sowers laudable Performances, which must have deeper Roots, Motions, and Instigations, to give them the Stamp of Vertues.

Tho humane Infirmity may betray thy heedless days into the popular ways of Extravagancy, yet let not thine own depravity, or the torrent of vicious Times, carry thee into desperate Enormities in Opinions, Manners, or Actions: if thou hast dip'd thy foot in the River, yet venture not over *Rubicon;*[101] run not into Extremities from whence there is no Regression, nor be ever so closely shut up within the holds of Vice and Iniquity, as not to find some Escape by a Postern of Recipiscency.[102]

Owe not thy Humility unto Humiliation by Adversity, but look humbly down in that State when others look upward upon thee: be patient in the Age of Pride and days of Will and

99. Literally 'not beyond' – i.e. the terminal point.

100. Interpretation (cf. above, p. 171, note 9).

101. The river whose crossing by Caesar in 49 B.C. marked the beginning of the civil war.

102. i.e. by a private door of repentance.

Impatiency, when Men live but by Intervals of Reason, under the Sovereignty of Humor and Passion, when 'tis in the Power of every one to transform thee out of thy self, and put thee into the short Madness.[103] If you cannot imitate *Job*, yet come not short of *Socrates*, and those patient Pagans, who tired the Tongues of their Enemies, while they perceiv'd they spet their Malice at brazen Walls and Statues.

Let Age, not Envy, draw Wrinkles on thy Cheeks: be content to be envied, but envy not. Emulation may be plausible, and Indignation allowable; but admit no Treaty with that Passion which no Circumstance can make good. A Displacency at[104] the good of others, because they enjoy it, altho we do not want it, is an absurd Depravity, sticking fast unto humane Nature from its primitive Corruption; which he that can well subdue, were a Christian of the first Magnitude, and for ought I know, may have one foot already in Heaven.

While thou so hotly disclaimst the Devil, be not guilty of Diabolism; fall not into one Name with that unclean Spirit; nor act his Nature whom thou so much abhorrest; that is, to accuse, calumniate, backbite, whisper, detract, or sinistrously interpret others; degenerous Depravities and narrow-minded Vices, not only below S. *Paul*'s noble Christian, but *Aristotle*'s true Gentleman.[105] Trust not with some, that the Epistle of S. *James* is Apocryphal,[106] and so read with less fear that stabbing truth, that in company with this Vice thy Religion is in vain. *Moses* broke the Tables without breaking of the Law; but where Charity is broke the Law it self is shattered, which cannot be whole without Love, that is the fulfilling of it. Look humbly upon thy Virtues, and tho thou art rich in some, yet think thy self poor and naked without that crowning Grace, which thinketh no Evil, which envieth not, which beareth, believeth,

---

103. 'Anger is short-lived madness' (Browne marg., quoting the Latin of Horace, *Epistles*, I, ii, 62).

104. Displeasure with.

105. In *Nicomachean Ethics*, IV, 5 (Browne marg.).

106. Protestants have not actually questioned the Epistle's canonical status, but many – especially Luther – disliked its emphasis on works at the expense of faith.

hopeth, endureth all things.[107] With these sure Graces, while busie Tongues are crying out for a drop of cold Water, Mutes may be in Happiness, and sing the *Trisagium*[108] in Heaven.

Let not the Sun in *Capricorn*[109] go down upon thy Wrath, but write thy Wrongs in Water; draw the Curtain of Night upon Injuries; shut them up in the Tower of Oblivion,[110] and let them be as tho they had not been. Forgive thine Enemies totally, and without any Reserve of hope, that however, God will revenge thee.

Be substantially great in thy self, and more than thou appearest unto others; and let the World be deceived in thee, as they are in the Lights of Heaven. Hang early Plummets upon the Heels of Pride, and let Ambition have but an Epicycle or narrow Circuit in thee. Measure not thy self by thy Morning shadow, but by the Extent of thy Grave; and reckon thy self above the Earth by the Line thou must be contented with under it. Spread not into boundless Expansions either of Designs or Desires. Think not that Mankind liveth but for a few, and that the rest are born but to serve the Ambition of those, who make but Flies of Men, and Wildernesses of whole Nations. Swell not into Actions which embroil and confound the Earth; but be one of those violent ones which force the Kingdom of Heaven.[111] If thou must needs reign, be *Zeno*'s King,[112] and enjoy that Empire which every Man gives himself. Certainly the iterated Injunctions of Christ unto Humility, Meekness, Patience, and

107. From St Paul's hymn to charity in 1 Corinthians 13.

108. 'Holy, Holy, Holy' (Browne marg.: as below, p. 423, note 21).

109. 'Even when the days are shortest' (Browne marg.: as below, p. 422, note 18). The paragraph amplifies Ephesians 4.26: 'Be ye angry, and sin not: let not the sun go down upon your wrath'.

110. 'Alluding to the Tower of Oblivion mentioned by *Procopius* [*History of the Wars*, I, 4–5], which was the name of a Tower of Imprisonment among the *Persians*: whosoever was put therein, he was as it were buried alive, and it was Death for any but to name him' (Browne marg.: as below, p. 422, note 19).

111. Matthew 11.12 (Browne marg.: as below, p. 424, note 26).

112. i.e. the ideal wise man as described by Zeno (in Cicero, *About the Ends*, III, 22).

that despised Train of Virtues, cannot but make pathetical Impressions upon those who have well considered the Affairs of all Ages, wherein Pride, Ambition, and Vain-glory, have led up the worst of Actions, and whereunto Confusion, Tragedies, and Acts denying all Religion, do owe their Originals.

Rest not in an Ovation,[113] but a Triumph over thy Passions; chain up the unruly Legion of thy Breast;[114] behold thy Trophies within thee, not without thee: Lead thine own Captivity captive, and be *Cæsar* unto thy self.

Give no quarter unto those Vices which are of thine inward Family: and having a Root in thy Temper, plead a Right and Propriety in thee. Examine well thy complexional[115] Inclinations. Raise early Batteries against those strong-holds built upon the Rock of Nature, and make this a great part of the Militia of thy Life. The politick Nature of Vice must be opposed by Policy, and therefore wiser Honesties Project and plot against Sin; wherein notwithstanding we are not to rest in Generals, or the trite Stratagems of Art: that may succeed with one Temper which may prove successless with another. There is no Community or Commonwealth of Virtue; every Man must study his own OEconomy,[116] and erect these Rules unto the Figure of himself.

Lastly, If length of Days be thy Portion, make it not thy Expectation: reckon not upon long Life, but live always beyond thy Account. He that so often surviveth his Expectation, lives many Lives, and will hardly complain of the shortness of his Days. Time past is gone like a shadow; make Times to come, present; conceive that near which may be far off; approximate thy last Times by present Apprehensions of them: live like a Neighbour unto Death, and think there is but little to come. And since there is something in us that must still live on, joyn

113. 'Ovation a petty and minor kind of Triumph' (Browne marg.: as below, p. 417, note 3).

114. Cf. '*Lucifer* keeps his court in my breast, *Legion* is revived in me' (above, p. 125).

115. Temperamental (cf. above, p. 69, note 37).

116. As above, p. 69, note 38.

both Lives together; unite them in thy Thoughts and Actions, and live in one but for the other. He who thus ordereth the Purposes of this Life, will never be far from the next; and is in some manner already in it, by an happy Conformity, and close Apprehension of it.

Christian Morals

[*Christian Morals* was first published posthumously in
1716, edited 'from the Original and Correct Manu-
script of the Author' by Archdeacon John Jeffery of
Norwich. Its authenticity was vouched in a prefatory
note by Jeffery as well as in the epistle dedicatory to the
Earl of Buchan by Elizabeth Littleton, Browne's
daughter. Its second edition was preceded by Dr
Johnson's *Life* (below, pp. 481 ff.).

The work repeats, with minor changes, parts of *A
Letter to a Friend* (above, pp. 389 ff.). The repeated
passages – all in Part I (Sections 1–5, 7–11, 13–16, 18–
19, 30) except for one in the last section of Part III –
are here bracketed so that the reader can establish the
nature of Browne's revisions (cf. §176). The extensive
variants in the extant manuscripts are listed in *M*, pp.
272–88.]

1. [Tread softly and circumspectly in this funambulatory Track and narrow Path of Goodness: Pursue Virtue virtuously: Leven not good Actions nor render Virtues disputable.][1] Stain not fair Acts with foul Intentions: Maim not Uprightness by halting Concomitances, nor circumstantially deprave substantial Goodness.

[Consider where about thou art in *Cebes*'s Table, or that old Philosophical Pinax of the Life of Man: whether thou art yet in the Road of uncertainties; whether thou hast yet entred the narrow Gate, got up the Hill and asperous way, which leadeth unto the House of Sanity, or taken that purifying Potion from the hand of sincere Erudition, which may send Thee clear and pure away unto a virtuous and happy Life.

In this virtuous Voyage of thy Life hull not about like the Ark without the use of Rudder, Mast, or Sail, and bound for no Port. Let not Disappointment cause Despondency, nor difficulty despair. Think not that you are Sailing from *Lima* to *Manillia* when you may fasten up the Rudder, and sleep before the Wind; but expect rough Seas, Flaws, and contrary Blasts, and 'tis well if by many cross Tacks and Veerings you arrive at the Port; for we sleep in Lyons Skins[2] in our Progress unto Virtue, and we slide not, but climb unto it.

Sit not down in the popular Forms and common Level of Virtues. Offer not only Peace Offerings but Holocausts unto God: where all is due make no reserve, and cut not a Cummin Seed with the Almighty: To serve Him singly to serve our selves were too partial a piece of Piety, not like to place us in the illustrious Mansions of Glory.]

2. [Rest not in an Ovation[3] but a Triumph over thy Passions.

1. Brackets designate the passages forming part of *A Letter to a Friend* (see headnote, above).

2. 'That is, in armour, in a state of military vigilance. One of the Grecian chiefs used to represent open force by the lion's skin, and policy by the fox's tail' (*SJ*).

3. 'Ovation a petty and minor Kind of Triumph' (Browne marg.; as above, p. 413, note 113).

Let Anger walk hanging down the head: Let Malice go Man-
icled, and Envy fetter'd after thee. Behold within thee the long
train of thy Trophies not without thee. Make the quarrelling
Lapithytes sleep, and Centaurs within lye quiet.⁴ Chain up the
unruly Legion of thy breast. Lead thine own captivity captive,
and be *Cæsar* within thy self.]

3. [He that is Chast and Continent not to impair his strength,
or honest for fear of Contagion, will hardly be Heroically
virtuous. Adjourn not this virtue untill that temper, when *Cato*
could lend out his Wife, and impotent Satyrs write Satyrs upon
Lust: But be chast in thy flaming Days, when *Alexander* dar'd
not trust his eyes upon the fair Sisters of *Darius*, and when so
many think there is no other way but *Origen*'s.]⁵

4. Show thy Art in Honesty, and loose not thy Virtue by the
bad Managery of it. [Be Temperate and Sober, not to preserve
your body in an ability for wanton ends, not to avoid the infamy
of common transgressors that way, and thereby to hope to
expiate or palliate obscure and closer vices, not to spare your
purse, nor simply to enjoy health; but in one word that thereby
you may truly serve God, which every sickness will tell you
cannot well do without health. The sick Man's Sacrifice is but a
lame Oblation. Pious Treasures lay'd up in healthful days plead
for sick non-performances: without which we must needs look
back with anxiety upon the lost opportunities of health, and
may have cause rather to envy than pity the ends of penitent
publick Sufferers, who go with healthful prayers unto the last
Scene of their lives, and in the Integrity of their faculties return
their Spirit unto God that gave it.]

5. [Be Charitable before wealth make thee covetous, and
loose not the glory of the Mite. If Riches encrease, let thy mind
hold pace with them, and think it not enough to be Liberal, but
Munificent. Though a Cup of cold water from some hand may
not be without it's reward, yet stick not thou for Wine and Oyl
for the Wounds of the Distressed, and treat the poor, as our

4. Cf. the violent conflict between the Lapiths and the Centaurs at the
marriage of Perithous.

5. 'Who is said to have Castrated himself' (Browne marg.: as above,
p. 408, note 97).

Saviour did the Multitude, to the reliques of some baskets.]
Diffuse thy beneficence early, and while thy Treasures call thee
Master: there may be an Atropos of thy Fortunes before that of
thy Life, and thy wealth cut off before that hour, when all Men
shall be poor; for the Justice of Death looks equally upon the
dead, and *Charon*[6] expects no more from *Alexander* than from
Irus.

6. Give not only unto seven, but also unto eight,[7] that is unto
more than many. Though to give unto every one that asketh[8]
may seem severe advice, yet give thou also before asking, that
is, where want is silently clamorous, and mens Necessities not
their Tongues do loudly call for thy Mercies. For though some-
times necessitousness be dumb, or misery speak not out, yet
true Charity is sagacious, and will find out hints for beneficence.
Acquaint thy self with the Physiognomy of Want, and let the
Dead colours and first lines of necessity suffise to tell thee there
is an object for thy bounty. Spare not where thou canst not
easily be prodigal, and fear not to be undone by mercy. For
since he who hath pity on the poor lendeth unto the Almighty
Rewarder,[9] who observes no Ides[10] but every day for his pay-
ments; Charity becomes pious Usury, Christian Liberality the
most thriving industry, and what we adventure in a Cockboat
may return in a Carrack unto us. He who thus casts his bread
upon the Water shall surely find it again; for though it falleth to
the bottom, it sinks but like the Ax of the Prophet,[11] to arise
again unto him.

7. [If Avarice be thy Vice, yet make it not thy Punishment.
Miserable men commiserate not themselves, bowelless unto
others, and merciless unto their own bowels. Let the fruition of
things bless the possession of them, and think it more satis-
faction to live richly than dye rich. For since thy good works,
not thy goods, will follow thee; since wealth is an appertinance

6. As above, p. 301, note 23.
7. Ecclesiastes 11.2 (Browne marg.).
8. Luke 6.30 (Browne marg.).
9. Proverbs 19.17.
10. 'the time when money lent out at interest was commonly repaid'
(*SJ*).
11. 2 Kings 6.5–7.

of life, and no dead Man is Rich; to famish in Plenty, and live
poorly to dye Rich, were a multiplying improvement in Mad-
ness, and use upon use in Folly.]

8. [Trust not to the Omnipotency of Gold, and say not unto
it Thou art my Confidence. Kiss not thy hand to that Terrestrial
Sun, not bore thy ear unto its servitude. A Slave unto Mammon
makes no servant unto God. Covetousness cracks the sinews of
Faith; nummes the apprehension of any thing above sense, and
only affected with the certainty of things present makes a perad-
venture of things to come; lives but unto one World, nor hopes
but fears another; makes their own death sweet unto others,
bitter unto themselves; brings formal sadness, scenical mourn-
ing, and no wet eyes at the grave.]

9. [Persons lightly dipt, not grain'd in generous Honesty, are
but pale in Goodness, and faint hued in Integrity. But be thou
what thou vertuously art, and let not the Ocean wash away thy
Tincture. Stand magnetically upon that Axis,[12] where prudent
simplicity hath fixt thee;[13] and let no attraction invert the Poles
of thy Honesty. That Vice may be uneasy and even monstrous
unto thee, let iterated good Acts and long confirmed habits
make Virtue almost natural, or a second nature in thee. Since
virtuous superstructions have commonly generous founda-
tions, dive into thy inclinations, and early discover what nature
bids thee to be, or tells thee thou may'st be. They who thus
timely descend into themselves, & cultivate the good seeds
which nature hath set in them, prove not shrubs but Cedars in
their generation. And to be in the form of the best of the Bad, or
the worst of the Good,[14] will be no satisfaction unto them.]

10. [Make not the consequence of Virtue the ends thereof.
Be not beneficent for a name or Cymbal of applause, nor exact
and just in Commerce for the advantages of Trust and Credit,
which attend the reputation of true and punctual dealing. For

12. 'That is, with a position as immutable as that of the magnetical
axis, which is popularly supposed to be invariably parallel to the meridian,
or to stand exactly north and south' (*SJ*).

13. 'where prudent Simplicity hath fix'd thee' (as above, p. 409): 'when
prudent simplicity hath fixt thee' (1716 ed.).

14. 'Optimi malorum pessimi bonorum' (Browne marg.). The dictum,
most likely proverbial, is translated in the text.

these Rewards, though unsought for, plain Virtue will bring with her. To have other by-ends in good actions sowers Laudable performances, which must have deeper roots, motives, and instigations, to give them the stamp of Virtues.]

11. [Let not the Law of thy Country be the non ultra of thy Honesty; nor think that always good enough which the Law will make good. Narrow not the Law of Charity, Equity, Mercy. Joyn Gospel Righteousness with Legal Right. Be not a mere *Gamaliel* in the Faith, but let the Sermon in the Mount be thy *Targum* unto the Law of *Sinah*.]

12. Live by old Ethicks and the classical Rules of Honesty. Put no new names or notions upon Authentick Virtues and Vices. Think not that Morality is Ambulatory;[15] that Vices in one age are not Vices in another; or that Virtues, which are under the everlasting Seal of right Reason, may be Stamped by Opinion. And therefore though vicious times invert the opinions of things, and set up a new Ethicks against Virtue, yet hold thou unto old Morality; and rather than follow a multitude to do evil, stand like *Pompey*'s Pillar[16] conspicuous by thy self, and single in Integrity. And since the worst of times afford imitable Examples of Virtue; since no Deluge of Vice is like to be so general, but more than eight will escape;[17] Eye well those Heroes who have held their Heads above Water, who have touched Pitch, and not been defiled, and in the common Contagion have remained uncorrupted.

13. [Let Age not Envy draw wrinkles on thy cheeks, be content to be envy'd, but envy not. Emulation may be plausible and Indignation allowable, but admit no treaty with that passion which no circumstance can make good. A displacency at the good of others because they enjoy it, though not unworthy of it, is an absurd depravity, sticking fast unto corrupted nature,] and often too hard for Humility and Charity, the great Suppressors of Envy. This surely is a Lyon not to be strangled but by *Hercules* himself, or the highest stress of our minds, and an

15. Mutable.
16. The monument in Alexandria commemorating the city's capture by Diocletian.
17. i.e. the eight members of Noah's family.

Atom of that power which subdueth all things unto it self.

14. [Owe not thy Humility unto humiliation from adversity, but look humbly down in that State when others look upwards upon thee. Think not thy own shadow longer than that of others, nor delight to take the Altitude of thy self. Be patient in the age of Pride, when Men live by short intervals of Reason under the dominion of Humor and Passion, when it's in the Power of every one to transform thee out of thy self, and run thee into the short madness. If you cannot imitate *Job*, yet come not short of *Socrates*, and those patient Pagans who tired the Tongues of their Enemies, while they perceived they spit their malice at brazen Walls and Statues.]

15. [Let not the Sun in Capricorn[18] go down upon thy wrath, but write thy wrongs in Ashes. Draw the Curtain of night upon injuries, shut them up in the Tower of Oblivion[19] and let them be as though they had not been. To forgive our Enemies, yet hope that God will punish them, is not to forgive enough. To forgive them our selves, and not to pray God to forgive them, is a partial piece of Charity. Forgive thine enemies totally, and without any reserve, that however God will revenge thee.]

16. [While thou so hotly disclaimest the Devil, be not guilty of Diabolism. Fall not into one name with that unclean Spirit, nor act his nature whom thou so much abhorrest; that is to Accuse, Calumniate, Backbite, Whisper, Detract, or sinistrously interpret others. Degenerous depravities, and narrow minded vices! not only below St. *Paul*'s noble Christian but *Aristotle*'s true Gentleman.[20] Trust not with some that the Epistle of St. *James* is Apocryphal, and so read with less fear that Stabbing Truth, that in company with this vice thy Religion is in vain. *Moses* broke the Tables without breaking of the Law; but where Charity is broke, the Law it self is shattered, which cannot be whole without Love, which is the fulfilling of it. Look humbly upon thy Virtues, and though thou art Rich in some, yet think thy self Poor and Naked without that Crowning

18. 'Even when the days are shortest' (Browne marg.: as above, p. 412, note 109).

19. See above, p. 412, note 110.

20. See above, p. 411, note 105.

Grace, which thinketh no evil, which envieth not, which beareth, hopeth, believeth, endureth all things. With these sure Graces, while busy Tongues are crying out for a drop of cold Water, mutes may be in happiness, and sing the *Trisagion*[21] in Heaven.]

17. However thy understanding may waver in the Theories of True and False, yet fasten the Rudder of thy Will, steer strait unto good and fall not foul on evil. Imagination is apt to rove and conjecture to keep no bounds. Some have run out so far, as to fancy the Stars might be but the light of the Crystalline Heaven shot through perforations on the bodies of the Orbs.[22] Others more Ingeniously doubt whether there hath not been a vast tract of Land in the *Atlantick* Ocean, which Earthquakes and violent causes have long ago devoured.[23] Speculative Misapprehensions may be innocuous, but immorality pernicious; Theoretical[24] mistakes and Physical Deviations may condemn our Judgments, not lead us into Judgment. But perversity of Will, immoral and sinfull enormities walk with *Adraste* and *Nemesis*[25] at their Backs, pursue us unto Judgment, and leave us viciously miserable.

18. [Bid early defiance unto those Vices which are of thine inward Family, and having a root in thy Temper plead a right and propriety in thee. Raise timely batteries against those strong holds built upon the Rock of Nature, and make this a great part of the Militia of thy life.] Delude not thy self into iniquities from participation or community, which abate the sense but not the obliquity of them. To conceive sins less, or less of sins, because others also Transgress, were Morally to commit that natural fallacy of Man, to take comfort from Society, and think adversities less, because others also suffer them. [The politick nature of Vice must be opposed by Policy. And therefore wiser Honesties project and plot against it. Wherein notwithstanding

21. 'Holy, Holy, Holy' (Browne marg.: as above, p. 412, note 108).

22. Cf. *The Garden of Cyrus* on the stars as 'rayes and flashing glimpses of the Empyreall light' etc. (above, p. 375).

23. On Atlantis, the mythical island 'vaster than Libya and Asia put together', see Plato, *Timaeus*, 24e.

24. Speculative.

25. 'The powers of vengeance' (*SJ*). Adrastea is an epithet of Nemesis.

we are not to rest in generals, or the trite Stratagems of Art.
That may succeed with one which may prove successless with
another: There is no community or commonweal of Virtue:
Every man must study his own oeconomy, and adapt such rules
unto the figure of himself.]

19. [Be substantially great in thy self, and more than thou
appearest unto others; and let the World be deceived in thee, as
they are in the Lights of Heaven. Hang early plummets upon
the heels of Pride, and let Ambition have but an Epicycle and
narrow circuit in thee. Measure not thy self by thy morning
shadow, but by the extent of thy grave, and Reckon thy self
above the Earth by the line thou must be contented with under
it. Spread not into boundless Expansions either of designs or
desires. Think not that mankind liveth but for a few, and that
the rest are born but to serve those Ambitions, which make but
flies of Men and wildernesses of whole Nations. Swell not into
vehement actions which imbroil and confound the Earth; but
be one of those violent ones which force the Kingdom of
Heaven.[26] If thou must needs Rule, be *Zeno*'s King, and enjoy
that Empire which every Man gives himself.] He who is thus
his own Monarch contentedly sways the Scepter of himself, not
envying the Glory of Crowned Heads and Elohims[27] of the
Earth. Could the World unite in the practise of that despised
train of Virtues, which the Divine Ethicks of our Saviour hath
so inculcated unto us, the furious face of things must disappear,
Eden would be yet to be found, and the Angels might look
down not with pity, but Joy upon us.

20. Though the Quickness of thine Ear were able to reach the
noise of the Moon, which some think it maketh in it's rapid
revolution;[28] though the number of thy Ears should equal
Argus his Eyes; yet stop them all with the wise man's wax,[29] and
be deaf unto the suggestions of Talebearers, Calumniators,

26. Matthew 11.12 (Browne marg.: as above, p. 412, note 111).

27. i.e. gods: rulers who imitate the Lord God (Elohim).

28. The moon's 'noise' was thought to have formed part of the music
of the spheres (above, p. 149).

29. 'Alluding to the story of Ulysses, who stopped the ears of his com-
panions with wax when they passed by the Sirens' (*SJ*): *Odyssey*, XII, 173.

Pickthank or Malevolent Delators,[30] who while quiet Men sleep, sowing the Tares of discord and division, distract the tranquillity of Charity and all friendly Society. These are the Tongues that set the world on fire, cankers of reputation, and, like that of *Jonas* his Gourd, wither a good name in a night.[31] Evil Spirits may sit still while these Spirits walk about, and perform the business of Hell. To speak more strictly, our corrupted hearts are the Factories of the Devil, which may be at work without his presence. For when that circumventing Spirit hath drawn Malice, Envy, and all unrighteousness unto well rooted habits in his disciples, iniquity then goes on upon its own legs, and if the gate of Hell were shut up for a time, Vice would still be fertile and produce the fruits of Hell. Thus when God forsakes us, Satan also leaves us. For such offenders he looks upon as sure and sealed up, and his temptations then needless unto them.

21. Annihilate not the Mercies of God by the Oblivion of Ingratitude. For Oblivion is a kind of Annihilation, and for things to be as though they had not been is like unto never being. Make not thy Head a Grave, but a Repository of God's mercies. Though thou hadst the Memory of *Seneca*, or *Simonides*, and Conscience, the punctual Memorist within us, yet trust not to thy Remembrance in things which need Phylacteries.[32] Register not only strange but merciful occurrences: Let *Ephemerides* not *Olympiads*[33] give thee account of his mercies. Let thy Diaries stand thick with dutiful Mementos and Asterisks of acknowledgment. And to be compleat and forget nothing, date not his mercy from thy nativity, Look beyond the World, and before the Æra of *Adam*.

22. Paint not the Sepulcher of thy self, and strive not to beautify thy corruption. Be not an Advocate for thy Vices, nor call for many Hour-Glasses to justify thy imperfections. Think

30. i.e. sycophants or malevolent accusers.

31. Jonah 4.6–10: 'the gourd . . . came up in a night, and perished in a night'.

32. i.e. which need to be preserved.

33. The time span of ephemerides (as above, p. 81, note 104) surpasses by far that of the quadrennial Olympic games.

not that always good which thou thinkest thou canst always make good, nor that concealed which the Sun doth not behold. That which the Sun doth not now see will be visible when the Sun is out, and the Stars are fallen from Heaven.[34] Mean while there is no darkness unto Conscience, which can see without Light, and in the deepest obscurity give a clear Draught of things, which the Cloud of dissimulation hath conceal'd from all eyes. There is a natural standing Court within us, examining, acquitting, and condemning at the Tribunal of our selves, wherein iniquities have their natural Theta's,[35] and no nocent[36] is absolved by the verdict of himself. And therefore although our transgressions shall be tryed at the last bar, the process need not be long: for the Judge of all knoweth all, and every Man will nakedly know himself. And when so few are like to plead not Guilty, the Assize must soon have an end.

23. Comply with some humors, bear with others, but serve none. Civil complacency consists with decent honesty: Flattery is a Juggler, and no Kin unto Sincerity. But while thou maintainest the plain path, and scornest to flatter others, fall not into self Adulation, and become not thine own Parasite. Be deaf unto thy self, and be not betrayed at home. Self-credulity, pride, and levity lead unto self-Idolatry. There is no *Damocles* like unto self opinion, nor any *Siren* to our own fawning Conceptions. To magnify our minor things, or hug our selves in our apparitions; to afford a credulous Ear unto the clawing suggestions of fancy; to pass our days in painted mistakes of our selves; and though we behold our own blood,[37] to think our selves the Sons of *Jupiter*;[38] are blandishments of self love, worse than outward delusion. By this Imposture Wise Men sometimes are Mistaken in their Elevation, and look above themselves. And Fools, which are Antipodes unto the Wise, conceive themselves

34. i.e. after the Last Judgement.

35. i.e. deaths. See above, p. 309, note 21.

36. i.e. no one who is guilty. The phrase echoes Juvenal, *Satires*, XIII, 2–3.

37. 'that is ... though we find in ourselves the imperfections of humanity' (*SJ*).

38. 'As *Alexander* the Great did' (Browne marg.).

to be but their *Periœci*,[39] and in the same parallel with them.

24. Be not a *Hercules furens*[40] abroad, and a Poltron[41] within thy self. To chase our Enemies out of the Field, and be led captive by our Vices; to beat down our Foes, and fall down to our Concupiscences; are Solecisms in Moral Schools, and no Laurel attends them. To well manage our Affections, and wild Horses of *Plato*,[42] are the highest Circenses;[43] and the noblest Digladiation[44] is in the Theater of our selves: for therein our inward Antagonists, not only like common Gladiators, with ordinary Weapons and down right Blows make at us, but also like Retiary and Laqueary Combatants,[45] with Nets, Frauds, and Entanglements fall upon us. Weapons for such combats are not to be forged at *Lipara*:[46] *Vulcan*'s Art doth nothing in this internal Militia: wherein not the Armour of *Achilles*, but the Armature of St. *Paul*,[47] gives the Glorious day, and Triumphs not Leading up into Capitols, but up into the highest Heavens. And therefore while so many think it the only valour to command and master others, study thou the Dominion of thy self, and quiet thine own Commotions. Let Right Reason be thy *Lycurgus*, and lift up thy hand unto the Law of it; move by the Intelligences[48] of the superiour Faculties, not by the Rapt[49] of Passion, not merely by that of Temper and Constitution. They who are merely carried on by the Wheel of such Inclinations, without the Hand and Guidance of Sovereign Reason, are but the Automatous part of mankind, rather lived than living, or at least underliving themselves.

39. 'Only placed at a distance in the same line' (*SJ*).
40. i.e. 'the mad Hercules', as in the title of Seneca's tragedy.
41. 'Knave, Rascal' (Blount).
42. i.e. the soul, represented in *Phaedrus* (246, 253) as two winged horses – one black, the other white – and a charioteer.
43. Chariot races (from *ludi circenses*: the games in Rome's Circus Maximus).
44. 'Fight, strife' (Cockeram).
45. Gladiators armed with a net and a noose respectively (cf. above, p. 336, note 17).
46. One of the Lipari Islands, Hiera, was Vulcan's abode.
47. Ephesians 6.13–17. Cf. above, p. 70, note 47.
48. Spiritual beings thought to have ruled the celestial spheres.
49. Ecstasy.

25. Let not Fortune, which hath no name in Scripture, have any in thy Divinity. Let Providence, not Chance, have the honour of thy acknowledgments, and be thy *Oedipus* in Contingences.[50] Mark well the Paths and winding Ways thereof; but be not too wise in the Construction, or sudden in the Application. The Hand of Providence writes often by Abbreviatures, Hieroglyphicks or short Characters,[51] which, like the Laconism on the Wall,[52] are not to be made out but by a Hint or Key from that Spirit which indited them. Leave future occurrences to their uncertainties, think that which is present thy own; And since 'tis easier to foretell an Eclipse, than a foul Day at some distance, Look for little Regular below. Attend with patience the uncertainty of Things, and what lieth yet unexerted[53] in the Chaos of Futurity. The uncertainty and ignorance of Things to come makes the World new unto us by unexpected Emergences, whereby we pass not our days in the trite road of affairs affording no Novity;[54] for the novellizing Spirit of Man lives by variety, and the new Faces of Things.

26. Though a contented Mind enlargeth the dimension of little things, and unto some 'tis Wealth enough not to be Poor, and others are well content, if they be but Rich enough to be Honest, and to give every Man his due: yet fall not into that obsolete Affectation of Bravery to throw away thy Money, and to reject all Honours or Honourable stations in this courtly and splendid World. Old Generosity is superannuated, and such contempt of the World out of date. No Man is now like to refuse the favour of great ones, or be content to say unto Princes, stand out of my Sun.[55] And if any there be of such antiquated Resolutions, they are not like to be tempted out of them by great ones; and 'tis fair if they escape the name of Hypocondriacks from the Genius of latter times, unto whom contempt

50. See above, p. 66, note 26.

51. See above, p. 31.

52. i.e. the words inscribed on it during Belshazzar's feast (Daniel 5.5–28).

53. Unrevealed.

54. i.e. novelty.

55. 'This was the answer made by Diogenes to Alexander, who asked him what he had to request' (*SJ*). So Plutarch, *Alexander*, XIV.

of the World is the most contemptible opinion, and to be able, like *Bias*, to carry all they have about them were to be the eighth Wise-man. However, the old tetrick[56] Philosophers look'd always with Indignation upon such a Face of Things, and observing the unnatural current of Riches, Power, and Honour in the World, and withall the imperfection and demerit of persons often advanced unto them, were tempted unto angry Opinions, that Affairs were ordered more by Stars than Reason, and that things went on rather by Lottery, than Election.

27. If thy Vessel be but small in the Ocean of this World, if Meanness of Possessions be thy allotment upon Earth, forget not those Virtues which the great disposer of all bids thee to entertain from thy Quality and Condition, that is, Submission, Humility, Content of mind, and Industry. Content may dwell in all Stations. To be low, but above contempt, may be high enough to be Happy. But many of low Degree may be higher than computed, and some Cubits above the common Commensuration;[57] for in all States Virtue gives Qualifications, and Allowances, which make out defects. Rough Diamonds are sometimes mistaken for Pebbles, and Meanness may be Rich in Accomplishments, which Riches in vain desire. If our merits be above our Stations, if our intrinsecal Value be greater than what we go for, or our Value than our Valuation, and if we stand higher in God's, than in the Censor's Book;[58] it may make some equitable balance in the inequalities of this World, and there may be no such vast Chasm or Gulph between disparities as common Measures determine. The Divine Eye looks upon high and low differently from that of Man.[59] They who seem to stand upon *Olympus*, and high mounted unto our eyes, may be but in the Valleys, and low Ground unto his; for he looks upon those as highest who nearest approach his Divinity, and upon those as lowest, who are farthest from it.

28. When thou lookest upon the Imperfections of others,

56. 'Severe, hard, sowre' (Cockeram).
57. i.e. measurement.
58. 'The book in which the Census, or account of every man's estate, was registered among the Romans' (*SJ*).
59. See above, pp. 28 and 51.

allow one Eye for what is Laudable in them, and the balance they have from some excellency, which may render them considerable. While we look with fear or hatred upon the Teeth of the Viper, we may behold his Eye with love.[60] In venemous Natures something may be amiable: Poysons afford Antipoysons:[61] nothing is totally, or altogether uselesly bad. Notable Virtues are sometimes dashed with notorious Vices, and in some vicious tempers have been found illustrious Acts of Virtue; which makes such observable worth in some actions of King *Demetrius*, *Antonius*, and *Ahab*, as are not to be found in the same kind in *Aristides*, *Numa*, or *David*. Constancy, Generosity, Clemency, and Liberality have been highly conspicuous in some Persons not markt out in other concerns for Example or Imitation. But since Goodness is exemplary in all, if others have not our Virtues, let us not be wanting in theirs, nor scorning them for their Vices whereof we are free, be condemned by their Virtues, wherein we are deficient. There is Dross, Alloy, and Embasement in all human Temper; and he flieth without Wings, who thinks to find Ophyr[62] or pure Metal in any. For perfection is not like Light center'd in any one Body, but like the dispersed Seminalities[63] of Vegetables at the Creation scattered through the whole Mass of the Earth, no place producing all and almost all some. So that 'tis well, if a perfect Man can be made out of many Men, and to the perfect Eye of God even out of Mankind. Time, which perfects some Things, imperfects also others. Could we intimately apprehend the Ideated Man,[64] and as he stood in the intellect of God upon

60. Cf. above, p. 133: 'at the sight of a Toad, or Viper, I finde in me no desire to take up a stone to destroy them'.

61. Cf. above, p. 152: 'I ground upon experience, that poysons containe within themselves their owne Antidote'.

62. Gold (see below, p. 529: Ophir).

63. Seminal principles (as above, p. 374, note 53).

64. i.e. the man created according to the Idea in the mind of God (above, p. 30). An earlier version of this passage in one of Browne's commonplace books reads: 'Could wee intimately apprehend the ideated man and as it primitively stood in the intellect of god upon the first exertion by creation, wee might more narrowlie apprehend our degeneration; & how widely wee are fallen from the pure exemplar & Idea of ourselves' (*K*, III, 293).

the first exertion by Creation, we might more narrowly comprehend our present Degeneration, and how widely we are fallen from the pure Exemplar and Idea of our Nature: for after this corruptive Elongation from a primitive and pure Creation, we are almost lost in Degeneration; and *Adam* hath not only fallen from his Creator, but we our selves from *Adam*, our Tycho and primary Generator.

29. Quarrel not rashly with Adversities not yet understood; and overlook not the Mercies often bound up in them. For we consider not sufficiently the good of Evils, nor fairly compute the Mercies of Providence in things afflictive at first hand. The famous *Andreas Doria* being invited to a Feast by *Aloysio Fieschi* with design to Kill him, just the night before fell mercifully into a fit of the Gout and so escaped that mischief. When *Cato* intended to Kill himself, from a blow which he gave his servant, who would not reach his Sword unto him, his Hand so swell'd that he had much ado to Effect his design. Hereby any one but a resolved Stoick might have taken a fair hint of consideration, and that some mercifull Genius[65] would have contrived his preservation. To be sagacious in such intercurrences[66] is not Superstition, but wary and pious Discretion, and to contemn such hints were to be deaf unto the speaking hand of God, wherein *Socrates* and *Cardan* would hardly have been mistaken.[67]

30. Break not open the gate of Destruction, and make no haste or bustle unto Ruin. Post not heedlessly on unto the *non ultra* of Folly, or precipice of Perdition. Let vicious ways have their Tropicks and Deflexions,[68] and swim in the Waters of Sin but as in the *Asphaltick* Lake,[69] though smeared and defiled, not to sink to the bottom. [If thou hast dipt thy foot in the Brink, yet venture not over *Rubicon*. Run not into Extremities from whence there is no regression.] In the vicious ways of the

65. Attendant spirit (see below, note 67).

66. i.e. intervening occurrences.

67. 'Socrates, and Cardan, perhaps, in imitation of him, talked of an attendant spirit or genius, that hinted from time to time how they should act' (*SJ*).

68. Turnings back and turnings aside (*M*).

69. i.e. the Dead Sea, called *lacus asphaltites* because of the bitumen floating on its surface. Cf. Milton's 'Asphaltic Pool' (*Paradise Lost*, I, 411).

World it mercifully falleth out that we become not extempore[70] wicked, but it taketh some time and pains to undo our selves. We fall not from Virtue, like *Vulcan* from Heaven,[71] in a day. Bad Dispositions require some time to grow into bad Habits, bad Habits must undermine good, and often repeated acts make us habitually evil: so that by gradual depravations, and while we are but staggeringly evil, we are not left without Parentheses of considerations, thoughtful rebukes, and merciful interventions, to recal us unto our selves. For the Wisdom of God hath methodiz'd the course of things unto the best advantage of goodness, and thinking Considerators overlook not the tract[72] thereof.

31. Since Men and Women have their proper Virtues and Vices, and even Twins of different sexes have not only distinct coverings in the Womb, but differing qualities and Virtuous Habits after; transplace not their Proprieties and confound not their Distinctions. Let Masculine and feminine accomplishments shine in their proper Orbs, and adorn their Respective subjects. However unite not the Vices of both Sexes in one; be not Monstrous in Iniquity, nor Hermaphroditically Vitious.

32. If generous Honesty, Valour, and plain Dealing, be the Cognisance of thy Family or Characteristick of thy Country, hold fast such inclinations suckt in with thy first Breath, and which lay in the Cradle with thee. Fall not into transforming degenerations, which under the old name create a new Nation. Be not an Alien in thine own Nation; bring not *Orontes* into *Tiber*;[73] learn the Virtues not the Vices of thy foreign Neighbours, and make thy imitation by discretion not contagion. Feel something of thy self in the noble Acts of thy Ancestors, and find in thine own Genius that of thy Predecessors. Rest not under the Expired merits of others, shine by those of thy own. Flame not like the central fire which enlightneth no Eyes, which no Man seeth, and most men think there's no such thing to be

70. 'sodaynly' (Elyot).

71. *Iliad*, I, 592.

72. Course, tendency.

73. So Juvenal – 'speaking of the confluence of foreigners to Rome' (*SJ*) – in *Satires*, III, 62.

seen. Add one Ray unto the common Lustre; add not only to the Number but the Note of thy Generation; and prove not a Cloud but an Asterisk[74] in thy Region.

33. Since thou hast an Alarum in thy Breast,[75] which tells thee thou hast a Living Spirit in thee above two thousand times in an hour; dull not away thy Days in sloathful supinity and the tediousness of doing nothing. To strenuous Minds there is an inquietude in overquietness, and no laboriousness in labour; and to tread a mile after the slow pace of a Snail, or the heavy measures of the Lazy of Brazilia, were a most tiring Pennance, and worse than a Race of some furlongs at the Olympicks. The rapid courses of the heavenly bodies are rather imitable by our Thoughts than our corporeal Motions; yet the solemn[76] motions of our lives amount unto a greater measure than is commonly apprehended. Some few men have surrounded the Globe of the Earth; yet many in the set Locomotions and movements of their days have measured the circuit of it, and twenty thousand miles have been exceeded by them. Move circumspectly not meticulously, and rather carefully sollicitous than anxiously sollicitudinous. Think not there is a Lyon in the way,[77] nor walk with Leaden Sandals in the paths of Goodness; but in all Virtuous motions let Prudence determine thy measures. Strive not to run like *Hercules*[78] a furlong in a breath: Festination[79] may prove Precipitation: Deliberating delay may be wise cunctation,[80] and slowness no sloathfulness.

34. Since Virtuous Actions have their own Trumpets, and without any noise from thy self will have their resound abroad; busy not thy best Member in the Encomium of thy self. Praise is a debt we owe unto the Virtues of others, and due unto our

74. i.e. small star.

75. 'The motion of the heart, which beats about sixty times in a minute; or, perhaps, the motion of respiration, which is nearer to the number mentioned' (*SJ*).

76. Customary (*E*).

77. Proverbs 22.13: 'The slothful man saith, There is a lion without, I shall be slain in the streets'.

78. In his pursuit of the hind of Keryneia.

79. 'Speed, haste' (Cockeram).

80. 'Slackness' (Cockeram).

own from all, whom Malice hath not made Mutes, or Envy struck Dumb. Fall not however into the common prevaricating way of self commendation and boasting, by denoting the imperfections of others. He who discommendeth others obliquely commendeth himself. He who whispers their infirmities proclaims his own Exemption from them, and consequently says, I am not as this Publican, or *Hic Niger*,[81] whom I talk of. Open ostentation and loud vain-glory is more tolerable than this obliquity, as but containing some Froath, no Ink, as but consisting of a personal piece of folly, nor complicated with uncharitableness. Superfluously we seek a precarious applause abroad: every good Man hath his plaudite[82] within himself; and though his Tongue be silent, is not without loud Cymbals in his Breast. Conscience will become his Panegyrist, and never forget to crown and extol him unto himself.

35. Bless not thy self only that thou wert born in *Athens*;[83] but among thy multiplyed acknowledgments lift up one hand unto Heaven, that thou wert born of Honest Parents, that Modesty, Humility, Patience, and Veracity lay in the same Egg, and came into the World with thee. From such foundations thou may'st be Happy in a Virtuous precocity, and make an early and long walk in Goodness; so may'st thou more naturally feel the contrariety of Vice unto Nature, and resist some by the Antidote of thy Temper. As Charity covers, so Modesty preventeth a multitude of sins; withholding from noon day Vices and brazen-brow'd Iniquities, from sinning on the house top, and painting our follies with the rays of the Sun. Where this Virtue reigneth, though Vice may show its Head, it cannot be in its Glory: where shame of sin sets, look not for Virtue to arise; for when Modesty taketh Wing, *Astræa*[84] goes soon after.

81. 'This blackhearted fellow' (Browne marg., quoting in Latin the full line of Horace, *Satires*, I, iv, 85).

82. 'the term by which the antient theatrical performers solicited a clap' (*SJ*).

83. 'As *Socrates* did. *Athens* a place of Learning and Civility' (Browne marg.). In Socrates's praise of the Athenians (Xenophon, *Memorabilia*, III, v, 3).

84. '*Astræa* Goddess of Justice and consequently of all Virtue' (Browne marg.).

36. The Heroical vein of Mankind runs much in the Souldiery, and couragious part of the World; and in that form we oftenest find Men above Men. History is full of the gallantry of that Tribe; and when we read their notable Acts, we easily find what a difference there is between a Life in *Plutarch* and in *Laërtius*.[85] Where true Fortitude dwells, Loyalty, Bounty, Friendship, and Fidelity, may be found. A man may confide in persons constituted for noble ends, who dare do and suffer, and who have a Hand to burn for their Country and their Friend.[86] Small and creeping things are the product of petty Souls. He is like to be mistaken, who makes choice of a covetous Man for a Friend, or relieth upon the Reed of narrow and poltron Friendship. Pityful things are only to be found in the cottages of such Breasts; but bright Thoughts, clear Deeds, Constancy, Fidelity, Bounty, and generous Honesty are the Gems of noble Minds; wherein, to derogate from none, the true Heroick English Gentleman hath no Peer.

PART II

1. Punish not thy self with Pleasure; Glut not thy sense with palative Delights; nor revenge the contempt of Temperance by the penalty of Satiety. Were there an Age of delight or any pleasure durable, who would not honour *Volupia*? but the Race of Delight is short, and Pleasures have mutable faces. The pleasures of one age are not pleasures in another, and their Lives fall short of our own. Even in our sensual days the strength of delight is in its seldomness or rarity, and sting in its satiety: Mediocrity is its Life, and immoderacy its Confusion. The Luxurious Emperors of old inconsiderately satiated themselves with the Dainties of Sea and Land, till, wearied through all varieties, their refections became a study unto them, and they were fain to feed by Invention. Novices in true Epicurism! which by mediocrity, paucity, quick and healthful Appetite, makes delights smartly acceptable; whereby *Epicurus* himself found *Jupiter*'s brain in a piece of Cytheridian Cheese, and the

85. The one wrote mostly of warriors; the other, of philosophers (*SJ*).
86. Like M. Scaevola (below, p. 532).

Tongues of Nightingals in a dish of Onyons.[1] Hereby healthful and temperate poverty hath the start of nauseating Luxury; unto whose clear and naked appetite every meal is a feast, and in one single dish the first course of *Metellus*;[2] who are cheaply hungry, and never loose their hunger, or advantage of a craving appetite, because obvious food contents it; while *Nero*[3] half famish'd could not feed upon a piece of Bread, and lingring after his snowed water, hardly got down an ordinary cup of Calda.[4] By such circumscriptions of pleasure the contemned Philosophers reserved unto themselves the secret of Delight, which the *Helluo*'s[5] of those days lost in their exorbitances. In vain we study Delight: It is at the command of every sober Mind, and in every sense born with us: but Nature, who teacheth us the rule of pleasure, instructeth also in the bounds thereof and where its line expireth. And therefore Temperate Minds, not pressing their pleasures until the sting appeareth, enjoy their contentations[6] contentedly, and without regret, and so escape the folly of excess, to be pleased unto displacency.[7]

2. Bring candid[8] Eyes unto the perusal of mens works, and let not *Zoilism* or Detraction[9] blast well intended labours. He that endureth no faults in mens writings must only read his own, wherein for the most part all appeareth White. Quotation mistakes, inadvertency, expedition, and human Lapses may make not only Moles but Warts in Learned Authors, who notwithstanding being judged by the capital matter admit not of

---

1. '*Jupiter's* brain': '*Cerebrum Jovis*, for a Delicious bit' (Browne marg.). 'Cytheridian cheese': the cheese of the island of Cythnus (?). 'Tongues of Nightingals': 'A dish used among the luxurious of antiquity' (*SJ*).

2. '*Metellus* his riotous Pontifical Supper, the great variety whereat is to be seen in *Macrobius*' (Browne marg.): *Saturnalia*, III, xiii, 10 ff.

3. '*Nero* in his flight': Suetonius, *Nero*, XLVIII, 4 (Browne marg.).

4. 'Tepid water, with which the ancients tempered their wine' (*apud G1*). So Juvenal, *Satires*, V, 63 (Browne marg.).

5. Gluttons.

6. i.e. contentments.

7. Cf. above, p. 411, note 104.

8. Favourably disposed (*OED*; *M*).

9. Zoilus: 'a poete, whych envied Homerus: and therefore the enviers of well lerned men are called Zoili' (Elyot, in §176).

disparagement. I should unwillingly affirm that *Cicero* was but slightly versed in *Homer*, because in his Work *de Gloria*[10] he ascribed those verses unto *Ajax*, which were delivered by *Hector*. What if *Plautus* in the account of *Hercules* mistaketh nativity for conception? Who would have mean thoughts of *Apollinaris Sidonius*, who seems to mistake the River *Tigris* for *Euphrates*, and though a good Historian and learned Bishop of *Auvergne* had the misfortune to be out in the Story of *David*, making mention of him when the Ark was sent back by the *Philistins* upon a Cart; which was before his time. Though I have no great opinion of *Machiavel*'s Learning, yet I shall not presently say, that he was but a Novice in Roman History, because he was mistaken in placing *Commodus* after the Emperour *Severus*. Capital Truths are to be narrowly eyed, collateral Lapses and circumstantial deliveries not to be too strictly sifted. And if the substantial subject be well forged out, we need not examine the sparks, which irregularly fly from it.

3. Let well weighed Considerations, not stiff and peremptory Assumptions, guide thy discourses, Pen, and Actions. To begin or continue our works like *Trismegistus* of old, *verum certè verum atque verissimum est*,[11] would sound arrogantly unto present Ears in this strict enquiring Age, wherein, for the most part, Probably, and Perhaps, will hardly serve to mollify the Spirit of captious Contradictors. If *Cardan* saith that a Parrot is a beautiful Bird, *Scaliger* will set his Wits o' work to prove it a deformed Animal. The Compage[12] of all Physical Truths is not so closely jointed, but opposition may find intrusion, nor always so closely maintained, as not to suffer attrition. Many Positions seem quodlibetically[13] constituted, and like a *Delphian* Blade[14] will cut on both sides. Some Truths seem almost Fals-

10. No longer extant; but the mistake is reported by Aulus Gellius.

11. 'In *Tabula Smaragdina*' (Browne marg.). The words from the 'Smaragdine Table' (as above, p. 74, note 71) mean: 'It is true, certainly true, true in the highest degree' (*SJ*).

12. Structure (cf. above, p. 250, note 3).

13. Scholastically. 'A "quodlibet" was a question in philosophy or theology proposed for scholastic disputation' (*SCR*).

14. i.e. like the ambiguous oracular pronouncements at Delphi.

hoods, and some Falshoods almost Truths; wherein Falshood and Truth seem almost æquilibriously stated, and but a few grains of distinction to bear down the ballance. Some have digged deep, yet glanced by the Royal Vein;[15] and a Man may come unto the *Pericardium*,[16] but not the Heart of Truth. Besides, many things are known, as some are seen, that is by Parallaxis, or at some distance from their true and proper beings, the superficial regard of things having a different aspect from their true and central Natures. And this moves sober Pens unto suspensory[17] and timorous assertions, nor presently to obtrude them as *Sibyls* leaves,[18] which after considerations may find to be but folious[19] apparences, and not the central and vital interiours of Truth.

4. Value the Judicious, and let not mere acquests[20] in minor parts of Learning gain they preexistimation.[21] 'Tis an unjust way of compute to magnify a weak Head for some Latin abilities and to under-value a solid Judgment, because he knows not the genealogy of *Hector*.[22] When that notable King of *France* would have his Son to know but one sentence in Latin,[23] had it been a good one, perhaps it had been enough. Natural parts and good Judgments rule the World. States are not governed by Ergotisms.[24] Many have Ruled well who could not perhaps define a Commonwealth, and they who understand not the Globe of the Earth command a great part of it. Where natural Logick

15. 'The *vena basilica* in the arm, one of the veins opened in bloodletting' (*M*).

16. 'a membrane or thin skin, involving the whole heart, like a case' (Blount).

17. Uncertain.

18. 'On which the Sibyl wrote her oracular answers' (*SJ*).

19. Leafy.

20. i.e. acquisitions.

21. Previous estimation.

22. The Emperor Tiberius used to exercise his grammarians by demanding the name of Hecuba's mother. See also above, p. 307, note 13.

23. 'Lewis the Eleventh: "He who knows not how to dissemble knows not how to reign" ' (Browne marg., quoted in Latin).

24. 'quiddities; from the Lat. (*Ergo*) a word much used in Syllogisms' (Blount).

prevails not, Artificial[25] too often faileth. Where Nature fills the
Sails, the Vessel goes smoothly on, and when Judgment is the
Pilot, the Ensurance need not be high. When Industry builds
upon Nature, we may exspect Pyramids: where that foundation
is wanting, the structure must be low. They do most by Books,
who could do much without them, and he that chiefly ows
himself unto himself is the substantial Man.

5. Let thy Studies be free as thy Thoughts and Contempla-
tions: but fly not only upon the wings of Imagination; Joyn
Sense unto Reason, and Experiment unto Speculation, and so
give life unto Embryon Truths, and Verities yet in their Chaos.
There is nothing more acceptable unto the Ingenious World,
than this noble Eluctation[26] of Truth; wherein, against the
tenacity of Prejudice and Prescription, this Century now pre-
vaileth. What Libraries of new Volumes aftertimes will behold,
and in what a new World of Knowledge the eyes of our Pos-
terity may be happy, a few Ages may joyfully declare; and is
but a cold thought unto those, who cannot hope to behold this
Exantlation[27] of Truth, or that obscured Virgin half out of the
Pit.[28] Which might make some content with a commutation of
the time of their lives, and to commend the Fancy of the
Pythagorean metempsychosis;[29] whereby they might hope to
enjoy this happiness in their third or fourth selves, and behold
that in *Pythagoras*, which they now but foresee in *Euphorbus*.[30]
The World, which took but six days to make, is like to take six
thousand [years] to make out:[31] mean while old Truths voted

25. Used in the pejorative sense, unlike its use in *Religio Medici* to
describe the art of God (above, p. 81).

26. 'Forcible eruption' (*SJ*).

27. As above, p. 184, note 49.

28. Cf. the proverb 'Truth lies at the bottom of a well' (*M*).

29. As above, p. 66, note 28.

30. 'I myself (for I well remember it) at the time of the Trojan war was
Euphorbus, son of Panthous' (Browne marg., quoting the Latin of Ovid,
Metamorphoses, XV, 160–61.)

31. The universe, commonly assumed to have been created in about
4000 B.C., was expected to terminate by the year A.D. 2000 – a period
usually divided into Three Eras of 2,000 years each, in accordance with the
'prophecy' of the 'school of Elijah' (*Sanhedrin*, 97a–b, in *The Babylonian
Talmud*, ed. I. Epstein [1935], Sanh. II). See §97.

down begin to resume their places, and new ones arise upon us; wherein there is no comfort in the happiness of *Tully*'s Elizium[32] or any satisfaction from the Ghosts of the Ancients, who knew so little of what is now well known. Men disparage not Antiquity, who prudently exalt new Enquiries, and make not them the Judges of Truth, who were but fellow Enquirers of it. Who can but magnify the Endeavors of *Aristotle*, and the noble start which Learning had under him; or less than pitty the slender progression made upon such advantages? While many Centuries were lost in repetitions and transcriptions sealing up the Book of Knowledge. And therefore rather than to swell the leaves of Learning by fruitless Repetitions, to sing the same Song in all Ages, nor adventure at Essays[33] beyond the attempt of others, many would be content that some would write like *Helmont* or *Paracelsus*; and be willing to endure the monstrosity of some opinions, for divers singular notions requiting such aberrations.

6. Despise not the obliquities of younger ways, nor despair of better things whereof there is yet no prospect. Who would imagine that *Diogenes*, who in his younger days was a falsifier of Money, should in the after course of his Life be so great a contemner of Metal? Some Negros, who believe the Resurrection, think that they shall Rise white.[34] Even in this life Regeneration may imitate Resurrection, our black and vitious tinctures may wear off, and goodness cloath us with candour. Good Admonitions Knock not always in vain. There will be signal Examples of God's mercy, and the Angels must not want their charitable Rejoyces for the conversion of lost Sinners. Figures of most Angles do nearest approach unto Circles, which have no Angles at all. Some may be near unto goodness, who are conceived far from it, and many things happen, not likely to ensue from any promises of Antecedencies. Culpable begin-

32. 'Who comforted himself that he should there converse with the old Philosophers' (Browne marg.). So Cicero, *On Old Age*, LXXXIV.

33. i.e. assays: attempts.

34. Mandelslo (Browne marg.) reported in his *Travels* (trans. 1662) that the inhabitants of Capo Verde 'believe the dead will rise again, but that they shall be white, and trade as the *Europeans* do' (*SCR*; *M*).

nings have found commendable conclusions, and infamous courses pious retractations. Detestable Sinners have proved exemplary Converts on Earth, and may be Glorious in the Apartment of *Mary Magdalen* in Heaven. Men are not the same through all divisions of their Ages. Time, Experience, self Reflexions, and God's mercies make in some well-temper'd minds a kind of translation before Death, and Men to differ from themselves as well as from other Persons. Hereof the old World afforded many Examples to the infamy of latter Ages, wherein Men too often live by the rule of their inclinations; so that, without any Astral prediction, the first day gives the last,[35] Men are commonly as they were, or rather, as bad dispositions run into worser habits, the Evening doth not crown, but sowerly conclude the Day.

7. If the Almighty will not spare us according to his merciful capitulation[36] at *Sodom*, if his Goodness please not to pass over a great deal of Bad for a small pittance of Good, or to look upon us in the Lump; there is slender hope for Mercy, or sound presumption of fulfilling half his Will, either in Persons or Nations: they who excel in some Virtues being so often defective in others; few Men driving at the extent and amplitude of Goodness, but computing themselves by their best parts, and others by their worst, are content to rest in those Virtues, which others commonly want. Which makes this speckled Face of Honesty in the World; and which was the imperfection of the old Philosophers and great pretenders unto Virtue, who well declining the gaping Vices of Intemperance, Incontinency, Violence and Oppression, were yet blindly peccant in iniquities of closer faces, were envious, malicious, contemners, scoffers, censurers, and stufft with Vizard Vices, no less depraving the Ethereal particle and diviner portion of Man. For Envy, Malice, Hatred are the qualities of *Satan*, close and dark like himself; and where such brands smoak the Soul cannot be White. Vice may be had at all prices; expensive and costly

35. 'Our first day fixed our last' (Browne marg., quoting the Latin of Seneca, *Oedipus*, 988).

36. Agreement – i.e. with Abraham (Genesis 18.20–32).

iniquities, which make the noise, cannot be every Man's sins: but the soul may be foully inquinated[37] at a very low rate, and a Man may be cheaply vitious, to the perdition of himself.

8. Opinion rides upon the neck of Reason, and Men are Happy, Wise, or Learned, according as that Empress shall set them down in the Register of Reputation. However weigh not thy self in the scales of thy own opinion, but let the Judgment of the Judicious be the Standard of thy Merit. Self-estimation is a flatterer too readily intitling us unto Knowledge and Abilities, which others sollicitously labour after, and doubtfully think they attain. Surely such confident tempers do pass their days in best tranquility, who, resting in the opinion of their own abilities, are happily gull'd by such contentation; wherein Pride, Self-conceit, Confidence, and Opiniatrity[38] will hardly suffer to complain of imperfection. To think themselves in the right, or all that right, or only that, which they do or think, is a fallacy of high content; though others laugh in their sleeves, and look upon them as in a deluded state of Judgment. Wherein notwithstanding 'twere but a civil piece of complacency to suffer them to sleep who would not wake, to let them rest in their securities, nor by dissent or opposition to stagger their contentments.

9. Since the Brow speaks often true, since Eyes and Noses have Tongues, and the countenance proclaims the Heart and inclinations; let observation so far instruct thee in Physiognomical lines, as to be some Rule for thy distinction, and Guide for thy affection unto such as look most like Men. Mankind, methinks, is comprehended in a few Faces, if we exclude all Visages, which any way participate of Symmetries and Schemes of Look common unto other Animals. For as though Man were the extract of the World, in whom all were *in coagulato*, which in their forms were *in soluto* and at Extension;[39] we often observe that Men do most act those Creatures, whose constitution, parts, and complexion do most predominate in their mixtures.

37. 'Defiled' (*SJ*).
38. 'obstinacy' (Blount).
39. *in coagulato*: 'in a congealed or compressed mass'; *in soluto:* 'in a state of expansion and separation' (*SJ*).

This is a corner-stone in Physiognomy, and holds some Truth not only in particular Persons but also in whole Nations. There are therefore Provincial Faces, National Lips and Noses, which testify not only the Natures of those Countries, but of those which have them elsewhere. Thus we may make *England* the whole Earth, dividing it not only into *Europe*, *Asia*, *Africa*, but the particular Regions thereof, and may in some latitude affirm, that there are *Ægyptians*, *Scythians*, *Indians* among us; who though born in *England*, yet carry the Faces and Air of those Countries, and are also agreeable and correspondent unto their Natures. Faces look uniformly unto our Eyes: How they appear unto some Animals of a more piercing or differing sight, who are able to discover the inequalities, rubbs, and hairiness of the Skin, is not without good doubt. And therefore in reference unto Man, *Cupid* is said to be blind. Affection should not be too sharp-Eyed, and Love is not to be made by magnifying Glasses. If things were seen as they truly are, the beauty of bodies would be much abridged. And therefore the wise Contriver hath drawn the pictures and outsides of things softly and amiably unto the natural Edge of our Eyes, not leaving them able to discover those uncomely asperities, which make Oyster-shells in good Faces, and Hedghoggs even in *Venus*'s moles.

10. Court not Felicity too far, and weary not the favorable hand of Fortune. Glorious actions have their times, extent and *non ultra*'s.[40] To put no end unto Attempts were to make prescription of Successes, and to bespeak unhappiness at the last. For the Line of our Lives is drawn with white and black vicissitudes, wherein the extremes hold seldom one complexion. That *Pompey* should obtain the sirname of Great at twenty five years, that Men in their young and active days should be fortunate and perform notable things, is no observation of deep wonder, they having the strength of their fates before them, nor yet acted their parts in the World, for which they were brought into it: whereas Men of years, matured for counsels and designs, seem to be beyond the vigour of their active fortunes, and high exploits of life, providentially ordained unto Ages best agreeable unto them. And therefore many brave men finding their fortune

40. As above, p. 410, note 99.

grow faint, and feeling its declination, have timely withdrawn themselves from great attempts, and so escaped the ends of mighty Men, disproportionable to their beginnings. But magnanimous Thoughts have so dimmed the Eyes of many, that forgetting the very essence of Fortune, and the vicissitude of good and evil, they apprehend no bottom in felicity; and so have been still tempted on unto mighty Actions, reserved for their destructions. For Fortune lays the Plot of our Adversities in the foundation of our Felicities, blessing us in the first quadrate,[41] to blast us more sharply in the last. And since in the highest felicities there lieth a capacity of the lowest miseries, she hath this advantage from our happiness to make us truly miserable. For to become acutely miserable we are to be first happy. Affliction smarts most in the most happy state, as having somewhat in it of *Bellisarius* at Beggers bush, or *Bajazet* in the grate.[42] And this the fallen Angels severely understand, who having acted their first part in Heaven, are made sharply miserable by transition, and more afflictively feel the contrary state of Hell.

11. Carry no careless Eye upon the unexpected scenes of things; but ponder the acts of Providence in the publick ends of great and notable Men, set out unto the view of all for no common *memorandums*. The Tragical Exits and unexpected periods of some eminent Persons cannot but amuse[43] considerate Observators; wherein notwithstanding most Men seem to see by extramission, without reception or self-reflexion,[44] and conceive themselves unconcerned by the fallacy of their own Exemption: Whereas the Mercy of God hath singled out but few to be the signals of his Justice, leaving the generality of

41. 'that is, in the first part of our time, alluding to the four quadratures of the moon' (*SJ*).

42. The one was reduced to poverty on having his eyes put out, the other while in captivity was placed in an iron cage. 'It may somewhat gratify those who deserve to be gratified, to inform them that both these stories are FALSE' (*SJ*).

43. 'amuse' (1716 ed.): 'amaze' (*MSS*.). But the former can also mean the latter (*E*).

44. 'Sight is made . . . by Extramission, by receiving the rayes of the object into the eye, and not by sending any out' (*Pseudodoxia Epidemica*, III, 7).

Mankind to the pædagogy of Example. But the inadvertency of our Natures not well apprehending this favorable method and merciful decimation, and that he sheweth in some what others also deserve; they entertain no sense of his Hand beyond the stroak of themselves. Whereupon the whole becomes necessarily punished, and the contracted Hand of God extended unto universal Judgments: from whence nevertheless the stupidity of our tempers receives but faint impressions, and in the most Tragical state of times holds but starts of good motions. So that to continue us in goodness there must be iterated returns of misery, and a circulation in afflictions is necessary. And since we cannot be wise by warnings, since Plagues are insignificant, except we be personally plagued, since also we cannot be punish'd unto Amendment by proxy or commutation, nor by vicinity, but contaction;[45] there is an unhappy necessity that we must smart in our own Skins, and the provoked arm of the Almighty must fall upon our selves. The capital sufferings of others are rather our monitions[46] than acquitments. There is but one who dyed salvifically for us,[47] and able to say unto Death, hitherto shalt thou go and no farther; only one enlivening Death, which makes Gardens of Graves, and that which was sowed in Corruption to arise and flourish in Glory: when Death it self shall dye, and living shall have no Period, when the damned shall mourn at the funeral of Death, when Life not Death shall be the wages of sin, when the second Death[48] shall prove a miserable Life, and destruction shall be courted.

12. Although their Thoughts may seem too severe, who think that few ill natur'd Men go to Heaven; yet it may be acknowledged that good natur'd Persons are best founded for that place; who enter the World with good Dispositions, and natural Graces, more ready to be advanced by impressions from above, and christianized unto pieties; who carry about them

45. i.e. direct contact.
46. i.e. admonitions.
47. i.e. for our salvation.
48. Revelation 20.14: 'death and hell were cast into the lake of fire. And this is the second death'. Cf. above, p. 313, note 46.

plain and down right dealing Minds, Humility, Mercy, Charity, and Virtues acceptable unto God and Man. But whatever success they may have as to Heaven, they are the acceptable Men on Earth, and happy is he who hath his quiver full of them for his Friends. These are not the Dens wherein Falshood lurks, and Hypocrisy hides its Head, wherein Frowardness makes its Nest, or where Malice, Hardheartedness, and Oppression love to dwell; not those by whom the Poor get little, and the Rich some times loose all; Men not of retracted Looks, but who carry their Hearts in their Faces, and need not to be look'd upon with perspectives;[49] not sordidly or mischievously ingrateful; who cannot learn to ride upon the neck of the afflicted, nor load the heavy laden, but who keep the Temple of *Janus* shut by peaceable and quiet tempers; who make not only the best Friends, but the best Enemies, as easier to forgive than offend, and ready to pass by the second offence, before they avenge the first; who make natural Royalists, obedient Subjects, kind and merciful Princes, verified in our own, one of the best natur'd Kings of this Throne.[50] Of the old Roman Emperours the best were the best natur'd; though they made but a small number, and might be writ in a Ring. Many of the rest were as bad Men as Princes; Humorists rather than of good humors, and of good natural parts, rather than of good natures: which did but arm their bad inclinations, and make them wittily wicked.

13. [With what strift[51] and pains we come into the World we remember not; but 'tis commonly found no easy matter to get out of it.] Many have studied to exasperate the ways of Death, but fewer hours have been spent to soften that necessity. That the smoothest way unto the grave is made by bleeding, as common opinion presumeth, beside the sick and fainting Languors which accompany that effusion, the experiment in *Lucan* and *Seneca*[52] will make us doubt; under which the noble Stoick so deeply laboured, that, to conceal his affliction, he was

49. Magnifying glasses.
50. i.e. Charles II.
51. 'strift' or striving (as above, p. 393): 'shift' (1716 ed.).
52. As above, p. 155, note 112.

fain to retire from the sight of his Wife, and not ashamed to implore the merciful hand of his Physician to shorten his misery therein. Ovid[53] the old Heroes,[54] and the Stoicks, who were so afraid of drowning, as dreading thereby, the extinction of their Soul, which they conceived to be a Fire, stood probably in fear of an easier way of Death; wherein the Water, entring the possessions of Air, makes a temperate suffocation, and kills as it were without a Fever. Surely many, who have had the Spirit to destroy themselves, have not been ingenious in the contrivance thereof. 'Twas a dull way practised by *Themistocles* to overwhelm himself with Bulls-blood,[55] who, being an *Athenian*, might have held an easier Theory of Death from the state potion of his Country; from which *Socrates* in *Plato*[56] seemed not to suffer much more than from the fit of an Ague. *Cato* is much to be pitied, who mangled himself with poyniards; And *Hannibal* seems more subtle, who carried his delivery not in the point, but the pummel[57] of his Sword.

The *Egyptians* were merciful contrivers, who destroyed their malefactors by Asps, charming their senses into an invincible sleep, and killing as it were with *Hermes* his Rod.[58] The Turkish Emperour, odious for other Cruelty, was herein a remarkable Master of Mercy, killing his Favorite in his sleep, and sending him from the shade into the house of darkness.[59] He who had been thus destroyed would hardly have bled at the presence of his destroyer; when Men are already dead by metaphor, and pass but from one sleep unto another, wanting herein the

53. 'Spare me from shipwreck; then death will be a boon' (Browne marg., quoting the Latin of Ovid, *Tristia*, I, ii, 52).

54. Cf. above, p. 271: 'the old Heroes in *Homer*, dreaded nothing more than water or drowning'.

55. So Plutarch, *Themistocles*, XXXI (Browne marg.).

56. *Phaedo*, 117–18.

57. 'Pummel, wherein he is said to have carried something, whereby upon a struggle or despair he might deliver himself from all misfortunes' (Browne marg.).

58. *Odyssey*, V, 47–8: 'the staff, with which [Hermes] mazes the eyes of those mortals whose eyes he would maze, or wakes again the sleepers'.

59. The murder of Ibrahim Pasha by Suleiman the Magnificent is related by Knolles (Browne marg.).

eminent part of severity, to feel themselves to dye, and escaping
the sharpest attendant of Death, the lively apprehension there-
of. But to learn to dye is better than to study the ways of dying.
Death will find some ways to unty or cut the most Gordian
Knots of Life, and make men's miseries as mortal as them-
selves: whereas evil Spirits, as undying Substances, are un-
separable from their calamities; and therefore they everlastingly
struggle under their *Augustia*'s,[60] and bound up with immor-
tality can never get out of themselves.

PART III

1. 'Tis hard to find a whole Age to imitate, or what Century to
propose for Example. Some have been far more approveable
than others: but Virtue and Vice, Panegyricks and Satyrs,[1]
scatteringly to be found in all. History sets down not only
things laudable, but abominable; things which should never
have been or never have been known: So that noble patterns
must be fetched here and there from single Persons, rather than
whole Nations, and from all Nations, rather than any one. The
World was early bad, and the first sin the most deplorable of
any.[2] The younger World afforded the oldest Men, and perhaps
the Best and the Worst, when length of days made virtuous
habits Heroical and immoveable, vitious, inveterate and irre-
claimable.[3] And since 'tis said that the imaginations of their
hearts were evil, only evil, and continually evil; it may be feared
that their sins held pace with their lives; and their Longevity
swelling their Impieties, the Longanimity[4] of God would no
longer endure such vivacious abominations. Their Impieties
were surely of a deep dye, which required the whole Element

60. 'Agonies' (*SJ*).

1. i.e. satires (see above, p. 408, note 96).

2. Man's first disobedience, according to Milton's theological treatise,
encompasses distrust, sacrilege, deceit, ingratitude, gluttony, and so on
(*Works*, Columbia ed., XV, 181–3).

3. Implacable.

4. 'lasting sufferance' (as above, p. 177).

of Water to wash them away,[5] and overwhelmed their memories with themselves; and so shut up the first Windows of Time, leaving no Histories of those longevous[6] generations, when Men might have been properly Historians, when *Adam* might have read long Lectures unto *Methuselah*, and *Methuselah* unto *Noah*.[7] For had we been happy in just Historical accounts of that unparallel'd World, we might have been acquainted with Wonders, and have understood not a little of the Acts and undertakings of *Moses* his mighty Men, and Men of renown of old; which might have enlarged our Thoughts, and made the World older unto us. For the unknown part of time shortens the estimation, if not the compute of it. What hath escaped our Knowledge falls not under our Consideration, and what is and will be latent is little better than non existent.

2. Some things are dictated for our Instruction, some acted for our Imitation, wherein 'tis best to ascend unto the highest conformity, and to the honour of the Exemplar. He honours God who imitates him. For what we virtuously imitate we approve and Admire; and since we delight not to imitate Inferiors, we aggrandize and magnify those we imitate; since also we are most apt to imitate those we love, we testify our affection in our imitation of the Inimitable. To affect to be like may be no imitation. To act, and not to be what we pretend to imitate, is but a mimical conformation, and carrieth no Virtue in it. *Lucifer* imitated not God, when he said he would be like the Highest,[8] and he[9] imitated not *Jupiter*, who counterfeited Thunder. Where Imitation can go no farther, let Admiration step on, whereof there is no end in the wisest form of Men. Even Angels and Spirits have enough to admire in their sublimer Natures, Admiration being the act of the Creature and not of God, who doth not Admire himself. Created Natures

5. i.e. during Noah's Flood.

6. Long-lived.

7. Methuselah was born before Adam died, and died after Noah was born.

8. Isaiah 14.12–15, where the reference to the King of Babylon was traditionally understood to apply to Satan.

9. Salmoneus in Virgil, *Aeneid*, VI, 585–6 (*SJ*).

allow of swelling Hyperboles; nothing can be said Hyperbolically of God, nor will his Attributes admit of expressions above their own Exuperances.[10] *Trismegistus* his Circle, whose center is every where, and circumference no where,[11] was no Hyperbole. Words cannot exceed, where they cannot express enough. Even the most winged Thoughts fall at the setting out, and reach not the portal of Divinity.

3. In Bivious[12] Theorems and *Janus*-faced Doctrines let Virtuous considerations state the determination. Look upon Opinions as thou doest upon the Moon, and chuse not the dark hemisphere for thy contemplation. Embrace not the opacous and blind side of Opinions, but that which looks most Luciferously[13] or influentially unto Goodness. 'Tis better to think that there are Guardian Spirits, than that there are no Spirits to Guard us; that vicious Persons are Slaves, than that there is any servitude in Virtue; that times past have been better than times present, than that times were always bad, and that to be Men it suffiseth to be no better than Men in all Ages, and so promiscuously to swim down the turbid stream, and make up the grand confusion. Sow not thy understanding with Opinions, which make nothing of Iniquities, and fallaciously extenuate Transgressions. Look upon Vices and vicious Objects with Hyperbolical Eyes, and rather enlarge their dimensions, that their unseen Deformities may not escape thy sense, and their Poysonous parts and stings may appear massy and monstrous unto thee; for the undiscerned Particles and Atoms of Evil deceive us, and we are undone by the Invisibles of seeming Goodness. We are only deceived in what is not discerned, and to Err is but to be Blind or Dim-sighted as to some Perceptions.

4. To be Honest in a right Line,[14] and Virtuous by Epitome, be firm unto such Principles of Goodness, as carry in them Volumes of instruction and may abridge thy Labour. And since

10. i.e. exsuperances: 'exaggerations' (*SJ*).

11. See above, p. 26.

12. Offering two courses.

13. Luminously.

14. 'A straight line is the shortest [i.e. most direct distance between two points]' (Browne marg., quoting the Latin of the proverbial utterance derived from Euclid).

instructions are many, hold close unto those, whereon the rest depend. So may we have all in a few, and the Law and the Prophets in a Rule, the Sacred Writ in Stenography,[15] and the Scripture in a Nut-Shell. To pursue the osseous[16] and solid part of Goodness, which gives Stability and Rectitude to all the rest; To settle on fundamental Virtues, and bid early defiance unto Mother-vices, which carry in their Bowels the seminals of other Iniquities, makes a short cut in Goodness, and strikes not off an Head but the whole Neck of *Hydra*. For we are carried into the dark Lake, like the *Ægyptian* River into the Sea, by seven principal Ostiaries.[17] The Mother-Sins of that number are the Deadly engins of Evil Spirits that undo us, and even evil Spirits themselves, and he who is under the Chains thereof is not without a possession. *Mary Magdalene* had more than seven Devils, if these with their Imps were in her, and he who is thus possessed may literally be named *Legion*.[18] Where such Plants grow and prosper, look for no Champian or Region void of Thorns, but productions like the Tree of *Goa*,[19] and Forrests of abomination.

5. Guide not the Hand of God, nor order the Finger of the Almighty, unto thy will and pleasure; but sit quiet in the soft showers of Providence, and Favorable distributions in this World, either to thy self or others. And since not only Judgments have their Errands, but Mercies their Commissions; snatch not at every Favour, nor think thy self passed by, if they fall upon thy Neighbour. Rake not up envious displacences at[20] things successful unto others, which the wise Disposer of all thinks not fit for thy self. Reconcile the events of things unto

15. As above, p. 74, note 69.

16. 'bonye, or of a bone' (Elyot).

17. The Seven Deadly Sins, here associated with the passage across the Styx (as above, p. 301, note 23), in turn related to the Nile with the obvious implications of God's judgements against the Egyptians.

18. As above, p. 125, note 324.

19. '*Arbor Goa* or *ficus Indica*, whose branches send down shoots which root in the ground, from whence there successively rise others, till one Tree becomes a wood' (Browne marg.). Milton's similar reference to the Indian fig-tree (*Paradise Lost*, IX, 1101–12) was doubtless adapted from its celebrated description by Ralegh (pp. 137–8).

20. Displeasures with (as above, p. 411, note 104).

both beings, that is, of this World and the next: So will there not seem so many Riddles in Providence, nor various inequalities in the dispensation of things below. If thou doest not anoint thy Face, yet put not on sackcloth at the felicities of others. Repining at the Good draws on rejoicing at the evils of others, and so falls into that inhumane Vice,[21] for which so few Languages have a name. The blessed Spirits above rejoice at our happiness below; but to be glad at the evils of one another is beyond the malignity of Hell, and falls not on evil Spirits, who, though they rejoice at our unhappiness, take no pleasure at the afflictions of their own Society or of their fellow Natures. Degenerous Heads! who must be fain to learn from such Examples, and to be Taught from the School of Hell.

6. Grain not thy vicious stains, nor deepen those swart[22] Tinctures, which Temper, Infirmity, or ill habits have set upon thee; and fix not by iterated depravations what time might Efface, or Virtuous washes expunge. He who thus still advanceth in Iniquity deepneth his deformed hue, turns a Shadow into Night, and makes himself a *Negro* in the black Jaundice; and so becomes one of those Lost ones, the disproportionate pores of whose Brains afford no entrance unto good Motions, but reflect and frustrate all Counsels, Deaf unto the Thunder of the Laws, and Rocks unto the Cries of charitable Commiserators. He who hath had the Patience of *Diogenes*, to make Orations unto Statues, may more sensibly apprehend how all Words fall to the Ground, spent upon such a surd[23] and Earless Generation of Men, stupid unto all Instruction, and rather requiring an Exorcist, than an Orator for their Conversion.

7. Burden not the back of *Aries*, *Leo*, or *Taurus*, with thy faults, nor make *Saturn*, *Mars*, or *Venus*, guilty of thy Follies. Think not to fasten thy imperfections on the Stars, and so despairingly conceive thy self under a fatality of being evil. Calculate thy self within, seek not thy self in the Moon, but in thine own Orb or Microcosmical Circumference. Let celestial

21. Ἐπιχαιρεκακία (Browne marg.). The vice is malignant delight at another's misfortune (Aristotle, *Nicomachean Ethics*, II, vi, 18, and vii, 15).
22. Dark; also malignant (below, note 24).
23. 'deaf' (Blount).

aspects admonish and advertise, not conclude and determine thy ways. For since good and bad Stars moralize not our Actions, and neither excuse or commend, acquit or condemn our Good or Bad Deeds at the present or last Bar, since some are Astrologically well disposed who are morally highly vicious; not Celestial Figures, but Virtuous Schemes must denominate and state our Actions. If we rightly understood the Names whereby God calleth the Stars, if we knew his Name for the Dog-Star,[24] or by what appellation *Jupiter*, *Mars*, and *Saturn* obey his Will, it might be a welcome accession unto Astrology, which speaks great things, and is fain to make use of appellations from Greek and Barbarick Systems. Whatever Influences, Impulsions, or Inclinations there be from the Lights above, it were a piece of wisdom to make one of those Wise men who overrule their Stars,[25] and with their own Militia contend with the Host of Heaven. Unto which attempt there want not Auxiliaries from the whole strength of Morality, supplies from Christian Ethicks, influences also and illuminations from above, more powerfull than the Lights of Heaven.

8. Confound not the distinctions of thy Life which Nature hath divided: that is, Youth, Adolescence, Manhood, and old Age, nor in these divided Periods, wherein thou art in a manner Four, conceive thy self but One. Let every division be happy in its proper Virtues, nor one Vice run through all. Let each distinction have its salutary transition, and critically deliver thee from the imperfections of the former, so ordering the whole, that Prudence and Virtue may have the largest Section. Do as a Child but when thou art a Child, and ride not on a Reed at twenty. He who hath not taken leave of the follies of his Youth, and in his maturer state scarce got out of that division, disproportionately divideth his Days, crowds up the latter part of his Life, and leaves too narrow a corner for the Age of Wisdom, and so hath room to be a Man scarce longer than he hath been a Youth. Rather than to make this confusion, antici-

24. Sirius – 'the swart Star' of Milton's *Lycidas* (l. 138: cf. above, note 22) – under whose malign influence vegetation was said to wither.

25. '*Sapiens dominabitur Astris*' (Browne marg.): a proverb, translated in the text.

pate the Virtues of Age, and live long without the infirmities of it. So may'st thou count up thy Days as some do *Adams*,[26] that is, by anticipation; so may'st thou be coetaneous[27] unto thy Elders, and a Father unto thy contemporaries.

9. While others are curious in the choice of good Air, and chiefly sollicitous for healthful habitations, Study thou Conversation, and be critical in thy Consortion.[28] The aspects, conjunctions, and configurations of the Stars, which mutually diversify, intend, or qualify their influences, are but the varieties of their nearer or farther conversation with one another, and like the Consortion of Men, whereby they become better or worse, and even Exchange their Natures. Since Men live by Examples, and will be imitating something; order thy imitation to thy Improvement, not thy Ruin. Look not for Roses in *Attalus* His Garden,[29] or wholesome Flowers in a venemous Plantation. And since there is scarce any one bad, but some others are the worse for him; tempt not Contagion by proximity and hazard not thy self in the shadow of Corruption. He who hath not early suffered this Shipwrack, and in his Younger Days escaped this *Charybdis*, may make a happy Voyage, and not come in with black Sails into the port.[30] Self conversation, or to be alone, is better than such Consortion. Some Schoolmen[31] tell us, that he is properly alone, with whom in the same place there is no other of the same Species. *Nabuchodonozor* was alone, though among the Beasts of the Field,[32] and a Wise Man may be tolerably said to be alone though with a Rabble of People, little better than Beasts about him. Unthinking Heads, who have not learn'd to be alone, are in a Prison to themselves,

26. '*Adam* thought to be created in the State of Man, about thirty years Old' (Browne marg.). Cf. above, p. 109: 'Some Divines count *Adam* 30 yeares old at his creation'.

27. 'Of one time and age' (Cockeram).

28. Company.

29. '*Attalus* made a Garden which contained only venemous Plants' (Browne marg.). Cf. above, p. 328.

30. Like Theseus, who on returning home forgot to change his black sails to white, and so caused the suicide of his father Aegeus.

31. i.e. medieval scholastic theologians (cf. above, p. 69, note 39).

32. Daniel 4.32.

if they be not also with others: Whereas on the contrary, they whose thoughts are in a fair, and hurry within, are sometimes fain to retire into Company, to be out of the crowd of themselves. He who must needs have Company, must needs have sometimes bad Company. Be able to be alone. Loose not the advantage of Solitude, and the Society of thy self, nor be only content, but delight to be alone and single with Omnipresency.[33] He who is thus prepared, the Day is not uneasy nor the Night black unto him. Darkness may bound his Eyes, not his Imagination. In his Bed he may ly, like *Pompey* and his Sons,[34] in all quarters of the Earth, may speculate the Universe, and enjoy the whole World in the Hermitage of himself. Thus the old *Ascetick* Christians found a Paradise in a Desert, and with little converse on Earth held a conversation in Heaven; thus they Astronomiz'd in Caves, and though they beheld not the Stars, had the Glory of Heaven before them.

10. Let the Characters of good things stand indelibly in thy Mind, and thy Thoughts be active on them. Trust not too much unto suggestions from Reminiscential Amulets, or Artificial *Memorandums*. Let the mortifying *Janus* of *Covarrubias*[35] be in thy daily Thoughts, not only on thy Hand and Signets. Rely not alone upon silent and dumb remembrances. Behold not Death's Heads till thou doest not see them, nor look upon mortifying Objects till thou overlook'st them. Forget not how assuefaction[36] unto any thing minorates[37] the passion from it, how constant Objects loose their hints, and steal an inadvertisement[38] upon us. There is no excuse to forget what every thing prompts unto us. To thoughtful Observators the whole World

33. i.e. with the ever-present God.

34. As above, p. 263, note 2.

35. '*Don Sebastian de Covarrubias* writ 3 Centuries [i.e. three hundred] of moral Emblems in *Spanish*. In the 88*th* of the second Century he sets down two Faces averse, and conjoined *Janus*-like, the one a Gallant Beautiful Face, the other a Death's Head Face, with this Motto out of Ovid's *Metamorphosis* [II, 551], *Quid fuerim quid simque vide*' – i.e. 'See what I used to be and what I am now' (Browne marg.).

36. 'attaining' (Blount).

37. Diminishes.

38. i.e. inadvertence: inattention.

is a Phylactery,[39] and every thing we see an Item of the Wisdom, Power, or Goodness of God. Happy are they who verify their Amulets, and make their Phylacteries speak in their Lives and Actions. To run on in despight of the Revulsions and Pul-backs of such Remora's[40] aggravates our transgressions. When Death's Heads on our Hands[41] have no influence upon our Heads, and fleshless Cadavers abate not the exorbitances of the Flesh; when Crucifixes upon Mens Hearts suppress not their bad commotions, and his Image who was murdered for us with-holds not from Blood and Murder; Phylacteries prove but formalities, and their despised hints sharpen our condemnations.

11. Look not for *Whales* in the *Euxine* Sea,[42] or expect great matters where they are not to be found. Seek not for Profundity in Shallowness, or Fertility in a Wilderness. Place not the expectation of great Happiness here below, or think to find Heaven on Earth; wherein we must be content with Embryon-felicities, and fruitions of doubtful Faces. For the Circle of our felicities makes but short Arches. In every clime we are in a periscian state,[43] and with our Light our Shadow and Darkness walk about us. Our Contentments stand upon the tops of Pyramids ready to fall off, and the insecurity of their enjoyments abrupteth our Tranquilities. What we magnify is Magnificent, but like to the *Colossus*, noble without, stuft with rubbidge and course[44] Metal within. Even the Sun, whose Glorious outside we behold, may have dark and smoaky Entrails. In vain we admire the Lustre of any thing seen: that which is truly glorious is invisible. *Paradise* was but a part of the Earth, lost not only to our Fruition but our Knowledge. And if, according to old

39. Cf. above, p. 425, note 32.
40. Impediments.
41. i.e. in rings.
42. i.e. the Black Sea.
43. i.e. 'with shadows all round us. The Periscii are those, who, living within the polar circle, see the sun move round them, and consequently project their shadows in all directions' (*SJ*).
44. i.e. coarse. The wondrous Colossus of Rhodes is described by Pliny, XXXIV, 18.

Dictates, no Man can be said to be happy before Death, the happiness of this Life goes for nothing before it be over, and while we think our selves happy we do but usurp that Name. Certainly true Beatitude groweth not on Earth, nor hath this World in it the Expectations we have of it. He Swims in Oyl, and can hardly avoid sinking, who hath such light Foundations to support him. 'Tis therefore happy that we have two Worlds to hold on. To enjoy true happiness we must travel into a very far Countrey, and even out of our selves; for the Pearl we seek for is not to be found in the *Indian*, but in the *Empyrean* Ocean.[45]

12. Answer not the Spur of Fury, and be not prodigal or prodigious in Revenge. Make not one in the *Historia Horribilis*;[46] Flay not thy Servant for a broken Glass, nor pound him in a Mortar who offendeth thee;[47] supererogate not in the worst sense, and overdo not the necessities of evil; humour not the injustice of Revenge. Be not Stoically mistaken in the equality of sins, nor commutatively iniquous[48] in the valuation of transgressions; but weigh them in the Scales of Heaven, and by the weights of righteous Reason. Think that Revenge too high, which is but level with the offence. Let thy Arrows of Revenge fly short, or be aimed like those of *Jonathan*, to fall beside the mark.[49] Too many there be to whom a Dead Enemy smells well, and who find Musk and Amber in Revenge. The ferity[50] of such minds holds no rule in Retaliations, requiring too often a Head for a Tooth, and the Supreme revenge for trespasses, which a night's rest should obliterate. But patient Meekness takes injuries like Pills, not chewing but swallowing them down,

45. Cf. Matthew 13.45: 'the kingdom of heaven is like unto a merchant-man seeking goodly pearls: who, when he had found one pearl of great price, went and sold all that he had, and bought it'.

46. 'A Book so entituled wherein are sundry horrid accounts' (Browne marg.). It was published in 1597.

47. Like the tyrants in the stories related by Seneca (*On Anger*, III, 40) and Diogenes Laertius (*Lives*, IX, 10), respectively.

48. i.e. iniquitous in commutative fashion. The phrase is opposed to 'commutative justice' (see above, p. 157, note 117).

49. 1 Samuel 20.20.

50. As above, p. 293, note 70.

Laconically suffering, and silently passing them over, while angred Pride makes a noise, like *Homerican Mars*,[51] at every scratch of offences. Since Women do most delight in Revenge, it may seem but feminine manhood to be vindicative. If thou must needs have thy Revenge of thine Enemy, with a soft Tongue break his Bones,[52] heap Coals of Fire on his Head, forgive him, and enjoy it. To forgive our Enemies is a charming way of Revenge, and a short *Cæsarian*[53] Conquest overcoming without a blow; laying our Enemies at our Feet, under sorrow, shame, and repentance; leaving our Foes our Friends, and solicitously inclined to grateful Retaliations. Thus to Return upon our Adversaries is a healing way of Revenge, and to do good for evil a soft and melting ultion,[54] a method Taught from Heaven to keep all smooth on Earth. Common forceable ways make not an end of Evil, but leave Hatred and Malice behind them. An Enemy thus reconciled is little to be trusted, as wanting the foundation of Love and Charity, and but for a time restrained by disadvantage or inability. If thou hast not Mercy for others, yet be not Cruel unto thy self. To ruminate upon evils, to make critical notes upon injuries, and be too acute in their apprehensions, is to add unto our own Tortures, to feather the Arrows of our Enemies, to lash our selves with the Scorpions of our Foes, and to resolve to sleep no more. For injuries long dreamt on take away at last all rest; and he sleeps but like *Regulus*, who busieth his Head about them.

13. Amuse not thy self about the Riddles of future things. Study Prophecies when they are become Histories, and past hovering in their causes. Eye well things past and present, and let conjectural sagacity suffise for things to come. There is a sober Latitude for prescience in contingences of discoverable Tempers, whereby discerning Heads see sometimes beyond

51. 'You may shout so as to outdo Stentor, or at least as loudly as Homer's Mars' (Browne marg., quoting the Latin of Juvenal, *Satires*, XIII, 112–13). Cf. *Iliad*, V, 785 and 858.

52. 'A soft Tongue breaketh the bones' (Browne marg.): Proverbs 25.15.

53. Pertaining to Caesar. Cf. above, p. 402, note 64.

54. 'vengeance' (Elyot).

their Eyes, and Wise Men become Prophetical. Leave Cloudy predictions to their Periods, and let appointed Seasons have the lot of their accomplishments. 'Tis too early to study such Prophecies before they have been long made, before some train of their causes have already taken Fire, laying open in part what lay obscure and before buryed unto us. For the voice of Prophecies is like that of Whispering-places: They who are near or at a little distance hear nothing, those at the farthest extremity will understand all. But a Retrograde cognition of times past, and things which have already been, is more satisfactory than a suspended Knowledge of what is yet unexistent. And the Greatest part of time being already wrapt up in things behind us;[55] it's now somewhat late to bait after things before us; for futurity still shortens, and time present sucks in time to come. What is Prophetical in one Age proves Historical in another, and so must hold on unto the last of time; when there will be no room for Prediction, when *Janus* shall loose one Face, and the long beard of time shall look like those of *David*'s Servants,[56] shorn away upon one side, and when, if the expected *Elias* should appear,[57] he might say much of what is past, not much of what's to come.

14. Live unto the Dignity of thy Nature, and leave it not disputable at last, whether thou hast been a Man, or since thou art a composition of Man and Beast, how thou hast predominantly passed thy days, to state the denomination. Un-man not therefore thy self by a Beastial transformation, nor realize old Fables.[58] Expose not thy self by four-footed manners unto monstrous draughts, and *Caricatura*[59] representations. Think not after the old *Pythagorean* conceit, what Beast thou may'st be after death. Be not under any Brutal *metempsychosis* while thou livest, and walkest about erectly under the scheme of Man. In thine own circumference, as in that of the Earth, let the Rational

55. i.e. in the sense that history's 6,000 years are about to expire (see above, p. 439, note 31).
56. 2 Samuel 10.4.
57. See above, p. 313, note 44.
58. Such as Circe's reduction of Odysseus's companions to swine (*Odyssey*, X, 237 ff.).
59. As above, p. 397, note 35.

Horizon be larger than the sensible, and the Circle of Reason than of Sense. Let the Divine part be upward, and the Region of Beast below. Otherwise, 'tis but to live invertedly, and with thy Head unto the Heels of thy *Antipodes*. Desert not thy title to a Divine particle and union with invisibles. Let true Knowledge and Virtue tell the lower World thou art a part of the higher. Let thy Thoughts be of things which have not entred into the Hearts of Beasts: Think of things long past, and long to come: Acquaint thy self with the *Choragium*[60] of the Stars, and consider the vast expansion beyond them. Let Intellectual Tubes[61] give thee a glance of things, which visive Organs[62] reach not. Have a glimpse of incomprehensibles, and Thoughts of things, which Thoughts but tenderly touch. Lodge immaterials in thy Head: ascend unto invisibles: fill thy Spirit with Spirituals, with the mysteries of Faith, the magnalities[63] of Religion, and thy Life with the Honour of God; without which, though Giants in Wealth and Dignity, we are but Dwarfs and Pygmies in Humanity, and may hold a pitiful rank in that triple division of mankind into Heroes, Men, and Beasts. For though human Souls are said to be equal, yet is there no small inequality in their operations; some maintain the allowable Station of Men; many are far below it; and some have been so divine, as to approach the *Apogeum*[64] of their Natures, and to be in the *Confinium*[65] of Spirits.

15. Behold thy self by inward Opticks and the Crystalline[66] of thy Soul. Strange it is that in the most perfect sense there should be so many fallacies, that we are fain to make a doctrine, and often to see by Art. But the greatest imperfection is in our inward sight, that is, to be Ghosts unto our own Eyes, and while we are so sharp-sighted as to look thorough others, to be invisible unto our selves; for the inward Eyes are more fallacious than the outward. The Vices we scoff at in others

60. Dancing area.
61. i.e. telescopes, here used metaphorically.
62. i.e. organs of vision.
63. As above, p. 351, note 51.
64. 'To the utmost point of distance from earth and earthly things' (*SJ*).
65. 'border' (Elyot).
66. i.e. the crystalline lens.

laugh at us within our selves. Avarice, Pride, Falshood lye undiscerned and blindly in us, even to the Age of blindness: and therefore, to see our selves interiourly, we are fain to borrow other Mens Eyes; wherein true Friends are good Informers, and Censurers no bad Friends. Conscience only, that can see without Light, sits in the *Areopagy*[67] and dark Tribunal of our Hearts, surveying our Thoughts and condemning their obliquities, Happy is that state of vision that can see without Light, though all should look as before the Creation when there was not an Eye to see, or Light to actuate a Vision: wherein notwithstanding obscurity is only imaginable respectively unto Eyes; for unto God there was none, Eternal Light was ever, created Light was for the creation, not himself, and as he saw before the Sun, may still also see without it. In the City of the new *Jerusalem* there is neither Sun nor Moon;[68] where glorifyed Eyes must see by the *Archetypal* Sun, or the Light of God, able to illuminate Intellectual Eyes, and make unknown Visions. Intuitive perceptions in Spiritual beings may perhaps hold some Analogy unto Vision: but yet how they see us, or one another, what Eye, what Light, or what perception is required unto their intuition, is yet dark unto our apprehension; and even how they see God, or how unto our glorified Eyes the Beatifical Vision[69] will be celebrated, another World must tell us, when perceptions will be new, and we may hope to behold invisibles.

16. When all looks fair about, and thou seest not a cloud so big as a Hand[70] to threaten thee, forget not the Wheel of things: Think of sullen vicissitudes, but beat not thy brains to foreknow them. Be armed against such obscurities rather by submission than fore-knowledge. The Knowledge of future evils mortifies present felicities, and there is more content in the uncertainty or ignorance of them. This favour our Saviour vouchsafed unto *Peter*,[71] when he fore-told not his Death in

67. Referring to the Areopagus near the Acropolis at Athens, established as a judicial tribunal in the seventh to sixth centuries B.C.

68. Revelation 21.23.

69. Our ultimate vision of God.

70. 1 Kings 18.44.   71. John 21.18–19.

plain terms, and so by an ambiguous and cloudy delivery dampt not the Spirit of his Disciples. But in the assured fore-know-ledge of the Deluge *Noah* lived many Years under the affliction of a Flood, and *Jerusalem* was taken unto *Jeremy* before it was besieged.[72] And therefore the Wisdom of Astrologers, who speak of future things, hath wisely softned the severity of their Doctrines; and even in their sad predictions, while they tell us of inclination not coaction from the Stars, they Kill us not with *Stygian* Oaths[73] and merciless necessity, but leave us hopes of evasion.

17. If thou hast the brow to endure the Name of Traytor, Perjur'd, or Oppressor, yet cover thy Face when Ingratitude is thrown at thee. If that degenerous Vice possess thee, hide thy self in the shadow of thy shame, and pollute not noble society. Grateful Ingenuities are content to be obliged within some compass of Retribution, and being depressed by the weight of iterated favours may so labour under their inabilities of Requital, as to abate the content from Kindnesses. But narrow self-ended Souls make prescription of good Offices, and obliged by often[74] favours think others still due unto them: whereas, if they but once fail, they prove so perversely ungrateful, as to make nothing of former courtesies, and to bury all that's past. Such tempers pervert the generous course of things; for they discourage the inclinations of noble minds, and make Bene-ficency cool unto acts of obligation, whereby the grateful World should subsist, and have their consolation. Common gratitude must be kept alive by the additionary fewel of new courtesies: but generous Gratitudes, though but once well obliged, without quickening repetitions or expectation of new Favours, have thankful minds for ever; for they write not their obligations in sandy but marble memories, which wear not out but with themselves.

18. Think not Silence the wisdom of Fools, but, if rightly timed, the honour of Wise Men, who have not the Infirmity, but the Virtue of Taciturnity, and speak not out of the abun-

72. i.e. in that he had prophesied its fall (Jeremiah 21.7).
73. Binding oaths 'by the Styx', as in *Iliad*, XV, 38 (*M*).
74. Few.

dance, but the well weighed thoughts of their Hearts. Such Silence may be Eloquence, and speak thy worth above the power of Words. Make such a one thy friend, in whom Princes may be happy, and great Councels successful. Let him have the Key of thy Heart, who hath the Lock of his own, which no Temptation can open; where thy Secrets may lastingly ly, like the Lamp in *Olybius* his Urn,[75] alive, and light, but close and invisible.

19. Let thy Oaths be sacred and Promises be made upon the Altar of thy Heart. Call not *Jove* to witness with a Stone in one Hand, and a Straw in another,[76] and so make Chaff and Stubble of thy Vows. Worldly Spirits, whose interest is their belief, make Cobwebs of Obligations, and, if they can find ways to elude the Urn of the *Prætor*,[77] will trust the Thunderbolt of *Jupiter*: And therefore if they should as deeply swear as *Osman* to *Bethlem Gabor*;[78] yet whether they would be bound by those chains, and not find ways to cut such *Gordian* Knots, we could have no just assurance. But Honest Mens Words are *Stygian* Oaths, and Promises inviolable. These are not the Men for whom the fetters of Law were first forged: they needed not the solemness of Oaths; by keeping their Faith they swear,[79] and evacuate such confirmations.

20. Though the World be Histrionical, and most Men live Ironically, yet be thou what thou singly art, and personate only thy self. Swim smoothly in the stream of thy Nature, and live but one Man. To single Hearts doubling is discruciating:[80] such tempers must sweat to dissemble, and prove but hypocritical Hypocrites. Simulation[81] must be short: Men do not easily

75. 'Which after many hundred years was found burning under ground, and went out as soon as the air came to it' (Browne marg.). The improbable lamp was unearthed *c.* 1500.

76. '*Jovem Lapidem jurare*' (Browne marg.): 'the person making the oath would throw the stone away, wishing he too might be cast out if the oath was not kept' (*M*).

77. 'The vessel, into which the ticket of condemnation or acquittal was cast' (*SJ*).

78. The hyperbolic oath is related by Knolles (Browne marg.).

79. So Quintus Curtius, VII, 8 (Browne marg.).

80. Tormenting.

81. 'dissimulation' (Elyot).

continue a counterfeiting Life, or dissemble unto Death. He who counterfeiteth, acts a part, and is as it were out of himself: which, if long, proves so ircksome, that Men are glad to pull of their Vizards, and resume themselves again; no practice being able to naturalize such unnaturals, or make a Man rest content not to be himself. And therefore since Sincerity is thy Temper, let veracity be thy Virtue in Words, Manners, and Actions. To offer at iniquities, which have so little foundations in thee, were to be vitious up hill, and strain for thy condemnation. Persons vitiously inclined want no Wheels to make them actively vitious, as having the Elater[82] and Spring of their own Natures to facilitate their Iniquities. And therefore so many, who are sinistrous unto Good Actions, are Ambi-dexterous unto bad, and *Vulcans* in virtuous Paths, *Achilleses* in vitious motions.

21. Rest not in the high strain'd Paradoxes of old Philosophy supported by naked Reason, and the reward of mortal Felicity, but labour in the Ethicks of Faith, built upon Heavenly assistance, and the happiness of both beings. Understand the Rules, but swear not unto the Doctrines of *Zeno* or *Epicurus*. Look beyond *Antoninus*, and terminate not thy Morals in *Seneca* or *Epictetus*. Let not the twelve, but the two Tables be thy Law:[83] Let *Pythagaras* be thy Remembrancer, not thy textuary and final Instructer; and learn the Vanity of the World rather from *Solomon* than *Phocylides*. Sleep not in the Dogma's of the *Peripatus*, Academy, or *Porticus*.[84] Be a moralist of the Mount,[85] an *Epictetus* in the Faith, and christianize thy Notions.

22. In seventy or eighty years a Man may have a deep Gust of the World, Know what it is, what it can afford, and what 'tis to have been a Man. Such a latitude of years may hold a considerable corner in the general Map of Time; and a Man may have a curt Epitome of the whole course thereof in the days of his own Life, may clearly see he hath but acted over his Fore-fathers,

82. Driving force (*M*).

83. i.e. not the Roman code (see above, p. 269, note 17) but the two tables of stone on which the Decalogue was engraven (Deuteronomy 34.1).

84. i.e. the followers of Plato, Aristotle, and the Stoics, respectively.

85. 'That is, according to the rules laid down in our SAVIOUR'S sermon on the mount' (*SJ*).

what it was to live in Ages past, and what living will be in all ages to come.

He is like to be the best judge of Time who hath lived to see about the sixtieth part thereof.[86] Persons of short times may Know what 'tis to live, but not the life of Man, who, having little behind them, are but *Januses* of one Face, and Know not singularities enough to raise Axioms of this World: but such a compass of Years will show new Examples of old Things, Parallelisms of occurrences through the whole course of Time, and nothing be monstrous unto him; who may in that time understand not only the varieties of Men, but the variation of himself, and how many Men he hath been in that extent of time.

He may have a close apprehension what it is to be forgotten, while he hath lived to find none who could remember his Father, or scarce the friends of his youth, and may sensibly see with what a face in no long time oblivion will look upon himself. His Progeny may never be his Posterity; he may go out of the World less related than he came into it, and considering the frequent mortality in Friends and Relations, in such a Term of Time, he may pass away divers years in sorrow and black habits, and leave none to mourn for himself; Orbity[87] may be his inheritance, and Riches his Repentance.

In such a thred of Time, and long observation of Men, he may acquire a *Physiognomical* intuitive Knowledge, Judge the interiors by the outside, and raise conjectures at first sight; and knowing what Men have been, what they are, what Children probably will be, may in the present Age behold a good part, and the temper of the next; and since so many live by the Rules of Constitution, and so few overcome their temperamental Inclinations, make no improbable predictions.

Such a portion of Time will afford a large prospect backward, and Authentick Reflections how far he hath performed the great intention of his Being, in the Honour of his Maker; whether he hath made good the Principles of his Nature and what he was made to be; what Characteristick and special

86. i.e. lived until his 100th year – 'the sixtieth part' of history's duration (as above, p. 439, note 31).

87. 'want or privation' (Blount).

Mark he hath left, to be observable in his Generation; whether he hath Lived to purpose or in vain, and what he hath added, acted, or performed, that might considerably speak him a Man.

In such an Age Delights will be undelightful and Pleasures grow stale unto him; Antiquated Theorems will revive, and *Solomon*'s Maxims[88] be Demonstrations unto him; Hopes or presumptions be over, and despair grow up of any satisfaction below. And having been long tossed in the Ocean of this World, he will by that time feel the In-draught of another, unto which this seems but preparatory, and without it of no high value. He will experimentally find the Emptiness of all things, and the nothing of what is past; and wisely grounding upon true Christian Expectations, finding so much past, will wholly fix upon what is to come. He will long for Perpetuity, and live as though he made haste to be happy. The last may prove the prime part of his Life, and those his best days which he lived nearest Heaven.

23. Live happy in the *Elizium* of a virtuously composed Mind, and let Intellectual Contents exceed the Delights wherein mere Pleasurists place their Paradise. Bear not too slack reins upon Pleasure, nor let complexion or contagion betray thee unto the exorbitancy of Delight. Make Pleasure thy Recreation or inter-missive Relaxation, not thy *Diana*, Life and Profession.[89] Volup-tuousness is as insatiable as Covetousness. Tranquility is better than Jollity, and to appease pain than to invent pleasure. Our hard entrance into the World, our miserable going out of it, our sicknesses, disturbances, and sad Rencounters[90] in it, do clamorously tell us we come not into the World to run a Race of Delight, but to perform the sober Acts and serious purposes of Man; which to omit were foully to miscarry in the advantage of humanity, to play away an uniterable[91] Life, and to have lived in vain. Forget not the capital end, and frustrate not the oppor-tunity of once Living. Dream not of any kind of *Metempsychosis*

88. e.g. 'all is vanity' (Ecclesiastes 1.2).
89. Demetrius, who made silver shrines for Diana at Ephesus, told his fellow craftsmen: 'by this craft we have our wealth' (Acts 19.24–5).
90. Conflicts.
91. Non-repeatable.

or transanimation, but into thine own body, and that after a long time, and then also unto wail or bliss, according to thy first and fundamental Life. Upon a curricle[92] in this World depends a long course of the next, and upon a narrow Scene here an endless expansion hereafter. In vain some think to have an end of their Beings with their Lives. Things cannot get out of their natures, or be or not be in despite of their constitutions. Rational existences in Heaven perish not at all, and but partially on Earth: That which is thus once will in some way be always: The first Living human Soul is still alive, and all *Adam* hath found no Period.

24. Since the Stars of Heaven do differ in Glory; since it hath pleased the Almighty hand to honour the North Pole with Lights above the South; since there are some Stars so bright, that they can hardly be looked on, some so dim that they can scarce be seen, and vast numbers not to be seen at all even by Artificial Eyes; Read thou the Earth in Heaven, and things below from above. Look contentedly upon the scattered difference of things, and expect not equality in lustre, dignity, or perfection, in Regions or Persons below; where numerous numbers must be content to stand like *Lacteous* or *Nebulous* Stars, little taken notice of, or dim in their generations. All which may be contentedly allowable in the affairs and ends of this World, and in suspension unto what will be in the order of things hereafter, and the new Systeme of Mankind which will be in the World to come; when the last may be the first and the first the last; when *Lazarus* may sit above *Cæsar*, and the just obscure on Earth shall shine like the Sun in Heaven; when personations[93] shall cease, and Histrionism[94] of happiness be over; when Reality shall rule, and all shall be as they shall be for ever.

25. When the *Stoick* said that life would not be accepted, if it were offered unto such as knew it,[95] he spoke too meanly of that

92. Short course (in racing).
93. i.e. impersonations (referring to play-acting: see next note).
94. Play-acting. Cf. above, p. 119: 'This is that one day' etc.
95. Seneca, *On Consolation to Marcia*, XXII, 3 (Browne marg., quoting the Latin).

state of being which placeth us in the form of Men. It more depreciates the value of this life, that Men would not live it over again; for although they would still live on, yet few or none can endure to think of being twice the same Men upon Earth, and some had rather never have lived than to tread over their days once more. *Cicero* in a prosperous state had not the patience to think of beginning in a cradle again.[96] *Job* would not only curse the day of his Nativity, but also of his Renascency, if he were to act over his Disasters, and the miseries of the Dunghil. But the greatest underweening of this Life is to undervalue that, unto which this is but Exordial or a Passage leading unto it. The great advantage of this mean life is thereby to stand in a capacity of a better; for the Colonies of Heaven must be drawn from Earth, and the Sons of the first *Adam* are only heirs unto the second. Thus *Adam* came into this World with the power also of another, nor only to replenish the Earth, but the ever-lasting Mansions of Heaven.[97] Where we were when the foundations of the Earth were lay'd, when the morning Stars sang together and all the Sons of God shouted for Joy,[98] He must answer who asked it; who understands Entities of preordination, and beings yet unbeing; who hath in his Intellect the Ideal Existences of things, and Entities before their Extances.[99] Though it looks but like an imaginary kind of existency to be before we are; yet since we are under the decree or prescience of a sure and Omnipotent Power, it may be somewhat more than a non-entity to be in that mind, unto which all things are present.[100]

26. If the end of the World shall have the same foregoing Signs, as the period of Empires, States, and Dominions in it, that is, Corruption of Manners, inhuman degenerations, and deluge of iniquities; it may be doubted whether that final time be so far of, of whose day and hour there can be no prescience.

96. *On Old Age*, XXIII.

97. On the commonplace notion that man was created to repair the 'detriment' of the expelled angels, see *Paradise Lost*, VII, 154–61. Cf. §95.

98. Job 38.4 and 7 (Browne marg.): the question God puts to Job.

99. Emergences – i.e. from non-being into being. 'Ideal' alludes as always to the Ideas in God's mind (above, p. 31).

100. Cf. above, pp. 131–2.

But while all men doubt and none can determine how long the World shall last, some may wonder that it hath spun out so long and unto our days. For if the Almighty had not determin'd a fixed duration unto it, according to his mighty and merciful designments in it, if he had not said unto it, as he did unto a part of it, hitherto shalt thou go and no farther; if we consider the incessant and cutting provocations from the Earth, it is not without amazement how his patience hath permitted so long a continuance unto it, how he, who cursed the Earth in the first days of the first Man, and drowned it in the tenth Generation after, should thus lastingly contend with Flesh and yet defer the last flames. For since he is sharply provoked every moment, yet punisheth to pardon, and forgives to forgive again; what patience could be content to act over such vicissitudes, or accept of repentances which must have after penitences, his goodness can only tell us. And surely if the patience of Heaven were not proportionable unto the provocations from Earth; there needed an Intercessor not only for the sins, but the duration of this World, and to lead it up unto the present computation. Without such a merciful Longanimity, the Heavens would never be so aged as to grow old like a Garment;[101] it were in vain to infer from the Doctrine of the Sphere, that the time might come when *Capella*, a noble Northern Star, would have its motion in the *Æquator*, that the Northern *Zodiacal* Signs would at length be the Southern, the Southern the Northern, and *Capricorn* become our *Cancer*. However therefore the Wisdom of the Creator hath ordered the duration of the World, yet since the end thereof brings the accomplishment of our happiness, since some would be content that it should have no end, since Evil Men and Spirits do fear it may be too short, since Good Men hope it may not be too long; the prayer of the Saints under the Altar[102] will be the supplication of the Righteous World. That his mercy would abridge their languishing Expectation and hasten the accomplishment of their happy state to come.

27. Though Good Men are often taken away from the Evil

101. Isaiah 51.6.
102. As above, p. 119. note 290.

to come, though some in evil days have been glad that they were old, nor long to behold the iniquities of a wicked World, or Judgments threatened by them; yet is it no small satisfaction unto honest minds to leave the World in virtuous well temper'd times, under a prospect of good to come, and continuation of worthy ways acceptable unto God and Man. Men who dye in deplorable days, which they regretfully behold, have not their Eyes closed with the like content; while they cannot avoid the thoughts of proceeding or growing enormities, displeasing unto that Spirit unto whom they are then going, whose honour they desire in all times and throughout all generations. If *Lucifer* could be freed from his dismal place, he would little care though the rest were left behind. Too many there may be of *Nero*'s mind, who, if their own turn were served, would not regard what became of others, and, when they dye themselves, care not if all perish.[103] But good Mens wishes extend beyond their lives, for the happiness of times to come, and never to be known unto them. And therefore while so many question prayers for the dead, they charitably pray for those who are not yet alive; they are not so enviously ambitious to go to Heaven by themselves; they cannot but humbly wish, that the little Flock[104] might be greater, the narrow Gate wider, and that, as many are called, so not a few might be chosen.

28. That a greater number of Angels remained in Heaven, than fell from it, the School-men will tell us;[105] that the number of blessed Souls will not come short of that vast number of fallen Spirits, we have the favorable calculation of others. What Age of Century hath sent most Souls unto Heaven, he can tell who vouchsafeth that honour unto them. Though the Number of the blessed must be compleat before the World can pass away, yet since the World it self seems in the wane, and we have no such comfortable prognosticks of Latter times, since a greater part of time is spun than is to come, and the blessed Roll

103. Suetonius, *Nero*, XXXVIII.

104. As above, p. 131, note 348.

105. Or indeed Milton: 'a third part of the gods' is said to have fallen (*Paradise Lost*, VI, 156), on the basis of the claim (in Revelation 12.4) that the dragon 'drew the third part of the stars'.

already much replenished; happy are those pieties, which solicitously look about, and hasten to make one of that already much filled and abbreviated List to come.

29. Think not thy time short in this World since the World it self is not long. The created World is but a small *Parenthesis* in Eternity, and a short interposition for a time between such a state of duration, as was before it and may be after it. And if we should allow of the old Tradition that the World should last Six Thousand years,[106] it could scarce have the name of old, since the first Man lived near a sixth part thereof, and seven *Methusela*'s would exceed its whole duration. However to palliate the shortness of our Lives, and somewhat to compensate our brief term in this World, it's good to know as much as we can of it, and also so far as possibly in us lieth to hold such a *Theory* of times past, as though we had seen the same. He who hath thus considered the World, as also how therein things long past have been answered by things present, how matters in one Age have been acted over in another, and how there is nothing new under the Sun, may conceive himself in some manner to have lived from the beginning, and to be as old as the World; and if he should still live on 'twould be but the same thing.

30. [Lastly, if length of Days be thy Portion, make it not thy Expectation. Reckon not upon long Life: think every day the last, and live always beyond thy account. He that so often surviveth his Expectation lives many Lives, and will scarce complain of the shortness of his days. Time past is gone like a Shadow; make time to come present. Approximate thy latter times by present apprehensions of them: be like a neighbour unto the Grave, and think there is but little to come. And since there is something of us that will still live on, join both lives together, and live in one but for the other. He who thus ordereth the purposes of this Life will never be far from the next, and is in some manner already in it, by a happy conformity, and close apprehension of it.][107] And if, as we have elsewhere

106. See above, p. 439, note 31.

107. The bracketed sentences are also in the concluding paragraph of *A Letter to a Friend*, above, pp. 413–14.

declared,[108] any have been so happy as personally to understand Christian Annihilation, Extasy, Exolution, Transformation, the Kiss of the Spouse, and Ingression into the Divine Shadow, according to Mystical Theology, they have already had an handsome Anticipation of Heaven; the World is in a manner over, and the Earth in Ashes unto them.

108. In the penultimate paragraph of *Hydriotaphia*, above, p. 314.

FROM THE SHORTER WORKS

On Dreams

[The date of composition of this short work is not known. The present text is from *K* (III, 230–33), as transcribed from a manuscript in the British Library.]

Half our dayes wee passe in the shadowe of the earth, and the brother of death[1] exacteth a third part of our lives. A good part of our sleepes is peeced out with visions, and phantasticall objects wherin wee are confessedly deceaved. The day supplyeth us with truths, the night with fictions and falshoods, which unconfortably divide the natural account of our beings. And therefore having passed the day in sober labours and rationall enquiries of truth, wee are fayne to betake ourselves unto such a state of being, wherin the soberest heads have acted all the monstrosities of melancholy, and which unto open eyes are no better then folly and madnesse.

Happy are they that go to bed with grave musick like Pythagoras, or have wayes to compose the phantasticall spirit, whose unrulie wandrings takes of inward sleepe, filling our heads with St. Antonies visions, and the dreams of Lipara[2] in the sober chambers of rest.

Virtuous thoughts of the day laye up good treasors for the night, whereby the impressions of imaginarie formes arise into sober similitudes, acceptable unto our slumbring selves, and preparatory unto divine impressions: hereby Solomons sleepe was happy. Thus prepared, Jacob might well dreame of Angells upon a pillowe of stone, and the first sleepe of Adam might bee the best of any after.[3]

That there should bee divine dreames seemes unreasonably doubted by Aristotle.[4] That there are demonicall dreames wee have little reason to doubt. Why may there not bee Angelicall? If there bee Guardian spirits, they may not bee unactively about

1. i.e. sleep. See above, p. 311, note 35.
2. 'somnia Liparitana, turbulent dreams as men have observed to have in the Isle of Lipara, abounding in sulphurous & minerall exhalations, sounds, smoakes & fires' (Browne marg.). Cf. above, p. 427, note 46.
3. On Solomon's sleep, see Proverbs 3.24; on Jacob's dream of the ladder to heaven: Genesis 28.11 ff.; and on Adam's sleep which resulted in Eve's creation: Genesis 2.21.
4. In his short treatise Of Prophecy in Sleep.

us in sleepe, butt may sometimes order our dreames, and many strange hints, instigations, or discoveries which are so amazing unto us, may arise from such foundations.

Butt the phantasmes of sleepe do commonly walk in the great roade of naturall & animal dreames; wherin the thoughts or actions of the day are acted over and ecchoed in the night. Who can therefore wonder that Chrysostome should dreame of St. Paul who dayly read his Epistles; or that Cardan whose head was so taken up about the starres should dreame that his soul was in the moone! Pious persons whose thoughts are dayly buisied about heaven & the blessed state thereof, can hardly escape the nightly phantasmes of it, which though sometimes taken for illuminations or divine dreames, yet rightly perpended may prove butt animal visions and naturall night scenes of their waking contemplations.

Many dreames are made out by sagacious exposition & from the signature of their subjects; carrying their interpretation in their fundamentall sence & mysterie of similitude, whereby hee that understands upon what naturall fundamentall every notionall dependeth, may by sumbolicall adaptation hold a readie way to read the characters of Morpheus. In dreames of such a nature Artemidorus, Achmet, and Astrampsychus, from Greeck, Ægyptian, and Arabian oneirocriticisme,[5] may hint some interpretation, who, while wee read of a ladder in Jacobs dreame, will tell us that ladders and scalarie ascents signifie preferment, & while wee consider the dreame of Pharaoh, do teach us, that rivers overflowing speake plentie, leane oxen famin and scarcitie, and therefore it was butt reasonable in Pharaoh to demand the interpretation from his magitians, who being Ægyptians, should have been well versed in symbols & the hieroglyphicall notions of things.[6] The greatest tyrant in such divinations was Nabuchodonosor, while beside the interpretation hee demanded the dreame itself;[7] which being prob-

5. On these authorities on oneirocriticism – the art of interpreting dreames – see the dictionary of names, below, pp. 513 ff.

6. Genesis 41.8. Browne's expectations of the Egyptians centres on his approbation of Hermes Trismegistus (above, p. 30).

7. Daniel 2.5.

ably determin'd by divine immission, might escape the common roade of phantasmes, that might have been traced by Satan.

When Alexander going to beseidge Tyre dreampt of a Satyre, it was no hard exposition for a Grecian to say, Tyre will bee thine.[8] Hee that dreamed that hee sawe his father washed by Jupiter and annoynted by the sunne, had cause to feare that hee might bee crucified, whereby his body would bee washed by the rayne & drop by the heat of the sunne. The dreame of Vespasian was of harder exposition, as also that of the Emperour Mauritius concerning his successor Phocas. And a man might have been hard putt to it to interpret the languadge of Æsculapius, when to a consumptive person hee held forth his fingers, implying thereby that his cure laye in dates, from the homonomie of the Greek which signifies dates & fingers.[9]

Wee owe unto dreames that Galen was a physitian, Dion an historian, and that the world hath seen some notable peeces of Cardan, yet hee that should order his affayres by dreames, or make the night a rule unto the day, might bee ridiculously deluded. Wherin Cicero is much to bee pittied; who having excellently discoursed of the vanitie of dreames, was yet undone by the flatterie of his owne, which urged him to apply himself unto Augustus.[10]

However dreames may bee fallacious concerning outward events, yet may they bee truly significant at home, & whereby wee may more sensibly understand ourselves. Men act in sleepe with some conformity unto their awaked senses, & consolations or discoureagments may bee drawne from dreames, which intimately tell us ourselves. Luther was not like to feare a spiritt in the night, when such an apparition would not terrifie him in the daye. Alexander would hardly have runne away in the sharpest combates of sleepe, nor Demosthenes have stood stoutly to it, who was scarce able to do it in his prepared senses. Persons of radicall integritie will not easily bee perverted in

8. A marginal note, in providing the Greek word σάτυρος (satyros), suggests the intended pun (sa-tyros, literally 'Tyre will be thine').

9. 'Dactylos' (Browne marg.) means – as the text makes clear – both finger and the fruit of the date-palm.

10. Plutarch, Cicero, XLIV.

their dreames, nor noble minds do pitifully things in sleepe. Crassus would have hardly been bountifull in a dreame, whose fist was so close awake. Butt a man might have lived all his life upon the sleeping hand of Antonius.[11]

There is an Art to make dreames as well as their interpretations, and physitians will tell us that some food makes turbulent, some gives quiet dreames. Cato who doated upon cabbadge might find the crude effects thereof in his sleepe; wherein the Ægyptians might find some advantage by their superstitious abstinence from onyons. Pythagoras might have more calmer sleepes if hee totally abstained from beanes. Even Daniel, that great interpreter of dreames, in his leguminous dyet seemes to have chosen no advantageous food for quiet sleepes according to Græcian physick.[12]

To adde unto the delusion of dreames, the phantasticall objects seeme greater then they are, and being beheld in the vaporous state of sleepe, enlarge their diameters unto us; whereby it may prove more easie to dreame of Gyants then pygmies. Democritus might seldome dreame of Atomes, who so often thought of them. Helmont might dreame himself a bubble extending unto the eigth sphere. A little water makes a sea, a small puff of wind a Tempest, a graine of sulphur kindled in the blood may make a flame like Ætna, and a small spark in the bowells of Olympias a lightning over all the chamber.

Butt beside these innocent delusions there is a sinfull state of dreames; death alone, not sleepe is able to putt an end unto sinne, & there may bee a night booke of our Iniquities; for beside the transgressions of the day, casuists will tell us of mortall sinnes in dreames arising from evill precogitations; meanewhile human lawe regards not noctambulos; and if a night walker should breacke his neck, or kill a man, takes no notice of it.

Dionysius was absurdly tyrannicall to kill a man for dreaming that hee had killed him, and really to take away his life who had butt fantastically taken away his.[13] Lamia was ridiculously un-

11. 'The reputation of Crassus for wealth and avariciousness was matched by that of Antony for liberality' (E).
12. Daniel 1.12–16.
13. Plutarch, Dion, IX.

just to sue a yong man for a reward, who had confessed that
pleasure from her in a dreame, wch shee had denyed unto his
awaking senses, conceaving that shee had merited somewhat
from his phantasticall fruition & shadowe of herself.[14] If there
bee such debts, wee owe deeply unto sympathies, butt the com-
mon spirit of the world must bee judg in such arreareges.[15]

If some have swounded[16] they may have also dyed in dreames
since death is butt a confirmed swounding. Whether Plato dyed
in a dreame, as some deliver,[17] hee must rise agayne to informe
us. That some have never dreamed is as improbable as that
some have never laughed. That children dreame not the first
half yeare, that men dreame not in some countries, with many
more, are unto mee sick mens dreames, dreames out of the
Ivorie gate, and visions before midnight.[18]

14. 'Plutarch' (Browne marg.) in *Demetrius*, XXVII.
15. i.e. arrears, payments due.
16. i.e. swooned, fainted.
17. e.g. Tertullian (Browne marg.).
18. '*Sunt geminæ somni portæ*. The Ivory & the horny gate; false dreames
out of the ivory gate, true out of the horny' (Browne marg.).

APPENDIX

Samuel Johnson
The Life of Sir Thomas Browne

[Dr Johnson's biography of Browne was first published in 1756, prefixed to an edition of *Christian Morals*. In addition to its historical value, it sheds light as much on Browne as on Johnson in that it is, according to Boswell at any rate, 'one of Johnson's best biographical performances' (*Life of Johnson*, ed. G. B. Hill [Oxford, 1934], I, 308). The reader may also wish to consider Pater's suggestion that Johnson was 'perhaps influenced' by Browne, not least in 'that slow Latinity which Johnson imitated from him' (§218; cf. §§212, 331, 341).]

Though the writer of the following Essays[1] seems to have had the fortune common among men of letters, of raising little curiosity after his private life, and has, therefore, few memorials preserved of his felicities or misfortunes; yet, because an edition of a posthumous work appears imperfect and neglected, without some account of the author, it was thought necessary to attempt the gratification of that curiosity which naturally inquires, by what peculiarities of nature or fortune eminent men have been distinguished, how uncommon attainments have been gained, and what influence learning has had on its possessors, or virtue on its teachers.

Sir Thomas Browne was born at London, in the parish of St. Michael in Cheapside, on the 19th of October, 1605. His father was a merchant of an antient family at Upton in Cheshire. Of the name or family of his mother, I find no account.[2]

Of his childhood or youth, there is little known; except that he lost his father very early; that he was, according to the common fate of orphans, defrauded by one of his guardians;[3] and that he was placed for his education at the school of Winchester.

His mother, having taken three thousand pounds, as the third part of her husband's property, left her son, by consequence, six thousand; a large fortune for a man destined to learning, at that time when commerce had not yet filled the nation with nominal riches. But it happened to him as to many others, to be made poorer by opulence; for his mother soon married Sir Thomas Dutton, probably by the inducement of

1. Browne's *Christian Morals* (see headnote, above).

2. Browne's mother Anne was the daughter of Paul Garroway of Acton, Middlesex.

3. The charge, made in Whitefoot's earlier sketch of Browne's life (below, note 34) and much exaggerated by Johnson, is no longer accepted. For the actual details, so far as they are known, consult N.J. Endicott, *UTQ*, XXX (1961), 180–210; cf. J.-J. Denonain, 'Le reître et le jouvenceau', *Caliban*, new series, I (1965), i, 7–20.

her fortune; and he was left to the rapacity of his guardian, deprived now of both his parents, and therefore helpless and unprotected.

He was removed in the beginning of the year 1623 from Winchester to Oxford; and entered a gentleman-commoner of Broadgate-Hall, which was soon afterwards endowed, and took the name of Pembroke-College, from the Earl of Pembroke then chancellor of the University. He was admitted to the degree of bachelor of arts, January 31, 1626/7; being, as Wood[4] remarks, the first man of eminence graduated from the new college, to which the zeal or gratitude of those that love it most, can wish little better, than that it may long proceed as it began.

Having afterwards taken his degree of master of arts, he turned his studies to physick,[5] and practised it for some time in Oxfordshire; but soon afterwards, either induced by curiosity, or invited by promises, he quitted his settlement, and accompanied his father-in-law, who had some employment in Ireland, in a visitation of the forts and castles, which the state of Ireland then made necessary.

He that has once prevailed on himself to break his connexions of acquaintance, and begin a wandering life, very easily continues it. Ireland had, at that time, very little to offer to the observation of a man of letters: he, therefore, passed into France and Italy; made some stay at Montpellier and Padua, which were then the celebrated schools of physick; and returning home through Holland, procured himself to be created Doctor of physick at Leyden.

When he began his travels, or when he concluded them, there is no certain account; nor do there remain any observations made by him in his passage through those countries which he visited. To consider, therefore, what pleasure or instruction might have been received from the remarks of a man so curious and diligent, would be voluntarily to indulge a painful reflection, and load the imagination with a wish, which, while it is formed, is known to be vain. It is, however, to be lamented,

4. Anthony à Wood, who had written a highly eclectic sketch of Browne's activities in *Athenæ Oxonienses* (ed. Philip Bliss [1820], IV, 56–9).
5. i.e. medicine.

that those who are most capable of improving mankind, very frequently neglect to communicate their knowledge; either because it is more pleasing to gather ideas than to impart them, or because to minds naturally great, few things appear of so much importance as to deserve the notice of the publick.

About the year 1634, he is supposed to have returned to London; and the next year to have written his celebrated treatise, called *Religio Medici*, 'The Religion of a Physician', which he declares himself never to have intended for the press, having composed it only for his own exercise and entertainment. It, indeed, contains many passages, which, relating merely to his own person, can be of no great importance to the publick: but when it was written, it happened to him as to others, he was too much pleased with his performance, not to think that it might please others as much; he, therefore, communicated it to his friends, and receiving, I suppose, that exuberant applause with which every man repays the grant of perusing a manuscript, he was not very diligent to obstruct his own praise by recalling his papers, but suffered them to wander from hand to hand, till at last, without his own consent, they were in 1642 given to a printer.[6]

This has, perhaps, sometimes befallen others; and this, I am willing to believe, did really happen to Dr. Browne: but there is, surely, some reason to doubt the truth of the complaint so frequently made of surreptitious editions. A song, or an epigram, may be easily printed without the author's knowledge; because it may be learned when it is repeated, or may be written out with very little trouble. But a long treatise, however elegant, is not often copied by mere zeal or curiosity, but may be worn out in passing from hand to hand, before it is multiplied by a transcript. It is easy to convey an imperfect book, by a distant hand, to the prefs, and plead the circulation of a false copy as an excuse for publishing the true, or to correct what is found faulty or offensive, and charge the errors on the transcriber's depravations.

This is a stratagem, by which an author panting for fame, and yet afraid of seeming to challenge it, may at once gratify his

6. The 'authorised' edition was published in 1643. See above, p. 57.

vanity, and preserve the appearance of modesty; may enter the lists, and secure a retreat: and this, candour might suffer to pass undetected as an innocent fraud, but that indeed no fraud is innocent; for the confidence which makes the happiness of society, is in some degree diminished by every man, whose practice is at variance with his words.

The *Religio Medici* was no sooner published than it excited the attention of the publick, by the novelty of paradoxes, the dignity of sentiment, the quick succession of images, the multitude of abstruse allusions, the subtlety of disquisition, and the strength of language.

What is much read, will be much criticised. The Earl of Dorset recommended this book to the perusal of Sir Kenelm Digby, who returned his judgment upon it, not in a letter, but a book;[7] in which, though mingled with some positions fabulous and uncertain, there are acute remarks, just censures, and profound speculations, yet its principal claim to admiration is, that it was written in twenty-four hours, of which part was spent in procuring Browne's book, and part in reading it.

Of these animadversions, when they were yet not all printed, either officiousness or malice informed Dr. Browne; who wrote to Sir Kenelm with much softness and ceremony, declaring the unworthiness of his work to engage such notice, the intended privacy of the composition, and the corruptions of the impression; and received an answer equally gentle and respectful, containing high commendations of the piece, pompous professions of reverence, meek acknowledgments of inability, and anxious apologies for the hastiness of his remarks.

The reciprocal civility of authors is one of the most risible scenes in the farce of life. Who would not have thought, that these two luminaries of their age had ceased to endeavour to grow bright by the obscuration of each other: yet the animadversions thus weak, thus precipitate, upon a book thus injured in the transcription, quickly passed the press; and *Religio Medici* was more accurately published, with an admonition prefixed

---

7. *Observations upon Religio Medici*, written at a single sitting on 22–23 December 1642, published in 1643, and usually bound with Browne's work from 1659. Cf. §343.

'to those who have or shall peruse the observations upon a former corrupt copy;' in which there is a severe censure, not upon Digby, who was to be used with ceremony, but upon the Observator who had usurped his name: nor was this invective written by Dr. Browne, who was supposed to be satisfied with his opponent's apology; but by some officious friend zealous for his honour, without his consent.[8]

Browne has, indeed, in his own preface, endeavoured to secure himself from rigorous examination, by alleging, that 'many things are delivered rhetorically, many expressions merely tropical, and therefore many things to be taken in a soft and flexible sense, and not to be called unto the rigid test of reason.' The first glance upon his book will indeed discover examples of this liberty of thought and expression: 'I could be content (says he) to be nothing almost to eternity, if I might enjoy my Saviour at the last.' He has little acquaintance with the acuteness of Browne, who suspects him of a serious opinion, that any thing can be 'almost eternal,' or that any time beginning and ending is not infinitely less than infinite duration.

In this book, he speaks much, and, in the opinion of Digby, too much of himself; but with such generality and conciseness as affords very little light to his biographer: he declares, that, besides the dialects of different provinces, he understood six languages; that he was no stranger to astronomy; and that he had seen several countries: but what most awakens curiosity, is his solemn assertion, that 'His life has been a miracle of thirty years; which to relate, were not history but a piece of poetry, and would sound like a fable.'

There is, undoubtedly, a sense, in which all life is miraculous; as it is an union of powers of which we can image no connexion, a succession of motions of which the first cause must be supernatural: but life, thus explained, whatever it may have of miracle, will have nothing of fable; and, therefore, the author

8. The 'severe censure', signed by 'A.B.', accuses Digby that *inter alia* he either 'mistaketh, or traduceth the intention, and (besides a parenthesis sometimes upon the Author) onely medleth with those points from whence he takes a hint to deliver his prepar'd conceptions'. The charges are not altogether unfair.

SAMUEL JOHNSON'S LIFE OF BROWNE

undoubtedly had regard to something, by which he imagined himself distinguished from the rest of mankind.

Of these wonders, however, the view that can be now taken of his life offers no appearance. The course of his education was like that of others, such as put him little in the way of extraordinary casualties. A scholastick and academical life is very uniform; and has, indeed, more safety than pleasure. A traveller has greater opportunities of adventure; but Browne traversed no unknown seas, or Arabian desarts: and, surely, a man may visit France and Italy, reside at Montpellier and Padua, and at last take his degree at Leyden, without any thing miraculous. What it was, that would, if it was related, sound so poetical and fabulous, we are left to guess; I believe, without hope of guessing rightly. The wonders probably were transacted in his own mind: self-love, co-operating with an imagination vigorous and fertile as that of Browne, will find or make objects of astonishment in every man's life: and, perhaps, there is no human being, however hid in the crowd from the observation of his fellow-mortals, who, if he has leisure and disposition to recollect his own thoughts and actions, will not conclude his life in some sort a miracle, and imagine himself distinguished from all the rest of his species by many discriminations of nature or of fortune.

The success of this performance was such, as might naturally encourage the author to new undertakings. A gentleman of Cambridge, whose name was Merryweather, turned it not inelegantly into Latin; and from his version it was again translated into Italian, German, Dutch, and French; and at Strasburg the Latin translation was published with large notes, by Lenuus Nicolaus Moltfarius. Of the English annotations, which in all the editions from 1644 accompany the book, the author is unknown.[9]

Of Merryweather, to whose zeal Browne was so much indebted for the sudden extension of his renown, I know nothing,

9. John Merryweather's Latin translation was published in 1644. The Dutch version appeared in 1665; the French, in 1668; the German, in 1746 – but the Italian is not extant. The English annotations were attempted by Thomas Keck (§ 257).

but that he published a small treatise for the instruction of young persons in the attainment of a Latin stile. He printed his translation in Holland with some difficulty. The first printer to whom he offered it, carried it to Salmasius,[10] 'who laid it by (says he) in state for three months,' and then discouraged its publication: it was afterwards rejected by two other printers, and at last was received by Hackius.

The peculiarities of this book raised the author, as is usual, many admirers and many enemies; but we know not of more than one professed answer, written under the title of 'Medicus medicatus,' by Alexander Ross, which was universally neglected by the world.[11]

At the time when this book was published, Dr. Browne resided at Norwich, where he had settled in 1636, by the persuasion of Dr. Lushington his tutor, who was then rector of Barnham Westgate in the neighbourhood. It is recorded by Wood, that his practice was very extensive, and that many patients resorted to him. In 1637 he was incorporated Doctor of physick in Oxford.

He married in 1641 Mrs. Mileham, of a good family in Norfolk; 'a lady (says Whitefoot)[12] of such symmetrical proportion to her worthy husband, both in the graces of her body and mind, that they seemed to come together by a kind of natural magnetism.'

This marriage could not but draw the raillery of contemporary wits upon a man, who had just been wishing in his new book, 'that we might procreate, like trees, without conjunction;' and had lately declared, that 'the whole world was made for man, but only the twelfth part of man for woman;' and, that 'man is the whole world, but woman only the rib or crooked part of man.'

Whether the lady had been yet informed of these contemptuous positions,[13] or whether she was pleased with the conquest

10. The French scholar with whom Milton was later to engage in a violent controversy (1651).

11. For the full title of Ross's work, see §265.

12. As below, p 501, note 28.

13. Cf. above, pp. 148–9.

of so formidable a rebel, and considered it as a double triumph, to attract so much merit, and overcome so powerful prejudices; or whether, like most others, she married upon mingled motives, between convenience and inclination; she had, however, no reason to repent: for she lived happily with him one and forty years; and bore him ten[14] children, of whom one son and three daughters outlived their parents: she survived him two years, and passed her widowhood in plenty, if not in opulence.

Browne having now entered the world as an author, and experienced the delights of praise and molestations of censure, probably found his dread of the publick eye diminished; and, therefore, was not long before he trusted his name to the criticks a second time: for in 1646 he printed *Enquiries into vulgar and common errors* [*Pseudodoxia Epidemica*]; a work, which as it arose not from fancy and invention, but from observation and books, and contained not a single discourse of one continued tenor, of which the latter part rose from the former, but an enumeration of many unconnected particulars, must have been the collection of years, and the effect of a design early formed and long persued, to which his remarks had been continually referred, and which arose gradually to its present bulk by the daily aggregation of new particles of knowledge. It is, indeed, to be wished, that he had longer delayed the publication, and added what the remaining part of his life might have furnished: the thirty-six years which he spent afterwards in study and experience, would doubtless have made large additions to an 'Enquiry into vulgar errors.' He published in 1672 the sixth edition, with some improvements; but I think rather with explications of what he had already written, than any new heads of disquisition.[15] But with the work, such as the author, whether hindered from continuing it by eagerness of praise, or weariness of labour, thought fit to give, we must be content; and remem-

14. Actually twelve.
15. Dr Johnson errs. The successive editions of *Pseudodoxia Epidemica* display substantial amendments in both matter and manner (see above, p. 33).

ber, that in all sublunary things, there is something to be wished, which we must wish in vain.

This book, like his former, was received with great applause, was answered by Alexander Ross, and translated into Dutch and German, and not many years ago into French.[16] It might now be proper, had not the favour with which it was at first received filled the kingdom with copies, to reprint it with notes partly supplemental and partly emendatory, to subjoin those discoveries which the industry of the last age has made, and correct those mistakes which the author has committed not by idleness or negligence, but for want of Boyle's and Newton's philosophy.

He appears, indeed, to have been willing to pay labour for truth. Having heard a flying rumour of sympathetick needles, by which, suspended over a circular alphabet, distant friends or lovers might correspond, he procured two such alphabets to be made, touched his needles with the same magnet, and placed them upon proper spindles: the result was, that when he moved one of his needles, the other, instead of taking by sympathy the same direction, 'stood like the pillars of Hercules.' That it continued motionless, will be easily believed; and most men would have been content to believe it, without the labour of so hopeless an experiment. Browne might himself have obtained the same conviction by a method less operose, if he had thrust his needles through corks, and then set them afloat in two basons of water.

Notwithstanding his zeal to detect old errors, he seems not very easy to admit new positions; for he never mentions the motion of the earth but with contempt and ridicule,[17] though the opinion, which admits it, was then growing popular, and was, surely, plausible, even before it was confirmed by later observations.

The reputation of Browne encouraged some low writer to

16. The Dutch version was published in 1688; the German, in 1680; the French, in 1733 – as well as an Italian one in 1737. For the full title of Ross's work, see §294.

17. Hardly: see above, p. 160, note 139.

publish, under his name, a book called 'Nature's cabinet un-locked,'[18] translated, according to Wood, from the physicks of Magirus; of which Browne took care to clear himself, by modestly advertising, that 'if any man had been benefited by it, he was not so ambitious as to challenge the honour thereof, as having no hand in that work.'

In 1658 the discovery of some antient urns in Norfolk gave him occasion to write *Hydriotaphia, Urnburial, or a discourse of Sepulchral urns*, in which he treats with his usual learning on the funeral rites of the antient nations; exhibits their various treat-ment of the dead; and examines the substances found in his Norfolcian urns. There is, perhaps, none of his works which better exemplifies his reading or memory. It is scarcely to be imagined, how many particulars he has amassed together, in a treatise which seems to have been occasionally written; and for which, therefore, no materials could have been previously collected. It is, indeed, like other treatises of antiquity, rather for curiosity than use; for it is of small importance to know which nation buried their dead in the ground, which threw them into the sea, or which gave them to birds and beasts; when the practice of cremation began, or when it was disused; whether the bones of different persons were mingled in the same urn; what oblations were thrown into the pyre; or how the ashes of the body were distinguished from those of other sub-stances. Of the uselesness of all these enquiries, Browne seems not to have been ignorant; and, therefore, concludes them with an observation which can never be too frequently recollected.

'All or most apprehensions rested in opinions of some future being, which ignorantly or coldly believed, begat those per-verted conceptions, ceremonies, sayings, which christians pity or laugh at. Happy are they, which live not in that dis-advantage of time, when men could say little for futurity, but from reason; whereby the noblest mind fell often upon doubt-ful deaths, and melancholy dissolutions: with these hopes Socrates warmed his doubtful spirits, against the cold potion; and Cato, before he durst give the fatal stroke, spent part of

18. The author is unknown.

the night in reading the Immortality of Plato, thereby confirming his wavering hand unto the animosity of that attempt.

It is the heaviest stone that melancholy can throw at man, to tell him he is at the end of his nature; or that there is no further state to come, unto which this seems progressional, and otherwise made in vain: without this accomplishment, the natural expectation and desire of such a state, were but a fallacy in nature; unsatisfied considerators would quarrel the justice of their constitution, and rest content that Adam had fallen lower, whereby, by knowing no other original, and deeper ignorance of themselves, they might have enjoyed the happiness of inferior creatures, who in tranquillity possess their constitutions, as having not the apprehension to deplore their own natures; and being framed below the circumference of these hopes or cognition of better things, the wisdom of God hath necessitated their contentment. But the superior ingredient and obscured part of ourselves, whereto all present felicities afford no resting contentment, will be able at last to tell us we are more than our present selves; and evacuate such hopes in the fruition of their own accomplishments.' (*above, pp. 305-6*).

To his treatise on *Urnburial* was added *The garden of Cyrus, or the quincunxial lozenge, or network plantation of the antients, artificially, naturally, mystically considered*. This discourse he begins with the Sacred Garden, in which the first man was placed; and deduces the practice of horticulture from the earliest accounts of antiquity to the time of the Persian Cyrus, the first man whom we actually know to have planted a Quincunx; which, however, our author is inclined to believe of longer date, and not only discovers it in the description of the hanging gardens of Babylon, but seems willing to believe, and to persuade his reader, that it was practised by the seeders on vegetables before the flood.

Some of the most pleasing performances have been produced by learning and genius exercised upon subjects of little importance. It seems to have been, in all ages, the pride of wit, to

shew how it could exalt the low, and amplify the little. To speak
not inadequately of things really and naturally great, is a task
not only difficult but disagreeable; because the writer is de-
graded in his own eyes by standing in comparison with his
subject, to which he can hope to add nothing from his imagi-
nation: but it is a perpetual triumph of fancy to expand a scanty
theme, to raise glittering ideas from obscure properties, and to
produce to the world an object of wonder to which nature had
contributed little. To this ambition, perhaps, we owe the Frogs
of Homer, the Gnat and the Bees of Virgil, the Butterfly of
Spenser, the Shadow of Wowerus,[19] and the Quincunx of
Browne.

In the prosecution of this sport of fancy, he considers every
production of art and nature, in which he could find any decussa-
tion or approaches to the form of a Quincunx; and as a man
once resolved upon ideal discoveries, seldom searches long in
vain, he finds his favourite figure in almost every thing, whether
natural or invented, antient or modern, rude or artificial, sacred
and civil; so that a reader, not watchful against the power of his
infusions, would imagine that decussation was the great business
of the world, and that nature and art had no other purpose than
to exemplify and imitate a Quincunx.

To shew the excellence of this figure, he enumerates all its
properties; and finds in it almost every thing of use or pleasure:
and to shew how readily he supplies what he cannot find, one
instance may be sufficient; 'though therein (says he) we meet
not with right angles, yet every rhombus containing four
angles equal unto two right, it virtually contains two right in
every one.'

The fanciful sports of great minds are never without some
advantage to knowledge. Browne has interspersed many
curious observations on the form of plants, and the laws of
vegetation; and appears to have been a very accurate observer
of the modes of germination, and to have watched with great

19. i.e. the parodic *Batrachomyomachia* usually attributed to Homer (as
above, p. 138, note 22), the *Culex* of Virgil, the *Muiopotmos* of Spenser,
and the *Dies Aestiva, sive de umbra paegnion* (1610) of Jan van de Wouwer.

nicety the evolution of the parts of plants from their feminal principles.

He is then naturally led to treat of the number five; and finds, that by this number many things are circumscribed; that there are five kinds of vegetable productions, five sections of a cone, five orders of architecture, and five acts of a play. And observing that five was the antient conjugal or wedding number, he proceeds to a speculation which I shall give in his own words; 'The antient numerists made out the conjugal number by two and three, the first parity and imparity, the active and passive digits, the material and formal principles in generative societies.'

These are all the tracts which he published: but many papers were found in his closet, 'Some of them, (says Whitefoot) designed for the press, were often transcribed and corrected by his own hand, after the fashion of great and curious writers.'

Of these, two collections have been published; one by Dr. Tennison, the other in 1722 by a nameless editor.[20] Whether the one or the other selected those pieces which the author would have preferred, cannot now be known: but they have both the merit of giving to mankind what was too valuable to be suppressed; and what might, without their interposition, have, perhaps, perished among other innumerable labours of learned men, or have been burnt in a scarcity of fuel like the papers of Pereskius.

The first of these posthumous treatises contains 'Observations upon several plants mentioned in Scripture.' These remarks, though they do not immediately either rectify the faith, or refine the morals of the reader, yet are by no means to be censured as superfluous niceties or useless speculations; for they often shew some propriety of description, or elegance of allusion, utterly undiscoverable to readers not skilled in oriental botany; and are often of more important use, as they remove some difficulty from narratives, or some obscurity from precepts.

The next is 'Of garlands, or coronary and garland plants;' a

20. The first, edited by Thomas Tenison, is the *Certain Miscellany Tracts* (1684); the other, the *Posthumous Works* (1712).

subject merely of learned curiosity, without any other end than the pleasure of reflecting on antient customs, or on the industry with which studious men have endeavoured to recover them.

The next is a letter, 'on the fishes eaten by our Saviour with his disciples, after his resurrection from the dead;' which contains no determinate resolution of the question, what they were, for indeed it cannot be determined. All the information that diligence or learning could supply, consists in an enumeration of the fishes produced in the waters of Judea.

Then follow 'Answers to certain queries about fishes, birds, and insects;' and 'A letter of hawks and falconry antient and modern:' in the first of which he gives the proper interpretation of some antient names of animals, commonly mistaken; and in the other has some curious observations on the art of hawking, which he considers as a practice unknown to the antients. I believe all our sports of the field are of Gothick original; the antients neither hunted by the scent, nor seem much to have practised horsemanship as an exercise; and though, in their works, there is mention of 'aucupium' and 'piscatio,'[21] they seem no more to have been considered as diversions, than agriculture or any other manual labour.

In two more letters he speaks of 'the cymbals of the Hebrews,' but without any satisfactory determination; and of 'repalick or gradual verses,' that is, of verses beginning with a word of one syllable, and proceeding by words of which each has a syllable more than the former; as,

O Deus, æternæ stationis conciliator.
Ausonius.

and, after his manner, pursuing the hint, he mentions many other restrained methods of versifying, to which industrious ignorance has sometimes voluntarily subjected itself.

His next attempt is 'On languages, and particularly the Saxon tongue.' He discourses with great learning, and generally with great justness, of the derivation and changes of languages; but, like other men of multifarious learning, he receives some notions without examination. Thus he observes, according to

21. 'fowling' and 'fishing'.

the popular opinion, that the Spaniards have retained so much Latin, as to be able to compose sentences that shall be at once gramatically Latin and Castilian: this will appear very unlikely to a man that considers the Spanish terminations; and Howel, who was eminently skilful in the three provincial languages, declares, that after many essays he never could effect it.[22]

The principal design of this letter, is to shew the affinity between the modern English and the antient Saxon; and he observes, very rightly, that 'though we have borrowed many substantives, adjectives, and some verbs, from the French; yet the great body of numerals, auxiliary verbs, articles, pronouns, adverbs, conjunctions, and prepositions, which are the distinguishing and lasting parts of a language, remain with us from the Saxon.'

To prove this position more evidently, he has drawn up a short discourse of six paragraphs, in Saxon and English; of which every word is the same in both languages, excepting the terminations and orthography. The words are, indeed, Saxon, but the phraseology is English; and, I think, would not have been understood by Bede or Ælfric, notwithstanding the confidence of our author. He has, however, sufficiently proved his position, that the English resembles its parental language, more than any modern European dialect.

There remain five tracts of this collection yet unmentioned; one 'Of artificial hills, mounts, or burrows, in England;' in reply to an interrogatory letter of E. D. whom the writers of *Biographia Britannica*[23] suppose to be, if rightly printed, W. D. or Sir William Dugdale, one of Browne's correspondents. These are declared by Browne, in concurrence, I think, with all other antiquarians, to be for the most part funeral monuments. He proves, that both the Danes and Saxons buried their men of eminence under piles of earth, 'which admitting (says he) neither ornament, epitaph, nor inscription, may, if earthquakes spare them, outlast other monuments: obelisks have their term, and pyramids will tumble; but these mountainous monuments

22. James Howell in *Instructions for Forreine Travell* (1642) actually supports Browne's contention, not Johnson's.
23. As below. p. 547.

may stand, and are like to have the same period with the earth.'

In the next, he answers two geographical questions; one concerning Troas, mentioned in the Acts and Epistles of St. Paul, which he determines to be the city built near the antient Ilium; and the other concerning the dead sea, of which he gives the same account with other writers.

Another letter treats 'Of the answers of the oracle of Apollo at Delphos, to Crœsus king of Lydia.' In this tract nothing deserves notice, more than that Browne considers the oracles as evidently and indubitably supernatural, and sounds all his disquisition upon that postulate. He wonders why the physiologists of old, having such means of instruction, did not inquire into the secrets of nature: but judiciously concludes, that such questions would probably have been vain; 'for, in matters cognoscible, and formed for our disquisition, our industry must be our oracle, and reason our Apollo.'

The pieces that remain are, 'A prophecy concerning the future state of several nations;' in which Browne plainly discovers his expectation to be the same with that entertained lately with more confidence by Dr. Berkley, 'that America will be the seat of the fifth empire:'[24] and 'Museum clausum, sive Bibliotheca abscondita;' in which the author amuses himself with imagining the existence of books and curiosities, either never in being, or irrecoverably lost.

These pieces I have recounted as they are ranged in Tennison's collection, because the editor has given no account of the time at which any of them were written. Some of them are of little value, more than as they gratify the mind with the picture of a great scholar, turning his learning into amusement; or shew, upon how great a variety of enquiries the same mind has been successfully employed.

The other collection of his posthumous pieces, published in octavo, London 1722, contains 'Repertorium; or some account of the tombs and monuments in the cathedral of Norwich;'

24. In the philosopher Berkeley's *Verses on the prospect of planting arts and learning in America* (1752), which include the celebrated line 'Westward the Course of Empire takes its way . . .'

where, as Tennison observes, there is not matter proportionate to the skill of the Antiquary.

The other pieces are, 'Answers to Sir William Dugdale's enquiries about the fens; A letter concerning Ireland; Another relating to urns newly discovered; Some short strictures on different subjects;' and 'A letter to a friend on the death of his intimate friend,' published singly by the author's son in 1690.

There is inserted, in the *Biographia Britannica*, 'A letter containing instructions for the study of physick;' which, with the Essays[25] here offered to the public, completes the works of Dr. Browne.

To the life of this learned man, there remains little to be added, but that in 1665 he was chosen honorary fellow of the college of physicians, as a man, 'Virtute et literis ornatissimus,— eminently embellished with literature and virtue:' and, in 1671, received, at Norwich, the honour of knighthood from Charles II; a prince, who with many frailties and vices, had yet skill to discover excellence, and virtue to reward it, with such honorary distinctions at least as cost him nothing, yet conferred by a king so judicious and so much beloved, had the power of giving merit new lustre and greater popularity.[26]

Thus he lived in high reputation; till in his seventy-sixth year he was seized with a colick, which, after having tortured him about a week, put an end to his life at Norwich, on his birthday, October 19, 1682. Some of his last words were expressions of submission to the will of God, and fearlesness of death.

He lies buried in the church of St. Peter, Mancroft, in Norwich, with this inscription on a mural monument, placed on the south pillar of the altar:

M. S.
Hic situs est THOMAS BROWNE, M. D.
Et Miles.
Aº 1605. Londini natus
Generosa Familia apud Upton
In agro Cestriensi oriundus.

25. i.e. *Christian Morals* (see headnote, above, p. 481).
26. Dr Johnson as an ardent royalist much exaggerates the king's perception. The true circumstances are noted above, p. 21.

Scholâ primum Wintoniensi, postea
In Coll. Pembr.
Apud Oxonienses bonis literis
Haud leviter imbutus
In urbe hâc Nordovicensi medicinam
Arte egregia, & fælici sussessu prosessus,
Scriptis quibus tituli, RELIGIO MEDICI
Et PSEUDODOXIA EPIDEMICA aliisque
Per Orbem notissimus.
Vir Prudentissimus, Integerrimus, Doctissimus;
Obiit Octobr. 19, 1682.
Pie posuit mæstissima Conjux
Dᵃ. Doroth. Br.

Near the Foot of this Pillar
Lies Sir Thomas Browne, Kt. and Doctor in Physick,
Author of Religio Medici, and other Learned Books,
Who practic'd Physick in this City 46 Years,
And died Octr. 1682, in the 77 Year of his Age.
In Memory of whom
Dame *Dorothy Browne*, who has bin his Affectionate Wife
47 Years, caused this Monument to be Erected.

Besides his lady, who died in 1685, he left a son and three daughters. Of the daughters nothing very remarkable is known; but his son, Edward Browne, requires a particular mention.

He was born about the year 1642; and after having passed through the classes of the school at Norwich, became bachelor of physick at Cambridge; and afterwards removing to Merton-College in Oxford, was admitted there to the same degree, and afterwards made a doctor. In 1668 he visited part of Germany; and in the year following made a wider excursion into Austria, Hungary, and Thessaly; where the Turkish Sultan then kept his court at Larissa. He afterwards passed through Italy. His skill in natural history made him particularly attentive to mines and metallurgy. Upon his return he published an account of the countries thro' which he had passed;[27] which I have heard commended by a learned traveller, who has visited many places after him, as written with scrupulous and exact veracity, such as is scarcely to be found in any other book of the same kind.

27. Published in 1677; see §334.

But whatever it may contribute to the instruction of a naturalist, I cannot recommend it as likely to give much pleasure to common readers: for whether it be, that the world is very uniform, and therefore he who is resolved to adhere to truth, will have few novelties to relate; or that Dr. Browne was, by the train of his studies, led to enquire most after those things, by which the greatest part of mankind is little affected; a great part of his book seems to contain very unimportant accounts of his passage from one place where he saw little, to another where he saw no more.

Upon his return, he practised physick in London; was made physician first to Charles II, and afterwards in 1682 to St. Bartholomew's hospital. About the same time he joined his name to those of many other eminent men, in 'A translation of Plutarch's lives.' He was first censor, then elect, and treasurer of the college of physicians; of which in 1705 he was chosen president, and held his office, till in 1708 he died in a degree of estimation suitable to a man so variously accomplished, that King Charles had honoured him with this panegyrick, that 'He was as learned as any of the college, and as well-bred as any of the court.'

Of every great and eminent character, part breaks forth into publick view, and part lies hid in domestick privacy. Those qualities which have been exerted in any known and lasting performances, may, at any distance of time, be traced and estimated; but silent excellencies are soon forgotten; and those minute peculiarities which discriminate every man from all others, if they are not recorded by those whom personal knowledge enabled to observe them, are irrecoverably lost. This mutilation of character must have happened, among many others, to Sir Thomas Browne, had it not been delineated by his friend Mr. Whitefoot, who 'esteemed it an especial favour of Providence, to have had a particular acquaintance with him for two thirds of his life.' Part of his observations I shall, therefore, copy.[28]

28. The ensuing paragraphs (to p. 505) reproduce nearly the sum of John Whitefoot's 'Some Minutes for the Life of Sir Thomas Browne', prefixed to Browne's *Posthumous Works* (1712), pp. xxvii–xxxi, xxxiii–

'For a character of his person, his complexion and hair was answerable to his name; his stature was moderate, and habit of body neither fat nor lean, but εὔσαρκος.[29]

In his habit of clothing, he had an aversion to all finery, and affected plainness, both in the fashion and ornaments. He ever wore a cloke, or boots, when few others did. He kept himself always very warm, and thought it most safe so to do, though he never loaded himself with such a multitude of garments, as Suetonius reports of Augustus, enough to clothe a good family.

The horizon of his understanding was much larger than the hemisphere of the world: All that was visible in the heavens he comprehended so well, that few that are under them knew so much: He could tell the number of the visible stars in his horizon, and call them all by their names that had any; and of the earth he had such a minute and exact geographical knowledge, as if he had been by Divine Providence ordained surveyor-general of the whole terrestrial orb, and its products, minerals, plants, and animals. He was so curious a botanist, that besides the specifical distinctions, he made nice and elaborate observations, equally useful as entertaining.

His memory, though not so eminent as that of Seneca or Scaliger, was capacious and tenacious, insomuch as he remembred all that was remarkable in any book that he had read; and not only knew all persons again that he had ever seen at any distance of time, but remembred the circumstances of their bodies, and their particular discourses and speeches.

In the latin poets he remembred every thing that was acute and pungent; he had read most of the historians, antient and modern, wherein his observations were singular, not taken

---

xxxvii. Browne himself spoke of the author as 'my learned and faithfull old freind Mr John Whitefoot, Rector of Heigham and very deserving clark of the convocation for Norfolk' (in *Repertorium*, K, III, 134).

29. i.e. possessing fullness of flesh, in good condition.

notice of by common readers; he was excellent company when he was at leisure, and expressed more light than heat in the temper of his brain.

He had no despotical power over his affections and passions, (that was a privilege of original perfection, forfeited by the neglect of the use of it;) but as large a political power over them, as any Stoick, or man of his time, whereof he gave so great experiment, that he hath very rarely been known to have been overcome with any of them. The strongest that were found in him, both of the irascible and concupiscible, were under the controul of his reason. Of admiration, which is one of them, being the only product, either of ignorance, or uncommon knowledge, he had more, and less, than other men, upon the same account of his knowing more than others; so that tho' he met with many rarities, he admired them not so much as others do.

He was never seen to be transported with mirth, or dejected with sadness; always chearful, but rarely merry, at any sensible rate; seldom heard to break a jest; and when he did, he would be apt to blush at the levity of it: his gravity was natural without affectation.

His modesty was visible in a natural habitual blush, which was increased upon the least occasion, and oft discovered without any observable cause.

They that knew no more of him than by the briskness of his writings, found themselves deceived in their expectation, when they came in his company, noting the gravity and sobriety of his aspect and conversation; so free from loquacity, or much talkativeness, that he was something difficult to be engaged in any discourse; though when he was so, it was always singular, and never trite or vulgar. Parsimonious in nothing but his time, whereof he made as much improvement, with as little loss as any man in it: when he had any to spare from his drudging practice, he was scarce patient of any diversion from his study; so impatient of sloth and idleness, that he would say, he could not do nothing.

Sir Thomas understood most of the European languages;

viz. all that are in Hutter's bible,[30] which he made use of. The Latin and Greek he understood critically; the Oriental languages, which never were vernacular in this part of the world, he thought the use of them would not answer the time and pains of learning them; yet had so great a veneration for the matrix of them, viz. the Hebrew, consecrated to the Oracles of God, that he was not content to be totally ignorant of it; tho' very little of his science is to be found in any books of that primitive language. And tho' much is said to be written in the derivative idioms of that tongue, especially the Arabick, yet he was satisfied with the translations, wherein he found nothing admirable.[31]

In his religion he continued in the same mind which he had declared in his first book, written when he was but thirty years old, his *Religio Medici*, wherein he fully assented to that of the church of England, preferring it before any in the world, as did the learned Grotius. He attended the publick service very constantly, when he was not withheld by his practice. Never missed the sacrament in his parish, if he were in town. Read the best English sermons he could hear of, with liberal applause; and delighted not in controversies. In his last sickness, wherein he continued about a week's time, enduring great pain of the cholick, besides a continual fever, with as much patience as hath been seen in any man, without any pretence of Stoical apathy, animosity, or vanity of not being concerned thereat, or suffering no impeachment of happiness. Nihil agis dolor.[32]

His patience was founded upon the christian philosophy, and a sound faith of God's Providence, and a meek and humble submission thereunto, which he expressed in few words: I visited him near his end, when he had not strength to hear or speak much; the last words which I heard from him, were, besides some expressions of dearness, that he did freely submit to the will of God, being without fear: He had

30. Elias Hutter's Nuremberg Polyglot Boble (1599), which included texts in Hebrew, Chaldee, Greek, Latin, German, and French.
31. i.e. surprising, utterly exceptional.
32. 'O grief, you do nothing': a common expression.

oft triumphed over the king of terrors in others, and given many repulses in the defence of patients; but when his own turn came, he submitted with a meek, rational, and religious courage.

He might have made good the old saying of Dat Galenus opes,[33] had he lived in a place that could have afforded it. But his indulgence and liberality to his children, especially in their travels, two of his sons in divers countries, and two of his daughters in France, spent him more than a little. He was liberal in his house entertainments, and in his charity; he left a comfortable, but no great estate, both to his lady and children, gained by his own industry.[34]

Such was his sagacity and knowledge of all history, antient and modern, and his observations thereupon so singular, that it hath been said by them that knew him best, that if his profession, and place of abode, would have suited his ability, he would have made an extraordinary man for the privy-council, not much inferior to the famous Padre, Paulo, the late oracle of the Venetian state.

Tho' he were no prophet, nor son of a prophet, yet in that faculty which comes nearest it, he excelled, *i.e.* the stochastick,[35] wherein he was seldom mistaken, as to future events, as well publick as private; but not apt to discover any presages or superstition.'

It is observable, that he who in his earlier years had read all the books against religion, was in the latter part of his life averse from controversies. To play with important truths, to disturb the repose of established tenets, to subtilize objections, and elude proof, is too often the sport of youthful vanity, of which maturer experience commonly repents. There is a time, when every wise man is weary of raising difficulties only to task himself with the solution, and desires to enjoy truth without the

33. 'Galen affords riches': a medical axiom.

34. Whitefoot's text adds, '. . . having spent the greatest Part of his Patrimony in his Travels'. A footnote further adds, 'He was likewise very much defrauded by one of his Guardians' (see above, p. 483, note 3).

35. The faculty of conjecturing.

labour or hazard of contest. There is, perhaps, no better method of encountering these troublesome irruptions of scepticism, with which inquisitive minds are frequently harrassed, than that which Browne declares himself to have taken: 'If there arise any doubts in my way, I do forget them; or at least defer them, till my better settled judgment and more manly reason be able to resolve them: for I perceive, every man's reason is his best Oedipus, and will, upon a reasonable truce, find a way to loose those bonds, wherewith the subtilties of error have enchained our more flexible and tender judgments.' (*above, p.* 66)

The foregoing character may be confirmed and enlarged, by many passages in the *Religio Medici*; in which it appears, from Whitefoot's testimony, that the author, though no very sparing panegyrist of himself, has not exceeded the truth, with respect to his attainments or visible qualities.

There are, indeed, some interior and secret virtues, which a man may sometimes have without the knowledge of others; and may sometimes assume to himself, without sufficient reasons for his opinion. It is charged upon Browne by Dr. Watts,[36] as an instance of arrogant temerity, that, after a long detail of his attainments, he declares himself to have escaped 'the first and father-sin of pride.' A perusal of the *Religio Medici* will not much contribute to produce a belief of the author's exemption from this father-sin: pride is a vice, which pride itself inclines every man to find in others, and to overlook in himself.

As easily may we be mistaken in estimating our own courage, as our own humility; and, therefore, when Browne shews himself persuaded, that 'he could lose an arm without a tear, or with a few groans be quartered to pieces,' I am not sure that he felt in himself any uncommon powers of endurance; or, indeed, any thing more than a sudden effervescence of imagination, which, uncertain and involuntary as it is, he mistook for settled resolution.

'That there were not many extant, that in a noble way feared the face of death less than himself,' he might likewise believe at

36. Isaac Watts, in *Reliquiae juveniles* (1734).

a very easy expence, while death was yet at a distance; but the time will come to every human being, when it must be known how well he can bear to die; and it has appeared, that our author's fortitude did not desert him in the great hour of trial.

It was observed by some of the remarkers on the *Religio Medici*, that 'the author was yet alive, and might grow worse as well as better:' it is, therefore, happy, that this suspicion can be obviated by a testimony given to the continuance of his virtue, at a time when death had set him free from danger of change, and his panegyrist from temptation to flattery.

But it is not on the praises of others, but on his own writings, that he is to depend for the esteem of posterity; of which he will not easily be deprived, while learning shall have any reverence among men: for there is no science, in which he does not discover some skill; and scarce any kind of knowledge, profane or sacred, abstruse or elegant, which he does not appear to have cultivated with success.

His exuberance of knowledge, and plenitude of ideas, sometimes obstruct the tendency of his reasoning, and the clearness of his decisions: on whatever subject he employed his mind, there started up immediately so many images before him, that he lost one by grasping another. His memory supplied him with so many illustrations, parallel or dependent notions, that he was always starting into collateral considerations: but the spirit and vigour of his persuit always gives delight; and the reader follows him, without reluctance, thro' his mazes, in themselves flowery and pleasing, and ending at the point originally in view.

To have great excellencies, and great faults, 'magnæ virtutes nec minora vitia, is the poesy,' says our author, 'of the best natures.' This poesy may be properly applied to the style of Browne: It is vigorous, but rugged; it is learned, but pedantick; it is deep, but obscure; it strikes, but does not please; it commands, but does not allure: his tropes are harsh, and his combinations uncouth. He fell into an age, in which our language began to lose the stability which it had obtained in the time of Elizabeth;[37] and was considered by every writer as a subject on

37. The reputed 'stability' did not become apparent until the later part of the seventeenth century.

which he might try his plastick[38] skill, by moulding it according to his own fancy. Milton, in consequence of this encroaching licence, began to introduce the Latin idiom: and Browne, though he gave less disturbance to our structures and phraseology, yet poured in a multitude of exotick words; many, indeed, useful and significant, which, if rejected, must be supplied by circumlocution, such as *commensality* for the state of many living at the same table; but many superfluous, as a *paralogical* for an unreasonable doubt; and some so obscure, that they conceal his meaning rather than explain it, as *arthritical analogies* for parts that serve some animals in the place of joints.[39]

His style is, indeed, a tissue of many languages; a mixture of heterogeneous words, brought together from distant regions, with terms originally appropriated to one art, and drawn by violence into the service of another.[40] He must, however, be confessed to have augmented our philosophical diction; and in defence of his uncommon words and expressions, we must consider, that he had uncommon sentiments, and was not content to express in many words that idea for which any language could supply a single term.

But his innovations are sometimes pleasing, and his temerities happy: he has many 'verba ardentia,' forcible expressions, which he would never have found, but by venturing to the utmost verge of propriety; and flights which would never have been reached, but by one who had very little fear of the shame of falling.

There remains yet an objection against the writings of Browne, more formidable than the animadversions of criticism. There are passages, from which some have taken occasion to rank him among Deists, and others among Atheists. It would be difficult to guess how any such conclusion should be formed,

38. i.e. modelling, shaping.

39. Both 'arthritical analogies' and 'paralogical' are now obsolete; but 'commensality' is still in use. Browne's other contributions to the language still current, include: antediluvian, electricity, hallucination, incontrovertible, literary, medical, precarious, retrogression, etc. (all in *Pseudodoxia Epidemica*).

40. Cf. above, p. 48, note 50.

had not experience shewn that there are two sorts of men willing to enlarge the catalogue of infidels.

It has been long observed, that an Atheist has no just reason for endeavouring conversions; and yet none harrass those minds which they can influence, with more importunity of solicitation to adopt their opinions. In proportion as they doubt the truth of their own doctrines, they are desirous to gain the attestation of another understanding; and industriously labour to win a proselyte, and eagerly catch at the slightest pretence to dignify their sect with a celebrated name.[41]

The others become friends to infidelity only by unskilful hostility: men of rigid orthodoxy, cautious conversation, and religious asperity. Among these, it is too frequently the practice, to make in their heat concessions to Atheism, or Deism, which their most confident advocates had never dared to claim or to hope. A sally of levity, an idle paradox, an indecent jest, an unseasonable objection, are sufficient, in the opinion of these men, to efface a name from the lists of Christianity, to exclude a soul from everlasting life. Such men are so watchful to censure, that they have seldom much care to look for favourable interpretations of ambiguities, to set the general tenor of life against single failures, or to know how soon any slip of inadvertency has been expiated by sorrow and retractation; but let fly their fulminations, without mercy or prudence, against slight offences or casual temerities, against crimes never committed, or immediately repented.

The Infidel knows well, what he is doing. He is endeavouring to supply, by authority, the deficiency of his arguments; and to make his cause less invidious, by shewing numbers on his side: he will, therefore, not change his conduct, till he reforms his principles. But the zealot should recollect, that he is labouring, by this frequency of excommunication, against his own cause;

41. Dr Johnson quotes in a footnote from Sir John Davies:

> Therefore no hereticks desire to spread
> Their wild opinions like these epicures.
> For so their stagg'ring thoughts are [comforted],
> And other men's assent their doubt assures.
>
> (*Nosce Teipsum*, ed. A.B. Grosart, 1876, I, 83)

and voluntarily adding strength to the enemies of truth. It must always be the condition of a great part of mankind, to reject and embrace tenets upon the authority of those whom they think wiser than themselves; and, therefore, the addition of every name to infidelity, in some degree invalidates that argument upon which the religion of multitudes is necessarily founded.

Men may differ from each other in many religious opinions, and yet all may retain the essentials of Christianity; men may sometimes eagerly dispute, and yet not differ much from one another: the rigorous persecutors of error, should, therefore, enlighten their zeal with knowledge, and temper their orthodoxy with Charity; that Charity, without which orthodoxy is vain; Charity that 'thinketh no evil,' but 'hopeth all things,' and 'endureth all things.'[42]

Whether Browne has been numbered among the contemners of religion, by the fury of its friends, or the artifice of its enemies, it is no difficult task to replace him among the most zealous Professors of Christianity. He may, perhaps, in the ardour of his imagination, have hazarded an expression, which a mind intent upon faults may interpret into heresy, if considered apart from the rest of his discourse; but a phrase is not to be opposed to volumes: there is scarcely a writer to be found, whose profession was not divinity, that has so frequently testified his belief of the Sacred Writings, has appealed to them with such unlimited submission, or mentioned them with such unvaried reverence.

It is, indeed, somewhat wonderful, that He should be placed without the pale of Christianity, who declares, that 'he assumes the honourable stile of A Christian,' not because it is 'the religion of his country,' but because 'having in his riper years and confirmed judgment seen and examined all, he finds himself obliged, by the principles of Grace, and the law of his own reason, to embrace no other name but this:' Who, to specify his persuasion yet more, tells us, that 'he is of the Reformed Religion: of the same belief our Saviour taught, the Apostles disseminated, the Fathers authorized, and the Martyrs con-

42. 1 Corinthians 13. 5 and 7.

firmed:' Who, tho' 'paradoxical in philosophy, loves in divinity to keep the beaten road;' and pleases himself, that 'he has no taint of heresy, schism, or error:' To whom 'where the Scripture is silent, the Church is a text; where that speaks, 'tis but a comment;' and who uses not 'the dictates of his own reason, but where there is a joint silence of both:' Who 'blesses himself, that he lived not in the days of miracles, when faith had been thrust upon him; but enjoys that greater blessing, pronounced to all that believe and saw not.' He cannot surely be charged with a defect of faith, who 'believes that our Saviour was dead, and buried, and rose again, and desires to see him in his glory:' and who affirms, that 'this is not much to believe;' that 'as we have reason, we owe this faith unto history;' and that 'they only had the advantage of a bold and noble faith, who lived before his coming; and, upon obscure prophecies and mystical types, could raise a belief.' Nor can contempt of the positive and ritual parts of religion be imputed to him, who doubts, whether a good man would refuse a poisoned eucharist; and 'who would violate his own arm, rather than a church.'

The opinions of every man must be learned from himself: concerning his practice, it is safest to trust the evidence of others. Where these testimonies concur, no higher degree of historical certainty can be obtained; and they apparently concur to prove, that Browne was a zealous adherent to the faith of Christ, that he lived in obedience to his laws, and died in confidence of his mercy.

A DICTIONARY OF NAMES

The entries include mythological and Biblical figures and places. The dates of historical figures are 'A.D.' unless otherwise stated.

Aaron: the brother of Moses (q.v.), and priest

Abel: second son of Adam (q.v.)

Abrabanel (Leo Hebraeus, d. 1535): Spanish Neoplatonist, author of *Dialogues of Love* (in Italian)

Abraham: Hebrew patriarch (see Genesis 11–25)

Abram, Nicolas (1589–1655): French classical and Biblical scholar

Abramas: see previous entry

Absalom: favourite son of and rebel against David (q.v.; see 2 Samuel 18)

Absolom: see previous entry

Acheron: the river in Hades (q.v.)

Achilles: the Greek hero of the Trojan war (for his armour see *Iliad*, XVIII, 478 ff.)

Achmet: see Ahmed ibn Sirin

Acosta, Christopher (d. 1580): Portuguese physician and naturalist

Actius: see p. 139, note 27

Adam: according to tradition, the first man (said to have been created *c.* 4000 B.C.)

Adrastea: see p. 423, note 25

Adrian(us): see Hadrian

Aegineta: see Paulus Aegineta

Aelfric (955?–1022?): English writer

Aelian (3rd cent. or earlier): Roman historian

Aeneas: the Trojan protagonist of Virgil's *Aeneid*

Aeschulapius (Asclepius): the god of medicine and healing

Aeson: restored to youth by Medea (q.v.)

Aesop (*c.* 620–560 B.C.): Greek fable writer

Aetius (fl. 500): Greek medical writer

Agamemnon: King of Argos, leader of the Greek host before Troy

Agostino, Antonio (1517–1586): Spanish numismatist and jurisprudent

Agricola, G. Julius (37–93): Roman general and statesman

Ahab: king of Israel, personification of wickedness (see 1 Kings 16 ff.)

Ahasuerus: see Artaxerxes I

Ahmed I: Ottoman emperor (1603–1617)

Ahmed ibn Sirin (fl. 820): Arab interpreter of dreams

Ajax (Aias) Oileus: leader of the Locrians at the siege of Troy

Ajax (Aias) Telamonian: the noble if obstinate Greek warrior at the siege of Troy (see *Iliad*, XVII, 279 ff.)

Alacci, Leone (1586–1669): Greek scholar and theologian

Alaric (*c.*370–410): Visigothic chief, conqueror of Rome

Alberti, Leandro (1479–1553?): Italian Dominican historian and geographer

Albertus Magnus, St (1193?–1280): scholastic philosopher, 'the universal Doctor'

Alchmena: see Alcmene

Alcinous: king of the Phaeacians (see *Odyssey*, VI, 12 ff.)

Alcmene: the mother of Hercules (q.v.)

Aldrovandi, Ulisse (1522–1604): Italian naturalist

Alexander (3rd cent.): Christian martyr

Alexander III the Great: king of Macedon (336–323 B.C.)

Alexander Severus: Roman emperor (222–235)

Allatius, Leo: see Alacci

Almanzor (Al Mansur): Caliph of Baghdad (754–775), patron of learning

Amandus, St (d. *c.* 675): Merovingian Apostle of Flanders

Amatus (1511–1568): Portuguese physician, anatomist, and botanist

Ambrose, St (*c.*339–397): Bishop of Milan, Doctor of the Church

Ammianus Marcelinus (fl. *c.* 390): Roman soldier and historian

Anastasius (fl. 869): Italian scholar and writer

Anaxagoras (500?–428 B.C.): Greek philosopher

Andreas: author of a lost treatise (see p. 167, note 7) as reported by Athenaeus (q.v.)

Andrewes, Lancelot (1555–1626): Bishop of Winchester, formative influence on Anglican theology

Angelo: see Michelangelo

Angelus Victorius: see Victorius

Annius (Giovanni Nanni, 1432–1502): Italian literary impostor

Ansgarius (801–865): Archbishop of Hamburg Bremen, Apostle of the North

Anthony, St: see Antony

Antipater (398?–319 B.C.): Macedonian general

Antoninus: see Marcus Aurelius

'Antonio the Rich': see p. 391, note 2

Antonius: see Mark Antony

Antony, St (251?–356): hermit

Antony, Mark: see Mark Antony

Apelles (4th cent. B.C.): Greek painter

Apollinaris Sidonius: see Sidonius

Apollo: Olympian god of music, poetry, and medicine

Apollo Daphnes: a prophetess according to Theodoret (*Eccl. History*, III, 6–7)

Apomazar: see Ahmed ibn Sirin

Aquapendente, Girolamo Fabrici d' (1533–1619): Italian biologist, surgeon, and medical writer

Arachne: challenged Minerva to a weaving contest and, for her pride, was transformed into a spider

Archangelus of Burgonovus (fl. late 16th cent.): Italian Hebraist and cabalist

Archemorus: the infant whose funeral honours are described in Statius, *Thebaid*, VI

Archimedes (287?–212 B.C.): Greek mathematician

'Arden': not identified (but according to Mr Robbins, he may be the early seventeenth-century chiliast Henry Arthington)

Areopagite, the: see Dionysius the Pseudo-Areopagite

Argus: the hundred-eyed giant ordered to watch Io

Aries: the first sign of the zodiac; also the constellation between Pisces and Taurus

Ariosto, Lodovico (1474–1533): Italian poet

Aristeus (Aristeas): legendary Greek epic poet and historian

Aristides the Just (530?–468? B.C.): Athenian statesman and general

Aristotle (384–322 B.C.): Greek philosopher

Arius (c. 250–c. 336): heresiarch, denied Christ's divinity

Arrian (fl. 2nd cent.): Greek historian and biographer

Artaxerxes I Longimanus: king of Persia (464–424 B.C.)

Artaxerxes II Mnemon: king of Persia (404–359 B.C.)

Artemidorus (late 2nd/early 3rd cent.): Ephesian author of *Oneirocritica*, the period's chief extant work on dream interpretation

Artemisia: wife of Mausolus (q.v.)

Arthur: legendary king of medieval Britain

Asa: king of Judah (see 2 Chronicles 14–16)

Ashurbanipal: king of Assyria (668–629? B.C.)

Asshur: i.e. Assyria, or its major city or principal god; also used of kings (e.g. Shalmaneser)

Assur: see previous entry

Astraea: see p. 434, note 84

Astrampsychus (3rd cent.?): occult writer on dreams: cf. Artemidorus

Athenaeus (late 2nd/early 3rd cent.): Greek scholar

Atlas: the giant obliged to support the earth on his shoulders

Atropos: one of the three Fates who cuts the thread of life

Attalus III Philometor: king of Pergamum (138–133 B.C.)

Aubrey, John (1626–1697): English antiquary

Augustine, St (354–430): Bishop of Hippo in Roman Africa, the greatest theologian of the early Latin Church

Augustine, St, of Canterbury (d. 604/5): missionary to Kent and first Archbishop of Canterbury

Augustus: first Roman emperor (27 B.C.–A.D. 14)

Aulus Gellius (fl. 117?–180?): Latin grammarian

Ausonius (310?–395): Roman poet and rhetorician

Austin: see Augustine

Averroes (Ibn Rushd, 1126–1198): Arabian philosopher

Avicenna (980–1037): Arabian philosopher

A DICTIONARY OF NAMES

Bacchus: the god of wine and revelry

Bacon, Sir Edmund: see p. 321, note 18

Bacon, Sir Francis (1561–1626): philosopher and essayist

Bacon, Nicholas (1623–1666): see p. 314, note 1

Bado Aureo, Johannes de (fl. late 14th cent.): the obscure author of the oldest British treatise on heraldry

Bajazet I: Ottoman emperor (1389–1403), captured by Timur (Tamburlaine)

Baldwin: the first king of Jerusalem (1100–1118)

Barcephas: see Moses Bar-Cepha

Barnabas: disciple of St Paul and missionary (Acts 4.36)

Baronius, Caesar Cardinal (1538–1607): Italian ecclesiastical historian

Basil the Great, St (c. 330–379): Bishop of Caesarea, Father of the Church

Bauhin, Jean (1541–1613): French physician and botanist

Beaumont, Francis (1584–1616): English dramatist

Becanus, Martinus (1550–1624): Jesuit from Brabant, theologian and exegete

Bede, St (c. 673–735): English scholar, 'Father of English History'

Bel: i.e. Baal, a great Babylonian deity; the efficacy of its statue is ridiculed in the apocryphal Bel and the Dragon

Belinus: British king (see Geoffrey of Monmouth, III, 1 ff.)

Belisarius (505 ?–565): general of the Eastern Roman Empire

Bellinus: see Belinus

Bellisarius: see Belisarius

Bellonius (Pierre Belon, 1517–1564): French physician and naturalist

Belus: see Bel

Bembus (Pietro Cardinal Bembo, 1470–1547): Italian historian, poet, scholar

Benedict III: Pope (855–858)

Benjamin: Jacob's youngest and favourite son (see Genesis 35.18); also the tribe

Berosus (3rd cent. B.C.): Babylonian historian

Besler, Basil (1561–1629): German naturalist

Bethlem Gábor: prince of Transylvania (1613–1629) and king of Hungary (1620–1629)

Bevis: hero of the medieval romance Sir Bevis of Hampton

Bias: one of the seven wise men of ancient Greece ('I carry everything with me' – i.e. in the head)

Biringuccio, Vanucci (1480–1539): Italian mathematician and military scientist

Blancanus, Josephus: Italian author of Aristotelis loca mathematica (1615)

Blount, Sir Henry (1602–1682): English traveller and author

Blount, Thomas (1618–1679): English scholar: see below, p. 537

Blunt, Sir Henry: see Blount

Boadicea (d. 62): British queen, revolted against Romans

Bochart, Samuel (1599–1667): French theologian and scholar

A DICTIONARY OF NAMES

Boethius (*c.* 480 – *c.* 524): Roman philosopher and statesman

Boorde, Andrew (1490?–1549): English physician and writer

Bosio, Antonio (d. 1629): Italian archaeologist

Bosio, Giacomo (fl. late 16th cent.): Italian historian and scholar

Bovillus (Charles Bouelles, 1470?–1553?): French mathematician and philosopher

Boyle, Robert (1627–1691): English physicist and chemist

Brennus: Brennius, British king, brother of Belinus (q.v.)

Britannicus (41–55): son of Claudius I (q.v.), set aside in favour of Nero

Browne, Edward (1644–1708): Sir Thomas's eldest son: physician and author; see above, pp. 499 ff.

Bullokar, John (fl. 1622): English lexicographer: see below, p. 537

Burton, Robert (1577–1640): English scholar, author of *Anatomy of Melancholy* (pseudonym: Democritus Junior)

Burton, William (1575–1645): English antiquary

Cabeus (Niccolo Cabeo, 1585–1650): Italian mathematician and philosopher

Cacus: see p. 406, note 81

Cadamustus (Alvise Cadamosto, 1432–1477): Venetian explorer and writer

Cadmus: legendary founder of Thebes, said to have introduced the art of writing from Phoenicia

Caesar, G. Julius: Roman dictator (49–44 B.C.) and author

Cain: eldest son of Adam and Eve

Cajetan, Tomasso de Vio Cardinal (1470–1534): Italian-Spanish theologian

Caligula: Roman emperor (37–41)

Calvin, John (1509–1564): French Reformer and theologian

Cambyses II: last Median king of Persia (d. 522 B.C.)

Camden, William (1551–1623): English antiquary and historian

Canute II the Great: king of England (1016–1035) and Denmark (1018–1035)

Caracalla: Roman emperor (211–217)

Cardan (Girolamo Cardano, 1501–1576): Italian physician and mathematician

Carew, Richard (1555–1620): English antiquary and translator

Cartaphilus: see p. 257

Casalius, Joannes Baptista (fl. mid 17th cent.): Italian antiquary and writer

Casaubon, Meric (1599–1671): English classical scholar

Cassiodorus (*c.* 485–*c.* 580): Roman author and monk

Cassius Longinus (d. 42): Roman tribune, one of Caesar's assassins

Castellus (Pietro Castelli, d. 1657): Italian physician and botanist

Castor: one of the Dioscuri ('sons of Zeus')

Cato the Elder (234–149 B.C.): Roman consul

Cato the Younger (Cato of Utica, 95–46 B.C.): Roman statesman and philosopher

Cebes: see p. 408, note 93

Cestius, Gaius (1st cent. B.C.): Roman praetor and tribune

Cham: see Ham

Charlemagne: Charles I the Great, king of the Franks (768–814) and emperor of the West (800–814)

Charles II: king of Great Britain (1660–1685)

Charles V: Holy Roman Emperor (1519–1556)

Charles the Great: see Charlemagne

Charles Wayne, the stars of: 'Certaine Starres winding about the North pole of the world, in fashion like foure wheeles and horses drawing it' (Bullokar)

Charon: see p. 301, note 23

Charybdis: the mythical whirlpool off the coast of Sicily (see *Odyssey*, XII)

Cheops: king of Egypt (*c.* 2900–2877 B.C.)

Chifflet, Jean Jacques (1588–1660): French medical and political writer

Childeric I: king of the Salian Franks (458?–481)

Chimaera: in Greek mythology, a fire-breathing female monster

Chiron: the wisest of the Centaurs, teacher of Achilles and Hercules

Christian IV: king of Denmark and Norway (1588–1648)

Christopher, St (3rd cent.): the patron of wayfarers

Chrysippus of Soli (*c.* 280–207 B.C.): Stoic philosopher

Chrysostom: see John Chrysostom

Chus: see Cush

Chymera: see Chimaera

Cicero (106–43 B.C.): Roman orator, philosopher and statesman

Cimon (507–449 B.C.): Athenian statesman and general

Claudian (d. *c.* 395): Latin poet

Claudius I: Roman emperor (9 B.C.–A.D. 54)

Clemens: see next entry

Clement of Alexandria, St (*c.* 150–*c.* 215): theologian

Cleobulus (fl. 560 B.C.): Greek lyric poet, one of the Seven Sages

Cleopatra: queen of Egypt (51–49 and 48–30 B.C.)

Clusius, Carolus (1526–1609): Dutch physician and botanist

Cockeram, Henry (fl. 1650): English lexicographer: see below, p. 537

Codrus: last king of Athens, said to have reigned *c.* 1068 B.C.

Colonna, Fabio (1567?–1650): Italian naturalist

Columbus, Christopher (1446?–1506): Italian explorer

Columbus, Realdus (d. 1577?): Italian anatomist

Columna: see Colonna

Commodus: Roman emperor (180–192)

Constans I: Roman emperor (337–350)

Constantine the Great: Roman emperor (306–337)

Copernicus, Nicolas (1473–1543): Polish astronomer, his heliocentric theory not confirmed much before the end of the 17th century; see p. 160, note 139

Cornelius Sylla: see Sulla

Costa, Christophorus a: see Acosta

Covarrubias y Orozco, Sebastián de (fl. early 17th cent.): Spanish scholar

Craesus: see Croesus

Crassus, Lucius Licinius (140–91 B.C.): Roman orator and statesman

Croesus (6th cent. B.C.): king of Lydia, celebrated for his wealth

Crucius (Alsario della Croce, fl. early 17th cent.): Italian physician and writer

Cupid (Eros): the god of love, son of Venus

Curtius: see Quintus Curtius

Curtius, Benedictus (Benoît Court, fl. 1533–1560): French jurist and writer on agriculture (*Horti*, 1560)

Curtius, Marcus (d. 362 B.C.): Roman knight, self-sacrificed for Rome (Livy, VII, 6)

Cush (Kush): the eldest son of Ham (see Genesis 10.6)

Cuthbert (d. 758): Archbishop of Canterbury

Cuthred: king of the West Saxons (740–754)

Cynthia: see p. 281, note 29

Cypraeus, Joannes Adolphus (16th cent.): German ecclesiastical historian

Cyprian, St (d. 258): Bishop of Carthage, pastoral theologian

Cyril, St (376–444): Bishop of Alexandria, Father of the Church

Cyrus the Elder: see next entry

Cyrus the Great: king of Persia (500–529 B.C.), founder of the Persian Empire

Cyrus the Younger (424?–401 B.C.): Persian prince and satrap, conspired against his brother Artaxerxes II (q.v.) with help of mercenaries under Xenophon (q.v.)

Damocles: courtier under Dionysius the Elder (q.v.) who sat him under a suspended sword to demonstrate the perils of a ruler's life

Damon and Pythias: 'loved each other so well, as that one offered to suffer death for the other' (Cockeram)

Dan: the son of Jacob by Bilhah, Rachel's maid (see Genesis 30.6); also the tribe – 'an adder' (Gen. 49.17) which, omitted from the list of tribes (Rev. 7.4–8), was expected to yield the Antichrist from its ranks

Daniel: 'prophet', protagonist of the homonymous Biblical book

Dante (1265–1321): Italian poet

Darius III Codomannus: king of Persia (336–330 B.C.)

David: the second king of Israel, accepted as author of Psalms

Dee, John (1527–1608): English mathematician and astrologer

Deiphobus: Trojan prince, Helen's husband after Paris's death (see *Aeneid*, VI, 495 ff.)

de Laet, Jean (1593–1649): Flemish geographer and naturalist

della Porta, Giovanni Battista (1538?–1615): Italian natural philosopher (*Villa*, 1592)

Demetrius: the silversmith of Ephesus (see Acts 19.23 ff.)

Demetrius I Poliorcetes: king of Macedon (294–283 B.C.)

A DICTIONARY OF NAMES

Democritus (late 5th/early 4th cent. B.C.): the Greek 'laughing philosopher', proverbially a mocker of human follies

Demosthenes (c. 385–322 B.C.): Athenian statesman, the greatest of Greek orators

Deucalion: the only survivor, with his wife Pyrrha, of the flood sent by Jupiter

Diana: Olympian goddess of hunting and virginity; also her great temple at Ephesus

Didymus (c. 65 B.C.–A.D. 10): Alexandrian scholar and commentator on Homer

Digby, Sir Kenelm (1603–1665): English author and diplomat

Dio Cassius: see Dion Cassius

Diocletian: Roman emperor (284–305)

Diodorus Siculus (late 1st cent. B.C.): Greek historian

Diogenes (412?–323 B.C.): Greek Cynic philosopher

Diogenes Laertius (2nd cent.): Greek author of *Lives of the Philosophers*

Diomedes: son of Tydeus, leader of Argos and Tiryns in the Trojan War

Dion Cassius (c.155–c.235): Greek historian.

Dionysius the Elder: tyrant of Syracuse (405–367 B.C.)

Dionysius the Younger: tyrant of Syracuse (367–356 and 347–344 B.C.)

Dionysius the Pseudo-Areopagite (c. 500): mystical theologian, often confused with St Paul's convert in Athens (Acts 17.34)

Dionysus: see previous entries

Dioscorides (4th cent. B.C.): Greek historian and moralist

Dioscorides Pedanius (fl. 1st cent. B.C.): Greek medical writer

Domitian: Roman emperor (81–96)

Doria, Andrea (1468?–1560): Genoese admiral and statesman

Dorset, Thomas Marquess of: see p. 295, note 82

Du Bellay, Joachim (1522?–1560): French poet and critic

Dugdale, Sir William (1605–1686): English antiquary and historian

Du Loir (fl. 1639–1654): French traveller and writer

Duns Scotus, Johannes (c. 1264–1308): medieval philosopher, 'Doctor of Subtlety'

Ecclesiastes: see Solomon

Elagabalus: see Heliogabalus

Eliah: see Elijah

Elias: see next entry

Elijah (9th cent. B.C.): Hebrew prophet, 'translated' into heaven (2 Kings 2.1–18) and so a type of the Resurrection

Elizium: see Elysium

Elyot, Sir Thomas (1490?–1546): English scholar: see below, p. 538

Elysium: abode of the blessed after death

Emanuel I the Great: king of Portugal (1495–1521)

Enoch: Hebrew patriarch, 'translated' into heaven (Genesis 5.24) and so a type of the Resurrection

Epaminondas (*c.* 418–362 B.C.): Theban statesman and general

Ephraim: the youngest son of Jacob (q.v.)

Epictetus (*c.* 60 – *post* 118): Greek Stoic philosopher

Epicurus (342?–270 B.C.): Greek philosopher

Epimenides (7th cent. B.C.): Cretan philosopher and poet-prophet, quoted by St Paul (Titus 1.12)

Epiphanius, St (*c.* 315–403): Bishop of Salamis, militant defender of orthodoxy

Erasmus, Desiderius (1467–1536): Dutch scholar and humanist

Esarhaddon: king of Assyria and Babylonia (681–669 B.C.), father of Ashurbanipal (q.v.)

Esdras: title of two books of the Septuagint (four of the Vulgate) in the Apocrypha; cf. Ezra

Esther: the Jewish wife of 'Ahasuerus' (q.v.); also the homonymous Biblical book

Euphorbus: the Trojan killed by Menelaus (see *Iliad*, XVII, 9 ff.)

Euripides (*c.* 480–406 B.C.): the last of the three greatest Attic tragedians

Eusebius (*c.* 260–340): Bishop of Caesarea, 'Father of Church History'

Eustathius: Bishop of Thessalonica (1175–*c.* 1192), commentator on Homer

Eve: according to tradition, the first woman

Evelyn, John (1620–1706): English diarist

Ezekiel (early 6th cent.? B.C.): Hebrew prophet; also the homonymous Biblical book

Ezra (5th/4th cent.? B.C.): Jewish reformer; also the homonymous Biblical book (cf. Esdras)

Favorinus (2nd cent.): Greek philosopher

Ferdinand II: German emperor (1619–1637)

Fernel, Jean (1497–1558): French physician, author of *De abditis rerum causis* (1548): see p. 77, note 85

Ferrarius, Omnibonus: German author of *De arte medica infantium* (1605)

Ficino, Marsilio (1433–1499): Florentine Neoplatonist and humanist

Fletcher, John (1579–1625): English dramatist

Fourcroy, A.F.: see p. 295, note 79

Francis I: king of France (1515–1547)

Frontinus, Sextus Julius (40?–104): praetor urbanus of Rome, soldier and author

Frotho the Great: legendary Danish king, probably the same as Unguinus (q.v.)

Fuchs(ius), Leonhard (1501–1566): German physician and botanist

Gad: a son of Jacob (see Genesis 30.9 ff.); also the tribe

Gaffarel, Jacques (1601–1681): French Hebraist and astrologer

Gaguinus: see Guagninus

Galba: Roman emperor (68–69)

Galen (fl. 2nd cent.): Greek physician and writer: see p. 77, note 85

A DICTIONARY OF NAMES

Galileo Galilei (1564–1642): the great Italian astronomer

Gallienus: Roman emperor (253–268)

Gamaliel: Jewish rabbi, teacher of St Paul in his pre-Christian days (Acts 5.34, 22.3)

Garcias ab Horto: see Orta

Gargantua: see Rabelais

Gassendus (Pierre Gassend, 1592–1655): French philospher, mathematician, and physician

Gauricus, Lucas (1476–1558): Italian mathematician and astrologer

Geber (fl. 721–776): Arabian alchemist

Gemistus Plethon (c. 1355–c. 1450): Byzantine Platonist, influential in Renaissance Florence

Geoffrey of Monmouth (c. 1100–1154): British inventive historian

George, St: patron saint of England

George, David: see Joris

Germanicus (15 B.C.–A.D. 19): Roman general, adopted son of Tiberius (q.v.)

Gesner(us), Konrad (1516–1565): Swiss naturalist, author of *History of Animals*

Geta: Roman emperor (211–212)

Gigas: see next entry

Giggei, Antonio (d. 1632): Italian orientalist, gave Aldrovandi (q.v.) a piece of peacock's flesh that was six years old

Giovio, Paolo (1530?–1585?): Italian Latin poet

Giraldi, Giglio (1479–1552): Italian poet and archaeologist

Giraldus Cambrensis (1147–c. 1223): Welsh historian

Goliah: see next entry

Goliath: the Philistine giant killed by David (see 1 Samuel 17)

Gomesius, Bernardinus: author of *Diascepseon de sale* (1605)

Gordianus: Roman emperor (238–244)

Goropius: see Becanus

Gregory XV: Pope (1621–1623)

Grotius, Hugo (1563–1645): Dutch scholar, statesman, authority on international law

Gruterus, Janus (d. 1607): Dutch scholar and educator

Guagninus, Alexander (1548?–1614): Italian historian

Guellius, Valentinus: annotator of Virgil (1575)

Guevara, Antonio de (1490–1544): Spanish chronicler and moralist

Gyraldus: see Giraldus

Habakkuk (Habbacuc): Hebrew prophet who also figures in the apocryphal Bel and the Dragon (33–39); also the homonymous Biblical book

Hades: the abode of the dead; also the ruler of the underworld (cf. Pluto)

Hadrian: Roman emperor (117–138)

Halicarnasseus: see Herodotus

A DICTIONARY OF NAMES

Ham: the youngest son of Noah (q.v.), regarded as forefather of the Egyptians

Hannibal (247–183 B.C.): the Carthaginian general who invaded Italy

Harald: i.e. Haraldr Hilditöhn (Wartooth), the semi-historical Danish king killed *c.* 775 by Ringo (q.v.)

Harpalus (d. 324? B.C.): Macedonian general and satrap of Babylonia

Harvey, William (1578–1657): English physician and naturalist, discovered the circulation of the blood

Hector: the foremost Trojan warrior, killed by Achilles (q.v.)

Hecuba: queen of Troy, mother of Hector

Helena, St (*c.* 255–*c.* 330): mother of Constantine the Great, reputed to have discovered the Cross

Heliogabalus: Roman emperor (218–222)

Helmont, Jean Baptiste van (1577–1644): Flemish physician and chemist

Henry II: king of England (1154–1189)

Henry III: king of England (1216–1272)

Henry VIII: king of England (1509–1547)

Heraclitus (6th/5th cent. B.C.): the Greek 'weeping philosopher'

Hercules (Heracles): the son of Jupiter and Alcmene, completed the twelve 'labours' imposed by Juno

Hermes: see Mercury

Hermes surnamed Trismegistus ('the thrice-greatest'): legendary author of Greek and Latin religious and philosophical writings

Hermias (fl. 350 B.C.): tyrant of Atarneus and patron of Aristotle

Hernandes, Francisco (1530–1587): Spanish physician and naturalist

Herod the Great: king of the Jews (37–4 B.C.)

Herodias: the second wife of Herod Antipas son of Herod the Great (see Mark 6.17 ff.)

Herodotus (484–425 B.C.): Greek historian

Herostratus: who in 356 B.C. burnt the Temple of Diana (q.v.) to make his name immortal

Hesiod (fl. 859–824 B.C.): Greek epic poet

Hester: see Esther

Heurnius, Johannes van (1543–1601): Dutch physician and writer

Hevelius, Johann (1611–1687): German astronomer

Hierusalem: i.e. Jerusalem

Hippocrates (460?–377? B.C.): Greek physician, 'the Father of Medicine'

Hippolytus, St (*c.* 170–*c.* 236): theologian of the Latin Church

Hippon (5th cent. B.C.): Greek philosopher

Hofmann(us), Caspar (1572–1648): German physician and prolific writer

Holinshed, Raphael (d. *c.* 1580): English chronicler

Holland, Philemon (1552–1637): English translator

Homer: understood as author of the two epics and the 'Homeric' hymns

Horace (65–8 B.C.): Roman poet

Horto, Garcias ab: see Orta

Horus: the Egyptian god of the sun, son of Osiris and Isis (q.v.), often conflated with Hermes Trismegistus (q.v.)

Howell, James (1594?–1666): English pamphleteer and letter-writer

Hubert, St (d. *c.* 727); Bishop of Maestricht and Liége

Hucher(i)us, Joannes: French physician of Montpellier, author of *De sterilitate* (1610)

Hugo, Johannes (fl. early 16th cent.): German humanist

Humbert, St: see Hubert

Huss, John (*c.* 1369–1415): Bohemian Reformer, burnt at the stake

Hutter, Elias (1553–1607?): German orientalist and Biblical scholar

Hyacinth: the youth beloved of Apollo; also the flower

Hydra: the nine-headed serpent slain by Hercules (q.v.)

Ibrahim Pasha: Ottoman grand vizier (1523–1536) under Suleiman (q.v.)

Icarus: escaping with his father Daedalus from Crete, flew close to the sun and fell to his death

Ignatius, St (*c.* 35–*c.* 107): Bishop of Antioch and author

Iphicrates (419?–348? B.C.): Athenian general

Iris: the goddess of the rainbow; also the flower

Irus: the beggar of Ithaca (*Odyssey*, XVIII)

Isaac: Hebrew patriarch (see Genesis 21–28)

Isidore, St (*c.* 560–636): Archbishop of Seville, encyclopedic scholar

Isis: the Egyptian goddess of fertility, sister and wife of Osiris (q.v.)

Ixion: the Centaurs' father, bound on a constantly revolving wheel on aspiring to love Juno (q.v.)

Jacob (Israel): Hebrew patriarch (see Genesis 25–49)

Jair: the eighth judge of Israel (see Judges 10.3–5)

Janus: the patron god of beginnings and endings, represented with two faces; the doors of his temple in Rome were open in wartime, closed in peacetime

Jeffery, John: Archdeacon of Norwich (1694–1720)

Jehoram: king of Judah, son of Jehoshaphat (see 2 Chronicles 21.1 ff.)

Jenny, Sir Arthur: one of Browne's patients (see *K*, III, 301)

Jephthah: a 'judge' of Israel (see Judges 11.30 ff.)

Jeremiah (7th cent. B.C.): Hebrew prophet, accepted as author of homonymous Biblical book and of the Lamentations

Jeremy: see previous entry

Jerome, St (*c.* 342–420): scholar, translator of the Bible (Vulgate), Doctor of the Church

Joan: the mythical Pope: see p. 258

Job: protagonist of the homonymous Biblical book, personification of patience

John the Baptist, St: the forerunner of Christ

John the Evangelist: accepted as the author of the Fourth Gospel, the Book of Revelation, and three of the Catholic Epistles

John Chrysostom, St (*c.* 347–407): Patriarch of Constantinople, Father of the Church

John Ernest: Duke of Saxony (1594–1626)

Johnstonus: see Jonston
Jonah: Hebrew 'prophet' who sojourned in the whale's belly and so a
  type of the Resurrection; also the homonymous Biblical book
Jonas: see previous entry
Jonathan: Saul's eldest son, David's close friend (see 1 Samuel 18–20)
Jones, Inigo (1573–1652): architect and stage designer
Jonston (Johnstone), John (1603–1675): Scottish naturalist
Jordandes (or Jordanes, 6th cent.): historian of the Goths
Joris, David (Jan Jorisz, c. 1501–1556): Anabaptist extremist
Joseph: Hebrew patriarch (see Genesis 30, 37–50)
Joseph, St: the husband of the Virgin Mary
Josephus, Flavius (38?–100?): Jewish historian
Joshua: the successor of Moses (q.v.), conqueror of Palestine
Josuah: see previous entry
Joubert, Laurent (1529–1582): French medical writer, author of *Erreurs
  populaires et propos vulgaires touchant la médicine et le régime de santé* (1579;
  Latin trans., *De vulgi erroribus*, 1600)
Jove: see Jupiter
Jovius, Paulus: see Giovio
Judah: the fourth son of Jacob (q.v.); also the most powerful of Israel's
  twelve tribes
Julian 'the Apostate': Eastern Roman emperor (361–363), attempted to
  restore paganism
Julius Caesar: see Caesar
Juno (Hera): queen of the Olympian gods, wife of Jupiter
Jupiter (Zeus): the supreme Olympian god; also the planet
Justin (3rd cent.?): Roman historian
Justin Martyr, St (c. 100–c. 165): Christian apologist
Juvenal (c. 60–c. 140): Roman lawyer and satirist

Keck, Thomas: see below, p. 552
Kepler, Johann (1571–1630): the great German astronomer
Kircher, Athanasius (1602–1680): German mathematician and scholar
Kirchmann, Johannes (1575–1643): German antiquary
Knolles, Richard (1550?–1610): English historian of the Turks

Lactantius (c. 240 – c. 320): Christian apologist: see p. 78, note 93
Laertes: the father of Ulysses (q.v.)
Laertius: see Diogenes Laertius
Lamia: a female man-devouring monster
Lamia (4th cent. B.C.): Athenian courtesan
Lampridius Aelius (fl. 300): Roman historian
Largus, Scribonius (fl. 47): Roman physician
Laurenberg, Peter (1585–1639): German botanist and anatomist
Lazarus: the intimate friend of Jesus who raised him from the dead (see
  John 11.1–44)

Lazarus: the beggar in the parable (see Luke 16.20 ff.)

Lazius, Wolfgang (1514–1565): Austrian physician and historian

Leandro: see Alberti

Leeuwenhoek, Antony van (1632–1723): Dutch microscopist

Le Gros, Thomas: see p. 263, note 1.

Leo: the constellation between Cancer and Virgo

Leo III: Pope (795–816)

Leo IV, St: Pope (847–855)

Leo X (Giovanni de' Medici): Pope (1513–1521)

Leo XI: Pope (1605)

Leo the Jew: see Abrabanel

Leon of Modena (1571–1648): Jewish scholar and rabbi

Leonardo da Vinci (1452–1519): Italian painter, scientist, natural philosopher, etc.

Lepidus (d. c. 77 B.C.): Roman triumvir

Leuenhoek: see Leeuwenhoek

Lewis: see Louis

Licinius: Roman emperor (308–324)

Linden, Johannes A. van der (1609–1664): Dutch physician and writer

Linschoten, Jan Hugh van (1563–1611): Dutch traveller and author

Lipsius, Justus (1547–1606): Flemish scholar

Livy (59 B.C.–A.D. 17): Roman historian

Lombard, Peter: see Peter Lombard

Lopes, Eduardo (late 16th cent.): Spanish (or Portuguese) explorer and author

Lot: Abraham's nephew who fled Sodom; his wife glanced back and was turned into a pillar of salt (see Genesis 19)

Louis I le Débonnaire: king of Aquitaine (from 781), and emperor (813–833, 835–840)

Louis II: king of Hungary (1516–1526)

Louis XI: king of France (1461–1483)

Loveday, Robert: see p. 389 (headnote)

Lucan (39–65): Roman poet

Lucian (c. 120–200): Greek satirist

Lucifer: Satan's name ('light-bearer') before his expulsion from Heaven

Lucilius (180–102 B.C.): Roman poet, creator of satire

Lucina: the Roman goddess of childbirth

Lucretius (96?–55 B.C.): Roman poet and philosopher

Ludovicus Pius: see Louis I

Luna: i.e. the moon

Luther, Martin (1483–1546): founder of the German Reformation

Lycosthenes (Konrad Wolffhart, 1518–1561): Swiss philosopher and theologian

Lycurgus: according to tradition, the foremost Spartan lawgiver

Lyser(us), Michael (fl. mid 17th cent.): German physician and writer

Machiavelli, Niccolò (1469–1527): Florentine statesman and political philosopher

Macrobius, Ambrosius Theodosius (fl. 395–423): Roman philosopher and grammarian

Magasthenes: see Megasthenes

Magdalen: see Mary Magdalen

Maginus (Giovanni Magini, 1555–1617): Italian mathematician

Magius, Hieronymus (Girolamo Maggi, 1523–1572): Italian engineer and author

Mahomet: see Mohammed

Maimonides, Moses (1135–1204): Jewish philosopher

Mammon: the false god of riches

Manasseh (Manasses): Joseph's eldest son (see Genesis 41.51); also the tribe

Mandelslo, Johann Albrecht von (1616–1644): German traveller and author

Manlius: Titus Manlius Torquatus, who had his son beheaded (Livy, VIII, 7)

Mantuan: see Virgil

Marcellus (268?–208 B.C.): Roman general and statesman

Marcus: see next entry

Marcus Aurelius: Roman emperor (161–180) and author

Marius (2nd cent.): Christian martyr

Marius, Gaius (155?–86 B.C.): Roman general and statesman

Mark Antony (83?–30 B.C.): Roman general and triumvir

Marlianus, Joannes Bartholomaeus (1490?–1560?): Milanese antiquary

Mars (Ares): Olympian god of war; also the planet

Martial (fl. 1st cent.): Roman writer of epigrams

Martialis, St (fl. 2nd cent.): first bishop of Limoges

Martinus Polonus (d. 1278): chronicler

Martyr, Peter: see Peter Martyr

Mary Magdalen, St: a follower of Christ who cast out of her 'seven devils' (Luke 8.2)

Mathiolus: see Mattioli

Matilda (1102–1167): queen of England and empress

Matthew of Miechów (1475–1523): Polish historian

Matthias: German emperor (1612–1619)

Mattioli, Pietro Andrea (1500–1577): Sienese physician and botanist

Maud: see Matilda

Mauricius: Byzantine emperor (582–602)

Mausolus: king of Caria, buried (353 B.C.) in a splendid monument erected by Artemisia (q.v.)

Medea: sorceress who helped Jason obtain the Golden Fleece

Megasthenes (fl. c. 300 B.C.): Greek geographer and historian

Mela, Pomponius (1st cent.): Latin geographer

Melissa: wife of Periander (q.v.)

Menoeceus: the hero self-killed for his country's welfare (Statius, *Thebaid*, X)

Menoeceus: the recipient of the letter of Epicurus (q.v.)

Mercurialis (Girolamo Mercuriale, 1530–1606): Italian physician and scholar

Mercurii (Girolamo Mercurio, 1550?–1615): Italian physician, author of *De gli errori popolari d'Italia* (1603)

Mercurius: see next entry

Mercury (Hermes): Olympian god of commerce, eloquence, etc.; also the planet

Mersenne, Marin (1588–1648): French mathematician and scholar

Metellus, L. Caecilius (d. 221 B.C.): Roman dictator

Methuselah: patriarch, died aged 969 (see Genesis 5.27)

Metrophanes (9th cent.): Bishop of Smyrna and theologian

Michelangelo (1475–1564): Italian sculptor, painter, poet

Michovius, Matthaeus: see Matthew of Miechów

Minerva (Athena): Olympian goddess of wisdom

Minutius Felix (fl. *c.* 270): Roman rhetor

Miszraim: see next entry

Mizraim: the second son of Ham (see Genesis 10.6)

Modena: see Leon of Modena

Mohammed (570–632): Arabian prophet, founder of Islam

Moloch: a Phoenician-Ammonite god to whom children were sacrificed by burning

Montacutius (Richard Montague, 1577–1641): English scholar and theologian, Bishop of Norwich from 1638

Montanus, Arnoldus (fl. 1657–1683): Dutch miscellaneous writer

More, Henry, the Cambridge Platonist (1614–1687): English philosopher

Morpheus: the god of dreams, son of the god of sleep

Morta: see p. 397, note 34

Moses: the founder and lawgiver of Israel, accepted as the author of the Pentateuch (Genesis through Deuteronomy)

Moses Bar-Cepha (*c.* 813–903): Syrian bishop and Biblican scholar

Muffetus (Thomas Moffett, 1553–1604): English physician and author

Murad IV: Ottoman emperor (1623–1640)

Mustapha I: Ottoman emperor (1617–1618, 1622–1623)

Nabuchodonosor: see Nebuchadnezzar

Naphthali: the sixth son of Jacob (see Genesis 49.21); also the tribe

Narses (478?–573): Byzantine general and statesman

Nebuchadnezzar II: king of Babylon (605–562 B.C.)

Nebuchodonosor: see previous entry

Nemesis: the Greek goddess of vengeance: see p. 423, note 25

Nero: Roman emperor (54–68)

Newton, Sir Isaac (1642–1717): English mathematician and scientist

A DICTIONARY OF NAMES

Nicephorus: obscure Byzantine writer on dreams: cf. Artemidorus
Nicholas of Damascus (1st cent. B.C.): Greek historian
Nieremberg, Juan (1595–1658): Spanish mystic
Nimrod: legendary founder of the Assyrian Empire (see Genesis 10.8–10)
Ninus: legendary founder of Nineveh
Nirembergius: see Nieremberg
Noah: tenth in descent from Adam; father of Shem, Ham and Japheth
Numa Pompilius: the legendary second king of Rome

Octavian: see Augustus
Oedipus: noted for solving riddles; became king of Thebes on murdering
his father and marrying his mother
Og: the giant king of Bashan (see Deuteronomy 3.11)
Olaus Magnus (1490–1558): Swedish historian
Oleaster, Hieronymus (d. 1563): Portuguese Biblical commentator
Olmo, Giovanni (late 16th cent.): Italian physician and writer
Olympias (d. 316 B.C.): mother of Alexander the Great
Ophir: famous for its gold (1 Kings 10.11, Isaiah 13.12, etc.)
Opimius (d. 100? B.C.): Roman consul
Oppianus of Apameia (fl. c. 210): Greek poet
Orcus: the underworld (see Hades)
Orestes: son of Agamemnon and Clytemnestra, murdered her and her
lover Aegisthus
Origen (c. 185–c. 254): Alexandrian Biblical scholar and theologian
Orion: the hunter beloved of Diana; also the constellation near Taurus
Orpheus: legendary pre-Homeric poet, founder of the mystic cult
Orphism
Orta, Garcia de (fl. mid 16th cent.): Portuguese naturalist
Ortelius, Abraham (1527–1598): Flemish cartographer and antiquary
Orus: see Horus
Osiris: the Egyptian god of the lower world (see Isis, Horus)
Osman II: Ottoman emperor (1618–1622)
Osorius (Jeronimo Osorio da Fonseca, 1506–1580): Portuguese bishop
and historian
Ostorius Scapula, P.: Roman governor in Britain (47–51)
Osyris: see Osiris
Ovid (43 B.C.–c. A.D. 17): Roman poet

Palaephatus (4th cent. B.C.): Greek grammarian who rationalised Greek
mythology
Palamedes: Greek warrior at the siege of Troy, said to have added several
letters to the alphabet
Pantagruel: see Rabelais
Paracelsus (Theophrastus Bombastus von Hohenheim, 1493–1541): Swiss
physician and chemist
Paré (Pareus), Ambrose (1510–1590): French surgeon

Pareus, Johann (1576–1648): German theologian and philologist

Paris: the Trojan prince who kidnapped Helen of Sparta causing the Trojan War

Patrick, St (c. 389–c. 461): the 'Apostle of the Irish'

Patroclus: friend of Achilles (q.v.), killed by Hector of Troy

Paul, St (d. c. A.D. 65): the 'Apostle of the Gentiles'

Paul V: Pope (1605–1621)

Paulinus: see Suetonius Paulinus

Paulo, Padre: see Sarpi

Paulus Aegineta (fl. *ante* 700): Greek medical writer

Pausanias (2nd cent.): Greek traveller and geographer

Peiresc, Nicolas de (1580–1637): French scholar and naturalist

Penelope: the faithful wife of Ulysses (q.v.)

Penthesilea: daughter of Mars and the queen of the Amazons

Pereskius: see Peiresc

Periander (625–585 B.C.): Greek statesman, one of the Seven Wise Men

Perithous: son of Ixion king of the Lapiths

Perseus: the son of Jupiter and Danaë, slayer of Medusa

Persius (34–62): Roman satiric poet

Perucci, Francesco: Italian author of *Pompe funebri* (1639)

Peter, St: the Prince of the Apostles

Peter Lombard (c. 1100–1160): author of the standard textbook of medieval theology, the 'Sentences'

Peter Martyr (Pietro Martire Vermigli, 1500–1562): Italian Reformer

Petrarch (Francesco Petrarca, 1304–1374): Italian poet and humanist

Petronius (d. c. 66): Roman satirist

Pettus, Sir John: see p. 389 (headnote)

Phaëton: struck down by Jupiter on borrowing the chariot of his father Sol (q.v.)

Phalaris: tyrant of Agrigento (570–554 B.C.); also the canary grass

Pharamond: the legendary first king of France

Phavorinus: see Favorinus

Philes, Manuel (1275?–1345): Byzantine poet

Philip: one of the seven 'deacons' chosen as missionaries (see Acts 6.3 ff., 8.26 ff.)

Philip II: king of Macedon (359–336 B.C.)

Philip II: king of Spain (1556–1598)

Philo (c. 20 B.C.–c. A.D. 50): Jewish thinker and exegete

Philopoemen (253–183 B.C.): Greek commander

Philoxenus (5th/6th cent.): Syriac writer

Phocas: Byzantine emperor (602–610)

Phocylides (fl. c. 560 B.C.): Greek philosopher and poet

Phoebus: see Apollo

Photius (c, 810–895): Patriarch of Constantinople

Pico della Mirandola, Giovanni (1463–1494): Florentine scholar and mystic

A DICTIONARY OF NAMES

Picotus (Pichotus), Petrus: French author of *De rheumatismo* (1577)
Pictiolus (Antonio Piccioli): Italian writer on chiromancy (1587)
Pierius: see Valerianus
Pilate, Pontius: Roman procurator (governor) of Judaea (26–36)
Pineda, Juan de (1558–1637): Spanish theologian and Biblical exegete
Pittacus of Mytilene (d. 570 B.C.): warrior and sage
Plato (427–347 B.C.): the foremost Greek philosopher
Plautus (254?–184 B.C.): Roman writer of comedies
Plempius, Vopiscus Fortunatus (1601–1671): Dutch medical writer
Plethon, Gemistus: see Gemistus Plethon
Pliny (23–79): Roman scholar, author of the uncritical encyclopedia *Natural History*
Plutarch (*c.* 46–*c.* 120): Greek biographer and philosopher
Pluto: the ruler of the infernal regions
Polonus, Martinus: see Martinus
Polydorus: see Vergil, P.
Polyphemus: the one-eyed Cyclops who imprisoned Ulysses and his companions (see *Odyssey*, IX, 105 ff.)
Pompey the Great (106–48 B.C.): Roman general and statesman
Pomponius Mela: see Mela
Poppaea (d. 65?): wife of Nero (q.v.)
Porphyry (*c.* 232–303): Neoplatonist philosopher
Porta: see della Porta
Porus (d. 321 B.C.): king of India
Posthumius: see next entry
Postumus: Gallic emperor (258–267)
Prasutagus (d. 61): king of the Iceni, husband of Boadicea (q.v.)
Prateolus (Gabriel Du Préau, 1511–1588): French theologian and translator
Prester John (i.e. 'Presbyter' John): legendary medieval Christian king of Asia (or 'Abyssinia', commonly confused with India)
Primerose, James (d. 1659): Scottish physician, author of *De vulgi erroribus in medicinae* (1639, trans. 1651)
Priscian (5th cent.): Latin grammarian
Procrustes: a mythical robber who mutilated his captives
Propertius (fl. *c.* 30–15 B.C.): Roman poet
Proteus: the sea god capable of changing his appearance at will
Psellus, Michael (*c.* 1019–*c.* 1078): Byzantine philosopher and historian
Ptolemy (2nd cent.): Alexandrian astronomer and geographer
Ptolemy II: king of Egypt (283–246 B.C.), commissioned the Septuagint for Alexandria's library
Ptolemy VI Philometor: king of Egypt (181–145 B.C.)
Ptolomy: see previous entries
Purchas, Samuel (1575?–1616): English author and collector of travel literature
Pythagoras (6th cent. B.C.): Greek philosopher and mathematician

Pythias: see Damon

Quintilian (1st cent.): Roman rhetorician and critic
Quintus Curtius (2nd cent.): Roman historian

Rabelais, François (1494?–1553): French satirist, author of *Gargantua et Pantagruel*
Radamanth: see Rhadamanth
Ralegh, Sir Walter (1552?–1618): English explorer, historian, poet, courtier
Ramusius (Giovanni Battista Ramusio, 1485–1557): Venetian diplomat and collector of travel literature
Rapha: the monstrous warrior described in 1 Chronicles 20.6
Raphael of Urbino (1483–1520): Italian painter and architect
Regiomontanus (Johann Müller of Königsberg, 1436–1476): see p. 78, note 90
Regulus, Marcus Atilius (d. 250 B.C.): Roman consul and general
Remus: twin brother of Romulus the founder of Rome
Reuben: Jacob's eldest son (see Genesis 29); also the tribe
Rhadamanth: a judge of the dead in Hades
Rhodiginus, Ludovicus (1450?–1525): Italian scholar
Ringo: i.e. Hringr Ingildsson, king of Sweden (cf. Harald)
Rollo (860?–931?): Norse chieftain, 1st Duke of Normandy
Romulus: the legendary founder of Rome; also, a Roman consul put to death by want of sleep
Rondelet(ius), Guillaume (1507–1566): French naturalist, professor of anatomy at Montpellier
Rudolph II: German emperor (1576–1612)

Salmanasser: see Shalmaneser
Salmasius, Claudius (1588–1653): French scholar
Salmoneus: see p. 449 note 9
Samaria: the capital of Northern Israel (to 722 B.C.)
Samson: the last of the great 'judges' (see Judges 13 ff.)
Sandys, George (1578–*c.* 1644): English poet and traveller
Sardanapalus (*c.* 822 B.C.): ruler of Assyria
Sarpi, Paolo (1552–1623): Venetian historian and theologian
Saturn (Cronos): the god of agriculture; also the planet
Saul: the first king of Israel
Saxo Grammaticus (1150?–1220?): Danish historian
Scaevola, G. Mucius: legendary Roman hero (6th cent. B.C.), 'saved his life by the patient tolleration of the burning of his hand' (Cockeram; see Livy, II, 12)
Scaliger, Joseph Justus (1540–1609): the great French scholar
Scaliger, Julius Caesar (1484–1558): Italian philosopher and scholar, father of the former
Scevola: see Scaevola

Scipio Major (237–183 B.C.): Roman general, defeated Hannibal in 202 B.C.

Scipio Mercurii: see Mercurii

Scribonius Largus: see Largus

Sedechias: see Zedekiah

Semiramis: legendary queen of Assyria

Sempronius: see Giggei

Seneca (c. 4 B.C.–A.D. 65): Roman statesman, philosopher and playwright

Seneca the Elder (54? B.C.–A.D. 39): Roman rhetorician, father of the former

Sennacherib: king of Assyria and Babylonia (705–681 B.C.), father of Esarhaddon (q.v.)

Septimius Severus: see Severus, Lucius Septimius

Serapis: a god of the lower world

Servius (4th cent.): Roman grammarian and commentator on Virgil

Seth: the third son of Adam

Severus, Lucius Septimius: Roman emperor (193–211)

Severus Alexander: see Alexander Severus

Shalmaneser V: king of Assyria (727–722 B.C.), besieged Samaria (q.v.)

Sibyl: any inspired prophetess

Sidney, Sir Philip (1554–1586): English courtier, poet and critic

Sidonius Apollinaris, St (c. 432 – c. 480): Bishop of Clermont, poet and letter-writer

Simonides (557?–467 B.C.): Greek lyric poet

Siren: any of the sea nymphs who lured sailors to their death by singing (see *Odyssey*, XII, 165 ff.)

Sisyphus: condemned to roll a stone uphill, only to have it roll back

Smith, John, the Cambridge Platonist (1618–1652): philosopher

Smyrnaeus: see Metrophanes

Socrates (470?–399 B.C.): Athenian philosopher and teacher

Sol (Helios): the sun god

Solinus, G. Julius (early 3rd cent.): Latin grammarian and encyclopedic author

Solomon: the third king of Israel, accepted as the author of Ecclesiastes, Proverbs, and Wisdom of Solomon

Solon (638?–558? B.C.): Athenian lawgiver

Solyman: see Suleiman

Somnus: i.e. Sleep

Starkatterus: i.e. Starkaòr the Old, a popular legendary figure

Statius (45?–96): Roman epic poet

Stentor: the herald of the loud voice (see *Iliad*, V, 785)

Stowe, John (1525–1605): English chronicler and antiquary

Strabo (c. 63 B.C.–c. A.D. 24): Greek geographer

Strebaeus (Jacques-Louis Strébée, fl. mid 16th cent.): French classical scholar

Suarez, Francisco de (1548–1617): Spanish Jesuit theologian, author of *Disputationes metaphysicae* (1597); see p. 77, note 85

A DICTIONARY OF NAMES

Sueno: see Sweyn Forkbeard
Suetonius (2nd cent.): Roman biographer and historian
Suetonius Paulinus, C.: Roman governor in Britain (59–61)
Suleiman 'the Magnificent': Ottoman emperor (1520–1566)
Sulla, Lucius Cornelius (138–78 B.C.): Roman general and dictator
Sweyn Forkbeard: king of Denmark (985?–1014) and conqueror of England
Sybilla: see Sibyl
Sydenham, Humphrey (1591–1650?): English divine and author
Sylla: see Sulla

Tacitus, Cornelius (52?–*post* 117): Roman orator, politician, historian
Tantalus: son of Jupiter; his punishment: eternal hunger and thirst
Tarquinius Priscus: the fifth king of Rome (617–578 B.C.)
Tartaret, Pierre (late 15th cent.): see p. 88, note 140
Tartarus: see Hades
Taurus: the northern constellation containing the Pleiades
Taylor, Jeremy (1613–1667): Anglican bishop and writer
Tellus: the Roman goddess of the earth
Tenison, Thomas: Archbishop of Canterbury (1694)
Tertullian (c. 160–c. 220): theologian, Father of the Latin Church
Tetricus: Gallic emperor (268–273), successor of Victorinus (q.v.)
Thales of Miletus (c. 640–546 B.C.): Greek philosopher and scientist
Themistocles (527?–460? B.C.): Athenian statesman and commander of the fleet at Salamis (480)
Theocritus (3rd cent. B.C.): Greek pastoral poet
Theodoret (c. 393–c. 458): Bishop of Cyrrhus, prolific exegete, historian, etc.
Theodoric: king of the Ostrogoths (475–526) and the Romans (493–526)
Theophrastus (d. c. 287 B.C.): Greek philosopher and naturalist
Thersites: the deformed and abusive Greek soldier (see *Iliad*, II, 212 ff.)
Theseus: the chief mythical hero of pre-classical Attica
Theudas: the leader of an unsuccessful Jewish insurrection (see Acts 5.36)
Thucydides (471?–400? B.C.): the greatest historian of antiquity
Tiberius: second emperor of Rome (14–37)
Tibullus, Albius (54?–18? B.C.): Roman elegiac poet
Timon (late 5th cent. B.C.): Athenian misanthrope
Tiresias: the blind Theban soothsayer
Tirinus, Jacobus (1580–1636): Flemish Jesuit ecclesiastical writer
Titius: see Tityus
Titus: Roman emperor (79–81)
Tityus: the giant punished by having vultures eat his liver
Trajan: Roman emperor (98–117)
Tremellius, Joannes Immanuel (1510–1580): Italian Hebrew scholar
Tricassus (Patricio Tricasso, 1480?–1550?): Italian chiromancer and physiognomist

Trismegistus: see Hermes Trismegistus
Tully: see Cicero
Twinus, J.: see next entry
Twyne, John (1501?–1581): English antiquary and author
Tycho: the god of chance (*tyche*)
Tzetzes, Joannes (12th cent.): Byzantine poet and grammarian

Ulfkell Snilling: leader of the East Anglian forces against Sweyn (q.v.) in 1004
Ulmus: see Olmo
Ulysses (Odysseus): the Greek warrior in *The Iliad*, and protagonist of *The Odyssey*
Unguinus: i.e. Yngvi, Swedish king, contemporary with Frotho (q.v.)
Upton, Nicholas (1400?–1457): English writer on heraldry and the art of war
Urban VIII: Pope (1623–1644)
Urbin: see Raphael

Valens: Eastern Roman emperor (364–378)
Valerianus (Piero Valeriano, 1477–1558): Italian scholar (*Hieroglyphica*, 1556 ff., etc.)
Valla, Lorenzo (*c.* 1406–1457): Italian scholar and humanist
van der Linden, Johannes: see Linden
Varro, Marcus Terentius (116–27 B.C.): Roman scholar
Vasthi (Vashti): wife of 'Ahasuerus' (see Esther 1.9 ff.)
Vegetius Renatus (fl. 385): Roman military writer
Venus (Aphrodite): Olympian goddess of love, beauty, etc.; also the planet
Vergil, Polydore (1470?–1555?): Italian historian of England
Vespasian: Roman emperor (69–79)
Victorinus: Gallic emperor (267–268), successor of Postumus (q.v.)
Victorius, Angelus: Italian author of *Medicae Consultationes* (1640)
Vigenère, Blaise de (1523–1596): French scholar
Virgil (70–19 B.C.): the greatest Roman poet
Virgil, Polydore: see Vergil
Virgilius, St (*c.* 700–784): Bishop of Salzburg and scholar; see p. 94, note 167
Vitruvius Pollio, Marcus (1st cent. B.C.): Roman architect and engineer
Volupia: the Roman goddess of sensual pleasure
Vulcan (Hephaestus): Olympian god of fire

Wayne, Charles: see Charles Wayne
William I (1027–1087): Norman duke, conqueror of England
Wormius, Olaus (1588–1654): Danish physician and scholar
Woverus (Johann von Wovern, 1574–1612): Dutch-German philologist

A DICTIONARY OF NAMES

Xenophon (*c.* 434–*c.* 355 B.C.): Greek historian and essayist
Xiphilinus, Joannes: Patriarch of Constantinople (1064–1075)

Zedekiah: king of Judah (see 2 Kings 24.17, Jeremiah 34.5 ff.)
Zeno of Citium (335–263 B.C.): founder of Stoicism
Zerubbabel: prince of Judah, restored God's worship (see Ezra 2.2., 3.2)
Zeus: see Jupiter
Zoilus: see p. 436, note 9
Zoroaster (fl. prob. 6th cent. B.C.): founder of Zoroastrianism, the religion of the ancient Persian peoples
Zorobabel: see Zerubbabel

BIBLIOGRAPHY

CONTENTS

ABBREVIATIONS

Biblical quotations are from *AV* unless otherwise indicated. Places of publication are given only if other than London or New York.

AV: The King James ('Authorised') Version of the Bible (1611)

BHM: *Bulletin of the History of Medicine*

Blount: Thomas Blount, *Glossographia: or a Dictionary* (1656)

Browne add.: Browne's marginal note, added in a later edition

Browne marg.: Browne's marginal note to the text

Browne suppl.: Browne's supplementary note to *Hydriotaphia* or *The Garden of Cyrus* (from the list appended to most copies of a reprint of the 1st edition later in 1658). The abbreviation concerns notes never reprinted; for those that were, see 'Browne add.'

BTB: Sir Geoffrey Keynes, *A Bibliography of Sir Thomas Browne*, 2nd rev. ed. (Oxford, 1968)

Bullokar: John Bullokar, *An English Expositor: . . . The Interpretation of the Hardest Words* (1616)

CJ: *Cambridge Journal*

Cockeram: Henry Cockeram, *The English Dictionarie* (1623)

Coleridge: *Coleridge on the Seventeenth Century*, ed. Roberta F. Brinkley (Durham, N.C., 1955), pp. 438–62

E: Norman J. Endicott (ed.), *The Prose of Sir Thomas Browne* (1967)

ELH: *Journal of English Literary History*

ELN: *English Language Notes*

ELR: *English Literary Renaissance*

Elyot: Sir Thomas Elyot, *Dictionary* (1538)

ES: *English Studies*

ESA: *English Studies in Africa*

G1: W. A. Greenhill (ed.), 'Religio Medici', 'A Letter to a Friend', 'Christian
   Morals' (1881)

G2: W. A. Greenhill (ed.), 'Hydriotaphia' and 'The Garden of Cyrus' (1896)

H: Frank L. Huntley (ed.), 'Hydriotaphia' and 'The Garden of Cyrus' (North-
   brook, Ill., 1966)

HLQ: *Huntington Library Quarterly*

HTR: *Harvard Theological Review*

JEGP: *Journal of English and German Philology*

JHI: *Journal of the History of Ideas*

JHM: *Journal of the History of Medicine and Allied Sciences*

K: Sir Geoffrey Keynes (ed.), *The Works of Sir Thomas Browne* (1964),
   4 vols.

Keck: (as below, p. 552)

M: L.C. Martin (ed.), 'Religio Medici' and Other Works (Oxford, 1964)

MLR: *Modern Language Review*

MP: *Modern Philology*

MSS.: The reading of one or more of the extant manuscripts

MSS. marg.: Marginal note to the text provided by one or more of the
   extant manuscripts

N&Q: *Notes and Queries*

OED: *The Oxford English Dictionary*

P: The Pembroke College manuscript of *Religio Medici* (ed. Jean-Jacques
   Denonain, *Une Version primitive de Religio Medici*, Paris, 1958)

PMLA: *Publications of the Modern Language Association*

PQ: *Philological Quarterly*

R: R. H. A. Robbins (ed.), 'Religio Medici', 'Hydriotaphia' and 'The Garden
   of Cyrus' (Oxford, 1972)

Ralegh: Sir Walter Ralegh, *The History of the World* (1614), ed. C.A.
   Patrides (1971)

RES: *Review of English Studies*

Ross: (as below, p. 552)

SCR: S. C. Roberts (as below, p. 556

SEL: *Studies in English Literature*

Septuagint: The Greek version of the Old Testament (3rd cent. B.C.?)

SJ: Dr Johnson's (?) notes to *Christian Morals*: see above, p. 11, note 3

SP: *Studies in Philology*

TLS: *Times Literary Supplement*

UA: The unauthorised edition of *Religio Medici* (1642)

UTQ: *University of Toronto Quarterly*

Vulgate: St Jerome's Latin version of the Bible (*c.* 384–404)

W: Simon Wilkin (ed.), *Sir Thomas Browne's Works* (1835–36), 4 vols.

A BIBLIOGRAPHICAL NOTE

For a general guide to studies of Browne and his contemporaries, consult the detailed entries in Douglas Bush (below, §20), pp. 461–668. The revised first volume of *The New Cambridge Bibliography of English Literature*, ed. George Watson (1974), is exhaustive but severely noncommittal. See further below, p. 547.

Annual bibliographies include: the English Association's *The Year's Work in English Studies* (1919 ff.); the Modern Humanities Research Association's *Annual Bibliography of English Language and Literature* (1920 ff.); *PMLA* (1922 ff.); *SP* (1922 ff.); and *SEL* (1961 ff.).

BACKGROUND STUDIES

§1. Allen, Don Cameron: *Doubt's Boundless Sea: Scepticism and Faith in the Renaissance* (Baltimore, 1964). With a chapter on 'atheism and atheists in the Renaissance'. Cf. §16.

§2. Allen, Don Cameron: *The Legend of Noah: Renaissance Rationalism in Art, Science and Letters* (Urbana, 1949).

§3. Allen, Phyllis: 'Medical Education in Seventeenth Century England', *JHM*, I (1946), 115–43.

§4. Allers, Rudolf: 'Microcosmus: From Anaximandros to Paracelsus', *Traditio*, II (1944), 319–407.

§5. Ashley, Maurice: *The Golden Century: Europe 1598–1715* (1969).

§6. Ashley, Maurice: *Life in Stuart England* (1964). Cf. §55.

§7. Ashton, Trevor (ed.): *Crisis in Europe 1560–1660* (1965).

§8. Aylmer, G.E.: *The Struggle for the Constitution 1603–1689* (1963; American edn: *A Short History of Seventeenth-Century England*).

§9. Baker, Herschel: *The Image of Man: A Study of the Idea of Human Dignity in Classical Antiquity, the Middle Ages, and the Renaissance* (1961; former title: *The Dignity of Man*, Cambridge, Mass., 1947), and *The Wars of Truth: Studies in the Decay of Christian Humanism in the Earlier Seventeenth Century* (1952).

§10. Baldwin, Thomas W.: *William Shakespeare's Small Latine and Lesse Greeke* (Urbana, 1944), 4 vols. Cf. §27.

§11. Bamborough, J. B.: *The Little World of Man* (1952). On Renaissance psychological theory.

§12. Bennett, H. S.: *English Books and Readers 1603 to 1640* (Cambridge, 1970).

§13. Bishop. W. J.: 'Some Medical Bibliophiles and their Libraries', *JHM*, III (1948), 229–62. Describes Browne's collection, pp. 255–8. Cf. §§181, 203.

§14. Blau, Joseph L.: *The Christian Interpretation of the Cabala in the Renaissance* (1944). Cf. W. J. Bouwsma, 'Postel and the Significance of Renaissance Cabalism', as below (§73), Ch. XI; also §§108, 109.

§15. Bolgar, R. R.: *The Classical Heritage and its Beneficiaries* (Cambridge, 1954).

§16. Bredvold, Louis I.: *The Intellectual Milieu of John Dryden* (Ann Arbor, 1934). On the traditions of scepticism; with some remarks on Browne, pp. 40–46. Cf. §1.

§17. Briggs, K. M.: *Pale Hecate's Team* (1962). On witchcraft during the English Renaissance. Cf. §88.

§18. Burns, Norman T.: *Christian Mortalism from Tyndale to Milton* (Cambridge, Mass., 1972). Cf. §§261, 272.

§19. Burtt, Edwin A.: *The Metaphysical Foundations of Modern Physical Science*, rev. ed. (1932). Cf. §70.

§20. Bush, Douglas: *English Literature in the Earlier Seventeenth Century*, 2nd rev. ed. (Oxford, 1962). The best single survey of Browne's age.

§21. Bush, Douglas: *The Renaissance and English Humanism* (Toronto, 1939).

§22. Bush, Douglas: 'Two Roads to Truth: Science and Religion in the Early Seventeenth Century', *ELH*, VIII (1941), 81–102. Cf. §§69, 127.

§23. Butler, Christopher: *Number Symbolism* (1970).

§24. Carré, Meyrick H.: 'The New Philosophy', in his *Phases of Thought in England* (Oxford, 1949), Ch. VII. A survey of seventeenth-century philosophy.

§25. Cassirer, Ernst: *The Platonic Renaissance in England*, trans. J. P. Pettegrove (1953). Cf. §98.

§26. Castiglioni, Arturo: *The Renaissance of Medicine in Italy* (Baltimore, 1934), and 'The Medical School at Padua and the Renaissance of Medicine', *Annals of Medical History*, n.s., VII (1935), 214–17.

§27. Charlton, Kenneth: *Education in Renaissance England* (1965). A comprehensive survey. Cf. §§10, 36, 67, 84.

§28. Clark, Sir George: *The Seventeenth Century*, 2nd ed. (Oxford, 1947).

§29. Clements, Robert J.: *Picta Poesis: Literary and Humanistic Theory in Renaissance Emblem Books* (Rome, 1960).

§30. Cochrane, Eric (ed.): *The Late Italian Renaissance 1525–1630* (1970).

§31. Colie, Rosalie L.: *Paradoxia Epidemica: The Renaissance Tradition of Paradox* (Princeton, 1966).

§32. Collinson, Patrick: *The Elizabethan Puritan Movement* (1967). Cf. §52.

§33. Craig, Hardin: *The Enchanted Glass: The Renaissance Mind in English Literature* (1936), and its sequel, *New Lamps for Old* (1960). Studies in the cross-currents of ideas.

§34. Crombie, A.C.: *Augustine to Galileo: The History of Science, A.D. 400–1650*, new ed. (1957). Cf. §50.

§35. Cruickshank, John (ed.): *French Literature and its Background*, Vol. II: *The Seventeenth Century* (Oxford, 1969). Cf. §§80, 119.

§36. Curtis, Mark H.: *Oxford and Cambridge in Transition, 1558–1642* (Oxford, 1959). Cf. §27.

§37. Davies, R. Trevor: *The Golden Century of Spain 1501–1621* (1937), and *Spain in Decline 1621–1700* (1957).

§38. Debus, G. Allen: *The English Paracelsians* (1965).

§39. Debus, G. Allen (ed.): *Medicine in 17th Century England* (Berkeley, 1974). With 15 comprehensive essays; on Browne see esp. pp. 116–17, 197–200, 343–5.

§40. Debus, G. Allen (ed.): *Science, Medicine and Society in the Renaissance* (1972), 2 vols. with 38 wide-ranging essays.

§41. Delany, Paul: *British Autobiography in the Seventeenth Century* (1969). Cf. §113.

§42. Dieckmann, Liselotte: *Hieroglyphics: The History of a Literary Symbol* (St Louis, 1970). With a section on Browne, pp. 109–15.

§43. Doran, Madeleine: 'On Elizabethan "Credulity", with some questions concerning the use of the marvelous in literature', *JHI*, I (1940), 151–76.

§44. Farmer, David L.: *Britain and the Stuarts* (1965).

§45. Finney, Gretchen L.: *Musical Backgrounds for English Literature: 1580–1650* (New Brunswick, N.J., 1962).

§46. Friedrich, Carl J.: *The Age of the Baroque 1610–1660* (1952).

§47. Garin, Eugenio: *Italian Humanism*, trans. Peter Munz (1965).

§48. Geyl, Peter: *The Netherlands in the Seventeenth Century* (1936–64), 2 vols.

§49. Grierson, Sir Herbert: *Cross-Currents in English Literature of the Seventeenth Century* (1929).

§50. Hall, A. Rupert: *From Galileo to Newton, 1630–1720* (1963). Cf. §34.

§51. Hall, Marie Boas: *The Scientific Renaissance 1450–1630* (1962). Cf. §34.

§52. Haller, William: *The Rise of Puritanism* (1938), and *Liberty and Reformation in the Puritan Revolution* (1955). Cf. §32.

§53. Harris, Victor: *All Coherence Gone* (Chicago, 1949). On the belief in nature's decay.

§54. Harrison, Charles T.: 'The Ancient Atomists and English Literature of the Seventeenth Century', *Harvard Studies in Classical Philology*, XLV (1934), 1–79.

§55. Hart, Roger: *English Life in the Seventeenth Century* (1970). Cf. §6.

§56. Heninger, S.K., Jr: *Touches of Sweet Harmony: Pythagorean Cosmology and Renaissance Poetics* (San Marino, Calif., 1974).

§57. Heninger, S.K., Jr: 'Tudor Literature of the Physical Sciences', *HLQ*, XXXII (1969), 101–33, 249–70.

§58. Hill, Christopher: *The Century of Revolution 1603–1714* (Edinburgh, 1961).

§59. Hoeninger, F.D. and J.F.M.: *The Growth of Natural History in Stuart England from Gerard to the Royal Society* ('Folger Booklets on Tudor and Stuart Civilization', 1969).

§60. Hoopes, Robert: *Right Reason in the English Renaissance* (Cambridge, Mass., 1962).

§61. Houghton, Walter E.: 'The English Virtuoso in the Seventeenth Century', *JHI*, III (1942), 51–73, 190–219.

§62. Howell, Wilbur S.: *Logic and Rhetoric in England, 1500–1700* (Princeton, 1956).

§63. Hunter, William B., Jr: 'The Seventeenth Century Doctrine of Plastic Nature', *HTR*, XLIII (1950), 197–213.

§64. Johnson, Francis R.: *Astronomical Thought in Renaissance England* (Baltimore, 1937); also, 'Astronomical Text-books in the Sixteenth Century', as below (§92), I, 285–302. Cf. §74.

§65. Jones, Richard F.: *Ancients and Moderns: A Study of the Rise of the Scientific Movement in Seventeenth-Century England*, 2nd ed. (1961).

§66. Jordan, Wilbur K.: *The Development of Religious Toleration in England* (1932–40), 4 vols. With a discussion of Browne, II, 446–53.

§67. Kearney, Hugh: *Scholars and Gentlemen: Universities and Society in Pre-Industrial Britain* (1970). Cf. §27.

§68. Knights, L.C.: *Drama and Society in the Age of Jonson* (1937).

§69. Kocher, Paul H.: *Science and Religion in Elizabethan England* (San Marino, Calif., 1953). Cf. §127.

§70. Koyré, Alexandre: *From the Closed World to the Infinite Universe* (Baltimore, 1957). Cf. §19.

§71. Kristeller, Paul O.: *Studies in Renaissance Thought and Letters* (Rome, 1956); also *Renaissance Thought: I* (1961) and *II* (1965).

§72. Kristeller, Paul O.: *The Philosophy of Marsilio Ficino*, trans. Virginia Conant (1943). Cf. §§56, 111, 135.

§73. Kristeller, Paul O., and Philip P. Weiner (eds.): *Renaissance Essays* (1968).

§74. Kuhn, Thomas S.: *The Copernican Revolution: Planetary Astronomy in the Development of Western Thought* (Cambridge, Mass., 1957), Cf. §64.

§75. Lewis, C.S.: *The Discarded Image: An Introduction to Medieval and Renaissance Literature* (Cambridge, 1964). Cf. §133.

§76. Lockyer, Roger: *Tudor and Stuart Britain 1471–1714* (1964).

§77. Lovejoy, Arthur O.: *The Great Chain of Being* (Cambridge, Mass., 1936). Cf. §94.

§78. McAdoo, H.R.: *The Spirit of Anglicanism: A Survey of Anglican Theological Method in the Seventeenth Century* (1965). Cf. §83.

§79. Macpherson, C.B.: *The Political Theory of Possessive Individualism: Hobbes to Locke* (Oxford, 1962). Cf. §82.

§80. Maland, David: *Culture and Society in Seventeenth Century France* (1970). Cf. §114.

§81. Mazzeo, Joseph A.: *Renaissance and Revolution: Backgrounds to Seventeenth-Century English Literature* (1965).

§82. Mintz, Samuel I.: *The Hunting of Leviathan: Seventeenth-Century Reactions to the Materialism and Moral Philosophy of Thomas Hobbes* (Cambridge, 1962).

§83. More, Paul E., and Frank L. Cross (eds.): *Anglicanism: The Thought and Practice of the Church of England* (1935). Cf. §78.

§84. Mulder, John R.: *The Temple of the Mind: Education and Literary Taste in Seventeenth-Century England* (1969). Cf. §27.

§85. Nicolson, Marjorie H.: *Science and Imagination* (Ithaca, N.Y., 1956).

§86. Nicolson, Marjorie H.: *The Breaking of the Circle: Studies in the Effect of the 'New Science' upon Seventeenth-Century Poetry*, rev. ed. (1960).

§87. Nicolson, Marjorie H.: 'The Early Stages of Cartesianism in England', *SP*, XXVI (1929), 356–74.

§88. Notestein, Wallace: *A History of Witchcraft in England* (Washington, 1911). Cf. §17.

§89. O'Connell, Marvin R.: *The Counter-Reformation, 1560–1610* (1974).

§90. Ogg, David: *Europe in the Seventeenth Century*, 8th ed. (1961).

§91. Ornstein, Martha: *The Rôle of Scientific Societies in the Seventeenth Century*, 3rd ed. (Chicago, 1938).

§92. Pagel, Walter: 'The Reaction to Aristotle in Seventeenth-Century Biological Thought', in *Science, Medicine and History*, ed. E. Ashworth Underwood (1953), I, 489–509.

§93. Patrides, C.A.: *The Grand Design of God: The Literary Form of the Christian View of History* (1972).

§94. Patrides, C.A.: 'Renaissance Thought on the Celestial Hierarchy', *JHI*, XX (1959), 155–66, and 'Hierarchy and Order', in *Dictionary of the History of Ideas*, ed. Philip P. Wiener (1973), II, 434–49. Cf. §77.

§95. Patrides, C.A.: *Milton and the Christian Tradition* (Oxford, 1966). On the period's theological horizons.

§96. Patrides, C.A.: 'Renaissance and Modern Thought on the Last Things: A Study in Changing Conceptions', *HTR*, LI (1958), 169–85; and 'Renaissance and Modern Views on Hell', *HTR*, LVII (1964), 217–36.

§97. Patrides, C.A.: 'Renaissance Estimates of the Year of Creation', *HLQ*, XXVI (1963), 315–22.

§98. Patrides, C.A. (ed.): *The Cambridge Platonists* (1969). Cf. §25.

§99. Pennington, D.H.: *Seventeenth Century Europe* (1970).

§100. Powell, Chilton L.: *English Domestic Relations 1487–1653* (1917).

§101. Quinones, Ricardo J.: *The Renaissance Discovery of Time* (Cambridge, Mass., 1972).

§102. Raven, Charles E.: *English Naturalists from Neckham to Ray* (Cambridge, 1947).

§103. Raven, Charles E.: *Natural Religion and Christian Theology*, 1st Series (Cambridge, 1953).

§104. Rhys, Hedley H. (ed.): *Seventeenth-Century Science and the Arts* (Princeton, 1961).

§105. Robb, Nesca: *Neoplatonism of the Italian Renaissance* (1935). Cf. §72.

§106. Roots, Ivan: *The Great Rebellion 1642–1660* (1966).

§107. Schmitt, Charles B.: 'Perennial Philosophy: From Agostino Steuco to Leibniz', *JHL*, XXVII (1966), 505–32.

§108. Scholem, Gershom G.: *Major Trends in Jewish Mysticism*, rev. ed. (1946), and *On the Kabbalah and its Symbolism*, trans. R. Manheim (1965). The best studies of cabbalistic thought. Cf. next entry.

§109. Secret, François: *Les Kabbalistes chrétiens de la Renaissance* (Paris, 1964). Cf. previous entry.

§110. Sells, Arthur L.: *The Paradise of Travellers: The Italian Influence on Englishmen in the Seventeenth Century* (1964). Cf. §114.

§111. Shumaker, Wayne: *The Occult Sciences in the Renaissance* (Berkeley, 1972).

§112. Smith, A.G.R.: *Science and Society in the Sixteenth and Seventeenth Centuries* (1972).

§113. Stauffer, Donald A.: *English Biography before 1700* (Cambridge, Mass., 1930). Cf. §41.

§114. Stoye, John W.: *English Travellers Abroad, 1604–1667: Their Influence in English Society and Politics* (1952). Cf. §110.

§115. Svendsen, Kester: *Milton and Science* (Cambridge, Mass., 1956). Cf. §§34, 51.

§116. Temkin, Owsei: *Galenism: Rise and Decline of a Medical Philosophy* (Ithaca, N.Y., 1973).

§117. Thorndike, Lynn: *A History of Magic and Experimental Science* (1941–1958), Vols. V–VIII. On the sixteenth and seventeenth centuries.

§118. Trapp, J.B. (ed.): *Background to the English Renaissance* (1974). Six lectures.

§119. Treasure, G.R.R.: *Seventeenth Century France* (1966). Cf. §80.

§120. Trinkaus, Charles: *In Our Image and Likeness: Humanity and Divinity in Italian Humanistic Thought* (1970), 2 vols.

§121. Tulloch, John: *Rational Theology and Christian Philosophy in England in the Seventeenth Century*, rev. ed. (Edinburgh, 1874), 2 vols. Still a reliable account.

§122. Walker, D.P.: *The Decline of Hell: Seventeenth-Century Discussions of Eternal Torment* (1964).

§123. Walker, D.P.: 'Orpheus the Theologian and Renaissance Platonism', *Journal of the Warburg and Courtauld Institutes*, XVI (1953), 100–20; repr. in his *The Ancient Theology* (1972), Ch. I.

§124. Warnke, Frank J.: *Versions of Baroque: European Literature in the 17th Century* (New Haven, 1972).

§125. Weidhorn, Manfred: *Dreams in Seventeenth-Century English Literature* (The Hague, 1970).

§126. West, Robert H.: *Milton and the Angels* (Athens, Ga., 1955). On the period's angelology.

§127. Westfall, Richard S.: *Science and Religion in Seventeenth-Century England* (New Haven, 1958), Cf. §69.

§128. Willey, Basil: *The Seventeenth-Century Background* (1934).

§129. Willey, Basil: 'The Touch of Cold Philosophy', as below (§155), pp. 369–76.

§130. Williams, Arnold: *The Common Expositor: An Account of the Commentaries on Genesis, 1527–1633* (Chapel Hill, 1948).

§131. Williamson, George: *Seventeenth Century Contexts* (1960).

§132. Wilson, Charles: *England's Apprenticeship 1603–1763* (1965).

§133. Wilson, F.P.: *Elizabethan and Jacobean* (Oxford, 1945). An introduction to the period of transition. Cf. §75.

§134. Wright, Louis B.: *Middle-Class Culture in Elizabethan England* (Chapel Hill, 1935).

§135. Yates, Frances A.: *Giordano Bruno and the Hermetic Tradition* (1964). The best survey of Renaissance hermetic thought.

§136. Zagorin, Perez: *The Court and the Country: The Beginnings of the English Revolution* (1969).

THE PROSE OF THE ENGLISH RENAISSANCE

General Studies

[The following list includes general as well as particular studies of representative prose writers from the late sixteenth to the late seventeenth centuries. For other studies of individual authors, consult the bibliographies in *Seventeenth Century English Prose*, ed. David Novarr (1967), pp. 485–527, and in Douglas Bush, as above, §20. For Milton, see the bibliography in his *Selected Prose*, ed. C.A. Patrides (Penguin Books, 1974), pp. 411 ff.]

§137. Adolph, Robert: *The Rise of Modern Prose Style* (Cambridge, Mass., 1968). With some remarks on *Religio Medici*, pp. 153–6.

§138. Babb, Lawrence: *Sanity in Bedlam: A Study of Robert Burton's 'Anatomy of Melancholy'* (East Lansing, 1959).

§139. Barish, Jonas A.: 'Baroque Prose in the Theater of Ben Jonson', *PMLA*, LXXIII (1958), 184–95.

§140. Barish, Jonas A.: 'The Prose Style of John Lyly', *ELH*, XXIII (1956), 14–35.

§141. Beum, Robert: 'The Scientific Affinities of English Baroque Prose', *English Miscellany*, XIII (1962), 59–80.

§142. Boughner, Daniel C.: 'Notes on Hooker's Prose', *RES*, XV (1939), 194–200. Cf. §153.

§143. Brinkley, Roberta F. (ed.): as above (p. 537), pp. 411–500. Coleridge's remarks on the period's prose style generally, but also on Browne, Bunyan, Burton, Donne, Milton, *et al.*

§144. Carey, John: 'Sixteenth and Seventeenth Century Prose', in *English Poetry and Prose, 1540–1674*, ed. Christopher Ricks (1970), Ch. XII.

§145. Crane, William G.: *Wit and Rhetoric in the Renaissance: The Formal Basis of Elizabethan Prose Style* (1973).

§146. Croll, Morris W.: *Style, Rhetoric, and Rhythm*, ed. J. Max Patrick *et al.* (Princeton, 1966). Important essays on Renaissance prose and rhetoric.

§147. Crook, Margaret B., *et al.*: *The Bible and its Literary Associations* (1937).

§148. Daiches, David: *The King James Version of the English Bible* (Chicago, 1941).

§149. Eliot, T.S.: 'Lancelot Andrewes' (1926), in his *Selected Essays* (1932), pp. 299–310. Cf. §162.

§150. Elton, Oliver: 'English Prose Numbers', in his *A Sheaf of Papers* (1922), pp. 130–63. Cf. §§209, 222, 229.

§151. Fish, Stanley (ed.): *Seventeenth-Century Prose: Modern Essays in Criticism* (1971).

§152. Gordon, Ian A.: *The Movement of English Prose* (1966), Ch. VII–XII.

§153. Hill, W. Speed: 'The Authority of Hooker's Style', *SP*, LXVII (1970), 328–38. Cf. §142.

§154. Howell, A.C.: '*Res et Verba*: Words and Things', *ELH*, XIII (1946), 131–43; repr. in §151.

§155. Jones, Richard F.: *The Seventeenth Century* (Stanford, 1951). With four essays on prose style, two of them repr. in §151.

§156. Kranidas, Thomas: 'Milton and the Rhetoric of Zeal', *Texas Studies in Literature and Language*, VI (1965), 423–32; also in his *The Fierce Equation* (The Hague, 1965).

§157. Krapp, George P.: *The Rise of English Literary Prose* (1915). An introductory historical survey.

§158. Lewis, C.S.: *The Literary Impact of the Authorized Version* (1950); repr. with other essays in *The Bible read as Literature*, ed. Mary E. Reid (Cleveland, 1959). Cf. §147.

§159. Lowes, John Livingston: 'The Noblest Monument of English Prose', in his *Essays in Appreciation* (Boston, 1936), pp. 3–31. On the King James version of the Bible (1611). Cf. previous entry.

§160. Mazzeo, Joseph A.: 'Seventeenth-Century English Prose Style: The Quest for a Natural Style', *Mosaic*, VI (1973), iii, 107–44. On Browne, pp. 124–8.

§161. Miner, Earl: 'Inclusive and Exclusive Decorums in Seventeenth-Century Prose', *Language and Style*, V (1972), 192–203.

§162. Mitchell, W. Fraser: *English Pulpit Oratory from Andrewes to Tillotson* (1932).

§163. Mueller, William R.: *John Donne: Preacher* (Princeton, 1962). Cf. previous entry.

§164. Sharrock, Roger: *John Bunyan* (1954).

§165. Stapleton, Laurence: 'John Donne: The Moment of the Sermon', in her *The Elected Circle: Studies in the Art of Prose* (Princeton, 1973), Ch. I. Cf. §§162, 163, 168.

§166. Stedmont, J.M.: 'English Prose of the Seventeenth Century', *Dalhousie Review*, XXX (1950), 269–78.

§167. Vickers, Brian: *Francis Bacon and Renaissance Prose* (Cambridge, 1968).

§168. Webber, Joan: *Contrary Music: The Prose Style of John Donne* (Madison, 1963).

§169. Webber, Joan: *The Eloquent 'I': Style and Self in Seventeenth-Century Prose* (Madison, 1968). Essays on Baxter, Browne, Bunyan, Burton, Donne, Lilburne, Milton, and Traherne.

§170. White, Helen C.: *English Devotional Literature, Prose, 1600–1640* (Madison, 1931). A survey.

§171. Williamson, George: *The Senecan Amble: A Study in Prose Form from Bacon to Collier* (1951).

§172. Williamson, George: 'Senecan Style in the Seventeenth Century', in his *Milton and Others* (1965), Ch. XII; repr. in §151.

§173. Wilson, F.P.: *Seventeenth Century Prose* (Berkeley, 1960). Lectures on Browne, Burton, biography, and the sermon. Cf. §133.

STUDIES OF BROWNE

The principal editions of the collated *Works* are *W* and *K*; and of selected writings: *M*, *E*, and Sir Geoffrey Keynes (1968). See also the entries below, pp. 551, 553, 554, 555.

The major bibliographical guides to Browne are: *BTB*; Olivier Leroy, *A French Bibliography of Sir Thomas Browne* (1931); and Dennis G. Donovan in *Elizabethan Supplements X* (1968) as well as in 'Recent Studies in Browne', *ELR*, II (1972), 271–9. See also above, p. 539.

Biographies rely in the first instance on John Whitefoot's 'Some Minutes for the Life of Sir Thomas Browne', in Browne's *Posthumous Works* (1712), pp. xxiv–xxxvii; quoted at length by Samuel Johnson, above, pp. 502–5. Between Whitefoot and Johnson intervened Andrew Kippis with an account in his *Biographia Britannica*, 2nd ed. (1730), II, 627–37, which superseded Anthony à Wood's earlier but highly eclectic sketch in *Athenæ Oxonienses* (ed. Philip Bliss [1820], IV, 56–9).

For modern biographies of Browne, see §§176, 190, 198. His birth on 19 October 1605 occurred, according to Johnstone Parr, between 8:11 and 9:02 a.m.! (*ELN*, XI [1973], 44–6). Miriam M. Tildesley's discussion of *Sir Thomas Browne: his Skull, Portraits, and Ancestry* (Cambridge, 1927) is reprinted from *Biometrica*, XV (1923), 3–76, and abstracted in the appendix to §190. What little is known of Browne at Leyden is cited by R.W. Innes Smith, *English-Speaking Students of Medicine at the University of Leyden* (Edinburgh, 1932); cf. Frank L. Huntley, 'Sir Thomas Browne's Leyden Thesis', *TLS*, 8 May 1953, p. 301. Jac. G. Riewald in 'Sir Thomas Browne's Supposed Visit to the Continent', *ES*, XXVIII (1947), 171–3, denies that Browne visited Holland in 1665. A more important and much misunderstood episode in his life is placed in its correct perspective by Malcolm Letts in 'Sir Thomas Browne and Witchcraft', *N&Q*, 11th Series, V (1912), 221–3, and especially by Dorothy Tyler in 'A Review of the Interpretation of Sir Thomas Browne's Part in a Witch Trial in 1664', *Anglia*, LIV (1930), 179–95. Finally, Margaret Toynbee considers 'Some Friends of Sir Thomas Browne', in *Norfolk Archaeology*, XXXI (1957), 377–94.

The most indispensable record of Browne's stupendous learning is *A Catalogue of the Libraries of the Learned Sir Thomas Brown, and Dr Edward Brown, his Son* (1711).

General Studies

[In addition to the studies listed below, see §§16, 20, 31, 42, 81, 88, 95, 96, 111, 115, 130, 151, 171, 173, etc.]

§174. Anderton, Basil: 'Sir Thomas Browne', in his *Sketches from a Library Window* (Cambridge, 1922), Ch. VIII. On the prose rhythm.

§175. Anon: 'Sir Thomas Browne', *TLS*, 24 May 1928 (pp. 365–86); partly reprinted in §214.

§176. Bennett, Joan: *Sir Thomas Browne* (Cambridge, 1962). Highly recommended.

§177. Bischoff, Dietrich: *Sir Thomas Browne als Stilkünstler: Ein Beitrag zur Deutung der englischen Barockliteratur* (Heidelberg, 1943).

§178. Blau, Joseph I.: 'Browne's Interest in Cabalism', *PMLA*, XLIX (1934), 963–64. Cf. §14.

§179. Brown, Huntington: *Rabelais in English Literature* (Cambridge, Mass., 1933), pp. 105–10.

§180. Bulwer-Lytton, Edward: 'Sir Thomas Browne', in his *Quarterly Essays* (1875), pp. 137–75. An appreciation.

§181. Cawley, Robert R.: 'Sir Thomas Browne and his Reading', in *Studies in Sir Thomas Browne*, ed. R.R. Cawley and G. Yost (Eugene, Oregon, 1965), pp. 104–66; revised from *PMLA*, XLVIII (1933), 426–70. Cf. §178.

§182. Chalmers, Gordon K.: 'Hieroglyphs and Sir Thomas Browne', *Virginia Quarterly Review*, XXI (1935), 547–60, and 'That Universal and Public Manuscript', ibid., XXVI (1950), 414–30. Cf. §§275–77.

§183. Coleridge, Samuel Taylor: as above (p. 537).

§184. Denonain, Jean-Jacques: *La Personnalité de Sir Thomas Browne: Essai d'application de la caractérologie à la critique et l'histoire littéraires* (Paris, 1959).

§185. De Quincey, Thomas: *Rhetoric*, in his *Collected Writings*, ed. David Masson (1897), X, esp. pp. 104–5, as well as in *De Quincey's Literary Criticism*, ed. Helen Darbishire (1909), esp. p. 55. Also in §174.

§186. Dowden, Edward: 'Sir Thomas Browne', in his *Puritan and Anglican: Studies in Literature* (1900), Ch. II.

§187. Dunn, William P.: *Sir Thomas Browne: A Study in Religious Philosophy*, 2nd ed. (Minneapolis, 1950).

§188. Dutt, William A.: 'Sir Thomas Browne and Bishop Hall', in his *Some Literary Associations of East Anglia* (1907), Ch. VIII. An appreciation.

§189. Finch, Jeremiah S.: 'The Humanity of Sir Thomas Browne', *Bulletin of the New York Academy of Medicine*, XXVII (1951), 521–30. An appreciation.

§190. Finch, Jeremiah S.: *Sir Thomas Browne: A Doctor's Life of Science and Faith* (1950, repr. 1961).

§191. Fisch, Harold: *Jerusalem and Albion: The Hebraic Factor in Seventeenth-Century Literature* (1964), pp. 46–8, 206–10.

§192. Gosse, Sir Edmund: *Sir Thomas Browne* (1905). Cf. Strachey's adverse review (§227).

§193. Green, Peter: *Sir Thomas Browne* ('Writers and their Work', 1959).

§194. Hazlitt, William: *Lectures chiefly on the Dramatic Literature of the Age of Elizabeth* (1820), pp. 292–306.

§195. Howell, A.C.: 'A note on Sir Thomas Browne's Knowledge of Languages', *SP*, XXII (1925), 412–17. See above, p. 147, note 64.

§196. Howell, A.C.: 'Sir Thomas Browne as Wit and Humorist', *SP*, XLII (1945), 564–77.

§197. Huntley, Frank L.: 'A Garland for Sir Thomas Browne, M.D., Knight', *Michigan Alumnus Quarterly Review*, LXIII (Dec. 1956), 23–33. An appreciation.

§198. Huntley, Frank L.: *Sir Thomas Browne: A Biographical and Critical Study* (Ann Arbor, 1962). Highly recommended.

§199. Huntley, Frank L.: 'Sir Thomas Browne, M.D., William Harvey, and the Metaphor of the Circle', *BHM*, XXV (1951), 236–47, and 'Sir Thomas Browne and the Metaphor of the Circle', *JHI*, XIV (1953), 353–64.

§200. Hutchinson, G.E.: 'Tuba mirum spargens sonum', in his *The Itinerant Ivory Tower: Scientific and Literary Essays* (New Haven, 1953), pp. 186–98.

§201. King, James Roy: 'Sir Thomas Browne: Scientific Data and Mystical Experience', in his *Studies in Six Seventeenth-Century Writers* (Athens, Ohio, 1966), Ch. III. Cf. §242.

§202. Leroy, Olivier: *Le Chevalier Thomas Browne (1605–82), médecin, styliste & métaphysicien* (Paris, 1931).

§203. Letts, M.: 'Sir Thomas Browne and his Books', *N&Q*, 11th Series, X (1914), 321–3, 342–4, 361–2. On the 1711 sale catalogue (above, p. 547).

§204. Löffler, Azno: *Sir Thomas Browne als Virtuoso: Die Bedeutung der Gelehrsamkeit für sein literarisches Alterswerk* (Nuremberg, 1972).

§205. Loiseau, J.: 'Sir Thomas Browne écrivain "métaphysique",' *Revue anglo-américaine*, X (1933), 385–98.

§206. Merton, Egon S.: *Science and Imagination in Sir Thomas Browne* (1949). Highly recommended, Cf. §§ 284–9

§207. Merton, E.S.: 'Sir Thomas Browne on Astronomy', *History of Ideas News Letter*, IV (1958), 83–6.

§208. Merton, E.S.: 'Sir Thomas Browne's Interpretation of Dreams', *PQ*, XXVIII (1949), 497–503.

§209. Moloney, Michael F.: 'Metres and *Cursus* in Sir Thomas Browne's Prose', *JEGP*, LVIII (1959), 60–67.

§210. Moran, Berna: 'Sir Thomas Browne's Reading on the Turks', *N&Q*, CXCVII (1952), 380–82, 403–6.

§211. More, Paul Elmer: 'Sir Thomas Browne', in his *Shelburne Essays*, 6th Series: *Studies of Religious Dualism* (1909), pp. 154–86.

§212. Morgan, Edwin: ' "Strong Lines" and Strong Minds: Reflections on the Prose of Browne and Johnson', *CJ*, IV (1951), 481–91.

§213. Nathanson, Leonard: *The Strategy of Truth: A Study of Sir Thomas Browne* (Chicago, 1967). The chapter on *Hydriotaphia* is reprinted in §151.

§214. Needham, Joseph: *The Great Amphibium: Four Lectures on the Position of Religion in a World Dominated by Science* (1931). With some remarks on Browne, pp. 45–50.

§215. Needham, Joseph: 'Thomas Browne and the Beginning of Chemical Embryology', in his *A History of Embryology* (Cambridge, 1934), pp. 110–12.

§216. Olivero, Federico: 'Sir Thomas Browne', in his *Studi britannici* (Turin, 1931), pp. 57–101.

§217. Osler, Sir William: 'Sir Thomas Browne', in his *An Alabama Student and Other Biographical Essays* (Oxford, 1908), pp. 248–77; also in his *Selected Writings* (1951), Ch. IV. An appreciation.

§218. Pater, Walter: 'Sir Thomas Browne', in his *Appreciations* (1889), pp. 127–66.

§219. Phelps, Gilbert: 'The Prose of Donne and Browne', in *From Donne to Marvell*, being *A Guide to English Literature*, ed. Boris Ford, III (1956), 116–30.

§220. Praz, Mario: 'Sir Thomas Browne', *ES*, XI (1929), 161–71.

§221. Raven, Charles E.: 'The Coming of Modern Man: *Religio Medici*', as above (§102), Ch. XVIII.

§222. Saintsbury, George: *A History of English Prose Rhythm* (1912), pp. 181–200. Cf. §174.

§223. Schultz, Howard: *Milton and Forbidden Knowledge* (1955), pp. 57–64.

§224. Sencourt, Robert: *Outflying Philosophy* (Hildesheim, 1925). 'A literary study of the religious element' in Donne, Browne, and Vaughan.

§225. Stapleton, Laurence: 'Sir Thomas Browne and Meditative Prose', as above (§165), Ch. II.

§226. Stephen, Sir Leslie: 'Sir Thomas Browne', in his *Hours in a Library*, 2nd Series (1876), Ch. I.

§227. Strachey, Lytton: 'Sir Thomas Browne', in his *Books and Characters French and English* (1922), pp. 31–44. Highly recommended.

§228. Symonds, John Addington: 'Sir Thomas Browne', in his edition of *Religio Medici* etc. (1886), pp. vii–xxxi.

§229. Tempest, Norton R.: 'Rhythm in the Prose of Sir Thomas Browne', *RES*, III (1927), 308–18. Cf. §307.

§230. Texte, Joseph: 'La descendance de Montaigne: Sir Thomas Browne', in his *Études de littérature européenne* (Paris, 1898), pp. 51–93. Cf. §16.

§231. Thaler, Alwin: 'Shakspere and Sir Thomas Browne', in his *Shakspere's Silences* (Cambridge, Mass., 1929), Ch. III. On Shakespeare's 'unmistakable influence' on Browne.

§232. Thaler, Alwin: 'Sir Thomas Browne and the Elizabethans', *SP*, XXVIII (1931), 87–117.

§233. Wallerstein, Ruth: *Studies in Seventeenth-Century Poetic* (Madison,

1950), pp. 244–56.

§234. Warren, Austin: 'The Style of Sir Thomas Browne', *Kenyon Review*, XIII (1951), 674–87; repr. in his *Connections* (Ann Arbor, 1970), pp. 11–23, and in §151. Highly recommended.

§235. Whallon, William: 'Hebraic Synonymy in Sir Thomas Browne', *ELH*, XXVIII (1961), 335–52. On the 'parallelism' of his prose.

§236. Whibley, Charles: 'Sir Thomas Browne', in his *Essays in Biography* (1913), pp. 277–311. An appreciation.

§237. Wiley, Margaret L.: 'Sir Thomas Browne and the Genesis of Paradox', *JHI*, IX (1948), 303–22; repr. in her *The Subtle Knot: Creative Scepticism in Seventeenth-Century England* (1952), Ch. V.

§238. Willey, Basil: 'A Note on Sir Thomas Browne as a Moralist', in his *The English Moralists* (1964), Ch. XII.

§239. Willey, Basil: 'Sir Thomas Browne', as above (§128). Ch. III–IV.

§240. Withington, Robert: 'Religio duorum medicorum', *International Journal of Ethics*, XLIII (1932–3), 413–28. An appreciation of Browne and Oliver Wendell Holmes.

§241. Yost, George: 'Sir Thomas Browne and Aristotle', in *Studies* (as above, §181), pp. 41–103.

§242. Ziegler, Dewey K.: *In Divided and Distinguished Worlds: Religion and Rhetoric in the Writings of Sir Thomas Browne* (Cambridge, Mass., 1943).

§243. Zolla, Elémire: 'Musica e Cabala in Sir Thomas Browne', *English Miscellany*, XVI (1965), 117–29.

On 'Religio Medici'

[1st unauthorised edition, 1642 (facsimile: ed. W.A. Greenhill, 1883). 2nd authorised edition, 1643 (facsimile: Scolar Press, 1970); edited by Greenhill (*W 1*) and, with full *apparatus criticus*, by Vittoria Sanna (Cagliari, 1958; followed by Sir Geoffrey Keynes, 1968). The reconstructed text by Jean-Jacques Denonain (with *apparatus criticus*, Cambridge, 1953; without it, 1963) incorporates several readings from the extant manuscripts, none authoritative. *M* (followed by *R*) and *E* are based on 1643; so is the present edition. Other editions of *Religio Medici* include Frank L. Huntley's (1968) and James Winny's (Cambridge, 1963); but the latter provides an unreliable text and displays, in both the introduction and notes, a positive dislike of Browne. On translations, see above, p. 488, note 9.

The eight extant manuscripts of *Religio Medici* are named by *M*, p. xii, and *K*, I, 5–6. The manuscript at Pembroke College, Oxford, has been edited by Jean-Jacques Denonain (*P*), who dates it much earlier than Frank L. Huntley does (*MP*, LVII [1959], 58–60).

In addition to the studies listed below, see §§18, 42, 53, 66, 93, 131, 137 176, 187, 190, 197–9, 206, 213, etc.]

§244. Abramson, Ernst: 'The Maid of Germany', *TLS*, 24 July 1948 (p. 415). See also C.H. Wilkinson, ibid., 21 August 1948 (p. 471). Cf. above, p. 98, note 186.

§245. Bensly, Edward: 'A Spanish Quotation in *Religio Medici*', *N&Q*, 12th series, XI (1922), 347. See above, p. 152, note 95.

§246. Bottrall, Margaret: 'Browne's *Religio Medici*', in her *Every Man a Phoenix: Studies in Seventeenth-Century Autobiography* (1958), Ch. III.

§247. Cook, Elizabeth: 'The First Edition of *Religio Medici*', *Harvard Library Bulletin*, II (1948), 22–31; cf. Sir Geoffrey Keynes, *TLS*, 18 April 1952 (p. 265). Discusses the two unauthorised issues of 1642.

§248. Croll, Morris W.: 'The Baroque Style in Prose', as above (§146), Ch. V; repr. in §151. Highly recommended.

§249. Denonain, J.-J.: 'Les Problèmes de l'honnête homme vers 1635: *Religio Medici* et les *Conférences* du Bureau d'Adresse', *Etudes Anglais*, XVIII (1965), 235–7.

§250. Digby, Sir Kenelm: *Observations upon Religio Medici* (1643). Usually bound with *Religio Medici* from 1659. Cf. §343.

§251. Edelstein, Ludwig: 'The Golden Chain of Homer', in *Studies in Intellectual History*, by G.G. Boas *et al.* (Baltimore, 1953), pp. 48–66. The background to Browne's reference (above, p. 84, note 116). Cf. next entry.

§252. 'Eirionnach': 'Aurea Catena Homeri', *N&Q*, 2nd Series, III (1857), 63–5, 81–4, 104–7, and XII (1861), 161–3, 181–3. Cf. previous entry.

§253. Endicott, N.J.: 'Some Aspects of Self-Revelation and Self-Portraiture in *Religio Medici*', in *Essays in English Literature*, ed. Millar MacLure and F.W. Watt (Toronto, 1964), pp. 85–102.

§254. Howell, A.C.: 'A Doctor Looks at Religion', *The University of North Carolina Extension Bulletin*, XXXIV (1954), ii, 45–69.

§255. Huntley, Frank L.: 'The Publication and Immediate Reception of *Religio Medici*', *Library Quarterly*, XXV (1955), 203–18; partly reprinted in §198 (Ch. VII and IX).

§256. Hutchinson, F.E.: '*Religio Medici*', *Theology*, L (1947), 423–6. An appreciation.

§257. Keck, Thomas: *Annotations upon Religio Medici*, first appended to the 'Fourth' edition of *Religio Medici* (1656), pp. 175–297.

§258. Low, Anthony: 'Sir Thomas Browne's Social Abacus', *N&Q*, new series, XV (1968), 98–9. Cf. above, p. 134, note 7.

§259. Mackenzie, Norman: 'The Concept of Baroque and its Relation to Sir Thomas Browne's *Religio Medici* and *Urn Burial*', *ESA*, X (1967), 147–66. Cf. §305.

§260. Mulder, John R.: '*Religio Medici:* Aristotle *versus* Moses', as above (§84), pp. 54–62. Highly recommended.

§261. Patrides, C.A.: 'Psychopannychism in Renaissance Europe', *SP*, LX (1963), 227–9. Cf. §§18, 272.

§262. Patrides, C.A.: ' "The Beast with Many Heads": Renaissance Views on the Multitude', *Shakespeare Quarterly*, XVI (1965), 241–6. Cf. above, p. 134, note 5.

§263. Patrides, C.A.: 'The Salvation of Satan', *JHI*, XXVIII (1967), 467–478. Cf. above, p. 67, note 32.

§264. Pritchard, Allan: 'Wither's *Motto* and Browne's *Religio Medici*', *PQ*, XL (1961), 302–7. On the possible influence of Wither's 'crude and naive' poem (1621).

§265. Ross, Alexander: *Medicus Medicatus: or the Physicians Religion cured, by a lenitive or gentle potion: With some Animadversions upon Sir Kenelme Digbie's Observations on Religio Medici* (1645). Cf. §343.

§266. Schneck, Jerome M.: 'Sir Thomas Browne, *Religio Medici*, and the History of Psychiatry', *American Journal of Psychiatry*, CXIV (1958), 657–60.

§267. Schonack, Wilhelm: *Sir Thomas Brownes 'Religio Medici': Ein verschollenes Denkmal des englischen Deismus* (Tübingen, 1911).

§268. Shaaber, M.A.: 'A Crux in *Religio Medici*', *ELN*, III (1966), 263–5. Cf. above, p. 343, note 130.

§269. Sloane, Cecile A.: 'Imagery of Conflict in *Religio Medici*', *ELN*, VIII (1971), 260–62.

§270. Ward, H.G.: 'Joachim du Bellay and Sir Thomas Browne', *RES*, V (1929), 59–60. See above, p. 139, note 30.

§271. Webber, Joan: 'Sir Thomas Browne: Art as Recreation', as above (§169), Ch. VI. Highly recommended.

§272. Williamson, George: 'Milton and the Mortalist Heresy', as above (§131), Ch. VII. Cf. Nathaniel H. Henry, 'Milton and Hobbes: Mortalism and the Intermediate State', *SP*, XLVIII (1951), 234–49, as well as §§18, 261. The intellectual context of Browne's reference (above, p. 67, note 31).

On 'Pseudodoxia Epidemica'

[1st edition, 1646 (facsimile: Scolar Press, with a textual preface by T.-L. Pebworth, 1972). Revised editions: 2nd, 1650; 3rd and 4th, 1658; 5th, 1659; and 6th, 1672. The present edition reproduces the text of 1650. On translations, see above, p. 491, note 16. A critical text with introduction and commentary is now being prepared for the Clarendon Press by Robin Robbins.

In addition to the studies listed below, see §§20, 43, 59, 176, 181, 187, 190, 198, 206, 210, 215, 241, 330, etc.]

§273. Bodemer, Charles W.: 'Embryological Thought in Seventeenth Century England', in Bodemer and L.S. King, *Medical Investigation in Seventeenth Century England* (Los Angeles, 1968), pp. 3–25.

§274. Cawley, Robert R.: 'The Timeliness of *Pseudodoxia Epidemica*', in *Studies* (as above, §181), pp. 1–40.

§275. Chalmers, Gordon K.: 'Sir Thomas Browne, True Scientist', *Osiris*, II (1936), 28–79. Highly recommended.

§276. Chalmers, Gordon K.: 'The Lodestone and the Understanding of Matter in Seventeenth Century England', *Philosophy of Science*, IV (1937), 75–95.

§277. Chalmers, Gordon K.: 'Three Terms of the Corpuscularian Philosophy', *MP*, XXXIII (1936), 243–60. Cf. §54.

§278. Colie, Rosalie L.: 'Dean Wren's Marginalia and Early Science at Oxford', *Bodleian Library Record*, VI (1960), 541–51.

§279. Debus, Allen G.: 'Sir Thomas Browne and the Study of Colour Indicators', *Ambix*, X (1962), 29–36.

§280. Gordon, George: 'Sir Thomas Browne', in his *The Lives of Authors* (1950), pp. 101–10.

§281. Guerlac, Henry: 'The Poet's Nitre', *Isis*, XLV (1954), 243–55. On Browne's 'earliest complete statement in English of the gunpowder theory' (*Pseud.*, II, 5).

§282. Howell, Almonte C.: 'Sir Thomas Browne and 17th Century Scientific Thought', *SP*, XXII (1925), 61–80.

§283. L'Estrange, Sir Hamon: *Observations on Pseudodoxia Epidemica*. Still in manuscript; summarised in *W*, II, 173–5.

§284. Merton, E.S.: 'Old and New Physiology in Sir Thomas Browne: Digestion and Some Other Functions', *Isis*, LVII (1966), 249–59. On *Pseud.*, III, 21–2.

§285. Merton, E.S.: 'Sir Thomas Browne as Zoologist', *Osiris*, IX (1950), 413–34.

§286. Merton, E.S.: 'Sir Thomas Browne's Embryological Theory', *JHM*, V (1950), 416–21.

§287. Merton, E.S.: 'Sir Thomas Browne's Scientific Quest', *JHM*, III (1948), 214–28; repr. in §206 (Ch. II). Highly recommended.

§288. Merton, E.S.: 'Sir Thomas Browne's Theories of Respiration and Combustion', *Osiris*, X (1952), 206–23.

§289. Merton, E.S.: 'The Botany of Sir Thomas Browne', *Isis*, XLVII (1956), 161–71.

§290. Oppenheimer, Jane M.: 'John Hunter, Sir Thomas Browne and the Experimental Method', *BHM*, XXI (1947), 17–32. Unfairly contrasted to Hunter in the eighteenth century, Browne is inevitably found wanting as a scientist.

§291. Patrides, C.A.: 'Renaissance Ideas on Man's Upright Form', *JHI*, XIX (1958), 256–8. See above, pp. 223 ff.

§292. Patrides, C.A.: 'The Cessation of the Oracles: The History of a Legend', *MLR*, LX (1965), 500–507. Cf. above, p. 97, note 176, and pp. 253 ff.

§293. Robinson, John: *A Calm Ventilation of Pseudodoxia Epidemica*, appended to his *Endoxa, or, Some probable Inquiries into Truth* (1658), pp. 105–51; translated by the author from his own Latin treatise (1656).

§294. Ross, Alexander: *Arcana Microcosmi: or, The Hid Secrets of Man's Body disclosed; ... with a Refutation of Doctor Browns Vulgar Errors, and the Ancient Opinions vindicated* (1651). Especially pp. 143 ff.

§295. South, Malcolm H.: 'A Note on Spenser and Sir Thomas Browne', *MLR*, LXII (1967), 14–16.

On 'Hydriotaphia' and 'The Garden of Cyrus'

[1st edition of the two works, 1658 (facsimile: Noel Douglas Replicas, 1927). Edited by Greenhill (*G2*), by Huntley (*H*), and by John Carter (with full *apparatus criticus*, 1932; without it, Cambridge, 1958; followed by Sir Geoffrey Keynes, 1968). *M* (followed by *R*) and *E* are based on 1658; so is the present edition. The first translation of the two works was into Dutch, in 1688.

In addition to the studies listed below, see §§23, 176, 187, 190, 198, 206, 213, 289, etc.]

§296. Barnes, William H.: 'Browne's *Hydriotaphia* with a Reference to Adipocere', *Isis*, XX (1933), 337–43. Cf. above, p. 295, note 79.

§297. Cline, James M.: '*Hydriotaphia*', in *Five Studies in Literature*, 'University of California Publications in English', VIII (1940), 73–100. Highly recommended.

§298. Evans, Sir John (ed.): *Hydriotaphia* (1893).

§299. Finch, Jeremiah S.: 'Early Drafts of *The Garden of Cyrus*', *PMLA*, LV (1940), 742–7.

§300. Finch, Jeremiah S.: 'Sir Thomas Browne and the Quincunx', *SP*, XXXVII (1940), 274–82.

§301. Grundy, Dominick: 'Skepticism in Two Essays by Montaigne and Sir Thomas Browne', *JHI*, XXXIV (1973), 529–42. Juxtaposes *De la vanité* and *Hydriotraphia*.

§302. Heideman, Margaret A.: '*Hydriotaphia* and *The Garden of Cyrus*: A Paradox and a Cosmic Vision', *UTQ*, XIX (1950), 235–46. Highly recommended.

§303. Huntley, Frank L.: 'Sir Thomas Browne: The Relationship of the *Urn Burial* and *The Garden of Cyrus*', *SP*, LIII (1956), 204–19; revised in §198 (Ch. XIII); repr. in §151. Highly recommended.

§304. Jaffé, Michael: 'Sir Thomas Browne at Midnight', *CJ*, II (1949), 752–7.

§305. Mackenzie, Norman: 'Sir Thomas Browne as a Man of Learning: A Discussion of *Urn Burial* and *The Garden of Cyrus*', *ESA*, X (1967), 67–86. Highly recommended. Cf. §259.

§306. Pande, R.P.: *Sir Thomas Browne, with a detailed study and text of 'Urn Burial'* (Allahabad etc., 1963).

§307. Parker, Edward L.: 'The Cursus in Sir Thomas Browne', *PMLA*, LIII (1938), 1037–53. Cf. §229.

§308. Patrides, C.A.: 'The Numerological Approach to Cosmic Order during the English Renaissance', *Isis*, XLIX (1958), 391–7.

§309. Williamson, George: 'The Purple of *Urn Burial*', *MP*, LXII (1964), 110–17.

On 'A Letter to a Friend', 'Christian Morals', the letters, and the minor works

[The present edition reproduces *A Letter to a Friend* from the 1st (posthumous) edition of 1690 (facsimile: Haslewood Press, 1924); *Christian Morals* (from the 1st (posthumous) edition of 1716 (ed. John Jeffery); and 'On Dreams' from the text transcribed by *K*. The first two are also edited by Greenhill (*G1*); and all three in *E*. For the letters, see *K*, vol. IV; and for the minor works both English and Latin: *K*, vol. III.

In addition to the studies listed below, see §§176, 187, 190, 198, 334, etc.]

§310. Ashton, Arthur.: 'Sir Thomas Browne *en famille*', *The English Review*, XLIII (1926), 693–707, and XLIV (1927), 59–68.

§311. Endicott, N.J.: 'Sir Thomas Browne, Montpellier, and the Tract "Of Languages" ', *TLS*, 24 August 1962 (p. 645).

§312. Endicott, N.J.: 'Sir Thomas Browne's *Letter to a Friend*', *UTQ*, XXXVI (1966), 68–86. Cf. §315.

§313. Harper, George M.: 'The Family Correspondence of Sir Thomas Browne', in his *Literary Appreciations* (Indianapolis, 1937), pp. 46–69.

§314. Huntley, Frank L.: 'Robert Loveday: Commonwealth Man of Letters', *RES*, new series, II (1951), 262–7. On the subject of *A Letter to a Friend*.

§315. Huntley, Frank L.: 'The Occasion and Date of Sir Thomas Browne's *A Letter to a Friend*', *MP*, XLVIII (1951), 157–71; revised in §198 (Ch. XI). See also N.J. Endicott's 'Browne's *A Letter to a Friend*', *TLS*, 15 September 1966 (p. 868), and Huntley's rejoinder, 9 February 1967 (p. 116); also Karl J. Höltgen, 20 October 1966 (p. 966) and 25 June 1970 (p. 687).

§316. Kane, Robert J.: 'James Crossley, Sir Thomas Browne, and the *Fragment on Mummies*', *RES*, IX (1933), 266–74. Argues that the *Fragment* is a forgery.

§317. Kellett, C.E.: 'Sir Thomas Browne and the Disease called the Morgellons', Annals of Medical History, n.s., VII (1935), 467–79. See above, p. 397, note 39.

§318. Löffler, Arno: 'Sir Thomas Browne at Work: An Unpublished Early Section of *Christian Morals*', *N&Q*, n.s., XX (1973), 391–2. Provides an addition to Part II, Sect. 5.

§319. Roberts, S.C. (ed.): *Christian Morals* (Cambridge, 1927). With Johnson's *Life*.

§320. Seaton, Ethel: *Literary Relations of England and Scandinavia in the Seventeenth Century* (Oxford, 1935), 182–4. On Browne's connections with Iceland.

§321. Wright, William A.: 'The Great Antonio', *N&Q*, 7th series, IV (1887), 386. See above, p. 391, note 2.

On Browne's reputation and influence

[In addition to the studies listed below, see above, pp. 548 ff. and 551 ff.]

§322. Bennett, Joan: 'A Note on *Religio Medici* and Some of its Critics', *Studies in the Renaissance*, III (1956), 175–84. Cf. §343.

§323. Childs, Herbert E.: 'Emily Dickinson and Sir Thomas Browne', *American Literature*, XXII (1951), 455–65.

§324. Coleridge, Samuel Taylor: as above (p. 537).

§325. Colie, Rosalie L.: 'Sir Thomas Browne's "Entertainment" in XVIIth Century Holland', *Neophilologus*, XXXVI (1952), 162–71. On Dutch attitudes to Browne.

§326. Cowles, Thomas: 'Dr. Henry Power, Disciple of Sir Thomas Browne', *Isis*, XX (1933–4), 345–66.

§327. Davis, Merrell R.: *Melville's 'Mardi': A Chartless Voyage* (New Haven, 1952), esp. pp. 64–6.

§328. de Beer, E.S.: 'The Correspondence between Sir Thomas Browne and John Evelyn', *Library*, 4th Series, XIX (1938–9), 103–6. See also the next entry.

§329. Evelyn, John: *Diary*, ed. E.S. de Beer (Oxford, 1955), III, 594–5 [entry for 17 October 1671]. On Evelyn's visit to Browne. For their correspondence, see *K*, IV, 273–81.

§330. Ewing, Majl: 'Mrs. Piozzi Peruses Dr. Thomas Browne', *PQ*, XXII (1943), 111–18. Mrs Thrale's annotations on *Pseudodoxia Epidemica* in 1811.

§331. Finch, Jeremiah S.: 'The Lasting Influence of Sir Thomas Browne', *Transactions and Studies of the College of Physicians of Philadelphia*, XXIV (1956), 59–69. Especially on Dr Johnson and Charles Lamb.

§332. Iseman, Joseph S.: *A Perfect Sympathy: Charles Lamb and Sir Thomas Browne* (Cambridge, Mass., 1937).

§333. Leroy, Olivier: 'Les Critiques', as above (§202), Part IV.

§334. Löffler, Arno: 'Sir Thomas Browne als Redaktor von Edward Brownes *Travels*', *Anglia*, LXXXVIII (1970), 337–40. Browne's contributions to his son's *Account of Several Travels through a great part of Germany* (1677).

§335. Matthiessen, F.O.: 'The Metaphysical Strain', in his *American Renaissance: Art and Expression in the Age of Emerson and Whitman* (1941), Ch. III.

§336. Newton-De Molina, David: 'A Note on Sir Thomas Browne and Jorge Luis Borges', *Antigonish Review*, II (1971), ii, 33–40.

§337. Pennel, Charles: 'The Learned Sir Thomas Browne: Some Seventeenth-Century Viewpoints', *Kansas Magazine* (Manhattan, Kansas, 1965), pp. 82–6. Cf. §343.

§338. Pepys, Samuel: *Diary*, ed. Robert Latham and William Matthews (1971), V, 27 [entry for 27 January 1663/4]. Reports that *Religio Medici*, together with Rochester's *Hudibras* and Osborne's *Advice to a Son*, are 'generally cried up for wit in the world'.

§339. Robertson, Stuart: 'Sir Thomas Browne and R.L. Stevenson', *JEGP*, XX (1921), 371-84.

§340. Vande Kieft, Ruth M.: ' "When Big Hearts Strike Together": The Concussion of Melville and Sir Thomas Browne', *Papers in Language and Literature*, V (1969), 39–50.

§341. Wagley, Mary F. and Philip F.: 'Comments on Johnson's Biography of Sir Thomas Browne', *BHM*, XXXI (1957), 318–26. Cf. above, pp. 481 ff.

§342. Williams, Mentor L.: 'Why "Nature Loves the Number Five": Emerson Toys with the Occult', *Papers of the Michigan Academy of Science, Art and Letters*, XXX (1944), 639–49.

§343. Wise, James N.: *Sir Thomas Browne's 'Religio Medici' and Two Seventeenth-Century Critics* (Columbia, Mo., 1972). On Digby (§250) and Ross (§265). Cf. §§322, 337.

§344. Woodbridge, Benjamin M., Jr: 'Sir Thomas Browne, Lamb, and Machado de Assis', *Modern Language Notes*, LXIX (1954), 188–9.

MORE ABOUT PENGUINS
AND PELICANS

Penguinews, which appears every month, contains details of all the new books issued by Penguins as they are published. From time to time it is supplemented by *Penguins in Print*, which is our complete list of almost 5,000 titles.

A specimen copy of *Penguinews* will be sent to you free on request. Please write to Dept EP, Penguin Books Ltd, Harmondsworth, Middlesex, for your copy.

In the U.S.A.: For a complete list of books available from Penguins in the United States write to Dept CS, Penguin Books, 625 Madison Avenue, New York, New York 10022.

In Canada: For a complete list of books available from Penguins in Canada write to Penguin Books Canada Ltd, 2801 John Street, Markham, Ontario L3R 1B4.